CRYPTIC CROSSWORD CLUEFINDER

CRYPTIC CROSSWORD CLUEFINDER

A DICTIONARY OF CROSSWORD CLUES

J.A.Coleman

Capella

This edition published in 2005 by Arcturus Publishing Limited
26/27 Bickels Yard, 151–153 Bermondsey Street,
London SE1 3HA

In Canada published for Indigo Books
468 King St W,
Suite 500,
Toronto,
Ontario M5V 1L8

ISBN 1-84193-347-3

Printed in India

INTRODUCTION

Thousands of crossword clues are published every day of the year and it would be an impossible task to cover even a fraction of this output in one dictionary. However, it is possible to recognise the general patterns used by compilers and such recognition is the first step on the road to solving a clue.

Typically, a clue in a cryptic crossword will contain a direct clue which is sufficient to provide the answer if you can recognise it, plus one or more indirect clues which will also provide the answer but may need to be manipulated for that purpose, and one or more pointers which will indicate how the indirect clues should be manipulated to provide the answer. An example might be **Carmen, perhaps, breaks into surgery(9)**. We could be looking for a solution for 'Carmen' (or 'carmen') or for a word meaning 'surgery' but since it is only 'perhaps Carmen' we should expect the direct clue to be 'surgery'. This might tell you the answer (OPERATION) but, if not, you can look at the indirect clue 'Carmen' (OPERA) and the pointer 'breaks' which invites you to rearrange the second indirect clue 'into' to form the anagram - TION, giving the same result.

The components of indirect clues are listed below:

Abbreviations - recognised ones such as SS for (steam)ship or 'compiler's language' forms such as NS for North Sea

Anagrams - letters, usually from given words, re-arranged to form another word, so that *'shattered* [arm]' becomes MAR or RAM

Articles such as 'a' and 'an', printed in the clue, may be used as part of the solution, but may be overlooked because they are so common; this includes foreign versions such as 'der', 'la', etc so that 'Continental articles' can be UNDER

Cockney expressions such as 'apples and pears' (STAIRS) and words from which the initial 'h' has been dropped so that *'Cockney* headgear' becomes (h)AT

Colloquialisms or careless speech such as 'ain't' or ''otter'

Compound words which should be read as two separate words so that 'legend' becomes 'leg' and 'end' meaning FOOT

Derived words are words derived from words given in the clue - as distinct from the given words themselves - so that, for example, SHE can be derived from the word 'female' given in the clue

Foreign words quite often appear, often combined with English words, so that *'French*man' requires HOMME

Given words are words printed in the clue which are sometimes used, as printed, in the solution, particularly in the case of Articles and Small words

Hidden words - words forming part of given words such as CHIN which can be found hidden in 'Fren/ch in/sults'

Homophones - words which sound the same as words given in the clue but which have different spelling and meaning as, for instance, WAIT and WEIGHT

Numbers, particularly Roman numerals, which are often used to represent letters, with C(100), D(500), L(50) and M(1000) standing for 'many'

Oblique descriptions are elaborately-worded or punning clues designed to disguise the required synonym rather as Churchill's 'terminological inexactitude' meant a plain old-fashioned LIE

Old words - obsolete and archaic words are used in crosswords, even though banned in other word games, so that 'the old' means YE

One of a class - here the clue gives a general class (eg: dog) and you are required to provide a particular example (eg: SETTER) or you may be given 'setter' as the particular specimen requiring the general class DOG

Opposite/negative clues require a solution which is the reverse of a given or derived word, so that 'face up' would yield BACK DOWN and 'not over' is more likely to mean UNDER than 'unfinished'

Part words - the clue may be so worded as to require the use of part of a given or derived word, so that 'some pepper' might mean PEP or PER

Poetic words - words used mainly by writers such as Spenser, Shakespeare, etc, so that 'poets' guild' might be GYELD

Proper nouns, including personal names, are sometimes used, often as the first word of the clue, so that the capital letter does not immediately indicate the use of a proper noun.

Quotations from literature, the Bible, the classics, history, etc often appear, sometimes unfairly, in that there are no indirect clues to give the solution to those unfamiliar with the quotation.

Rhymes - the solution in such cases is a word which rhymes with an indirect clue, so that 'her. . .' might require CUR, SIR, PURR, etc

Selected letters - letters from given words may be retained, so that 'initially my eye' gives ME, or they may be omitted so that *decapitated* (w)omen' becomes OMEN

Singulars and plurals - a 'singular' word may be half of another singular word, such as SING-SING, which has two identical parts, and 'plural words' may require the repeated use of a singular word such as IS to give ISIS

Small words - insignificant given words such as 'at', 'on', etc which, like articles, can easily be overlooked; 'pass on' may give COLON rather than 'hand over' or 'die'

Split words - any word may be split to allow another word to be written inside so that 'put *in* de-ed' becomes DEPUTED and, using abbreviations in the same way, 'highest *in* ship' give STOPS

Stuttered words - an indication that you need to double the stuttered letter so that 'a *stuttering peal*' becomes APPEAL

Synonyms are words having the same meaning but spelt differently and in some cases more than two meanings may be used; eg: 'able to', 'chimney', 'container' and 'prison' would all be satisfied with CAN

Any of these components can be combined to form the solution by adding words or parts, including words or parts within others, omitting parts of words or letters, reversing words or parts, substituting words or letters for others, or by using combinations of these devices such as writing part of one word backwards inside another. How you are to use these various components will be indicated by the pointers provided, which may be as devious as the clues themselves.

In this book you will find examples of all these various forms together with many tips and hints. In some cases the solution is not a recognisable word but the example is there to illustrate a point and the letters of the suggested solution can form part of a required answer. Some words have a number of entries, each relating to a different use and identified by a superscript number. When looking up a particular word, it is worth while checking all entries; 'the first . . . T' will be found under the entry dealing with uses of 'the' itself, whereas 'the first ball . . . B' is under the entry that deals with 'the' in its normal role as an article attached to a noun.

All the above formed the introduction to the original *Cluefinder* which was published in 1995 by Cassells. Since that date, additional material has been added, increasing the size of the book by some 60%. This is that book, *Cryptic Crossword Cluefinder*, which may perhaps prove to be 60% more useful than its parent.

KEY

The following list gives details of the symbols, etc used above and in the following pages:

anagram	[cat]
any word included or omitted	*
beginnings	IGN-
direct clue	<u>cat</u>
endings	-ING
examples	•
hidden word	/cat/
implied-additions	(on)
-inclusions	(in)
letter replaced	\c\at
pointers	*out*
selected letters-omitted	(a)
-retained	<u>a</u>
word-split for inclusion	B-ED
-used in Down clue	(D)
-written backwards-across	<
-down	^

The list of words printed in bold at the head of each section gives words for which that letter can be used as an abbreviation. Compilers' versions, as distinct from normal usage, are given in italics.

A

Academician, accepted, ace, ack, acre, active, adult, advanced, afternoon, aleph, alpha, alto, amateur, America, ampere, an, ana, ane, angström, annus, ante, answer, are, argon, associate, atomic, atto-, Austria, *ay*, *aye*, before (ante), blood group, bomb, effect, electric current, examination, film, fifty, five hundred, five thousand, *first character*, first-class, first letter, *high class*, it, key, level, mass number, note, nucleon number, one, paper, road, string, *top grade*, *top mark*, un, vitamin, year (annus)

a¹

as 'a' – English:

a	AN, I, ONE, UNIT
a *deficient*	omit A
a *dialect*	HE, IT, SHE, THEY
a *follower*	B
a *for example*	VOWEL
a *loss*	omit A
a *missing*	omit A
a turn to . . .	AUTO

a²

as 'a' – other languages:

a *Continental* . . .	UN, UNE
a *French* . . .	UN, UNE
• a *French* composer	UNRAVEL
• a *French* dressing	UNROBING
• a *French* pirate	UNHOOK
a *German* . . .	EIN
a *Greek* . . .	ALPHA
a *Hebrew* . . .	ALEPH
a *Parisian* . . .	UN, UNE
a *Scottish* . . .	ANE
a *Spanish* . . .	UN, UNA, UNO
an *Italian* . . .	UN, UNA, UNO

a³

as an inclusion:

• a *break in* the se–t	SEAT
• be–t *about* a . . .	BEAT
• colour *including* a . . .	READ, TAINT
• fl–y *around* a . . .	FLAY
• me–t *round* a . . .	MEAT

a⁴

as a 'prefix':

• A50	–AL
• a 2p . . .	APP–
• a 50-50 . . .	ALL
• a bank	ADRIFT
• a billow	AWAVE
• a bit of money	–AL
• a boat	ASS

• a book	ANT
• a border	AHEM
• a bounder, Scot	ACADIAN
• a cat	ATOM
• a Celt	ASCOT
• a cereal	ACORN
• a character here, *say*	ACARDIA
• a chimney	ALUM
• a church	ACE
• a church feature	ASPIRE
• a cleaner	ACHAR
• a climbing plant	AVINE
• a colliery	AMINE
• a competitor, *say*	ARRIVAL
• a container	AJAR
• a container like this	ACANTHUS
• a cricket club	ACC–
• a cricketer you are, *say*	ABATURE
• a decoy	ALURE
• a defender	ABACK
• a deficiency	ALACK
• a desire	AITCH, ALONG
• a disguise	AVAIL
• a doctor in front	AMBLED
• a drink	APORT
• a drink	ARUM
• a drunken father, *say*	APATITE
• a drupe, *say*	APLUMB
• a face cover, *say*	AVAIL
• a faint beat	APPULSE
• a fall	ATRIP
• a feast	ASPREAD
• a few, *say*	SUM
• a fiddle	AGUE
• a fight	ABOUT
• a fine fellow	AGENT
• a fish	ACHAR
• a fish	AGAR, AIDE
• a flower	AROSE
• a foot	AFT

Anag [cat]; Any *; Begin IGN–; Endings –ING; eg •; Hidden /cat/; Implied add (on); Implied in (in); Letter replaced \c\at; Omit (a); Pointers *out*; Retain a̲; Split B_ED; Down (D); Backwards <or ^

• a foot ailment	ACORN	• a note	ATONE
• a four	AFORESAID	• a number take exercise, *say*	TENDRIL
• a friend	AMATE	• a pace	ASTRIDE
• a frock, *say*	ADDRESS	• a pamphlet, *say*	ATTRACT
• a fruit, *say*	APLOMB, APPEAR	• a paper handkerchief, *say*	ATISHOO
• a funeral vigil	AWAKE	• a parrot performing	APOLLYON
• a gambler	ABETTER	• a party circle	ADORING
• a game point	APOLOGIST	• a path, *say*	AWEIGH
• a general	ALEE	• a pause, *say*	ARREST
• a giant	AGOG	• a pick-me-up, *say*	ATONIC
• a girl	AMISS	• a pig, *say*	ABHOR
• a girl might, *say*	ADAMITE	• a peer, *say*	ASHORE
• a girl severed, *say*	ANICUT	• a pilaster, *say*	APPEAR
• a goddess	AMUSE	• a pit	AMINE
• a grating	ARACK	• a plague	AT EASE
• a harbour	APORT	• a ploy	ATACTIC
• a <u>head</u>start	AH	• a poem	ANODE, AVERSE
• a horse	AMOUNT	• a poet	ANDANTE
• a hundredweight	ACTON	• a Pole scoffed	APOSTATE
• a husk	APOD	• a policeman	ACOP
• a journey	ATRIP	• a priesthood, *say*	ACCURACY
• a jump	ABOUND	• a prison	ASTIR
• a labyrinth	AMAZE	• a prize	ATROPHY
• a large drink, *say*	ABIGAIL	• a profit	AGAIN
• a large meal	ABIGEAT	• a promontory	AHEAD
• a large quantity, *say*	ALLOT	• a quiet man	APRON
• a leader	ACID	• a quiet sitter	APPOSER
• a leader-worker	ABEYANT	• a raid, *say*	ARRAYED
• a learner	–AL	• a ray, *say*	ABEAM
• a legume, *say*	APPULSE	• a reason, *say*	AGROUND
• a light touch, *say*	ATICAL	• a religious heretic	APIARIAN
• a lightweight	ACT	• a rendezvous	AVENUE
• a lightweight, *say*	ANNOUNCE	• a reward	ATROPHY
• a line	–ARY	• a right	ALIEN
• a lintel, *say*	ABEAM	• a ring, *say*	APPEAL
• a little porcelain, *say*	SUMMING	• a river	ANILE
• a load, *say*	AWAIT	• a road	AWAY
• a loose woman	ABROAD	• a road to the hill	AVIATOR
• a loud tale	AFFABLE	• a row, *say*	ALIGN
• a married . . .	AWED	• a rule, *say*	ARRAIGN
• a mask, *say*	AVAIL	• a ruler, *say*	ACHING
• a match	ABOUT	• a sailor, *say*	ATTAR
• a measure	AFOOT	• a saint, *say*	APPAL
• a meeting place	AVENUE	• a sanctimonious heretic	APIARIAN
• a member	AMP	• a savage . . .	ACCRUAL
• a method	AWAY	• a screw	AWARDER
• a method, *say*	AWEIGH	• a service	AMASS, ARAF
• a minor road	ABROAD	• a sex, *say*	AGENDA
• a mole, *say*	APPEAR	• a share	ARATION
• a mother	ADAM	• a shelf, *say*	ALLEGE
• a mother-worker	ADAMANT	• a ship	AHOY, ASS
• a mountain range	AURAL	• a silly tax	ADUMBRATE
• a niece is, *say*	ANESIS	• a singer	AWAIT
• a noble, *say*	ACCOUNT, APPEAR	• a sitter, *say*	APPOSER
• a Norseman, *say*	JOCKEY, RIDER	• a sixpence	AVID
• a Northern . . .	AN	• a skin, *say*	APPEAL
• a note	ADO, ALA, ARE, ATE	• a soft fruit	APPEACH

Anag [cat]; Any *; Begin IGN–; Endings –ING; eg •; Hidden /cat/; Implied add (on); Implied in (in);

• a sound	ATONE	**AAA**	DASHBOARD
• a sound, *say*	ANNOYS	**abandon**[1]	
• a spanner	ABRIDGE	indicating omission:	
• a spell in this place, *say*	APHASIA	*abandon* a . . .	omit A
• a spirit	ARUM	*abandon* daughter	omit D
• a stain, *say*	ATTAINT	*abandon* husband	omit H
• a step	APACE	*abandon* one . . .	omit A or I
• a step	ASTRIDE	*abandon* ship	omit SS
• a stone fruit, *say*	APPEACH	*abandon* son	omit S
• a strong group	AFFORCE	*abandon* wife	omit W
• a stud	ASTABLE	*abandon* *	omit *
• a stye	ABOIL	• sen(try) *abandons* attempt	SEN
• a superior	ABETTER	*abandoned by* *	omit *
• a tax	ATOLL	• cab(le) *abandoned by* the *French*	CAB
• a team, *say*	ASIDE	quietly *abandons* . . .	omit P
• a tenet, *say*	ADRIFT	**abandon**[2]	
• a valley, *say*	AVAIL	abandon fight	SCRAP
• a very quiet dog	APPROVER	abandon sin	SHE-DEVIL
• a vice	AGREED	*abandoned* [claim]	MALIC
• a wager	ABET, ALPHABET	abandons colours	MAROONS
• a wanderer, *say*	AROMA	abandons trenches	DITCHES
• a warden	ARRANGER	[dance] *with abandon*	CANED
• a waterpipe	AMAIN	**abbess/abbot/abbey**	ABB
• a weight	ACT	**abbreviate**	
• a wicked fellow	ABADDON	*abbreviate* boo(k)	BOO
• a woman (US)	ABROAD	*abbreviated* period	TIM(e)
• a writer	ASCRIBE	*abbreviation of* par(t)	PAR
• a Yugoslav, *say*	ACERB	**abdicated**	ABD
and		**Abel**	ADAMSON
• a leopard	ANNOUNCE	**aberration**	
• a poem	ANODE	*aberrant* [tones]	NOTES, ONSET, SETON
• a poet	ANDANTE	*aberration of* [mental] . . .	LAMENT
• a twitch	ANTIC	**ablative**	ABL
• a weight	ANNOUNCE	**able**	
and		able seaman	AB
• leave *after* a . . .	AGO	able-bodied seaman, *say*	WHOLESALER
• man *behind* a . . .	AGENT	*able to be* [used]	DUES, SUED
• obliged to *follow* a . . .	ABOUND	(*see also* sailor)	
and		**abnormal**	
• an angry insect, *say*	ACROSTIC	*abnormal* [lump]	PLUM
• an opening	AGATE	*abnormally* [low]	OWL
• an urge	AITCH	**aboard**	
	(*see also* an)	aboard	(in) S–S
		• work *aboard*	SOPS
a[5]		aboard	incl SS
as a 'suffix':		• Ma–e *aboard*	MASSE
• a boy *and* a . . .	ERICA	aboard	ON
• feature article	CHINA	• lady's *aboard*	HERON
• fish *with* a . . .	CODA	*aboard* ket/ch ar/riving . . .	CHAR
• one *joining* a . . .	PERSONA	(*see also* on[6])	
• barrel *having* a . . .	TUNA		
a[6]		**abolish**	
a bit of ca/ke en/closed	KEEN	*abolish* a . . .	omit A
a little m/an tic/ked . . .	ANTIC	*abolish* *	omit *
a share of he/r est/ate	REST	• fa(the)r *abolishes* the . . .	FAR
A		• franc *abolished* in (F)inland	INLAND
AA man	AARON, ARCHIE	**abominable**	
AA gun	ARCHIE	abominable snowman	YETI

abominable [taste]	TEATS, TESTA
abominably [evil]	LIVE
abort	
aborted [sea trip]	TRAIPSE
abortive [try, Pa]	PARTY
about¹	
about (=approximately)	
about	C
• about a boy	CALF, CANDY
	CANTON, CERIC
• about a girl	CANNA, CLASS
• about a member	CAMP
• about an old king	CLEAR
• about an old ship	CARGO
• about fifty	CL–
• about right	CR–
• about this *Latin* . . .	CHIC
• about time	CAGE
• about *to be removed*	omit C
• about *to leave*	omit C
• about *twice*	CRE–
about	CA
• about 500	CAD
• about about	CARE
• about *about*<	AC
• about about about *about*	CAREER
• about right	CAR, CART
• about time	CAT
• about *twice*	CARE
• about *to be removed*	omit CA
• about to get up	CAROUSE
• about *to leave*	omit CA
about	CIRC(A)
• about East	CIRCE
• about the *French* . . .	CIRCLE
• about you and me	CIRCUS
about²	
about (=concerning)	
about	RE
• about a boy	REASON
• about *about*<	ER
• about fifty	REL–
• about money	RECENT
• about now	REPRESENT
• about over	REPAST
• about poetry	REVERSE
• about some quarters	REPARTEE
• about sea	REMAIN
• about tax	RECESS
• about *to be removed*	omit RE
• about *to leave*	omit RE
• about *twice*	CARE, CRE–
• I *take* about . . .	IRE
• leave about . . .	GORE
• snake, one about . . .	ASPIRE
about *retirement*<	–ER
about *to return*<	–ER

about *to rise*(D)^	–ER
	(*see also* touching)
about³	
indicating inclusion:	
about a . . .	incl A
about a hundred	incl C, AC
about fifty	incl L
about five	incl V
about four	incl IV
about nine	incl IX
about one	incl A, I
about right	incl R, RT
about six	incl VI
about ten	incl X
about time	incl T
about turn	incl U
about *	incl *
• talk *about* scabies	CHITCHAT
about⁴	
other uses:	
about face<	LAID
about [now]	OWN, WON
about time<	ARE, EMIT
about turn	U
about turn at . . .<	TA
enthusiastic *about*<	DAM
above	
above	SUP(RA)
above(D)	(*see* over³)
above ten	ELEVEN, TENT
above zero	NOTICE(D)
Abrahamville	LINCOLN
abridge	
abridged	ABD
abridged boo(k)	BOO
abridged st(or)y	STY
abroad	
abroad [in gold] . . .	DOLING
abroad	
indicating use of a	
foreign language:	
• *Continental* house	CASA, MAISON
• *cross-channel* bridge	PONT
• go *abroad*	ALLER
• *overseas* contract	APPALTO
• walk *on the Continent*	MARCHER
• work *overseas*	LAVORO, TRAVAIL
[travel] *abroad*	VARLET
	(*see also* continent, cross⁴, foreign)
absent	
absence of	NO
–approval	NOOK
–friend	NOPAL
–hooter	NONOSE
–males	NOMEN
–medicine	NODOSE
–stomach	NOTUM

Anag [cat]; Any *; Begin IGN–; Endings –ING; eg •; Hidden /cat/; Implied add (on); Implied in (in);

–wickedness	NOVICE	• girl *accommodated by* a–n..	AMAIN
absent	AWOL	accommodating a . . .	incl A
absent king	omit K, R	*accommodating* *	incl *
absent worker	OFFHAND	• Ab–e *accommodating* us	ABUSE
absent *	omit *	*accommodating* ma/ny, ala/s	NYALA
• ap(pal) *absent* friend	AP	accommodation rented	FLATLET
absentee	omit EE	**accompany**	
an *absent* . . .	omit AN	accompanying	WITH
absolute		–gangster	WITHAL
absolute	ABS	–woman	WITHER
absolutely transparent	SHEER	–you, *say*	WITHE, WITHY
absorb		accompanying page	ATTENDANT
absorb eggs, *say*	SUCCEED	*accompanied by*	incl AND
absorb oxygen	incl O	• Henry *accompanied by* son	HANDS
absorbed in *	incl in *	**accomplished**	
• saint *absorbed in* music	ASTIR	accomplished actors	OVERCAST
absorbing a . . .	incl A	accomplished country girl	DONEGAL
absorbing *	incl *	accomplished explorer	OVERCOOK
• music *absorbing* saint	ASTIR	accomplished, *say*	VERST
absorbs mu/ch I li/ke	CHILI	**according**	
abstainer	RECHABITE, TT	according to	
abstract		–art	SA
abstract	ABS	–law	SEC LEG
abstract a . . .	omit A	–nature	SN
abstract form	REMOVE	–rule	SEC REG
abstract money	omit L	–value	AD VAL(OREM)
abstract *	omit *	according to some (=dialect)	
• Greek so *abstracted*	(so)CRATES	• *according to some*, swift . . .	WIGHT
absurd		• information *according to some*	WITTING
absurd [idea]	AIDE	accordingly legal	SOLICIT
absurdly [used]	DUSE, SUED	**account**	
abuse		account	AC(C), ACCT, BILL
abuse [slave]	SALVE, VALES	account clerk	BILLPOSTER
abused [animal]	LAMINA	account for	
abusing [dogs]	GODS	–cutlery	SPOONBILL
academic		–footwear	SHOEBILL
academic	MA, PROF	–instrument	HORNBILL
academic appointment	CHAIR	account outstanding	BILLOWED
academic stream	CAM, ISIS		BILLOWING
academician	A, ARA, PRA, RA	accountant	AC, ACA, CA, FCA
academy	RA, RADA	accountants	CAS, SAA
accept		• accountant's girl	CASSANDRA
acceptable	OK, ON, U	• accountant's note	CASE
accepted	A, INSET, U	**accurate**	
accepted by t/he m/ajority	HEM	accurate imitator	DEAD PARROT
accepted by *	incl in *	accurate shot	(ANNIE) OAKLEY, TELL
• we are *accepted by* group	SWEET	accurately (=to the letter)	
accepting a . . .	incl A	• absolutely *accurately*	DEAD LETTER
accepting *	incl *	ace	A, EXPERT, I, NOI–
• b–at *accepting* nothing	BOAT		ONE, PRO, WINNER
accident			*(see also* expert)
accident	HAP	**achievement quotient**	AQ
accident in [plane]	PANEL	**acid test**	PH
accidentally [spilt]	SPLIT	**acknowledge**	
after accident [rider] . . .	DRIER	acknowledge worker	AVOWANT
accommodate		acknowledged debts	–IOUS
accommodated by *	incl in *	acknowledgement	ROGER

Letter replaced \c\at; Omit (a); Pointers *out*; Retain a̲; Split B_ED; Down (D); Backwards <or ^

acoustic
acoustic wave	WAIVE
acoustics, *say*	ECOSYSTEM

acquire leverage	PURCHASE
acre	A

across
across (=a cross)	X
• across fish	X-RAY
• get monkey across	APEX
• put the man across	HEX
across the Channel (=in French)	
• swim *across the Channel*	NAGER
• bridge *across the Channel*	PONT
• fly *across the Channel*	MOUCHE
• *across the Channel*, men . . .	HOMMES
	(*see also* abroad)
across	TRANS–
across a street	SAT
across the Atlantic	–TOUS
fl–y *across* a . . .	FLAY
run *across<*	NUR

act¹
[act]	WILDCAT
[act] *peculiarly*	CAT
[acted] *strangely*	CADET
	(*see also* indeed)

act²
act	BILL, TAKE APART
act	
–fraudulently	BEACON
–gallantly	BENIGHT
–impishly	BEDEVIL
–legally	PROSECUTE, SUE
–like	
a dog *say*	BEAKER
a stone *say*	BEJEWEL
–more rashly	BEWILDER
–of	
union	MARRIAGE, WEDDING
war	DORA
act as	
–consumer	EAT
–publisher	BEADMAN
–ruler	BEAKING
–sentry	BEGUARD
–sentry, *say*	BEGGARRED, BEGHARD
–starter, *say*	SAGO
–swindler	BEACON
–telephone	BEARING
acting	ON
acting as	QUA
–a pig	QUAHOG
–monarch	QUAKING
acts collectively	DRAMA, PLAY

activate
activate [plot]	POLT
activated [a model] . . .	LOAMED

active
active	A, ACT
• active people	AMEN
• active railway	ALINE
• not active	NOTA
active Communist	LIVERED
active [life]	FILE
[great] *activity*	GRATE
[stride] *actively*	DIREST

actor
actor	PLAYER, TREE
actor's remuneration	PART PAYMENT
actors	EQUITY, RADA
actors on tour	CASTAWAY
[actors] *on tour*	CROATS
actors' wages	CASTRATE

actuaries	FA
acute lamentation	KEEN

Adam
Adam	FIRST MAN, FIRST MATE
Adam (and Eve)	BELIEVE
Adam's ale	WATER
Adam's first wife	LILITH
Adam's wine	WATER
Adam*son*	ABEL, CAIN, SETH

adapt
adaptable [sort]	TORS
adaptation of [recent] . . .	CENTRE
adapted [an old] . . .	NODAL
adapting [another's] . . .	SHERATON

add
add	
–garnish	ATTACH
–it on, *say*	SUMMON
–it up, *say*	SUMMIT
–letters, *say*	COUNTESSES
add	
–an ode	ANODE
–pound *to* fee	FEEL
–weight *to* dreadful . . .	DIRECT
added weight	EXTRACT

additional
additional	
–award	BAR
–additional message	PS
–additional postscript	PPS
additional	MORE
–beer, *say*	MORALE
–directions, *say*	MOREEN
–donkeys, *say*	MORASSES
–Scotsman, *say*	MORMON
additional	EXTRA
–parties, *say*	EXTRADOS
–weight	EXTRACT
additional premium	AP

address
address in America	GETTYSBURG

Anag [cat]; Any *; Begin IGN–; Endings –ING; eg •; Hidden /cat/; Implied add (on); Implied in (in);

address	
indicating mode of address:	
ambassador's address	HE, EXCELLENCY
archdeacon's address	(VEN)ERABLE
bishop's address	GRACE
cardinal's address	EMINENCE
–old	MOST ILLUSTRIOUS
dean's address	VERY REV(EREND)
duke's address	GRACE
earl's address	LORD
judge's address	LORD
king's address	MAJESTY
knight's address	SIR
magistrate's address	HONOUR
mayor's address	WORSHIP
member's address	HON(OURABLE)
pope's address	HOLINESS
prince's address	HIGHNESS
queen's address	MAJESTY
teacher's address	MISS, SIR
vicar's address	REV(EREND)
	(see also previous)
address	
indicating place of residence:	
ambassador's address	EMBASSY
clergyman's address	MANSE, PARSONAGE, RECTORY, VICARAGE
monk's address	FRIARY, MONASTERY, PRIORY
PM's address	NUMBER TEN, DOWNING STREET
Pope's address	VATICAN
adherent	BUR(R), FAN
adjective	ADJ
adjoin	
adjoining (=ad – joining other words or letters)	
• adjoining m–e	MADE
• adjoining s–ly . . .	SADLY
• adjoining student and the German . . .	LADDER
adjourned	ADJ
adjust	
adjust harmony	TUNE
adjustable [seat is] . . .	SIESTA
adjustable spanner	DRAWBRIDGE
adjusted [Kit's] . . .	SKIT
adjusting [strap]	PARTS, SPRAT, TRAPS
adjustment	ADJ
adjustment [let us] . . .	TUSSLE
Adjutant-general	AG
adman	PRO
administer	MANAGE, RUN
administer, say	MANEGE
admiral	
admiral	ADM
	BUTTERFLY

	DRAKE, HOOD, NELSON
Admiral of the Fleet	AF
admire	
admirer, say	SUTOR
admit¹	
admitted	IN
• admitted dog	INCUR
• admitted group	INSECT, INCULT
• admitted to hospital	INWARD
admitting	AM
• admitting essayist	AMELIA
• admitting girl	AMRITA
• admitting one ship	AMISS
admitting	IM–
• admitting journalists	IMPRESS
• admitting two	IMPAIR
• admitting working	IMPLYING
and	
• I am an attendant	IMPAGE
• I am out of date	IMPASSE
• I am wan	IMPALE
admitting	IAM
• admission of age	IAMAGED
• admitting vehicle	IAMBUS
• admitting wind	IAMBISE
• I am second-class	IAMB
admit	OWN
• admit queen	OWNER
• many admit . . .	MOWN
• transport company admits . . .	BROWNS
admitted by mo/st ar/my . . .	STAR
admitting tha/t he n/ever . . .	THEN
	(see also claim, confess, declare)
admit²	
indicating inclusion:	
admitted by *	incl in *
• men admitted by wrong . . .	TORMENT
admitting a . . .	incl A
admitting nothing	incl O
admitting *	incl *
• wrong, admitting men . . .	TORMENT
adopt	
adopt children	TAKE ISSUE
adopted by *	incl in *
• daughter adopted by Ma–e	MADE
adopting a . . .	incl A
adopting *	incl *
• Ma–e adopting daughter	MADE
adore	
adore Communist	LOVERED
adore, say	A DOOR
adrift	
adrift [in the] . . .	THINE
[came] adrift	ACME, MACE
[ship] adrift	HIPS, PISH
adult	
adult	A

Letter replaced \c\at; Omit (a); Pointers out; Retain a̲; Split B_ED; Down (D); Backwards <or ^

• adult people	AMEN
adult film	X
adult worker, *say*	MATURANT
adulterate	
adulterate [wines]	SINEW, SWINE
adulteration of [meat]	MATE, TAME, TEAM
advance	
advance	SUB
• advance for fruit	SUBLIME
• advance *to* position	SUBSTATION
• advance with *German*	SUBMIT
advance, *say*	COMMON
advanced	A
advanced fast	LENT
advantage	VAN
advent	ADV
adventure	
adventurous girl	ALICE
adventurous [girl in] . . .	RULING
adverb	ADV
adverse	
adverse	ANTHONY
adversely affected rats<	STAR
adversely affected [rats]	ARTS, STAR
	TARS
advertise	
advertise	AIR
• advertise room	AIRSPACE
• advertise sportswear	AIRSTRIP
• advertises tours	AIRSTRIPS
advertisement	AD, BILL, PLUG
	POSTER, PUFF
	(*see also* notice)
advise	
advice centre	CAB
ad<u>vice</u> *centre*	VI
advise, *say*	COUNCIL
advisor	CABMAN
advocate	ADV
advocates	BAR
Aero Club	AC
aeroplane	JET, MIG, etc
affect	
affect [large] . . .	LAGER, REGAL
affected [animal]	LAMINA, MANILA
affected settlement	CAMP
affecting [lots] . . .	SLOT
affectionate	
affectionate	FOND
• boy	FONDLES
• relative, *say*	FONDANT
• worker	FONDANT
affectionate	KIND
• boy	KINDLES
• Communist	KINDRED
afflict	
afflicted [by a lone] . . .	BALONEY

affliction [she 'ad] . . .	HEADS, SHADE
afloat	(in) S–S
aforesaid	
aforesaid	DITTO, DO
afore*said*	A FOUR
African	
African capital	RAND
<u>A</u>frican *capital*	A
African *flower*	ZAMBESI
African heathland	MOOR
African lives	BERBERIS
<u>A</u>frican *leader*	A
African, *say*	CREW
after	
after	POST
• after a time	POSTAGE
• after some hesitation	POSTER
• after teacher	POSTMASTER
• after the fruit	POSTDATE
• after the Italian . . .	POSTIL
• after the river . . .	POSTURE
after²	
indicating one word written	
after another word or letter:	
• *after* all the *old return*<	ALLEY
• *after* he married	HEM, HEWED
• *after* mid<u>night</u> I'll . . .	GILL
• almost ful(l) *after*taste	TASTEFUL
• dine *after* noon	NEAT
• many *after* the . . .	THEM
• not so much *after*care	CARELESS
• Scot *after*guard	GUARDIAN
• space *after*ward	WARDROOM
after³	
other uses:	
after accident [men are] . . .	MEANER
after all	LAST, REARMOST, STERNMOST
	TAIL-END CHARLIE
	TAIL-ENDER
after all	(in) EN–D
after analysis [it was] . . .	WAIST, WAITS
after dark, *say*	TONITE
after date	AD
after death	PM
after five, *say*	SEX
after me, *say*	FAH
after midnight	AM, –IAM
after one, *say*	TO(O)
after opening	omit 1st letter
• *after opening* wine	(t)OKAY, (g)RAVES
after seven, *say*	ATE, AIT, EYOT
after reform [it was] . . .	WAIST, WAITS
after retirement	(in) B–ED, (in) C–OT
• bird, *after retirement* . . .	BOWLED
• *after retirement*, learner . . .	CLOT
after retreat, ogre< . . .	ERGO
after review [army] . . .	MARY, MYRA

after tax	NET(T)	*agitated* [waters]	WASTER
after the style of	ALA	*agitatedly* [paces]	CAPES, SPACE
after the start	omit 1st letter	*agitation of* [men at] . . .	MEANT
• *after the start of* bad weather	(w)INTER	**agree**	
• (l)eaves *after the start*	EAVES	agree *with* directors	SIDEBOARD
after three, *say*	FOR(E)	agree total	TALLY
after twelve	PM	agreed	ATONE
afterlife		agreement	AY, AYE, YEA
afterlife, *say*	WENDED	–Franco–German	OUIJA
afternoon		–French	OUI
afternoon	A, EXAM, PM	–German	JA
afternoon	after AM	–Italian	SI
• *quiet afternoon*	AMP	–Russian	DA
afternoon	after N	–Spanish	SI
• a quiet *afternoon*	NAP	agreement in writing	CORRESPONDENCE
afternoon service	TEA-SET	agreement, *say*	PACKED
afterthought	PS	**aggravate**	
again	RE	*aggravate* [parent]	ENTRAP
against		[it was] aggravating	WAIST
against	CON	**aggressive**	
• against dogs	CONCURS	aggressive	
• against poetry	CONVERSE	–American	DOUGHBOY, GI
• against the edge	CONVERGE	–Frenchman	SOLDAT
against	V	–German	SOLDAT
• against drink	VALE	–Italian	SOLDATO
• against one and . . .	VIAND	–Spaniard	SOLDADO
• against the current	VAMPS	aggressor's weapon	HAWKSBILL
against, *say*	AUNTIE	(*see also* belligerent)	
age		**agriculture**	
age of		agriculture	AGR, EARTHWORK
–building	HALLAGE	agricultural collection	FLOCK, HERD
–building, *say*	HAULAGE		STABLE
–vehicle, *say*	CABBAGE, CARRIAGE	agricultural policy	CAP
–vessel, *say*	PANNAGE	**ahead**	
age *of backwardness*<	ARE, EGA	*ahead* with	W
age of womanhood, *say*	GESTATING	*went ahead*	W
aged	AE, AET	**aide-de-camp**	ADC
aged head	OLDNESS	**ail**	
aged judge	REFOLD	ail, *say*	ALE, BEER
agent		*ailing* [king is] . . .	SKIING
agent	AGT	*what ails* [thee, Ms] . . .	THEMES
agent	BOND	**aimless**	
• agent's boss	M	*aimless* [stroll]	TROLLS
agent	REP	[saunter] *aimlessly*	NATURES
• agent *has* a bit	REPORT	**ain't**	
• agent *has* a chimney	REPLUM	ain't, *say*	ARNOT
• agent *with* paintings	REPART	**air**	
agent	SPY	air *and* sea	GAS-MAIN
• agent is aware, *say*	SPINOSE	[air]-*conditioned*	RIA
agile		air controllers	CAA
agile [animal]	LAMINA, MANILA	air expeller	COUGHER
agility of [apes]	PEAS	air expeller *say*	COFFER
agitate		air filter	STRAIN
agitate	STIR	Air Force	
• agitate Communist	STIRRED	–flew	RAFFLED
• agitate prison	STIR	–in front, *say*	RAFFLED
• agitate, *say*	STIRRUP	–instruments	ANEMOMETERS

Letter replaced \c\at; Omit (a); Pointers *out*; Retain <u>a</u>; Split B_ED; Down (D); Backwards <or ^

air-hose	WINDSOCK	**alert runners**	WAKEFIELD
air passage	FLIGHT	**alfresco party**	OUTDO
air *terminal*	R	**algebra**	ALG
Air Traffic Control	ATC	**alias**	
air traffic control	AILERON, ELEVATOR,	alias	AKA
	JOYSTICK, RUDDER	*alias* [given to] . . .	VETOING
Air Training Corps	ATC	**alien**	
air trip	WINDFALL	alien	ET
airborne	(in) F–LIGHT	• alien deity	ETHEL
• a number airborne	FANLIGHT	• alien roué	CADET
airborne nanny	FLYING BUTTRESS	• offer alien . . .	BIDET
airborne policeman	BLUEBOTTLE	alien (=foreign)	
aircraft compartment, *say*	BOMBAY	• *alien* ship	BATEAU
aircraftsman	AC, ERK, LAC	• *alien* soldiers	SOLDATEN
	COMPOSER, VERDI et al	• *alien* woman	DONNA
airman	FO, PO	**all¹**	
airway	LARYNX, THROAT, WINDPIPE	*after* all	begin with ALL
in the air	(in) SK–Y	• cure *after* all	ALLHEAL
• *air*sick	SKILLY	• unknown *after* all	ALLY
air transport	CARRIAGE	all-*embracing*	incl ALL
aired beforehand	PREVENTED	• sh–ow all-*embracing* . . .	SHALLOW
airy fairy	BLITHE SPIRIT	all *finished*	L
airline¹		all *gone*	omit ALL
airline	BA	• m(all)ow all *gone*	MOW
• airline fashion	BATON	all *in*	incl ALL
• airline girl	BASAL, BALASS	• sh–ow all *in* . . .	SHALLOW
• airline study	BACON	• s–ow *includes* all . . .	SALLOW
• airline toilet	BALOO	al(l) *not finished*	AL
airline	BAC	all *out*	omit ALL
• airline above . . .	BACON	all round	'ALLO
• airline delicacy	BACCATE	all *round<*	LLA
• to airline company	TOBACCO	all *round*	AL–L
airline	BEA	• go al–l *round*	ALGOL
• airline, a *French* one	BEAUNE	*almost* al(l)	AL
• airline buildings	BEASTIES	**all²**	
• airline students	BE-ALL	other uses:	
• airline study	BEACON	all *and* part	WHOLESOME
airline	TWA	*all but* a . . .	omit A
• airline in . . .	TWAIN	*all but* one	omit A, I
• airline not known	TWANK	all dead	OLIVE
• airline unknown	TWAY	all-[English]	SHINGLE
airline²		all off	NOON
airline	GAS PIPE, ISOBAR	all out	GENERAL STRIKE
airline dessert	PIE IN THE SKY	*all over the place* [I went]	TWINE
airline *terminal*	E	all right	NONE LEFT, OK(AY)
airlines	LYRICS	all round	EIGHTEEN HOLES
aisle		*all round*	
aisle, *say*	ILL, ISLE	• one with wa–ter *all round*	WAITER
Albert		all-round achievement	HOME RUN, HOMER
Albert	WATCH-CHAIN	all round(er)	BALL, BAND, BELT
Albert's place	HALL		DRAKE, FRANCIS, MAGELLAN
alcoholic state	DT(S)		O, ORB, SPHERE
alderman	ALD	all, *say*	AWL, HOLE
Alderney	GBA	All Souls	NOBODY
ale		all types	FO(U)NT
ale, *say*	AIL, BIER	all women	NOMEN, OMEN
aleph	A	all wrong, *say*	NORITE

Anag [cat]; Any *; Begin IGN–; Endings –ING; eg •; Hidden /cat/; Implied add (on); Implied in (in);

allow

allow	LET
• allow Henry	LETHAL
• Malcolm allowed . . .	MALLET

alloy

alloy of [iron]	NOIR
[silver] *alloy*	LIVERS, SLIVER

allude

allude to, *say*	REEFER

almost¹

almost al(l)	AL
almost all gone	–GON, ONE
almost crazy	CRACKER(s)
almost dressed	ROBIN(g)
almost fully-developed	ADUL(t)
almost left	POR(t)
almost lose sight	GOBLIN(d)
almost pointless	NEEDLES(s)
almost succeed	DOWEL(l)
almost the finest . . .	THEBES(t)
almost unnecessary	NEEDLES(s)
almost wholly bad	BA, AD

almost²

almost fal/l ove/r	LOVE
almost left	NEAR
almost the last of the . . .	H
almost the last of the wi<u>ne</u>	N

aloft

aloft, sailor . . .(D)^	BA, RAT
go *aloft*(D)^	OG

alone

alone, *say*	A LOAN, SOUL

alongside HYPOTENUSE

alpha A

Alpine

Alpine Club	AC
[Alpine] *resort*	NEPALI

also

also	AND
• also alter, *say*	ANDVARI
• also lift, *say*	ANDRASE
• also metal	ANDIRON
also known as	AKA, ALIAS

altar REV COUNTER

alter

alter [a trend]	RANTED
alter dress	SHIFT
alter, *say*	ALTAR
alteration to [route]	OUTER, OUTRE
alter	RATEL

alternate

alternate	ALT
alter[nate]	NEAT
alternate time intervals	TM, IE
alternating current	AC

alternative

alternative	OR
• alternative cereal	ORRICE
• alternative cut	ORLOP
• alternative energy	ORE
• alternative entrance	OR-GATE
• alternative note	ORC, ORE
• alternative piece	ORBIT
• alternative timber	ORDEAL, ORPINE
• alternative trade	ORDEAL

and

• alternative coins	DORP, LORD
• alternative letters	BORN, CORD, FORM, HORN, WORD etc
• alternative directions	NORE, SORE, WORE, WORN

and

• alternative *to* decay	ROTOR
• choose alternative	ELECTOR
• man *with* alternative . . .	MANOR
• out-of-date alternative	PASTOR
• fellow *with* alternative . . .	DONOR
alternative solution to [clue]	LUCE
alternative technology	AT
alternative [to her] . . .	OTHER, THROE

altitude

altitude	ALT
altitude, *say*	HIGHT

alto ALT

alumnus OB

always

always	AY, AYE, EVER
• learner always . . .	LAY
• always *in* the way	RAYED
• always *in debt*	REVERED
always	FORAY

amalgamate

amalgamate [ores]	ROES, SORE
amalgamating [teams]	MATES, STEAM
amalgamation of [parties]	PASTIER

amateur

amateur	A
amateur	HAM
• amateur bandsman	(RADIO) HAM
• amateur lost blood	HAMBLED
• amateur town, *say*	HAMBURG
amateur	LAY
• amateur circles	LAIC, LAITY
• amateur cricket side	LAY OFF
• quiet amateur	PLAY
amateur's department	DIY

amazing

amazed [by a] . . .	BAY
Amazing [Grace]	CAGER
amazing [thing]	NIGHT

ambassador

ambassador	HE
• ambassador attending	HEAT
• ambassador speaks	HEADDRESSES

Letter replaced \c\at; Omit (a); Pointers *out*; Retain <u>a</u>; Split B_ED; Down (D); Backwards <or ^

• ambassador's residence	HEADDRESS	American sports pitch	SCREWBALL
ambiguous		American tug	YANK
ambiguous [words]	SWORD	**amid**	
ambiguously [said]	DAIS	*amid* t/he w/aves	HEW
ambition		*amid*ship	(in) S–S
ambition at the age of		*amid* *	incl in *
–three, *say*	BEFORE	• many *amid* trees	FIRMS
–eight	BENIGN	* *amid*	incl *
–nine, *say*	BEATEN	• I *am amid* breakers	WAIVES
ambivalent		**amiss**	
ambivalence [over] . . .	ROVE	[goes] *amiss*	EGOS
ambivalent [male]	LAME, MEAL	[went] *amiss*	NEWT
ambivalent person	NOYES	**ammunition supplier**	MAGAZINE,
amend			ROUNDSMAN
amend [speech]	CHEEPS	**among**	
amended [later]	ALTER	among Berbers	MIDRIFFS
amendment of [law]	AWL	among peopl/e at a	
America(n)[1]		ble/ak . . .	EATABLE
American	AM	*among* *	incl in *
• American employed	AMUSED	• she *is among* ma–d . . .	MASHED
• American in charge		* *among*	incl *
can . . .	AMICABLE	• is *among* engineers	RISE
• American shrub	AMBUSH	**amount**	
• American woman	AMRITA	amount of metrication	LITRE
American	AMER	*amount of* metri/cat/ion	CAT
• American church	AMERCE	**ampere**	A
• American in Germany	AMERIND	**amphibian**	
American	US	amphibian, *say*	TOED
• American can . . .	USABLE	amphibian leg	NEWTON
• American journalist	USED	amphibian working	NEWTON
• American period	USAGE	**amputate**	
• American woman	USHER	amputate feet	DOCKYARD
and		*amputate* fee(t)	FEE
• American beauty queen	MISSUS	*amputate* th(e) . . .	TH
• American sailors	TARSUS	*amputation of* to(e)	TO
• American school period	TERMINUS	**amplitude modulation**	AM
• born American	BUS	**amusing**	
• round America	–OUS	amusing detour	DIVERSION
• this *Latin*-American	HOCUS	amusing fellow	FUNGUS
and		amusing fellow, *say*	FUNGI
• American *in* Abe's . . .	ABUSES	amusing, *say*	HUMERUS
• American *in* acid test	PUSH	**an**	
• American *in* me	MUSE	an	A
and		–abscess	ABOIL
• *in* America	U–S	–assignation, *say*	ATTRIST
American[2]		–attic	ALOFT
American address	GETTYSBURG	–empty space	AVOID
American banker	MISSISSIPPI, etc	–entrance	AGATE
American capital	DOLLAR	–entrance, *say*	ADORE
American *capital*	A	–incursion, *say*	ARRAYED
American citizen	STATESMAN	–infection, *say*	ATTAINT
American doctrine	MONROE	–insect, *say*	ATTIC
American drag	YANK	–interval, *say*	ARREST
American exclamation	OGEE	–Italian leader, *say*	ADDUCE
American *flower*	MISSISSIPPI, etc	–objection	ABUT
American *leader*	A	–ocean	AMAIN
American saloon	SEDAN	–opening	AGAT

Anag [cat]; Any *; Begin IGN–; Endings –ING; eg •; Hidden /cat/; Implied add (on); Implied in (in);

–orchestra	ALSO	angel	BACKER
–orchestra playing	ABANDON		MICHAEL, RAPHAEL et al
–ulcer	ABOIL	**anger**	
–upright state	APICAL	anger, *say*	BHYLE, CALLER, COLLAR
–urge	AITCH	angry	*(see separate entry)*
an *absent*	omit AN	**angle**	
• a dog *with* an *absent*	SP(an)IEL	angle	FISH
an *Italian* . . .	UNA, UNO	• angle iron	FISH CLUB, FISH-PRESS
an *uprising*(D)^	NA	angle	L
	(see also a)	**Anglican worship**	CE
anaesthetic		**Anglo-**	
anaesthetic	NUMBER	Anglo-American	EAM
anaesthetic, *say*	EITHER	Anglo-French waters	SEAMER
analysis		Anglo-Saxon	AS
analyse failure	BREAKDOWN	**angry**	
analysed [ores]	EROS, ROES, SORE	*angrily* [throw]	WORTH
analysis of [soil]	OILS, SILO	angry	CROSS
analyst's bike, *say*	PSYCHICAL	• angry allusion	CROSS-REFERENCE
anarchist		• angry European, *say*	CROSS-CHECK
anarchist	RED		CROSS CHEQUE
• anarchist dead, *say*	REDDED	• angry lawyers	CROSSBAR
• anarchist lair	REDDEN	• angry man CROSS-PARTY, GEORGE CROSS	
• anarchist ring	REDO	• angry wound	CROSSCUT
	(see also communist)	angry	HOT
ancestral tree	ELDER	• angry footballer	HOTSPUR
anchor-worm	FLUKE	• angry soldiers	HOTFOOT
ancient		angry	SORE
ancient	ANC, FLAG	• angry man, *say* SORAL, SORDES, SORTED	
ancient	AGED	• angry saint	SOREST
• ancient mother	DAMAGED	• angry soldiers	FOOTSORE
• ancient orchestra	BANDAGED	*angry* [lion]	LOIN, NOIL
ancient		angry motorist	HORNBLOWER
indicating old words:		[pace] *angrily*	CAPE
• *ancient* goat	GATE	**angström**	A
• *ancient* friend	INGLE	**animal¹**	
• *ancient* poet-laureate	ARCH-POET	animal	
	(see also old³)	–attacks say	BULRUSHES
ancient city	TROY, UR	–club	PIG–IRON
ancient hunter	OLD TIMER	–cunning	ASSART
Ancient Mariner	NOAH, SHELLBACK	–devoured	BULLATE
ancient, *say*	ANTIC	–family	DOGSKIN
ancient times	BC	–fastener, *say*	BULLOCK
ancient vessel	ARK	–fodder	CATHAY
ancient weapon	PISTOL	–fur	CATNAP
and		–got up	DOG–ROSE
and *French* . . .	ET	–*has* a right . . .	ASSART
and *German* . . .	UND	–joint	DOGSHIP
and not	NOR	–king	WOLFER
and *Roman* . . .	ET	–painting	ASSART
and *without* a . . .	(a)ND	–sees	OX–EYES
ane	A, I	–sleeps	BULLDOZES
anent	ON, RE	–speculator	STAG
	(see about²)	–talk	YAK
anew		–torment	BADGER
[made] *anew*	DAME, EDAM, MEAD	–trail	DOG, PIGTAIL
[men hope] *anew*	PHENOME	–trap	PIGGIN
		–with	

Letter replaced \c\at; Omit (a); Pointers *out*; Retain <u>a</u>; Split B_ED; Down (D); Backwards <or ^

mother	DOGMA
nothing on	RATOON
–would wander, *say*	HIPPODROME
animals mounted	CATSUP
animal's teacher, *say*	COWSHED
animal²	
[Animal] *Crackers*	LAMINA, MANILA
Animal Farm	RANCH, STUD
animal feet, *say*	PAUSE
animal friend, *say*	BRUTALLY
animal group, *say*	HEARD
animal rescuer	NOAH
animal, *say*	BARE, HOARSE,
	LAMA, LAM
	LINKS, STERE, WHORES,
	YEW, YOU
animal *sound*	BRUIT
animal's home	INSTALL
animate	
animated [scene I] . . .	NIECES
animation of [animal]	LAMINA, MANILA
[spoke] *animatedly*	POKES
Anitra	
[Anitra's] *Dance*	ARTISAN
Annie Oakley	MISFIRING
announce	
announce their . . .	THERE
announce you and me, *say*	STATUS
announcement of time	THYME
annoy	
annoy informer	NARK
annoying habit	HAIR SHIRT
annual	
annual	PA
• annual camp	PATENT
• annual payment	PARENT
• annual right	PART
• annual *return<*	AP
annual meeting	AGM
anoint	
anoint, *say*	ANNEAL
anonymous	
anonymous	AN
• *anonymous* queen	ANER
anonymous	omit N
• *anonymous* ma(n)	MA
another	
another form of male . . .	LAME, MEAL
another husband	SECOND MATE
another order for [lamb]	BALM
another order [given to] . . .	VETOING
another order given to [army]	MARY, MYRA
another shape [I drew]	WEIRD
another spell of weather	W(H)ETHER
another way of	
putting [things]	NIGHTS
another way to [put] . . .	TUP
answer	
answer	ANS
• answer *back<*	SNA–
• one answer	–IANS
answer	KEY
• answer letter	KEY-NOTE
• answer telephone	KEY-RING
answer	LIGHT
• answer head	LIGHTNESS
• teacher *with* the answer	HEADLIGHT
• team answer	SIDELIGHT
ante	A
antelope	
antelope	BUCK
• antelope has been, *say*	BUCKBEAN
• antelope is warm	BUCKSHOT
• antelope *with* sheep	BUCKRAM
• antelope's family	BUCKSKIN
antelope	DOE
• antelope's family	DOESKIN
• *old* does	DOTH
antelope, *say*	KNEW, NEW
antelopes, *say*	NEWS
anti-	
anti-aircraft	AA, ARCHIE
anti-aircraft fire	UPSHOT
anti-American	NOUS
anti-ballistic missile	ABM
anti-tetanus serum	ATS
anticipate	
anticipate no share	EXPECTORATION
anticipating	(in) HOP–E
antiquarian	FAS, SAS
any	
any other business	AOB
any, *say*	NE
any [sort]	ORTS, TORS
[any] *sort*	NAY
anybody	ALL, ONE
anyhow [I am] . . .	AIM, AMI
any[thing]	NIGHT
anyway	
indicating a palindrome:	
• *anyway*, a flop	DUD
• father *anyway* . . .	DAD, POP
anyway [let us] . . .	LUTES
in any *case*	AN–Y
aorist	AOR
apart	
apart [from] . . .	FORM
apart from a . . .	omit A
apart from a new . . .	omit AN
apart from the front	omit 1st letter
apart from the leader	omit 1st letter
apart from name	omit N
apart from *	omit *
• fa(the)r *apart from* the . . .	FAR

Anag [cat]; Any *; Begin IGN–; Endings –ING; eg •; Hidden /cat/; Implied add (on); Implied in (in);

[tear] *apart*	RATE, TARE	apply conditioning	BRAINWASH
apiary		**apportion**	
apiary, *say*	APRE	*apportion* [blame]	MABEL
apogee	APO	*apportionment of* [shares]	SHEARS
apoplectic		**appreciate**	
apoplectic [general]	ENLARGE	appreciate	DIG
apoplectically [rave]	AVER	• appreciate it	DIGIT
apostle		• appreciates lodgings	DIGS
apostle, *say*	LOOK, MARC	appreciate	GROW
appal		• appreciate new	GROWN
appalling [thing]	NIGHT	• appreciate trousers	GROW-BAGS
appallingly [made]	DAME, EDAM, MEAD	**apprehend**	
apparent		*apprehend* a . . .	incl A
apparent, *say*	APP	*apprehend* *	incl *
apparent in t/he w/ay . . .	HEW	• police *apprehended* husband	CHOPS
apparently	APP	*apprehended by* *	incl in *
apparently not	KNOT	• husband *apprehended* by police	CHOPS
appeal		**apprentice**	
appeal	IT	apprentice	APP, L
appeal	O	apprentice cook	DEVIL
• appeal for fish, *say*	OBLIQUE	(*see also* learner)	
• appeal for insects, *say*	OBESE, OBIS		
• appeal for money	OGIVE	**appropriate**	
• appeal to cog	OPINION	appropriate the lady's,	
• appeal to costume, *say*	OLIVARY	say	KNICKERS
• appeal to friends	OPALS	appropriate title	NICKNAME
• appeal to girl, *say*	ODORINE	**approve**	
• appeal to governor	OBEY	approval	OK(AY)
• appeal to Kenneth, *say*	OAKEN	approve wine	PASSPORT
• appeal to make	OCREATE	**approx**	C, CA, CIRC
• appeal to make, *say*	OCHREATE		SOME
• appeal to male sex	OMEN		(*see* about[1])
• appeal to purchase, *say*	OCELLUS	**APRE**	APIARY
• appeal to sailor	ORATING	**April**	
• appeal to vendor, *say*	OCELLAR	April *1st*	A
appeal	SA, SOS	April 1st	MARCH-PAST
appealing	CUTE	**apron**	
appear		apron manufacturer	STAGE MANAGER
appear smaller, *say*	SEAMLESS	apron producer	FIG-TREE
appear [untidy]	NUDITY	**aquiver**	
appearance in tw/ice ni/ghtly...	ICENI	*aquiver* [over sin]	VERSION
appeared injured	BLED	[he's] *aquiver*	SHE
appeared loud	TURNED UP	**Arab**	
appears in . . .	incl *	Arab	AR
• it *appears in* an opening	AGITATE	• Arab adversary	ARRIVAL
appears in We/st End s/how	STENDS	• Arab girl	ARENA, ARGAL
appears to be weak	WEEK	• Arab *on* camel	ARRIDING
appears to be [worse]	SWORE	• Arab torture	ARRACK
appears to have so/me tal/l...	METAL	and	
apple		• Arab *in* Maine	MARE
apple *core*	P	• man *embracing* Arab	DARES
apple juice, *say*	SIDER	• soldiers *surround* Arab	RARE
apple *peel*	AE	Arab	HORSE
apple picker	EVE	• Arab drama	HORSE OPERA, HORSEPLAY
apple tree	OAK	• Arab fight	HORSE BOX
apples (and pears)	STAIRS	• Arab money	HORSE BRASS
apply		Arab chieftain, *say*	CHIC, SHAKE
		Arab's cry	NEIGH, WHINNY

Letter replaced \c\at; Omit (a); Pointers *out*; Retain a; Split B_ED; Down (D); Backwards <or ^

Arab's cry, *say*	NAY, WINNIE	• argumentative oarsman	ROWER
Arabia	UAR	• quiet argument	PROW
arable land	LEA, LEY	• th(e) *short* argument	THROW
Aramaic	SYRIAC	**aright**	AR, ART
arbitrary		**Arion's rescuer**	DOLPHIN
arbitrary [rules]	LURES	**arise**	
[demand] *arbitrarily*	DAMNED	*arise*, Sir . . .(D)^	RIS-
arch		*arising* as an . . .(D)^	NASA
arch	CHIEF	*arising from* [a new] . . .	WANE, WEAN
• chief method	ARCHWAY	*arising from* se/a dept/ths	ADEPT
• chief queen	ARCHER	may *arise*(D)^	YAM
• novice chief	LARCH	**aristocrat**	
archaeopteryx	EARLY BIRD	aristocratic	U
archaic	ARCH	aristocrat's carriage	TUMBREL, TUMBRIL
	(*see also* old³)	**arm**	
archangel	GABRIEL, MICHAEL et al	arm-lock	(HALF-)NELSON
	RECORDING HEAD	arm rest	SLING
archbishop	ABP	[arm]-*twisting*	MAR, RAM
	CANTUAR, EBOR, LAMBETH	[arm]-*wrestling*	MAR, RAM
	LANG, LAUD et al	armed female	BRITANNIA
archdeacon	VEN	armed timer	WRISTWATCH
arched flyover	RAINBOW, VIADUCT	armless female	VENUS
archer	CUPID, EROS	arms limitation	STRAIT JACKET
	HOOD, TELL	**Armenian**	ARM, HAIKH
architect		**armour**	
architect	PLANGENT	armour-*plated*	(in) M–AIL
architect	ADAM, WREN, WRIGHT et al	armour, *say*	MALE
• architect *and* worker	ADAMANT	**army**	
• architect, honoured	WRENCH	army	TA
• high-flying architect	WRIGHT	• army advanced	TALENT
architect's office	DRAWING-ROOM	• army engineer	TARE
architecture	ARCH	• army man	TAKEN, TALES
Arctic animal	POLAR BEAR, POLECAT	• army family, *say*	TAKE-IN
ardent		• army leader	TAKING
ardent, *say*	EAGRE	• army minstrel	TABARD
arduous		• army team	TAXI
arduous [task 'e] . . .	SKATE	and	
[slog] *arduously*	LOGS	• Dad's Army	PASTA
are		• farewell to army	VALETA
are, *say*	R	• fight an army	SPARTA
are (metric)	A	army chaplain	HCF, OCF
are not	ANT	army command	ATTENTION, SHUN
are you *and* I *said* . . .	RUI–	army dentists	RADC
are spotted, *say*	ARSINE	army doctors	RAMC
area		army entertainer	HOST
area	A	army group devoured	UNITATE
• area *behind* fish	CODA	army jumper	PARATROOPER
• area *in front of church*	ACE, ARC	army MC	HOST
• area *to* left	AL(T)	army paymasters	RAPC
• area *to* right	ALIEN, AR(T)	army rations	WARFARE
• area transport	ABUSES	army, *say*	HOAST
argentine		army teachers	RAEC
argentine	SILVER	army technicians	REME
Argentine cast	INGOT	army vets	RAVC
argonaut	JASON		(*see also* reserve, soldier)
argument		**around**[1]	
argument	ROW	meaning: about	

approximately	
roughly, etc	(see about¹)
around²	
around (=a round)	O
• around following doctor	VETO
• around in ho–t . . .	HOOT
• around on soldiers . . .	OMEN
around [town]	WONT
around a . . .	incl A
around *	incl *
• run around one . . .	RUIN
run around<	NUR
arrange	
arrange board	PLAN TABLE, PLANTABLE
arrange, say	MARTIAL
arrange [table]	BLATE, BLEAT
arranged	ARR
arranged [a new] . . .	WANE, WEAN
arranged rose	GOT UP
arrangement of locks	COIFFURE, HAIR-DO
arrangement of roses	BOUQUET, POSY
arrangement of [roses]	SORES
[secret] arrangement	RESECT
arrest	
arrest a . . .	incl A
arrest one group	CO-PILOT
arrest head	COP
arrest suspect	APPREHEND
arrest *	incl *
• police arrest king	CORPS
arrested by *	incl in *
• king arrested by police	CORPS
arrested, say	COPT
arrive	
arrival	AR, ARR
arrive	AR, ARR
arrived finally	D
arrived frequently, say	CAMELOT
arrived with an artist	CAMERA
arrow	
arrowhead	A
arrow-maker	FLETCHER
ars	RR
arsenal	
Arsenal's journal	MAGAZINE
Arsenal's shots	GUNFIRE
arsonist's case	MATCHBOX
art	
art class	GENRE
art committee	DRAWING-BOARD
[art] form	RAT, TAR
[Art] Nouveau	RAT, TAR
art of potter	ONEUPMANSHIP
art school, say	SLAYED
artful place	MUSEUM, STUDIO
artless	NORA
[art]work	RAT, TAR

arty, say	RT
artery	
artery, say	JUGGLER
Arthur's place	CAMELOT
article	
article	ART
English article	A, AN, IT, THE
• article on poetry	AVERSE
	ANODE
• article in church	CITE
• artist has article . . .	RATHE
French article	LE, LA, LES, UN, UNE
French/English articles	LATHE
French/German articles	UNDER
German article	DAS, DER, DIE, EIN, EINE
Italian article	IL, LA, LE, UNA, UNO
Spanish article	EL, LA, LAS, LO
	LOS, UNA, UNO
Spanish/Italian articles	ELLA
articulate	
articulation of bone	BEAUNE
articulated aloud	ALLOWED
articulated one . . .	WON
articulated lorry	LAURIE
artificial	
artificial	ART
artificial diamond	SHAMROCK
artificial flowers	CANALS
artificial stone	SHAMROCK
artificial [stone]	NOTES, ONSET
	SETON, TONES
artillery	ART(Y), HA, HAC, RA
artisan	
artisan, say	RIGHT, RITE, WRITE
artist	
artist	ARA
• artist-fellow	ARAF
• artist-graduate	ARABA
• artist is English	ARISE
artist	PRA
• artist I exalt	PRAISING
• artist not known	PRANK
• artist unknown	PRAY
artist	RA
• artist ran	RASPED
• artist wearing a jacket	RAINCOAT
• artist with complaint	RAGOUT, RASORES
• Cockney artist	RAINBOW
and	
• horse artist	COBRA
• male artist	HERA
• police artist	COPRA
artist	CLAUDE, ETTY, LELY et al
artist, say	–TITION
artist, Turner<	REWARD
artist's board, say	PALATE
	(see also painter)

as

as	AS
• as an indication	ASSIGN
• as below	ASUNDER
• as quiet	ASP
as	LIKE
• as a baby	CHILDLIKE
• as divine . . .	GODLIKE
• as Edward	LIKENED
as	QUA
• as king	QUAKING
• as light	QUAVERY
• as unknown	QUAY
and	
• like a building	QUASHED
• like a caravan	QUATRAIN
• like the *Italian*	QUAIL
as	SO
• as below	SOUNDER
• as deep, *say*	SOLO
• as far, *say*	SOFA
• as thick, *say*	SOTHIC
as a [rule]	LURE
as above	US, UT SUPRA
as arranged, [Alsatians] . . .	ASSAILANT
as before	
indicating an old word:	
• roast, *as before*	ROST
• *as before*, in another	
way OTHERGATES, OTHERGUESS	
as if he would	HEED
as if some on . . .	SUMMON
as far as I'm concerned	TOME
as it happens	LIVE
as it turns out [her top] . . .	POTHER
as said	UT DICT(UM)
as said by a . . .	BUYER
as stated, he'll . . .	HEAL, HEEL
as the poet said	(*see* poetic)
as the writer put it	SIC, STET
as you like it	AYLI
as you say, we'll . . .	WEAL, WHEEL
ash dispenser	ETNA etc VOLCANO

Asian

Asian	E
• Asian study	EDEN
• Asian treaty	EPACT
• faint Asian . . .	DIME
Asian (in East)	INE
• Asian training	INEPT
• fellow *with* Asian . . .	FINE
• swindle Asian	CONINE
Asian adder	INDIAN SUMMER
Asian *flower*	MEKONG etc
<u>A</u>sian *leader*	A

ask

ask	BEG
• ask a person	BEGONE
• ask Barnaby	BEGRUDGE
• ask for fish	BEGGAR
• ask in	BEGIN
ask for . . .	FORE, FOUR
asked aloud	ALLOWED
asking for tea	FORTY

askew

askew, *say*	RILEY
[goes] *askew*	EGOS
[it was] *askew*	WAIST, WAITS
[went] *askew*	NEWT

asleep

asparagus

OUT	
asparagus tip	SPEARHEAD
<u>a</u>sparagu<u>s</u> *tips*	AS

aspect

aspect, *say*	GUYS

asphyxiate

asphyxiate	GAS
• asphyxiate family	GASKIN
• asphyxiate lad, *say*	GAS-BUOY

aspiration

aspiration	H
aspirations	HH

assail

assail, *say*	COURSE, JIB, SHEET
	SPINNAKER etc
assail a number, *say*	PELTATE

assassin

assassin	BOOTH, OSWALD
assassinate	KILL
• assassinate Edward	KILLED, KILTED
• assassinate ruler	KILLER
• assassinate that man, *say*	KHILIM

assault

assault course	PUNCH LINE
assault man	MUGGENT
assault, *say*	SAILOR

assemble

a rum *assembly*	ARUM
assembled [ratings]	STARING
assembly [line]	LIEN, NEIL, NILE
assembly, *say*	COUNSEL
[General] *Assembly*	ENLARGE

assign

assign [blame]	AMBLE, MABEL
assign property	ATTRIBUTE

assimilate

assimilate a rum	ARUM
assimilate a . . .	incl A
assimilate *	incl *
• companion *assimilates* rum	CRUMB
assimilated by *	incl in *
• rum *assimilated by*	
companion	CRUMB

assistant

assistant	ASST

associate	A
associate fellow	AF
associate member	AM
associate of Bacon	EGGS
associate of drunk	DISORDERLY
associated with tart, *say*	HOARD, HORDE
association	ASS(N)
assort	
assorted [nuts]	STUN, TUNS
assortment of [hooks]	SHOOK
assume	
assume	DON
assume a . . .	incl A
assume *	incl *
• P–a *assumes* it . . .	PITA
assume, *say*	HARROGATE
assume title	DON
assumed by *	incl in *
• it *is assumed by* P–a . . .	PITA
assure	
assurance company	PRU
assured, *say*	CONFIDANT(E)
astern	
astern was . . . <	SAW
follow *astern*<	GOD
astray	
astray [in the] . . .	THINE
[doesn't go] *astray*	STEGODON
[went] *astray*	NEWT
astride	
girl *astride* a horse	JACOBEAN
pa–ge *astride* a donkey	PASSAGE
astronaut's pub	SPACE-BAR
astronomical unit	AU
astute	
[astute] *move*	STATUE
astutely [I sold] . . .	SOLID
asylum	CRANKCASE
at¹	AT
a̲t first	A
at *first*	start with AT
• male at *first*	ATMAN
at *first* s̲ight	S
at *heart*	incl AT
• h–e at *heart*	HATE
at *last*	end with AT
• shape at *last*	FORMAT
a̲t *last*	T
(a)t *losing* a . . .	T
at one on	–ATION
at one point	ATE, ATS
a̲t *the back*	T
at *the back*	end with AT
• be at *the back*	BEAT
a̲t *the beginning*	A
at *the beginning*	start with AT
• pamphlet at *the beginning*	ATTRACT
at *the bottom*(D)^	T
at *the centre*	incl AT
• at *the centre of the* Civil Service . . .	CATS
a̲t *the end*	T
at th̲e *end*	ATE
at *the end* . . .	end with AT
• flourished at *the end* . . .	FLAT
a̲t *the front*	A
at *the front*	start with AT
• tear at *the front*	ATRIP
at *the middle*	incl AT
• we *with* her at	
the middle	WEATHER
a̲t *the rear*	T
at th̲e *rear*	ATE
at *the rear*	end with AT
• about at *the rear*	CAT
a̲t *the start*	A
at *the start*	start with AT
• one at *the start*	ATONE
at²	
indicating origins:	
at Cardiff Arms Park (=Welsh)	
• fervour *at Cardiff Arms Park*	HWYL
at Hampden Park (=Scottish)	
• game *at St Andrews*	GOWF
at Longchamps (=French)	
• horse *at Longchamps*	CHEVAL
at sea (=nautical expression)	
• behind *at sea*	ABAFT, ASTERN
• change course *at sea*	TACK
• stop *at sea*	AVAST, BELAY
at³	
other uses:	
at cross purposes	VOTING
at fault [when] . . .	HEWN
at first	incl –IST
• almost pur(r) *at first*	PURIST
at first s̲ight	S
at heart s/he w/was . . .	HEW
at heart *	incl *
• young *at heart*	INCUBUS
at home	IN, (in) N–EST
at last, winter . . .	R
at odds [over] . . .	ROVE
at one time	(see old)
at pleasure	AD LIB(ITUM)
at random, [cast] . . .	CATS, SCAT
at rest	(in) B–ED, (in) C–OT
at sea [all the] . . .	LETHAL
at suit of	ATS
at the bottom of(D)	
• about *at the bottom of*	
the river	PORE
at the bottom of th̲e . . .(D)	E
at the double	(in) HAST–E
at the end	AD FINIT(UM)

Letter replaced \c\at; Omit (a); Pointers *out*; Retain a̲; Split B_ED; Down (D); Backwards <or ^

at the finish	(in) EN–D
at the heart of *	incl in *
• one *at the heart of* he–r . . .	HEIR
at the heart of a/ny ala/rm system	NYALA
at the outset she told youth	STY
at the place	AD LOC(UM)
at the police-station	OFF-BEAT
at the wicket	BATTING, IN
at this place	AHL
at this word	AHV
at university	UP
at war	(in) AC–TION, INACTION
at what place?, *say*	WARE, WEAR
	WEIGHER
at what time?, *say*	WEN
at work	(in) HAR–NESS, INFIRM
at work, [boredom] . . .	BEDROOM
[ship] *at sea*	HIPS, PISH
* *at first*	start with *
• detectives ran *at first*	RANCID
* *at heart*	incl *
• sick *at heart*	SILLY
• wax is *at heart*	CERISE
* *at last*	end with *
• credit one *at last* . . .	CRONE
* *at the beginning*	start with *
• sweet, not *at the beginning*	NOTICE
* *at the end*	end with *
• quiet in *the end*	SHIN
* *at the middle*	incl *
• be *at the middle*	ABED, ABET
ate	
ate *about* . . .	A–TE
• ate *about* 51 . . .	ALITE
ate *up* (D)^	DEF–, ETA
ate bird	BITTERN
ate, *say*	AIT, EIGHT, EYOT
ate tea, *say*	EIGHTY
ate twice, *say*	PECTATE
Athenian	TIMON
athlete	
athlete	BLUE
• athlete understands, *say*	BLUENOSE
athletic team	ALLOA, CHARLTON
Atlantic	POND
atmosphere	ATM
atom	
atomic	A
atomic number	Z
atomised [town]	WONT
atomising [spray]	PRAYS
attach	
attached to a . . .	incl A
• *attached to* a stake	ABET, BETA
• stake *attached to* a . . .	ABET, BETA
attached to *	incl *
• animal *attached to* her . . .	RATHER

attack	
attack	GOAT
• attack animals	GOATHERD
• attack fish	GOATLING
attack equipment	CLOBBER
attack spirits	MUGGINS
attack worker	ASSAILANT
attacking bat	DRACULA
attend	
attend	BEAT
attend	SERVE
• attend Scotsman, *say*	SERVIAN
• attend worker, *say*	SERVANT
attendant	PAGE
• attendant insect	PAGEANT
• attendant worker	PAGEANT
attending	AT
• attending ceremony, *say*	ATTRITE
• attending cricket match	ATTEST
• attending robbery	ATHEIST
• attending trial	ATTEST
attending lesson	(in) FOR–M, INFORM
attorney	ATT
Attorney-General	AG
attract	
attract	DRAW
• attract fish	DRAWLING
• attract game	DRAWBRIDGE
attractive	CUTE, DISHY
attractive	WITHDRAW
• attractive artist	DRAWER
• attractive artwork	DRAWING
attractive bar	MAGNET
attractive binding	ENGAGING
attractive girl	BELLE, CUTIE, DISH
	DOLLY, PEACH, STUNNER
attractive instrument	GLAMORGAN
attractive rock	LODESTONE
attractive strip	MAGNETIC TAPE
au pair	FOREIGN EXCHANGE
auction	
auction, *say*	SAIL
audio-	
audible beat	BEET, TIC
audible pause	PAWS
audibly weak	WEEK, FEINT
audience hears a noise	ANNOYS
audio frequency	AF
audio-visual	AV
auditor adds	ADZE
auditors	EARS, SAA
augmentative	AUG
August	AUG
aunt	
Auntie Jennifer, *say*	ANTIGEN
aunt's pain	AGONY
aureole	HEADLIGHT, O

Anag [cat]; Any *; Begin IGN–; Endings –ING; eg •; Hidden /cat/; Implied add (on); Implied in (in);

Australia	
Australia	AUS, DOWN UNDER, OZ
Australian *capital*	A
Australian *flower*	DARLING etc
Australian *leader*	A
author	
author	STERNE, WELLS et al
author, *say*	REITER
author's *opening* . . .	A
author's place	WELLS
author's statement, *say*	IRITE
authorise	
authorisation	OK(AY)
authorise embargo	SANCTION
authorise penalty	SANCTION
Authorised Version	AV
autobiography	
autobiography	CV
autobiographical subject	I, ME
automatic	
automatic data processing	ADP
automatic pilot	GEORGE
automatic, *say*	HANDGUN
autumn	
autumn	FALL
• autumn trip	FALL
• wet autumn	RAINFALL, WATERFALL
available	
available *in* [shop]	HOPS, POSH
available *in* so/me sh/ops	MESH
avenue	AV(E)
average	
average	AVE(R)
• about average	CAVE(R)
• average state	AVER
• right average	RAVE(R)
average	MEAN
• average period	MEANTIME
• average square	MEANT
• the *Camptown* average	DEMEAN
average	MED
• army *has* average . . .	TAMED
• "Average", I state	MEDICAL
• average man	MEDAL
average	PAR
• average man	PARED, PARIAN, PARTED
• average ruler	PARKING
• average sum	PARAMOUNT
average entertainment	FAIR
average, *say*	MIEN
avert	
aversion therapy, *say*	COUNTERPANE
averted [crash]	CHARS
Avogadro's number	N
avoid[1]	
avoid	DUCK
• avoid fish	DUCKLING

• avoid payment	DUCKBILL
avoid city	DODGE
avoid container	SKIP
avoid surgery	BYPASS
avoid talons, *say*	ESCAPE CLAUSE
avoided issue	CHILDLESS
avoids carrier	SLIPSHOD
avoid[2]	
indicating omission:	
avoid a . . .	omit A
avoid drug	omit E
avoid extremes of (h)ea(t)	EA
avoid one not drinking	omit TT
avoid publicity	omit AD
avoid students	omit LL, LS
avoid *	omit *
• mon(k)ey *avoids* king	MONEY
I'd *avoided*	omit ID
Avonville	BATH
award	
award	CH
• award a member	CHAMP, CHARM
• each award . . .	PERCH
award	MEDAL
• award *to* star	MEDALLION
award	OBE
• award *to* animal	OBELION
• award *to* man	OBERON
• royal award	ROBE
award	OM
• award an . . .	OMAN
• h–e *grabs* award	HOME
(*see also* honour, order)	
away	
away (=a way)	–ARD
• away *with* our . . .	ARDOUR
• many away	CARD, LARD
• away *in* h–er . . .	HARDER
away (=a way)	–AST
• away *in* sea	MASTED
• Away *with* king!	ASTER
• many away	CAST, LAST
away	OUT
• away in Greece	OUTING
• Away *with* work!	OUTPOST
• many away	CLOUT, LOUT
away result	OFFEND
away south	omit S
away with a . . .	omit A
away *	omit *
miles *away*	omit M
awful	
awful display of [art]	TAR
awful [part]	PRAT, TRAP
awful people, *say*	DIATRIBE
awful weight	DIRECT
awfully [tired]	TRIED

Letter replaced \c\at; Omit (a); Pointers *out*; Retain <u>a</u>; Split B_ED; Down (D); Backwards <or ^

awkward		[pole]-*axed*	LOPE
awkward angle	OBTUSE	**axiom**	AX
awkward [sort]	ORTS, ROTS, TORS	**ay**	
[I creep] *awkwardly*	PIERCE	ay(e)	A, I
axe		ay(e)s	AS, IS
axed [a fir]	FAIR	**azimuth**	AZ

B

a follower, Bach, bachelor, baron, bass, bay, bed-bug, *bee*, Beethoven, bel, Belgium, beta, beth, billion, binary, bishop, black, blessed, bloodgroup, *bloody*, book, born, boron, bowled, boy, Brahms, breadth, Britain, British, *inferior*, key, magnetic flux, note, *paper*, *road*, *second*, *second-class*, second letter, three hundred, three thousand, vitamin

B	
B–	BLESS
B9	BENIGN
B10	BEATEN
B minor	BLESS
B minus	BLESS
B row	BRACKET
babe	RUTH
baby	
baby bird	STORK
baby-carriage	GESTATION
baby slept	KIDNAPPED
Babylonian	URGENT
bachelor	
bachelor	B
• bachelor *has* study	BLAIR
• bachelor is *French*	BEST
• strike bachelor	LAMB
bachelor	BA
• bachelor *has* study	BACON
• bachelor *with* jolly . . .	BARM
• strange bachelor	RUMBA
bachelor of	
–Arts	AB, BA
–Civil Law	BCL
–Commerce	BCOM(M)
–Dental Surgery	BDS
–Divinity	BD
–Education	BED, EDB
–Engineering	BAI, BE, BENG
–Law	BL, LLB
–Letters	BL
–Literature	BLITT
–Medicine	BM, MB
–Music	BMUS
–Philosophy	PHB
–Science	BS, BSC, SCB
–Surgery	BCH, BS, CHB
Bach's works	S
back¹	
indicating reversal:	
back again<	ER

back-cloth<	ERIC, MINED
back door<	ROOD
back-drop<	PROD
back-end of year<	CED
back entry<	ROOD
back-flow<	WOLF
back-heel<	TAR
back line<	KNAR
back number<	NET, ON
back pay<	YAP
back room<	MOOR
back street<	DR, TS
back stretch<	EMIT
back to . . .<	OT
back to front bat<	TAB
back trouble<	LIA
back-up<	PU
back-up may . . .<	YAM
back way<	DR, TS, YAW
back way in<	NI
back-yard<	DRAY
*back*bite<	PIN, WANG
*back*fall<	PROD
*back*firing guns<	SNUG
*back*hand<	RAT
backing horse<	RECAP
*back*saw<	WAS
*back*side<	IX, NO
*back*sliding VIPs<	SPIV
*back*spin<	NIPS
*back*stop<	POTS
*back*tracking deer<	REED
*back*water<	LOOP
pay *back*<	YAP
back²	
back	BET
• back leg	BETON
back	REAR
• back China	REARMING
• back number	REARM
• back row of violins	REARGUES
• back to sea	REARMED

Letter replaced \c\at; Omit (a); Pointers *out*; Retain <u>a</u>; Split B_ED; Down (D); Backwards <or ^

back biter	MOLAR, WISDOM TOOTH	bad speller	MAGICIAN, WARLOCK
back bite<u>r</u>	R		WITCH, WIZARD
back down	FACE UP	bad spelling	CHARMING
back dow<u>n</u>	N	bad tempered man	CROSSPIECE
back end of yea<u>r</u>	R	*badly affected* [by a] . . .	BAY
back in front	RUMPLED	*badly constructed* [table]	BLATE, BLEAT
back number	EPIDURAL, SPINAL	*badly designed* [town]	WONT
back numbe<u>r</u>	R	*badly missed*	omit ILL
back of beyon<u>d</u>	D	• *badly missed* fr(ill)y . . .	FRY
back of lorry	TAILBOARD	*badly* [organised]	GRANDIOSE
back of lorr<u>y</u>	Y	*badly organised* [trips]	SPIRT, SPRIT
back of neck	NAPE		STRIP
back of nec<u>k</u>	K	*badly treated* [men at] . . .	MEANT
back of truc<u>k</u> <u>he</u> ra<u>n</u>	KEN	*badly written* [letters]	SETTLER
back row	REARRANGE	[gone] *bad*	–GEON
back ro<u>w</u>	W	**badger**	
back seat	SADDLE	badger bait	TEASE
back sea<u>t</u>	T	badger's home in front	SETTLED
back to front	RUMPLED	**Badminton performer**	SHOW-JUMPER
back track	PASTRY	**baffle**	
back trac<u>k</u>	K	*baffle* [noises]	ESSOIN
backing hors<u>e</u>	E	*baffled* [by her] . . .	HERBY
backmarker in rac<u>e</u>	E	*bafflement of* [all the] . . .	LETHAL
backsid<u>e</u>	E	**bag**	
backward		bag	DOROTHY
backward<	DRAW	bag clasp	CATCH
backward boy<	NOD, NOR et al	bag of lettuce, *say*	SACCOS
	DAL, NOS, YOB	*bags* a . . .	incl A
backward glance<	KEEP	*bags* *	incl *
backward island<	ABLE	• m–an *bags* a duck	MOAN
backward school-boys<	SLIP-UP	baggage control	GRIP, PIMP
backward-looking boy<	NOD, NOR et al	*bagged by* *	incl in *
	DAL, NOS, YOB	• duck *bagged by* m–an	MOAN
bad		baggy	KNEED
bad	OFF	baggy, *say*	KNEAD, NEED
• bad finish	OFFEND	bagman	GLADSTONE
• bad season	OFFSPRING	**Bahamas**	BS
• bad worker	OFFHAND	*in the* Bahamas	B–S
bad actor	HAM	**bail**	
bad [actor]	CROAT	[bail] *out*	BALI
bad *back*<	DAB, LIVE	bailiff, *say*	BAY-LEAF, CAESAR
bad feeling	ILLNESS	bailsman	WICKET-KEEPER
bad fish	RANKLING	[can bail] *out*	CALIBAN
bad *French*	MAL	**baker**	SUNBATHER
• bad *French* relatives	MALKIN	**balance**	BAL
• bad *French* ruler	MALAGA	balance, *say*	WAY
• bad *French* sweet	MALICE	balance sheet	BS
and		balanced, *say*	WADE
• for bad *French* . . .	FORMAL	**bald**	
• neither bad *French* . . .	NORMAL	bald	DISTRESSED, UNLOCKED
• the *German with* bad *French*	DERMAL	bald, *say*	AIRLESS, HEIRLESS
bad hand	SCRAWL, SCRIBBLE	<u>b</u>ald-*headed*	B
bad ignition	ARSON	bald patch	O
bad man	CHRONICLES	• doctor *has* bald patch	VETO
bad mark	CROSS, SCAR	**bale**	
bad spell	CHARM	bale	BL

[bale] *out*	ABLE, ELBA	• hat-band	CAPO
in bales	B–LS	• string band	BO, CO, DO, GO
ball		band leader	CONDUCTOR, ROBIN HOOD
ball	O	b<u>a</u>nd *leader*	B
• ball-bearing	ONE(S), –OSE	band, *say*	BANNED
	OWE(S), OWN(S)	(b)and *without a leader*	AND
• ball-boy	OLEO, OVAL	bands of rock *and* stone	STRATAGEM
• ball *on* the green	OVERT	**bandy**	
• ball-point	OE, ON, OS, OW	*bandied about* [names]	MANES, MEANS
• ball-points	ONE(S), OWN(S)	*bandy* [legs]	GELS
ball	YORKER	bandy words	BOW-LEGGED
ball-game, *say*	CROAKY	*bandy* [words]	SWORD
ballpoint manufacturer,		**bang**	
say	PENOLOGIST	bang-like	POPISH
Baltic		bang on	CORRECT, RIGHT
Baltic journalist	LAPPED	bang *on* time	REPORTAGE
Baltic queen	LETTER	banger	FIREWORK, TNT
ban			SAUSAGE
ban a . . .	omit A	**banish**	
ban beauty, *say*	BARBEL	*banish* a . . .	omit A
ban bishopric, *say*	BARELY	*banish* king	omit K, R
ban box, *say*	BANK-RATE	*banish* *	omit *
ban colour	BARRED	• *banish* wife *from* (W)ales	ALES
ban Communist	BARRED	**banjo**	BARMAID
ban firm	BANCO	**bank**	
ban first-<u>b</u>orn	omit B	bank	BK
ban gambling, *say*	BARBETTES	bank attacker	ALLIGATOR, CROCODILE
ban gangster	BANAL	bank go-between	FERRYMAN, RIVER
ban on lake, *say*	BARMIER	Bank of Scotland	BRAE
ban		bank rate	BR
–one building	BANISHED	banker	RIVER
–one colour	BARITONE	• English banker	THAMES etc
ban private eye, *say*	BARDIC	• French banker	SEINE etc
ban profits	BARGAIN	• German banker	RHINE etc
ban song, *say*	BANDITTI		(*see also* flower, river)
ban sweetheart	BANJO	banker's statement	IDEAL
ban wire, *say*	BANKABLE	banking	BKG
ban woman, *say*	BANSHEE	*banks* of <u>r</u>iver	RR
ban *	omit *	**baptise**	
• *ban* learner *from* c(l)ub	CUB	baptise child	CALL-GIRL
banned, *say*	BAND	baptised	BAP(T)
banned girl, *say*	BANDANNA	Baptist	BAP(T)
banned service	BARDLET	**bar**	
banned woman	BRIDE	bar	SILKS
bans weeder	BAR-SHOE	*bar closing*	omit last letter
parking *banned*	omit P	• *bar closing* tim(e)	TIM
parking *banned* in A(p)ril	ARIL	bar fees	COUNTERCHARGES
	(*see also* bar)	bar gangster	BANAL
banana		bar on letter	BARONESS
b<u>a</u>nan<u>a</u> *skin*	BA	*bar opening*	omit 1st letter
banana *split*	BAN, ANA	• *bar opening* (h)ours	OURS
bananas	CRAZY, MAD, NUTS	bar ornament	GRACE NOTE
bananas [I sold]	SOLID		MORDENT, TRILL
band		bar profits	BARGAIN
band	O	bar purchase	LEVERAGE
• band *together with* archdeacons	OVENS	barmaid	BANJO, HEBE, PORTIA

Letter replaced \c\at; Omit (a); Pointers *out*; Retain <u>a</u>; Split B_ED; Down (D); Backwards <or ^

barman	BARRISTER, COUNSEL	barristers	BAR
	GANYMEDE	**barter**	
barred fight, *say*	BANDBOX	barter hawk	SELL
barred Scot	BANDIAN	barter vehicle	TRUCK
barred the *old*, *say*	BANDAGED	**base**	
	(*see also* ban)	base abandoned	FOOTLOOSE
Barbados	BS	base fellow	FOOTMAN
in Barbados	B–S	*base of* tre<u>e</u>(D)	E
barbarian		base, *say*	LO, VIAL
barbarian	HUN	basic, *say*	ALIMENTARY
barbaric [rite]	TIER, TIRE	basic subject(s)	R(R)
barbarous [Huns]	SHUN	nava<u>l</u> *base*(D)	L
barbecue		**bashful**	
barbecue	OUTDO	bashful head	SHYNESS
barbecues, *say*	GRILSE	<u>b</u>ashful *head*	B
bard	WILL	**Basil**	
bare		basil	HERB
bare (=with nothing on)		• Basil's book	HERBAL
• bare arm	LIMBO	Basil	BRUSH
• bare tree	MAYO	**basking**	
	(*see also* naked)	bask, *say*	PYRENEAN
bare	OUT OF GEAR	basking	(in) SU–N
bare, *say*	BEAR, CARRY, DELIVER	**basket**	
	GRIZZLY, POOH	basket	BKT
bare skin, *with* nothing on	BUFFOON	basket-maker	OSIER, WICKER
bareback rider	GODIVA	basketry	RUSH JOB
barefaced	NONOSE	**bass**	
barely frozen	JUSTICE	bass	B
barely seen	NAKED, NUDE	bass note, *say*	DEEP SEA
barely true	JUST	**bat**	
barer	LESSON	bat	CRICKET CLUB
bargain		bats	(*see separate entry*)
bargain	SNIP	batsman	OPENER
bargain crop	SNIP	<u>b</u>atsman's *first* run	BR
bargain price	SONG	batsman's position	INCREASE,
baritone	BAR		STANCE
bark		batter	(*see separate entry*)
bark	BK, WOOF, WOW	batting	IN, INCREASE
bark of tree	BAY	batting side	INSET, OFF, ON, ONSET
barker, *say*	COFFER		
barker's pitch	DOGSTAR	**bathe**	
barn		bathe queen	WASHER
[barn]*storm*	BRAN	**bats**	
demolish [barn]	BRAN	bats	CRAZY, MAD, NUTS
baron		*bats* [can see]	SEANCE
baron	BN	*batty* [idea]	AIDE
Baron Munchausen, *say*	LIKING	**battalion**	BAT(T), BN
baronet	BART, BT	**batter**	
baroque		batter	EYELID
baroque [art]	RAT, TAR	*batter* [wives]	VIEWS
baroquely [coiled]	DOCILE	battered cooker	STOVE
barrel		*battered* [crate]	CATER, REACT
barrel	BL	*battering* [ram]	ARM, MAR
in barrels	B–LS	**battery**	
barrister		battery	BAT(T)
barrister	SILK	battery-powered warship	GUNBOAT

battle

battle	WAR
• battle *at* sea	WARMER
• battle casualties, *say*	WARDED
• battle circuit	WARRING
• battle-gear	WARDRESS
• battle has started	WARISON
• battle rations	WARFARE
• battle shout	WARRANT
• battle study	WARDEN
battle	WATERLOO etc
battle call	ENGAGEMENT RING
battle-dress	BALACLAVA
battle scene	ACTION PAINTING
battle station	WATERLOO
battlefield	ACRE
[great] *battles*	GRATE
battling [over] . . .	ROVE

bay

bay	B
• bay tree	BASH
bay, *say*	BITE, BYTE
bayleaf, *say*	BAILIFF
BBC	AUNTIE, BEEB
b-bird	BEAGLE, BOWL
BD	
BD, *say*	BEADY

be

be fastened, *say*	BETIDE
be drunk	BELIT
be female	BEHEN
be *heard*	BEE
be keeper	HAVE, OWN
be my telephone, *say*	BEMIRING
be pierced, *say*	BEHOLD
be positive	LIVE
be prepared	BP
be quick	EXIST, LIVE
be sullen at this point	SULKIER
being smart	PERSONABLE

beach

beach artist	SANDRA
beach fibre	STRAND
beach, *say*	SURE
Beachy *Head*	B

bead

bead counter	ABACUS
beady, *say*	BD

beam

beam-arm	RAY-GUN
beam, *say*	MANTLE
beams, *say*	RAISE

bear

bear	BRUIN, POOH, RUSSIAN
bear in front, *say*	POOLED
bear company	STAND FIRM
bear punishment	STICK
bear, *say*	BARE, NAKED, NUDE
	OUT OF GEAR, UNDRESSED GRISLY
bear twin	POOH-POOH
bear up	THE GREAT BEAR, URSA MAJOR
	URSA MINOR
bear *up*(D)^	HOOP
bear wine	PORT
bears scorn	POOH-POOH
bears suffer	HASLET
<u>bear</u>skin	BR

bearing

bearing	AIR
• bearing left	AIRPORT
• bearing wine	AIRPORT
• strong bearing	FAIR
bearing	N, S, E, W
• bearing poems	NODES
• bearing wine	SHOCK
• bearing flower	EASTER
• bearing one each	WIPER
	(*see* also directions)
bearing	DEMEANOUR
bearing a . . .	incl A
bearing, *say*	MEAN
bearing *	incl *
• ship *bearing* German . . .	SHUNS
borne by *	incl in *
• German *borne by* ship	SHUNS

beastly

beastly driver	SHEEPDOG, TOAD
beastly fighter	GLADIATOR, PICADOR
	TOREADOR, TORERO
beastly lot	ZOO
beastly man	CENTAUR, SATYR
beastly mother	DAM, MARE
beastly overheads	ANTLERS, HORNS

beat

beat	PIP
• beat Edward	PIPED
• Beat it!	PIPIT
• beat queen	PIPER
beat	TAN
• beat fellow	TANGENT
• beat Nicholas, *say*	TANNIC
• beat ruler	TANKING
beat [all the] . . .	LETHAL
beat bottom	WORST
beat cloth	WORSTED
beat favourite	WHIPPET
beat player	BATTER
beat seed	PULSE
beat time	TEMPO
beat tramp	LAYABOUT
beat *up*(D)^	GOLF, MAL
beat up [sorbet]	STROBE

Letter replaced \c\at; Omit (a); Pointers *out*; Retain <u>a</u>; Split B_ED; Down (D); Backwards <or ^

beaten club	FLAT-IRON	[it was] *bedraggled*	WAIST
beaten [silver]	LIVERS, SLIVER	**bee**	
beater	CONDUCTOR	bee	B
	HEADMASTER, TANNER	bee *in* <u>b</u>onnet	B, FIRST LETTER
	HEART, PACEMAKER, PULSE	beekeeper	HIVE
beau	ADONIS, DANDY	beekeeper, *say*	HAVE, OWN
beautiful		bees	BB, BS
beautiful blonde	FAIR	**beef**	
beautiful country	FAIRGROUND	beef consultant	OMBUDSMAN
beauty queen	MISSUS	beef entrée	CARPENTRY
because	AS, COS, FOR, SINCE	<u>b</u>eef *entrée*	B
become		beef not available	BULLY OFF
become angry, *say*	CERED	**beer**	
become calm	ENDANGER	beer container	BELLY, STOMACH
become embarrassed	GORED	beer *container*	DALEK, WALER, WHALES
become father	BEDAD	beer, *say*	AIL, BIER, LAAGER
become fit	GETABLE	beer strike	WALLOP
become less civilised	BEWILDER	beer with fish	ALEGAR
become older	PASSAGE	beer *with* head	STOUTNESS
become quiet	GOSH	**Beethoven**	
become [quiet]	QUITE	Beethoven quartet	BEET, HOVE, OVEN
become solvent	ENDOWING	Beethoven's *finish*	OVEN, VEN
become tense, *say*	TITAN	B<u>ee</u>thoven's *Third*	E
become taller	STRETCH ONE'S LEGS	**beetle**	
becomes [tired]	TRIED	beetle	OVERHANG, PROJECT
becomes warm	GET SHOT	beetle design	PROJECT
becoming respectable	PROPER	*wings of* <u>beetle</u>	BE
bed		**befog**	
bed	COT, GARDEN, PLOT	befogged	(in) M–IST
bed factory	PLANT	• a king *is befogged*	MARIST
bed maker	GARDENER	• Ron *loses* his head *when befogged*	MONIST
bed makers	PLANTS, ROSES etc	**before**	
bed of nails	QUICK	before	A, AN, ANTE, BEF, ER, OR
bed of nail<u>s</u>(D)	S	before	ERE
bed, *say*	LAIR	• before transport	EREBUS
bedfellow	PROCRUSTES	• before the children	EREMITES
<u>bed</u>*head*	B	• before the court	ERECT
bedridden	(in) BE–D, (in)B–ED	before	PRE
• *bedridden*	BILLED	• before *and* after	PRELATE
• *bedridden* king	BRED	• before Herb, *say*	PRESAGE
bedridden	(in) CO–T, (in) C–OT	before Christ	AC, BC
• son *is bedridden*	COST	before delivery	ANTE-NATAL
• *bedridden* learner	CLOT	before five, *say*	FOR(E)
bedridden (=laid up)(D)^	DIAL	before nine, *say*	AIT, ATE, EYOT
bedroom	DORMITORY, WARD	before noon	AM
bedsitter	OYSTER	*before* noon	in front of N
bedspread	MULCH	• see *before* noon	SEEN
[bed]*spread*	DEB	before the bench	UP
bedevil		before the day	AD
bedevil [his] . . .	–ISH	before three, *say*	TO(O)
bedevilled [by a] . . .	BAY	before twelve	AM
bedlam		*before*hand	in front of L, LT, R, RT
Bedlam [in the] . . .	THINE	• appeared *before*hand	CAMEL
[like] *Bedlam*	KIEL	• me *before*hand	MELT
bedraggled		• contribute *before*hand	GIVER
bedraggled [mare]	REAM	• he *has* one *before*hand	HEART

Anag [cat]; Any *; Begin IGN–; Endings –ING; eg •; Hidden /cat/; Implied add (on); Implied in (in);

befuddle
befuddled [by a gin] . . .	BAYING
befuddling [wines]	SINEW, SWINE

beg
beg, *say*	PREY
begged, *say*	PREYED

begin
[begin] *afresh*	BINGE
begin to e̲at	E
begin t̲o eat	TEAT
begin to fight	SET-TO

beginning
beginning	A, ALPHA
beginning	PARTI–
• beginning *with* friend	PARTIALLY
• beginning *by*	
breaking [into]	PARTITION
beginning *in Greece*	ALPHA
beginning *in Israel*	ALEPH
beginning of April	MARCH-PAST
beginning of A̲pril	A
beginning of l̲ast . . .	L
beginning of last month	DEC(I)–
beginning of play	ACTI–, KICK-OFF
beginning of p̲lay	P
beginning of t̲he . . .	T
beginning of t̲ime	T
beginning will, *say*	STARTLE
(m)eat beginning *to go off*	EAT

begone
beg*one*	omit BE
• Beg*one!* Beg*one!*	GONE
• Beg*one,* (b)rid(e)	RID

begotten
begotten [in anger]	EARNING, NEARING
[woe]-*begotten*	OWE

behead
behead	omit 1st letter
• *behead* (g)oats	OATS, (b)UTTERS
• *beheaded* (t)he (b)ad	
(a)long . . .	HEADLONG
• *beheaded* (w)omen	OMEN

behind
behind	
indicating one word written after another word or letter:	
• daughter *behind the* times	AGED
• directions *behind*hand	TARES
• girl *behind* the lines	BREVE
• man *behind*hand	HANDED
• put directions *behind* tree	ASHEN
behind bars	(in) C–AGE, (in) PE–N
behind family	BUMKIN
behind the times	PASSE

behold
be*holding*	incl in B–E
• be*holding* a saint	BASTE
• be*holding* clear . . .	BRIDE
• be*holding* notice	BADE

being
being drawn	UNDERTOW
being human	ERRING
being human, *say*	HERRING

Belgian   LIEGEMAN

belittle
belittle country	FRANC(e)
belittle countrymen	IRIS(h)

belligerent
belligerent American	GI
belligerent poet	MARTIAL
(*see also* aggressive)	

bellringer   CAMPANOLOGIST
                 CLAPPER

belong
belong	LIVELONG
belonging in Fir/st Ar/my	STAR
belonging to the pub/lic e/nemy	LICE
belonging to you, *say*	YORE

below
below	ASUNDER
below	
indicating one word written under another:	
• live *below* soldier(D)	GIBE
below forty	FOR, FORT
below freezing	OFFICE
below seven	SIX
below (s)even	EVEN

belt
belt *up*(D)^	MAL

bemuse
bemuse [all the] . . .	LETHAL
bemused [by all] . . .	BALLY

bend
bend	S, U, Z
bend a knee	KNEEL
bend a [knee]	KEEN
bend before hill	TURNPIKE
bend fastener	BUCKLE
bend oar	SWEEP
bend piece	ARCHBISHOP
bend [rules]	LURES
bender	ELBOW, JOINT, KNEE
bending [low]	OWL
bent into [shape]	HEAPS, PHASE
bent [nail]	ANIL, LAIN
bent striker, *say*	CURLICUE

beneath
beneath	UNDER
• beneath fish	UNDERLING
• beneath mammal	UNDERSEAL
• beneath trees	UNDERSTAND

benevolent Communist	KINDRED
Benjamin	
Benjamin is working	BENISON
Benjamin is complete, *say*	BENZOLE
bent	(*see* bend)
bequeath	
bequeath it, *say*	WILLET
bequeath *to* alien	WILLET
bequeath *to* Edward, *say*	WILTED
Berlin division	WALL
berserk	
berserk [slayer]	LAYERS, RELAYS
[goes] *berserk*	EGOS
berth	WATER-BED
beset	
beset a . . .	incl A
beset *	incl *
• runner's *besetting* sin	COSINES
beset by *	incl in *
• king *beset by* wo–e	WOKE, WORE
beside	
father *beside* himself	PAPA
man *beside* himself	TOM-TOM
mother *beside* herself	MAMA
soldier *beside* himself	GIGI
besiege	
besieged by *	incl in *
• island *besieged by* engineers	RISE
besieged Lady	SMITH
besieging *	incl *
• engineers *besieging* island	RISE
besotted	(in) LO–VE
bespatter	
bespatter [door]	ROOD
bespattered [car she] . . .	SEARCH
bespectacled	
bespectacled	incl in O–O
• *bespectacled* bishop *in* right . . .	ROBOT
• *bespectacled* king *in* the Merchant Navy	MORON
bespoke	
bespoke [T-shirt]	THIRST
best	
best	WORST
best china	CHUM, MATE, SOULMATE
best club	ACE
best diamond	ACE, ICE CREAM
best man	CHAMPION, WINNER
best parliamentarian	WHIP
best part of the . . .	TH
best part of the meat	EAT
[best] *possible*	BETS
best spade	ACE
best suit	TRUMPS
best time	PLUMAGE

best type	ELITE
best writing	FIRST HAND
bet	
bet frequently, *say*	OFFENBACH
bet in Germany	BACKING
bet *on* a fight	LAYABOUT
betting levy, *say*	SYNTAX
beta	B
betray	
betray disciple	FINGERMARK
betray store	SHOP
better	
better	GAMBLER, PUNTER
better bed	LAYER
better half	RIB, WIFE
better *half*	BET, TER
better sportsman	GAMBLER, PUNTER
better teacher	MASTER
better workman	FITTER
between	
between bends	S–S
between ol/d and y/oung	DANDY
between the sheets	(in) B–ED, (in) C–OT
between us	U–S
bewilder	
bewildered [men at] . . .	MEANT
bewildering [speed I] . . .	ESPIED
[I am] *bewildered*	AIM
beyond	
beyond reason	OTT, OVER THE TOP
beyond the mouth	omit 1st letter
• river *beyond the mouth*	(h)UMBER
	(o)USE, (t)RENT etc
beyond the river	PASTURE
bias	
bias in [test]	SETT
biased [umpire]	IMPURE
bible	
bible	AV, BIB, NT, OT, RV
• bible queen	AVER
• bible records	BIBLISTS
• nothing *in* the Bible	NOT
• bible-woman	OTHER
• last word *about* the Bible	CURVE
bible classes	RE, RI
big¹	BIG
big-*hearted*	I
big-*end*	G
Big *Top*(D)	B
big*head*	B
big*mouth*	B
big²	
big	OS
• big flower	OSIRIS
• big sheep	OSRAM
• big-time girl	OSMOSIS

Anag [cat]; Any *; Begin IGN–; Endings –ING; eg •; Hidden /cat/; Implied add (on); Implied in (in);

and
- very large bird   OSTEAL
- very large vehicle   OSCAR
- very large victim   OSPREY

and
- big-*hearted* flower   HOSTA
- big-*hearted* M–oe   MOOSE
- th–e big-*hearted*   THOSE

big³
Big Bang time   REPORTAGE
big banger   TNT
Big Ben   NEVIS
big build-up   SKYSCRAPER, TOWER
big drinker   FISH
big fiddle   CELLO
big fight   BATTLE
big game   FINAL
big guns   RA
big issue   GRANDCHILD(REN)
big landlords   BLOCK LETTERS
big letter   ENLARGE, LARGESSE
big lie   ONER
big luminary   SUN
big man   BEN, FATAL
big match, *say*   FATTEST
big noise   BOOM, VIP
big *noise*   GRATE
big officer   MAJOR
big picture   CLOSE-UP
big race   GIANTS, TITANS
   MARATHON
big, *say*   GRATE
big ship   LARGESS
big sum   IMPOUNDS
big timer   BEN
big toes, *say*   POLICIES
big way   M, MI
bigger area, *say*   MOORLAND
bigger offer, *say*   MORBID

bike
bike riders, *say*   CYCLAMEN

bikini
bikini   ATOLL
bikini top   BRA
bikini *top*(D)   B

bilabial
bi-labial, *say*   TULIPS

bilingual
bilingual agreement   OUIJA
bilingual articles   ELLA, LATHE, UNDER

bill¹
bill   AC
- Bill Hill   ACTOR
- Bill Price   ACCOST
- Bill *with* another man   ACED, ACERIC,
   ACHE, ACRON, ACTED

bill   AD
- Bill *is in* front   FACADE
- Bill *is on* time   ADAGE
- bill it   ADIT

bill²
bill of exchange   BE
bill of lading   BL
bill of parcels   BP
bill of sale   BS
bill payable   BP
bill receivable   BREC
Bill's companion   BEN, COO

billow
billow, *say*   WAIVE
billowing   OVERDUE ACCOUNT
billowing [robes]   BOERS, BORES, SOBER
[sails] *billowing*   SILAS

biochemical oxygen demand   BOD
biography   BIOG, LIFE
biology   BIOL
biology class(es)   TAXON(TAXA)

bird
bird   COCK, CROW, TERN, TIT etc
- bird *and* animal   TITMOUSE
- bird *and* fish   REELING, TITLING
- bird ate . . .   HAWKBIT, TERNATE, TITBIT
- bird-boy   RUFFIAN
- bird complaint   GROUSE
- bird disease   THRUSH
- bird-dog   COCKTAIL, HARRIER
- bird exists   MARTINIS
- bird expired, *say*   CROWDED, REEDED
- bird flying, *say*   TITUP
- bird follows   DOVETAILS
- bird food   PIE
- bird helps, *say*   COCKADES
- bird in front   COCKLED, REELED,
   RUFFLED, TITLED
- bird is cooked, *say*   DUCK-SHOT
- bird joint, *say*   COCKNEY
- bird nuts   CUCKOO
- bird painter   WHISTLER
- bird pecks   MOABITES
- bird-ring   MAGPIE
- bird ruler   REEKING
- bird, *say*   TURN, WIDER
- bird speed   TITRATE
- bird-table, *say*   TURNTABLE
- bird-talk   CHAT
- bird trap   CROWNET
- bird *under* vehicle (D)   CAROUSEL
- bird walking   CROWFOOT
- bird will, *say*   TITTLE
- birdman   COCKED, COCKLES, RUFFIAN,
   TERNAL, TITHE, TITLES
- birds arrive, *say*   COXCOMB

• bird's difficulties	KNOTS	bits of paper	CONFETTI
• bird's perch	CROWBAR	*bit out of* so/me re/d . . .	MERE
• bird's recreation	HOBBY	*bits out of* a/n ap/ple	NAP
• birdshot	SNIPE	bitty, *say*	BITE
• birdsong	PENCHANT	**bitch**	DOGMA
• blackbird	BEAGLE, BOWL, BROOK	**bite**	
bird	PRISON	bit her, *say*	BITTER, NIPTER
bird fancier	CAT	bite *back*<	GNAT, PANS, PIN
bird house	HAREM	bite biscuit	SNAP
bird noise, *say*	CHEAP	*bite out of* a/n ap/ple	NAP
bird sanctuary	NEST	biting cold	NIPPY
bird settling down	NESTLING	biting pastry	TART
bird watcher	EAGLE EYE, GAOLER	**bitter**	
	JAILER, SCREW, WARDER	bitter	BEER
bird's nest	CLUTCH HOUSING	bitter *end*	R
birth		bitter fish, *say*	RILING
birthday	PRESENT DAY	bitter fluid, *say*	BHYLE
birthplace	BED, BP, NATAL	bitter-money	SOURDOUGH
biscuit man	GARIBALDI	bitter prostitute	TART
bishop		bitter, *say*	BIT HER, NIPTER
bishop	B, BP, RR	bitter turnover	TART
	ABBA, ANSELM, ODO	**bizarre**	
bishop's chair, *say*	THROWN	*bizarre* [affair]	RAFFIA
bishop's letters	RR	*bizarrely* [robed man]	DOBERMAN
bissextile	BIS	**black**	
bisexuals	HEBRIDES	black	B
bit		• a black deed	ABACTION
a bit pale	PAL(e), WHIT(e)	• a black mark	ABSTAIN
bit ahead	CRUMBLED	• a black tree	ABASH
bit her, *say*	BITTER, NIPTER	and	
bit of a bloomer	PETAL, SEPAL etc	• black cat	BOUNCE
bit of a boob	NIPPLE	• Black Death	BEND
bit of a habit	MONKSHOOD	• black hole	BO
bit of a laugh	HO	• black fish	BANGLE, BROACH
bit of character	C	• black rage	BANGER
bit of character	SERIF	• blackball	BO
bit of crest	C	• blackbird	BEAGLE, BOWL, BROOK
bit of crest	PARTRIDGE	• blackspots	BRASH
bit of fish	F	and	
bit of fish	FIN	• black*head*	B
bit of fun	F	• black*out*	omit B
bit of fun	JAPE, JOKE, LARK	black	DARK
bit of litter	L	• black fish	DARKLING
bit of l/it/ter	IT	• black queen	DARKER
bit of litter	KITTEN, PIGLET, PUP(PY)	• blackhead	DARKNESS
bit of luck	L, LU	black	JET
bit of luc/k I sh/all . . .	KISH	• black art	JETCRAFT
bit of paper	P	• black convict	JET LAG
bit of paper	ARTICLE, FEATURE, LEADER	• black cravats	JETTIES
bit of pig	P	• black fashion	JETTON
bit of pig	BACON, RASHER	• black dog	JET-SETTER
bit of pride	P	• Black *has* much weight	JETTON
bit of p/rid/e	RID	• black sheep	RAMJET
bit of pride	LION CUB	• black Uncle	JETSAM
bi(t) *short*	BI	• black weight	JETTON
bits of paper	PA	• Blackburn	JET STREAM

Anag [cat]; Any *; Begin IGN–; Endings –ING; eg •; Hidden /cat/; Implied add (on); Implied in (in);

• blackish offspring, *say*	JETTISON
black	PITCH
• black hose	PITCH PIPES
• black journalist	PITCHED
• black king	PITCHER
black	TAR
• Black *and* Tan	TARTAN
• black glue	TARGUM
• black sailor	TAR, TARTAR
• black salt	TAR, TARTAR
black and blue	DIRTY
black and white players	PIANISTS
black art	NECROMANCY, NIGROMANCY
Black Beauty	DARK HORSE, NIGHTMARE
black belt	DAN
black country	JAPAN
black gold	OIL
black lead	OTHELLO
black mole	JETTY
black note	FLAT, SHARP
black paint brush	SABLE
black sailor	COALTAR
black stuff	COAL, OIL, TAR
black suit	C, S
blade	
blade, *say*	VAIN, VEIN
blame	RAP
blanket coverage	BEDSPREAD, DUVET, EIDERDOWN, SHEET
blast	
blast of [air]	IRA, RIA
blast rocks, *say*	CURSORES
blast swan, *say*	DAMPEN
blasted [pest]	PETS, STEP
blazing	
blazing [fire]	RIFE
blazing [row]	WOR–
[guns] *blazing*	GNUS, SNUG, SUNG
blemish	
blemish	SCAR
• blemish *on* metropolis	SCARCITY
• blemish *on* female	SCARF
• circular blemish	OSCAR
blend	
blend here, *say*	NEEDIER
blend it, *say*	WISKET, WHISKET
blend of [teas]	EATS, SATE, SEAT
blend, *say*	KNEED, NEED
blended [wines]	SINEW, SWINE
blending [into sea]	ESTONIA
blending into th/e land/scape	ELAND
blessed	
blessed	B
blessed one	DONOR, GIVER, SAINT, TAKER
blessed sacrament	BS
Blessed Virgin (Mary)	BV(M)

blind	
blind [dates]	SATED
blind (man)	VENETIAN
blind gangster	HOOD
blind mic(e)	MIC
blissful state	IGNORANCE
Blithe Spirit	AIRY FAIRY, (SKY) LARK
blitz	
blitz [town]	WONT
blitz[krieg]	GRIKE
blizzard	
blizzard [in Ayr]	RAINY
[in a] *blizzard*	AIN
[rode] *in a blizzard*	DOER
blob	O
block	
block a view	DAMASCENE
block shoe	CLOG
block *	incl in *
• stone *blocking* river	TASTY
block flooring, *say*	PARKY
blocked by *	incl *
• river *blocked by* stone	TASTY
blockbuster	SCULPTOR
blockhouse	IGLOO
blood	
blood count	DRACULA
blood factor	RH
blood letter	MOSQUITO
blood money	ERIC
blood pump, *say*	HART
blood sucker	BAT, LEECH, VAMPIRE
blood-sucking grasshopper	CRICKET BAT
bloodgroup	A, AB, B, O FAMILY, KIN
bloody	B
• bloody cheek	BLIP
• bloody fool	BASS
• bloody wet	BRAINY
bloody	RARE
• bloody diocese, *say*	RARELY
• bloody king	RARER
• bloody saint	RAREST
bloody	RED
• bloody battle	REDACTION
• bloody, *say*	READY
• English *in* bloody . . .	REED
• lawyer *has* blood . . .	DARED
bloody channel	AORTA, ARTERY, VEIN
bloody channel, *say*	VAIN, VANE
bloody fool	BF
bloody scarce	RARE
bloody tube	AORTA, ARTERY, VEIN
bloody tube, *say*	VAIN, VANE
bloom	
bloomer	FLOWER

Letter replaced \c\at; Omit (a); Pointers *out*; Retain a̲; Split B_ED; Down (D); Backwards <or ^

blooming	OUT	board game	GOSPORT
blooming female	IRIS, ROSE et al	board meeting	CHESS MATCH
	(*see also* flower¹)		DINNER PARTY
blow		board member	CHESS PIECE, PAWN etc
blow	ONER, WIND		DIRECTOR
blow apart [outer] . . .	OUTRE	• board-members' dance	PAWNSHOP
blow at this point, *say*	WINDIER	• board-member's joint	DIRECTORSHIP
blow open [door]	ODOR, ROOD	Board of . . .	
blow-pipe	OCARINA, WHISTLE etc	–Control	BC
blow *to the ear*	GAEL	–Education	BE
blow up	DYNAMITE	–Trade	BOT
	EXAGGERATE	board, *say*	BORED, DRILLED
	UPPERCUT		WEARIED
blow *up*(D)^	PAR	board weight	PLANKTON
blow up building	PUMPHOUSE	*boarded by* a . . .	incl A
blow up [dam]	MAD	*boarded by* *	incl *
blow ill, *say*	TOOTLE	• bri–g *boarded by* number . . .	BRING
blower	TELEPHONE, WIND	boarder	PG
blowing about [in the] . . .	THINE	*boarding* *	incl in *
blowing up [a ship]	APHIS	• number *boarding* bri–g	BRING
blown [about]	U-BOAT	boards	STAGE
blown about [by a] . . .	BAY	• boards train	STAGECOACH(ES)
blue		**boast**	
blue	DOWN, OFF COLOUR, SAD	boast *about*<	GARB
	SPEND	boastful relation	TALL STORY
blue-blooded boys	REGAL, ROYAL	boasting	AM, IAM, IM
blue-blooded line	VEIN	(*see also* admit, claim, confess, declare)	
blue film	ANGEL, MAX	boasting	SNAKE-BITE
blue fish, *say*	BLUE-EYED, SADDLING	**boat**	TUB
blue flower	DANUBE, NILE	boat builder	ARKWRIGHT, NOAH
blue jumper	ATHLETE		SHIPWRIGHT
blue pencil wielder, *say*	CENSER, SENSOR	boat in front	SCOWLED
blue ships	NAVY	boat propeller	GONDOLIER, OARSMAN
blue water	DANUBE, NILE		ROWER, SAIL
blues	CAMBRIDGE, OXFORD	boat, *say*	WAILER, WALER
blues rhythm	STROKE	boat shelter	DUGOUT
bluestocking	MALADY	boat strike	SMACK
bluff king	HAL	boater	STRAW
blunder		boatman	JEROME, KERN
blunder [made] . . .	DAME, EDAM, MEAD	book boats	VOLCANOES
blundering [steps]	PESTS	**bob**	
blunt point	ROUNDHEAD	bob	S
biur		Bob's producer	BELLRINGER
blurred [letters]	SETTLER		CAMPANOLOGIST
[saw it] *in a blur*	WAIST, WAITS	*short of* a bob	omit S
blush		**body**	
blush	GORED	body-builder	STEROID
blushing	RED	body odour	BO
BMA dance	MEDICINE BALL	body support	BIER, BONE, SPINE
Boadicea's people	ICENI	body support, *say*	BEAUNE, BEER
boar		bodyshop worker	EMBALMER
boar, *say*	CARRIED, DELIVERED	bodywork decay	CARROT
	BORE, DRILL	**bogged down**	(in) FE–N, (in) MAR–SH
	EAGRE		(in) MU–D
board		**bogus**	
board	BD, DIRECTORS	bogus journalist	SHAMED

bogus [priest]	RIPEST, STRIPE	• books *about*< . . .	TO
[claimed] *bogus* . . .	DECIMAL, MEDICAL	Books *I & III*	BO
Bohemian	BOH	book-store	RESERVE
boil	FURUNCLE	handbook	MANUAL
boil beer	WALLOP	**book²**	
boil [beer at] . . .	BERATE	indicating character in	
boiled [over]	ROVE	or title of novel, etc:	
boiler-fuel overlord, *say*	COKING	• *booked*	
	COAKING	–3	MEN IN A BOAT
boiling point	BP	–4	JUST MEN
boiling *point*	B	–5	FAMOUS
boiling [point]	PINTO	–7	PILLARS (OF WISDOM)
boiling [swede]	SEWED, WEEDS	–10	LITTLE INDIANS
boisterous		–39	STEPS
boisterous [gale]	GAEL	• *booked* as thief	(ARTFUL) DODGER
[throw] *boisterously*	WORTH	• *booked* captain . . .	AHAB, HORNBLOWER
bond	SPY		NEMO
bond lover	SCRIPOPHILE	• *booked* Finn	HUCKLEBERRY
Bond's boss	M	• *booked* traveller	GULLIVER
Bond's club	STICK	• *booked* woman	SHE
bondsman	ERNIE	**boor**	
bone		boor, *say*	BOAR, BORE
bone	T		EAGRE
• a bone	AT	boorish, *say*	RUED
• girl *with* bone	SUET	**boot**	
bone, *say*	BEAUNE, WINE	boot unavailable	KICK-OFF
bonehead	SKULL	boots	(SAM) WELLER
bone*head*	B	**Booth**	ASSASSIN
[bone]*shaking*	EBON	**boozy**	
bony digit, *say*	BONITO	*boozy* [male]	LAME, MEAL
bony impediment	GAUNTLET	[man is] *on the booze*	MAINS
book¹		**border**	
book	B, BK, LIB, TOME	border dispute	HEDGEROW
Book *I*	B	border *flower*	RIO GRANDE, TWEED etc
book	VOL	border poet	SIDEBURNS
• book boats	VOLCANOES	border restriction	LIMIT
• book insect	VOLANT	border security	HEMLOCK
• book worker	VOLANT	*borders of* Hungary	HY
book cover	COPYRIGHT	*borders of* the . . .	TE
book *covers*	BK		(*see also* boundary)
book-*ends*	BK	**bore**	
book matches	NOVELTIES	bore ape	DRILL
book production	GENESIS	bore cloth	DRILL
book reviewer	AUDITOR	bore, *say*	BOAR, BOOR
book turns	ACTS		EAGRE
bookcase	SATCHEL	bored, *say*	BOARD, MANAGEMENT
bookmaker	AMOS, JOB, EZRA, etc	boring	DRY
	AUTHOR(ESS), EDITOR	• boring advertisement	DRYAD
bookmaker's work	NOVEL	• boring head	DRYNESS
bookkeeper	LIBRARIAN	• boring holes	DRY CELLS
bookmaker	PAPER	• boring period	DRYAD
books	BB	• boring publicity	DRYAD
books	NT, OT	boring drink	GIMLET
• about books	CANT, RENT	boring group, *say*	DULCET
• about books	COT	boring job	WELL-TO-DO
• books *about* . . .	N–T, O–T	boring part	BIT, DRILL

Letter replaced \c\at; Omit (a); Pointers *out*; Retain a; Split B_ED; Down (D); Backwards <or ^

born

born	B
• born a monarch	BAKING
• born *and* bred	BRAISED
• born fool	BASS
born	N
• born in New York	NINNY
born	NAT
• born right on . . .	NATRON
born	NE, NEE
• born at hospital	NEATH
• born dead, *say*	NEEDED
born fool	GOD'S APE
born free	DELIVERED
[Born] *Free*	BRNO
born *in France*	NE(E)

borne

borne by al/l oth/er . . .	LOTH
borne, *say*	BORN, BOURNE

borough   BOR

bosom

bosom	BUST
• bosom in front	BUSTLED
• bosom will, *say*	BUSTLE
• monarch *has* no bosom	ROBUST

boss

boss	NOI–
• boss *has* a few . . .	NOISOME
• boss *is given* directions	NOISE(S)
boss	STUD
• boss expired, *say*	STUDIED
• boss *has* ten . . .	STUDIO
• boss *has* debts	STUDIOUS
• boss I love	STUDIO
boss of	
–British Airways	BAKING
–MI6, *say*	SPIKING

botany   BOT

botch

botched [task Ed] . . .	SKATED
botching [all the] . . .	LETHAL

both

both directions	
indicating a palindrome:	
• flat *in both directions*	LEVEL
both ends of the . . .	TE
both ends of the candle	CE
both sides	LR, RL
• copper *on* both sides	CURL
• girl *in* both sides	LEVER, REVEL
both sides	
indicating an inclusion:	
• river *on both sides of* road	TARDY
both ways	
indicating a palindrome:	
• look *both ways*	PEEP
both ways	
indicating reversal:	
• played *both ways*	STRAD

bother

[a bit] of *bother*	BAIT
bother [about] . . .	U-BOAT
bothering to [write a] . . .	WAITER

bottle

bottle	BOT, NERVE
bottle fruit	GOURD
bottle-*opener*	B
bottle-party	PINTADO
bottle-*top*(D)	B
bottled	(in) VI–AL
bottled spirit	GENIE
bottling a . . .	incl A
bottling *	incl *
• wa–s *bottling* in . . .	WAINS
bottling premises	CHATEAU
* *bottled*	incl *
• drink *bottled in* the	
outskirts of souk	STEAK

bottom

bottom gear	KNICKERS, PANTS
bottom of all the big . . .(D)	LEG
bottom of foot	SOLE
bottom of foot(D)	T
mug, *bottom up*(D)^	GUM

bought   BT, BOT

bounce

bouncer	BALL
bouncing [babe]	ABBE

bound

bound	BD
bounding [over]	ROVE
bounds of possibility	PY

boundary

boundary	FOUR, IV, SIX, VI
• boundary out of date	FOUR SQUARE
boundaries of Surrey	SY
boundaries of the . . .	TE
boundary dispute	HEDGEROW
boundary restriction	LIMIT
boundary trees	LIMES
(*see also* border)	

bounder

bounder	CAD
• bounder expires	CADDIES
• bounder states . . .	CADAVERS

bovine

bovine cheek	COWSLIP, OXLIP
bovine part	COWSLIP, OXLIP
bovine part, *say*	COWSHED

bow

Bow (=Cockney)	
• Bowman's (h)ouse	OUSE

	(see also Cockney)		ROYALLY
bow of liner	L		*(see also* friend)
bow-legged bird, *say*	BANDICOOT	boy gets up, *say*	SUNRISES
bowed woman	VIOLA	boy *has* support, *say*	ALGEBRA
bowman	ARCHER, CUPID, EROS, TELL	boy *meets* maiden	ANTONYM
	CELLIST, VIOLINIST	boy *on* one side, *say*	REGICIDE
	COCKNEY	boy, *say*	SUNNI, SUNNY
bows	FIDDLESTICKS	boy scoffed	MALATE
bow of ship	PROW	boy *with* trophy	SIDCUP
bow of ship	S	boy wipes up, *say*	SUNDRIES
bows of ship	SH	boy-worker	PAGEANT
bows in front	PROWLED	**bra**	
bowtie	CABLE, HAWSER, PAINTER	bra	FALSIE
bowl		bra-burning ceremony, *say*	FALSIFIER
bowl this way, *say*	SOBOLE	**brace of peacock**	STRUT
bowled	B	**bracket**	
bowled out	omit B	*bracket* a . . .	incl A
• (b)elatedly *bowled out*	ELATEDLY	*bracket* *	incl *
bowler	DRAKE	• gunners *bracket* carrier	RHODA
bowling	ON, TOM	*bracketed by* *	incl in *
bowls rent	YORKSHIRE	• carrier *bracketed by* gunners	RHODA
box		**braggart**	PISTOL
box-kite	CRATE	**brain**	
box, *say*	KRAIT	brain treatment	ECG
box, see	SPARELY	[brain] *treatment*	BAIRN
boxed	(in) CR-ATE	brainy case	CRANIUM, HEAD, SKULL
boxed in by *	incl in *	**branch**	
• is *boxed in by* r–ing	RISING	branch	BR
boxer	ALI, CLAY	branch deposit	BIRDLIME
boxer	DOG	branch office	BO
• boxer's supporter	DOG-LEG	**brand**	
boxer	PUG(ILIST)	brand, *say*	MARC, MARQUE
• boxer understands, *say*	PUG-NOSE	branding-iron statement, *say*	ICIER
boxers	ABA, WBA, WBC	**brandish**	
boxer's diary	SCRAPBOOK	brandish	CEREAL, OATMEAL
boxing a . . .	incl A	brandish roller	WAVE
boxing belt	CROSS, HOOK, LEFT	brandish, *say*	WAIVE, WEALD
	RIGHT, SWING, UPPERCUT	**brandy**	
boxing champion	SPARKING	brandy and soda	BANDS
Boxing Club	ABA	brandy, *say*	MARK, MARQUE
Boxing Day duo	TURTLE DOVES	*in* brandy and soda	B–S
boxing, *say*	PHAETON	**brass**	
boxing venue, *say*	SQUARING	brass animal	RHINO
boxing *	incl *	brass band	MONEY-BELT
• r–ing-*boxing* is . . .	RISING	brass rubber	ALADDIN
boy		**brave**	
affectionate boy	FONDLES	brave	INDIAN, REDSKIN
boy	B, LAD, SON	brave child	PAPOOSE
boy *and* girl	BENGAL, LEONORA	brave fellow, *say*	MANDARIN
	PATELLA, PATINA, REGINA	brave group	INDIAN CLUB, TRIBE
	REGNANCY, VICUNA	brave wife	SQUAW
	THEOSOPHY	brave opponent	PALEFACE
	(see also girl and boy)	brave, *say*	BOWLED
boy *and* a girl	LENA	brave set-up	TOTEM POLE
boy editor	TIMED	**Brazil(ian)**	
boy-friend	NORMALLY, REGALLY	Brazil	NUT

Letter replaced \c\at; Omit (a); Pointers *out*; Retain a̲; Split B_ED; Down (D); Backwards <or ^

Brazilian	BR
• Brazilian drunk	BROILED
• Brazilian wears spectacles *at* church	BROOCH
• Brazilian with different . . .	BROTHER
Brazilian	BRA
• Brazilian square	BRAT
• Brazilian *with* the *Italian* . . .	BRAIL
• company *has* Brazilian...	COBRA
Brazilian *flower*	AMAZON
Brazilian *leader*	B
Brazilian steps	SAMBA

breach

breach *	include in *
• I breach he–er	HEIR
breach [wall of] . . .	FALLOW
breaching [wall by a] . . .	WALLABY

bread

[bread] *crumbs*	BARED, DEBAR
bread *crusts*	BD
bread round	DOORSTEP
bread, *say*	DOE, DOH
	BRED, REARED
breadmaker	FINANCIER, FLOUR
slice of bread	BR

breadth   B

break¹

indicating anagram:

break down [result]	ULSTER
break [into] . . .	–TION
break [into a] . . .	–ATION
break out of [Broadmoor]	BOARDROOM
break [plate]	PETAL
break up [town]	WONT
break [the law]	WEALTH
break the [law]	AWL
break[down]	WOND–
breakdown of [law]	AWL
break[fast]	FATS
breaking [rules]	LURES
[break]*out*	BAKER, BRAKE
break[out]	TOU
breakout [last]	SLAT
breakthrough [in art]	TRAIN
broken down [van I] . . .	IVAN, VAIN
broken [leg]	GEL, –GLE
broken [romance]	CREMONA
broken up [by a] . . .	BAY
broken[hearted]	EARTHED, RED HEAT
brokenly [I moan] . . .	NAOMI
[code]-*breaking*	CO–ED, DECO
[horse]-*breaking*	SHORE

break²

indicating inclusion:

break into *	incl in *
• all *break into* sh–op	SHALLOP

break open	incl *
• English master *breaks open* cr–ate	CREMATE
breaks *	incl in *
• war *breaks* flier	BEWARE
broken by a . . .	incl A
broken by *	incl *
• flier *broken by* war	BEWARE
broken into by a . . .	incl A
broken into by *	incl *
• sh–op *broken into by* all	SHALLOP

break³

indicating omission:

break end off shove(l)	SHOVE
break ends off (s)hove(l)	HOVE
break ends off bran(ch)	BRAN
break head off (f)lower	LOWER
break tip off (s)pear	PEAR

break⁴

other uses:

break	HOL, WE
break of day	D
break point	SNAPS
break the ice	DEFROST
break vessel	CRACKPOT
breakdown specialist	ANALYST
	COUNSELLOR, PSYCHIATRIST
	SHRINK
breaking into sa/fe at/ night	FEAT
broken romance	SERIAL
broken statue	BUST
short break	HOL, WE
	(*see also* broke)

breakfast

break[fast]	FATS
breakfast (cereal)	BRANDISH
breakfast food, *say*	SERIAL

breakwater

breakwater, *say*	GROIN
break[waters]	WASTER

breast

breast-fed rodent	TITMOUSE
breast feeding	TITRATION

breather

breather	GILL, LUNG
breathing space	PORE

bred

bred, *say*	BREAD, DOE, DOH, DOUGH

breed

breed aliens	HATCHETS
breed fish, *say*	RAISE
breed it, *say*	HATCHET
breeding dogs, *say*	PUPATION, PUPPETRY

brew

brew of [ale]	LEA
brewed [tea]	ATE

brewing [ales]	LEAS, SALE, SEAL	*bring back* new<	WEN
brews, *say*	BRUISE	*bring in* a	incl A
[trouble] *brewing*	BOULTER	*bring in* *	incl *
bribe(ry)	PALM-OIL	• pun–t *brings in* girl	PUNDIT
brick		• Bill *brought in* the *French* . . .	LACE
brick carrier	HOD, STRETCHER	*bring round* a . . .	incl A
brickmaker	CLAY	*bring round* *	incl *
bride		• king *brought round* the . . .	LEATHER
bridal train	HONEYMOON EXPRESS	*bring up* boy(D)^	YOB
Brides*head*	B	bring up sentry	REARGUARD
bridle-path, *say*	AISLE	brings in rent	ISLET
bridge		*brought about by* [a new] . . .	WANE, WEAN
bridge	BR	brought forward	BF
• bridge *has* different . . .	BROTHER	*brought round* [his pal]	PHIALS
• bridge in East	BRINE	brought together	ATI, ATONE
• bridge that is . . .	BRIE	*brought up* [a lot] . . .(D)^	TOLA
bridge	SPAN	**Britain**	B, BR, GB
• bridge champion	SPANKING	**British**	
• bridge *enclosing* one . . .	SPAIN	British	B
• bridge that is long	SPANIEL	• British are good horsemen	BRIDEWELL
bridge builder, *say*	ARCHAEOLOGIST	• British nationality	BRACE
bridge game	PONTOON	• British weather	BRAIN
bridge opponents	NE, NW, SE, SW	British	BR
bridge partners	EW, NS, SN, WE	• British and *French*	BRET
bridge player, *say*	CARDIOLOGIST	• British fish	BRANGLE, BRIDE
bridge players	E, N, S, W	• British landlord	BROWNER
Bridg*end*	G	• British philosopher	BRAYER
bridge*head*	B	• British service women	BRATS
bridle	(*see* bride)	• British state	BRAVER
brief		• British tree	BRASH
brief		British	
indicating abbreviation:		–Academy	BA
• *brief* manuscript	MS	–Airways	BA
• *brief* period	MIN, MO, HR, SEC	–America	BA
• *brief* reply	ANS	–Association	BA
brief agreement	COMPACT	–Columbia	BC
brief attire	LAW SUIT	–Empire Medal	BEM
brief-case	SHORT SUIT	–Home Stores	BHS
brief farewell	SOLON(g)	–Institute of	
brief flutter	SHORT WAVE	Management	BIM
brief season	SHORTFALL	Radiology	BIR
brief trip	SHORTFALL	–Legion	BL
brief*case*	BF	–Library	BL
briefly writ(e)	WRIT	–Medical Journal	BMJ
brig	BR	–Museum	BM
brigade		–Library	BML
brigade	BDE	–Optical Association	BOA
brigade-major	BM	–Oxygen Company	BOC
bright		–Petroleum	BP
bright boy	RAY	–Pharmacopoeia	BP
bright land	WEST	–Pharmaceutical Codex	BPC
brightly coloured	(in) R–ED, RED	–Printing Corporation	BPC
brilliant champion	STARCH	–Rail	BR
brimstone	S, SULPHUR	–Red Cross Society	RCS
bring		–Road Services	BRS
bring about [a new] . . .	WANE, WEAN	–Shipbuilders	BS

–Standards (Institution)	BS(I)	• brown and . . .	BRAND
–Steel (Corporation)	BS(C)	• Brown drunk	BROILED
–Sugar Corporation	BSC	• brown insect	BRANT
–Summer Time	BST	brown	TAN
–Thermal Unit	BT(H)U	• brown hats	CAPSTAN
–United Provident Association	BUPA	• brown man	TANGENT
British capital	STERLING	• brown potassium	TANK
British *capital*	B	brown bread	TOAST
British company	BL	brown schoolboy	TOM
British country		browned off	SUNBURNED, TANNED
music	GOD SAVE THE QUEEN	**browse**	
	NATIONAL ANTHEM	browse, *say*	BROWS, GREYS
British *flower*	SEVERN, THAMES etc	**bruise**	
British Honduras	BH	bruise, *say*	BREWS, WAIL, WHALE
British *leader*	B		WHEAL, WHEEL
broach		**brush**	BASIL, SAGE
broach *	incl in *	**bubble**	
• I *broach* h–er . . .	HEIR	*bubbling* [stream]	MASTER, REMAST
• barrel *broached by* a . . .	TUAN	*bubbly* [girl in] . . .	RILING
broad		**buckle**	
Broad Street	LARGEST, WIDEST	*buckled* [post]	POTS, SPOT, STOP, TOPS
broader, *say*	WHIDAH, WHYDAH	*buckles,* [gold pair]	PRODIGAL
broadcast		*buckling* [down 'e] . . .	OWNED
[broad]*cast*	BOARD	**budding**	
broadcast [news]	WENS	*budding* of (f)lowers	LOWERS
broadcast news	GNUS	*budding* writer	PE(n)
broadcast race	RELAY	**Buenos Aires**	BA
broadcast [race]	ACER, ACRE, CARE	**buffet**	
broadcast, *say*	SEW, SEWN, SO	*buffet* [car]	ARC
broadcast seed again, *say*	RECEDED	*buffeting* [gale]	GAEL
broadcast twice, *say*	SO-SO	**buggy type**	BACTERIOLOGIST
broadcaster	SOWER	**build**	
broadcasting organisation	AUNTIE, BEEB	builder	JACK, JERRY
broadcasting, *say*	SEWING	*builders of*	
[live] *broadcast*	EVIL, VILE	[Kew longed]	KNOWLEDGE
[outside] *broadcast*	TEDIOUS	building	BDG
Broadmoor	CRANK CASE	building area, *say*	HALLIARD, HALLYARD
broke		building at this point, *say*	HAULIER
broke	NOCENT	building charges	HALLIONS
broken sculpture	BUST	*building* [Ma used]	MEDUSA
	(*see also* break)	*builds* [town]	WONT
broker	UNCLE	*built of* [stone]	NOTES, ONSET, TONES
bronchitic		*built-up* [shoe]	HOES, HOSE
bronchitic, *say*	COFFER	[empire]-*building*	PREMIER
bronchitic lungs	ANCIENT LIGHTS	[master]-*builder*	REMAST, STREAM
broth		**bulk**	
broth [made in] . . .	MAIDEN	*bulk of* grain	GRA, RAIN
broth of a [boy]	YOB	bulk service	MASS
[stale] *broth*	LEATS, STEAL	bulkhead	B
	TALES, TEALS	**bull**	
brother		bullhead	B
brother	BILLY, BR, BRO	bully	COWER, FLASHMAN, HECTOR
brotherhood	COWL	bully	OXY–
brought	(*see* bring)	bully beef	WARFARE
brown		bully prince	HECTOR
brown	BR	**bulletin**	LOADED, SHOT

Anag [cat]; Any *; Begin IGN–; Endings –ING; eg •; Hidden /cat/; Implied add (on); Implied in (in);

bum
bum-boat — TRAMP
bum-[boats] — SABOT
bum rap — SPANKING
bum [steer] — RESET
bump
bump into attendant — RAMPAGE
bumpy [lane] — LEAN
bumpy [ride] — DIRE
bunch
bunch of fives — FIST
bunch of keys — ACE, AGE, BAD, GAB
     AGED, BADE, CAFE, DEAF,
     EDGE, EGAD, FACE
     DEFACE, FACADE
bundle
bundle of [papers] — SAPPER
bundle [was tied] — WAISTED
bundled up [in rags] — RASING
bungle
bungle [each] ... — ACHE
bungling [all the] ... — LETHAL
bunker — WARDEN
bunter — BILLY, GOAT, SANDSTONE
buoyant actress — MAE WEST
Burlington House — RA
Burmese
Burmese — SHAN
• Burmese tea, *say* — SHANTY
burn
burn church — SEARCE, SEARCH
bu<u>rn</u> *both ends* — BN
burn fish — CHAR
burn fuel — CHARCOAL
burn planes, *say* — GLOWING
burn, *say* — FLAIR
burn them, *say* — SERUM
burn vehicle, *say* — GLOBOSE, GLOBOUS
burned incense, *say* — SENSED
burning — (in) FI–RE
burning desire — ARSON, PYROMANIA
burning issue — FIRE-ENGINE
burning land — ALIGHT
burning ring — FLAMINGO
burnt bones, *say* — BEAU NASH
burst
burst [into] ... — –TION
burst [into a] ... — –ATION
burst [into tears] — STATIONER
burst into * — incl in *
• he *bursts into* mas–s — MASHES
burst [open] — NOPE, PEON
bursting [vein] — VINE
Burundi
Burundi — RU
capital of Burundi — B

leader of Burundi — B
bury
buried — INTOMB
buried in /a gar/den — AGAR
bury — INTER
• bury Edward — INTERNED
• bury girl — INTERVAL
• bury *up to* the knees, *say* — INTERNEES
bury a ... — incl A
bury * — incl *
• *bury* saint in ha–y — HASTY
burying * — incl in *
• ha–y *burying* saint — HASTY
bush
bushman — TOPIARIST
bushwhacker — TOPIARIST
bushel — BU, BUS(H)
business
business — ADO
• business about ... — ADORE
• business exercise — ADOPT
• business *with* the Navy — ADORN
business — BIZ
business — CO
• Brown on business ... — BRONCO
• business event — COINCIDENT
• business friend — COPAL
• business support — COBRA
• business woman — COW
• businessman — CODAN, CODON,
     CODES, COGENT
business — FIRM
• a loud business — AFFIRM
• in business *with* a line ... — INFIRMARY
• study business — CONFIRM
business area — EC, SHOPFLOOR
business
subscription — YOURS FAITHFULLY
busybody — ANT
bust
bust [bust] — BUTS, STUB
[bust] *bust* — BUTS, STUB
bust in [marble] — RAMBLE
bust up [over] ... — ROVE
busted [gut] — TUG
bust, *say* — KISSED
but
but French ... — MAIS
but *once* — SED
butcher
butcher [cows] — SCOW
butcher's complaint — BEEF
butcher's (hook) — LOOK, SEE
butchery of [tribe] — BITER, TIBER
[lamb] butchered — BALM
butler — JEEVES, RAB, RHET

butt

butt in(to) *	incl in *
• I *butted into* he–r . . .	HEIR
butter	GOAT, RAM
butter-paper	RAMPAGE(S)
butter-*up*(D)^	MAR
buttress	NANNY-GOAT

buy

buy dog, *say*	BIKER
buy parts for radio, *say*	BIVALVES
buy *sound* . . .	BY(E)
buyer's option	BO

buzz

buzzed, *say*	WORD
buzzer	BEE, FLY

by

by	PER
• by a boy	PERSON
• by cutting	PERSEVERANCE
• by *returning*<	REP
• by *turning over*<	REP
by (=times)	X
• nothing by . . .	OX
by *accident* [spilt] . . .	SPLIT
by *all accounts* might . . .	MITE
by *arrangement* [I went] . . .	TWINE
by canopy	ATTESTER
by *ear*, Handel . . .	HANDLE
by *half*	B, Y
by loch (=Scottish)	
• by *loch*, one . . .	ANE
• church *by loch*	KIRK
by [means] . . .	MANES, NAMES
by means of, *say*	THREW

by *mistake* [I went] . . .	TWINE
by name	SC
by *no means* al(l)	AL
by-pass	COLOSTOMY, ILEOSTOMY
by-*passed by* *	incl in *
• city *by-passed by* r–ing	RELYING
by-*passing* a . . .	incl A
by-*passing* *	incl *
• r–ing *by-passing* city	RELYING
by proxy	PP
by, *say*	BUY, BYE
by *the ears* I'll . . .	AISLE, ISLE
by *the mouth* were . . .	WHIRR
by the river, *say*	DECIDE
by *the sound* of her . . .	OFFER
by *the sound of it*	BUY, BYE
by the way	ROADSIDE
by the way	incl RD or ST
• the man, *by* the way	HERD
• a Red, *by* the way	STARED
• the *French, by* the way	LAST, LEST
by the way	incl N, S, E, W
	incl RD, ST
by turning [over]	ROVE
by using [miracles]	RECLAIMS
by *word of mouth* passed	PAST
eaten *by mouth*	ETON

bye

bye	B
bye-bye	BB

Byzantine

Byzantine [art is] . . .	STAIR
<u>B</u>yzantine *capital*	B
<u>B</u>yzantine *leader*	B

Anag [cat]; Any *; Begin IGN–; Endings –ING; eg •; Hidden /cat/; Implied add (on); Implied in (in);

C

about, approximately, Caesarian, calorie, canine, cape, caput, capacitance, carat, carbon, cargo, castle, Catholic, caught, cedi, cee, Celsius, cent, centi-, centigrade, centime, century, chapter, Charles, circa, city, cloudy, club, clef, cold, college, colony, colt, common time, complex numbers, compliance, computer language, Conservative, constant, contralto, copyright, coulomb, Cuba, cubic, electrical capacitance, horizon, hundred, hundred thousand, key, *lot*, *many*, note, *number*, roughly, san, *sea*, *see*, social class, speed of light, spring, tap, third grade, vitamin

---

cab
cab, *say*	HANDSOME
cabs, *say*	TAXES

cabbage
cabbage, *say*	KAIL

cabinet
cabinet enquiry	CASE STUDY
cabinet-maker	ADAM, CHIPPENDALE
	HEPPLEWHITE, SHERATON
	EBENISTE
	KINGWOOD, ROSEWOOD,
	SATINWOOD
	PRIME MINISTER

Caesar
Caesar's (=Latin or Roman)	
• *Caesar's* clemency	LATIN QUARTER
• *Caesar's* cloak	TOGA

cage
cage seagull	MEW
caged in *	incl in *
• cat *caged in* pen	SCATTY
cagey, *say*	KG
caging a . . .	incl A
caging *	incl *
• pen *caging* a cat	SCATTY
cagy, *say*	KG

cake
cake	BUN
• cake container, *say*	BUNKAGE
• cake firm	BUNCO
• cake particle	BUNION
cake burner	ALFRED
Cakesville	ECCLES

calamity
calamitous [drop]	PROD
calamity [when] . . .	HEWN
[it was] *calamitous*	WAIST

Caledonian

Caledonian (=Scottish)
• *Caledonian* oxen	OWSEN
• fat *Caledonian*	FOZY
	(*see also* Scottish)

calf
calf	CF, STOCKING FILLER
calf, *perhaps*	NEW JERSEY
calfskin	LOWER CASE

California
Californian city	LA
Californian tree, *say*	RED-WUD

call
call *about*	R–ING
call *about*<	BUD, –ETIC
call at pub	BARRING
call *back*<	BUD, –ETIC
callboy	RINGED
call for prayer	COLLECT
call from Tom	MIAOW
call from Queen	MIAOW
call *on* debtor	YELLOWER
call round	RING
call *round*	R–ING
call *to* grub	RINGWORM
call to prayer, *say*	NEIL
call up	TALLY-HO, YOICKS
call *up*(D)^	BUD, –ETIC
called, *say*	SIGHTED, SITED
called cops	COPSE
called in a . . .	incl A
called in *	incl *
• Le–n *called in* doctor	LEMON
called into question [all the]...	LETHAL
callgirl	CALLUNA
calling for . . .	FORE, FOUR

calm
calm down	ENDANGER
calm, *say*	PIECE

Letter replaced \c\at; Omit (a); Pointers *out*; Retain a̲; Split B_ED; Down (D); Backwards <or ^

calorie	CAL	*can't keep* *	omit *
Cambodia		• fat(her) *can't keep* her	FAT
Cambodia	KA	*can't spell* too *well*	TO, TU–, TWO
capital of Cambodia	C	*can't spell* too *well*	TOWEL
leader of Cambodia	C	**Canada**	CDN
Cambridge university	HARVARD	**Canadian**	
came		Canadian Air Force	RCAF
came here by boat, *say*	ROE-DEER	Canadian *capital*	C
	ROWDIER	Canadian *flower*	ST LAWRENCE etc
came here on a horse, *say*	ROE-DEER	Canadian *leader*	C
	ROWDIER	Canadian National Railway	CNR
came to a point, *say*	PIQUED	Canadian navy	RCN
	(*see also* come)	Canadian Pacific Railway	CPR
camouflage		Canadian police force	MOUNTIES, RCMP
camouflaged [tanks]	STANK	Canadian Royal Academy	CRA
camouflaging [guns]	GNUS, SNUG	Canadian sailors	RCN
[desert] *camouflage*	RESTED	Canadian soldiers	CEF
camp		**Canary Islands**	E
camp child	STALAGMITE	**cancel**	
camp helper	AIDE	cancel	omit DO
camping	(in) T–ENT, INTENT	• *cancel* door	OR
camping holiday	INTENT	cancel score	SCRATCH
campanologist		cancelled	incl O
campanologist, *say*	WRINGER	• *cancelled* match	OWED
	YOUTH HOSTELLER	• *cancelled* race	ORAN
can¹		• *cancelled* soldiers' . . .	OMEN
can	–ABLE	**candela**	CD
can be prosecuted	ISSUABLE	**candle**	
• can I?	AMIABLE	candle point	TAPER
can	MAY	candlemaker	STEARIN, TALLOW, WAX
• can a European . . . ?	MAYPOLE	candlepower	CP
• can cough	MAYHEM	**canine**	
• this can, *say*	DISMAY	canine affliction	TOOTHACHE
can	TIN	canine letter	R
• can sell, *say*	TINSEL	canine racer	LAPDOG
• can state	TINCAL	**cannibal**	
• cans will, *say*	TINSEL	cannibal, *say*	MASSETER
can²		*cannibalised* [cars]	ARCS, SCAR
can be heard coughing	COFFIN	*cannibalising* [parts]	SPRAT, TRAPS
can be [leased]	SEALED	**canon**	CAN
can be said aloud	ALLOWED	**canoodle**	
can be said to . . .	TOO, TWO, TU–	canoodle	BILL (AND COO)
can be said to be . . .	TUBE	• canoodle with Chinese	
can become [angry]	RANGY	gang, *say*	BILTONG
can he, *say*	CANNY	canoodle	NECK
can opener	PRISON GATE	• canoodle with sailor, *say*	NECTAR
can opener	C	canoodle	SPOON
canned	(in) CA–N, (in) T–IN	• canoodle twice	SPOONBILL
• no *tinned* . . .	CANON	**can't**	(*see* can, unable)
• *canned* beef	TOXIN	**cant**	TINT
canned	BLIND (DRUNK), TIGHT		(*see* can, unable)
• canned fruit	BLIND DATE	**canter**	
• liquid canned	WATERTIGHT	*cantered* [into] . . .	–TION
can't	TINT	*cantering* [horse]	SHORE
can't keep a . . .	omit A	**canto**	CAN
can't keep quiet	omit P	**canvas**	
• do(p)e *can't keep* quiet	DOE	canvas	PAINTING

Anag [cat]; Any *; Begin IGN–; Endings –ING; eg •; Hidden /cat/; Implied add (on); Implied in (in);

canvas support	EASEL
canvassed area	CAMP SITE
canvassed views	LANDSCAPES, SEASCAPES
	TOWNSCAPES etc
cap	
cap	HAT
• cap colour	HATRED
• cap fit	HATABLE
capless (m)ale(D)	ALE
capped	BLUE, INTERNATIONAL
capability	BROWN
cape	C, HORN
Capek's play	RUR
caper	
caper, *say*	ANTIQUE
capital¹	
capital	AI
• capital fish	AILING
• capital money	AID, AIL
• capital *return<*	–IA
• *raise* capital(D)^	–IA
capital (=first letter)	
• *capital loss* in (S)pain	PAIN
• *capital of* Spain	S
• *capital punishment*	
for (s)entry	ENTRY
• state *capital*	S
capital *missing*	omit 1st letter
• capital *missing*	
from (t)ill	ILL
capital *withdrawn*	omit 1st letter
• capital withdrawn	
from (B)erne	ERNE
capital²	
capital	HEAD
capital cover	HAT, HAIR, SCALP
capital flat	TEMPLE
capital improvement	HAIR-DO
	PERM(ANENT WAVE)
capital investment	HEADDRESS
capital issue	BEARD, HAIR, WHISKERS
capital³	
capital (=chief city)	
capital authority	GLC
capital footwear	WELLINGTON
capital players	LSO
capital type	BERLINER, LONDONER
	NEW YORKER, PARISIAN, ROMAN
capital⁴	
other uses:	
Capital Gains Tax	CGT
capital letter	ENLARGE, LARGESSE
capital letters	TOPAZ
capital punishment	FINE, STOCKS
Capital Transfer Tax	CTT
capricious	
[act] *capriciously*	CAT

capricious [mood]	DOOM
capriciously [makes] . . .	KAMES
capsize	
capsized [ship]	HIPS, PISH
capsized vessel<	TOP
[it was] *capsizing*	WAIST
captain	
captain	CID, OLD MAN
captain	SKIP(PER)
• captain with sailor	SKIPJACK
captain's place	BRIDGE
captivate	
captivate a . . .	incl A
captivate *	incl *
• ma–n *captivates* one . . .	MAIN
captivated by gent/le har/mony	LEHAR
captivated by *	incl in *
• one *captivated by* ma–n	MAIN
captive	
captive	incl in *
• no–ted *captive* bird	NOMINATED
captive	(in) C–AGE, (in) GA–OL
capture	
capture	BAG
• capture animal, *say*	BAGASSE
• capture the Tube	BAGPIPE
• press captures . . .	PAPER BAGS
capture king	SECURER
captured, *say*	COPT
captured by *	incl in *
• queen *captured by* PM	PERM
captured in larg/e vil/la	EVIL
captures a . . .	incl A
captures, *say*	COPSE
captures *	incl *
• PM *captures* queen	PERM
car	
car	AUTO
• car dealer	AUTOCHANGER
• car driver	AUTOPILOT
• car indicator	AUTOCUE
• cars in front	AUTO-SLED
car	GT
• nothing *in* car	GOT
car	MINI
• car *on* motorway	MINIM
• cars go	MINISTRY
car	RR
• girl *in* car	RADAR
car club	AA, RAC
car driver	PETROL
car key, *say*	KHAKI
car lifter	JACK
car rug	AUTOMAT
car salesman's technique	AUTO-SUGGESTION
car-test	MOT
(c)ar *won't start*	AR

Letter replaced \c\at; Omit (a); Pointers *out*; Retain a̲; Split B_ED; Down (D); Backwards <or ^

carat	CAR, CT	• carried Portuguese noble	BOREDOM
carbon		• carried, *say*	BOAR
carbon	C	carried by	ON
• carbon copy	CAPE	• carried by Scot	–ONIAN
• carbon-dating	CAGING	• club carried by . . .	BATON
• carbon fibre	CHAIR	carried on	
• remains of carbon	CASH	–in error, *say*	SINDON
card		–snogging, *say*	NEKTON
card	A, ACE, J, K, Q	carried, *say*	BORN, BOURNE, WARN
card	CHARACTER	*carried by* (D)	
• card player	CHARACTER ACTOR	• mother *carried by* boy	DAMSON
card	DENRY MACHIN	*carried by* mo/st ar/tists	STAR
card game, *say*	PEAKY, PICKET, WIST	*carried by* *	incl in *
card player	DECKHAND	• log *carried by* ship	SLOGS
card players	NEWS, SEWN, WENS	*carried out* [a test]	TASTE
cards	HAND, TALON	carried papers	PIPE-DREAM
cardinal		*carries*(D)	
cardinal	CARD, RED, WOLSEY	• boy *carries* mother	DAMSON
cardinal point	EMINENCE	*carries* a . . .	incl A
cardinal points	NEWS, SEWN, WENS	*carries* cross	incl X
cardiograph	TICKER TAPE	carries on	
care		–signalling	WAVESON
care of	CO	–staunching	STEMSON
care for, *say*	WRECK	carries sailor, *say*	LODESTAR
[care] *free*	ACER, ACRE, RACE	*carries* *	incl *
careless bonds	CASUALTIES	• ship *carries* log	SLOGS
careless (h)ost	OST	carry	BEAR
careless [metering]	REGIMENT	• carry money	BEARD
carelessly [done]	NODE	*carry back in* a/erop/lane<	PORE
carer, *say*	WRECKER	*carry* money	incl L, P
cares, *say*	REX, WRECKS	• carry money *in* s–ack	SLACK
[rank] *carelessness*	KNAR, NARK	• he *carries* money	HEP
career		carry on	
career people	RACE	–diving	PLUNGEON
careering [over]	ROVE	–fighting, *say*	PUNCHEON
careers [about]	U-BOAT	–playing	BATON
[cars] *careered*	ARCS, SCAR	–pushing	SURGEON
cargo boats	MN	–*say*	CARRION
Caribbean islands	WI	–teasing, *say*	RIBBON
carpenter		carry revolver	CARTWHEEL
carpenter	CHIPPY	*carry* round	incl O
carpenter's mate	WALRUS	carry, *say*	BARE, WARE
carpentry	CARP	carrying hose	STOCKING
carpet	REPRIMAND	**cart**	
carriage		[cart]*wheels*	–CRAT
carriage, *say* ACNE, FIGHTING, HANDSOME		[he's] *in the cart*	SHE
carriage paid	CP	**Cartesian**	
carried	(*see* carry)	[Cartesian] *formula*	ASCERTAIN
carrier		**cartoon fish**	STRIPLING
carrier	BARKIS, BR, RY, RLY	**carve**	
carrier for hooligan	ROUGHSHOD	carve accent	GRAVE
carrier, *say*	BARER	carve insect	ETCHANT
carrier's confession	IMPORTER	*carved up* [meat]	MATE, TAME, TEAM
carry		*carving* [lamb]	BALM
carried	BORE	**case**	
• carried corpses, *say*	BOARDED	case of pins and needles	ETUI
• carried drill	BORE	*case of* _w_hisky	WY

Anag [cat]; Any *; Begin IGN–; Endings –ING; eg •; Hidden /cat/; Implied add (on); Implied in (in);

cased in a . . .	incl A	casual worker	TEMP
cased in *	incl *	• casual worker *with* one . . .	TEMPI
• gold *cased in* iron	FORE	• casual worker in front	TEMPLED
cases	CA	• casual worker overdue	TEMPLATE
casing in *	incl in *	and	
• iron *casing in* gold	FORE	• worker is *French*	TEMPEST
in any *case*	AN–Y	• worker, the *French* . . .	TEMPLE
in case of wine	H–OCK, VI–N	• worker *with* ring	TEMPO
pastry *case*	PY	casually dressed	UNSUITED
cash		*casualty* [ward]	DRAW
cash	BRASS	**cat**	
• cash collapses	BRASSFOUNDERS	cat	CAT
• cash that is about . . .	BRASSIERE	• cat family	CATKIN
cash	BREAD	• cat fur	CATNAP
• cash crop	BREADFRUIT	• cat goes to church	CATCH
• cash *given to* journalist	BREADED	cat	FELIX, MOG, REX
cash	L	cat	OUNCE
• cash *in the* bag	SLACK	• black cat	BOUNCE
• paid *in* cash? *The reverse*	PLAID	• flourished cat	FLOUNCE
cash	READY, RHINO	• girl *with* cat	ANNOUNCE
cash	TIN	cat	TABBY
• cash *in* saint's . . .	STINTS	• cat chewed, *say*	TABITUDE
• cash, for example *returns*	TINGE	• cat trap *say*	TAB(B)INET
cash against documents	CAD	cat	TOM
cash on delivery	COD	• a cat	ATOM
	MATERNITY GRANT	• catbird	TOMTIT
cash present	COINHERE	• catfish	TOMCOD
cash registers	NOTES	• cats	TOM-TOM
cash with order	CWO	cat-o'-nine-tails	BACKMARKER
cashless	omit L	cat rouses, *say*	KITTIWAKES
• cash*less* Lapp	APP–	cat will, *say*	CATTLE
casserole		catcall	MEW, MIAU, MIAOW
casserole of [meat]	MATE, TAME, TEAM	cat's home, *say*	MEWS
casseroled [lamb]	BALM	cat's paw	PUSSYFOOT
cast		catty utterance	PURR
cast [a net]	NEAT	catty utterance, *say*	PER
cast about ten< . . .	NET	**catalogue**	CAT
cast about [ten]	–ENT, ENT–, NET	**catch**	
c(as)t as *not wanted*	CT	catch	NET
cast down	MOULT(ED)	• catch spirit	NETRUM
cast off	EXEUNT	• catch woman's . . .	NETHER
[cast] *off*	ACTS, CATS, SCAT	• good catch	BONNET
cast off here	GREEN ROOM	catch	TRIP
cast out here	STAGE DOOR	• catch fish	TRIPLING
cast, *say*	THROUGH	• catch insect, *say*	TRIPPANT
cast skin	omit 1st and last letters	*catch* cold	incl C
• (p)up(a) *casts skin*	UP	catch game	CONTRACT
[cast] *spell*	ACTS, CATS, SCAT	catch Joy	GLEE
*cast*a[way]	YAW	catch model	SITTER
casting director	PLASTERER	catch *up*(D)^	BAN, TEN
castle		catches fish	TAKE SIDES
castle	R(OOK)	*catching* a . . .	incl A
castle in the air	FLYING FORTRESS	*catching some* fi/sh or e/els	SHORE
	ROOK	*catching* the one-five	incl IV
casual		*catching* *	incl *
casual [remark]	MARKER	• ma–n *catching* one . . .	MAIN
casual trousers, *say*	GENES	*caught* a . . .	incl A

Letter replaced \c\at; Omit (a); Pointers *out*; Retain a; Split B_ED; Down (D); Backwards <or ^

caught *	incl *
• ma–n *caught* one	MAIN
caught by *	incl in *
• one *caught by* ma–n	MAIN
caught in m/an t/rap	ANT
	(*see also* caught)
catechism	CAT
cathedral	ELY
cathode-ray	
cathode-ray oscillograph	CRO
cathode-ray tube	CRT
catholic	RC
cattle	
cattle	KINE, NEAT
cattle complaint	BEEF
cattle dealing	STOCK EXCHANGE
cattle drive	STEER
cattle not watered	NEAT
cattle-truck	STOCK-CAR
caught	
caught	C
• caught a married . . .	CAWED
• caught an anthropoid	CANAPE
• caught at church	CATCH
• caught bird	CRAVEN, CROOK
• caught *by* leg	CLIMB
• caught fish	CLING
• caught man	CALF, CHAL, CLEW
• caught *on* branch	CLIMB
• caught *with* nothing on	COON
• caught *with* stolen goods	CLOOT
caught	CT
caught *in*	incl C
caught *out*	omit C
caught spirit	SNARE-DRUM
	(*see also* catch)
cause	
cause [alarm]	MALAR
cause of quarrel	ARROWROOT
cause for complaint	BACILLUS, BACTERIUM
	GERM, VIRUS etc
cause relief	EMBOSS
cause, *say*	CAWS
caused by [germ in a] . . .	REAMING
causes pain, *say*	HERTZ
caution	
caution, *say*	FOUR, WEAR, WORN
cautious sign(al)	AMBER
cave	
cave, *say*	KV
caveman	DEN
	POTHOLER, SPELEOLOGIST
cavy, *say*	KV
cavity	
cavity	O
• cavity *in* b–at	BOAT
• p–ut *round* cavity	POUT

cavort	
cavorted [like] . . .	KIEL
cavorting [lamb]	BALM
celebrate	
celebrate	SING
celebrated	CEL
celebrated dynasty	SUNG
celebration	DO, GALA
• celebration tea, *perhaps*	DOT, DOTE
• celebration drink	GALATEA
celebrity	LION, STAR, VIP
Celtic	
Celt, *say*	GALE
Celtic tax	SCOT
censor	CATO, EDIT
cent	C, CT
centilitre	CL
centime	C, CT
centimetre	CM
centipede	CLIMBS
central	
Central	
–African Republic	CAR, RCA
–America	CUS
–European Time	CET, MEZ
–Standard Time	CST
central	CEN
Central America	(s)TATE(s)
central character in Tosca	S
central de<u>fend</u>er	FEND
central heating	CH
central hea<u>t</u>ing	T
central letters	M, N
central le<u>t</u>ters	T
central nervous system	CNS
central processing unit	CPU
central Wales	ALE, L
centre	
Centre <u>Cou</u>rt	U
centre-forwards, *say*	HOSPITAL
centre-*half*	CEN, TRE
centre-<u>h</u>alf	AL
centre of gravity	CG
centre of gra<u>v</u>ity	V
centre of Paris	R
centre of *	incl in *
• the *centre of* scared . . .	FEATHERED
centre<u>fold</u>	OL
centrepiece	K, KING, Q, QU, QUEEN
*centre*pie<u>c</u>e	E
centrepiece of deco<u>rat</u>ions	RAT
Centre Point	MIDDLE EAST
Centre Po<u>i</u>nt	I
centre, *say*	NAVAL
s<u>e</u>lf-*centred*	EL
shop<u>p</u>ing-*centre*	PP
s<u>o</u>ft-*centred*	OF

Anag [cat]; Any *; Begin IGN–; Endings –ING; eg •; Hidden /cat/; Implied add (on); Implied in (in);

to<u>w</u>n-*centre*	OW
(l)OUT(h), (n)EAT(h) etc	
century	C, CEN
ceremony	
ceremony, *say*	RIGHT, WRIGHT, WRITE
cereal	
cereal	BRAN
• cereal bowl	BRANDISH
certain	
certain	SURE
• certain sack	SURE-FIRE
certain amount of beer	PINT
certain amount of <u>bee</u>r	BEE
certain amount of bee/r I se/nt	RISE
certain m/en rol/ling . . .	ENROL
certain parts of c/ar c/an . . .	ARC
certain person	DOGMATIST
certain, *say*	SHORE
certainly	YES, SURE
certainly *not*	omit SURE
• Pleasure? Certainly *not*	PLEA
certificate	
certificate	A, B, U, X
Certificated Master	CM
chain	
chain-letters	MAIL
chain parts, *say*	LYNX
chair	
chair is hard, *say*	CHERISH
chairman	ADAM, CHIPPENDALE
	HEPPLEWHITE, SHERATON
	PROFESSOR
chairman of	
–British Airways, *say*	BAKING
–RAC, *say*	RACKING
–TUC, *say*	TUCKING
chaldron	CH
champion	
champion	ACE
• champion	
water-sportsman	SURFACE
• fine champion	FACE
• formidable champion	GRIMACE
champion	CH
• champion members	CHARMS
• champion *with* style	CHAIR
• supreme champion	STARCH
champion boxer	SPARKING, TOP-DOG
chance	EARTHLY, HAP
change¹	
indicating anagram:	
• *change* [bowler]	BLOWER
• *change* [coins]	ICONS, SONIC
• *change* [into]	–TION
• *change* [into a]	–ATION
• *change of* [heart]	EARTH, HATER, RATHE
• *change of* [scene]	CENSE, –SENCE

• *change*-[over]	ROVE
• *change-over of* [duties]	SUITED
• *changeable* [weather]	WREATHE
• *changing* [gear]	RAGE
• [gear]-*change*	RAGE
• [ship] *changes course*	HIPS, PISH
change²	
indicating substitution:	
change ends of *	
• *change ends of* \l\eve\r\	REVEL
change leader	change 1st letter
• *change* \F\rench	
leader	DRENCH, TRENCH, WRENCH
• \p\arty *changes leader*	TARTY, WARTY
change of hear\t\	HEARS
change of heart	change middle letter(s)
• *change of heart* for T\or\y	TROY
• le\p\er has *change of heart*	LEVER
change of sc\e\ne	SCONE
change partners	change E for W, W for E
	change N for S, S for N
change polarity	change N for S
	change S for N
change sides	change L to R, R to L
• *change* side of \r\oad	LOAD
• *changing* side of \l\oom	ROOM
• gent\l\y *changing sides*	GENTRY
• pee\r\ *changes side*	PEEL
changing character	
of \w\eather	HEATHER, LEATHER
\O\ *for* \a\ *change in* vogue	VAGUE
change³	
other uses:	
change bowler	MONEY-SPINNER
change direction of road<	DR, EVA, IA, IM, TS
change directors	SWITCHBOARD
change gear	RECLOTHE, REDRESS
change girls, *say*	ALTERCATES
change in	
–America	CENT
–France	CENTIME
–Germany	PFENNIG
–Italy	CENTESIMO
–Spain	PESETA
–UK	PENNY
change into suit	BECOME
change its colour, *say*	DIET
change of heart	TRANSPLANT
change, *say*	ALTAR
change sides	RAT
changes	PEAL
changes clothes	SHIFTS
changes colour	TURNSTONE
changes, *say*	PEEL
changing gear	TRANSVESTISM
changing place	CREWE etc
	JUNCTION

Letter replaced \c\at; Omit (a); Pointers *out*; Retain <u>a</u>; Split B_ED; Down (D); Backwards <or ^

changing-room	BANK
channel	
Channel Islands	CI
channelled into [thin] . . .	HINT
chaos	
chaos [in the] . . .	THINE
chaotic [mess on] . . .	MESONS
[it was] *chaotic*	WAIST
chap	
chap in charge	MANIC
chaps	(*see* men, two²)
chapel	
chapel, *presumably*	NOTCH
chaplain	CF, CHAP, HCF, OCF, REV(D)
chaps	(*see* men, two²)
chapter	C, CAP, CH, CHAP
Chapter I	CHI
chapters	CC
Chapters *I & III*	CA
char	
char	DAILY
• char paper	DAILY
• chars wages	DAILY BREAD
char	TEA
• char got up	TEA-ROSE
• char *has* money	TEAL
character	
[all the] *characters*	LETHAL
character	CARD
• character-actor	CARD PLAYER
• character in Greek . . .	CARDING
• port authority *has* character	PLACARD
character	LETTER
character-forming	PRINTING, TYPING, WRITING
character impression	STAMP
character, *say*	ROLL
characters in [play]	PALY
character's size	POINT
Greek characters	ALPHA, BETA etc
Hebrew characters	ALEPH etc
charge	
charge	BILL
• angry charge	CROSSBILL
• charge alien	BILLET
• charge directors	BILLBOARD
charge	FEE
• charge a man, *say*	FEMALE
• charge circuit	FEERING
• charge circuit, *say*	FEARING
• charge family, *say*	FELINE
• charge nothing, *say*	PHOENIX
• charge *on* the bus, *say*	PHOEBUS
• charge *to* fish	FEELING
• charges, *say*	FEEZE
charge girl	COSTMARY
charge moderate	RUSHLIGHT

charge per session, *say*	CITRATE
charge *up*(D)^	NOI–
charge, *say*	INDITE, LODE
charged	LIVE
charged particle	ION
charged *up*(D)^	EVIL
charged with a . . .	incl A
charged with *	incl *
• iron *charged with* current	FACE
Charles	
Charles (king)	CR
• Charles I	CRONE
Charles *I*	C
Charles *II*	H
Charlie's better	FOOLSCAP
charm	
charm Scot	MAGICIAN
charmer	MUSIC
[charming] *disposition*	MARCHING
charming islander	CIRCE
charming man	WARLOCK
charming woman	WITCH
chart	
chart showing errors, *say*	SYNGRAPH
chase	
chased police	RANCID
chasing prostitutes, *say*	OARING
chased, *say*	CHASTE
chaste	
chaste	PURE
• chaste saint	PUREST
chaste, *say*	CHASED
chat	
chatting aloud	ALLOWED
not *chatting*	KNOT
chatterbox	TELEPHONE KIOSK
cheap	
cheap	ID, IP
cheap drink	FARTHINGALE
cheap floor	KNOCKDOWN
cheap ring	LOCAL CALL
cheap, *say*	CHEEP
cheap shelter, *say*	PENITENT
cheap transport	PENNY-FARTHING
cheat	
cheat	BEACON
cheat	CON
• cheat two boys	CONVICTED
cheat	DO
• cheat people	DONATION
• cheat soldiers	DOOR
• cheat twice	DODO
• cheats family	DOESKIN
cheating player	FIDDLER
check	
check	REIN
• check certain . . .	REINSURE

• check condition	REINSTATE
• check garment	REINVEST
• check, *say*	RAIN, REIGN
	(*see also* control)
check mate	TEST MATCH, TRIAL MARRIAGE
check performance	STUNT
check, *say*	CHEQUE, CZECH
checked *out*	SE–EN
• 5 checked *out*	SEVEN
checked, *say*	RAINED, REIGNED
checking again	REVETTING
checks sound, *say*	KERBSTONE

cheek

cheek	LIP
• cheeky	LIPOID
• loud cheek	FLIP
cheek	NECK
• cheek allowed	NECKLET
checks men	CHAPS
cheeky	MALAR
cheeky drop	TEAR
cheeky novel	FRESH

cheer

cheer up(D)^	HAR
cheering up	STANDING OVATION
cheerleader	HIP
cheer*leader*	C
cheers	TOAST

cheese

cheese container	ROLL
cheese insect	BRIEFLY
cheesemaker	RENNET
hard cheese	BAD LUCK
indifferent cheese	MOUSETRAP
say cheese	SMILE
chef's whiskers	BLENDERS, EGG BEATERS

chemical

chemical	NITRE
Chemical Society	CS
chemist	MPS
chemists	CS

chess

chess player	BLACK, WHITE
chessman, *say*	NIGHT

chest

chest, *say*	COUGHER
chest expander	MEDAL
chevron	V

chew

chew fly, *say*	GNAWING
chew lips, *say*	TULIPS
chewed [meat]	MATE, TAME, TEAM
chewing up [bone]	EBON
chews, *say*	CHOOSE
chi	X

chief

chief	ARCH
• chief Cornish saint	ARCHIVES
• chief financial backer	ARCHANGEL
• chief journalist	ARCHED
chief	CH, CID
chief	KING
• chief architect	PLANKING
• chief boxer	SPARKING
• chief censor	BANKING
• chief debt collector	DUNKING
• chief herring-packer	CRANKING
• chief invoice-clerk *say*	BILKING
• chief pastry-cook	BUNKING
• chief lavatory attendant	LOOKING
• chief leather-dresser	TANKING
• chief of tribe	CLANKING
• chief sun-god	RAKING
chief accountant	MAJORCA
chief manufacturer	KINGMAKER
chief mason	MASTER BUILDER

child

child	BOY
• child *after* cat	TOMBOY
• child put to bed	BOYCOTTED
• childhood, *say*	BUOYAGE
child	BRAT
child	CH
• child with guns	CHARMED
• child *in* horses' . . .	MARCHES
• strike child	HITCH
child	IMP
• child displays	IMPAIRS
child	KID
• child *on* knee, *say*	KIDNEY
• one *local* child	UNKID
• child slept	KIDNAPPED
• child *with* joint, *say*	KIDNEY
• child's family	KIDSKIN
child	TOT
• child *has* energy	TOTE
• child *with* friend	TOTALLY
• child *with* letter	TOTEM
Child Guidance Officer	JUNIOR COUNSEL
childish habits	LAYETTE, ROMPER SUITS
childish relation	BEDTIME STORY
	FAIRY STORY
childless	SP
childless	omit SON
• child*less* cleric	PAR(son)
• child*less* individual	PER(son)
• child*less* worker	MA(son)
children	ISSUE, SEED
children, *say*	BREWED
child's	
–drink	TOT
–play	PANTOMIME, PETER PAN etc
–toy, *say*	WHOOP
Chile	RCH

Letter replaced \c\at; Omit (a); Pointers *out*; Retain <u>a</u>; Split B_ED; Down (D); Backwards <or ^

chill
chill at this place, *say* — FREESIA
chill, *say* — FRIEZE
chime
chiming (=rhyming)
- *chiming* bell — CELL, DELL, FELL, HELL, SELL, TELL, WELL, YELL
- *chiming* sound — BOUND, FOUND, HOUND MOUND, POUND, ROUND
- *chiming* merrily — VERILY
chimney
chimney — LUM
- base of chimney, *say* — BEDLAM
- cowl *on* chimney — HOODLUM
chimney-pot — CAN
chin
[chin]*wag* — INCH
china
china — PORCELAIN, POTTERY SERVICE
china (plate) — MATE, PAL
china tea — MATE
China
China — CATHAY, CH, CHIN MIDDLE KINGDOM
China area (Far East) — FARE
Chinese *capital* — C
Chinese *flower* — YANGTSE
Chinese fruit — MANDARIN
Chinese *leader* — C
Chinese, *say* — CYNIC
Chinese takeaway — SHANGHAI
river in China — PLATE
chip
chip — UPSHOT
chip bag — KNAPSACK
chips — OLD MASTER
chips *without* fish — (carp)ENTER
chipshot — COUNTERSTROKE
chiropodist — CORN MERCHANT, FOOTMAN
chisel
chiselled [bust] — BUTS, STUB
chiselling [marble] — RAMBLE
choice
choice — OR
- choice cut — ORLOP
- choice of directions — NORE, NORSE SORE, SORN WORE, WORN, WORSE
- make choice *with* pin — ORPIN
chomp
chomp [oats] — STOA
chomping [roots] — TORSO
[horse] *chomped* — SHORE
choose
choose — ELECT
- choose artist — ELECTRA

- choose *by* word of mouth — ELECTORALLY
- choose particle — ELECTION
- choose *to* speak — ELECTORATE
- choosy individual — ELECTOR
choose — OPT
- choose one hundred — OPTIC
- choose one mother — OPTIMUM
- choose worker — OPTANT
choose — PICK
- choose a heretic *say* — PICARIAN
- choose an entrance, *say* — PICADOR
- choose bed, *say* — PICOTTE
- choose correctly, *say* — PICRITE
- choose fish — PICKLING
- choose foolish *Australian, say* — PICCADILLY
- choose prison, *say* — PICCAGE
- chose 'your', *say* — PICTURE
choose passage — EXTRACT
chop
chop down pin(e) — PIN
chop off bran(ch) — BRAN
chopstick — CLEAVE
chopped spice — CLOVE
chopped [spice] — EPICS
chopped (s)pice — PICE
chopper *up*(D)^ — EXA–
chopping [logs] — SLOG
Chopin lover — SAND
choreograph
choreograph [dance] — CANED
choreography of [Act IV] — VATIC
chorus girl — SHOWPIECE
chow-chow — DOG'S DINNER
Christ — CHR, X, XT
Christian — CHR, XN
Christian endeavour — CE
Christian era — AD
Christian men — MUTINEERS
Christian service — CS
Christmas
Christmas — PRESENT DAY, XM(AS)
Christmas girl — CAROL
Christmas hangover — MISTLETOE
Christmas period — DEC
Christmas present — FRANKINCENSE, GOLD MYRRH PARTRIDGE etc
Christmas present drawer — REINDEER
Christmas spirit — MARLEY'S GHOST
chromosome — X, Y
chronic patient — LONG-SUFFERING
chuck
chuck out a . . . — omit a
chuck out * — omit *
- ma(s)ter *chucked out* son — MATER
I chucked out. . . — omit I

church		**CID member**	YARDARM
church	CE	**cigar(ette)**	
• a church	ACE	[cigar]-*maker*	CRAIG
• a church ruler	ACER	cigarett<u>e</u>-*end*	E
• a church gallery	ACETATE	cigarette, *say*	REFER
and		**cinema director**	USHERETTE
• American church	AMERCE	**cipher**	
• city church	ESSENCE	cipher	O
• Italian church	ROMANCE	*ciphered* [signal]	ALIGNS
• many in church	MINCE	**circle**	
• mother church	MACE	[arty] *circles*	TRAY
• when at church . . .	WHENCE	*broken* [circle]	CLERIC
and		circle	DISC
• hurried *in* church	CRANE	• circle above . . .	DISCOVER
• man *in* church	CHIME	• circle America	DISCUS
• rodent *in* church	CRATE	• circle drops	DISCLOSES
and		• circle or ball	DISCORDANCE
• church keys	CEDE	circle	O
• church scriptures	CENT	• Circle line	OL, –ORY
• Church Street	CEST	• circle of friends	OPALS
church	CH	• circle round	OO
• church examination	CHORAL	• circles the globe	OOSPHERE
• church like St Paul's	WRENCH	• circular letter	OMISSIVE
• church militant	CHARMED, CHARMING	• dress-circle	GARBO
• church music (writer)	CHAIR(MAN)	• lady's circle	HERO
• church painter	CHARTIST	• race *in* circles	OTTO
• church songs	CHAIRS	circle	RING
• church vessel	CHURN	• a race *in* circle	RATTING
• church-woman	CHALICE	• circle permitted	RINGLET
• church work	CHOP	• circle, *say*	WRING
• church-worker	CHANT	• lady's circle	HERRING
and		*circle* a . . .	incl A
• church *on* the hill	TORCH	[circle] *around* . . .	CLERIC
• Egyptian church	ETCH	Circle Line	CHORD, CIRCUMFERENCE
• German church	HUNCH		DIAMETER, EQUATOR, INNER TUBE
• in church	INCH		MERIDIAN, NOOSE, RADIUS
• low church	MOOCH	circle of rocks	ETERNITY RING
• mother church	MACH	circle roughly	ROUNDABOUT
• stone church	PITCH	*circle* *	incl *
• which church?	THATCH	• rodent *circles* it	CAVITY
church	RC	* *circled by* . . .	incl in *
• a church (house)	ARC(H)	• it is *circled by* rodent	CAVITY
• church *has* enemies *all round*	FORCES	circles	DISCO, RING-DIAL
• spies *surround* church	CIRCA	*circling* [plane]	PANEL
church leader	LANG, HUME etc	Inner Circle	BULL'S EYE, GOLD, RED
<u>c</u>hurch *leader*	C	**circuit**	
churchman inside, *say*	DOMINEER	circuit	O
churchwarden's home	PIPE-RACK	circuit	RING
Churchill		• circuit rented	RINGLET
Churchill	WINNIE		(*see also* circle)
Churchill, *say*	WHINNY	*circuit of* [town]	WONT
churl		**circular**	
churl	CARL	circular letter	O, OMICRON, OMISSIVE
churlish, *say*	RUED	circular objects	DISCO, RING-DIAL
churn			(*see also* circle)
churning [a pint]	PAINT	**circulate**	
churning up [earth]	HATER, HEART, RATHE	*circulate* [news or] . . .	OWNERS

Letter replaced \c\at; Omit (a); Pointers *out*; Retain <u>a</u>; Split B_ED; Down (D); Backwards <or ^

circulating [in the] . . .	THINE
circulating note<	ETON
flat *remains in circulation*	LEVEL
[news in] *in circulation*	SEWN, WENS
circumnavigate	
circumnavigate a . . .	incl A
circumnavigate *	incl *
• help *circumnavigate* cape	ACID
circumnavigated by * . . .	incl in *
• cape *circumnavigated with*	
help	ACID
circus character	EROS
circumvent	
circumvent a . . .	incl A
circumvent *	incl *
• writing *circumvents* end . . .	MENDS
circumvented by *	incl in *
• end *circumvented by*	
writing . . .	MENDS
cite	
citation	CIT
cite, *say*	SIGHT, SITE
cites pain, *say*	NAMESAKE
city	
Abrahamville	LINCOLN
Cakesville	ECCLES
citizen	CIT
city	EC
• city house	ECHO
• city retreat	ECLAIR
• res–t *outside* the city	RESECT
city	ELY
• a king *in* city	EARLY
• as I *entered* the city	EASILY
• city diocese	ELYSEE
city	LA
• city representative	LAMP
• city street	LARD, LAST
city	NY
• big *in* New York	NOSY
• tin city	CANNY
city	LA, NY
city church	ESSENCE
city feature	URCHIN
city girl	ADELAIDE, ALICE, CONSTANCE,
	FLORENCE, NANCY, VICTORIA
city judge	TRIER
city (old)	TROY, UR
city press	SHANGHAI
city road	ANCHORAGE
city sailors	BATH SALTS
city, *say*	CITE
city slum	STOKEHOLE
c(it)y *with no centre*	CY
eternal city	ROME
granite city	ABERDEEN
holy city	JERUSALEM, MEDINA

	MECCA, ROME
New York	BIG APPLE, GOTHAM
old city	TROY, UR
Witchville	SALEM
Wyeville	ROSS
civic	
civic *leader*	C
civic leader, *say*	MARE
civil	
civil defence	ARP, CD
civil engineer	CE
civil servant	(in) C–S
civil service	CS
civilian	CIV
civilian dress	MUFTI
clad	
clad in ragg/ed gar/ments	EDGAR
clad with *	incl in *
• gold *clad with* i–vy	IVORY
cladding a . . .	incl A
cladding *	incl *
• I–vy *cladding* for gold . . .	IVORY
claim	
claim	AM
• claiming *French* father	AMPERE
• claiming lamb	AMELIA
• claiming our . . .	AMOUR
• claiming to be essayist	AMELIA
claim	IAM
• claiming *to have* vehicle	IAMBUS
• two claiming . . .	PRIAM
claim	IM–
• claiming goodness	IMPIETY
	IMPIOUSNESS, IMPURITY
• claiming some . . .	IMPART
• claiming to be Bill	IMPOSTER
claim	ME
• claim to be Edward	METED
• claim to be Indian	MEUTE
• claim *to* father	MESON
claim *say*	RITE, WRIGHT, WRITE
	(*see also* admit, confess, declare)
clash	
clashing [sound]	NODUS
[red] *clashes with* [pink]	PRINKED
clasp	
clasp, *say*	BUCCAL
clasped in /her b/reast	HERB
class	
class	CL
• Class 1	CLONE
• class always . . .	CLEVER
• class has...	CLOWNS
classic	
Classic races	DERBY, GUINEAS
	OAKS, ST LEGER
classic trees	OAKS

Anag [cat]; Any *; Begin IGN–; Endings –ING; eg •; Hidden /cat/; Implied add (on); Implied in (in);

Classics (examination)	GREATS	clear	PLAIN
classical		• clear air	PLAINSONG
classical (=Greek or Roman)		clear	RID
• classical art	ES	• clear note	RIDE
• classical god	DEUS	clear bargain	NEGOTIATE
• classical labourer	HERACLES, HERCULES	[clear] out	CLARE
• classical man	VIR	clear out [drawers]	REWARDS
• classical musician	ORPHEUS	clear photograph	TRANSPARENCY
• classical place	LOCUS	clear the table	DELAY
• classical power	VIS	clearance [granted]	DRAGNET
• classical skill	ARS	clearer run	BALDERDASH
• classical supporter	ATLAS	clearing [snow]	OWNS
classical character (=Greek letter)		**Cleopatra**	NEEDLEWOMAN
• classical character	ALPHA etc	**clergy**	
• classical character following a . . .	BETA	clergyman's address	SERMON
• first classical character	ALPHA		FATHER, RECTOR, VICAR
classify			MANSE, RECTORY, VICARAGE
classified	AD, ADVERT(ISEMENT)	clergyman *and* I celebrate	REVISING
classified item	ROAD	**cleric**	
classified [item]	EMIT, MITE, TIME	cleric	BD, DD
classified [papers]	SAPPER	clerical error	SPOONERISM
classification of cabs, *say*	TAXIS	clerical gangster	PRIESTHOOD
classmate	FORMALLY	*disguised* [cleric]	CIRCLE
classy	U	**clerk**	
clause		Clerk of the Peace	CP
clause	CL	Clerk to the Signet	CS
clause, *say*	CLAWS	**clever**	
clay		clever Dick	KNOW-ALL, SMART ALEC
clay	ALI	clever person	BA, MA
clay-pigeon	FLYING SAUCER	clever way	STREETWISE
clean		*cleverly* [made]	DAME, EDAM, MEAD
clean her, *say*	GUTTER	**climb**	
clean if I, *say*	PURIFY	climber	AMPELOPSIS, IVY
clean it up, *say*	MOPPET	climber's aid	TRELLIS
[clean] *out*	LANCE	*climbing* party(D)^	OD
cleaner	CHAR	*climbing* rose(D)^	DER
• cleaner fuel	CHARCOAL	*climbing* tor(D)^	ROT
• cleaner hair	CHARLOCK	**clinch**	
• cleaner *in* clear . . .	RICHARD	*clinch* a . . .	incl A
• cleaner porcelain	CHARMING	*clinch* *	incl *
cleaner entertainment	SOAP	• *clinch* deal *in* fog	MISDEALT
cleaner flag	DUSTER	*clinched by* *	incl in *
cleaner paper	DAILY	• deal *clinched in* fog	MISDEALT
clear		**cling**	
clear	`JUMP	*cling* to a . . .	incl A
• clear case	JUMP SUIT	*cling* to money	incl L
• clear crypt	VAULT	*cling* to *	incl *
clear	MANIFEST	• bo-y *clings to* ship	BOSSY
• clear round	MANIFESTO	**clip**	
clear	NET	*clip from* fil/m or n/egative	MORN
• clear round	NETBALL	clip wool, *say*	SHEER
• clear spirit	NETRUM	*clip* win(g)	WIN
• clear *up*(D)^	TEN	*clip wings of* (s)nip(e)	NIP
clear	OVERT	clipper	TOPIARIST
• clear cut	OVERTRUMP	**cloak**	
• clear lubricant	OVERTOIL	cloak, *say*	MANTEL, VALE
• clear water	OVERTRAIN	*cloaked in* secre/cy, St/ella . . .	CYST

cloaked in *	incl in *
• hollow *cloaked in* m–ist	MOIST
cloaking a . . .	incl A
cloaking *	incl *
• m–ist *cloaking* hollow	MOIST
clobber	
clobber [one] . . .	NEO–
[get] *clobbered*	TEG
clock	
clock	DIAL
• clock *on* city square	DIALECT
clock	TIMER
• clock *up*(D)^	REMIT
clock cover	VEIL, YASHMAK
clock cover, *say*	VALE
clock repair	FACE LIFT
clock repairer	COSMETIC SURGEON
clockwise	HOROLOGIST
close	
close	NIGH
• close connections	NIGHTIES
• close junction	NIGHT
• close relation	NIGHTIE
close average	MEAN
close boo<u>k</u>	K
close call	HANG UP, RING OFF
	TALLY-HO
close early	omit last letter
• ban(k) *closes early*	BAN
• *early closing* of gallery	TAT(e)
close friend	NEIGHBOUR
close of pla<u>y</u>	Y
close, *say*	MIEN
close to Cain's brother, *say*	BUYABLE
close watch	SHUT-EYE
closed	TO
closing of mil<u>l</u>	L
closing remar<u>k</u>	K
closure of min<u>e</u>	E
cloth	
cloth	CLERGY
• cloth-worker	CLERGYMAN
cloth	SERGE
• cloth-worker	SERGEANT
cloth	TWEED
• cloth in front	TWEEDLED
• cloth runner	TWEED
cloth cap	BIRETTA, MITRE
cloth-worker	VICAR etc
clothed	(in) GE–AR, IN GEAR
clothed by H/art/nell	ART
clothed by *	incl in *
• man *clothed in* re–d	REMAND
clothed in blu/e den/im	EDEN
clothes expert	HABITABLE
clothes fit . . .	SUIT
clothing a . . .	incl A

clothing strike	CLOBBER
clothing workers	SHIFT
clothing *	incl *
• re–d *clothing* man	REMAND
sh/e we/ars *clothing*	EWE
cloud	
cloud nine	EUPHORIA
[cloud]*burst*	COULD
cloudless plain	CLEAR
club	
club	C
club	IRON
• club functions	IRONWORKS
• club team	IRONSIDE
club	MACE
• club charges	MACERATES
• club servant	MACE-BEARER
club	RAC
club	SUIT
club	WOOD
• club talk	WOOD CHAT
• flower club	ROSEWOOD
club-house	VILLA
club magazine	ARSENAL
club sandwich	WEDGE
clubman	CADDY, GOLFER
	HERACLES, HERCULES
	PICKWICK
clubwoman	BATHER
clucking female	HEN, LAYER
clumsy	
clumsily [treads]	TRADES
clumsy [oafs]	SOFA
clutch	
clutch control	GRASP
clutch housing	BIRD'S NEST
clutching a . . .	incl A
clutching *	incl *
• Ra–y *clutching* £50	RALLY
clutched by *	incl in *
• £50 *clutched by* Ra–y	RALLY
CO$_2$	SECOND-IN-COMMAND
coach	
coach	TRAIN
• coach party	TRAINBAND
• second coach	STRAIN
coach bearing	CARRIAGE
coach building	SCHOOL
coach industry	DILIGENCE
coach look-out	TRAINSPOTTER
coach operator	BUSKING
coach shoe	TRAINER
coach worker	STAGEHAND
coaches	TRAIN
• coaches *aboard* ship	STRAINS
• coaches clayworker	TRAINSPOTTER
coal-hole	MINE, PIT

coalesce

coalescence of a mass	AMASS
fluorine *coalesces with* it	FLIT

coarse

coarse actors	BROADCAST
coarse aggregate	GROSS
coarse grade	RANK
coarse saint	CRUDEST
coarse, *say*	COURSE, RUFF

coast

coast erosion	BEACHWEAR
[coast] *erosion*	ATOCS, COATS
coastal billet	DRIFTWOOD

coat

coat of p<u>aint</u>	PT
coat, *say*	JERKING
coating a . . .	incl A
coating *	incl *
• frost *coating* tree	RIMFIRE
coated by *	incl in *
• tree *coated by* frost	RIMFIRE

cobbler

cobbler, *say*	SUITOR
cobble<u>r</u>'s *last*	R
cobbling together [yarn]	NARY

cocaine   CRACK, SNOW

cock

cock an ear(D)^	GUL, RAE
cocked a [snook]	NOOKS
cocked up [great] . . .	GRATE
cocked up an . . .(D)^	NA
cockerels, *say*	COX

Cockney

Cockney	omit H
• *Cockney* dwelling	(h)OUSE
• *Cockney* fence	(h)EDGE
• *Cockney* girl	(h)ER
• *Cockney* woodman	(h)EWER
• *East Ender's* (h)aunt	AUNT
• *East London* school	(h)ARROW
• *Eliza* getting better	(h)EALING
• fireplace *in Bow*	(h)EARTH
• hirsute *Bowman*	(h)AIRY
• *Londoner's* fish	(h)ERRING
• thin *Cockney*	(h)AIRLINE

Cockney
indicating pronunciation:

• *Cockney* abrasive	SANDPIPER
• *Cockney* behaves	BEE-HIVES
• *Cockney* daily	PIPER
• *Cockney* luggage tag	LIBEL
• *Cockney* rogues	KNIVES

Cockney
indicating rhyming slang:

• apples (and pears)	STAIRS
• china (plate)	MATE
• trouble (and strife)	WIFE

Cockney artist	RAINBOW
	(*see also* bow)

cocktail

cock<u>t</u>ail	K
cocktail of [gin]	–ING

code

[code]-*breaking*	CO-ED, DECO
code-name	LAWN
code [words]	SWORD
coded [remark]	MARKER
[German] *code*	MANGER

codex   COD

codicil   PS

coffee time   ELEVEN(TH HOUR)

coffer

coffer, *say*	COUGHER, KISSED

coffin

coffin carrier, *say*	BEER
coffin, *say*	COUGHING

cohabitants   ITEM

coil

coil here, *say*	WINDIER
coiled [rope]	PORE
coiling [adder]	DREAD

coin

coin a [phrase]	SHAPER, SHERPA
coin factory working	MINTON
coin remains . . .	SOUREST
coin, *say*	GILDER, MILL-RACE
	S(C)ENT, SUE
coin-trick, *say*	DIMETRIC
counterfeit coin	SLIP, STUMER

cold

catch cold	incl C
• Pa–t *catches* cold	PACT
cold	C
• cold earth	CLOAM
• cold meat	CHAM
• cold on . . .	CON–
cold bird, *say*	CHILDREN
cold buffet	ICE-BOX
cold environment	(in) I–CE
c<u>old</u> *front*	C
cold greeting	HAIL
cold look	DEAD-EYE
cold, *say*	CHILE, CHILLI, PARQUET
	KOFF
Cold War missile	SNOWBALL
cold-blooded poisoner	ADDER, ASP, SNAKE
cold-*hearted*	incl C
c<u>old</u>-*hearted*	OL

collage

collage made of [silver] . . .	LIVERS, SLIVER
c<u>o</u>llage *of* [flowers]	REFLOWS

collapse

collapse of [dais]	AIDS, SAID
collapsed [arch]	CHAR

Letter replaced \c\at; Omit (a); Pointers *out*; Retain <u>a</u>; S_plit B_ED; Down (D); Backwards <or ^

collapsible [seat]	EATS, SATE, TEAS	• colour stained, say	RED-EYED
collar		colour	FLAG
collar	TORC	• colour bar	FLAG-POLE, FLAG-STAFF
• collar, say	TALK, TORQUE	• colours fade	FLAG
• collar turning force, say	TORQUE	• without colour	OFLAG
collar fastener, say	TYPE-IN	colour	TAN
colleague	COLL	• colour goes, say	TANGOS
collect		• coloured man	TANGENT
collect	REAP	• coloured them, say	TANDEM
• collect directions	REAPPOINTS	colour	TONE
• collect fruit	REAPPEAR(S)	• colour of fruit	LIMESTONE
collect many	incl D, C, L, M	• fish colour	TROUTSTONE
collect money	incl D, L, P	• sun colour	STONE
• ti–ler collects money	TIDDLER	colour bar	LIPSTICK
	TILLER. TIPPLER	colour blind	SHADE
collect *	incl *	colour-sergeant	FLAMENCO
• ma–n collects one . . .	MAIN	colour signal	MAROON
collected animals	FAUNA	colour television	CHOCOLATE BOX
collected plants	FLORA	colour up(D)^	DER
collected [poems]	MOPES	coloured	(in) R–ED
collection	ANA	coloured	
collection of stories	SKYSCRAPER	–cheese	BRIERED
	TOWER BLOCK	–defender	GREENBACK
collector	COLL	–fish, say	BLUE-EYED
	GRASS-BOX, RAKE,	–gown, say	REDRESS
	TAXMAN	–people	ORANGEMEN
collectors	IR, TAXMEN	–sailor	BLACKJACK
college		–study	REDDEN
college	COLL, ETON, POLY	colourful article	REDAN
• college that is . . .	COLLIE	colourless	omit RED
• railway college	BRETON	• cove(red) colourless . . .	COVE
• college training	POLYPE	colourless prairie	PLAIN
college girl	CLARE, MAGDALEN(E)	colourless, say	PAIL, PLANE
college president	LINCOLN	**column**	
college window	ORIEL	column	COL
colliery area	MINEFIELD	columnist	NELSON
collision		columns, say	PEERS, PIERCE
collision [made] . . .	DAME, EDAM, MEAD	**combat jacket**	WARDRESS
collision of [heads]	HADES, SHADE	**combine**	
[slight] collision	LIGHTS	combination of [pills]	SPILL
colloquial		Combined Forces	RARE
colloquial	COLL	combined [ops]	SOP
colloquially cannot	CANT	Combined Universities	OXBRIDGE
is not colloquial	AINT	combines ponds	POOLS
Colombia	CO	combining [pairs]	PARIS
colonel	COL	**come**	
colony	C	come a cropper [in the] . . .	THINE
colonial building	ANTHILL	come down	(see comedown below)
Colonial Office	CO	come down in this fashion	SOLAND
colonial worker	ANT	come to halt(D)^	WARD
colonist	ANT	come to a conclusion	end with A
colony chief	GO-AHEAD	• he comes to a conclusion	MANA
colour		come up	
colour	DYE	• animal comes up(D)^	REED
• colour a scarf, say	DIASTOLE	• come up on . . .(D)^	NO
• colour-meter, say	DIMETER	come-uppance	
• colour rope, say	DICHORD	• come-uppance of prima-donna(D)^	AVID

Anag [cat]; Any *; Begin IGN–; Endings –ING; eg •; Hidden /cat/; Implied add (on); Implied in (in);

• fool's *come-uppance* (D)^	LOOF
comes from N/ew E/ngland	EWE
comes from [Spain]	PAINS
* *comes off* . . .	omit *
• motor *comes off* (car)ousel	OUSEL
comes out of [court on] . . .	CROUTON
comes out of [past]	PATS, TAPS
comes out of th/e ra/in	ERA
comes to grief in [race]	ACER, ACRE
	CARE
comes to light in s/ear/ch	EAR
comes to surface	
• sub *comes to surface*(D)^	BUS
comes to [terms in] . . .	MINSTER
comes through *	incl in *
• heat *comes through*	
opening of <u>sh</u>ed . . .	SHEATH
comedown HAIL, RAIN, SLEET, SNOW	
comeback	ECHO
comeback dance	GIG
comeback made< . . .	EDAM
comes to grief [on court]	CROUTON
coming from Jamai/ca t/o London	CAT
coming into Lon/don ate/evening	DONATE
coming out of thea/tre at/night	TREAT
coming *to* river	ADVENTURE
	(*see also* came)
comedy	COM
comic	
comic [acts]	CATS, SCAT
comic	FUN
• comic fellow	FUNGUS
• comic figure	FUND
• comic soldier	FUNGI
comic	WIT
• comic head	WITNESS
• comic success	WITH-IT
• lavatory humour, *say*	PEEWIT
comic Rugby player	HARLEQUIN
command	
command sequence	ORDER
commander AGA, CINC, CO, COM, OC	
• commander *batting*	AGAIN
• commander *has* hard . . .	CINCH
• Commander, Royal Navy	CORN
• commander *has*	
French father	COMPERE
• commander *with* dog	OCCUR
commander	CBE, CDR
commanding officer	CO, OC
commemorative meal	REPAST
commence	
commence <u>t</u>o . . .	T
commencement of <u>h</u>er . . .	H
commencing <u>w</u>ork	W
commerce	
commerce	COM

commercial	AD
• commercial address	ADORATION
• commercial break	ADRIFT
• commercial leader	ADDUCE
commercial traveller CARGO SHIP	
FREIGHT PLANE, GOODS TRAIN,	
	REP
commit	
commit (=put into)	
• *commit* little girl *to* car–e	CARMINE
committed me to war-d	WARMED
• I *am committed to* prison	CAIN, PEIN
committee	COM
commissioner	COM
common	
common	COM
common	
indicating colloquialism:	
• *common* (h)aunt	AUNT
• *commonly* (h)as . . .	AS
• will not *commonly* . . .	WONT
common haunt	FREQUENT
common man BLOKE, BO(D), CHAP	
GEEZER, PROLE	
common metre	CM
common pleas	CP
common salt AB, RATING, SAILOR, TAR	
commons FARE, HC, HOUSE	
Commonwealth (Relations)	
Office	C(R)O
commotion	
commotion	ADO, TODO
commotion [in street]	INTEREST
commune	COM
communication system	GRAPEVINE
communion	HC
communist	
communist	COM
• communist *apparently*	
intended	COMMENT
• communist *has* strong *French* . . .COMFORT	
• communist ruler	COMER
communist	RED
• anarchist deed	REDACT
• communist-*backed* . . .<	DER
• Communist club	REDWOOD
• Communist ring	REDO
• Communist study	REDDEN
• Communist's arrived, *say*	RED-SEAR
• Communist's family	REDSKIN
• Russian food	REDDISH
• tender Communist	KINDRED
communist	TROT
• communist *has* hard . . .	TROTH
• one *in* communist . . .	TAROT
• turn *in* communist . . .	TROUT
Communist Party	CP

Letter replaced \c\at; Omit (a); Pointers *out*; Retain <u>a</u>; Split B_ED; Down (D); Backwards <or ^

community

community	EC
• community home	ECLAIR
• community house	ECHO
• community standing	ECSTATIC
community centre	ABBEY
community *centre*	U
community *leader*	C
community payment	SETTLEMENT
Community Service Order	CSO
Community Service Volunteer	CSV

commute

commute [to an] . . .	NOTA
commuting (= going back and forth)	
• *commuting* to flat	LEVEL
commuting [daily]	LYDIA

compact

compact disc	CD
compact disc	O
compact house	H(O), HSE

companion

companion	CBE
companion	CH
• companion has weapons	CHARMED
• companion in a . . .	CHINA
• see companion	LOCH
companion for	
–Bacon	EGGS
–Bill	COO
–Daisy	BUTTERCUP
–Gilbert	SULLIVAN

company

company	CO
• company doctor	COMB
• company uniform	COHABIT
• company work	COOP
company	FIRM
• company cost	FIRM PRICE
• company employed . . .	FIRM HAND
• company position	FIRM STANCE
company	TWO
• company car	TWO-SEATER
• company *has* a few . . .	TWOSOME
• company work	TWO-PLY
company board	GANGPLANK
company director	IMPRESARIO
company *dismissed*	omit CO
• (co)aching company *dismissed* . . .	ACHING

compare

compare	CF, CP
comparatively cold	COLDER
comparatively cold	
(=cold as)	CHARITY, ICE
compared with Edward	LIKENED

compel

compelled a bird, *say*	MAIDEN
compelled terrorists . . .	MADEIRA

compile

compilation of [news]	SEWN, WENS
compiled [list]	SLIT

complain

complain	CARP
• complain *to* editor	CARPED
• complain *to* queen	CARPER
complain *at* meal	BEEF-TEA
complain, *say*	WINE

complete

complete meal	THOROUGHFARE
completed twice	OVERDONE
completely avian, *say*	AWL-BIRD
c(ompletel)y *gutted*	CY
completion of wor*k*	K
half-*completed*	F

complex

complex [design]	SIGNED
complex man	OEDIPUS
complex number	C
complex woman	ELECTRA
complexity of [ideas]	AIDES, SADIE

complicate

complicate [matters]	SMATTER
complicated [affair]	RAFFIA

component

components in mo/tors o/r . . .	TORSO
components of [cars]	ARCS, SCAR

compose

compose poetry	SING
compose some popul/ar son/gs	ARSON
composed by [Elgar]	GLARE, LAGER
	LARGE, REGAL
composed [of nuts]	FOUNTS
composed of [nuts]	STUN
composer	ARNE et al
	SCORER
composer's girl, *say*	MISHANDLE
composer's material	NOTEPAPER
composing music	CRADLE-SONG, LULLABY
composite [alloy]	LOYAL
[later] *composition*	ALTER, RATEL

compost

compost [heaps]	PHASE, SHAPE
compost of [dead] . . .	EDDA

compound

compound of [tin he] . . .	THINE
compound, *say*	OX-EYED, OX-HIDE
compounded [lots] . . .	SLOT

comprehend

comprehend (=take in)	
comprehend a . . .	incl A
comprehend *	incl *
• m–an *comprehends* always	MAYAN
comprehended by *	incl in *
• always *comprehended by* m–an	MAYAN
comprehensive case	SCHOOL-BAG

compress

compressed	PENT
• compressed fish	PENTANGLE
• compressed toes, *say*	PENTOSE
• second compressed . . .	SPENT
	(see also confine)

comprise

comprised in *	incl in *
• the *French comprised in* s–et	SLEET
comprises [all the] . . .	LETHAL
comprising a . . .	incl A
comprising *	incl *
• s–et *comprising* the French . . .	SLEET

computer

computer aided	
–design	CAD
–typesetting	CAT
computer assisted	
–instruction	CAI
–learning	CAL
computer club	BCS
computer firm	BIG BLUE
computer integrated	
–business	CIB
–manufacturing	CIM
computer language	
–recorder	CLR
–translator	CLT
computer managed instruction	CMI
computer oriented language	COL
computer output microfilm	COM
computerised scanner	CAT, CT
computers	IT

conceal

conceal	HIDE
• conceal boy, *say*	HYDRON
• conceal spring	HIDEBOUND
• conceal warden, *say*	HYDRANGEA
conceal head	omit 1st letter
• (n)ail *has concealed head*	AIL
conceal a . . .	incl A
conceal money	incl D, L, P
conceal one can	PALMITIN
concealed by camoufla/ge ne/t	GENE
concealed by *	incl in *
• it is *concealed by* m–e	MITE
concealed in [Dorset]	STORED
concealed in h/er go/wn	ERGO
concealed lair	HIDDEN
concealing a . . .	incl A
concealing, *say*	HAYDN
concealing *	incl *
• m–e *concealing* it	MITE

concern

concern	CO, FIRM
	(see company)
concerning	ON, RE

	(see about[2])

conclude

concluding remar<u>k</u>	K
conclusion	CON
conclusion h<u>e</u> *came to*	E
conclusion of pla<u>y</u>	Y
conclusions th<u>e</u> pane<u>l</u>	
had made after . . .	ELDER
conclusive proo<u>f</u>	F
fina<u>l</u> *conclusion*	L

concoct

concoct it, *say*	HATCHET
concoction of [report]	PORTER
concocted [recipe]	PIERCE
concubine	SULTANA

condemn

condemnation of [those] . . .	ETHOS
condemned [to die in] . . .	EDITION
[liar] *condemned*	ARIL, LIRA, RAIL

condition

condition	IF, STATE
conditioned [to heat]	HOT TEA
conductor	BUSBAR, CABLE, WIRE

confection

[a new] *confection*	WANE, WEAN
confection of [meats]	MATES, STEAM
	TEAMS

conference

conference	PEAK
conf<u>e</u>rence *centre*	ER

confess

confess	AM–
• confess aims	AMENDS
• confess to being	
right wing	AMATORY
• *confessing* I can	AMIABLE
confess	IAM
• *begin to* <u>l</u>earn confession	LIAM
• Bob *confessing*	SIAM
• confess *to* bishop in charge	IAMBIC
confess	IM–
• confess age	IMAGE
• *confessing* weight	IMPOUND
• *confessing before* jury	IMPANEL
confession of timidity	MESHY
confessor	COUGHER, EDWARD
confessor, *say*	COFFER
	(see also admit, claim, declare)

confide

confidante	GATE POST, YOU
confidential hint	INTIMATE

confine

confine	PEN
• confine drug-dealer	PEN-PUSHER
• confine sheep	PENT-UP
• confines charged	
particles	PENSIONS

Letter replaced \c\at; Omit (a); Pointers *out*; Retain <u>a</u>; Split B_ED; Down (D); Backwards <or ^

confined	PENT
• confined notice	PENTAD
• confined one *Scottish* . . .	PENTANE
• confined verse	PENTODE
	(see also compress)
confined by ste/el ba/rs	ELBA
confined by *	incl in A
• winner *confined* by two . . .	PACER
confined, *say*	DAMNED
confined to bed	(in) B–ED, (in) CO–T
• confined to bed	BILLED
confined to bed(=laid up)(D)^	DIAL
confined to hospital	INWARD
confining a . . .	incl A
confining *	incl *
• two *confining* winner	PACER
w/e we/re *confined*	EWE
conflict	
conflict of [wills]	SWILL
conflict, *say*	WORE
conflicted [with her] . . .	WRITHE
conflicting [ways]	SWAY, YAWS
conflicting ways	EW, NS, SN, WE
conforming	INSTEP
confound	
confound [devil]	LIVED
confounding [evil] . . .	LIVE, VILE
confront	
confront	C
confront man	FACETED
confronting	start with CON
• *confronting* dog	CONCUR
confuse	
confuse, *say*	JUMBAL
confused [ideas]	AIDES, SADIE
confusing [item]	EMIT, MITE, TIME
[no greater] *confusion*...	GENERATOR
confute	
confute [all the] . . .	LETHAL
confutation of [rules]	LURES
conglomerate	
conglomerate of [large] . . .	ELGAR, GLARE
	LAGER, REGAL
conglomeration of [things]	NIGHTS
Congo	RCB
congregation	INCE, (in) C–E
	INCH, (in) C–H
conjure	
conjure up [devil]	LIVED
conjuring up [evil] . . .	LIVE, VILE
connect	
indicating addition:	
• father is *connected*	
with church	PACE
• member *connected to* hard . . .	HARM
conquered	
conquered *by Caesar*	VICI
conqueror	WILLIAM
conscientious objector	CO
conservationist	
conservationist	GREEN
• conservationist	
support	GREENBACK
• conservationist wing	GREENFLY
conservationists	GREENS, NT
conservative	
Conservative	BLUE, C, CON, TORY
• conservative dress	BLUEGOWN
• Conservative majority	COVERAGE
• Conservative whip	CLASH
• Conservative state	CONGA
• six hundred	
Conservative . . .	VICTORY
conservative	U
conserve	
conserve *	incl *
• m–an *conserves* energy	MEAN
consider	
consider it, *say*	MULLET
consider summary	DIGEST
considerable	TIDY
conspirator	CADE, CASCA, FAWKES, OATES
Constable's house	ART GALLERY
constant	
constant	C
constant	PI
• constant speed	PIRATE
constant concern	FIRM
constant interference	STATIC
constant suffering	ABIDING
constipated	MOTIONLESS
constitute	
constituent of *	incl in *
• new *constituent of* ba–d . . .	BAND
constituent part of sal/address/ing	ADDRESS
constitute [my bases] . . .	EMBASSY
constitutional support	WALKING-STICK
[his] *constituents*	–ISH
[those] *constituents*	ETHOS
construct	
construct [a redoubt]	OBDURATE
constructed from [clay]	LACY
constructing [a new] . . .	WANE, WEAN
construction of [town]	WONT
constructors of [cars]	ARCS, SCAR
construe	
construe [a line]	ALIEN, ANILE
construing [odes]	DOES
consult	
consult lively *Scots*, *say*	SECANT
consulting room	INSPECTION CHAMBER
consume	
consumed by *	incl in *
• six *consumed* by o–ne	OVINE

Anag [cat]; Any *; Begin IGN–; Endings –ING; eg •; Hidden /cat/; Implied add (on); Implied in (in);

consumed [peas]	APES, APSE	–beaming	RAYON
consumer protection	NAPKIN, OVERALL	–burning	TORCHON
	SERVIETTE	–carrying	CARTON
consuming a . . .	incl A	–chatting	CHATON, YAPON
consuming interest	EATING	–decaying	ROTON
consuming *	incl *	–digging	PITON
• o–ne *consuming* six	OVINE	–drawing	DRAGON

contact

contact blue	TOUCH DOWN	–drilling, *say*	BORON
contagious disease	CD	–drooping	WILTON

contain

contain, *say*	HOLED	–for a long time	DRAGON
contained in [soup]	OPUS	–greeting, *say*	HALON
contained in st/ewe/d lamb	EWE	–heaping, *say*	PYLON
contained in *	incl in *	–informing, *say*	TALON
• number *contained in* tin	CANON	–innings	BATON
container for pistols, *say*	JEWEL-BOX	–interfering, *say*	PRION
container missing, *say*	JARGON	–ironing	PRESS ON
container ship	BIN LINER	–irritating	GALLON
containing a . . .	incl A	–miaouing	MUON
containing *	incl *	–mixing, *say*	MELON
• tin *containing* number	CANON	–moving	GOON
containing some th/in k/ind	INK	–nursing	TENDON
contents of new/spa/per	SPA	–playing	ACTON, BAT(T)ON
contents of crate	RAT	–pulling	DRAGON
contents of [crate]	REACT	–pushing	SURGEON
contents of lar/ge ne/w . . .	GENE	–rasping, *say*	PHYLON
contents of text with . . .	EXIT	–rushing	SURGEON
contents of the bad egg	HAG	–shaking	WAGON

contaminate

contaminate [pure soil]	PERILOUS	–signalling	FLAGON
contaminated [meat]	MATE, TAME, TEAM	–talking	CHATON, YAPON
contamination of [wines]	SINEW, SWINE	–the war, *say*	PHYTON

contemporary

contemporary	AD	–walking	GOON
• contemporary churchman	ADMINISTER	–waving	WAGON
• contemporary poetry	ADVERSE	–wearing hat	CAPON
• contemporary with *German* . . .	ADMIT	–working	ACTON
contemptible fellow	CAD, TWERP	continue reading	PTO

contentious

		continue summary	RESUME
contentious [idea]	AIDE	continued to indulge, *say*	SINDON
[speak] *contentiously*	PEAKS, SPAKE	continuing story, *say*	CEREAL

contents (*see* contain)

contort

		contorted [face]	CAFE
		contortions of [animal]	LAMINA
		[weird] *contortions*	WIDER, WIRED

continent ASIA, EUR

contract

Continental	M	contract	
continental (=French etc)		indicating abbreviation:	
• *continental* art	ES	• always *contracted*	EER
• *continental* articles	UNDER	• boys *contracted*	TIMED
• *continental* shelf	ANAQUEL	• *contract* bridge	BR
continental head	FRENCH BEAN	• *contract* cannot . . .	CANT
continental *head*	C	• *contract* illness	FLU
continental head	TETE	• *contract* written . . .	WRIT
(*see also* abroad, cross⁴, foreign)		• *contractor's word for* finished	OER
		(*see also* short¹)	

continue

		contract debts	INCURIOUS
continue	GOON	contract manager	BRIDGEMASTER
continue		*contracted* le(g)	LE
–attacking, *say*	RADON	contracted out	CAUGHT

contradict

contradiction of all . . .	SOME
contradiction of young . . .	OLD
contradictions	E–W, N–S, S–N, W–E
contradictory answer	NOYES

contrary

contrariwise, May . . .	YAM
contrary girl	MARY
contrary speech	CONVERSE
contrary way<	YAW

contribute

contribution from te/nor, Man/rico	NORMAN
contributing to t/he ed/itor's . . .	HEED
contribution t/o a f/und	OAF

contrive

[a new] *contrivance*	WANE, WEAN
contrived [a plot]	PLATO
contriving to [get a] . . .	GATE

control

control	REIN
• control animals	REINDEER
• control certain . . .	REINSURE
• control country	REINSTATE
• control violence	REINFORCE
• control what is said	REINSTATEMENT
	(see also check)
control animal	STEER
control clutch	GRASP
control knob	BOSS
control of corporation	DIETING
control, *say*	GUYED, RAIN, REIGN
controller of locks	ALICE BAND
	HAIR NET, KIRBIGRIP
	KIRBY-GRIP, SLIDE

controversy

controversial [remark]	MARKER
controversy in [Dail]	DIAL, LAID

convenient

convenience	CON
convenient headgear, *say*	HANDICAP

converse

adults *converse*	CHILDREN
conversation	CON
converse of all . . .	SOME
converse of old . . .	NEW, YOUNG
converse quietly	LOUDLY
conversing aloud	ALLOWED
heard *in conversation*	HERD
heard *in conversation* by . . .	BUY

convert

conversion of [sinner]	INNERS
convert [into] . . .	–TION
convert [into a] . . .	–ATION
convert [lire]	LIER, RILE
convert money	CHANGE
converted [infidel]	INFIELD
convertible [coins]	ICONS, SONIC

convey

convey delight	TRANSPORT
conveyed beforehand	PRESENT
conveyed herd	DROVE
conveying wa/ter ne/ar . . .	TERNE

convict

convict	CON
convict	LAG
• convict *with* nothing on	LAGOON
• fellow-convict	FLAG
• old convict	GREYLAY
	(see also criminal)

convulse

convulsed [with anger]	WREATHING
convulsion of [face]	CAFE
convulsive [leap]	PALE, PEAL, PLEA

convolute

convoluted [ideas]	AIDES, SADIE
convolutions of [dance]	CANED

cook

cook [meal]	LAME, MALE
cook, *say*	GRILLE
cook young fish	FRY
cooked [sausage]	ASSUAGE
cooker	POACHER
cooking [pots]	OPTS, SPOT, STOP, TOPS
Cook's craft	ENDEAVOUR
Cook's vessel	ENDEAVOUR
cook's weapon	MACE
cook's whiskers	EGG-BEATERS, BLENDERS
cooks fruit	STEAMSHIP
cooks insects	FIDDLESTICKS
cooks joint	STEAMSHIP
[over]*cooked*	ROVE
undercooked	RARE
[under]*cooked*	RUNED

cool

cool	FAN
• cool cat, *say*	PHANTOM
• cool city	FANNY
• cool food	FANFARE

co-ordinate

co-ordinate	X, Y
co-ordinated [with his] . . .	WHITISH
co-ordination of [arms]	MARS, RAMS

copper

copper	CU
• copper can	CUT IN
• copper (coin)	CUD, CUP
• copper colour	CURED
• copper embargo	CUBAN
• copper ring	CURING
• copper's helmet	CUSHAT
copper	D
• copper *and* unknown . . .	DANDY
• copper I dropped	DISHED
• copper I threw	DICAST

Anag [cat]; Any *; Begin IGN–; Endings –ING; eg •; Hidden /cat/; Implied add (on); Implied in (in);

copper	P
• copper *and* a . . .	PANDA
• copper fields	PLEAS
• copper I valued	PIRATED
copper	PC
copper disc	POLICE RECORD
copper-skinner	PEELER
coppers	PENNY-FARTHING
copy	
copy soldier	GIGI
	(*see also* double²)
copy some . . .	SUM
copy strip	TAKE OFF
copy Turner	REVOLVE, ROTATE
copying speed	CRIBRATE
*copy*right	RITE, WRIGHT
copyright	APER, C
cor	BLIMEY, FRENCH HORN
core	
apple *core*	P
core	omit centre
• *core* a(ppl)e	AE
• f(rui)t *cored*	FT
core of reactor	C
corn	
corn	EARS, FOOTPAD
corn cracker	(WIND)MILL
corn-Indian	CORNUTE
corn plaster	FOOTPAD
corned beef can, *say*	BULLETIN
corner	
corner	L
corner fish	ANGLE
corner man	CASTLE, ROOK
Cornwall	SW
coroner	COR
corporal	CPL, NYM, TRIM
corporate	
corporate state	FATNESS, OBESITY
corporation	BEEB, CO, INC, TUM
correct	
correct	OK
correct	TICK
• correct marks	TICKS
• correct sovereign	TICKER
• shilling is correct	STICK
correct [fare]	FEAR
correct *pronunciation*	RITE, WRIGHT
	WRITE
correct, *say*	RITE, WRIGHT
	WRITE
corrected [angle]	GLEAN
correction of [skid]	KIDS
correspond	
correspond completely	FITFULLY
correspond *with* king	WRITER
correspondence of [lovers]	SOLVER

correspondent, *say*	PENALLY
corresponding liquid	INK
corresponding member	CM
corresponding sheet	NOTEPAPER
corresponding to [German] . . .	MANGER
corrupt	
corrupt [dealer]	LEADER
corrupted [all the] . . .	LETHAL
corruption of [leader]	DEALER
corset	
corseted in cali/co st/uff	COST
corseted in *	incl in *
* *in corsets*	incl *
• a king *in* iron *corsets*	FAKE, FARE
cost	
cost, insurance, freight	CIF
cost of	
–leather, *say*	HYDRATE
–ride, *say*	FAIR, PHARE
–trimming	LACERATE
costs nothing	omit O
Costa Rica	
Costa Rica	CR
capital of C͟osta Rica	C
leaders of C͟osta R͟ica	CR
co-tangent	COT
could	
could be [Easter]	SEATER
could be Easter	FEAST
could be found in sup/erst/ore	ERST
could be feast	EASTER
could be said aloud	ALLOWED
could be said to . . .	TOO, TWO, TU–
could be said to be . . .	TUBE
could be [worse]	SWORE
could become [easy]	AYES, YEAS
could go into [Leith]	LITHE
could, *say*	MITE
coulomb	C
council	
Council of	
–Engineering Institutions	CEI
–Europe	CE
–Industrial Design	CID
c͟ouncil *leader*	C
councillor	CR
count	
count	TOT
• count gangster	TOTAL
• count them, *say*	TOTEM
• good count	BIENTOT
counts coins	NOBLES
counter	
counter	GEIGER, GM
[counter]-*move*	RECOUNT, TROUNCE
[counter]-*productive*	RECOUNT, TROUNCE
[counter]-*revolutionary*	RECOUNT, TROUNCE

Letter replaced \c\at; Omit (a); Pointers *out*; Retain a͟; Split B_ED; Down (D); Backwards <or ^

counter strike	BUFFET
counter stroke	BUFFET, CHIP-SHOT
countermarcher	SHOPWALKER
counterfeit	
counterfeit	SHAM
• counterfeit article	SHAMAN
• counterfeit bear, *say*	SHAMPOO
counterfeit [coin]	ICON
counterfeit [note]	ETON, TONE
counterfeit note	DUDE
country	
country	CHINA
• country dishes	CHINA
• country friend	CHINA
• country town	CHINAWARE
country	LAND
• country accent	LANDGRAVE
• country bar	LANDRAIL
• country folk	LANDRACE
country (=dialect)	
• country girl	GAL
• country-lover	SWAIN
• country worker	EMMET
country air	NATIONAL ANTHEM
country food	FIELDFARE
country girl	PERUSAL
country man	JOHN BULL, UNCLE SAM
country music	NATIONAL ANTHEM
country seat	SHOOTING STICK
country style (=dialect)	(*see above*)
country ways	LANES
country woman	BRITANNIA
county	
county	AVON, SOM etc
county	CO
• county exercises	COPE
• county side	COL, COR
• county woman	COW
county	DOWN
• county coach	DOWN STAGE
• county players	DOWNCAST
• county side	DOWNRIGHT
county alderman	CA
county borders	BEDS
county *borders*	CY
county coach	SURREY
county council	CC
county seat	SHOOTING STICK
county's team	CORKSCREW
couple	PAIR, PR, TWAIN
couple of	
−boys	REGAL, ROYAL
−days	WE
−fellows	CHAPMAN
−people	EVADES, SALTED
−times	TT
	(*see also* two)

couples starting <u>love</u> <u>a</u>ffairs	LOAF
first couple	ADAM, EVE
last couples ma<u>ke</u> rot<u>ten</u> . . .	KEEN
couplet	TT
course	
course	N, S, E, W
• all courses	NEWS, WENS
• course books	SENT, WENT
	SNOT, SWOT
• three courses	EWE, NEW, SEE, WEN etc
course	RIVER
• course *in* Ne/w Ye/ar	WYE
• course on border	TWEED
• course *of* for/ty ne/w . . .	TYNE
course (=golf, etc)	
• colour of course	GREEN
• course inspected, *say*	LYNX-EYED
• cry of course	FORE, OFF
• end of course	EIGHTEENTH, LINE, TAPE
• side of course	RAILS
• start of course	TEE
course (=part of meal)	PIECEMEAL
• course for beginners	STARTERS
• dampcourse	SOUP
• introduction to course	ENTREE
• main course	SEA-FOOD
course controller	HELM, RUDDER
course fee	REFRESHER
course official	MARSHAL, STARTER
course record	LOG BOOK, SCORECARD30
court	
court	CT
court	WOO
• court beginner	WOOL
• court daughter	WOOD
• court Satan	WOOD-EVIL
court actions	SUITCASE
court activity	BADMINTON, TENNIS etc
court martial	CM
court meeting	DATE
court *say*	SITTING-ROOM
court sessions	CS
courtly animal	KANGAROO
courtly lord	LUD
courtesan	SULTANA
cover	
cover	CAP
• cover cereal	CAPRICE
• cover girl	CAPELLA
• useful cover, *say*	HANDICAP
cover	HOOD
• clergyman *takes* cover	PRIESTHOOD
• cover chimney	HOODLUM
• cover journalist	HOODED
cover charge	PREMIUM
cover-stone	SKINFLINT
coverage in Daily Mirr/or fe/ature	ORFE

Anag [cat]; Any *; Begin IGN–; Endings –ING; eg •; Hidden /cat/; Implied add (on); Implied in (in);

covered by *	incl in *	*crackpot* [idea]	AIDE
• one *covered by* British . . .	BONER	crackshot	ANNIE (OAKLEY), TELL
covered in sn/ow, Ed/ward . . .	OWED		SURE-FIRE
covering a . . .	incl A	*crack*[shot]	HOST, HOTS
covering brood	HATCH	**cradle song**	LULLABY, ROCK MUSIC
covering fire	SHELL	**craft**	
covering mu/ch op/era	CHOP	craft	ART
covering of <u>c</u>loth	CH	• crafty deed, *say*	ARTEFACT, ARTIFACT
covering *	incl *	• crafty girl, *say*	ARTEMIS
• British *covering* one . . .	BONER	• hard craft	HART
cover-*up*(D)^	DIL, POT	craft	SS
covers lar/ge ar/ea	GEAR	craft of wickerwork	CORACLE
covers of <u>magazine</u>	ME	*craft* [she saw] . . .	WASHES
cow		*craftily* [sneaks] . . .	SNAKES
cow	LOWER	crafty director	CAPTAIN, NAVIGATOR,
• cowhide	LOWER CASE		HELM, RUDDER
• cowshed	LOWER HOUSE	crafty fellow	ARTISAN, TRADESMAN
• fine cow	FLOWER	crafty group	FLEET, NAVY, SQUADRON
cow pasture	OXLAND	crafty operator	BOATMAN, PUNTER
cowboy	STEERSMAN	*crafty* [seer]	ERSE, SERE
cowgirl	IO	**cram**	
cowman, *say*	COWARD, COWERED	cram cloth	STUFF
cowshed	STOCK ROOM, STOCKHOLDER	cram food	TUCK
coward		**cramp**	
coward, *say*	COWERED, COWHERD	*cramped by* a c/rowd y/ou . . .	ROWDY
cowardly defender	YELLOWBACK	*cramped by* *	incl in *
cowardly show	CAVALCADE	• individual *cramped by* man . . .	MAIN
cowl		*cramping* a . . .	incl A
cowl	HOOD	*cramping* *	incl *
• cowl *on* chimney	HOODLUM	• ma–n *cramping* individual . . .	MAIN
• stealing cowl, *say*	ROBIN HOOD	**crank**	
cox		crank case	ASYLUM, BROADMOOR
coxed pair	THREE MEN IN A BOAT	*crank* [case]	ACES, AESC
coxswain, *say*	COCKS	*cranky* [tutor]	TROUT
crack		**crash**	
[Animal] *Crackers*	LAMINA	*crashed* [car]	ARC
crack	ACE	*crashing* [bore]	EBOR, ROBE
• crack king	ACER	**crave**	
• crack note	ACETONE	crave, *say*	PREY
crack	DAB	craving drink	LUSTRUM
• crack rear, *almost*	DABSTER	**craze**	
• crack-*up*(D)^	BAD	*crazed* [china]	CHAIN
crack	PRO	crazy	MAD
• crack discovered...	PROFOUND	• crazier plant	MADDER
• crack dossier	PROFILE	• crazy about the girl, *say*	MADONNA
crack n–ut *with* a . . .	NAUT–	• crazy ruler, say	MADDER
crack [nuts]	STUN, TUNS	crazy fellow	HATTER
crack of dawn	DAYBREAK	*Crazy* [Horse]	SHORE
crack journalist	REPORTED	crazy proposal	LOCOMOTION
crack picture	SNAP	**crease**	
crack up	EXTOL	crease dresses	RUCKSACKS
crack up [when I] . . .	WHINE	crease us, *say*	CROESUS
cracked heads	NUTS	*creased* [sheet]	THESE
cracked [heads]	SHADE	**create**	
crackers [in the] . . .	THINE	*create* [anew]	WANE, WEAN
cracking [code in] . . .	COINED	create interest	INVEST
crack[pot]	OPT, TOP	creation	HAT

Letter replaced \c\at; Omit (a); Pointers *out*; Retain <u>a</u>; Split B_ED; Down (D); Backwards <or ^

creation of [life]	FILE, LIEF
credit	
credit	CR
• credit cut	CREDITED
• credit due	CROWED, CROWING
• credit State	CRAVER
credit notes	–IOUS
creditor	CR
creed	–ISM
creeper	IVY, SNAKE
crematorium	
crematorium	CREM
crematorium refuse, *say*	BEAU NASH
crew	
crew	BOASTED
	FOUR, EIGHT
crew weight, *say*	CROUTON
crewed	HANDS-ON
crewed, *say*	COARSE, CRUDE
crewed her, *say*	COARSER, CRUDER
cricket	
cricket boycott	TEST BAN
cricket club	BAT, CC
cricket ground	HEARTH
cricket ground, *say*	LAUDS
cricket side	LEG, OFF, ON, XI
cricket spectator	OVERSEER
cricket stroke	BATSWING
cricketer	BATMAN
cricketer's hat	BOWLER
home of cricket	HEARTH
criminal	
criminal	CON
• criminal evidence	CONSIGNS
• criminal punished	CONFINED
• criminal type	CONSORT
criminal	CROOK
criminal	HOOD
• criminal circles	HOODOO
• criminal journalist	HOODED
• sister *with* criminal	NUNHOOD
criminal error	CLUE
criminal procrastinator	THIEF
criminal pursuit	MANHUNT
Criminal (Records) Office	C(R)O
criminal [stole so] . . .	LOOSEST
	(*see also* convict)
crimson	
crimson-*clad*	(in) R–ED
• crimson-*clad* article	READ
cripple	
cripple [master]	REMAST, STREAM
crippled [man is] . . .	MAINS
crippling [trade]	RATED
criticise	
criticise	PAN
• criticise girl	PANADA
• criticise teacher, *say*	PANZER
• criticise test	PANTRY
criticise cook	ROAST
criticise fish	CARP
criticise, *say*	REVUE
crock	
crock [player]	REPLAY
crocked [a winger]	WEARING
crook	
crook	CRIMINAL
	CROSIER, CROZIER
crook [is not an] . . .	NATIONS
crooked [leg]	GEL
[details] *crook*	INSTEAD
crooner	
crooner	BING
in crooner's . . .	B–INGS
• energy *in* crooner's . . .	BEINGS
crop	
come a *cropper* [in the] . . .	THINE
crop *up*(D)^	NOTE, PINS, POL–
sort of crop	ETON
cross¹	
cross	IO
• cross *in* right . . .	RIOT
• dog crosses . . .	CURIOS
• five cross fifty . . .	VIOL
cross	ROOD
• cross *inside* b–y . . .	BROODY
• cross-*over*<	DOOR
cross	TAU
• cross a number	TAUTEN
• cross to grand . . .	TAUTOG
• cross *with* cross	TAUTEN
cross	TEN
• cross a town	TENACITY
• cross-bones	TENTS
• cross legs	TEN-PINS
• cross over	TENON
• cross the river	TENURE
cross	X
• cross-beam	X-RAY
• cross one . . .	ELEVEN, XI
• monkey-cross	APEX
cross islander	MALTESE
cross *over the* Channel	CROIX, KREUZ
French Cross	CROIX
German Cross	KREUZ
cross²	
cross	ANGRY
cross *over the* Atlantic	ORNERY
cross *over the* Channel	FURIEUSE
	FURIEUX
cross³	
indicating inclusion:	
cross a	incl A
cross river	incl R

Anag [cat]; Any *; Begin IGN–; Endings –ING; eg •; Hidden /cat/; Implied add (on); Implied in (in);

cross street	incl RD or ST
cross *	incl *
• saint *crosses* friend	SPALT
crossed by *	incl*
• friend *crossed by* saint	SPALT

cross⁴

other uses:	
cross-channel (=French etc)	
• *cross-channel* bridge	PONT
(*see also* abroad, continent, foreign)	
cross-country runner	RIVER
• cross-country runner	
changes [line]	NILE
• former English cross-country runner	EXE
• French cross-country runner	LOIRE
• German cross-country runner	RHINE
cross-examiner	SCRUTINEER
cross-maker	ELECTOR, VOTER
crossing	PANDA, PELICAN
cross[road]	DORA
cross[words]	SWORD

crowd

crowd	THREE
crowd crowed	CREW
crowded street, *say*	RUEFUL

crown

crown	CR
crown commission	MAJORITY, ROYALTY
crown jewels	TIARA
crown of head(D)	H
crowned	
indicating one word written	
below another word or letter:	
• man *crowned with* gold(D)	ORAL
crowned officer	MAJOR

crude

crude container	OIL DRUM
crude form of [words]	SWORD
crude [ore]	ROE
crude signature	X
crudely [made] . . .	DAME, EDAM, MEAD
crudely made [table]	BLEAT
cruder *say*	COURSER, RUFFER

cruel

cruel cut	FELL
cruelly [used]	DUES, DUSE, SUED

crumble

crumbling [ruins Ed] . . .	INSURED
crumbly [bread]	BARED

crumple

crumpled	INCREASES
crumpled [papers]	SAPPER

crunch

crunched [under a] . . .	UNREAD
crunching [nuts]	STUN

crush

crush newspapers	PRESS
crush pen	POUND
crush spirit	SCOTCH
crushed fabric	WORSTED
crushed [orange]	ONAGER
crushing [ores]	EROS, ROES, ROSE, SORE

crust

bread *crusts*	BD
crust on port	PT
crustless (p)or(t)	OR

cry

[cried] *off*	DICER
[cries] *out*	SERIC
cry aloud	ALLOWED
cry 'Foul!'	FOWL
cry of delight	OLE
cry of triumph	IO
cry out	YELLOW
cry *over*<	BULB
cry, *say*	W(H)ALE
crying 'Fore!'	FOR, FOUR
crying, say	W(HΛ)LING

cryptic

cryptic [clue]	LUCE
cryptically [signal]	ALIGNS

crystal box   SPAR

Cuba

Cuba	C
Cuban *capital*	C
Cuban *leader*	C
Cuban steps	RUMBA

cube

cube root	SUGAR BEET
cubic	CU, CUB
cubic feet per	
—minute	CUMIN
—second	CUSEC
cubic metre, *say*	STEER

cuckold   ACTAEON

cuckoo

cuckoo [in nest]	TENNIS
[man is] *cuckoo*	MAINS

cue

cue, *say*	Q, QUEUE

cull

[deer] *cull*	REDE, REED
culling [seal]	ALES, LEAS, SALE

cult

cult	SECT
• cult worker	SECTANT
• member of a cult	INSECT
• two cults	BISECTS

cultivate

cultivate stars	PLOUGH
cultivate [stars]	TRASS
cultivated dwarf	BONSAI
cultivated products	BACTERIA, PEARLS
cultivating [soil]	OILS, SILO

culture
culture of [animal] . . .   LAMINA, MANILA
cultured [pearl]   PALER
cunning
cunning man, *say*   ARCHBISHOP
cunning [ruse]   RUES, SURE
cunningly [plied]   PILED
cup
cup-bearer   GANYMEDE, HEBE
    SAUCER
Cup *Final*   P
Cup game   TIDDLY-WINKS
Cup round   TASSO
cupholder   GANYMEDE, HEBE
cure
cure [my pet]   EMPTY
cure, *say*   HEEL, HE'LL
cure your, *say*   HEALTHY
cured [bacon]   BANCO
cured, *say*   HEALD, HEELED
curie   CI
curious
curious book   ODDJOB
curious, *say*   KNICKNACKS
curious [thing]   NIGHT
curiously [shaped]   PHASED
curiously shaped [roots]   TORSO
curl
curl it up, *say*   PERMIT
curling [iron]   NOIR, ROIN
curly [beard]   BARED, BREAD, DEBAR
c̲urly *head*   C
current¹
current   AC
• current price   ACCOST
• current tax   ACCESS
• current usage   ACCUSTOM
current   AMPS
• 150 current . . .   CLAMPS
• c–current   CAMPS
• junction *with* current   TAMPS
current   DC
current   I
• current state   –ICAL
• current representative   IMP
• highest current   MAXI
current account   ELECTRICITY BILL
current-carrying   incl AC
• current-*carrying* lines   RACY
current unit   A, AMP, COULOMB
    KWH(R), VOLT
current²
current   TIDE
• current *recession*<   EDIT
• current recession   EBB-TIDE
• current usage   TIDEWAY
current drop   EBB(-TIDE)

current management
    structure   BREAKWATER, GROYNE
current, *say*   TIED
    (*see also* current³)
current³
current   RIVER
• current in London   THAMES
• current team   RIVERSIDE
• Indian current   GANGES
current control   WEIR
current drop   CATARACT, FORCE
    WATERFALL
current management
    structure   DAM, EMBANKMENT
current stoppage   DAM
    (*see also* current²)
current⁴
current cost accounting   CCA
current purchasing power   CPP
current success   WINNOW
current (this month)   CUR(T)
curse
curse   DAMN
• curse China, *say*   DAMMING
• curse people, *say*   DAMNATION
• English curse, *say*   EDAM
curse gentleman, *say*   BLAST-OFF
curse people   CONDEMNATION
curt greeting   SHORTWAVE
curtail
curtailed tri(p)   TRI–
curtailing journey   TRI(p)
curtain
curtain material   BAMBOO, IRON
curtains   DEATH
custom
customer   (in) SHO–P
customs   HMC
customs assigned number   CAN
cut¹
cut   AX(E)
• cut *back*<   EXA–
• cut leg   AXON
• cut *up*(D)^   EXA–
• cut*back*<   EXA–
cut   CUT
• cut *back*<   TUC
• cut note   CUTE
• cut *up*(D)^   TUC
• cut*back*<   TUC
cut   DOCK
• cut it off, *say*   DOCKET
• cut off three feet   DOCKYARD
• cut short   DOCK BRIEF
cut   HACK
• cut joint, *say*   HACKNEY
• cut objections   HACKBUTS

Anag [cat]; Any *; Begin IGN–; Endings –ING; eg •; Hidden /cat/; Implied add (on); Implied in (in);

• second cut	SHACK		DAIS(y), PANS(y), PEON(y)
cut	LOP	*cut* law(n)	LAW
• 100 cuts	CLOPS	*cut off* part . . .	ART, PAR
• cut *up*(D)^	POL	*cut*-price	COS(t)
• cut*back*<	POL	cut *say*	MOAN, MODE
cut	MOW		PAIR, PEAR
• cut name	MOWN	cu(t) *short*	CU
• cut journalist	MOWED	*cut* sh(ort)	SH
• cut, *say*	MOAN, MODE	*cut short* journey	TOU(r), TRI(p)
cut	NIP	cut skin	FELL
• cut at this point, *say*	NIPPIER	cut twice, *say*	MAU-MAU
• cut her, *say*	NIPPER, NIPTER	*cut out* a . . .	omit A
• cut support	NIPPIER	*cut out* *	omit *
cut	PRUNE	• le(ad)er *cuts out* notice	LEER
• cut fruit	PRUNE	*cut out odd bits* of (t)w(e)e(d)	WE
• cut monarch	PRUNER	*cut* *	omit *
• cut you and me, *say*	PRUNUS	*cutting* (h)edge	EDGE
cut	SAW	*cutting* *	omit *
• cut *at* angle	SAWFISH	I *cut*	omit I
• cut new . . .	SAWN	• ma(i)ze I *cut*	MAZE
• cut *up*(D)^	WAS	**cut⁴**	
• cut*back*<	WAS	other uses:	
cut	SEVER	cut a dash	HYPHENATE
• cut Edward	SEVERED	*cut down* afternoon . . .	PM
• cut friend	SEVERALLY	cut down drink	RATIONALE
• cut gangster	SEVERAL	cut-down ship	RAZEE
cut	SNIP	cut down tree	FELL
• cut animal	SNIPPET	*cut* [finger]	FRINGE
• cut favourite . . .	SNIPPET	cut grass	SPLIT
• cut*back*<	PINS	cut greeting	SHORTWAVE
cut²		cut later...	GASHOLDER
indicating inclusion:		cut production	CROP
cut *	incl in *	cut senior . . .	GASHOLDER
• king *cuts* corners	ANGLERS	cut staff	CLEFT STICK
cut by a . . .	incl A	cut the aged . . .	GASHOLDER
cut by *	incl *	*cut up* [steak]	SKATE, STAKE, TAKES
• corners *cut by* king	ANGLERS	cut whip	CROP
cut from woo/den se/at	DENSE	cut woman	SLITHER
cut into juic/y ap/ple	YAP	cuts face	CHOPS
cut t/he len/gth . . .	HELEN	**cute**	¯
cutting the grass	RE–ED	cutie	DISH
cut³		cutie, *say*	QT
indicating omission:		**cycles per second**	CPS, CS, HERTZ
a *cut*	omit A	cyclists	CTC
• a *cut* in me(a)t	MET	cyclopaedia	CYC(LO)
• he(a)l a *cut*	HEL	**Cymric**	CYM
cut cloth	CLOT, LOTH	**Cyprus**	CY
cut down ratio(n)	RATIO	**Czech**	
cut down (s)hip	HIP	Czech, *say*	CHECK, CHEQUE
cut down tree	TRE–, REE	Czechoslovakia	CS
cut fibre	SLIVER	*capital* of Czechoslovakia	C
cut flower	(b)LOOM, (f)LOWER	Czech (oslovak) *leader*	C

Letter replaced \c\at; Omit (a); Pointers *out*; Retain a̲; Split B_ED; Down (D); Backwards <or ^

D

damn, *date*, *daughter*, day, dead, deci, *Dee*, degree, dele, delete, delta, Democrat, denarius, density, department, departs, depth, deserted, deus, deuterium, Deutsch(land), diameter, diamond, died, differential operator, dimension, dinar, director, discantus, doctor, dominant, dominus, duke, Dutch, electrical flux, five hundred, four, four thousand, Germany, had, key, *lot*, many, mark, note, notice, *number*, old penny, penny, ring, Schubert's works, string, vitamin, would

Dad		**damn**	
Dad's Army	HG, PASTA	damn, *say*	DAM
Dad's double	PAPA	damned lucky	BLESSED
daft		**damp**	
daft [idea]	AIDE	damp course	SOUP
[I am] *daft*	AIM	damp environment	(in) MO–IST, (in) WE–T
daggers drawn	OBELI	damp-proof course	DPC
Dahomey	DY	damp-proof membrane	DPM
in Dahomey	D–Y	damp, *say*	WHET
Dai		**damsel**	
Dai's (=Welsh)		[damsel] *in distress*	MEDALS
• *Dai's* violin	CRWTH	**dance**	
home *for Dai*	CARTREF	dance	BALL
daily		• dance poster	BALLAD
daily	PAPER	• dance *on* tiptoe	BALLPOINTS
• daily job	PAPERWORK	• dance *with* alien	BALLET
• daily wager	PAPERBACK	• dance *with* nothing on	BALLOON
daily	CHAR	dance composer	HAYMAKER
• daily paper	CHARMS	dance dress	BOLERO
• one *in* daily . . .	CHAIR	dance in front	TRIPLED
• *put* shirt *on* daily . . .	CHART	(d)ance *not started*	–ANCE
daily	NEWSPAPER	Dance of The Tins	CANCAN
	SUN, TIMES	dance, *say*	HEY, REAL
daily job	REPORTER	dance tour	TRIP
dairy		*dancing* [bear]	BARE, BRAE
dairy girl	MARY	dancing girl	ALMA, ALME(H), GEISHA,
[dairy] *produce*	DIARY		NAUTCH, PAVLOVA, SALOME,
Daisy's transport	BICYCLE		SPINNING JENNY
dam			(WALTZING) MATILDA
dam, *say*	DAMN, WERE	*dancing* [shoe]	HOES, HOSE
dam river, *say*	SEA-LOUSE	[sun] *dance*	NUS, UNS–
damage		[tap]-*dancing*	APT, PAT
damage	MAR	**dandy**	ADONIS, BEAU, MACARONI
• damage container	MARTIN	**Dane**	HAMLET
• damage *in* a way	SMART	**danger**	
• damage key, *say*	MARQUEE, MARQUIS	danger at this point, *say*	RISKIER
damage *limitation*	COS(t), HAR(m)	dangerous driver	ROAD-HOG, TOAD
damage [vase]	SAVE	dangerous man	DAN
damaged [pear]	PARE, RAPE, REAP	dangerous, *say*	RISQUE
damaging footwear, *say*	SOUL DESTROYING	**Danish**	
damaging [remark]	MARKER	Danish	DAN

Anag [cat]; Any *; Begin IGN–; Endings –ING; eg •; Hidden /cat/; Implied add (on); Implied in (in);

Danish capital	KRONE
Danish *capital*	D
Danish *leader*	D
	(see also Denmark)
dark	
Dark [Ages]	SAGE
dark dress	NIGHTGOWN
dark blue	OXONIAN
dark horse	BLACK BEAUTY, NIGHTMARE,
	BLACK BESS
Dark Lady	NEGRESS
dark bird, *say*	BLACKEN
dark sportsman	NIGHTCAP
dark suit	CLUBS, NIGHT CLUB, SPADES
darkness, *say*	KNIGHT
darling girl	GRACE
dart	
dart *back<*	PIN, TRAD
[dart] *playing*	DRAT, TRAD
darts man	CUPID, EROS
dash	
dash about	DARTRE
dashing [about]	U-BOAT
dashing about [town]	WONT
data	
data processing	ADP, DP, EDP
data transfer	DT
date	D
date of birth	DOB
dative	DAT
daughter	
daughter	D
• daughter is hard . . .	DISH
• daughters-*in*-law	RUDDLE
• grand-daughter	GD
• twin daughters	DD
daughter born, *say*	MISBEGOTTEN
David's work	PSALMS
dawn	
dawn (=sun-up)(D)^	NUS
dawn of _c_ivilisation	C
dawns _o_n _p_eople _e_ntering _n_ew . . .	OPEN
day¹	DAY
[day] *off*	–ADY
[day] *out*	–ADY
[day] *trip*	–ADY
[day]*break*	–ADY
day²	
day	D
• day *after*	end with D
day after day	DD
day *before*	start with D
da_y_ *centre*	A
day *off*	omit D
• ban(d) *took* day *off*	BAN
day *out*	omit D
• la(d)y *had* day *out*	LAY

_d_aybreak	D
days	DD, DS
days after	
–date	DD
–sight	DS
day's date	DD
day³	
day in	incl D
• day in Wye, *say*	WIDE
day in	
–Berlin	TAG
–Paris	JOUR
–Rome	GIORNO
day *return<*	DEW
daybreak	DAWN, SHORT LEAVE
days, *say*	DAZE
daze	
daze, *say*	DAYS
dazed [reaction]	CREATION
in a daze [he was] . . .	HAWSE
d-duster	DRAG
dead	
dead	D
• dead bird, *say*	DOWEL
• dead keen	DAVID
• dead reckoning	DR
• dead right	DR–
dead	LATE
• dead bird	EMULATE
• dead saint	LATEST
• dead space	LATEEN
• deadhead	LATENESS
dead	OBIT
[dead] *beat*	–ADED, EDDA
dead-centre	CEMETERY, CHURCH YARD
	CREMATORIUM
	FUNERAL PARLOUR
dead *centre*	EA
[dead] *drunk*	–ADED, EDDA
dead end	CEMETERY, CHURCHYARD.
	GRAVE, TOMB
dead *end*	D
dead on arrival	DOA
dead policeman	BUSYBODY
dead language	OBIT(UARY)
_d_ead*head*	D
deadheaded (f)lower	(f)LOWER
deadheaded flower	(f)LAG, (v)ETCH etc
deal	
deal with [all the] . . .	LETHAL
dealt with [evil] . . .	LIVE, VILE
dean	
dean	INGE
Dean of Faculty	DF
dean's house, *say*	DENARY
dear	
[dear] . . .	READ-OUT

Letter replaced \c\at; Omit (a); Pointers *out*; Retain a̲; Split B_ED; Down (D); Backwards <or ^

dear *French* . . .	CHER(E)
dear money	SWEETBREAD
death	
death certificate	END PAPER
death lines	EPITAPH, OBIT(UARY), RIP
death of deity	GODSEND
Death Row, *say*	DICLINIC, DYELINE
[death] *throes*	HATED
death-wish	RIP
deathly words	EPITAPH, OBIT(UARY), RIP
debase	
debased [idea]	AIDE
[quite] *debased*	QUIET
debar	
debar dog, *say*	BANKER, BARKER
debar Scot	BANIAN
debris	
debris of the . . .	ETH, HET
debris [piled] . . .	PLIED
[much] *debris*	CHUM
debt	
debt	IOU
debt collector	DUNKING
debtor	DR–
debtor's documents	–IOUS
debts	–IOUS
debut	
debut of socialite	S
debut performance	P
decapitate	
decapitate	omit 1st letter
• *decapitated* (k)ing	–ING
• *decapitated* (w)oman	OMAN
decay	
decay	ROT
• decay a number	ROTTEN
• decay of jetty	PIERROT
• decay of woman, *say*	ROTTER
decay	RUST
• decay at this point, *say*	RUSTIER
• decay *in* article	THRUSTING
• decay in front	RUSTLED
decayed [leaf]	FLEA
decayed, *say*	DECADE
decaying bodywork	CÁRROT
decaying [tree is] . . .	RESITE
deceased	
deceased	D, DEC
deceased's title	DEAD MAN'S HANDLE
deceive	
deceitful [tinker]	REKNIT
deceive	COD
• deceive fish	COD, CODLING
• deceive *in* river	DECODE
• deceive journalist	CODED
deceive	CON
• deceive company	CONFIRM

• deceive leader	CONDUCE
• deceive top player, *say*	CONCEDE
deceive	GULL
• deceive alien	GULLET
• deceive bird	GULL
• deceive unknown . . .	GULLY
deceive	FOX
• deceive Communist	FOX-TROT
• deceive cricketer	FOX-BAT
• deceive follower	FOXTAIL
deceiver of policeman	SUPER-DUPER
deceiving [master]	REMAST, STREAM
December	DEC
decentralise	
decentralise	CORE
decentralise m(inistr)y	MY
deci-	
decigramme	DG
decilitre	DL
decimetre	DM
decider	ARBITRATOR, JUDGE, REFEREE
	UMPIRE, JUMP-OFF
	PLAY-OFF, TIE-BREAK
decimal	
decimal	OFTEN
decimal point	(IN)TENSE
decimal, *say*	INTENSE
[decimal] *system*	CLAIMED, DECLAIM,
	MEDICAL
decimally	INTENS–
decimate	
decimate [army]	MARY, MYRA
decimated [by a] . . .	BAY
decipher	
decipher [signal]	ALIGNS
deciphering [letters]	SETTLER
declare	
declaration	DEC
declaration of friendship	IMAMATE
declaration of	
–some . . .	SUM
–spirits	RHUMB
–war	WORE
declare	AM–
• declaring our . . .	AMOUR
• declaring rightist views	AMATORY
• declaring the result	AMEND
declare	IAM
• declaring vehicle . . .	IAMBUS
• pair declaring . . .	PRIAM
• son declaring directions	SIAMESE
declare	IM–
• declaring agreement	IMPACT
• declaring some . . .	IMPART
• declaring wine	IMPORT
	(*see also* admit, claim, confess)
declare perfect	UTTER

Anag [cat]; Any *; Begin IGN–; Endings –ING; eg •; Hidden /cat/; Implied add (on); Implied in (in);

declaring wine	WHINE	**deep**		
decline		deep	MAIN	
decline *old* gamebird	QUAIL	• continental *has* deep . . .	SPANISH MAIN	
declension	DEC	• deep surround	MAIN-FRAME	
decode		• make deep . . .	DOMAIN	
decode [signal]	ALIGNS	deep	SEA	
decoded [German] . . .	MANGER	• deep breath	SEA BREEZE	
decompose		• deep pink	SEA-ROSE	
decomposed [meat]	MATE, TAME, TEAM	• deep tone	SEARING	
decomposing [flesh]	SHELF	deep blue	LOW	
decomposition of [fibres]	BRIEFS	deep fish	BASS	
deconstruct		deep freezer	ICEBERG	
deconstruct [verse]	SEVER	deep consideration	OCEANOGRAPHY	
[later] *deconstruction*	ALTER	Deep South	ANTARCTIC OCEAN	
decorate¹		**deer**		
decorate	DECK	deer	BUCK	
• decorate cards	DECKHAND	• deer have a few, *say*	BUXOM	
• decorate journalist	DECKED	• deer in front	BUCKLED	
• decorate part of ship	DECK	• deer's relatives	BUCKSKIN	
decorated [plate]	PLEAT	deer	DOE	
decoration of [room]	MOOR	• deer-king	DOER	
decoration, *say*	MEDDLE	• deer's relatives	DOESKIN	
decorative border, *say*	FREEZE	• *invest* money *in* deer	DOLE	
indicating use of		deer	ROE	
abbreviation such as OBE:		• deer-dog, *say*	ROAD-HOG	
• company *has* decoration	COMBE	• deer, *say*	ROW(DIER)	
• decorated queen	OMER	deer	HIND	
• King *with* no decoration	ROOM	• deer *has* the greatest . . .	HINDMOST	
• decorated unknown . . .	OBEY	• deer spots . . .	HINDSIGHTS	
• King decorated . . .	ROBE	deer, *say*	DEAR, EXPENSIVE	
decrease		**deface**		
decrease	GODOWN	deface	MAR	
decreasing (ret)urns	URNS	• deface lines	MARRY	
decrepit		• deface ruler	MARKING	
decrepit [cars]	ARCS, SCAR	• deface script	MARTEXT	
decrepit girl, *say*	RUSTICATE	**defeat**		
decrepit vehicle, *say*	RUSTICA	defeat	PIP	
decrepit, *say*	TATTIE	• defeat boy	PIPERIC	
deduct		• defeat family	PIPKIN	
deduct from bill	(ac)COUNT, (b)ILL	• defeat girl	PIP-EMMA	
deduct one point	omit N, S, E or W	defeat Brown	TAN	
deduction from salary	(s)ALARY, (w)AGES	defeat champion	BEST	
deduction from r/igor/ous . . .	IGOR	defeat party	THRASH	
deduct two points	omit NE, SE etc	**defect**		
• *deduct* two points *from* (s)cor(e)	COR	*defect* [of nut]	FOUNT	
• *deduct* two points *from* gam(es)	GAM	defective hearing	MISTRIAL	
Dee		*defective* [tap]	APT, PAT	
Dee	D	[mental] *defective*	LAMENT	
Dee passed away, *say*	DEEDED	**defend**		
Dee's predecessor	C	defend Scot	GUARDIAN	
Deeside, *say*	DECIDE	defendant	DEF, DFT	
Deeside tartan	DEEP-LAID	defender	BACK	
deed		Defender of the Faith	DF	
deed of separation	CUT(TING), PARTING	defenders drinking	BACKSLAPPING	
	PARTITION, SEVERANCE	**deficient**		
	SEVERING	*deficient of* a . . .	omit A	
	(*see also* indeed)	deficient of, *say*	LAX	

Letter replaced \c\at; Omit (a); Pointers *out*; Retain a̲; Split B_ED; Down (D); Backwards <or ^

deficient of *	omit *	*delete* a line	omit AL
• Left *deficient of* part . . .	DE(part)ED	• *delete* a line *from* p(al)er . . .	PER
extremely deficient	omit end(s)	*delete* line	omit L
• crow(d) is *extremely deficient*	CROW	• Wa(l)ter *deletes* line	WATER
• (c)row(d) is *extremely deficient*	ROW	delete part of (p)age	AGE
very *deficient*	omit V	delete score	SCRATCH
• hal(v)e very *deficient* . . .	HALE	*delete* *	omit *
defile		**delicate**	
defile [art]	RAT, TAR	delicate	FINE
defiling [chapel]	PLEACH	• delicate lines	FINERY
defilement of [virgin]	RIVING	• soldier has delicate . . .	REFINE
define		**delightful drawing**	FETCHING
defining [words]	SWORD	**Delilah's (handi)work**	(D)EPILATION
definitely [was] . . .	SAW		HAIR-CUTTING
definition	DEF	**delinquent**	
deflect		*delinquency of* [boys]	YOBS
deflect [blade]	BALED	*delinquent* [kids]	SKID
deflection of [sword]	WORDS	**delirium**	
deform		*delirious* [chatter]	RATCHET
deformed [feet]	FETE	delirium tremens	DT(S)
deformity of [arms]	MARS, RAMS	**deliver**	
defrost	TAKE OFFICE	deliver children, *say*	BARE
degrade		deliver up(D)^	REVILED
degradable [type A] . . .	PEATY	*delivered from* hand/s of	
degradation of [art]	RAT, TAR	a/ vandal	SOFA
degrade [oils]	LOIS, SILO	deliveries	OVER
degree		• 150 deliveries	CLOVER
degree	BA	• deliveries *by* spinner	OVERTOP
• degree students	BALL	• deliveries expected	OVERDUE
• degree *with* honour	BACH	delivers fish	HANDSHAKE
• mother *has* degree	MAMBA	delivery	BALL
degree	D, DEG	delivery date	DOB
degree	MA	deliveryman	BOWLER, GYNAECOLOGIST
• degree students	MALL		LIBERATOR, SPEAKER
• degree *with* honour	MACH	**delta**	D
• school *with* degree . . .	GAMMA	**delusions**	DT(S)
degree of f/reed/om	REED	**demand style**	CALL
degree of hop(e)	HOP	**demented**	
deity		*demented* [Greek in] . . .	REEKING
deity	GOD	[made] *demented*	DAME, EDAM, MEAD
• deity appears	GODSON	**demi**	
• deity has urinated	GODSPEED	*demi*-cannon	CAN, NON
• deity knew . . .	GODWIT	*demi*john	JO
delay		**Democrat**	D, DEM
delay charge	STALLION	**demolish**	
delay exhibit	HOLD UP	demolish, *say*	RAISE, RAYS, RECK
delay permit	LET	*demolished* [barn]	BRAN
delay, *say*	PAWS	*demolition of* [shed in] . . .	SHINED
delay-switch, *say*	LIGHTWEIGHT	**demonstrate**	
delayed	LATE	demonstrate	SHOW
• delayed ceremony	LATERITE	• demonstrate a bit	SHOWPIECE
• delayed recovery	LATERALLY	• demonstrate concern	SHOW BUSINESS
• son delayed	SLATE	demonstrated (fabric)	SATIN
delegate	DEL	**Denmark**	
delete		Denmark	DK
delete	D	• a name *in* Denmark	DANK
delete a . . .	omit A	• smuggle *into* Denmark	DRUNK

Anag [cat]; Any *; Begin IGN–; Endings –ING; eg •; Hidden /cat/; Implied add (on); Implied in (in);

• we *in* Denmark	DUSK	**depose**	
	(*see also* Danish)	*depose leader*	omit 1st letter
dentist		• *depose leader* of (S)cots	COTS
dentist	BDS, DDS, LDS, MDS	depose monarch	SPURNER
	DRILLER, FILLER, STOPPER	depose monarch, *say*	SACKING
dentist's chair	DRILLING SITE	deposed	DEP
dentist's friend	EXTRACTOR FAN	**deposit**	
dentist's surgery	DRAWING ROOM	*deposit in* *	incl in *
	FILLING STATION	• *deposit* money *in* b–ank	BLANK
dentists	BDA	deposit, *say*	LOAD
deny		deposited, *say*	LADE
denial of her . . .	HIS	* *deposited in* . . .	incl *
denying right . . .	LEFT	• money *deposited in* b–ank	BLANK
depart		**depress**	
depart to . . .	GOAT	depressed fence	HAHA
departed saint	LATEST	depressing outcome	KEYSTROKE
departs quietly	omit P	depression	COL
• (p)arson *departs quietly*	ARSON	**deprive**	
departure	DEP	*deprive of* a . . .	omit A
departure of *	omit *	*deprive of* leader	omit 1st letter
• *departure of* king *from* par(k)	PAR	• (p)arty *deprived of* leader	ARTY
departure platform	BIER	*deprive of* love	omit O
* *departing*	omit *	*deprive of* money	omit L
• King *departing from* No(r)way	NO WAY	*deprived of* *	omit *
department		• (tot)ally *deprived of* drink	ALLY
department	DEPT, DPT	• (p)irate *deprived of* power	IRATE
Department of		**deputy**	
–Economic Affairs	DEA	deputy	DEP, LOCUM
–Education and Science	DES	deputy	STAND-IN
–Employment (and Productivity)	DE, DEP	• deputy stableman	STANDING-ROOM
–the Environment	DOE	*deputy head*	D
–Trade (and Industry)	DOT, DTI	deputy-lieutenant	DL
depend		**derail**	
depend	RELY	*derail* [Engine D]	NEEDING
• depend *on* woman, *say*	RELIEVE	*derailment of* [trucks]	STRUCK
• depend *on* worker, *say*	RELIANT	**derange**	
indicating one word written		*derange* [mental] . . .	LAMENT
below another word or letter:		*deranged* [or insane]	IN REASON
• Conservative *depends*		**deregulate**	
on his . . .(D)	HISTORY	*deregulating* [more] . . .	OMER, ROME
• expert *depends on* money(D)	LACE	*deregulation of* [Norse] . . .	SNORE
depict		**derelict**	
depicted in larg/e pic/ture	EPIC	*derelict* [chapel]	PLEACH
depicted in [orange]	ONAGER	*dereliction of* [duties]	SUITED
depicting [a last] . . .	ATLAS	[made] *derelict*	DAME, EDAM, MEAD
deplete		**derive**	
depleted (s)tor(e)	TOR	derivation	DER
depletion of (s)oil	OIL	*derivative of* Israe/li ve/rb	LIVE
deplorable		*derivative of* [German] . . .	MANGER
deplorable [lapse]	PALES, PEALS	derived	DER
deplorably [late]	LEAT, TALE, TEAL	*derived from* [one Red's] . . .	ENDORSE
deploy		*derived from* o/ur ge/nes	URGE
deploy [tanks]	STANK	**descend**	GODOWN
deployed in *	incl in *	**desert**	
• soldiers *deployed in*		desert	RAT
exercises	PORE, PORT	• desert animal	RAT
deployment of [guns]	GNUS, SNUG	• desert fighter	RAT

Letter replaced \c\at; Omit (a); Pointers *out*; Retain <u>a</u>; Split B_ED; Down (D); Backwards <or ^

• desert in the East	RATINE	destroy listeners	ENDEARS
• desert man	RATHE	*destruction of* [Troy]	TORY
• desert tribe	RAT RACE	destructive beauty	SMASHER
desert animal	RAT	*destructive* [blow Seb] . . .	WOBBLES
desert band	QUITO	**desultory**	
desert fault	DEFECT	*desultorily* [read] . . .	DARE, DEAR
desert holiday	LEAVE	*desultory* [try at] . . .	RATTY
desert ship	CAMEL	**detach**	
[Desert] *Storm*	RESTED	*detach* a . . .	omit A
deserted	D	*detach* *	omit *
deserted by a . . .	omit A	• Set(h) has *detached* house	SET
deserted by *	omit *	*detached* [retina]	RETAIN
• pa(la)ce *deserted by* the *French* . . .	PACE	detached territory	ISLAND
deserted sailor	LEFT-HAND	**detail**	
deserter	RAT	detail	DOCK
• deserter in front, *say*	RATTLED	*detail of* Picas/so p/ainting	SOP
• deserter will, *say*	RATTLE	*detailed* ca(t)	CA
• deserter X	RATTEN	*detailed* drawin(g)	DRAW-IN
* *deserting*	omit *	**detain**	
• princess *deserting* (di)vine . . .	VINE	*detain* a . . .	incl A
design		*detain* *	incl *
design	PLAN	• las–s *detains* her . . .	LASHERS
• design alien	PLANET	detain suspect	APPREHEND
• design church	PLANCH	*detained by* detecti/ve al/though . . .	VEAL
• design furniture	PLANTABLE	*detained by* *	incl in *
Design [Centre]	RECENT	• see her *detained by* las–s	LASHERS
Design Council	CID	**detect**	
designed [table]	BLATE, BLEAT	detect	SPY
desire		• detect Communist, *say*	SPIRED
desire	LUST	• detect hooligan, *say*	SPITED
• desire at this point	LUSTIER	• detect the *German, say*	SPIDER
• desire spirits	LUSTRUM	detective	BLOODHOUND, DET, EYE, TEC
desire merely . . .	WANTONLY	detectives	BUSIES, CID, YARD
despatch		detectives give	
despatch a . . .	omit A	information, *say*	EYE-STALK
despatch money	omit L	detective's joke, *say*	HOMESPUN
• p(l)an to *despatch* money	PAN	**deteriorate**	
despatched, *say*	SCENT	*deteriorate* [in water]	TINWARE
desperate		deteriorated, *say*	DECADE
Desperate [Dan]	AND	*deteriorating* [state]	TASTE, TEATS
desperate man	DAN	*deterioration of* [life]	FILE, LIEF
desperate [shriek]	HIKERS, SHRIKE	**determine**	
desperately [tired]	TRIED	determine, *say*	DEESIDE
despoil		determined attack	SET ON
despoiled, *say*	PRAYED	**detour**	
despoiler *say*	PRAYER	*detour* [made in] . . .	MAIDEN
dessert		[wider] *detour*	WEIRD, WIRED
dessert	AFTERS	**Deutsch**	D
• dessert wine	AFTERSHOCK	**devastate**	
• desserts have . . .	AFTERSHAVE	*devastate* [region D]	ERODING
• king *takes* desserts	RAFTERS	*devastated* [realm]	LAMER
dessert	FOOL, PUD etc	*devastation of* [forest]	FOSTER
destabilise		**develop**	
destabilise [regime]	EMIGRE	*developed* [a new] . . .	WANE, WEAN
destabilising [Roman] . . .	MANOR	*development of* [site]	TIES
destroy		**device**	
destroyed [castle]	CLEATS	*device* [may be] . . .	BEAMY

Anag [cat]; Any *; Begin IGN–; Endings –ING; eg •; Hidden /cat/; Implied add (on); Implied in (in);

[simple] *device*	IMPELS
devil	
devil	ABADDON, APOLLYON, BELIAL,
	CLOOT(IE), DAVY-JONES
	NICKNAME, (OLD) SCRATCH
	RAGMAN
devil	IMP
• 50 devils	LIMPS
• devil consumed us, *say*	IMPETUS
• devil performed	IMPACTED
• *give* the devil credit	CRIMP
• wandering devil	IMPROVING
devil, *say*	JUICE
devilish control	POSSESSION
devilish skill	IMPART
devilish [skill]	KILLS
devilled [lamb]	BALM
devious	
devious *ends*	DS
deviously [went] . . .	NEWT
[men are] *devious*	MEANER
devise	
devised [name]	MANE, MEAN
devising [means]	MANES, NAMES
Devon	SW
devote	
devoted [to her] . . .	THROE
[it was] *devoted* . . .	WAIST, WAITS
devour	
devour animals	WOLF-CUBS
devoured by *	incl in *
• one *devoured by* men	MEAN, MIEN
devouring a . . .	incl A
devouring, *say*	GOBELIN, GOBLIN
devouring *	incl *
• men devouring one . . .	MEAN, MIEN
devours, *say*	TOCSIN
devout	PI
diabolic	
diabolic [idea]	AIDE
diabolically [evil]	LIVE
[it was] *diabolic*	WAIST
dial	
dial	O
dial(D)^	LAID UP
dial girl, *say*	DILEMMA
dialling system	STD
diamond	
diamond(s)	ICE
• diamond case	ICEBOX
• diamond factory	ICE-PLANT
• diamonds only . . .	JUSTICE
diamond	ROCK
• 100 diamonds	CROCKS
• diamond ring	ROCK BAND
• *give* diamond to alien	ROCKET
diamond ring	ENGAGED SIGNAL

diameter	D
diarist	EVELYN, NOBODY, PEPYS
Dickens	
[Dickens] *novel*	SNICKED
Dickensian dance	TWIST
dicky	ILL
Dicky, [Sue] *and* [Sam]	ASSUME
dictate	
dictate tail	TALE
dictator's reign	RAIN, REIN
dictionary	OED
did	
Did expert . . . ?	ACCOMPLISHED
did it	FEC(IT), FF
Did you say 'No'?	KNOW
die	
die *from* . . .	omit D
• die *from* col(d)	COL
die *in* Germany	DEFINITE ARTICLE
die of cold	ICE-CUBE
[die] *off*	IDE, –IED
[die] *out*	IDE, –IED
die, *say*	GOADED, PASSOVER
died	D
• died later	DAFTER
• died young	DEARLY
• woman died	SHED
died	OB(IT)
died *out*	omit D
died without children	OSP
dieting	FAST WORK
differ	
differ [from anil]	FORMALIN
differ from [others]	THROES
difference [in the] . . .	THINE
different *conclusion*	T
different head	change 1st letter
• \f\ lower has *different*	
head	GLOWER
different [one]	NEO–
different position	
of [letters]	SETTLER
different role for [actress]	RECASTS
different spell of witch	WHICH
different way to draw<	WARD
different way [to fry]	FORTY
different way(s)	N, S, E, W
• *in* different ways, girl . . .	ENSUES
• \N\ orse have *a different way* . . .	WORSE
different [ways]	SWAY, YAWS
differential [gear]	RAGE
differently constructed	
[steel] . . .	LEETS, STELE
differing [points]	PINTOS
difficult	
difficult at this point, *say*	HARDIER
difficult [time]	EMIT, MITE

Letter replaced \c\at; Omit (a); Pointers *out*; Retain a̲; Split B_ED; Down (D); Backwards <or ^

difficult manoeuvre	HARD TACK	–sister	SIS
difficulty	ADO, ER, NET		(see also small[2])
difficulty [in art]	TRAIN	**dip cloth**	DUCK
difficulty, *say*	NOT	**dinar**	D
diffuse		**dine**	
diffuse [gases]	SAGES	[dine] *out*	ENID, NIDE
diffused [glow in] . . .	LOWING	dine *with* china	MESSMATE
diffusion of [air]	RIA	dined *after* match	TESTATE
dig		dined *out*	F–ED
dig it	UNDERSTAND	**diploma**	
dig *up*(D)^	GID	diploma	DIP
dig up food	GRUB	Diploma of Art	DA
dig up [trees]	RESET, TERSE	–of the Imperial College	DIC
digging up [soil]	OILS, SILO	–in Industrial Health	DIP
digs with hands	GRUB-SCREW	–in Public Health	DPH
	(see also dug)	–in Ophthalmic Medicine and Surgery	DOMS
digest		–in Psychological Medicine	DPM
digest *	incl *	**diplomat**	
• h–e *digested* the Bible	HAVE	diplomatic retreat	CONSULATE, EMBASSY
digest, *say*	SUMMERY	diplomatic sign	CD
digested [meal]	LAME, MALE	diplomats	CD, FO, UN
digestion of [oats]	STOA	**Dirac's constant**	H
digit		**dire**	
digit expires, *say*	TOADIES	*dire* [need]	DENE, EDEN
digit, *say*	UNDERSTAND	dire straits	(in) NE–ED
digital recording	BRAILLE	*direly* [felt, not] . . .	FLETTON
	DAT	**direct**	
	FINGERPRINT	direct current	DC
digits, *say*	TOSE, TOZE	direct speech	ADDRESS
dilute		*directed* [fire]	RIFE
dilute liquid	WATER	**direction**	
[diluted] *mixture*	LUDDITE	direction-finder	COMPASS, GUIDE
diluted sp(i)rit	SPRIT		(ROAD-)MAP
dim		directions	E, N, S, W
[dimmer] *switch*	RIMMED	• directions *to* the gallery	ESTATE
dim[wit]	TWI–	• in all directions	NEWS, SEWN, WENS
[saw it] *dimly*	WAIST, WAITS		(see also ways)
dime	IOC	directions from the staff (=musical directions)	
diminish		• *directions from the staff* to all . . .	TUTTI
diminish th(e) . . .	TH	• *directions from the*	
diminish the girt(h)	GIRT	staff quickly . . .	ALLEGRO, PRESTO
diminish t/he len/gth	HELEN	• loud *directions from the staff*	FORTE
diminishing asset	ASS, SET	**director**	
diminution of		change directors	SWITCHBOARD
–height	H	director	ARROW, DIR, POINTER
–interest	INT	Director of Public Prosecutions	DPP
–power	P	directors	BOARDBOARD
diminutive		directors *are after* money	BREAD
–footballer	HALF	director's dog	POINTER
–general	(TOM) THUMB	directors embark	BOARD
–man	CHAPLET	directors of astronomy	STARBOARD
–mother	MINIMUM	directors, *say*	BORED
diminutive		**dirty**	
–father	DAD, FR, PA, POP	*dirty* [dogs]	GODS
–girl	DI, G	dirty film	DUST, SCUM
–mother	MA(M), MUM	dirty gorge	DEFILE
–Senator	SEN	dirty old man	DOM

Anag [cat]; Any *; Begin IGN–; Endings –ING; eg •; Hidden /cat/; Implied add (on); Implied in (in);

dirty opening, *say*	MESSIDOR	• prohibit discharge, *say*	BARSAC
dirty, *say*	FOWL	**discharge²**	
dis-		*discharge* a . . .	omit A
many words beginning with		*discharge* *	omit *
dis-, some of which follow,		• fat(her) *discharges* her	FAT
are used to indicate anagrams		discharge debts	ENDOWING
disabled		discharge sailor	TURNABOUT
disabled (income group)	DIG	discharge soldiers	FOOT
disabled [poor Ted] . . .	TORPEDO	discharge *to* river	VENTURE
disadvantage		*finally discharged*	omit last letter
disadvantage (=draw*back*<)	WARD	• deb(t) *finally discharged*	DEB
disagree			*(see also* dismiss)
disagree with all . . .	PART, SOME	**disclose**	
disagree with many	FEW	*disclose* [secret]	RESECT
disappear		*disclosed in* no/vel vet/ted by . . .	VELVET
disappearance of a . . .	omit A	*disclosed in* [novels] . . .	SLOVEN
disappearance of *	omit *	*disclosure of* [news]	SEWN, WENS
• *disappearance of* shilling from pur(s)e	PURE	discoloured figures	LIVID
disappearing drink	EBB-TIDE, SEA-GOING	**discomfit**	
start *to* d̲isappear	D	*discomfitted* [king is] . . .	SKIING
start *to disappear*	omit 1st letter	*discomfiture of* [king at]...	TAKING
• flowers start *to disappear*	(f)LAGS	**discompose**	
	(f)LOWERS, (v)ETCHES etc	*discompose* [all the] . . .	LETHAL
disapprove	BOO	*discomposed* [by no] . . .	BONY
disarmers	CND	**disconnect**	
disarray		*disconnect* [lamp]	PALM
army *in disarray*	MARY, MYRA	*disconnected by* a . . .	incl A
disarray in [team]	MATE, MEAT, TAME	*disconnected by* *	incl *
disarray [in team]	INMATE	• r–ing *disconnected by* former	
disaster		pupil	ROBING
[American] *disaster*	CINERAMA	* *disconnects*	incl *
disaster [in the] . . .	THINE	• former pupil *disconnects*	
disastrous [fire]	RIFE	r–ing	ROBING
disastrous court	DIRECT	*disconnection of* [wires]	SWIRE
disastrously [I sailed] . . .	LIAISED	**disconcert**	
disband		*disconcert* [her fat] . . .	FATHER
disband [side]	DIES, IDES	*disconcerted* [by a] . . .	BAY
disbandment of [squad]	QUADS	[it was] *disconcerting*	WAIST
disc		**discontented**	
disc	O	*discontented*	omit centre
disc-jockey	DJ	• *discontented* m(al)e	ME
disc-jockey, *say*	COMPARE	• d(aughte)r *is discontented*	DR
discard		**discontinue**	
discard a . . .	omit A	*discontinuance of* man(y) . . .	MAN
discard hat	omit 1st letter	discontinue diet	PROROGUE
• parent *discards* hat	(m)OTHER	discontinued	DIS
discard reserves	SCRAP-BOOKS	*discontinued* mode(l)	MODE
discard *	omit *	**discord**	
• Wh(it)e, N, *discards* it	WHEN	*discord* [results] . . .	LUSTRES
discharge¹		*discordant* [notes]	ONSET, SETON
discharge	FIRE		STONE, TONES
• certain discharge	SURE-FIRE	**discount**	
• discharge soldier	FIREMAN	20% *discount on* (c)lock	LOCK
• discharges fish	FIRESIDE	50% *discount on* tic(ket)	TIC
discharge	SACK	**discourage**	
• discharge journalist	SACKED	discourage	DETER
• discharge girl, *say*	SACELLA	• discourage digging	DETERMINE

• discourage man	DETERGENT
discover	
discover gnomes	SEE-SAWS
dis*covered by* *	incl DIS
• dis*covered by* an Old English . . .	ANODISE
discovered in Sou/th Eir/e	THEIR
discovered in *	incl in *
• one *discovered in* m–y . . .	MONEY
discovered journalist	FOUNDED
dis*covering* . . .	incl in DI–S
• dis*covering* me . . .	DIMES
discovering [lost] . . .	LOTS
discuss	
discuss ways	WEIGHS
discussion group	GAS-RING
great *discussion*	GRATE
disease	
disease in [China]	CHAIN
diseased [trees]	RESET, STEER, TERSE
disembody	
disembodied [souls]	SOLUS
disembodiment of [flesh]	SHELF
disentangle	
disentangle [threads]	HARDEST
disentangled [nets]	STEN
disfigure	
disfiguration of [Roman] . . .	MANOR
	NORMA, RAMON
disfigure	MAR
• disfigure girl	MARINA
• disfigure leader	MARCID
• disfigure Scot	MARIAN
disfigure [a large] . . .	LAAGER
disfiguring [icon]	COIN
disgraceful	
disgraceful [scene, a] . . .	SENECA
disgracefully [used]	DUES, DUSE, SUED
disguise	
disguised [as priest]	PIASTRES
disguised by *	incl in *
• a king *disguised by* man	LEARN
disguising a . . .	incl A
disguising *	incl *
• man *disguising* a king	LEARN
disguising m/any how/itzers	ANYHOW
dish	
dish covered with yolks	BOW-LEGGED
dish out [gruel]	LUGER
dish-*up*(D)^	TOP
dishing out [wages]	SWAGE
dishearten	
dishearten	omit centre
• *disheartened* b(o)y	BY
disheartened	CORED
	(*see also* core)
dishevelled	
dishevelled [robes]	BORES, SOBER

[I am] *dishevelled*	AIM
dishonest	
dishonest [ruse]	RUES, SURE, USER
dishonest tendency	BENT
disinclined	HELL-BENT
disintegrate	
disintegrating [meteor]	REMOTE
disintegrations per minute	DPM
disinter	
disinterment of [bone]	EBON
disinterred [remains]	MARINES
dislike	
dislike	THING
dislike	OFF
• dislike gangster	OFFAL
• dislike her ring, *say*	OFFERING
• *disliking* queen	OFFER
disjointed	
disjointed [speech]	CHEEPS
[elbow] *disjointed*	BELOW
dislocate	
dislocate [knee]	KEEN
dislocated [elbow]	BELOW, BOWEL
dislocation of [arm]	MAR, RAM
dislodge	
dislodge [bails]	BASIL
dislodging [grit in] . . .	TIRING
dismal	
dismal prisoner	GREYLAG
dismally [failed]	AFIELD
dismantle	
dismantle	UNDRESS
dismantle [crane]	CANER, NACRE
dismantling [ship]	HIPS, PISH
dismember	
dismembered [cats]	SCAT
dismemberment of [deer]	REED
dismiss	
dismiss clergy	SACKCLOTH
dismiss, *say*	SAGO
dismiss team	FIRESIDE
dismissed	OFF, OUT
dismissed, *say*	BOLD
dismissing a	omit A
dismissing *	omit *
• co(lone)l *dismissed* single . . .	COL
finally dismissed	omit last letter
• soldier *finally dismissed*	PAR(a)
one's *dismissed*	omit I
	(*see also* discharge)
disorder	
disorder [I cannot] . . .	CONTAIN
disorder of [bowels]	ELBOWS
disorderly guerrillas	IRREGULARS
disorderly [trainer]	RETRAIN, TERRAIN
disorganise	
disorganise [seminar]	REMAINS

Anag [cat]; Any *; Begin IGN–; Endings –ING; eg •; Hidden /cat/; Implied add (on); Implied in (in);

disorganised [army]	MARY, MYRA
disorient	
disorientation of [brain]	BAIRN
disoriented [by all] . . .	BALLY
dispatch	(*see* despatch)
dispel	
dispel [fears]	FARES
dispelling [gloom in] . . .	LOOMING
dispense	
[all remedies] *dispensed*	EMERALD ISLE
dispensation [granted]	DRAGNET
dispense with a . . .	omit A
dispense with *	omit *
• pa(ye)r *dispenses with* the *old* . . .	PAR
dispensed [pills]	SPILL
disperse	
dispersed [much] . . .	CHUM
dispersing [a mob]	BOMA, MOAB
dispersion of [gas]	SAG
dispirited	DISPOSSESSED, EXORCISED
displace	
displace a . . .	omit A
displace *	omit *
• (k)night *displaces* king	NIGHT
displace [silent] . . .	ENLIST, LISTEN
displaced [by a] . . .	BAY
displaced person	DP
displacement of ship	TONNAGE
displacement of [ship]	HIPS, PISH
display	
display	AIR
• display slyness	AIRCRAFT
• display tolerated	AIRBORNE
• displayed beer	AIREDALE
• displays ship's company	AIRSCREW
• displays speed	AIRSPACE
display	SHOW
• display feathers	SHOWDOWN
• display pullovers	SHOW-JUMPERS
• displays headgear and	SHOW-STOPPER
• display a pasture, *say*	SHOALY
• display a shirt, *say*	SHOAT
• display weapon, *say*	SHOGUN
display of [art]	RAT, TAR
displayed in Ta/te g/allery	TEG
displaying [wares]	SWEAR, WEARS
displaying wa/res in/side . . .	RESIN
display wound	SPORTS CAR
dispose	
dispose of a . . .	omit A
dispose of bodies, *say*	BARIUM
dispose of leader	omit 1st letter
dispose of money	omit D, L, P
dispose of *	omit *
• moth(er) *disposed of* queen	MOTH

disposed [to rent]	ROTTEN
disposition [of latest],	FALSETTO
disposition, *say*	MOOED
[waste] *disposal*	SWEAT, TAWSE
[ill]-*disposed*	LIL
dispossess	DISPIRIT, EXORCISE
dispute	
disputatious mathematician	WRANGLER
dispute [over] . . .	ROVE
disputed [point]	PINTO
disquiet	
disquiet	omit P or SH
• *disquiet* (P)otter	OTTER
• *disquieted* tram(p)	TRAM
• *disquieting* mar(sh)y . . .	MARY
disrupt	
disrupted [lives]	EVILS
disrupting [life]	FILE, LIEF
disruption [entails] . . .	SALIENT
dissect	
dissect [bird]	DRIB
dissection of [rats]	ARTS, STAR, TARS
disseminate	
disseminate [news]	WENS
disseminated sclerosis	DS
dissipate	
dissipate [boredom]	BEDROOM
dissipated [Poles]	LOPES, SLOPE
dissipating [asset]	SEATS
dissipation of [gas]	SAG
dissolve	
dissolution of [later] . . .	ALTER, RATEL
dissolve into [tears]	RATES, RESAT
	STARE, TARES
dissolving [a gel]	GALE, GAEL
[it was] *dissolved*	WAIST
distant	
distant	FAR
• distant China	FARMING
• distant church	FARCE
• distant object	FARTHING
• distant grass-cutter, *say*	FARCICAL
• distant sea	FARMED, FARMER
distil	
distillation of [oils]	SILO, SOIL
distilled [scent]	CENTS
distiller, *say*	JINKING
distillers	DCL
distilling [gin]	–ING
distinguished	
Distinguished Conduct Medal	DCM
Distinguished Flying	
–Cross	DFC
–Medal	DFM
distinguished member	MBE
Distinguished Service	
–Cross	DSC

Letter replaced \c\at; Omit (a); Pointers *out*; Retain a; Split B_ED; Down (D); Backwards <or ^

–Medal	DSM
–Order	DSO
distort	
distorted [faces]	CAFES
distorted fish, *say*	RILING
distortedly, *say*	RILEY
distorting [views]	WIVES
distortion of [arch]	CHAR
distract	
distracted [all the] . . .	LETHAL
distractedly [paces]	CAPES, SPACE
distraction [of a] . . .	OAF
distraught	
distraught [as one is] . . .	ANOESIS
distraught [parent I] . . .	PAINTER
distress	
distress [signal]	ALIGNS
distressed	BALD, SHORN, UNLOCKED
distressed [wives]	VIEWS
distressing	HAIRCUT(TING)
distressing [news I] . . .	SINEW
distribute	
distribute [alms]	SLAM
distribute children	ISSUE
distributed [alms on] . . .	SALMON
distribution of [rice]	ERIC
distributor, *say*	PO(O)RER
district	
District Attorney	DA
District Commissioner	DC
District of Columbia	DC
District Officer Commanding	DOC
district prize	SEAWARD
disturb	
disturb, *say*	SHEIK
disturbed [sleep]	PEELS
disturbing [reports]	PORTERS
[recent] *disturbance*	CENTRE
disunite	
disunited [team]	MATE, MEAT, TAME
disunity of [friends]	FINDERS
ditch	
ditch	HAHA
ditch digger	OFFA
ditch, *say*	MOTE
ditch worker	TRENCHANT
dither	
dithered [when I] . . .	WHINE
dithering [over] . . .	ROVE
divers	
divers	SOME, SUNDRY
divers [races]	ACERS, ACRES, CARES, SCARE
diverse	
diverse [ways]	SWAY, YAWS
diversely [sent]	NETS, STEN
divert	
[a new] *diversion*	WANE, WEAN

diversion into Turin]	NUTRITION
divert	TURN
• divert canon	TURN ROUND
• divert fish	TURNPIKE, TURNSOLE
• diverts relatives	TURNSKIN
diverted [stream]	MASTER, REMAST
divide	
a *divided* . . .	incl A
• a *divided* group	SEAT
divide	DIV
divide country	SUNDERLAND
divide workers	QUARTERSTAFF
divided by a . . .	incl A
• group *divided by* a . . .	SEAT
divided by *	incl *
• Hull, *say*, *divided by* ten	PORTENT
divided skirt	TU–
divides accommodation	QUARTERS
dividing place	DIVORCE COURT, RENO
dividing *	incl in *
• ten *dividing* Hull, *say*	PORTENT
one *divided by* five	SOLVE
divine	
divine	DD
• divine *intervention*	
in Cole's . . .	CODDLES
divine substance	SENSE
divorce	
divorced	DIV
divorced husband	omit H
divorced spouse	EX, TIE-BREAKER
divorced wife	omit W
divorcee	EX, TIE-BREAKER
dizzy	
dizzy city	SWIMMING BATH
dizzy [turn]	RUNT
do	
do	DO
• do a *turn<*	OD
• do nothing	DOO–
• do shake her, *say*	DOWAGER
• do *wrong*	OD
• d–o *without*	incl in D–O
do badly	SWINDLE
do entertain us, *say*	PLEASING
do *fully*	DITTO
do gooder	S, ST
do in	HOUSE PARTY
do relief work	EMBOSS
do some drawing	ATTRACT
do without a . . .	omit A
do without money	omit L
do without *	omit *
do you, *say*	JU–
• Do you haver?, *say*	JUDICA
• Do you know?	JUNO
• Do you rave?, *say*	JURANT

Anag [cat]; Any *; Begin IGN–; Endings –ING; eg •; Hidden /cat/; Implied add (on); Implied in (in);

• Do you see?, *say*	JUICY	document *about* . . .	DE–ED, M–S
Do you say so?	SEW, SOUGH	document case, *say*	PHIAL
doing a roll, dog< . . .	GOD	*in* document	DE–ED, M–S
doing a roll, [plane] . . .	PANEL	*written in* document	DE–ED, M–S
doing aerobatics, *say*	LUPIN	**doddering**	
doing the rounds [near the] . . .	EARTHEN	*doddering* [old men]	DOLMEN
dock		*doddering* [into a] . . .	–ATION
dock brief	CUT SHORT	**dodge**	
dock closing	PORTENDING	*dodge* [past]	PATS, STAP, TAPS
dock management	CLIPBOARD	*dodged* [issues]	SUISSE
docked animal	DO(g)	*dodging* [rain]	IRAN, RANI
docked wages	PA(y)	*dodgy* [sort]	ORTS, ROTS, TORS
docker's work	DETAILING	**doe**	
ship *docked*	LINE(r)	doe, *say*	BUCKSHEE
doctor			DOH, DOUGH
doctor	BM	**doesn't**	
doctor	DR	*doesn't close*	omit last letter
• doctor copying	DRAPING	• *doesn't close* gat(e)	GAT
• doctor not well	DRILL	• doo(r) *doesn't close*	DOO–
• doctor *with* one . . .	DRONE	doesn't go	REMAINS, STAYS, STOPS
• doctor works . . .	DROPS	*doesn't get* a . . .	omit A
doctor	GP, LEECH	*doesn't get* on	omit ON
doctor	MB	*doesn't get* *	omit *
• 51 doctors	LIMBS	• B(ill)y *doesn't get* ill	BY
• 151 *have* doctor	CLIMB	*doesn't include* a . . .	omit A
• a doctor *to* the queen	AMBER	*doesn't include* *	omit *
doctor	MO	• fa(the)r *doesn't include* the . . .	FAR
• Doctor Hill	MOTOR	*doesn't make* amen(ds)	AMEN
• doctor on unknown . . .	MOONY	*doesn't start* (p)lay	LAY
• doctor with your *old* . . .	MOTHY	**dog¹**	
doctor	MD	Darwin's dog	BEAGLE
doctor	NO, WHO	director's dog	POINTER
Doctor [Cameron] CREMONA, ROMANCE		dog	BARKER
Doctor of		dog	CUR
–Canon and Civil Law	JUD, UJD	• dog at home	INCUR
–Civil Law	DCL, JCD	• dog-basket	CURBED
–Dental Surgery	DDS	• dog devoured	CURATE
–Divinity	DD	• dog-end	CURTAIL
–Education	DED	• dog-fish	CURLING
–Engineering	DENG, DING	• dog on hill	CURATOR
–Law	LLD	• dog trial	CURTEST
–Letters	DLIT, LHD, LITD	• dogged, *say*	CURD, KURD
–Literature	DLIT, LITD	• levy on dogs, *say*	CURT-AXE
–Medicine	MD	• rear of dog	CURTAIL
–Music	DMUS	• dog-bowl, *say*	KIRPAN
–Philosophy	DPH, PHD	• dog droppings, *say*	KERMESS
–Science	DSC, SCD	dog	MUTT
–Theology	DTH, THD	• dog performing	MUTTON
doctored [wines]	SINEW, SWINE	dog	PUG
doctors	BMA	• dog-bird	PUGREE
doctor's bag	SAC	• dog understands, *say*	PUG NOSE
doctors' dance	MEDICINE BALL	dog blanket	AFGHAN
doctor's paper-knife	LANCET	dog devoured . . .	PUPATE
unpopular doctor	FELL	dog does	ENDING
doctrine	–ISM	dog-food	CHOW
document		dog gnawed, *say*	LASSITUDE
document	MS	dog-lead	D

Letter replaced \c\at; Omit (a); Pointers *out*; Retain a̲; Split B_ED; Down (D); Backwards <or ^

Dog star	POINTER, SIRIUS	[he's] *done a runner*	SHE
dog tracks	COLLIERY	**donkey**	
dog unit	TALBOT	donkey	ASS
dogfight	BLENHEIM	• donkey always	
dogged policeman	HANDLER	ate . . .	ASSEVERATE
dogma	BITCH	• donkey-hire, *say*	ASSUAGE
dogs' dinner	CHOW-CHOW	• donkey is ill	ASSAILS
dogs notice them, *say*	COLISEUM	• donkey's optics, *say*	ASSIZE
guide dog	POINTER	donkey	NEDDY
dog²		**don't**	
dog	FOLLOW	*don't begin* (t)o . . .	O
• dog in <u>G</u>ates*head*	FOLLOWING	don't change it	STET
• dog *with* queen	FOLLOWER	don't declare	BATON
dog	TAIL	*don't finish* son(g)	SON
• dog food	TAIL-BOARD	don't give up	GOON
• dog breed	TAIL-RACE	*don't open* (t)he . . .	HE
• dog killer	TAILENDER	don't stand	SIT
• dog parts	TAILPIECES	*don't start* (t)o . . .	O
• Dog Star	TAIL-LIGHT	don't stop	GOON
dog	TRAIL	*don't take* a . . .	omit A
• dogfish, *say*	TRAILING	*don't take* *	omit *
• dog jacket	TRAIL-BLAZER	• so(me) *don't take* me . . .	SO
dole money	UB	don't tear off . . .	RIPON
dolichocephalic	HEADLONG	**doodlebug**	VI
doll		**door**	
dolled up [tart is] . . .	ARTIST	*back* door<	ROOD
[she was] *all dolled up*	WASHES	door catch	WICKET
dollar		doo<u>r</u> *closer*	R
a dollar (100 cents)	ACCENTS	door-handle	NAMEPLATE
dollar	BUCK	door-keeper	LATCH, LOCK, TILER
• dollar *and* a quarter	BUCKS	door-knocker	BATTERING RAM
• dollar sign	BUCKRAM	<u>d</u>oor *opening*	D
• noticed dollar	SAWBUCK	**dope**	ASS
dollar	DOL, S	**Dora**	
dollar pieces	CENTS, DIMES, NICKELS	[Dora]	CROSSROAD
domestic		**Doric**	DOR
domestic boiler	(TEA-)KETTLE	**dormitory**	
domestic rows	INDOOR FIREWORKS	dormitory feast	BEDSPREAD
domesticated saint	TAMEST	dormitory suburb	LAND OF NOD
dominate		**dotty character**	I, J
dominate		**double¹**	
indicating one word written		double	BI–
above another word or letter:		• double carriageway	BIRD
• tree *dominates*		• double *the* French	BILE
loch(D)	SPRUCENESS	• Doubleday	BID
dominant bird	TOPKNOT	double	DI–
dominant general	PREVAILING	• Doubleday	DID
don		• double double	DIKA, KADI
don *	incl in *	• double poem	DIODE
• king *dons* ha–t	HART	double	DUAL
donned by *	incl *	• double eyes, *say*	DUALISE
• ha–t *donned by* king	HART	• double, *say*	JEWEL
Donald Duck	MANDRAKE	• double tables, *say*	DUELLISTS
done		double	KA
done	OVER	• double double	DIKA, KADI
• done twice	OVERDONE	• double-talk	KAYAK
done [in fat]	FAINT	• double the *French* . . .	KALE

Anag [cat]; Any *; Begin IGN–; Endings –ING; eg •; Hidden /cat/; Implied add (on); Implied in (in);

double²			SHOWER, SNOW
double act	DODO	*downfall of* [kings I] . . .	SKIING
double chant	SING–SING	Downtown	NEWRY
double carriageway	MIMI	**drachma**	DR
double dose of sulphur	SS	**Draconian measure**	STERNWAY
double feature	CHIN-CHIN	**draft**	
double grave	STERN-CHASE	draft	DFT
double impact	SMASH-HIT	*drafted* [into]	–TION
double life	ISIS	**drag**	
double meat ration	CHOP-CHOP	drag	DRAW
double negative	NEVER-NEVER	• drag *back*<	WARD
double note	MIMI	• drag lake	DRAWL
double parking	PP	• drag *up*(D)^	WARD
double rations	CHOW-CHOW	drag	LUG
double share of profits	DIVI-DIVI	• drag *back*<	GUL
double stitch, *say*	SO-SO	• drag *up*<(D)^	GUL
double stomach	CRAW-CRAW	• second drag	SLUG
double your money	LL	*drag-*[race]	ACRE, ACER, CARE
	(see also two²)	drag-race	TRANSVESTITES
double³		drag swag	HAUL
double bend	Z	*dragging* [a log]	GAOL, GOAL
double cross	TWENTY, TWO TIMES	**drain**	
double eyes, *say*	DUALISE	drain rod, *say*	LOOP-HOLE
d_ouble-*header*	D	drainpipe	EXHAUST
double, *say*	WRINGER	**dram**	DR
double table, *say*	DUELLIST	**drama writer**	PLAYPEN
double tea, *say*	DOUBLET	**drank**	
double vision	DOPPELGANGER, LOOK-SEE	drank	TOPED
*double*t	TT	drank heartily, *say*	COIFFED
doubly		drank *up*(D)^	DEPOT
doubly deep	SEA-BASS		(*see also* drink, drunk)
doubly depressed	LOW-DOWN	**drastic**	
doubly finished	OVERDONE	drastic method	STERNWAY
doubly good	BON-BON	*drastic* [step]	PEST, PETS
doubly hard	HH	*drastically* [alter]	LATER
doubly healthy, *say*	WELL-HOLE	**draught**	
doubly loud	FF	draught beer	OUT OF THE WOOD
doubly low	DOWN UNDER	draughty passage	FLUE
doubly mute, *say*	DUM-DUM	**draw**	
doubly quiet	HUSH-HUSH, PP	draw	TIE
doubt		• draw game	TIEPOLO
doubt	ER, UM	• draw*back*<	EIT
doubter	THOMAS	draw	X
doubtful [result]	LUSTRE	draw at this point, *say*	HAULIER
doughboy	GI, GRUNT	draw fee	TOWAGE
down		*draw from* t/he r/anks	HER
down container	BLUEBOTTLE	draw hooligan, *say*	PULL-OUT
down-hearted	incl LOW	*draw in* a . . .	incl A
• s–ing down*heart*edly	SLOWING	*draw in* *	incl *
d_own-*hearted*	OW	• sh–ow *draws in* everybody	SHALLOW
Down here	IRELAND	draw knight, *say*	TOWSER
down-market bird	EIDER(DUCK)	draw male . . .	PULLMAN
down the pit, *say*	INDAMINE	*drawn in by* *	incl in *
downcast	MOULT(ED)	• everybody *drawn in*	
downfall	AVALANCHE	by sh–ow	SHALLOW
	CATARACT, RAPIDS, WATERFALL	*drawn into**	incl in *
	HAIL, RAIN, SLEET,	• woman *drawn into*	

Letter replaced \c\at; Omit (a); Pointers *out*; Retain a_; Split B_ED; Down (D); Backwards <or ^

wicked . . .	BASHED	• drill for coal, say	BORECOLE
[draw] out	WARD	drill	PE, PT
draw up(D)^	EIT, WARD	drill, say	AUGUR, BOAR
drawback<	EIT, WARD	drill [sergeant]	ESTRANGE
drawback part . . .<	TRAP	drilled, say	AUGURED, BOARD
drawer	ARTIST, DR	drilling rig	BRACE
	MAGNET	drilling site	DENTIST'S CHAIR
drawer overturned<	RD, REWARD		PARADE GROUND
drawing material	TOBACCO	**drink**	
drawing-room	STUDIO	drink	HOCK
drawn from fa/r an/d wide	RAN	• 100 drinks	CHOCKS
dreadful		• drink joint	HOCK
dreadful [rage]	GEAR	• second drink	SHOCK
dreadful service	BADMINTON	drink	LAP
dreadfully [made]	DAME, EDAM, MEAD	• drink to favourite	LAPPET
dreamer	JOSEPH	• drink when flying (=on wing)	LAPWING
dress		• fine drink	FLAP
dress	DON	drink	PORTER
dress	GARB	• claim drink	IMPORTER
• dress circle	GARBO	• drink before time	PORTERAGE
• dress in front . . .	GARBLED	• drink stout	SUPPORTER
• dress lubricant	GARBOIL	drink	SHORT
dress	GEAR	• drink before time	SHORTAGE
• dress adjustment	GEAR SHIFT	• drink with food	SHORTBREAD
• dress journalist	GEARED	• round of drinks	SHORT CIRCUIT
• dressed	IN GEAR	drink	SUP
dress	HABIT	• drink beer	SUPPORTER
• dress custom	HABIT	• drink to model	SUPPOSE
• dress-making	HABIT-FORMING	• drink wine	SUPPORT
• dressed	INHABIT	drink	TEA
dress business	SHIFTWORK	• drink alone	TEASINGLY
dress [circle]	CLERIC	• drink feature	TEACH-IN
dress-maker	CLOTH, FABRIC	• drink increased	TEA-ROSE
	NEEDLE, SATIN, WOOL etc	drink dispenser	GANYMEDE, HEBE
dress [sense]	ESSEN	drink manufacturer	STILL
dress up(D)^	EBOR	drink pop	HOCK
dressed by *	incl in *	drink problem	DT(S)
• fish dressed by ma–n	MAIDEN	drink round	LAP
dressed hair, say	QUAFFED	drink round<	EMIL, PAL, PIN, PUS
dressed [hare]	HEAR, RHEA	drink, say	(D)JINN, WHINE
dressed up [in gown]	OWNING		TAKES UP
dressed up in *	incl in *	drink too much	OVERLAP
• king dressed up in robe	GROWN	drink up	STIRRUP-CUP
dresses Arab	CLOTHES HORSE	drink up(D)^	EMIL, PAL, PIN, PUS
dressing a . . .	incl A	drink wallop	PUNCH
dressing-table	PLASTERBOARD	drink *	incl *
dressing-[table]	BLATE, BLEAT	• wa–g drinks gin	WAGING
dressing *	incl *	drinking, say	WHINING
• ma–n dressing a fish	MAIDEN	(see also drank, drunk)	
drift		**drive**	
drift into [port so] . . .	TROOPS	drive	DR
drifter	TRAMP STEAMER	drive sheep	RAM
drifting [ship]	HIPS, PISH	drive up motorway(D)^	IM–
drill		drivers	AA, RAC
drill	BORE	driver's place	TEE
• drill at a spot, say	BORACITE	driving	(in) CA–R
• drill deeper, say	BORON	• award driving . . .	CAMBER

driving force	HIGHWAY PATROL	drove	(see drive)
	POLICE CAR(S)	drown	
	TRAFFIC POLICE	drowned in *	incl in *
driving instructor	COACHMAN	• learner drowned in river	CLAM
driving [rain]	IRAN, RANI	drowning a . . .	incl A
drove one mad	SENTIMENTAL	drowning *	incl *
drop¹		• river drowning learner	CLAM
indicating inclusion:		**drug**	
dropping in a...	incl A	drug-taking	incl E
dropping in *	incl *	• drug-taking m–an	MEAN
• dropping students in river	TALLY	drug	ACID
drop²		• drug I see, say	ACIDIC
indicating omission:		• drug trial	ACID TEST
drop a . . .	omit A	• p(a)l without a drug	PLACID
drop a line	omit AL, ARY	drug	SPEED
drop a note	omit A, B, C, D, E, F, G	• drug dealer	SPEED MERCHANT
drop a point	omit N, S, E, W	• drug in college	SPEED UP
drop dead	omit D	• drug rate	SPEED
drop end of plan(k)	PLAN	• drug source	SPEEDWELL
drop money	omit L	drug	UPPER
drop off a . . .	omit A	• drug container	UPPER CASE
drop off *	omit *	• drug worker	UPPER HAND
drop out *	omit *	• second drug	SUPPER
drop quietly off	omit P, SH	drug dispenser	CHEMIST
drop *	omit *	drug excess	OD
• ski(p) and drop coin	SKI	drug, say	COCKAIGNE
drophead	omit 1st letter	drug supplier	POPPY, PUSHER
• drophead (c)ar with my . . .	ARMY	**drum**	
dropped letter		drum music	REEL
• Pat has dropped letter	AT, PA	drummer	DR
dropped letter	H	**drunk**	
dropping a . . .	omit A	[dead] drunk	–ADED, EDDA
dropping in	omit IN	drunk	(in) AL–E
• pa(in)ter dropping in	PATER	• drunk at . . .	ALATE
dropping out	omit OUT	• drunk on . . .	ALONE
• nearly dropping out	AB(out)	• four drunken . . .	ALIVE
dropping *	omit *	drunk	HIGH
• (p)arty dropping leader	ARTY	• drunken Communist, say	HIRED
drop³		• drunken friend, say	HIEMATE
other uses:		• drunken people, say	HYMEN
drop a little . . .	TASTE	• drunken sailor, say	HIGHJACK, HIJACK
drop building	SHED	• drunken woman, say	HY(A)ENA, HYGIENE
drop discrimination	TASTE	drunk	LIT
drop in current	CASCADE, WATERFALL	• drunk about . . .	LITRE
drop in the ocean	EBB(-TIDE), LOW TIDE	• drunken man	LITHE
drop litter	FARROW, WHELP	• saint in drunken . . .	LIST
drop note	MINIM	drunk	OILED
drop of water	W	• 100 drunken . . .	COILED
drop of water	EBB(-TIDE), WATERFALL	• drunken counsel	OILED SILK
drop off	SLEEP	• second drunk	SOILED
[drop]-off	DORP, PROD	drunk	TIGHT
[drop]-out	DORP, PROD	• drunk on H₂O	WATERTIGHT
drop rent	TEAR	• drunk on hemp	TIGHTROPE
dropped letter	H	• drunken head	TIGHTNESS
dropping stones	HAIL	drunk and disorderly [men at] . . .	MEANT
dropping zone	PARASITE	drunk by *	incl in *
drops of water	FALLS, RAIN, RAPIDS	• gin drunk by wa–g	WAGING

Letter replaced \c\at; Omit (a); Pointers out; Retain a; Split B_ED; Down (D); Backwards <or ^

drunk on [gin]	–ING	duly performed	DP
drunken characters from		**duff**	
[Leeds are] . . .	RELEASED	*duff* [part]	RAPT, TRAP
drunken nap	TIDDLYWINKS	[lamp] *is duff*	PALM
drunken [sots]	TOSS	[treacle] *duff*	ELECTRA
drunken [speech]	CHEEPS	**dug**	
drunken speech		dug	MINED
substitute SH for S		*dug out of* ear/th in G/ermany	THING
• *drunkard's* sort . . .	SHORT	dug, *say*	MIND
• *drunken* sort	SHORT	dug *up*(D)^	DEMIN
• selfish *in the pub*	SHELLFISH	[dug]*out*	–UDG–
(*see also* drank, drink)		(*see also* dig)	
dry		**duke**	FIST
dried grape, *say*	RAISING	duke's handwriting	FIST
dry	AIR	duke's protector	KNUCKLE-DUSTER
• dry *up*(D)^	RIA	**dull**	
• dry wine	AIRPORT	dull	DIM
dry	SEC	• dull eater, *say*	DIMETER
• dry *up*(D)^	CES	• dull porcelain	DIMMING
• dry worker	SECANT	dull	FLAT
dry	TT	• dull accommodation	FLAT
dry in the open air	SUNDRY	• dull man	FLATTED
dual carriageway	MIMI	• dull trial	FLATTEST
dubious		dull *and* fat, *say*	DULLARD
dubious [dealing]	LEADING	dull film	TARNISH
dubious dealing in [lira]	ARIL, LAIR	dull hooter	GREY-OWL
	LIAR, RAIL	**dumb man**	MALEMUTE
dubious [fate]	FEAT	**dunderhead**	
[stare] *dubiously*	ASTER, RATES	dunderhead	D
	TARES, TEARS	*dunder*headed boy	DREG
ducal footwear	WELLINGTONS	*dunder*headed [male]	LAME, MEAL
duck		**duplicate**	
Donald Duck	MANDRAKE	duplicate essays	GOGO
duck	O	duplicate *French* word	MOT-MOT
• duck feathers	OPINIONS	duplicate keys	AA, BB, CC
• duck-house	OCELLAR, OPEN		DD, EE, FF, GG
• duck liver	OLIVER	duplicate sounds	HUM-HUM
• duck's eggs	OO	duplicate tests	MOT-MOT
• portion of duck	ORATION	*duplicating* your . . .	YORE
and		(*see also* double, two)	
• duck *in* the mud	MOIRE	**Durham area**	NE
• duck *in* the road	SOT	**during**	
• eat meal *including* duck	SOUP	*during* he/r ear/ly . . .	REAR
and		during March	INFRINGE
• duck *on* her . . .	HERO	during Prohibition	(in) DO–NT
• father-duck	DADO	during race	(in) T–T
• leg of duck	LIMBO	during, *say*	WILE
• shoot at duck	POTATO	during school	(in) TER–M
duck á l'orange	MANDARIN	*during* *	incl in *
duck *eaten* . . .	incl O	• fiddle *during* pla–y	PLAGUEY
duck-farm, *say*	QUACKERY	(*see also* in²)	
duck shooter, *say*	FOULER	**Dutch**	
ducked	UNDERWENT	Dutch	DU
duck-*keeping*	incl O	Dutch capital	GUILDER, GULDEN
due		Dutch *capital*	D
[due] *for conversion*	EDU, –UDE	Dutch *leader*	D
due, *say*	DUE	Dutch ship, *say*	COUGH

Anag [cat]; Any *; Begin IGN–; Endings –ING; eg •; Hidden /cat/; Implied add (on); Implied in (in);

dwarf		**dynamic**		
dwarf	DOC, MINUTEMAN	*dynamic* [action]		CATION
dwarf fish	TROLL	*dynamically* [leads]		DALES, DEALS
dwarf's sayings	GNOMES			LADES, SLADE
dwindle		**dynamo(meter)**		DYN
dwindling hop(e)	HOP	**dyne**		DYN
(s)tore(s) *dwindled*	TORE			

E

Asian, Balearic Islands, boat, bridge player, Canary Islands, Earth, east, Easter, eastern, Ecstasy, Edward, eight, eight thousand, electromotive force, electron charge, electronic, Elizabeth, energy, England, English, epsilon, eta, European, exa-, five, five thousand, food additive, key, layer, logarithm base, *low-grade*, *mail*, natural base, note, *Orient*, *Oriental*, region, Spain, Spanish Guinea, Spanish Sahara, string, two hundred and fifty (thousand), universal set, vitamin.

---

each
each	AHEAD, EA
each	PER
• each change	PERMUTATION
• each letterhead	PERMISSIVENESS
• each employer	PERUSER
each side of . . .	
indicating inclusion:	
• *put* on *each side of* one	ONION
• ways *on each side of* pond	SPONDEE
each way	
indicating a palindrome:	
• blow *each way*	TOOT
• look *each way*	PEEP
• looks *each way*	SEES
• time *each way*	NOON
each year	PA

ear
ear, nose and throat	ENT
ear ornament, *say*	HEARING
ear, *say*	ORACLE
ears burning	EARSHOT

earl — COUNT
earl's daughter, *say*	MISCOUNT

early
earlier, *say*	PRIER, PRYER
early bath	BAPTISM
early bird	ARCHAEOPTERYX, PTERODACTYL
	EVE
	SATELLITE
early <u>b</u>irds	BI
early examples of <u>R</u>oman <u>a</u>rt	
form <u>t</u>o . . .	RAFT
early flier	ARCHAEOPTERYX, PTERODACTYL
	ICARUS, WRIGHT
early landfall	ARARAT
early letters	ATOC
early morning	IAM
early picture	FRONTISPIECE
early riser	SUN

early risers	FIRST STEPS
early <u>s</u>ign	S
early sign of <u>s</u>pring	S
early stage	BUD
early <u>s</u>tage	S
early stages of <u>his</u> <u>li</u>fe	HL
early transport	PERAMBULATOR, PRAM
	PUSH-CHAIR
early warning system	DEW

earn — NET

earth
[earth]-*moving*	HATER, HEART, RATHE
[earth]-*shattering*	HATER, HEART, RATHE
earthling	GLOBE-FISH
[earth]*quake*	HATER, HEART, RATHE
[earth]*work*	HATER, HEART, RATHE

ease
ease burden	CONTENT
ease, *say*	EE, ES
easily [won]	NOW, OWN
Easy	MIDSHIPMAN
easy remedy	SIMPLE

east
east	E
• East River	–ER
• h–ar<u>d</u> *out* East	HEARD
• in the East	–INE
East Africa	EA
East Central	EC
Eas<u>t</u> *End*	T
east end of tow<u>n</u>	N
East Ender	(see Cockney)
Eas<u>t</u> *Ender*	T
East *French*	EST
East *German*	OST
east-north-east	ENE
east *of Berlin*	OST
east *of Paris*	EST
East River	GANGES
east-south-east	ESE

Anag [cat]; Any *; Begin IGN–; Endings –ING; eg •; Hidden /cat/; Implied add (on); Implied in (in);

out East	omit E	eccentric	CRANK
out [East]	SATE, SEAT	• eccentric suit	CRANKCASE
eastwards	TOE	• eccentric will, *say*	CRANKLE
from East	TOW	• eccentric's handle . . .	CRANKSHAFT
eastern		eccentric	NUT
eastern	E	• eccentric *and* mad	NUT-CRACKERS
• Eastern agent	ESPY	• eccentric breed	NUTHATCH
• Eastern country	ESTATE	• eccentric woman	NUTMEG
• Eastern property	EQUALITY	eccentric	RUM
• Eastern ruler	EKING	• eccentric in workers' . . .	RUMINANTS
• Eastern traveller	EMIGRANT	• eccentric, *say*	RHUMB
and		• eccentrics' dance	RUM-SHOP
• in Eastern . . .	–INE	*eccentric* [teacher]	CHEATER
eastern dish	HOURI	**ecclesiastical member**	CHARM
eastern garment, *say*	JIBBER	**echo**	
Eastern Standard Time	EST	*echo* of guns<	SNUG
easy		*echoing* a noise	ANNOYS
easy, *say*	EEC	echoing sound	RHYME
		echoist	PARROT
(*see* ease)		**economy**	
eat		economical bowl	MAIDEN
eat	WOLF	economise	USELESS
• eat animals	WOLF-CUBS	economist	MILL, SMITH, *et al*
• eat fish, *say*	WOLFISH	**ecstatic**	
• eat sheep	WOLFRAM	Ecstasy (drug)	E
• eat *with* family	WOLFKIN	ecstatic	SENT
eat a . . .	incl A	*ecstatic* [state]	TEATS
eat, *say*	BIGHT, BYTE	**Ecuador**	
	IN JEST	Ecuador	EC
eat turkey	GOBBLE	*capital of* E̲cuador	E
eat vegetables	SUPPLANTS	*leader of* E̲cuador	E
eat *	incl *	**eddy**	NELSON
• man *eats* roll	TROLLED	**edge**	
eaten by *	incl in A	edge cut	RIMSAW
• roll *eaten by* man	TROLLED	edge of cliff	LANDSLIP
eaten by mo/st Ar/menians	STAR	*edge of* c̲liff	C
eating away part of (c)oast	OAST	edge of court	ADVANTAGE
eating fish	FINISHING SCHOOL	*edge of* c̲ourt	C
eating into *	incl in *	edge of pine	SIDELONG
• the *French eat into* foo–d	FOOLED	*edge of* p̲ine	P
eau de Cologne	RHINE	*edged by* *	incl in *
eavesdrop		• feature *edged by* silver	ACHING
eavesdropper	ICICLE	*edging* a . . .	incl A
eavesdropping on one		*edging* *	incl *
who interferes	MEDLAR	• silver *edging* to feature	ACHING
two *eavesdropping*	PEAR, TU–, TOO	*edges of* tabl̲e	TE
ebb		**edit**	
ebb-tide	WATERFALL	edit<	TIDE OVER
ebbing sea<	DEM–, REM–	edited	ED, EDIT
ebbing tide<	EDIT	*edited* [indent]	INTEND, TINNED
eccentric		editing instruction	STET
eccentric	CAM	*editing* [text or] . . .	EXTORT
• eccentric age	CAMERA	edition	ED, EDIT
• eccentric fool	CAMASS	*edition of* [a last] . . .	ATLAS
• eccentric man	CAMBRIAN	editor	ED
eccentric	CARD	[editor] *edited*	RIOTED
• eccentric's instrument	CARDSHARP	editor of 'Playboy'	FUNKING

Letter replaced \c\at; Omit (a); Pointers *out*; Retain a̲; Split B_ED; Down (D); Backwards <or ^

editor, *say*	CENSER, SENSOR	• charge Egypt . . .	BILLET
editor [wrote]	TOWER	• odds in Egypt	SPINET
educate		Egyptian capital	PIASTRES
educated man	MA	Egyptian *capital*	E
• educated Scot	MASCOT	Egyptian *flower*	NILE
educational centre	MIDDLE SCHOOL	Egyptian *leader*	E
educational *centre*	T	Egyptian king, *say*	FARO
educational journal	TES	Egyptian kings, *say*	FAROES
educational establishment	ETON, U	**eight**	
educational skill	R	eight Christmas presents	MILKMAIDS
educational supplement	TES	eight hundred	O, OMEGA
educationalist	BED	eight hundred thousand	O, OMEGA
educationally subnormal	ESN	eight-nil	EIGHTY
educationist	BED	eight-nil, *say*	ATE TEA
educationists	DES	eight notes	OCTAVE
English education	RRR	eight rowers	CREW
Edward		eight, *say*	AIT, ATE, EYOT
Edward II	SECONDER	one over the eight	DRUNK, NINE
Edward II	D	**eighteen**	
Edward expired	EDDIED	eighteen	MAJORITY, MANAGE
Edward Knight	SIRED	eighteen holes	ALL ROUND
Edward made, *say*	EDDIED		GOLF COURSE
Edward struck her, *say*	EDITOR	eighteen in team	AUSTRALIAN RULES
EEC		eighteen leaves	
EEC	TWELVE	per sheet	EIGHTEENMO
EEC, *say*	EASY		OCTODECIMO
e–emperor	EKING	eighteen letters	–ATOR
effort		**eighth**	
effortless	omit TRY	eighth note	QUAVER
• effort*less* indus(try)	INDUS	eighth part of circle	OCTANT
effortless flight	ESCALATOR	**eighty**	
egg		eighty	P, PI, R
egg	O, OVAL, SPUR	eighty-eight	PIANO
egg container	NEST, SHELL	eighty, *say*	ATE TEA
egg-making, *say*	OVATION	eighty thousand	P, PI, R
egg supplier	HEN, OVARY	**either**	
egg-*topping*(D)	E	*either end of* <u>house</u>	HE
egg white, *say*	GLARE	either way	
egg yellow, *say*	LUTINE	indicating a palindrome:	
*egg*head	E	• blow *either way*	TOOT
scrambled [eggs]	SEGG	• *either way*, it's flat	LEVEL
ego		• look *either way*	PEEP
[ego]-*trip*	GEO–	(*see also* each)	
egoism, *perhaps*	EYE TROUBLE	**eject**	
Egypt		*eject* a . . .	omit A
Egypt	ET	eject Turner	SPIT
• Egypt *almost* alon(e)	ETALON	*eject* *	omit *
• Egypt *and* her . . .	ETHER	• escort *ejects* hard . . .	US(h)ER
• Egypt *joins with*		• man *ejected by* small(les)t . . .	SMALT
North America	ETNA	*ejected from* mee/tin/g	TIN
and		**El Salvador**	ES
• archdeacon *in* Egypt	EVENT	**elaborate**	
• father *in* Egypt	EPOPT	*elaborate* [robes]	BOERS, BORES, SOBER
• I study *in* Egypt	EIDENT	*elaboration of* [ideas]	AIDES, SADIE
• the record is *in* Egypt	ELOGIST	**el**	
and		el	L
• draw Egypt . . .	PULLET	els	LL, LS

Anag [cat]; Any *; Begin IGN–; Endings –ING; eg •; Hidden /cat/; Implied add (on); Implied in (in);

elastic	
elastic [rope]	PORE
elasticated [edges]	SEDGE
elbow bender	BICEPS
elderly convict	GREYLAG
elect	
elected	IN
• *elected* friend	INMATE
• *elected* officer	IN GENERAL
• steal from *elected* . . .	ROBIN
election day, *say*	TUESDAY
election fever, *say*	BALLETOMANIA
electoral system	PR
electric	
electrical charge	Q
electric current	AC, DC, I
electric fence	RADIO RECEIVER
electric *lead*	E
electric unit	AH, AMP, VOLT
electrical capacity	C
electrical unit, *say*	WHAT, WOT
electricity	AC
• electricity *in* iron	FACE
• electricity money	ACCENTS
• price of electricity	ACCOSTS
electricity bill	CURRENT ACCOUNT
	(*see also* current)
electro-	
electro-cardiogram	ECG
electro-convulsive therapy	ECT
electro-encephalogram	ECG
electro-magnetic unit	EMU
electromotive force	EMF
electro-plated	EP
electrostatic unit	ESU
electron	
electron-volt	EV
electronic data processing	EDP
elegant	
elegant beasts	NEAT
elegant cape	NEATNESS
elegant, *say*	SHEIK(H)
element[1]	
ancient	AIR, EARTH, FIRE, WATER
modern	
commonly used names:	
argon	A
barium	BA
calcium	CA
carbon	C
chlorine	CL
chromium	CR
cobalt	CO
copper	CU
fluorine	F
gold	AU, OR
helium	HE

hydrogen	H
iodine	I
iridium	IR
iron	FE
krypton	KR
lead	PB
magnesium	MG
manganese	MN
mercury	AZOTH, HG
neon	NE
nickel	NI
nitrogen	AZOTE, N
oxygen	O
phosphorus	P
platinum	PT
plutonium	PU
potassium	K
radium	RA
radon	RN
silicon	SI
silver	AG, ARGENTUM
sodium	NA
strontium	SR
sulphur	S
tin	SN
titanium	TI
tungsten	W
uranium	U
zinc	ZN
elements	–IC, –CK, SC etc
element[2]	
element in mo/st ar/ticles	STAR
element of trage/dy in g/reat . . .	DYING
elevated	
elevated land	UP COUNTRY
elevated railway	EL
elevated road	EL
elevated road(D)^	DR, EVA, IM, TS
eleven	
eleven	LEGS, O, TEAM, XI
eleven	SIDE
• eleven children	SIDE ISSUE
eleven Christmas presents	PIPERS
eleven hundred	MC
eleven thousand	O
elevens(es)	SNACK
eleventh	
eleventh hour	COFFEE TIME
eleventh hour revival	LATERALLY
eliminate	
eliminate a . . .	omit A
eliminate about . . .	omit C, CA, RE
eliminate *	omit *
• pur(g)e *eliminates* 1000	PURE
• (p)urge *eliminates* leader	URGE
Eliza	
Eliza (=Cockney)	

Letter replaced \c\at; Omit (a); Pointers *out*; Retain <u>a</u>; Split B_ED; Down (D); Backwards <or ^

• *Eliza's* (h)at	AT
• (h)old *for Eliza*	OLD
	(see also Cockney)
Elizabeth	
Elizabeth II	SECONDER
Elizabeth II	L
ell	L
ells	LL, LS
elocution	
elocution heard	HERD
maid *in elocution*	MADE
elsewhere	
elsewhere, say	KNOTTIER
elusive	
elusive [bird]	DRIB
[act] *elusively*	CAT, TAC–
em	
em	M
ems	MM, MS
emaciated ruler	THINKING
emancipated worker	FREE HAND
embargo	
embargo	BAN
• embargo *expired*	BANDIED
• embargo *on* 500 . . .	BAND
• embargo *on* one building	BANISHED
embark	
embark on journey	J
embarkation of troops	T
embarrass	
be embarrassed	GORED
embarrassed	RED
• embarrassed player	REDACTOR
embarrassed [all the] . . .	LETHAL
embarrassing [remark]	MARKER
embed	
embedded in so/lid o/nyx	LIDO
embedded in *	incl in *
• queen *embedded in* stones	ROCKERS
embedding a . . .	incl A
embedding *	incl *
• stones *embedding* queen..	ROCKERS
embody	
embodied in *	incl in *
• old *embodied in* attempt . . .	TRAGEDY
embodied in o/ne st/atute	NEST
embody a . . .	incl A
embodying *	incl *
• attempt *embodying* old . . .	TRAGEDY
embrace	
all-*embracing*	incl ALL
• m–et all-*embracing* . . .	MALLET
embraced by *	incl in *
• you, *say, embraced by* b–oy	BUOY
embraced in stron/g ar/ms	GAR
embracing a . . .	incl A

embracing *	incl*
• b–oy *embracing* you, *say*	BUOY
embroider	
[altar] *embroidery*	TALAR
embroider [T-shirt]	THIRST
embroidered yarn	TALL STORY
embroil	
embroiled in *	incl in *
• a king *embroiled in* row	TARIFF
embroiling a . . .	incl A
embroiling *	incl *
• row *embroiling* a king	TARIFF
emend	
emendation of [line]	LIEN, NEIL, NILE
emended [phrase]	SHAPER
emending [verses]	SERVES
emerge	
emerging from mi/st at e/nd . . .	STATE
eminent pupil	BIG APPLE
emit	
emit fire	SHOOT
emit, *say*	POOR, PORE
emperor	
emperor	EMP, NERO, OTTO
emperor, *say*	SEIZE HER, SEIZER, SEIZOR
empire	
empire state	NY
empire woman	DBE
employ	
employ a . . .	incl A
employ *	incl *
• student *employed in* b–and	BLAND
employ painter	MOOR, TIE-UP
employ, *say*	EWES, YEWS
employed	INFIRM, INWORK
employed by manu/fact/urer	FACT
employed in m/unit/ions	UNIT
Employment Exchange	TRADE
empty	
empty	O
• *empty,* empty space	OVOID
• *empty* space	OZONE
• *empty* wood	OPINE
empty	incl O
• *empty* bed	COOT
• *empty* container	–TION
• *empty* ship	SOS
empty drain	EXHAUST
empty-*headed*	start with O
• *empty-headed* boy	ODES
• *empty-headed* girl	OKAY
• *empty-headed* teacher is . . .	OSIRIS
empty-*headed*	E
• empty-*headed* agent	ESPY
• empty-*headed* boy	EVICTOR
• empty-*headed* girl	EROSE
empty net	CLEAR

Anag [cat]; Any *; Begin IGN–; Endings –ING; eg •; Hidden /cat/; Implied add (on); Implied in (in);

empty, *say*	VANE, VEIN
empty vault	CLEAR
indicating omission	
of middle:	
• *emptied* m(agazin)e	ME
• *empty* h(ous)e	HE
• *empty* b(a)r	BR
• r(apidl)y *emptied*	RY

en

en	N
en route	(in) CA–R, (in) R–D, (in) S–T
en voyage	(in)S–S
ens	NN, NS

encage

encaged	(in) C–AGE
encaged by *	incl in *
• owl *encaged by* B–ing	BOWLING
encaged in ste/el m/esh	ELM
encaging a . . .	incl A
encaging *	incl *
• B–ing *encaging* owl	BOWLING

encapsulate

encapsulated in word/s	
of a/ sage	SOFA
hi/s word/s *encapsulated*	SWORD

encase

encased in concre/te ar/ound . . .	TEAR
encased in *	incl in *
• gold *encased in* iron	FORE
encasing a . . .	incl A
encasing *	incl *
• iron *encasing* gold	FORE
enchanting insect	SPELLING BEE

encipher

encipher [signal]	ALIGNS
encipherment of [all the] . . .	LETHAL

encircle

encircle a . . .	incl A
encircle *	incl *
• water *encircles* rat	DERATE
encircled by *	incl in *
• rat *encircled by* water	DERATE

enclose

enclose nerve	BOTTLENECK
enclosed in a b/ig loo/p	IGLOO
enclosed in *	incl in *
• auditor *enclosed in* sh–ed	SHEARED
enclosed, *say* BLOCK-TIN, WAULED, WAWLED	
enclosing a . . .	incl A
enclosing *	incl *
• sh–ed *enclosing* auditor	SHEARED
enclosure in wi/de cor/ral	DECOR
large *enclosure*	BI–G
• family in large *enclosure*	BIKING

encompass

encompass a . . .	incl A
encompass *	incl *
• pla–n *encompassing* one . . .	PLAIN
encompassed by *	incl in *
• one *encompassed by* pla–n	PLAIN
encompassed in Engli/sh ed/ition	SHED

encounter

encounter (=run into)	
• run *into* BT . . .	BRUNT
encounter, *say*	MEAT, METE
	POULTRY-KEEPER
encountered	MET
• *encountered* a number,	
say	METAPHOR
• *encountered* a road	
marker, *say*	METACONE
• *encountered* engineer	METRE
• *encountered*	
previously, *say*	METAPHOR
encountered in mo/st	
art/ists . . .	START

encrypt

encrypted [verses]	SEVERS
encryption of [German] . . .	MANGER

end

end of/*end of*	
–cake	ROLLOVER
–cak<u>e</u>	E
–crossing	PASSOVER
–crossin<u>g</u>	G
–go	TURNOVER
–g<u>o</u>	O
–draw	PULLOVER
–dra<u>w</u>	W
–filming	TAKEOVER
–filmin<u>g</u>	G
–June	THIRTIETH
–Jun<u>e</u>	E
–line	BUFFERS
–lin<u>e</u>	E
–music	CODA
–musi<u>c</u>	C
–prayer	AMEN
–praye<u>r</u>	R
–quarrel	ARROWHEAD
–quarre<u>l</u>	L
–race	TAPE
–rac<u>e</u>	E
–season	(sum)MER, (win)TER
–seaso<u>n</u>	N
–th<u>e</u> . . .	E
–the roa<u>d</u>	D
–the war	VE, VJ
–the wa<u>r</u>	R
–the world	ARMAGEDDON, RAGNAROK
–the worl<u>d</u>	D
–training	TERMINUS
–trainin<u>g</u>	G
end paper	DEATH CERTIFICATE

end protest	OBJECT	• English clergyman	ERECTOR
end-to-end lever	REVEL	• English country	ELAND, ESTATE
end *up*(D)^	MIA, PIT, POT, POTS	• English flower	EASTER
endless bel(t)	BEL	• English landowner	ESQUIRE
endless (f)light	LIGHT	• English team	EXI–
endlessly talk	DISCUS(s)	• English trees	EYEWASH
ends of <u>Ma</u>y and <u>A</u>pril	MYAL	• English woman	EPAULETTE
ends off th(e) ree(d)	THREE	• Englishmen	EVICTED
ends *up*(D)^	SPIT, SPOT, SPOTS	English	ENG
loose [ends]	DENS, SEND	• English nation	ENGRACE
<u>loos</u><u>e</u> *ends*	LE	• English period	ENGAGE
endear	LOBE	• English waterfall	ENGRAIN
enemy		• English lunatic	ENGRAVING
enemy	TIME	English banker	THAMES etc
• enemy *retreating*<	EMIT	English capital	STERLING
<u>e</u>nemy *front*	E	English *capital*	E
energy		English country music	NATIONAL ANTHEM
energy	E	English *flower*	THAMES etc
energy figures	VIM	English *leader*	E
engage		English linesman	KEATS et al
engaged in [war]	RAW	[English] *resort*	SHINGLE
engaged in w/ar t/o . . .	ART	English vale	FAREWELL, GOODBYE
engaged in *	incl in *	**English²**	
• chief *engaged in* de–ed	DECIDED	English as a	
engagement ring	ARENA, WARRING	–foreign language	EFL
	(*see also* battle)	–second language	ESL
engaging a . . .	incl A	English Chamber Orchestra	ECO
engaging *	incl *	English Church Union	ECU
• de–ed *engaging* the		English Dialect Society	EDS
chief . . .	DECIDED	English Golf Union	EGU
engender		English language teaching	ELT
engender [fear]	FARE	English Speaking Union	ESU
engendered by [lots] . . .	SLOT	**engrave**	
engendering [hate]	HEAT	engrave	BURY, INTER
engine		engrave worker	ETCHANT
engine driver	STEAM	engraved line, *say*	HATCHER
engine noise	CARPING	engraver	ENG
engineman	STEPHENSON, WATT		FUNERAL DIRECTOR
engineer			UNDERTAKER
engineer(s)	CE	engravers	RE
• engineers *almost* well off	CERIC (h)	engraving	ENG
• engineer *gets* wage increase	CERISE	**engulf**	
• engineer learners *have* nothing	CELLO	*engulfed by* *	incl in *
engineer	ENG	• one *engulfed by* wa–ve	WAIVE
engineer(s)	RE	*engulfed in* re/bell/ion	BELL
• engineer designs	REDRAWS	*engulfing* a . . .	incl A
• engineer *with a* vehicle	REBUS	*engulfing* *	incl *
• engineer's gallery	RESTATE	• wa–ve *engulfing* one . . .	WAIVE
• engineers teach . . .	RESTRAIN	**enigma**	
engineer(s)	REME	*enigma* [of Al] . . .	FOAL, LOAF
• engineer's graduated scale	REMEDIAL	[Enigma] *Variation*	GAMINE
• engineer's unknown quantity	REMEX	[real] *enigma*	LEAR
• test engineers, *say*	TRIREME	**enjoying hot weather**	(in) SU–N
engineer [has to] . . .	OATHS, SHOAT	**enlist**	
English¹		*enlist* a . . .	incl A
<u>Eng</u>land's *opening pair*	EN	*enlist* *	incl *
English	E	• navy *enlists* first-class . . .	RAIN

enlisted by *	incl in *		*(see also* entrance)
• I've *been enlisted by*		**entertain**	
the navy	RIVEN	*entertain* a . . .	incl A
enliven		*entertain* *	incl *
enliven [dance]	CANED	• drink *to entertain* judge	ALLUDE
enlivened [by a] . . .	BAY	• ho–st *entertains* beginner	HOLST
enlarge paper	REAM	• I am *entertained by* par–ty	PARITY
enough		entertainment finished	SHOW-OFF
enough for [all the] . . .	LETHAL	**enthrall**	
enough to make [many] . . .	MYNA	*enthralled by* *	incl in *
enrol		• see me *enthralled by* state	CAMEL
enrol a . . .	incl A	*enthralled by* cine/ma st/ars	MAST
enrol student(s)	incl L(L)	*enthralls* a . . .	incl A
enrol *	incl *	*enthralls* *	incl *
• I *enrol in* par–ty	PARITY	• state *enthralled* me	CAMEL
ensconce		**enthusiast**	
ensconced in ch/ape/l	APE	enthusiast	FAN
ensconced in *	incl in *	• enthusiast follows	FANTAILS
• Premier *has* queen		• enthusiast *grabs* money	FLAN
ensconced in..	PERM	• enthusiast's food	FANFARE
ensemble		cnthusiastic	HOT
ensemble [she saw] . . .	WASHES	• enthusiastic soldiers	HOTFOOT
[German] *ensemble*	MANGER	• enthusiastic trial	HOTTEST
enshrine		• enthusiastic, urges . . .	HOTSPURS
enshrine a . . .	incl A	enthusiastic *about*< . . .	DAM
enshrine *	incl *	enthusiastic girl	NANKEEN
• church *enshrines* a saint	CASTE	**entire**	
enshrined by *	incl in *	entire	STALLION
• a saint *enshrined by* church	CASTE	entire, *say*	IIOLE
enshrined by wor/ship/pers	SHIP	**entomology**	ENT
ensign	ENS	**entrance¹**	
enslave	DELIBERATE	entrance money	INCOME
ensnare		*entrance to* building	B
ensnare a . . .	incl A	entrance, *say*	WEIGH-IN, WEIGHING
ensnare *	incl *	*entry* form	F
• rustic *ensnares* learner	PLEASANT	*Entry of the* Gladiators	G
ensnared by *	incl in *	entry to profession	ADMISSION
• learner *ensnared by* rustic	PLEASANT	*entry to* profession	P
ensnared in pl/ot her s/on . . .	OTHERS	No *Entry*	N
entangle			*(see also* enter)
entangle a . . .	incl A	**entrance²**	
entangle *	incl *	entranced, *say*	WRAPPED
• re–ed-*entangled* fin	REFINED	entrancing flier	WITCH
entangled in *	incl in *	entrancing flier, *say*	WHICH
• fin *entangled in* re–ed	REFINED	**entreat**	
entangled [nets]	STEN	entreat	BEG
enter		• entreat a single . . .	BEGONE
enter in/to a st/and	TOAST	• entreat Barnaby	BEGRUDGE
enter plant	(in) RE–ED	• entreat Clark	BEGGABLE
entered	INGOT	entreat	PRAY
entered by *	incl *	• entreated, *say*	PREYED
• animals had *entered*	SHADOWS	• entreats, *say*	PRAISE
• the river *entered by* stream	THRILLER	• entreaty, *say*	PREYER
entered in da/ta b/ank	TAB	entreaty	PLEA
I *enter*	incl I	• entreaty finished, *say*	PLEADED
* *enters*	incl *	• entreaty *to* daughter	PLEAD
• stream *enters* th–e river	THRILLER	• entreaty *to* Edward	PLEATED

Letter replaced \c\at; Omit (a); Pointers *out*; Retain a̲; Split B_ED; Down (D); Backwards <or ^

entry	(*see* enter)
entwine	
entwine [arms]	MARS, RAMS
entwined by *	incl in *
• a king *entwined by* st–ring	STARRING
entwined in fi/bre d/rawn . . .	BRED
entwining a . . .	incl A
entwining *	incl *
• st–ring *entwining* a king	STARRING
entwining [roots]	TORSO
enunciate	
enunciated clause	CLAWS
enunciation of phrase	FRAYS
envelop	
envelop a . . .	incl A
envelop *	incl *
• f–og *envelops* king	FROG
enveloped by *	incl in *
• king *enveloped by* f–og	FROG
environment	
environment of Lond/on set/tlement	ONSET
* *environment*	incl in *
• a king *in* city *environment*	EARLY
environmentalists	GREENS
envy	
envious	GREEN
envy, *say*	NV
epistle	EP
epsilon	E
equal	
equal	PAR
• equal bargain	PARSNIP
• equal monarch	PARKING
• equal shares	PARTAKES
equal contest	MATCH
equal manufacturer	MATCHMAKER
Equal Opportunities Commission	EOC
equal *returns*	LEVEL
equal to or more than, *say*	KNOTLESS
equalise scales	BALANCE
equality, *say*	PARROTTY
equally	AS
• equally determined	ASSET
• equally hot	ASWARM
• equally sharp	ASTART
equals, *say*	PIERCE, PIERS
equestrian	
equestrian appendage	RIDER
equestrian humour	HORSE LAUGH
equestrienne	GODIVA
equitation, *say*	MANAGE
eradicate	
eradicate a . . .	omit a
eradicate *	omit *
• fat(her) *eradicates* her . . .	FAT
is *eradicated*	omit IS
• r(is)e is *eradicated*	RE
Erato	
Erato, *say*	AMUSE, MUSE
erect	
are *erected*(D)^	ERA
erect bat(D)^	TAB
erect cooker	REARRANGE
erected dam(D)^	MAD
erection of part(D)^	TRAP
was *erected*(D)^	SAW
ergo	SO
erode	
erode, *say*	WARE
eroded [coastline]	SECTIONAL
eroded, *say*	WARN
eroding [slope]	LOPES, POLES
erosion of coast	BEACHWEAR
erosion of [coast]	ATOCS, COATS
erosion, *say*	LANDWEHR
errant	
errant character	MISPRINT, TYPO
errant [Poles]	LOPES, SLOPE
erratic	
erratic [drive]	DIVER
[spoke] *erratically*	POKES
error	
erred in Italy, *say*	SYNDROME
erroneous [step]	PEST, PETS
error	SIN
• error by family	SINK IN
• error-trap	SINNET
• error unusual, *say*	SYNOD
error [in the] . . .	THINE
errors excepted	EE
errors and omissions excepted	EOE
[human] *error*	NAHUM
[on a quite] *erroneous* . . .	EQUATION
erupt	
erupt [in a] . . .	AIN, –IAN, INA
erupting [like] . . .	KIEL
eruption of [Etna]	NATE, NEAT
escape	
escape route	FLIGHT PATH
escaped a . . .	omit A
escaped [deer]	REED, REDE
escaped from Ber/lin g/aol	LING
escaped king	omit R
escaped queen	omit ER
I *escaped*	omit I
one *escaped*	omit A, I
* *escaped*	omit *
• she *escaped* ma(she)r	MAR
escudo	ESC
Eskimo	
Eskimo	HUSKY, IN(N)UIT
Eskimo *leader*	E

especially	ESP	European fashion, *say*	UROSTYLE
esquire	ESQ	European friend, *say*	CHECKMATE
essay		European journalist	POLISHED
essay, *say*	SA	European *leader*	E
essayist	ELIA, LAMB	European measure	POLE
essayist's claim	AMELIA	European on strike, *say*	CHECK-OUT
Essen		European property	SLAVE STATE
[Essen] *demolished*	SENSE	European, *say*	CHECK, CHEQUE, DEIGN
Essen, *say*	SN	**Evangelical Union**	EU
essence		**even**	
essence of ro_ses_	S	*even characters abandon* p(l)a(y)	PA
vani_lla essence_	I	*even characters in* pl_ay_	LY
essential		eve(n) *less*	EVE
essential in bre/ad mix/ture	ADMIX	even match	FLATTEST
essential part of en/gin/e	GIN	even number	FLATTEN, PLAINSONG
essentially sou_nd_	U	fai_rly even_	–ARY
Essex		**evening**	
Essex, *perhaps*	COUNTY	evening air	NOCTURNE, SERENADE
Essex, *say*	SX	evening dress, *say*	TALES
establish		evening journey, *say*	NITRIDE
established	EST, PROVEN	evening out	IRONING, PLANING, PRESSING
• *established* at eastern . . .	ESTATE	evening sun	RED SETTER
• *established* state	PROVENCAL	evening work	IRONING, PLANING, PRESSING
established church	EC, CE	**eventually**	
established company	FIRM	eventually	(in) EN–D
* *established*	incl *	• *certain eventually*	ENSURED
• *one established in* pos–t	POSIT	**ever**	
estate agent		ever	AY, AYE, ER, EER
Estate	VIRGINIA etc	[ever]-*changing*	REVE
estate agent	STEWARD	*ever*more	EVERT, LEVER, NEVER
estate agent's brochure	SEMI-CIRCULAR	evermore	NEVERTHELESS
estimated		**every**	
estimated time of		every evening, *say*	KNIGHTLY
–arrival	ETA	every other day	EOD
–departure	ETD	*every other part* of Spain	PI, SAN
eta	E	every player	TUTTI
etchers	RE	every year	PA
Ethiopia	ETH	everyone	ALL, EACH
etymology	ETY	everyone *up*^ North(D)	LLAN–
European[1]		everything does	ENDING
European	E, EUR	everything due	ALLOWING
European Broadcasting Union	EBU	**evict**	
European Council	CE, EC	*evict* a	omit A
European Defence Community	EDC	*evict* people	omit MEN
European Development Fund	EDF	*evict* *	omit *
European (Economic)		• *evict* girl *from* sor(di)d . . .	SORD
Commission	E(E)C	**evident**	
European (Economic)		evident *in* hi/s ap/proach	SAP
Community	E(E)C	**evil**	
European Monetary Agreement	EMA	evil boy	VICEROY
European Payments Union	EPU	evil ruler	SINKING
European Productivity Agreement	EPA	**evolve**	
European[2]		*evolution of* [man is] . . .	MAINS
European agreement	JA, OUI, OUIJA, SI	*evolve* [a new] . . .	WANE, WEAN
European articles	ELLA, LATHE, UNDER	*evolving from* [past] . . .	PATS, TAPS
E_uropean capital_	E	**ewe**	
European country, *say*	OSTREA	ewe, *say*	U, YEW, YOU

Letter replaced \c\at; Omit (a); Pointers *out*; Retain a_; Split B_ED; Down (D); Backwards <or ^

ewes, *say*	US, UU, YEWS, YOUSE	excellent	SUPER
ex-		• excellent book	SUPERB
ex-	X	• excellent disguise	SUPERVISOR
ex-captain	MAJOR	• excellent eyesight	SUPERVISION
ex-pupil	GRADUATE, OB	excellent	VG
ex-works	incl OP	excellent brandy	FINE
• *ex*-works sl–ed	SLOPED	excellent character	CAPITAL
exact		excellent drug	CRACKPOT
exact money	BLACKMAIL	excellent guess	DIVINE
exactly (=to a T)		excellent ruler	SOVEREIGN
• ten *exactly*	TENT	**except**	
• meet *exactly*	JOINT	*except* a . . .	omit A
• *exactly* to his . . .	HIST, THIS	except Edward	BUTTED
exact time	DEAD MARCH	*except* *	omit *
exalt		• *except* the fa(the)r	FAR
exaltation of new . . .(D)^	WEN	exception	EX(C)
exalted cleric *has* order(D)^	MOVER	*exceptional* [talent]	LATENT
examine		**exemplary**	EG
examination	ORAL, TEST, VIVA	**excess**	
• spring exam	MAYORAL	excess weight	GLUTTON
• try examination	TEST	excessive love	MANIA
• examination town	VIVACITY	*excessive rise*(D)^	OOT, REVO
examination	A-LEVEL, CSE, GCE	excessively	OTT
	O-LEVEL	**exchange**	
examination level	A, O	exchange currency	TRADEMARKS
examination paper	SEARCH WARRANT	exchange of letters	ANAGRAM
examine	CON	*exchange of* [letters]	SETTLER
• examine bivouacs	CONTENTS	*exchange* [rate]	TARE, TEAR
• examine evidence	CONSIGN(S)	exchanging punches	HORSE-TRADING
• examine punishments	CONFINES	[heat] *exchange*	HATE, THEA
examine	TEST	*in exchange for* [lira]	ARIL, LIAR, RAIL
• examine *after* warm . . .	HOTTEST	stock exchange	CATTLE MARKET
• examine river	TEST	**excise**	
• examine vessel, *say*	TESTERN	*excise* a	omit A
examine	PRY	*excise* one . . .	omit A, I
• examine friend, *say*	PRIMATE	*excise* some t(um)ours	TOURS
• examine lad	PRISON	*excise* *	omit *
• examine porcelain, *say*	PRIMING	• fa(the)r *excised* the . . .	FAR
examine	TRY	**excite**	
• examine cereal, *say*	TRICORN	excite dogs	FANTAILS
• examine cult, *say*	TRISECT	*excited* [dogs]	GODS
examined	EX	*excitement of* [atoms]	MOATS, STOMA
examines, *say*	CHEQUES, CZECHS	*exciting* [times]	EMITS, SMITE
example	EX	[great] *excitement*	GRATE
excavate		**exclude**	
excavate(=dig up)(D)^	GID	*exclude* outsiders	omit 1st and last
excavated boat	DUGOUT	• (b)oar(d) *excludes outsiders*	OAR
excavated from de/ep ic/e	EPIC	*excluding* a . . .	omit A
excavated, *say*	HOLLOAED, MIND	*excluding* nothing	incl ALL
excel		• wicked *excluding* nothing	BALLAD
excel, *say*	XL	*excluding* nothing	omit O
excellency	HE	• l(o)ad *excluding nothing*	LAD
excellency, *say*	XLNC	*excluding* *	omit *
excellent	AI	• Char(le)s *excluding*	
• excellent wine	AIRED	the *French*	CHARS
• excellent ball	AIDANCE	**excruciate**	
• excellent fish	AILING	*excruciating* [pains]	SPAIN

Anag [cat]; Any *; Begin IGN–; Endings –ING; eg •; Hidden /cat/; Implied add (on); Implied in (in);

excruciatingly [sharp]	HARPS	• existing lines	LIVERY
excursion		existing place	HOME, RESIDENCE
excursion [by bus]	BUSBY	existing present	TENSE, TENURE
excursion route	TRIPLANE	existing rate	COST OF LIVING
excursus	EX	existing, *say*	REEL
Exe	X	existing state	ASIS
execute		exists *on* earth	ISLAND
execute agent	IMPLEMENT	**exit**	
execute player	HANG BACK	exit permit	OUTLET
executed (k)ing	–ING	exit, *say*	WEIGH-OUT
executioner	KETCH, TOPPER	exits	OUTDOORS
executive	EX	**Exodus**	EX
executive officer	HANGMAN	**exonerate**	
executor	EXR, EXOR	exonerate	CLEAR
exemplified	EG	• exonerate journalist	CLEARED
exempt		• exonerate king	CLEARCOLE, CLEARER
exempt at the end	omit last letter	**exorcise**	
▪ mat(c) *exempt at the end*	MAT	exorcise	DISPOSSESS
exempt at the start	omit 1st letter	*exorcise* a . . .	omit A
• (m)ate *exempt at the start*	ATE	*exorcise* alien . . .	omit ET
exercise		*exorcise* one . . .	omit A, I
exercise	PE	exorcise, *say*	EXERCISE, PE, PT
• artillery exercise	RAPE	*exorcise* *	omit *
• company exercise	COPE	• p(ri)est *exorcises*	
• exercise books	PENT	king-emperor	PEST
exercise	PT	**exotic**	
• artillery exercise	RAPT	exotic (=foreign language)	
• company exercise	COPT	• *exotic* flower	FLEUR
• field exercise	LEAPT	• *exotic* friend	KAMERAD
exercise [dogs]	GODS	• *exotic* girl	SENORITA
exercise sequence	TRAIN	• *exotic* garden	GIARDINO
exercising [men at] . . .	MEANT	exotic	ALIEN, ET
exhaust pipe	DRAIN	exotic character (=letter from a	
exhibit		foreign language)	
exhibit	HANG	• first *exotic character*	ALEPH, ALPHA
• exhibit in Greece	HANGING	• *exotic character is*	
• exhibit pet	HANGDOG	*after* a . . .	BETA, BETH
• exhibit sack	HANG FIRE	*exotic* [trees]	STEER, STERE
exhibit	SHOW	**expand**	
• exhibit county . . .	SHOWDOWN	indicating an abbreviation	
• exhibit garments	SHOWJUMPERS	to be written in full:	
• exhibit *before* queen	SHOWER	• *expanded* her . . .	HERALDRY
exhibited by *	incl in *	• it *expanded*	ITALIAN
• spectacles *exhibited by*		• no *expansion*	NOBELIUM
musician	BOOM	**expect**	
exhibiting a . . .	incl A	expectant mother	LADY-IN-WAITING
exhibiting ar/t at T/ate	TATT	expected, *say*	JEW
exhibiting *	incl *	**expel**	
• musician *exhibiting*		*expel* a . . .	omit A
spectacles	BOOM	expel those present	TURNOUT
exhibition of wa/res t/ of . . .	REST	*expel* *	omit *
exhibitor	ARTIST, RA	• *expel* head of (c)lass	LASS
exist		• Henry *expelled from* school	(h)ARROW
exist in this way	SOLIVE	• (l)over *expels* student . . .	OVER
existing	LIVE	**experiment**	
• an existing . . .	ALIVE	*experiment* [in the] . . .	THINE
• existing king	LIVER	*experimental* [plane]	PANEL

[painter] *experimented*	REPAINT	**express**	
expert		express condition	STATE
expert	ABLE	express fare	FAST FOOD
• expert *has* square . . .	ABLET	expressions of regret, *say*	SIZE
• good man *has* expert . . .	STABLE	**expurgate**	
• run expert . . .	MANAGEABLE	*expurgated* t/ext end/ing . . .	EXTEND
expert	ACE	*expurgation* b/y obs/erving . . .	YOBS
• expert *with* twitch	ACETIC	**extend**	
• expert sound	ACETONE	extend plan	PROJECT
and		extend time	STRETCH
• British expert	BRACE	*extended* her . . .	HERALDRY
• friend and expert	PALACE	extended play	EP
• quiet expert	PACE	extended speech	DRAWL
• stern expert	GRIMACE	extension	EXT
and		extent, *say*	SIGHS
• fifty experts	LACES	it *extended* . . .	ITALIAN
• many experts	MACES	**exterior**	
expert	DAB	*exterior* of <u>cabin</u>	CAN
• expert *goes round* the bend	DAUB	* *exterior*	incl in *
• expert lost blood	DABBLED	• animal has re–d *exterior*	REAPED
• expert worker	DAB HAND	**external**	
expert	PRO	external measurements	OUTSIZE
• expert examination	PROTEST	*external* *	incl in *
• expert in good shape	PROFIT	• university's *external* entrance	AUDIT
• expert remedy	PROCURE	externally	EXT
expert did . . .	ACCOMPLISHED	**extinct**	EXT
expert oarsman	MASTERSTROKE	**extinguish**	
expert's knowledge	ONIONS	*extinguish* a . . .	omit A
	(*see also* ace, profess)	*extinguish* *	omit *
expire		• fa(the)r *extinguished* the . . .	FAR
expire	DIE	• fir(e) *finally extinguished*	FIR
• expire, *say*	DAI, DYE	**extol**	
expire	PASSOVER	extol queen	PUFFER
expired persons, *say*	WEEDED	extol summer	PUFF-ADDER
expiration of leas<u>e</u>	E	**extort**	
explode		[crude] *extortion*	CURED
explode	GOBANG	*extort* [ransom]	MANORS
exploding [mine]	MIEN	extort, *say*	RING
explosion of [rage]	GEAR	**extra**	
explosive	HE, TNT	extra	BYE
• explosive mixture	HEBREW	• extra reading	BY-ELECTION
• I *put in* explosive	TINT	• extra rules	BYE-LAWS
explosive finale	KO	• extras	BYE-BYE
explosiv<u>e</u> *finale*	E	extra	EXT
explosive [rate]	TARE, TEAR	• extra bit	EXTORT
explosive, *say*	TONIGHT	• extra boorish	EXTRUDE
exploit		• extra worker	EXTANT
exploit [forests]	FOSTERS	extra	MORE
exploit, *say*	FEET	• cut extra, *say*	HUMOR
exploitation of [slaves]	SALVES	• extra cut, *say*	MORLOP
exploits fish	MILKSHAKE	• extra flower, *say*	MOROSE
exponential	EXP	extra	NO-BALL
export	EX(P)	extra	WIDE
expose		• extra child	WIDE-BOY
expose some l/aye/rs	AYE	• extra food	WIDESPREAD
exposing hid/den t/alent	DENT	• extra run	WIDER
exposition of cle/ver ge/neral	VERGE	extra damage	SURCHARGE

Anag [cat]; Any *; Begin IGN–; Endings –ING; eg •; Hidden /cat/; Implied add (on); Implied in (in);

extra delivery	NO-BALL, WIDE
extra large	EXCEL, XL, OS
extra-sensory perception	ESP
extra-terrestrial	ALIEN
• extra-terrestrial scoffed	ALIENATE
extra-terrestrial	ET
	(*see also* alien)
extra thought	PS

extract

extract a . . .	omit A
extract a/n oun/ce	NOUN
extract from fun/gus t/ype	GUST
extract of [roe]	ORE
extract *	omit *
• *extract* lubricant *from* b(oil)ed...	BED
extracted from par/t of fee/t	TOFFEE
extracted from [skin]	INKS, SINK
extraction of bit/ter m/elon	TERM

extraordinary

extraordinarily [like] . . .	KIEL
extraordinary [caper]	PACER

extravagant

extravagant [claim]	MALIC
extravagantly [used]	DUES, DUSE, SUED
[Irish] *extravaganza*	RISHI

extreme

extreme characters	AZ
extreme characters in play	PY
extreme *left*	E
extreme left	L, T
extreme *right*	E
extreme right	R, T
extreme state	UTTER
extremely handy	FINGERTIP
extremely handy	HY
extremely light	VERY

extremely light	LT
extremes	N–S
extremes of paranoia	PA, PANDA
extremists abandoned (W)ale(s)	ALE
extremists in Paris	PS
extremities	N, S
extremities of endurance	EE
extremity	TOE
pedal *extremities*	PL

extricate

extricate from [a mesh]	HAMES, SHAME
extricate from ditc/h aft/er . . .	HAFT

exuberant

[act] *exuberantly*	CAT
exuberant [dancer]	CRANED

eye

eye of needle	E
eye, *say*	AYE, I
eye-dropper	TEAR
eye-liner	RETINA
eye-opener	ALARM (CLOCK), COCKEREL
	LID
eye-opener	E
eye-opener	start with I
• member has eye-*opener*	IMP
eye trouble, *say*	EGOMANIA, EGO(T)ISM
eyeball	ORB
eyeblack, *say*	COAL
eye*less*	omit I
eyelid	SHUTTER
eyepiece	CORNEA, IRIS, LENS
	RETINA
eyes at the back, *say*	REARISE
eyes, *say*	II, IS, –ISE, –IZE
eyesore	STYE
Ezra	EZ

F

clef, Fahrenheit, farad, Faraday's constant, farthing, fathom, fellow, female, feminine, femto-, fighter plane, filial generation, filly, *fine*, fluorine, folio, following, foot, force, forte, forty (thousand), franc, France, e, frequency, Friday, Helmholtz free energy, hole, key, layer, loud, *noisy*, note, number, stop, vitamin, word

---

fabricate

fabricate	LIE
• fabricate opening, *say*	LIGATE
• fabrication speed, *say*	LYRATE
• fabricator, *say*	LYRE
fabricate [cruel] . . .	LUCRE
fabricated song	LIED
fabrication of [steel]	LEETS, STELE

fabulous

fabulous bird	ROC
fabulous country, *say*	COCAINE
fabulous loser	HARE
fabulous place	COCKAIGNE, ELDORADO
fabulous supporter	UNICORN
fabulous winner	TORTOISE

facade

facade of <u>r</u>espectability	R
<u>i</u>mposing *facade*	I

face

face	DIAL
• engineer's face	REMEDIAL
• face shock treatment	DIALECT
• face with eyes, *say*	DIALISE
• face *up*(D)^	MUG, LAID
face job	CLOCKWORK
face lift(D)^	GUM
face pain	PANACHE
face saver	MASK, VISOR
face up	BACK DOWN
face wall	PLASTER, RENDER
• *faces of* the <u>old</u> <u>women</u>	TOW

facing

–east	TOE
–north	TON
–west	TOW
facing the other way, tip	
was< . . .	SAW PIT
rats *faced the other way*<	STAR

fact

facts	DATA, GEN
facts, *say*	FAX

(*see also* indeed)

factory

factory dance	WORKSHOP
factory output	RUN OF THE MILL
factory owner, *say*	MILKING

Faculty of Actuaries — FA

fade

[fade] *out*	DEAF
fade, *say*	WAIN
fadeout of final ac(t)	AC

Faeroe Islands — FR

fag-end

fag-*end*	G
fag-end of join<u>t</u>	T

Fahrenheit — F

fail

fail, *say*	WAIN
fail to declare	BATON
fail to finish	omit last letter
• a girl *fails to finish*	ALAS(s)
• *fail to finish* bee(r)	BEE
• sh(e) *fails to finish*	SH
fail to get a . . .	omit A
fail to get money	omit L
fail to get *	omit *
• *fail to get* son out of vessel	(s)HIP
• the(y) *fail to get* unknown . . .	THE
fail to open	omit 1st letter
• *fail to open* (g)ate	ATE
failed	CAMEO
failed [in the] . . .	THINE
failed, *say*	MIST
failing a . . .	omit A
failing *	omit *
• *failing* her fat(her)	FAT
failing [test]	SETT, STET
fails to start	omit first letter
• (b)us *fails to start*	US
• *fails to start* (r)ace	ACE
failure of [arch]	CHAR
failure to decide, *say*	ETHERISM

Anag [cat]; Any *; Begin IGN–; Endings –ING; eg •; Hidden /cat/; Implied add (on); Implied in (in);

Clue	Answer
[heart] *failure*	EARTH, HATER, RATHE
one *failing*	omit I
[renal] *failure*	LEARN
faint	
faint boundary	PALE
faint *heart*	I
faint letter	WEAKEN
faint point	WANE
faint *sound*	FEINT
fair	
fair	F
• fair, always	FEVER
• Fair Isle	FIONA
• mark *on* fair . . .	SCARF
fair account	EXPOSITION
fair *and* square	EVENT
fair game	AUNT SALLY, HOOPLA, SKITTLES, etc
fair location	PLEASURE GROUND
fair punishment	FINE
fair *shares*	FA, IR
fair treatment	BLEACH(ING), PEROXIDE
fairy	
fairy	HOB, IMP, PERI, PUCK
• fairy ring	HOBO
• fairy tales	IMPLORE
• fairy fish	PERICARP
• fairy queen	PUCKER
fairy dance	MOTH BALL
fairy king	OBERON
fairy queen	MAB
falcon	
falcon, *say*	JERKING
falconer's pastime	HOBBY
fake	
fake	SHAM
• fake article	SHAMAN
• fake diamonds	SHAMROCK
• fake drug	SHAME
fake ache, *say*	CHAMPAGNE
fall	
fall	HAIL, RAIN, SLEET, SNOW SLIPOVER
fall *for a Frenchman*	AUTOMNE
fall *for American* . . .	AUTUMN
fall from *	omit from *
• he *falls from* t(he) . . .	T
• he *falls from* (he)avens	AVENS
fall in *	incl in *
• rat *falling in* river	DERATE
fall short of targe(t)	TARGE
fall short of th(e) . . .	TH
fallen [angel]	ANGLE, GLEAN
falling about [in the] . . .	THINE
falling apart [when I] . . .	WHINE
falling house	USHER
falling out [over] . . .	ROVE
falling over [step]	PEST, PETS
falling [star]	ARTS, RATS, TARS
* *falls off*	omit *
• nose *falls off* (p)lane	LANE
falls over carrier	SLIPSHOD
false	
false [or true]	ROUTER, TOURER
false [start]	TARTS
false *start*	F
falsely [said] . . .	AIDS, DAIS
falsifies marks	FIDDLESTICKS
falsify [report]	PORTER
Falstaff's tipple	SACK
falter	
falter [over]	ROVE
faltering [steps]	PESTS, PETS
familiar	
familiar	FAM
indicating: colloquial	
diminutive	
slang	
familiar face	MUG
familiarity with Philip	PIP
familiarly eccentric	LOOPY
family	
family	BLOOD
• athlete's family	BLUE BLOOD
• family *with* unknown . . .	BLOODY
• family row	BLOOD BANK
family	FAM
• bovine family	OXFAM
• family in the East	FAMINE
• family *takes* drug	FAME
family	KIN
• feline family	CATKIN
• interrogate family	PUMPKIN
• odd family	RUMKIN
family	LINE
• incorporated family . . .	INCLINE
• family friend	LINEALLY
• family *has* king's . . .	LINERS
Family Income Supplement	FIS
family mess	LITTER
Family Planning Association	FPA
family story	RELATION
family works	HOUSE PLANT
famous	
famous day	VE
famous fish	STARLING
famous saw	NOTED
fancy	
fanciful [ideas]	AIDES, SADIE
fancy catalogue	IDEALIST
fancy food shop	DELI
fancy heel	IDEALIST
fancy [I can] . . .	CAIN
fancy man/woman	SUSPECT

Letter replaced \c\at; Omit (a); Pointers *out*; Retain <u>a</u>; Split B_ED; Down (D); Backwards <or ^

fancy table	IDEALIST
fancy [table]	BLATE, BLEAT
fanlight	BLOW-TORCH
fantasy	
fantastic aircraft	BROOMSTICK
fantastic relation	FABLE, FAIRY STORY
fantastic [scene I] . . .	NIECES
fantasy [in B]	BIN, NIB
far	
[far] *away*	FRA, RAF
far-fetched [idea]	AIDE
[far]-*flung*	FRA, RAF
far-flung [clime]	MELIC
[far] *off*	FRA, RAF
far side of road	D
farad	F
fare	
fare-carrier	LUNCH-BOX
	PICNIC HAMPER
fare from China	CHOW-MEIN
fare from Italy	PASTA
fare from Spain	PAELLA
farewell	
farewell	BV, SUCCEED
farewell speech	A BIENTOT, ARRIVEDERCI,
	ADIEU, ADIOS, ALOHA, AU REVOIR,
	AUF WIEDERSEHEN, CIAO, CHEERIO,
	GOODBYE, HASTA LA VISTA,
	SAYONARA, SO LONG, TATA, VALE
farm	
farm boss	STUD
farm butter	GOAT, RAM
farm victims	MIC(e)
farmer	GILES, YEOMAN
farmer's punch	HAYMAKER
farmhouse victims	MIC(e)
farming	(on) LAND
• fish*farming*	GARLAND
farming policy	CAP
farthing	F, Q
fashion	
fashion	ALA
• fashion *in* South Dakota	SALAD
• fashion lines	ALARY
• note fashion	BALA, GALA
fashion	RAGE
• current *in* fashion	RAMPAGE
• note fashion	MIRAGE
• see company bend *to* fashion	COURAGE
fashion	TON
• fashion *in* Home Counties	STONE
• fashion notes	TONDO, TONGA
• South American fashion	SAT ON
fashion	
indicating use of foreign	
language:	
• a *Greek fashion*	ALPHA

• leader *in Italian fashion*	DUCE
• new *French fashion*	NOUVEAU
• older *Spanish fashion*	MAYOR
• *Paris fashion* is . . .	EST
• sweet *American fashion*	CANDY
• the *German fashion*	DAS, DER, DIE
fashion bench	FORM
fashion city	BRISTOL
fashion class	FORM
fashion models	FORMS, MAKES, SHAPES
fashion [models]	SELDOM
fashion, *say*	MOWED
fashion shop	BOUTIQUE
fashion [shop]	HOPS, POSH
fashion that is . . .	CUTIE
fashion you and me, *say*	STYLUS
fashioned, *say*	MAID
[old]-*fashioned*	DOL, LOD
fashionable	
fashionable	CHIC
• fashionable fellow	CHICKEN
• fashionable girl	CHICHESTER
• fashionable in the past	CHICAGO
fashionable	HIP
• fashionable curves	HIPS
• kin(g)s *almost* fashionable...	KINSHIP
• woman *with* fashionable . . .	WHIP
fashionable	IN
• fashionable dress	INHABIT
• fashionable group	INSECT, INSET
• fashionable sound	INTONE, INVOICE
fashionable	U
• fashionable *and* quiet	UP
• fashionable evening, *say*	UNITE
• fashionable fur	USABLE
fashionable [gear]	RAGE
[not] *fashionable*	ONT, TON
fast	
fast	LENT
• fast one	LENTI
• in so fast . . .	INSOLENT
fast buck	DEER, HARE, RABBIT
fast car	GT, ROD
fast company	FIRM
fast delivery	CHATTER
fast finish	EASTER
fas*t finish*	T
fast freeze	STARVE
fast mover	CLAPPER
fast ships	FLEET
fast start	F
fast work	DIETING, STARVATION
fasten	
fasten	PIN
• fasten a number, *say*	PINNATE
• fasten to	PINTO
• fasten *to* land	TERRAPIN

Anag [cat]; Any *; Begin IGN–; Endings –ING; eg •; Hidden /cat/; Implied add (on); Implied in (in);

fasten	TIE
• fasten correctly, *say*	TYRITE
• fasten joint, *say*	TINY
• fasten, *say*	THAI
fasten	LOCK
• 100 fasten . . .	CLOCK
• fasten hair	LOCK
• fasten it, *say*	LOCKET
fasten folder	NAIL FILE
fasten in this way	SOLACE
fasten marine animal	SEAL
fasten opening	BOLT-HOLE
fastened a weight	PENTAGRAM
fastened [gates]	STAGE
fastened in *	incl in *
• four *fastened in* str–ing	STRIVING
fastened thus	SOLACED
fastening in a . . .	incl A
fastening in *	incl *
• str–ing *fastening in* four . . .	STRIVING
fastener	LOCK
• fastener for flat	PADLOCK
• fine fastener	FLOCK
• fastener *with* eccentric . . .	LOCKNUT
fastener, *say*	BUCCAL
fat	
fat	LARD
• cut *back*< fat . . .	POLLARD
• fat boy	LARDED
• fat monarch	LARDER
fat	
• fat goat	BUTTER
• fat prize	BUTTERCUP
fat	GREASE
• a fat, *say*	AGREES
• fat, *say*	GREECE, GREES
• fat Scot, *say*	GRECIAN
fat people	ROUND FIGURES
fat porter	STOUT
fat ruler	STOUTER, UNTHINKING
fat, *say*	OBIES, PICNIC
fathead	BROAD BEAN, BUTTERNUT
fathead	F
fattening food	BLOATER
fatted calf	STOCKING FILLER
fatter, *say*	GROCER
father	
father	ABBA
father	DAD
• father *has* cut . . .	DADDOCK
• father *with* a . . .	DADA
• father *with* nothing	DADO
father	FR
• father at church	FRATCH
• father should . . .	FRAUGHT
• father *with* East *German*	FROST
father	PA

• father-figure	PAD, PAL, PAM
• father married	PAWED
• Father Thomas	PATHOS
and	
• father's amusement	PASSPORT
• father's beer-mug, *say*	PASTE-IN
• father's wise	PASSAGE
father	POP
• father *after* money, *say*	LOLLIPOP
• father examined . . .	POP-EYED
• father is hot	POPISH
father	THAMES, TIME
father of pride	HELION
father, *say*	SIGHER
father*less*	omit PA
• father*less* (Pa)than	THAN
fatherless gangster	ORPHANHOOD
father's letters	PA, PANDA
fathom	F, FTH, FTHM
fatuous	
fatuous	
• *fatuous* [grin is] . . .	RISING
• [smile] *fatuously*	LIMES, MILES
fault	
fault*less* ser(vice)	SER
faulty hearing	MISTRIAL
faulty head	BADNESS
faulty [sign]	GINS, SING
[his] *fault*	–ISH
favour	
favour sage	LIKEWISE
favoured	IN
favourite	PET
• favourite man	PETAL, PETTED
• favourite ruler	PETER
• transport favourite . . .	CARPET
fear	
fear of Germans, *say*	HUNDRED
fearful [rage]	GEAR
fearfully [tried]	TIRED
feature	
feature	CHIN
• feature article	CHINA
• feature monarch	CHINK
• firm feature	COCHIN
feature a . . .	incl A
feature directors	STARBOARD
feature editor	COSMETIC SURGEON
feature of t/he be/st	HEBE
feature *	incl *
• *feature* article *in* story	LIANE
featured in [all the] . . .	LETHAL
featured in cine/ma ne/ar . . .	MANE
features in n/ew e/xperiment	EWE
featuring *	incl in *
• story *featuring* article	LIANE
featuring remarka/ble st/unt	BLEST

Letter replaced \c\at; Omit (a); Pointers *out*; Retain a; Split B_ED; Down (D); Backwards <or ^

February	FEB	–British Academy	FBA
feed		–Chartered Accountants	FCA
fed *up*(D)^	DEF	–Historical Society	FHS
feed*back*<	DEEF	–Institute of Journalists	FJI
feeding, *say*	FAIRING	–Royal Society	FRS
feel		–Society of Antiquaries	FAS
feel sad	BELOW, TOUCHDOWN	–Society of Arts	FAS
feel the weight	TOUCHSTONE	**female**	
feeling fit	INFORM	female	DI
[feeling] *poorly*	FLEEING	• female journalist	DIED
felt, *say*	CENSED	• female poet	DISPENSER
feet		• female sign	DIARIES
feet	FT	female	F
feet *up*(D)^	DRAY	• female duck	FO
FEG	EFFIGY	• female *has* no spirit	FORUM
fell		• female is ill	FAILS
fell	DOWN, MOOR, HILL	female	GAL
• fell *back*<	ROOM	• engineer *with* female . . .	REGAL
• fell down	MOOR, HILL	• female insects	GALLICE
• fell *over*<	ROOM	• female *with* money	GALL
• fell *up*(D)^	ROOM	female	HEN
• fell twice	DOWNHILL	• female *at* church	HENCE, HENCH
fell *back*<	DENNIS	• female line	HENRY
fell over	HIDE-OUT	• female part	HENBIT
fell sergeant	DEATH	female	HER
fellow¹		• female *and* male	HERM
fellow	CO–	• female with *German* . . .	HERMIT
• fellow-archdeacon	COVEN	• female working	HERON
• fellow-European	COBALT	female	MISS
• fellow fellow	CODON	• engineer *with* female . . .	REMISS
• fellow-friend	COPAL	• female gangster	MISSAL
fellow	COVE	• female journalist	MISSED
• a *French* fellow *with* king	UNCOVER	and	
• fellow Russian	COVERED	• female bank clerk, *say*	MISCALCULATING
• gangster fellow	ALCOVE	• female flatfish, *say*	MISPLACE
fellow	DON	• female magistrate, *say*	MISJUDGE
• fellow *at* tea, *say*	DONT	female	SHE
• fellow dined	DONATE	• female and *French* . . .	SHEET
• fellow fellow	CODON	• female antelope, *say*	BUCKSHEE
• fellow soldiers	DONOR	• female Berber	SHERIFF
• fellow *with* a Conservative	DONATORY	• female flies	SHEWINGS
fellow	F	• female monarch	SHEER
• fellow *has* a cow	FLOWER	female adviser	EGERIA
• fellow is not . . .	FAINT	female bookmaker	AUTHORESS, RUTH
• fellow *with* spectacular fish	FOOLING	female cat	ANNOUNCE
fellow	GENT	female donkey, *say*	ASSESS
• brown fellow	TANGENT	female figurehead, *say*	PROWESS
• fellow the *French* . . .	GENTLE	female friend, *say*	PALETTE
• fellow *with* Scots boy	GENTIAN	female gangster	ANNEAL, MISSAL, SHEAL
fellow	MAN	female graduates	MALADIES
• fellow is *back* < on	MANSION	female horse, *say*	MAYOR
• fellow-man	MANAL, MANED	female lawyer	BARMAID
• the *French* fellow	LEMAN	female mouse, *say*	MINI
fellows, *say*	FELLOES, GUISE	female *lead*	F
Fellow²		female relative, *say*	ANTI
Fellow of the		female supporter	BRA(SSIERE)
–Antiquarian Society	FAS		(*see also* girl)

feminine		*made of* [fibre]	BRIEF
feminine	F	**fickle**	
• feminine appearance	FLOOK	*fickle* [friend]	FINDER
• feminine limbs	FARMS	[man is] *fickle*	MAINS
• feminine usefulness	FUTILIY	**fiction**	
feminine	FEM	*fictional* [giant he] . . .	HEATING
femme fatale	MURDERESS	*fictionalised* [life] . . .	FILE, LIEF
fence		**fiddle**	AMATI, CREMONA
fenced in by *	incl in *		STRAD(IVARIUS)
• animal *fenced by* saints	SCOWS	*fiddled* [a lot]	TOLA
fencing in a . . .	incl A	fiddler	NERO
fencing in *	incl *	fiddlesticks	BOWS
• saints *fencing in* animal	SCOWS	*fiddling* [takings]	SKATING, STAKING
ferment		**field**	
fermentation of [wines]	SINEW, SWINE	field division	FENCE, HEDGE
fermented [in a glass]	ASSAILING	field-dressing	FERTILISER
fermenting [cask]	SACK		NITRE, POTASH
ferryman	CHARON	[field]-*dressing*	FILED
fertile		field-effect transistor	FET
fertile crescent	GROWING	field frog	PADDOCK
fertiliser	NITRE, STAMEN	Field-marshal	FM
fester		field of beans	RUNNERS
festered [like] . . .	KIEL	Field Officer	FO
festering [sore]	EROS, ORES, ROES, ROSE	field sport	MEADOW LARK
[it was] *festering*	WAIST	[field] *sport*	FILED
festival		field study	LEADEN, LEYDEN
festival	GALA	fieldfare	GRASS, GRAZING
• festival drink	GALATEA		PICNIC
• festival had . . .	GALAHAD	fielding side	ONSET
• festival writings	GALANT	**fiery**	
fetch		fiery mount	ETNA, VOLCANO
fetch companion	CARRY	fiery revolutionary	IXION
fetch, *say*	GOPHER	**fifteen**	RU TEAM
fête		**fifth**	
fête *say*	FATE	*fifth of* circle	L
fête tea	GALATEA	November *Fifth*	M
fetter		**fifty**	
fetters donkey	CHAIN–SMOKE	50% of people	PEO, PLE
fever		fifty	A
fever [I ran] . . .	RAIN, RANI	fifty	L
feverish [turn]	RUNT	• 50-50	LL
[hay]-*fever*	YAH	• fifties	LL, LS
few		• fifty copies	LIMITATIONS
few fish	SCANTLING	• fifty experts	LACES
few, *say*	FU–	• fifty I know	LIKEN
• few lay floors, *say*	FUTILE	• fifty I know, *say*	LINO
• few vocalise, *say*	FUSING	• fifty in cage, *say*	LINKAGE
• few *will have* me, *say*	FUME	• fifty in store	LINSTOCK
fewer clothes	LESSON	• fifty or five hundred	LORD
fewer directions	LESSEE(S),	• fifty points	–LES(S), –LESSNESS
	LESSEN(S)	• fifty-first	LIST
fewer fowl, *say*	LESSENS	• fifty refuse	LASH
fewer net serves	MOREOVER	fifty	N, NU, V
f–fish	FEEL, FIDE, FLING	fifty cents	DOL, LAR
fibre		• fifty-cent note	DOLE
fibre diet	BRANDISH	• fifty cents a thousand	LARK
fibre*tip*	F or E	fifty-fifty	EVENS

Letter replaced \c\at; Omit (a); Pointers *out*; Retain a̲; Split B_ED; Down (D); Backwards <or ^

fifty one	LI, LONE
• fifty-one can . . .	LIABLE
• fifty-one directions	LINES
• fifty-one doctors	LIMBS
• fifty-one extremely . . .	LIVERY
• fifty-one iron ships	LIFEBOATS
• fifty-one on	LION
• fifty-one pounds	LIQUIDS
• fifty-one ran	LISPED
• fifty-one support . . .	LIBRA
• fifty-one swindle . . .	LISTING
fifty-nine	LIX
Fifties	LL, LS
fifty States	US, USA
fifty thousand	L, N, NU, V
fight	
fight	BOX
• fight churchman	BOX-ELDER
• fight *with* mother	BOX-DAM
• ready *to* fight	MONEY-BOX
fight	SPAR
• fight *and* beat	SPARTAN
• fight Brown	SPARTAN
• fight Communist	SPARRED
• fight with Territorials	SPARTA
fight*back<*	RAW
fighter	MIG
• fighter raves	MIGRANTS
• fighter speed	MIGRATE
fighter	GI, MAN, SOLDIER
fighter in the ring	PICADOR, TOREADOR
	TORERO
fighter register	TERRIER
fighting	(in) AC–TION, INACTION
fighting	WAR
• fighting China	WARMING
• fighting Communist	WARRED
• fighting *in* Communist . . .	REWARD
fighting	
–American	DOUGHBOY, GI, GRUNT
–Frenchman	SOLDAT
–German	SOLDAT
–Italian	SOLDATO
–Spaniard	SOLDADO
fighting figure	MARS
fighting situation	BATTLEFIELD
	(BOXING) RING
fighting weight	WARRINGTON
fighting woman	AMAZON, ATS
fighting worker	COMBATANT
figure	
figuratively	FIG
figure	FIG
figure-*hugging*	incl number
• figure-*hugging* p–ants	PLANTS
figure of eight	OCTAGON
figure *out*	omit number

• (c)an figure *out*	AN
• figure *out* c(l)ues	CUES
figure *out*	CON–E, F–IVE, N–INE
	ON–E, TE–N
figures (in Rome)	C, D, L, M
	CI, CL, DI, LI, MI, MM
• cut a figure	SLICED
• figure eight, *say*	CATE, DATE
	LATE, MATE
• figure on	CON, DON, LION, MON
• figure out	CLOUT, LOUT
figures *out*	incl in numbers
• girl figures *out*	MADAM
• man figures *out*	CALL
figurehead	BUST
figure*head*	F
file	
[file]	WILDLIFE
file one class, *say*	FILIFORM
file poem, *say*	PHYLLODE
file them, *say*	PHYLUM
filing assistant	MANICURIST
filial claim	MESON
fill	
fill coach	CRAMBUS
fill the gap in *	incl in *
• always *fill the gap in* r–ed . . .	REVERED
fill the gap with *	incl *
• *fill gap in* bo–rder *with* a . . .	BOARDER
fill the sea	CRAMMED, CRAMMER
filled bread roll, *say*	BURGHER
filled with a . . .	incl A
filled with *	incl *
• a *French* bed *filled with*	
men	ALIMENT
filling *	incl in *
• men *filling* a *French* bed	ALIMENT
	(*see also* full)
film	
dull film	DUST, TARNISH
film	A, ET, U, X
film distributor	AEROSOL, SPRAY(-GUN)
film girl	GIGI
film sponsor	GODFATHER
filmed	(*see* picture)
filming	(on) SET
filming high ground	SET-DOWN
• scholars *filming*	BASSET
old film	PATINA
filter	
filter tip	SMOKESCREEN
filter *tip*	F
filter [wines]	SINEW, SWINE
final	
final blow	KO
final blow	W
final drink	LAST LAP

final drin<u>k</u>	K
final examination	ENDPAPER
final examinatio<u>n</u>	N
final home	GRAVE, TOMB
final hom<u>e</u>	E
final judgement	EPITAPH, OBIT(UARY)
final judgemen<u>t</u>	T
final letter	OMEGA, Z
final lette<u>r</u>	R
final mark	FULL STOP
final mar<u>k</u>	K
final message	OBIT(UARY), RIP
final messag<u>e</u>	E
final piece of evidenc<u>e</u>	E
final point	LANDS END
final poin<u>t</u>	T
final odds	SP
final odd<u>s</u>	S
final venue	ARMAGEDDON, RAGNAROK
	TWICKENHAM, WEMBLEY
final venu<u>e</u>	E
final word	AMEN, GOODBYE
final wor<u>d</u>	D
final words	EPITAPH, OBIT(UARY), RIP
finalists at Wimbled<u>on</u>	ON
finally	(in) EN–D
• *finally* certain	ENSURED
finally arrive<u>d</u>	D
finally failing	omit last letter
• hear(t) *finally failing*	HEAR
finally left	end with L
• Al *finally* left	ALL
finally left	omit last letter
• the(y) finally *left*	THE
finally lost	omit last letter
• Franc(e) finally *lost*	FRANC
finally, *say*	ATTEND
losing *finalist*	G
	(*see also* last)
finale	
finale of concer<u>t</u>	T
gran<u>d</u> *finale*	D
finance	
finance company	BRASS BAND
finance record	BACKLOG
financial liabilities	–IOUS
Financial Times	FT
find	
find a [log, ruin] . . .	LOURING
find [a log], *ruin* . . .	GAOL, GOAL
find another way to [drive] . . .	DIVER
find another way to say so	SEW, SOW
finding a synonym	LOCATING
finds it in ver/y ear/ly . . .	YEAR
	(*see also* found)
fine	
fine	AI

fine	F
• fine book	FACTS
• fine wine	FASTI
fine boy	ERIC
fine breed	GOODS TRAIN
fine	NOBLE
• directions *to* fine . . .	ENNOBLE
• fine coin	NOBLE
• fine fellows	NOBLEMEN
• fine queen	NOBLER
fine	OK, SCOT
fine fellow	JUDGE, MAGISTRATE
[fine] *form*	FEIN
fine leisure, *say*	GRANDEES
fine man	JUDGE, MAGISTRATE
fine manservant	GOOD FRIDAY
fine note	SHARP
fine scholar	GRANDMA
fine spring	WELL
finer, *say*	MORPHINE
finest *accommodation for* . . .	(in) B–EST
finest agent, *say*	SPIKING
finest mount	BESTRIDE
finest trip	BESTRIDE
finesse	
finesse [by Dan]	BANDY
finessing [in game]	GAMINE
finger	
fingerbowl	TOUCHWOOD
fingered fabric	FELT
fingerprint expert	DAB
finial	
finial of <u>s</u>pire(D)	S
<u>t</u>all *finial*(D)	T
finish	
al<u>l</u> *finished*	L
finish at Epsom	(THE) LINE
finish at Epso<u>m</u>	M
finish	END
• finish club	ENDIRON
• finish cross	ENDANGERED
finish game	MATE
finish gam<u>e</u>	E
finish needlework	CLOSEKNIT
finish *off*	omit last letter
• finish *off* boo(k)	BOO
finish of<u>f</u>	F
finish off pudding	G
finish shed	OVERSPILL
finished she<u>d</u>	D
finish work	RETIRE
finish wor<u>k</u>	K
finished exam	PASTORAL
finished gardening	HOEDOWN
finished gardening	G
finished skating	OFFICE
finishes letter	DIESEL

Letter replaced \c\at; Omit (a); Pointers *out*; Retain <u>a</u>; Split B_ED; Down (D); Backwards <or ^

finishing touc**h**	H
mat**t** *finish*	T
Finland	SF
Finnish	
Finnish author	TWAIN
Finnish *capital*	F
Finish *leader*	F
fir	
[fir-cone] *producer*	CONIFER
fir rod, *say*	FIRST HALF
fir, *say*	FUR
firs, *say*	FURS, FURZE
fire	
fire	SACK
• fire clergy	SACKCLOTH
• fire people	SACKRACE
• fire rifle	SACK
[fire]-*fighting*	RIFE
fire hydrant	FH
fire plug	FP
fire-ship	LIGHTER
fired	LIT
• fired engineer	LITRE
• fired man	LITHE
• son fired . . .	SLIT
firelighter	ARSONIST
fireman	GUNNER
firemen	GUNNERS, RA
firm	
firm	CO
• firm agreement	COOK
• firm friend	COPAL
• firm support(er)	COBRA, COPIER
• firm's a . . .	COCOA
firm agreement	COMPACT
firm building	STABLE
firm control	HOUSEHOLD, STRONGHOLD
firm grasp	STRONGHOLD
firm hand	IRON DUKE
fir**m**-*hearted*	IR
firm-*hearted*	incl CO
• a firm-*hearted* saint	ASCOT
• firm-*hearted* i–n . . .	ICON
firm ruler	HARDER, (MANAGING) DIRECTOR
firm undertaking	FUNERAL CONTRACTORS
first¹	
first	A
• first man	AGENT
• first team	ASIDE
• girl first	GALA
first	–IST
• fat man first	FATALIST
• first *after* many . . .	LIST, MIST
• first the *French*	ISTLE
first	NOI
• first *back*<	ION
• first directions	NOISE
• first *to return*<	ION
first²	
First XI	E
First-**a**id	A
first-born	start with NE, NEE
• *first*-born intend . . .	NEMEAN
• *first*-born died	NEED
first **b**atsman	B
first-**b**orn	B
first *character in* **H**amlet	H
first character *to*	
leave	omit 1st letter
• first character *to leave* (p)lay	LAY
first-**c**lass	C
first *couple on* **st**age **en**tered	STEN
first **h**alf	H
first *half of* **ga**me	GA
first-**h**and	H
first *item in* **s**ale	S
First **L**ady	L
first *letter*	L
first *light*	L
first **m**an	M
first man	start with MAN
• man *has* appointment	MANDATE
first **m**ate	M
first *of all*	A
first *of* **A**pril	A
first *of* **t**he . . .	T
first *of the* **m**onth	M
first **o**ffender	O
first **p**erson	P
first **p**ost	P
first **p**rize	P
first **q**uality	Q
first **r**ate	R
first **r**ound	R
first **s**ervice	S
first *showings of* **p**lay *in* **N**eath	PIN
first *sightings of* **W**est **I**ndies	WI
first *sign of* **S**pring	S
first **s**lice	S
first *slice of* **c**ake	C
first **s**tage	S
first *stage of* **r**ocket	R
first *to* **w**in	W
first *to* win	TWIN
first³	
first act of play	BREAK, FACE-OFF, KICK-OFF, SERV(IC)E
first-aid station	DRESSING-ROOM
first *American*	FOIST
first and foremost	A
first batsman	OPENER
first cardinal	ONE
first chance	OPENING
first character	A, ADAM, ALPHA

first character *to leave*	omit A
• first character *to leave* pl(a)y	PLY
first-class	(*see* first-class)
first clue	–IAC
first-day cover	AMNION, AMNIOTIC SAC
	BIRTHDAY SUIT, CAUL
	FIG-LEAF, SKIN
first drink	ADAM'S ALE, ADAM'S WINE
first gear	FIG-LEAF, LAYETTE
first generation	FRONTAGE
first in, first out	FIFO
first item in sale	LOTI
First Lady	EVE
first letter	A, ALPHA
first light	ONE ACROSS
first man	ADAM
first mate	ADAM, EVE
first mother	EVE
first mover	WHITE
first murderer	CAIN
first nine characters *returned*<	IOTA
first novel	ORIGINAL
first object	LEADING ARTICLE
first of April	MARCH PAST
first offender	ADAM, EVE
first opportunity	OPENING
first person	ADAM, I, ME
first place	EDEN
first prize	GOLD, PALM
first quality	A, AI
first question	QI
first reading book	ABC, ABCEE, ABSEY
	PRIMER
first sign	INITIAL
first slip	(ORIGINAL) SIN
first string	A, HEADLINE
first to be struck	PENNY BLACK
first victim	ABEL
first water	ADAM'S ALE, ADAM'S WINE
first wife	EVE

first-class

first-class	A
• father *has* first-class . . .	DADA
• first-class degrees	ADD
• fish *with* first-class . . .	CODA
first-class	AI
• first-class ball	AIDANCE
• first-class fish	AILING
• first-class *return*<	–IA
first-class	ACE
• first-class flower	ACEROSE
• first-class gallery	ACETATE
• fist-class sound	ACETONE
first-class	PRO
• first-class colliery	PROMINE
• first-class degree	PROD
• first-class match	PROTEST

first-class	CRACK, SMASHING
first class	KINDERGARTEN, NURSERY
	PLAYSCHOOL
first class attender	KINDERGARTENER
	INFANT

fish[1]

fish	ANGLE
• black fish	BANGLE
• fish-club	ANGLE-IRON
• many fish	MANGLE
fish	BASS
• fish caught, *say*	BASSINET
• fish devoured, *say*	BASSETTE
• fish-kettle	BASS-DRUM
fish	CARP
• criticise fish	CARP
• fish arrives	CARPENTERS
• fish-container	CAR PARK
fish	CHAR
• cleaner fish	CHAR
• fish cleaner	CHAR(LADY), CHARLOTTE
• fish tea	CHAR
fish	COD
• fish-stream	CO-DRIVER
• fish strike	CODSWALLOP
• fish freezes	CODICES
fish	DAB
• fish expert	DAB
• fish *rising*(D)^	BAD
• fish-worker	DAB HAND
fish	EEL
• female fish	FEEL
• fish *rising*(D)^	LEE
• k–ing *without* fish	KEELING
fish	GAR
• *bring* fish *to* shore	GARLAND
• fish lost blood	GARBLED
• fish trap	GARNET
fish	ID(E)
• flaccid fish	LIMPID
• kingfish	KID
• square fish	SQUID
and	
• hot fish	HID(E)
• kingfish	RID(E)
• sunfish	SID(E)
fish	RUDD
• fish at this spot, *say*	RUDDIER
• fish in front	RUDDLED
• fish unknown	RUDDY
fish	LING
• few fish	SCANTLING
• fine fish	FLING
• sunfish	SLING
fish	SHAD
• fish here, *say*	SHADIER
• fish unknown	SHADY

Letter replaced \c\at; Omit (a); Pointers *out*; Retain a̲; Split B_ED; Down (D); Backwards <or ^

• fish *with* journalist	SHADED	five hundred	D
fish	SKATE	• 501	DI
• Fish Authority	SKATEBOARD	• five hundred in time	DINT
• inexpensive fish	CHEAPSKATE	• five hundred is, ,	DIS–
• fish died	SKATED	• five hundred pounds	DL
fish	PIKE	five in Magnet (comic)	FAMOUS
• divert fish	TURNPIKE	five iron	MASHIE
• fishes Welsh river	PIKESTAFF	five lines	STAVE
• sunfish	SPIKE	five nil	FIFTY
fish²		five-star	FIRST CLASS
fish	SWIMMER	five thousand	A, V
fish		five-year olds	FIRST CLASS
–at sea	CLAMMED	five year prison sentence	HANDFUL
–at the seaside	PORTRAY	**fix**	
–at this point, *say*	RUDDIER, SHADIER	fix	PIN
fish-boat	DORY	• fix flower	PINASTER
fish-boy	SCHOOLMASTER	• fix in front, *say*	PINAFORE
fish cake	POMFRET	• fix puncture	PIN-PRICK
fish eggs, *say*	RHO, ROSE, ROW(S)	fix	SET
fish-house	BLEAK	• fix *up*(D)^	TES
fish-like	OFFISH	• fixed pay	SET SCREW
fish roost	PERCH	• scholars fixed . . .	BASSET
fish, *say*	ERRING, POLLEN, SOUL	fixed course	RUT
fish-spear	PIKE	fixed stud	STABLE
fish-spear, *say*	GAFFE	*fixed up* [a new] . . .	WANE, WEAN
fish stank	SMELT	fixed wages	SETSCREW
fish struggles	FLOUNDERS	*fixing* [tiles]	STILE
fish vessel	CAR PARK	**fizzy**	
fish-woman	SALMONELLA	fizzy wines	CHAMPAGNE, PERRY
fish worker	CLAMANT	*fizzy* [wines]	SWINE, SWINE
fisherman	PEDRO, PETER	**flabbergast**	
fisherman's problem	NONET	*flabbergast* [all the] . . .	LETHAL
fisherman's tale	BANK ACCOUNT	*flabbergasted* [when I] . . .	WHINE
fishing (industry)	NETWORK	**flag**	
fishmonger	SOLE AGENT	flag	IRIS, LIS
fishplate	SCALE	flag *on* fleet	COLOUR-FAST
fishing rod	PIKESTAFF	flag in front	SETTLED
two fish	CODLING, IDLING	flag officer	ENSIGN
	TROUTLING	flags *to* rent	WILTSHIRE
two fish, *say*	EALING	**flail**	
fit		*flail* [oats]	STOA
fit clothing	SUIT	*flailing* [arms]	MARS, RAMS
fit condition	AGUE, EPILEPSY	**flak**	AA
fitness competition	NATURAL SELECTION	**flaky**	
five		*flaky* [skin]	SINK
five	CINQUE	flaky stuff	SNOW
five	V	**flame**	
• 5 x 50	VIOL	flaming desire	ARSON, PYROMANIA
• five drinks	VALES	*flaming* [desire]	RESIDE
• five I lease	VIRENT	flaming redhead	MATCH, VESTA
• five in debt	VOWING	**flank**	
• five *in* low island	CAVY	*flankers of* pla<u>too</u>n	PN
• five *to* nine	VIX	*flanking* <u>army</u>	AY
• five *with* no instrument	VOLUTE	**flap**	
• five *with* one German . . .	VEIN	[emerge in a] *flap*	MENAGERIE
five Christmas presents	GOLD RINGS	flapper	BIRD
five hundred	A	*flapping* [about]	U-BOAT

Anag [cat]; Any *; Begin IGN–; Endings –ING; eg •; Hidden /cat/; Implied add (on); Implied in (in);

in a flap [over] . . .	ROVE
[sails] *flapping*	SILAS
flare	
flared trousers	HOTPANTS
flaring [gas]	SAG
flash	
flashing character	ROBOT
flashy boat	LIGHTSHIP
flashy building	LIGHTHOUSE
flat	
flat	UNNATURAL
Flat 10	FLATTEN
flat-*bottomed*(D)	T
flat dweller	PLAINSMAN
flat *opposite*	HILLY, SHARP, UNEVEN
flat-finding agency	SPIRIT LEVEL
flat fish, *say*	PLACE, SOUL
flattens note	IRONSTONE, SANDSTONE
flatter	
–animal	FAWN
–fabric	FLANNEL
flaunt	
flaunting [a new] . . .	WANE, WEAN
[was it] *flaunting* . . .	WAIST
flaw	
flaw in [glass]	SLAGS
flawed [sense]	ESSEN
flay	
flay pirate	SKINFLINT
flay [steer]	REEST, RESET, TREES
flea	
flea *in the ear*	FLEE
fleas jump	TICK-SHOP
jumping [flea]	LEAF
fleet	RN
flesh	
flesh, *say*	MEET, METE
flesh wound	SCRATCH
	SHOT IN THE ARM
flexible	
flexible [friend]	FINDER
flexing [arms]	MARS, RAM
flick	
flick [over]	ROVE
flicker of [life]	FILE, LIEF
flickering [lamps]	PALMS
flier	
flier, *say*	BURRED
fliers	RAF
	(*see also* fly)
flies	(*see* fly)
flight	
flight	HEGIRA, HEJ(I)RA, HIJRA(H)
flight cover	STAIR CARPET
flight demonstrator	SHOWER
flight of [swan I] . . .	SWAIN, WAINS
flight member	RISER, STAIR, TREAD

flight of locks	ALOPECIA, BALDNESS
flight path	STAIRCASE
flight unit	STAIR
flight, *say*	STARES
flighted delivery	AIRLIFT, AIRMAIL
flightless	OWING
flighty poet	HOMER
flighty [sort]	ROTS, TORS
fling	
[dance] *fling*	CANED
fling frill	FLOUNCE
fling [stone]	NOTES, ONSET, TONES
flint	
flint breaking, *say*	NAPPING
flint breaker, *say*	NAPPER
flip	
flipside	RECORD TURNOVER
flip over LP<	PL
flipping lid<	DIL
flit	
[bats] *flitting*	STAB, TABS
flitted [about]	U-BOAT
float	
flotation of [ship]	HIPS, PISH
floating	(in)S–S
floating about [lake]	KALE
floating [voter]	TROVE
flog	
flog queen, *say*	WHIPPER
flog twice	WHIPLASH
flood	
flood of [tears]	RATES, STARE, TARES
flood survivor	HAM, JAPHET, NOAH
florin	FN, SS, TWOS
flounder	
flounder [in sea in] . . .	ASININE
floundering [in sea]	ANISE
flourish	
flourished [when I] . . .	WHINE
flourished	FL
flourishing [guns]	GNUS, SNUG
flow	
[flow]	WILDFOWL
flow *over*<	NUR
flow, *say*	PEARL
flow through *	incl in *
• river *flows through* Sp–ain	SPRAIN
flowing [ale]	LEA
flowing through wa/ter m/eadow	TERM
flower[1]	
flower	ARUM, ROSE etc
flower arrangement	BOUQUET, GARLAND
	WREATH
[flower] *arrangement*	FOWLER, REFLOW
flower-bird	POPPYCOCK
flower-cutters	CLEAVERS
flower girl	DAISY, ROSE, etc

Letter replaced \c\at; Omit (a); Pointers *out*; Retain <u>a</u>; Split B_ED; Down (D); Backwards <or ^

flower, *say*	FLOCKS, LOOPING, ROWS
flower seed, *say*	POLLAN
flower spray	ROSE, WATERING-CAN
flower stores	STOCKS
flowers	LEI
flower's colour	FLAGSTONE
flowery item	PETAL, SEPAL
flowering shrub, *say*	FUTURE

flower²

flower	RIVER
• blue and white flower	NILE
• blue flower	DANUBE
• border flower	TWEED
• flower experiment	INDUSTRY
• flower for each . . .	CAMPER
• flower of France	RHONE, SEINE
• flower of Hades	STYX
• flower of oblivion	LETHE
• flower seen in Ireland	SHANNON
• German flower	RHINE
• that *French* flower	CELADON
flower-cutter, *say*	DREDGER
flower-power	HYDRO-ELECTRICITY
	(*see also* river)

fluctuate

fluctuating [beat is not] . . .	OBSTINATE
fluctuation of [tide]	EDIT, TIED

fluff

fluff [lines 'e] . . .	SENILE
fluffed [it when] . . .	WHITEN

fluid

fluid	FL
• fluid *has* unknown . . .	FLY
• fluid measure	FLINCH
• fluid style	FLAIR
fluid extract, *say*	DEUCE
fluid loss	SEEPAGE, SPILLAGE
fluid [made to] . . .	MOATED
fluidity of [style 'e] . . .	SLEETY

flurry

flurry of [snow]	OWNS, SOWN
flurried [man or] . . .	ROMAN

flush

flush	GORED
flush toilet	WATERLOO
flushed	RED
• flushed *out*	R–ED

fluster

flustered [and red]	DANDER
[never] *flustered*	NERVE

flutter

flutter of [wings]	SWING
fluttering [lids]	SLID
[heart] *aflutter*	EARTH, HATER, RATHE

fly

flies *up*(D)^	STANG, STOB
fly *about*	F–LY, W–ING
fly *about*<	TANG
fly bird	CRANE, DRAKE
fly *buzzing around*<	TANG
fly-by-night	BAT, MOTH
fly high, *say*	SORE
fly in this fashion	SOWING
fly saint	WIDEST
fly spider	SPINNER
fly *to*	
–France	MOUCHE, VOLER
–Germany	FLIEGE(N)
–Italy	MOSCA, PILOTARE
–Spain	MOSCA, VOLAR
fly *up*^(D)	TANG, TOB
flying	(in) SK–Y
• a king *flying*	SARKY
• sick, *flying*	SKILLY
flying	(on) PLANE
• test *flying*, *say*	TRIPLANE
• *flying* time	PLANET
flying	(on) WING
• about *flying*	CAWING
• father *flying*	PAWING
flying animal	BULLDOG, CAMEL
flying [animal]	LAMINA, MANILA
flying [ants]	STAN, TANS
flying around a . . .	incl A
• *b–ird flying around* a . . .	BAIRD
flying around [China]	CHAIN
flying around E, isle<	ELSIE
flying around *	incl *
• ti–t *flying around* pole	TINT
flying [bluetits]	SUB-TITLE
flying broomstick	WITCHCRAFT
flying club	BAT
flying fish	PILOT
flying fortress	CASTLE-IN-THE-AIR
flying machine, *say*	PLAIN
flying officer	ENSIGN, FO
flying out [airman]	MARINA
flying saucer	CLAY PIGEON
flying *start*	F
flying up on an(D)^ . . .	NANO–
flyover	HIGH ROAD

focus

focus of attention	N
focus of *	incl in *
• learner *is focus of* mu–ch . . .	MULCH

fog

fog, *say*	MISSED
foggy [day]	–ADY

fogey

	SQUARE

foil

['e soon] *foiled*	NOOSE
foiled [a gun raid]	GUARDIAN

fold

fold [diaper]	REPAID

fold knife	CREASE
fold linen	CRASH
fold net	TUCK
fold over [ends]	DENS, SEND
fold over top<	POT
fold you and me, *say*	CROESUS
folded [sheet]	THESE
folding [arms]	MARS, RAMS

folio

folio	F, FO, FOL
• First Folio *in front*	FIBT
folios	FF

follow

a *follower*	B
follow	DOG
• follow *up*(D)^	GOD
• follow hunter	DOG-WATCH
• follows sailor	DOG-STAR
follow	TAIL
• follow *after* bird	COCKTAIL
• follow dog	TAIL
• follow soldiers	TAILOR
follow	TRACK
• followed a Conservative, *say*	TRACTATORY
• followed a number, *say*	TRACTATE
• followed girl, *say*	TRACTOR
follow <u>my</u> *leader*	1st letter M
I'll follow <u>my</u> *leader*	MILL
follow win	SUCCEED
followed, *say*	CHASTE
followers	
—*of* ABC	DE
—*of* CND	DOE
—*of* star	TUBS
following	AFTER
• following mathematics	AFTER MATHS
• following smack	AFTERTASTE
• king *has* following	RAFTER
following	F
• following behind	FRUMP
• following deed	FACT
• mark following . . .	SCARF
following	SQ, SEQ, SEQUENS
following <u>his</u> *leader*	1st letter H
• little Arthur *following* <u>his</u> *leader*	HART
how *to follow* teams	SIDESHOW
	(*see also* dog²)

foment

foment [riots]	TRIOS
fomenting [revolt]	TROVER

food

Food and Agriculture Organisation	FAO
food container	EGGSHELL, NUTSHELL STOMACH, TUM(MY)

food crusher	MOLAR, TOOTH
food for supporter	FANFARE
food of the gods	PANCAKES, RADISHES
food processor	STOMACH, TUM(MY)
food purveyor	GULLET, OESOPHAGUS
food raiser	CHOPSTICK, FORK, SPOON
food, *say*	FAIR
• food pulverised, *say*	FAIRGROUND
• food unknown	FAIRY
food, *say*	PHARE
food store, *say*	DELHI
food tokens	CHIPS

fool

fool about	NITRE
fool *around*	AS-S
fool will, *say*	PRATTLE
fooling around [in the] . . .	THINE
foolish [boy]	YOB
foolish creature	FONDANT
foolish girl, *say*	SILICATE
foolishly [I went] . . .	TWINE
[general] *foolishness*	ENLARGE

foot

foot	DANCE
foot	F
• nothing *on* foot	OF
• one *on* foot	IF
• pertaining to foot	OFF
foot	FT
• man *on* foot	HEFT
• see US state *on* foot	RIFT
• the *French* foot	LEFT
foot fault	BUNION, CORN, HAMMER TOE
foot joint, *say*	PAWNEE
foot lever, *say*	PEDDLE
foot-pound-second	FPS
footpad	CORN PLASTER
footman	CHIROPODIST, PEDESTRIAN
footnote	PS
footwear, *say*	SHOO
footwear *with* spikes	BOOTLACES SHOELACES

football

football	FA
• football in square	FAINT
• football near church	FACE
• football on street	FAST
Football Association	FA
football club	AFA, FA
football club-house	VILLA
football club incentives	SPURS
football	RU
• football *in* these islands	GRUB
• football match	RUB OUT
• football revival	RURALLY
footballers	FA, RU
footballers' magazine	ARSENAL

Letter replaced \c\at; Omit (a); Pointers *out*; Retain <u>a</u>; Split B_ED; Down (D); Backwards <or ^

footwear   (*see* foot)

for¹

for example, for instance, maybe, perhaps, possibly and say are largely interchangeable and are used to indicate anagrams, homophones and one of a class

for²

for	FOR
• for a friend	FORMATE
• for me	FOREGO
• for teacher, *say*	FORCER
for	PRO
• for and against	PROV–
• for good measure	PROTON
• for one	PROA
for and against	NOYES
for and on behalf of	PP
for each	PER
• for each boy	PERSON
• for each king	PERK
• meat for each . . .	HAMPER
for example	EG, VG
	(*see also* for³)
for starters have egg mayonnaise	HEM
for the ear, I . . .	AY(E), EYE
for the family	OVERSTRAIN

for³

indicating a foreign language:

• boy *for Benito*	RAGAZZO
• dog *for Hans*	HUND
• house *for René*	MAISON
• sing *for Emilio*	CANTAR

indicating a homophone:

• *for example*, a weight	AWAIT
• *for instance*, hire	HIGHER
• *for the ear*-wax	WHACKS

indicating one of a class:

• *for example*, it . . .	PRONOUN
• *for example*, Jeeves	SERVANT
• *for example*, she'll	ELISION
• *for instance*, servant	JEEVES
• *for one*, Constable	PAINTER

indicating substitution:

• \p\enny *for* \s\on sent . . .	PENT
• \t\ime *for* \c\old chicken	TOWARD

forbid

forbidden in future, *say*	TABULATOR
forbidden *to speak*	BAND, BARD

force

force	F
• force cow	FLOWER
• one force	IF
• story *about* force	LIFE
force	G
• force oar	GROWER
• force out	GOUT
• out in force	OUTING
force of gravity	GRATE
force of law	POSSE
forced	FZ
forced [into] . . .	–TION
forced [into a]	–ATION
forced into [action]	CATION
forced, *say*	RESTED
forceful reportage	TELLING
forcibly break into	ENTERPRISING
forcibly remove	TEARAWAY

fore

fore and aft	1st and last letters
• *fore and aft of* the . . .	TE
• *fore and aft of* ship	SP
fore part of ship	S

forefront

forefront	F
forefront of the army group	TAG
soldiers in battledress *at the forefront*	SIB
the *forefront*	T

forego

forego a	omit A
forego money	omit L
forego, *say*	WAVE
forego *	omit *
• mot(her) *foregoes* her . . .	MOT

forehead

forehead	F
forehead	H
foreheads, *say*	BROWSE

foreshorten

foreshorten girl	(m)ARIA
for(e)*shortened*	FOR
foreshortened, *say*	THREE

foreign¹

indicating use of other languages:

• *foreign* castle	SCHLOSS
• *foreign* character	ALPHA
• *foreign* field	CHAMP
• *foreign* man	HOMBRE
• *Foreign* Office	BUREAU
• *foreign* town	VILLE
• *foreign* wine	VIN(O)
	(*see also* abroad, cross⁴, continent)

foreign²

foreign (= not English)	NOTE
Foreign (and Commonwealth) Office	F(C)O
foreign *capital*	F
foreign company	AG
foreign exchange	AU PAIR
foreign goddess	ALIENATE

foreign [to me]	MOTE
foreign warship	USS
foreign wife	DUTCH
foremost	
foremost <u>a</u>uthority	A
foremost character in <u>p</u>arty	P
foremost in <u>a</u>ny good <u>E</u>nglish . . .	AGE
foresters	AOF
forfeit	
forfeit a . . .	omit A
forfeit (a) hundred	omit (A)C
forfeit a pound	omit AL
forfeit money	omit D, L, P
forfeit *	omit *
• mate(lot) *forfeits* much . . .	MATE
forge	
forge money	MAKE READY
forged [coin]	ICON
forger's art	METALWORK
forger's shop	SMITHY
forging [note]	ETON, TONE
forget	
forget a . . .	omit A
forget money	omit D, L, P
forget name	omit N
forget nothing	omit O
forget *	omit *
• (To)by *forgets* to . . .	BY
half-*forgotten* parent	PAR, ENT
fork	
fork out *	omit*
• cut(l)er *forks out* pound	CUTER
• m(al)e *forks out* a pound	ME
forlorn	
[Ted is] *forlorn*	SITED
forlorn [but not] . . .	BUTTON
form	
Form [One]	EON, NEO–
form [a line]	ANILE
form of [stapler]	PLASTER
form of worship	PEW
form queue	BRAID, PLAIT
form round a . . .	incl a
form round *	incl *
• r–ing *forms round* a king	RAKING
form union	WED
forming [words]	SWORD
formal	
formal	PRIM
• formal park	PRIMP
• formal period	PRIMAGE
• formal states	PRIMUS
formal body	STIFF
formal garden, *say*	NOT
formal *introduction*	F
formally attired	(in) TA–ILS
formally dressed	INVESTMENT

format	
format [disk]	KIDS, SKID
formation of [planes]	PANELS
[page] *format*	GAPE, PEAG
[place in] *formation*	PELICAN
former	
former	
indicating old words:	
• *former* housewife	HUSSY
• *former* queen	PRINCE
• sailor *formerly*	SHIPMAN
former	EX
• former coins, *say*	EXPENSE
• former nurse	EXTEND
• former model	EXPOSE(R)
• former player	EXACTOR
• former position, *say*	EXCITE
• formerly a miner	EXAMINER
• formerly healthy	EXHALE
• formerly plenty	EXAMPLE
former	LATE
• engineer's former . . .	RELATE
• former ceremony	LATERITE
• former meeting	LATERALLY
former copper	D
former monk	OUT OF ORDER
	PRIOR
former painter	OLD ROPE
former pupil	FP, GRADUATE
former pupil	OB
• 100 former pupils	COBS
• former pupil *takes* exam	OBTEST
• former pupils' meeting	OBSESSION
former, *say*	YOUR
formerly	NE, NEE
	(*see also* old)
formidable champion	GRIMACE
formulate	
formula for [Cartesian] . . .	ASCERTAIN
formulate [his new] . . .	WHINES
formulation of [idea]	AIDE
fort	FT
forte	
forte	F
forte-piano	FP
forte, *say*	FOR TEA, FORTY
fortissimo	FF
forty	
Forties	ROARING, SEA AREA
forty	F, M, MU, XL
forty, *say*	EXCEL, FOR TEA, FORTE
forty days	LENT
forty-five	DISC, EP, RECORD
forty-five minutes	(h)OUR, HOU(r)
forty-nine	IL
forty-niner	GOLD-SEEKER, PROSPECTOR
forty, *say*	FOR TEA, FORTE

forty thousand	F, M, MU	• four have left, *say*	FOREGONE
forty winks	NAP	• four seas, *say*	FORESEES
forward		• four toys, *say*	FORETOPS
forward-looking	L	**fourth**	
forward part of ship	BOW, FOCSLE	fourth	D, QUARTER, UNPLACED
	FORECASTLE, PROW	fourth dimension	TIME
forward part of ship	S	fourth man	SETH
forwards of Arsenal play		*fourth of* December	DE, CE, MB, ER
together	APT	*fourth of* December	E
forzando/forzato	FZ	*fourth of* July	Y
foul		fourth part of play	ACTIV–
foul-mouthed	F	*fourth part of* play	Y
foul punch	LOWLANDER	**fowl**	
foul, *say*	FOWL	fowl	HEN
fouled [nest]	NETS, SENT, STEN	• fowl part	HENBIT
found		• fowlpest	HENBANE
found	CAST	• woman *with* fowl	WHEN
• found gold	CASTOR	fowl, *say*	FOUL
• found out	CASTAWAY	**fox**	
• found the *French* ...	CASTLE	fox	TOD
found abroad		• fox devoured	TO-DATE
indicating use of		fox, *say*	RUSTLE
foreign word:		**fracas**	
• coin *found in Spain*	PESETA	*fracas* in the	THINE
• flower *found in France*	FLEUR	[she saw] *fracas*	WASHES
• girl *found in Italy*	RAGAZZA	*start of* fracas	F
• I *found in Germany* ...	ICH	**fraction**	
• man *found abroad*	HOMME, HOMBRE	*fraction of* the	T, HE
	UOMO, MANN	*fraction of* t/he len/gth	HELEN
found at last	COBBLER, SHOEMAKER	*fractionate* [oils]	LOIS, SILO
found in S/anti/ago	ANTI–	proper *fraction*	PROP
found in *	incl in *	**fractious**	
• we are *found in* building	SHEWED	*fractious* [babe]	ABBE
found out [why it] ...	WITHY	[spoke] *fractiously*	POKES
found vessel	LAUNCH	**fracture**	
	(*see also* find)	*badly fractured*	BALDLY
founder		*fracture* [hip]	PHI
foundering [yacht]	CATHY	*fracturing* [arm]	MAR, RAM
[ship] *founders*	HIPS, PISH	**fragile**	
foundation		*fragile* [plate]	PETAL, PLEAT
foundation of house (D)	E	fragile, *say*	WEEK
strong *foundation*(D)	G	fragile vessel	TENDER
four		[quite] *fragile*	QUIET
four	IV, TWO-BY-TWO	**fragment**	
four Christmas presents	CALLING BIRDS	fragment	FR
four-in-hand	COACH, FINGERS, NECKTIE	*fragmented* [bone]	EBON
four-letter word	TETRAGRAM	*fragments of* petals	PEAL
four-nil	FORTY	*fragments of* [petals]	PLEATS, STAPLE
four of hearts	HEAR	**frail**	
four of the best	ACES	*frail* [prince]	PINCER
four points	NEWS, SEWN, WENS	frail, *say*	WEEK
	TRY	*frailty of* [old Ed] ...	DOLED
four, *say*	FOR	**frame**	
• four airs, *say*	FORTUNES	*framed by* ug/ly re/mains	LYRE
• four feet, *say*	FORFEIT	*framed by* *	incl in *
• four old people, *say*	FORAGED	• aim *framed by* manuscript	MENDS
four, *say*	FORE	*framed in* fi/ne st/eel	NEST

Anag [cat]; Any *; Begin IGN–; Endings –ING; eg •; Hidden /cat/; Implied add (on); Implied in (in);

framing a . . .	incl A	**free³**	
framing *	incl *	other uses:	
• manuscript *framing* aim	MENDS	*free* a . . .	omit A
franc	FR	free alongside ship	FAS
France		free of charge	GRATIS, NEUTRAL
France	FR, RF		UNLOADED, VINDICATE
France, *say*	GALL	free of charge	FOC
Franco-British articles	LATHE, LETHE	free on board	FOB
Franco-German agreement	OUIJA	free on rail	FOR
Franco-German articles	UNDER	Free Presbyterian	FP
	(see also French)	free publication	RELEASE
Frank		free-range eggs	LAID OUT
frank character	STAMP	free supply	DELIVER
Frank scoffed	CANDIDATE	free TV	AUNTIE, BEEB
Frank's deception	BLUFF	*free* *	omit *
frantic		• *free* her from fat(her)'s . . .	FATS
frantic [leap]	PALE, PEAL	insect-*free*	omit FLY
[stare] *frantically*	RATES, TARES, TEARS	• (f)air(ly) insect-*free*	AIR
fraudulent		**freeze**	
[act] *fraudulently*	CAT	freezing	ATOC, TEMPO
fraudulent [deal]	DALE, LADE, LEAD	freezing-point	FP, OC
fraudulently [alter]	LATER	freezing-*point*	F
[he's] *fraudulent*	SHE	freezing waterfall	HAIL(STORM)
fray		frozen bird, *say*	CHILDREN
frayed [nerves]	SEVERN	frozen vegetable	CORNICE
fraying [rope]	PORE	**French**	
freak		French	FR
freak [show]	HOWS	• a French help	AFRAID
freakish [result]	LUSTRE	• French caper	FRANTIC
free¹		• French crew	FREIGHT
free	RID	French and English money	SOUL,
• exist *without* free . . .	BRIDE		SOUP
• free ball	RIDDANCE	*French* art gallery	ESTATE
• free *return, for example*<	RIDGE	French banker	LOIRE, SEINE etc
• free-*standing*(D)^	DIR	French brother	JACQUES
• free study	RIDDEN	French capital	EURO, FRANC
free *admission*	incl RID	*French* *capital*	F
• free *admission to*		French capitalist	PARISIEN(NE)
Geological Society	GRIDS	*French* fort	STRONG
free²		French friend	AMI(E)
indicating anagram:		• French friend can . . .	AMIABLE
[Born] *Free*	BRNO	• French friend *in* the	
[dust]-*free*	STUD	Louvre *initially*	TAMIL
free-[for-all]	FLORAL	• French friend with 500 . . .	AMID
[free] *movement*	REEF	*French* horn	COR
free movement of [cars]	ARCS, SCAR	*French* *leader*	F
[free]-*range* . . .	REEF	*French* manger	EAT
free-[range I] . . .	GAINER, REGAIN	*French* private	ENTRE NOUS
free [slaves]	SALVES, VALSES	*French-speaking* girl	FILLE(TTE)
free-style [event seen] . . .	SEVENTEEN	French underground	MAQUIS, METRO
free [trade]	RATED, TREAD	Frenchman	M, RENE
free transfer for [player]	REPLAY	• Frenchman married	RENEWED
free [vote]	VETO	Frenchmen	MM
free[dom]	MOD		(*see also* France)
free[lance]	CLEAN	**frenetic**	
freely [as her] . . .	HARES, HEARS, SHARE	*frenetic* [pace]	CAPE
freely occurring [in the] . . .	THINE	[it was] *frenetic*	WAIST, WAITS

Letter replaced \c\at; Omit (a); Pointers *out*; Retain a̲; Split B_ED; Down (D); Backwards <or ^

frenzy

frenzied [dash]	SHAD
frenzy of [swine]	SINEW, WINES

frequent

frequency	F
frequency modulation	FM
frequently	FR

fresh

fresh	NEW
• fresh deposit	NEW-LAID EGG
• fresh people	NEWGATE
• fresh weight	NEWTON
and	
• fresh choler, *say*	NUBILE
• fresh song, *say*	NUDITY
• fresh work, *say*	NUT-OIL
and	
• fresh mother, *say*	PNEUMA
• freshly cut here, *say*	PNEUMONIA
fresh [bread]	BARED, BEARD, DEBAR
fresh edition	GREENED
fresh impression	REISSUE
fresh oar	CLEAN SWEEP
fresh spell of rain	REIGN, REIN
fresh start for boy	COY, GOY, HOY
	ROY, SOY, TOY
fresh support	GREENBACK
freshly cut [flowers]	FOWLERS
freshly gathered [grapes]	PAGERS, SPARGE
freshly [made]	DAME, EDAM, MEAD
freshly made [bread]	BARED, BEARD, DEBAR
freshness of [dawn]	WAND
	(*see also* new)

friar

friar	TUCK
• friar fights . . .	TUCK-BOXES
• friar's dance	TUCKSHOP
• son *with* friar	STUCK

Friday

Friday	F, FR, FRI
• Friday's child	FRISSON
Friday	MAN

friend

friend	ALLY
• alternative friend	ORALLY
• boy-friend	REGALLY, ROYALLY
• little boy friend	TOTALLY
• stout friend	FATALLY
• support friend	LEGALLY
friend	CHINA
• friend *on* island, *say*	CHINAMAN
• friend wears, *say*	CHINAWARES
friend	OPPO
• friend's height, *say*	OPPOSITE
• friend's ways	OPPOSES
friend	MATE
• deceives friend	FOOL'S MATE

• European friend, *say*	CHECKMATE
• friend *with* much . . .	MATELOT
friend	PAL
• friend *and* expert	PALACE
• friend *at* sea	PALMED, PALMER
• friend ate nothing, *say*	PALMETTO
• friendless	OPALS
• girl-friend	PALMARY, PALMYRA
• good friend	PIPAL
• no friend	OPAL
friend*less*	omit ALLY
• truly friend*less*	RE(ally)
friend*less*	omit PAL
• (pal)try, friend*less* . . .	TRY
friendly	PALLY
• friendly animal, *say*	PALLIASSE
• friendly father	PAPALLY
• friendly language, *say*	PALI
friendly cat	FAMILIAR
friendly *converse*	HOSTILE
friendly Russian	KINDRED
Friendly Society	OUTGOINGS
Friends of Europe	FOE
Friends of the Earth	FOE

fright

frighten	AWE
• frighten a few	AWESOME
• frighten completely, *say*	AWFULLY
• frightening, *say*	AURIFIC
• learner frightens, *say*	LAWS
frighten	COW
• frighten fish	COWLING
• frighten writer	COWPEN
• son frightens . . .	SCOWS
frightful [time]	EMIT, MITE
frightfully [ugly, Nott] . . .	GLUTTONY

fringe

fringe report	BANG
fringed by *	incl in *
• motorway *fringed by* tre–es	TREMIES
fringes a . . .	incl A
fringes *	incl *
• tre–es *fringe* motorway	TREMIES
fringes of society	SY

frisk

frisky [horse]	SHORE
[lamb] *frisking* . . .	BALM

fritter

fritter [asset]	TESSA
fritter, *say*	WAIST

Fritz

Fritz (=German)	
• *Fritz's* house	HAUS
• with *Fritz's* . . .	MIT

frog

frog	FRENCHMAN
frog clearer	AHEM

Anag [cat]; Any *; Begin IGN–; Endings –ING; eg •; Hidden /cat/; Implied add (on); Implied in (in);

frog march	MARCHE MILITAIRE	from London	DOWN
	MARSEILLAISE	*from* [Mali]	MAIL
frolic		from North-west	TOSE
frolic [in sea in] . . .	ASININE	from point to point (= between N, S, E, W)	
frolic about [in nude]	UNDINE	• Bill King *goes from*	
frolicking [lionesses]	NOISELESS	*point to point*	NACRE
from¹		• goddess *goes from*	
from	EX	*point to point*	EATEN
• from a pit	EXAMINE	• Hal *goes from point to point*	WHALE
• from shelter	EXTENT	from South	TON
• from the first	EXIST	from South-west	TONE
from	OFF	*from* Sou/th-ea/st	THEA
• from the freezer	OFFICE	from the air (=song)	
• from worker	OFFHAND	• *from the air*, London	
• shirt from . . .	TOFF	river	OLD FATHER THAMES
from *French*	DE	• *from the air*, Surrey feature	FRINGE
• from *French* girl	DECLARE	*from the back of* beyond	
• from *French* islands	DECAYS	they came	DYE
• from *French* records	DEFILES	from the beginning	AB INIT(IO)
from *Latin*	AB	*from the beginning of* time	
• from *Latin* customs	ABUSES	on Earth	TOE
• from *Latin* scholar	ABBA	*from the end of* the Big	
• from *Latin* spoken . . .	ABORAL	Bang	EGG
from the *French*	DELA, DES, DU	*from the finish of* play	
• from the *French*	DELAMINATE	he went	YET
bird, note		*from the front* he is sure . . .	HIS
• from the *French* in the East	DELAINE	*from the heart of* t/he be/ast	HEBE
• from the *French* youth	DELATED	*from the mouth of*	
and		• heard *from the mouth of* . . .	HERD
• from the *French* city	DESTROY	from the queen	OFFER
• from the *French* couple	DESPAIR	*from the rear of* the parade Al	EEL
• from the *French* I call	DESIRING	*from the rear* rank<	KNAR
and		*from the start of* the old year	TOY
• from the *French* church	DUCE	from West	TOE
• from the *French* scholar	DUMA	*from what we hear*, he'll . . .	HEAL, HEEL
• from the *French* members	DUMPS	*from what's said*, I'd . . .	EYED, IDE
from²		**front**	
indicating omission:		Brighton *front*	B
• alternative *from* the(or)y	THEY	cold *front*	C
• doctor *from* Bor(d)e(r)s	BORES	enemy *front*	E
• letter *from* (m)other	OTHER	front	BOW
from³		• artist in front	RAINBOW
indicating origins:		• front learner	BOWL
• agreement *from Moscow*	DA	• front letter	BOWESS
• boy *from Milan*	RAGAZZO	front cover	APRON
• *Cairngorm*-stone	STANE	*front* cover	C
• children *from Germany*	KINDER	*front* door	D
• dog *from Lyons*	CHIEN	front line	POLE POSITION
• girl *from Perth*	SHEILA	*front* line	L
• man *from Ayr*	MON	front of house	FACADE
• uncle *from Pretoria*	OOM	*front of* house	H
• woman *from Malaga*	SENORA	front of vehicle	CARNOSE
from⁴		front of vehicle	V
other uses:		front page	PI, RECTO
from A-K and M-Z	NOEL	*front* page	P
from Bir/ming/ham	MING	front runner	ADAM
from East	TOW	*front* runner	R

Letter replaced \c\at; Omit (a); Pointers *out*; Retain a; Split B_ED; Down (D); Backwards <or ^

front-runner in Derby	D
sea-*front*	S
warm *front*	W
frontier	
frontier of Russia	R
frontier restriction	LIMIT
Russian *frontiers*	RN
frost	
frost	DAVID
	HOAR, JACK, RIME
frost, *say*	RHYME, WHORE
froth	
frothing [over]	ROVE
frothy [surf]	FURS
frozen	(*see* freeze)
fruit	
fruit	LIME
• fruit flavour	LIMESTONE
• fruit underweight, *say*	LIMELIGHT
• second fruit	SLIME
• under fruit . . .	SUBLIME
fruit	PEAR
• a soft fruit	APPEAR
• fruit *and* fish	PEARLING
• fruit *carried in* ship	SPEARS
• fruit, *say*	PARE, PAIR
• harvest fruit	REAPPEAR(S)
fruit	PLUM
• fruit-fly	PLUMPEST
• fruit garden	PLUMBED
• fruit, *say*	PLUMB
• fruit season	PLUMAGE
fruit and veg, *say*	MELANCHOLY
fruit-bats	BANANAS
fruit dish	FOOL
fruit only	LEMON SOLE
fruit pulp	SQUASH
fruitful area	ORCHARD, ORANGE GROVE
	VINEYARD
fruitful, *say*	TEAMING
frustrate	
frustrate [action]	CATION
[it was] *frustrated*	WAIST, WAITS
fuddled	
fuddled [in bar]	BAIRN, BRAIN
fuddling [ales]	LEAS, SALE
fudge	
fudged [issue]	SUSIE
[lemon] *fudge*	MELON
full	
full	DRUNK, FED, STONED, TIGHT
full-*back*<	DEF
full board	THOROUGHFARE
full length	
indicating abbreviation	
to be expanded:	
• Al, *full-length* . . .	ALUMINIUM

• *full-length* cot	COTTAGE
full meal	THOROUGHFARE
full moon	O
full of *	incl *
• bo–x *full of* gunners' . . .	BORAX
Full Organ	FO
full rank	ABUNDANT
full version of	
indicating abbreviation to be expanded:	
• *full version of* sect	SECTION
• *full version of* Mass	MASSACHUSETTS
fully	
indicating abbreviation to be expanded:	
• do *fully*	DITTO
• *fully* met	METEOROLOGICAL
fumble	
fumble [about]	U-BOAT
fumbling [in the] . . .	THINE
function	
function	PI
• function *in* city	EPIC
• function noted, *say*	PICENE
• second function, *say*	SPY
function	SIN(E)
• firm function	COSINE
• function, *say*	SIGN
• function-like, *say*	CYNICAL
funeral	
funeral contractors	FIRM UNDERTAKING
funeral party	GRAVEDO
funky	
funky [notes]	SETON, STONE, TONES
[quite] *funky*	QUIET
funny	
funny-bone	
operation, *say*	HYSTERECTOMY
funny cry	SCREAM
funny-[face]	CAFE
funny [idea]	AIDE
funny [thing]	NIGHT
funny [turn]	RUNT
[How] *funny*!	WHO
[it was] *funny*	WAIST, WAITS
fur	
fur, *say*	FIR
furs, *say*	FIR, FURZE, MINX
local fur	FAR
furious	
furious [rage]	GEAR
furious woman	ALECTO, MEGAERA
	TISIPHONE
furious women	ERINYES, EUMENIDES
furiously [blame] . . .	MABEL
furl	
furled [sails]	SILAS
furling [tops'l]	PLOTS
furlong	FUR

Anag [cat]; Any *; Begin IGN–; Endings –ING; eg •; Hidden /cat/; Implied add (on); Implied in (in);

furniture

furniture maker	ADAM, CHIPPENDALE
	SHERATON el al
	MAHOGANY, OAK etc
furniture remover	CASTOR
furniture remover's garment	SHIFT
furrowed brow	HEADLINES

further

further	MORE
• further money	MOREL
• further *round* the bend	MORSE
• no further	NEVERMORE
furthest part of Chin<u>a</u>	A

furtive

furtive [leer]	REEL
[I creep] *furtively*	PIERCE

fury

furious [when I] . . .	WHINE
[I am] *furious*	AIM, AMI
in a fury [over] . . .	ROVE
[in a] *fury*	AIN, –IAN

furze

furze	GORSE, WHIN
furze, *say*	FIRS, FURS, WIN

fuse

fused [lights]	SLIGHT
fusion of [alloy]	LOYAL
[nuclear] *fusion*	UNCLEAR

fuss

fuss	ADO
• fuss about	ADORE
• fuss *about* one . . .	ADIO
• fuss *in* the Navy	RADON
fuss [about] . . .	U-BOAT
fussy [gown in] . . .	OWNING
fussy individual	PARTICULAR
[get] *fussed*	TEG
futile	(in) VA–IN
future	FUT

Letter replaced \c\at; Omit (a); Pointers *out*; Retain <u>a</u>; Split B_ED; Down (D); Backwards <or ^

G

acceleration, agent, clef, conductance, four hundred (thousand), gallon, gamma, gamut, gauss, gee, gelding, general intelligence, George, German, Germany, Gibb's function, giga-, girl, good, gram, gram(me), grand, gravity, group, guinea, gulf, key, man, note, shear modulus, spot, string, suit

G-man's son	GLAD	**game**	
gabble		game	BRIDGE
gabbled [words]	SWORD	• attract game	DRAWBRIDGE
[stop] gabbling	POTS, SPOT, TOPS	• game follows animal . . .	OXBRIDGE
gad		• game on river	CAMBRIDGE
gadabout	GA–D	game	LOO
gadabout<	DAG	• game with king's . . .	LOOKS
gadding about [in the] . . .	THINE	• give directions after game	LOOSE
gain		• I have grand game	IGLOO
gain admission to *	incl in *	game	POLO
• I gain admission to club	BAIT	• draw game	TIEPOLO
• we gain admission to s–et	SWEET	• game near city	POLONY
gain honour	APPRECIATE	game	RU, RUGBY
gain points	WINTRY	• game at home	RUIN
gain, say	PROPHET	• game fish	RULING
gained weight	WONTON	• game, second-class	RUB
gained weight, say	WANTON	game bird	HOBBY
Galatians	GAL	game birds	DUCKS AND DRAKES
gale	WINDLASS	game couple	TWOSOME
gallery		game leader	BRIDGEHEAD
gallery	TATE	game leader	G
• second gallery	STATE	game over<	UR
• gallery-owner's daughter	MISSTATE	game redhead	MATCH
gallery idols	GODS	game reserve	SUBSTITUTE, TWELFTH MAN
galley	PROOF	game reserves	POOL
Gallic king	ROI, SM	**gamma**	G
gallon	GAL(L)	**gang**	
gallop		gang-girl	BANDANNA
gallop [off in Reg's] . . .	OFFERINGS	gang leader	FOREMAN
gallop, say	CHOREA	gang leader	G
galloping [horse]	SHORE	gangster	AL
Gallup poll	GP	• gangster fellow	ALCOVE
Gambia	WAG	• gangster with President	ALIKE
gamble		• gangster with weapon	ALARMED
gamble	BET	gangster	HOOD
• gamble a small amount	BETA PARTICLE	• gangster bats an eye	HOODWINKS
• gamble on unknown . . .	BETONY	• gangster's moll	GIRLHOOD
• gamble with a monarch	BETAKING	• second gangster, say	SHOULD
gamblers	BETTER AND BETTER	**gaol**	
gambling theorist	SPECULATOR	[gaol]-break(ing)	GOAL, OLGA
gambol		gaol disturbance	STIR
gambol [in the] . . .	THINE	[gaol] disturbance	GOAL, OLGA
gambol, say	BET, SPECULATE	gaoled	(in) C–AGE, (in) PE–N
gambolling [lambs]	BALMS	riot in [gaol]	GOAL, OLGA

Anag [cat]; Any *; Begin IGN–; Endings –ING; eg •; Hidden /cat/; Implied add (on); Implied in (in);

gap
gap-filler	ER, UM
gap, *say*	WHOLE

garage
garage for vintage car, *say*	CARPORT
garage, *say*	CARCASE

garbage in, garbage out   GIGO

garble
garbled [speech]	CHEEPS
garbling [words]	SWORD

Garbo   DRESS CIRCLE

garden
garden	BED
• garden refuse	BEDASH
• gardener	BEDMAKER
• tool *used in* garden	BAWLED
garden	EDEN
garden	PLOT
• garden plan	PLOT
ga<u>rd</u>en *centre*	RD
garden maker	ADAM
[garden] *maker*	DANGER
garden-party	OUTDO
garden tool, *say*	SEA-DRAKE
gardener	ADAM, BEDFELLOW
gardener's share	ALLOTMENT

garrison dance   BASEBALL

gas
gas consumed	NEONATE
gas-cooled reactor	AGR
gas main	NORTH SEA
gas ring	DISCUSSION GROUP
	SEMINAR

gate
gate-crasher	BATTERING-RAM
[gate]-*crashing*	–TAGE
gateman	WICKET-KEEPER

Gateshead
<u>G</u>ateshead	G
• <u>G</u>ateshead owns . . .	GOWNS
• in <u>G</u>ateshead	–ING

gather
gather a . . .	incl A
gather food	TUCK
gather fruit	REAPPEAR(S)
gather round	incl O
gather [nuts]	STUN, TUNS
gather *	incl *
• bo–y *gathers* weight	BOOZY
gathered by *	incl in *
• weight *gathered* by bo–y	BOOZY
gathering	DO
gathering of [men at] . . .	MEANT
gathering of shea/ves t/aken . . .	VEST

gaunt
gaunt bird	HAGGARD
gaunt writer	HAGGARD

gauss   G

gazette(er)   GAZ

gear   FIRST, SECOND, THIRD
FOURTH, NEUTRAL, REVERSE
gear change	NEW SUIT
[gear] *change*	GARE, RAGE
gear changing	TRANSVESTISM
gearbox	SUITCASE

gee   G

gelignite   JELLY

gem
gem merchant, *say*	DUELLIST
gem, *say*	PURL
gem study, *say*	RUBICON
gem weight	STONE
gem weight, *say*	CARROT

gender   GEN

general[1]
general	BOOTH
• general stall	BOOTH
• general *swaps* book for shirt	TOOTH
general	GRANT
• general assistance	GRANT-AID
• my general, *say*	MIGRANT
general	LEE
• general's introduction	MELEE
• *in* general	LE–E
general	GEN(L)
• general *has* square . . .	GENT
• general *in* boat	PUNGENT
• general name	GENEVA
general	GORDON
[General] *Assembly*	ENLARGE
[general's] *order*	ENLARGES
order from [general]	ENLARGE

general[2]
General Assembly	GA
[General] *Assembly*	ENLARGE
general certificate	U
General Certificate of Education	GCE
General Court Martial	GCM
General Electric Company	GEC
general issue	GI
General Medical Council	GMC
General Motors	GM
General Officer Commanding	GOC
general paralysis of the insane	GPI
General Post Office	GPO
general practitioner	GP
general-service	GS
General staff	GS
General staff officer	GSO
[general] *surgery*	ENLARGE
General Teaching Certificate	GTC

generate
generate [steam]	MATES, MEATS, TAMES
generation	ERA

Letter replaced \c\at; Omit (a); Pointers *out*; Retain <u>a</u>; Split B_ED; Down (D); Backwards <or ^

generation of [heat]	HATE, THEA	• fear of Germans, *say*	HUNDRED
genesis		• German church	HUNCH
Genesis	GEN	• German dogs, *say*	HUNKERS
Genesis *I and II*	GE	• German youth	HUNTED
genesis of life	L	German	JERRY
genitive	GEN	• German is able, *say*	JERRICAN
genius	ID, KA	German	KRAUT, TEUTON
gentle		German *banker*	ODER, RHINE etc
gentle death	EASY GOING	German capital	(DEUTSCH)MARK, EURO
gentle game	LIGHTHOUSE	German *capital*	G
gentle type	KIND, MAGGOT	German capitalist	BERLINER
gently	P	[German] *dancing*	MANGER
very gently	PP	German fellow	OTTOMAN
	(*see also* quiet, soft)	German flower	ODER, RHINE etc
gentleman		German *leader*	G
gentleman Scot	GENTIAN	German linesman	GOETHE
gentleman's home	VERONA	German shell (WWI)	PIPSQUEAK
genuine		*German-speaking* woman	FRAU
genuine	REAL	German trooper, *say*	WRITER
• genuine fish	REALGAR	German way	AUTOBAHN
• genuine document	REALMS	two Germans	HUNGER
• genuine table, *say*	REALIST	**Germany**	D, GER
• over genuine . . .	SURREAL	**gerund**	GER
genuine, *say*	REEL	**get¹**	GET
• 100 genuine, *say*	CREEL	[Get] *lost!*	TEG
• genuine fish, *say*	REELING	[get] *organised*	TEG
genus	GEN	get *out*	GE–T
geology		[Get] *out!*	TEG
Geological Society	GS	get-*up*(D)^	TEG
geologist's work	FAULT-FINDING	**get²**	
Geordie		indicating implied inclusion:	
Geordie	NE	getting a tan	(in) SU–N
Geordie-land	NE	getting wet	(in) RA–IN
George		**get³**	
George I	GRACE	indicating inclusion:	
George *I*	G	*get into* t/he ar/my	HEAR
George Bernard Shaw	GBS	*get into* *	incl in *
George Cross	GC	• we *get into* sea	MEWED
George Medal	GM	*get* left *in* . . .	incl L or LT
germ		*get on*	incl ON
germ	BUG	• I *get on* both sides	ONION
• germ carries . . .	BUGBEARS	*get out for* a duck	incl O
• germ deficiency	BUGLOSS	• h–e *gets out for a* duck	HOE
• germ *with* the *French* . . .	BUGLE	*get out of* a . . .	incl A
• sound germ	HUMBUG	*get out of* brea/th an/d . . .	THAN
germ, *say*	CEDE	*get out of* line	incl I or L
German¹		• he–m *gets out of* line	HELM
German	BOCHE, FRITZ	• ma–n *gets out of* line	MAIN
German	G	*get out of* *	incl *
• German landlord	GHOST	• German soldier *gets*	
• German rage	GANGER	*out of* car	SCARS
• German state	GUTTER	*get right in* . . .	incl R or RT
German	GER	*get round* a . . .	incl A
• German and *German*	GERUND	*get round* *	incl *
• German *follows* male . . .	MANGER	• soldier *gets round* it	RITE
• German transport system	GERRY	**get⁴**	
German	HUN	indicating omission:	

Anag [cat]; Any *; Begin IGN–; Endings –ING; eg •; Hidden /cat/; Implied add (on); Implied in (in);

get out of a	omit A	• giant, *say*	TIGHTEN
get out of *	omit *	giant-killer	DAVID, JACK
• (Ch)arles *gets out*		**Gibraltar**	GIB, GBZ
of church	ARLES	**giddy**	
get rid of a . . .	omit A	*giddy* [goat]	TOGA
get rid of money	omit L	[spin] *giddily*	NIPS, SNIP
get rid of *	omit *	**gift**	
• the(y) *get rid of* unknown . . .	THE	gift	GAB
• *get rid of odd members*		gift coin	TALENT
of (p)a(r)t(i)e(s) . . .	ATE	gift of money	TALENT
get[5]		gift-*wrapped*	(in) PRES–ENT
other uses:		• I'd *gift-wrapped* . . .	PRESIDENT
get a big haul, *say*	CACHALOT	gifted father	SANTA CLAUS
get a good result	PASSABLY	**giga-electron-volt**	GEV
get a rise(D)^		**Gilbert and Sullivan**	GS, GANDS
• before *getting a rise*	ETNA	**gilded**	(in) O–R
get aboard, *say*	COMMON	**gilt**	
get awkward [and not] . . .	DANTON	gilt	OR
get cracking	DECIPHER, DECODE	gilt-*edged*	O–R
get down	DUCK	**gimmick**	
get drunk	BESOTTED	*gimmick* [used]	DUES, DUSE, SUED
get drunk [on ale]	ALONE	*gimmicky* [means]	MANES, NAMES
get from e/vide/nce	VIDE	**gin**	
get in a mess [over] . . .	ROVE	[gin] *cocktail*	IGN–, –ING, NIG
get [into] *shape*	–TION	gin mixer	ATONIC
get involved in [war]	RAW	[gin] *sling*	IGN–, –ING, NIG
get lost in [forest]	FOSTER	gin user	TRAPPER
get married, *say*	TAKE AMISS	**girdle**	
get moving [when I] . . .	WHINE	*girdles* a . . .	incl A
get out of bed	DIG UP	*girdles* *	incl *
get out of [breath]	BATHER	• staple *girdling* the . . .	BREATHED
get over it<	TI	**girl[1]**	
get ready	(EN)CASH, REALISE	commonly used names:	
get ready [to pin] . . .	PINTO, POINT	girl	ADA
get shot	SNAP, TAKE PICTURE	• girl *in* millions	MADAM
get to work [in car]	CAIRN	• girl *takes* exercise	ADAPT
get to work on [time]	EMIT, MITE	girl	ALMA
get up mad(D)^	DAM	• girl *has* a joke, *say*	ALMAGEST
get very 'ot	OVEREAT	• quiet girl	PALMA
gets help	GAINSAID	girl	ANN
getting better sport	RALLYING	• black girl, *say*	BAN(N)
getting firsts in Science,		• girl *in* sea in France	MANNER
English and Maths	SEAM	• girl *overweight*(D)	ANNOUNCE
getting on train	BOARDING SCHOOL	girl	ANNA
getting warm	NOTICED	• 100 girls	CANNAS
ghastly		• girl *in* telecommunications	BANNAT
ghastly [green end]	ENGENDER	• girl *puts on* pounds	ANNALS
[paints] ghastly . . .	PINTAS	girl	ANNE
ghost		• girl *in* transport	BANNER
ghost, *say*	GOAL	• girl *with* hat *on*	ANNELID
ghost-writer	IBSEN	• quiet girl	PANNE
ghostly remains, *say*	GOULASH	girl	ANNIE
in ghost, *say*	INSPECTOR	• girl lost, *say*	ANIMIST
giant		• girl married, *say*	ANIMATED
giant	ATLAS	• Greek girl, *say*	GRANNIE
giant	TITAN	girl	AVA
• giant in charge	TITANIC	• girl *takes* cereal	AVARICE

Letter replaced \c\at; Omit (a); Pointers *out*; Retain a; Split B_ED; Down (D); Backwards <or ^

• learner *takes* girl . . .	LAVA	• girl *with* dog	SALCHOW
• quiet girl *has* name . . .	PAVAN	• girl working	SALON
girl	DI	girl	SUE
• girl employees	DISTAFF	• girl died	SUED
• rotter *with* girl's . . .	CADDIS	• girl *without* right . . .	SURE
• spoil girl	MARDI	• is the girl?	ISSUE
girl	DINAH	girl	TESS
• girl might, *say*	DYNAMITE	• girl *takes* time	TESSERA
• girl, *say*	DINER	• girl *with* boy, *say*	TESTED
girl	ENA	• shouts *to* girl	HOSTESS
• girl *goes to* court	ENACT	girl	UNA
• girl *in* Lebanon	RENAL	• girl *in* sides	LUNAR
girl	EVE	• girl-struck	UNABASHED
• girl *after* transport	BREVE	• square girl	TUNA
• girl *has square*	EVET	girl	VERA
• girl *in* sides	LEVER	• girl *in* time . . .	AVERAGE
girl	IDA	• girl *reaches* big town	VERACITY
• *girl has* a call	IDAHO	• girl with a . . . , *say*	VERANDA
• girl *without* energy	IDEA	girl	VI
girl	JOY	• a girl died	AVID
• girl *almost* complete	JOYFUL	• girl has arrived, *say*	VISCUM
• girl *has* name, *say*	JOIN		VISIER, VIZIER
• girl's credit	JOYSTICK	• girl poses	VISITS
girl	KATE	**girl²**	
• girl out of practice, *say*	RUSTICATE	girl	DEB
• girl performed, *say*	KATYDID	• a royal girl	ARDEB
• second girl	SKATE	• girl broadcasting	DEBONAIR
girl	MAY	• girl *goes to* America	DEBUS
• girl *has* spoken	MAYORAL	girl	G
• girl *on* river, *say*	MAYFLOWER	• girl in . . .	GIN
• this girl, *say*	DISMAY	• girl *in* the money	COIGN
girl	MEG	• in girl	–ING
• girl *and* a boy	MEGARON	girl	GAL
• girl *on* the edge	MEGRIM	• girl runner	GALLOPER
• girl *with* a . . .	MEGA–	• girl *with* nothing on	GALOON
girl	MONA	• girl *with* one lion	GALILEO
• girl died	MONAD	girl	LASS
• girl's twitch	MONASTIC	• 100 girls	CLASSES
• off-white girl, *say*	CREMONA	• ginger-*headed* girl	GLASS
girl	PAT	• girl took action, *say*	LASSOED
• former girl	EXPAT	girl	MAID(EN)
• girl fastens . . .	PATTIES	• girl gangster	MAIDENHOOD
• second girl	SPAT	• girl *has* a point	MAIDENHEAD
girl	PEG	• worker *with* girl	HANDMAID
• girl like you and me	PEGASUS	girl	MISS
• girl on . . .	PEGLEG	• composer's girl, *say*	MISHANDLE
• girl spinner	PEGTOP	• girl and French . . .	MIS-SET
girl	ROSE	• girl locked up	MISSPENT
• girl devoured . . .	ROSEATE	**girl³**	
• girl is prepared, *say*	ROSEWOOD	girl *and* boy	ANNEAL, BETHANK, DIJON,
• quiet girl	PROSE		DIARCHY, DINED, GALLEON,
girl	RUBY		MISSAL, PATRON, PATTED,
• girl devoured *say*	RUBIATE		SALIAN, SALTED
• girl *with* criminal, *say*	RUBICON	girl *and* man	SALMON
• girl is prepared, *say*	RUBYWOOD	girl *and* two boys	BETRAYAL
girl	SAL		(*see also* boy and girl)
• girl from South America	PERUSAL	girl can handle gun	PEARL

Anag [cat]; Any *; Begin IGN–; Endings –ING; eg •; Hidden /cat/; Implied add (on); Implied in (in);

girl carrying camera	DOLLY
girl cyclist	DAISY
girl-friend	MANDATE, PALMARY
	PALMYRA, SALAMI
girl from	
–America	BROAD
–Australia	ADELAIDE, ALICE, SHEILA
–France	FILLE(TTE), NANCY
–Germany	FRAULEIN
–Ireland	COLLEEN
–Italy	RAGAZZA, SIGNORINA
–Picardy	ROSE
–Scotland	CUMMER
–Spain	MUCHACHA, NINA, SENORITA
–Tralee	ROSE
–Troy	HELEN
–Wales	MEGAN
–Wessex	TESS
Girl Guide	USHERETTE
girl in	
–[gaol]	OLGA
–opera	AIDA, CARMEN, MIMI
	NORMA, TOSCA
–[silo]	LOIS
–the [army]	MARY, MYRA
–the drink	OLIVE
–the garden	MAUD
–the shrubbery	MYRTLE, VERONICA etc
–Wonderland	ALICE
girl *making* [coral] . . .	CAROL
girl of the soft left	MILDRED
girl, *say*	GENE, MAIDAN
girl who	
–did	KATIE
–gets gun	ANNIE
–sparkles	BERYL, RUBY
–takes issue	SUE
–*took the* [blame]	MABEL, MELBA
girl with cold hands	MIMI
girl *working the* [oracle]	CAROLE
girlish *denial*	BOYISH
girl's	HER
• girl's love	HERO
• girl's ring in . . .	HEROIN
girl's claim	AMRITA
girl's best friend	DIAMOND
growing girl	DAISY, ERICA, ROSE etc
	(*see also* female)

give¹
indicating inclusion:

give key to . . .	incl A, B, C, D, E, F, G
give money to	incl D, L, P
give oxygen to	incl O
give shelter to a . . .	incl A
give shelter to *	incl *
• sh–ed *gives shelter to*	
English queen	SHEERED

give voice *about*	S–ING
given a . . .	incl A
given his head	incl H
given shelter by *	incl in *
• English queen *given*	
shelter by sh–ed	SHEERED
given *	incl *
• she *is given* £50	SHELL

give²
indicating omission:

give away a . . .	omit A
give away money	omit D, L, P
give away *	omit *
• (p)layer *gives away* pawn	LAYER
give nothing *away*	omit O
give out a . . .	omit a
give out *	omit *
• fat(her) *gives out* her . . .	FAT
give up a . . .	omit A
give up leader	omit 1st letter
give up *	omit *
• mot(her) *gives up* her . . .	MOT

give³
other uses:

give	HAND
• give at this point, *say*	HANDIER
• give the sack	HANDBAG
• support *and* give . . .	BACKHAND
	SECONDHAND
give a lift to diva(D)^	AVID
give attention to	EAR
give birth	
–at one,, *say*	LITERATI
–to eight, *say*	LITERATE
give girl a weapon	ARMADA
give no indication	SHAKE ONE'S HEAD
give nothing *for* a . . .	
• Chin\a\ *gives* nothing *for* a . . .	CHINO
give rise to [leer]	REEL
give rise to leer(D)^	REEL
give up, *say*	SEED
give worker a break	RESTANT
given a hearing, Paul . . .	PALL, PAWL
given a lift, boy(D)^	YOB
given in hi/s pare/nts' . . .	SPARE
gives [praise]	ASPIRE
giving away purchases	SHOPPING
giving consultation	CONFERRING
giving [her a] . . .	HARE, HEAR
giving up drink	(on) WAGON

Gladstone

Gladstone	BAGMAN, GOM
Gladstone's admission	ALIBI

glamour

glamour	IT
• glamour-queen dined	ITERATE
glamour	SA

Letter replaced \c\at; Omit (a); Pointers *out*; Retain a̲; Split B_ED; Down (D); Backwards <or ^

• glamour-girl	SAGENE, SAUNA

glass

acrobat's glass	TUMBLER
glass-maker	QUARTZ
glass of beer, *say*	PINTAIL
glass-paper	MIRROR
glass vessel	SCHOONER
stranger glass	RUMMER

gleaner RUTH
glider SNAKE
gloat

gloat *over<*	LEVER

globe

globe	O
globe-fish	EARTHLING

gloomy crypt GRAVE
gloria HEADLIGHT, O
glovemaker BUCKSKIN, DOESKIN
KID, LEATHER

gnarled

gnarled [oaks]	SOAK
gnarly [trees]	REEST, RESET, STEER

go¹ GO

go *a bit* silly	GOLLY
go *abroad*	ALLER
go *and* cut	GOSNICK
go *and* throw	GOSLING
go *back<*	OG
[go] *out*	OG
go *over<*	OG
go *round<*	OG
[go] *round*	OG
[go] *wrong*	OG
[goes] *funny*	EGOS
[gone] *bad*	–GEON

go²

go	PEP
• go *and* do wrong	PEPSIN
• go both ways	PEP
• go *with* the tide	PEPTIDE
go	TRY
• directions *to go* . . .	ENTRY
• go *by* road	TRYST
• succeed with go	WINTRY
go	TURN
• go *on* board	TURNTABLE
• go *to* fish	TURNPIKE
• go *to* university	U-TURN

go³

indicating anagram:

go astray [in the] . . .	THINE
go bad [in keg]	EKING
go into [slide]	IDLES, SIDLE
go off [meat]	MATE, TAME, TEAM
go off with [a tenor]	ORNATE
go to the dogs [or be] . . .	BORE, ROBE
go wild [over]	ROVE

go wrong [over an] . . .	VERONA

go⁴

indicating inclusion:

go round the bend	incl S, U
going about a . . .	incl A
going about *	incl *
• fish *going about* the . . .	GATHER
going around a . . .	incl A
going around *	incl *
• i–s *going around* a square	ITS
going inside *	incl in *
• he, *going inside,* swat–s . . .	SWATHES
going outside a . . .	incl A
going outside *	incl *
• w–ere *going outside* house	WHERE
go–ing outside-right	GORING
going round a . . .	incl A
going round *	incl *
• c–at *going round* circle	COAT
going through *	incl in *
• Scot *going through* Per–th	PERIANTH
going without a . . .	incl A
going without *	incl *
• w–e are *going without* her	WHERE

go⁵

indicating omission:

go away from	omit N, S, E, W
go East from	omit E
go North from	omit N
go off a . . .	omit A
go off *	omit *
• brother *goes off* the edge	(br)INK
* *goes*	omit *
• win(k) when king *goes*	WIN
go South from	omit S
go West from	omit W
going without a . . .	omit A
going without *	omit *
• fat(her) *going without* her	FAT

go⁶

other uses:

go	GREEN
go against it, *say*	BUCKET
Go *back,* fool!<	PAS
go before	PREDECEASE
go by sea, *say*	CREWS, SALE
go crazy	DEPARTMENTAL
go fishing	CASTANET
go into action	PROSECUTE, SUE
go mad	DEPARTMENTAL
go metric	SCRAPYARD
go north	QUITS
go on	RIDE
go on a bender	KNEEL
go over	(*see* over)
go over plot	CROSSPATCH
go to pot [when I] . . .	WHINE

Anag [cat]; Any *; Begin IGN–; Endings –ING; eg •; Hidden /cat/; Implied add (on); Implied in (in);

go upstairs	TAKE FLIGHT
go west	QUITE
goes in front, *say*	LEEDS
going around <u>s</u>lowl<u>y</u>	SLY
going around [there]	ETHER
* *going about*	
• saw *going about*<	WAS
* *going around*	
• gnat *going around*<	TANG
going astray, *say*	HERRING
going by air (=in a song)	
• cyclist, *going by air*	DAISY
• *going by air*, sailorman . . .	POPEYE
going north, walker . . . (D)^	RECAP
* *going round*	
• bus *going round* . . . <	SUB
going rate	MPH, SPEED, VELOCITY
going *to* a dance	WORKSHOP
going up step(D)^	PETS
goad her	NEEDLEWOMAN
goal	
[goal]	GAOLBREAK
goal-less draw	O–O
goat	
⁹ goat	BUTTER
• female goat	BUTTRESS
• goat's milk	BUTTERMILK
• goat-fat	BUTTER
goat	KID
• goat expires	KIDDIES
• goat family	KIDSKIN
• goat in ship	SKIDS
goat tender	NANNY
god	
god	LAR
• god is dead, *say*	LARDED
• god-like	LAROID
• river-god	POLAR
god	PAN
• god does his best	PANTRIES
• god fastens . . .	PANTIES
• god knows, *say*	PANNOSE
god	RA
• god *has* many . . .	RAM
• god *in* th–e . . .	THRAE
• horse-god	COBRA
god	RE
• god exists	REIS
• god *in* th–e . . .	THREE
• son to god	STORE
goddess	DEVI
• goddess devoured . . .	DEVIATE
• goddess in front	DEVILED
• goddess said, *say*	DEVISED
goddess, *say*	HEARER, MEWS, SERIES
godfather	CAPO, DON
godsend	GOTTERDAMMERUNG, RAGNAROK

going	(*see* go)
gold	
gold	AU
• gold *and* potassium	AUK
• gold cross in . . .	AUXIN
• gold rocks, *say*	AUROCHS
• gold the *French* . . .	AULA
gold	OR
• gold *and* iron	ORFE
• gold key	ORE
• gold coin	ORBIT
• gold letters	ORLANDO
• gold trade	ORDEAL
and	
• gold *in* church	CORE
• gold *in* iron	FORE
• gold sh–e *took in*	SHORE
and	
• measure gold	METEOR
• old gold	PASTOR
• win gold	SUCCESSOR
gold-*bearing*	incl AU, OR
• gold-*bearing* race	TAUT
• gold-*bearing* river	TORRENT
gold-bearing, *say*	HORRIFIC
gold coloured, *say*	GUILT
gold-*covered*	(in) O–R
gold-*edged*	(in) O–R
gold mint	BULL'S-EYE
gold-*mounted*	(in) O–R
gold-*mounted*(D)^	RO, UA
gold painter, *say*	GUILDER
gold-*plated*	(in) O–R
gold sovereign	MIDAS
gold-*wrapped*	(in) O–R
• the *old* gold-*wrapped* . . .	OYER
gold *wrapped in* . . .	incl AU, OR
• gold *wrapped in* pound note	LAUD, LORD
golden colour, *say*	GUILT
golden handshake	MIDAS TOUCH
golden retriever	ARGONAUT, JASON
golf	
golf course, *say*	LYNX
golf suit	CLUBS
golfer's curse	ROUND OATH
golfers	PGA
poor golfer	RABBIT
gone	(*see* go)
good[1]	
good	A
• good journey	ATRIP
• good relations	AKIN
• good team	ASIDE
good	AI
• good colour	AIRED
• good contest	AIR-ACE
• good fish	AILING

Letter replaced \c\at; Omit (a); Pointers *out*; Retain <u>a</u>; Split B_ED; Down (D); Backwards <or ^

good	BON	goose	
• good figure	BOND	gooselike	ANSERINE
• good note	BONA, BOND, BONE, BONG	gooselike, *say*	ANSWERING
• good *to* us	BONUS	Gort's men	BEF
good	FAIR	Gospels	NT
• good distance	FAIRWAY	got	(*see* get)
• good head	FAIRNESS	Gotham	NY
• *put* animal *to* good . . .	HORSE-FAIR	Gotterdammerung	GODSEND
good	G	gouge	
• embarge *has* good . . .	BANG	*gouged out* e(ye)s	ES
• good lad	GLAD	m(iddl)e *gouged out*	ME
• good-*hearted* roué	ROGUE	w(it)h *middle gouged out*	WH
good	OK	w(rass)e *with middle gouged out*	WE
• good always	OKAY	govern	
• good-*hearted* man	BLOKE	governed by policy	UNDERLINE
• behold good . . .	LOOK	governess	ANNA
good	PI	government	GOV(T)
• good friend	PIPAL	government controlled	UNDERSTATE
• good laugh, *say*	PILAFF	government house, *say*	STATOHM
• good value	PIRATE	government issue	GI
good *French*	BON	government	
• good *French* beef	RIBBON	representatives, *say*	CONSOL(E)S
• good *French* journalist	BONED	government	
• good *French* vehicle	CARBON	securities, *say*	CONSOLES,
good²			CONSULS
good book	BIBLE, NT, OT	governor	GOV, HE
good butter	GOAT	governor of Paris	PRIAM
good-bye	TATA, VALE	governor's position	OVERSTATE
good chap	JAKE, S, ST	grab	
good flan, *say*	OKAPI	*grab* a . . .	incl A
Good Food Guide	DIETICIAN	*grab* *	incl *
good friend(D)^	LAP UP	• do–g *grabs* a tin	DOTING
good friends(D)^	SLAP-UP	*grabbed by* *	incl *
good golfer	BOGEY MAN	• tin *grabbed by* do–g	DOTING
good-*hearted*	OO	**gradually**	ERIC
good looker	DISH, PEACH	**graduate**	
	SEARCHER, SPOTTER	graduate	BA
good looking, *say*	HANSOM	• graduate circle	BARING
good man	DEAN	• graduate fool, *say*	BASILIAN
good man	S, ST	• graduates are late	BASTARDY
• good man is not well	STILL	• graduates *have a* hair-cut	BASS-HORN
• good man *in* first class . . .	ASTI	• wicked graduate	BASINFUL
• see a good man	LOST	and	
good number	ANAESTHETIC, ANTHEM,	• mother *and* graduate	MAMBA
	HYMN	• peculiar graduate	RUMBA
good people	SS	• Uncle *with* graduate	SAMBA
good reading	BIBLE, NT. OT	graduate	MA
good rhyme	COULD, WOOD etc	• graduate queuing	MAINLINE
good score	PAR	• graduate's quarrel	MASTIFF
Good Service Pension	GSP	• graduates are wise	MASSAGE
good sort	KIND	• graduates celebrate	MASSING
good speller	MAGICIAN, WARLOCK	(*see also* scholar)	
	WITCH	**grain**	
good writing	BIBLE, NT, OT	grain	GR
goodness	MY, WELL-HEAD	grain, *say*	SERIAL
goodnight, *say*	GALAHAD	grain vessel	BRANDISH
goods, *say*	WEAR, WEIGHER, WHERE	**gram(me)**	G, GM, GR

Anag [cat]; Any *; Begin IGN–; Endings –ING; eg •; Hidden /cat/; Implied add (on); Implied in (in);

grammar	GR	**gravity**	
gran turismo	GT	gravity	G
grand		gravity-*free*	omit G
grand	G	• gravity-*free* (g)lobe	LOBE
• grand circle	GO	**graze**	
• grand entrance	GENTRY	graze, *say*	BROWS
• grand total	GADDING	grazing	FIELDFARE
• grand tour	GRANGE	**great**	
grand *deficiency*	omit G	great	GT, MEGA–, OS
grand	IMPOUNDS	great artist	TOP DRAWER
gran*d finale*	D	Great Britain	GB
Grand Old Man	GOM	great city	WEN
grand *opening*	G	great composer	TOP SCORER
Grand Union	MARRIAGE, WEDDING,	great conductor	COPPER, CU
	WEDLOCK	great craft	LARGESS
grandfather clock	OLD TIMER	Great Dane	HAMLET
graphite	KISH	great deal	BAGS, LOTS
grasp		great deceiver	SUPER-DUPER
grasp, *say*	HOLED	great dog	DANE
grasped by *	incl in *	great fiddle	CELLO
• king *grasped by* duke	FIRST	great flier	AUK, TIT
grasp twig	REALISE, UNDERSTAND	great flow(er) (=large river)	
grasp woman, *say*	CAESAR	• great flow of German . . .	RHINE
grasping a . . .	incl A	• great flower in South America	AMAZON
grasping compact	TIGHT	• Indian's great flower	GANGES
grasping hi/s hand, y/oung . . .	SHANDY	great fool	BF
grasping , *say*	CEASING	great healer	TIME
grasping *	incl *	great lady	BIGAMY
• duke *grasping* a king	FIRST	great letter	CAPITAL, LARGESS(E)
grass		great names	ALEXANDER, ALFRED
grass	FIELDFARE		CATHERINE
	MARIJUANA, POT(-PLANT)	great physician	TIME
grass	BETRAY, INFORM	great sea	MEDITERRANEAN
	SQUEAL, TELL	great swimmer	WHALE
grass	SING	great town	YARMOUTH
• grass and ecstasy	SINGE	Great Universal Stores	GUS
• grass twice	SINGLETON	Great Western Railway	GWR
• tea-grass	TEASING	greater alarm, *say*	MORPHIA
grass brush	FOXTAIL	Greater London Council	GLC
grass-covered	(in) RE–ED	greater, *say*	GRATER, MOOR
grasser	BETRAYER, INFORMER	greatness	BIGHEAD
	SQUEALER, TELLER	**Greece**	GR
grate		**Greek**	
grate [on her] . . .	HONER, RHONE	Greek	GK
grating [noises]	ESSOIN	Greek	GR
grating *sound*	GRILL	• Greek in debt	GROWER, GROWING
gratings in pighouse, *say*	STYRAX	• Greek river	GROUSE
gratings, *say*	GRILSE	• Greek state	GRAVER
gratitude	TA	Greek bedroom	ATTIC
grave		Greek capital	DRACHMA
grave description	DEAD END, TOMB	Gree_k *capital*	G
grave-digger, *say*	CRYPTOLOGIST	Greek capitalist	ATHENIAN
grave, *say*	CEREOUS	Greek character (=Greek letter)	
grave situation	CEMETERY, CHURCHYARD	• 3rd character in Greek . . .	GAMMA
	CREMATORIUM	• Greek character *has* no large . . .	OMEGA
gravestone	CARVE, SCULPT	Greek garret	ATTIC
grave testimonial	HEADSTONE	Greek judge, *say*	DIE-CAST

Letter replaced \c\at; Omit (a); Pointers *out*; Retain <u>a</u>; Split B_ED; Down (D); Backwards <or ^

Greek labourer	HERACLES, HERCULES	grip, *say*	BIGHT, BYTE
Greek *leader*	G	*grip* *	incl *
Greek story	ATTIC	• a v–ice *grips* a king	AVARICE
green		*gripped by* wa/ter m/onster	TERM
green	GO, NAIVE, RAW	*gripped by* *	incl in *
[green] *bananas*	GENRE, NEGRE	• a king *gripped by* a v–ice	AVARICE
green city	LINCOLN	gripper	CLAM(P), VICE, VISE
green cotton	LAWN	gripping article	CLAM(P), VICE, VISE
green-eyed monster	ENVY	lo/ve st/ory *is gripping*	VEST
green light	PERMISSION	**gritty fellow**	SANDY
[Green] *Movement*	GENRE, NEGRE	**groggy**	
[green] *salad*	GENRE, NEGRE	*groggily* [rise]	SIRE
greenkeeper	CONSERVATIONIST	*groggy* [males]	LAMES, MEALS
	EVERGREEN, LAUREL etc	**gross national product**	GNP
greenstuff	LAWN	**grotesque**	
Greenwich Mean Time	GMT	*grotesque* [icon]	COIN
greet		*grotesquely* [fat]	AFT
greet icily	HAIL	**ground**	
greeting	AVE	ground control approach	GCA
• greeting king	AVER	ground plan	PLOT
• greeting *with* anger	AVERAGE	ground rent	CREVASSE, FISSURE
• woman greeting . . .	WAVE	ground rent deposit	LAVA
greeting	HI	*ground* [rice]	CIRE, ERIC
• greeting Asian	HIMALAYAN	**group**	
• greeting child, *say*	HYSON	group	BAND
• greeting sailor	HIJACK	• group noticed	BAND-SAW
greet	HAIL	• group rented	BANDLET
• greet, *say*	HALE	• group, *say*	BANNED
• greets Franchot	HAILSTONE	group	CLASS
• second greeting, *say*	SHALE	• group directions	CLASSES
Grenada	WG	• group in charge	CLASSIC
Grenadines	WV	• group *with* fewer . . .	CLASSLESS
grey		group	GANG
grey suit	SLATE CLUBS	• function *in* group	GAPING
greyish carpet	SLATE	• group considers, *say*	GANGWAYS
greylag	GAOLBIRD	group	SECT
grievous		• belonging to group	INSECT
grievous bodily harm	GBH	• group insects	SECTANTS
grievous [hurt]	RUTH	• two groups	BISECTS
grievously [stinted]	DENTIST	group	SET
grill		• group of fliers	POSSET
grill for breakfast, *say*	FRIARLY	• group of graduates	BASSET
grill [lamb]	BALM	• group of officers	COSSET
grilled [sole]	LOSE	group of workers	BEE
grilling [steak]	SKATE, STAKE, TAKES	groups of sheep, *say*	PHLOX
grim		**grouse**	
grim	GRIZZLY	grouse	GR
grim situation	STERNPOST	grouse-meat	BEEF
grimace	MOUE, MOW	**grow**	
grind		grow back	REAR
grind coin	POUND	growing attractive	BECOMING
grind [into]	–TION	growing division	HEDGE
grind [into a] . . .	–ATION	growing girl	MYRTLE, ROSE, VIOLA et al
grind it, *say*	MILLET	growing incentive	CARROT
grinding [oats]	STOA	growing wrinkled	INCREASES
grip		growth industry	FARMING, FORESTRY
grip a . . .	incl A		MARKET GARDENING

Anag [cat]; Any *; Begin IGN–; Endings –ING; eg •; Hidden /cat/; Implied add (on); Implied in (in);

guard	
guard	SCREW
• follow guard	DOG-WATCH
• guard alien	WATCHET
• guard timepiece	WATCH
guarding a . . .	incl A
guarding *	incl *
• do–g *guarding* a tin	DOTING
guarded by *	incl in *
• tin *guarded by* a do–g	DOTING
Guatemala	GCA
Guernsey	GBG
guide	
guide animal	STEER
guide animal, *say*	STEAR, STERE
guide dog	POINTER
guide, *say*	GUYED
	LIEDER, PILATE
	STEAR(E), STERE
guide to cinema	USHERETTE
guilder	GLD
guile	
guile of [devil]	LIVED
guileful [ways]	SWAY, YAWS
[slid] *guilefully*	LIDS, SILD
guillotine	
guillotine	omit 1st letter
• *guillotine* cleric	(p)ARSON
• Marie's *guillotined* . . .	ARIES
guinea	G, GU
gules	GU
gulf	G
gullible fool	CHARLEY, CHARLIE
gulp	
gulp (=knock back)	
• *gulp* brandy<	CRAM

• *gulping* bun<	NUB
gum	
gum(D)^	MUG-UP
gum-*up*(D)^	MUG
gun	
gun	ARM
	BREN, GAT, LEWIS
	MAXIM, ROD, STEN
gun carrier	HOLSTER
gun-dogs	POMPOM
gun-running	PASSAGE OF ARMS
[gun]-*running*	GNU
[gun]-*whip*	GNU
[gun]*maker*	GNU
gunman	COLT, WEBLEY et al
gunmen	GRS, RA
gunner	FIREMAN, GR
gunners	FIREMEN, GRS, RA
guns	GRS, RA
gut	
c(ompletel)y *gutted*	CY
gut fish	STRIPLING
gutted h(ak)e	HE
gutless m(al)e	ME
Guy	
Guy	FAWKES, PLOTTER
Guy's companions	DOLLS
Guy's part	WARD
Guy's partner	DOLL
Guy's revolver	CATHERINE WHEEL
Guyana	GUY
gyrate	
gyrate [orb]	ROB
gyrating [top]	OPT, POT
gyration of [centre]	RECENT

Letter replaced \c\at; Omit (a); Pointers *out*; Retain <u>a</u>; Split B_ED; Down (D); Backwards <or ^

H

beam, bomb, complex cube root, Dirac's constant, enthalpy, Hamiltonian, hand, hard, heart, heat content, hearts, hecto-, height, Helmholtz free energy, henry, heroin, *horse*, hospital, hot, hotel, hour, house, Hungary, husband, hydrant, hydrogen, magnetic field strength, Planck's constant, tap, total energy, two hundred (thousand), vitamin

Habakkuk	HAB
habit	
annoying habit	HAIR SHIRT
habit-forming	DRESSMAKING, TAILORING
habitat	
habitat for *	incl *
• garden *habitat for* steer	BOXED
• organ *found in* dr–y *habitat*	DREARY
had confessed	OWNED
Haggai	HAG
Haggard girl	SHE
hail	
hail	AVE
• hail *after* sun	SAVE
• hail king	AVER
• hailstorms	AVERAGES
hail Mary	AM
hailing from Rome	ROAM
hair	
hair	FUR
• hair in front	FURLED
• hairline	FURROW
• made of hair, *say*	OFFER
Hair	MUSICAL
hair-*covered*	(in) MAN–E
hair fasteners	LOCKS
ha<u>ir</u>-*piece*	AIR
hair-remover	BARBER, HAIRDRESSER,
	RAZOR, SCISSORS
hair shirt	ANNOYING HABIT
hair-style	
–for the beach	SHINGLE
–report	BANG
–report, *say*	BHANG
hair*cut*	(h)AIR
hairdresser	COMB(ER)
hairdressers' dance	BARBERSHOP
hairy	DANGEROUS, LOCKED
hairy	(in) FU–R
hairy, *say*	INFER
Haiti	RH
half[1]	

half	DEMI–
• half egg	DEMIURGE
• half square	DEMIT
• half-way	DEMIST
half	HF
half	SEMI–
• half-*back*<	–IMES
• half-cold	SEMIC
• half-note	SEMITE
• half *with* no . . .	SEMINARY
half a score	TEN, X
half alphabet	ATOM
half-century	L
half-*cut*	ALF, HAL
half-day	AM, PM
half-dozen	VI
ha<u>lf</u>-*hearted*	AL
half-inch	PINCH, STEAL
half-minute	MO
half moon	FORTNIGHT
half *of France*	DEMI
half open	AJAR
half time	AM, PM
half[2]	
comm<u>only</u> *halved*	ONLY
half a jiffy	OND, SEC
half afraid	AID, AFR
*half*back	BA, CK
half-baked	COO, KED
half day	FRI, MON, SUN
• *half*-day closing	FRIEND
• *half*-day early	MONSOON
• *half*-day *and* night, *say*	SUNNITE
half days	DA, YS
half dead	AD, DE
half dry	T
half-*forgotten* parent	ENT, PAR
	FAT, HER
	HER, MOT
half full	FU, LL
half-hearted bel(l)ow	BELOW
half <u>length</u>	LEN

Anag [cat]; Any *; Begin IGN–; Endings –ING; eg •; Hidden /cat/; Implied add (on); Implied in (in);

half length of tunnel	TUN, NEL	• hands	PAWPAW
half-mast	MA, ST	• hands *back<*	SWAP
half mile	MI, LE	• hands *over<*	SWAP
half minute	MIN, UTE	• hands *to ears*	PAUSE
half-moon	MO, ON	• hands *up*(D)^	SWAP
half Nelson	NEL, SON	hand	PALM
half of bitter	BIT, TER	• hand ate, *say*	PALMETTE
half of ditch	HA	• hand ate nothing, *say*	PALMETTO
half of th/e ar/c	EAR	• name a hand	NAPALM
half open	EN, OP	hand in . . .	incl L, R
half-sister	SIS, TER	• had hand *in* ma–king	MARKING
half-sovereign	ARD, EDW	• hand *in* f–ew . . .	FLEW
	KI, NG	hand-*out*	omit L, R
half the capital	DON, LON	• (l)a(r)ge hand-*out*	AGE
half-time	TI, ME	**hand²**	
half volume	OK, BO	*hand over* [reins]	RESIN
*half*way	PA, TH	hand, *say*	SIGHED
	AD, RO	handbook, *say*	MANUEL
	EET, STR	*handed out* [dole]	LODE
half-witted	TED, WIT	*handover of* loot<	TOOL
halo	AUREOLE, GLORIA	hands down	SIX-THIRTY
	HEADLIGHT, NIMBUS, O	hands up	MIDNIGHT, NOON, TWELVE
ham		handy	
ham	OVERACT	–cleaner	NAILBRUSH
ham [actor]	CROAT, –OCRAT	–cover	GLOVE
Hamlet		–fitter	GLOVE
Hamlet, *say*	DEIGN	-fruit	BANANAS
Hamlet's agreement	SETTLEMENT	–joke, *say*	REDIGEST
Hamlet's rest	SILENCE	–pair	THUMBS
hammer		–sketch	THUMBNAIL
hammered [with] . . .	WHIT	–way	CLOCKWISE
<u>h</u>ammer*head*	H	**handicap**	
hammering [nails]	SLAIN	handicap	EBOR
Hampton		*handicapped* [male]	MEAL, LAME
[Hampton] *maze*	PHANTOM	**handle**	
hand¹		handle	EAR
hand	AB	• 150m handles	CLEARS
• hand-loom	ABLOOM	• handle money	EARMARK(S)
• hand-out	ABOUT	• long handle	LEAR
• hands pamphlet . . .	ABSTRACT	handle eyes, *say*	TREATISE
hand	FLUSH, FULL HOUSE	handle, *say*	EWES, YEWS
	STRAIGHT		HANDEL
hand	H	handle stores	STOCK
• hand fish . . .	HEEL, HID, HIDE	*handled* [adroitly]	IDOLATRY
• hand permits . . .	HALLOWS	handled fabric	FELT
• hand-work	HOP	*handling* [dogs]	GODS
hand	L, R	**hang**	
• bird *in* hands	LEMUR	hang alien	LYNCHET
• copper hands	CURL	*hang over* a lot(D)^	TOLA
• hands *round* girl	LANNER	hang-up	CLOSE CALL, MOBILE
	LEVER, REVEL	hanger-on	BARNACLE,
hand	MAN		CLAM, ICICLE,
• colour *round* hand	HUMANE		STALAGMITE
• hand *has* army . . .	MANTA	hangman	(JACK) KETCH
• warning *to* hand	FOREMAN	**haphazard**	
hand	PAW	*haphazard* [sort]	ORTS, ROTS, TORS
• hand-*out*	PA–W	[picks] *haphazardly*	SPICK

Letter replaced \c\at; Omit (a); Pointers *out*; Retain <u>a</u>; Split B_ED; Down (D); Backwards <or ^

happy

happier, *say*	MORGAY
happy few	GLADSOME
happy fish, *say*	MERICARP
happy ignorance	BLISS
happy members	CONTENT
happy people, *say*	MERIONES

harass

harassed [teacher]	CHEATER
harassment of [all the] . . .	LETHAL
[it was] *harassing*	WAIST

harbour

harbour a . . .	incl A
harbour	PORT
• harbour charges	PORTIONS
• harbour fruit	MULBERRY
• harbour lights	PORTRAYS
harbour *	incl *
• ship *harbouring* convict	SLAGS
harboured by *	
• convict *harboured by* ship	SLAGS

hard¹

hard	H
• hard and fast	HANDFAST
• hard ground	HEARTH
• hard *to* say	HAVER
• hard work	HOP
• hardwood	HASH, HELM
hard black	HB
hard *for outsiders* . . .	H–H
• as hard *for outsiders* . . .	HASH
• hard *going*	omit H
hard-*headed*	H
hard-*hearted*	incl H
• hard-*hearted* c–ad	CHAD
hard *to avoid*	omit H
• *hard to avoid* t(h)e . . .	TE
hard*top*(D)	H
very hard	HH

hard²

hard bed	STRATUM
hard case	SAFE, SHELL
hard drop	HAILSTONE
ha*rd*-*hearted*	AR
hard job	STERNPOST
hard, *say*	TUFF
hard tack	WARFARE
hard time	ROUGHAGE
hard times, *say*	CORSAGE
hard water	GLACIER, ICE, ICICLE
hardback	STERN
harden tablet	CAKE
hardly credible	TALL
hardly [human]	NAHUM
hardtop	CARAPACE, HELMET, SKULL

hardy

Hardy girl	TESS
Hardy companion	LAUREL
Hardy's superior	NELSON

harm

harm [a fly]	FLAY
harmless female, *say*	VENUS
harmless glider	GRASS SNAKE
[not] *harmed*	TON

harness

harness	TACK
• can harness . . .	TINTACK
• harness in front	TACKLED
• harness *in* ship	STACKS

harry

harried [master]	REMAST, STREAM
Harry [lived] . . .	DEVIL
harry [deer]	REDE, REED

harsh name — BITTERN

harvest

harvest	REAP
• harvest conference, *say*	REAPPEAR
• harvest fruit	REAPPEARS
• *use* a hundred *in* harvest	RECAP
harvested, *say*	MOAN, MODE

has¹

has	HAS
[has] *difficulty*	ASH
h–as gone out	HA–S
has leased	HASLET
has *to be made smaller*	HA, AS
[has] *trouble*	ASH

has²

has a role in T/he M/ousetrap	HEM
has a way with	incl N, S, E, W
• he *has a way with* . . .	HEN, HEW
has a way with	incl RD, ST
• she *has a way with* . . .	SHERD
has arrived	NOWHERE
[has made] *mistakes*	ASHAMED
has no . . .	incl NO
has *no* money	omit L
has *no* time	omit T
has no *	omit *
• I(r)an *has no* king	IAN
has nothing	incl O
has nothing *on*	end in O
has nothing on	incl OON
has on	incl ON
* *has gone off*	omit *
• clot(he)s he *has gone off*	CLOTS
hasn't a . . .	omit A
hasn't left	omit L
• p(l)ane *hasn't left*	PANE
hasn't married	omit M
• (m)an *hasn't* married	AN
hasn't *	omit *

hash

hash of [meal]	MALE, LAME

Anag [cat]; Any *; Begin IGN–; Endings –ING; eg •; Hidden /cat/; Implied add (on); Implied in (in);

hashy [mess a] . . .	SEAMS
made a hash of [it when] . . .	WHITEN
hassle	
[badly] *hassled*	BALDY
hassle [players]	REPLAYS
hasty	
hasty [words]	SWORD
hastily [hide]	HIED
[speak] *in haste*	PEAKS, SPAKE
hat	
hat maker	FELT, STRAW
hat measurement	CAPSIZE
hatless black woman(D)	(n)EGRESS
hatch	
[eggs] *hatching*	SEGG
hatch [new] . . .	WEN
hatching [plot]	POLT
haughty clique	UPSET
haul	
haul it, *say*	PULLET
haul on	PULLOVER
haul sail	LUG
haul, *say*	HALL, VESTIBULE
have	
(h)ave *an hour off*	AVE
have an hour *off*	omit H
• Cat(h) has an hour *off*	CAT
have it *at heart*	incl IT
having	WITH
• having base . . .	WITHSTAND
• having bear	WITHSTAND
• having drug	WITHE
• having *nearly* al(l)	WITHAL
• they are having, *say*	THEREWITH
having a . . .	incl A
having a run	LADDERED
having a row	OARING, SCULLING
having *a synonym*	OWNING
having an edge, *say*	RIMMON
having an overdraft	(in)R–ED
having changed [a note]	ATONE
having eyes, *say*	CITED, SITED
having keys, *say*	QUAYED
having large eyes, *say*	OX(H)IDE
having money	incl D, L, P
having mosquitoes, *say*	NATTY
having small fruit, *say*	BURIED
having wharves, *say*	KEYED
having wheels, *say*	WEALD, WIELD
having *	incl *
• s–py *having* cut . . .	SLOPPY
hawk	
hawk, *say*	TARSAL
hawker, *say*	PEDALLER
Haworth residence	PARSONAGE
hay	
[hay] *fever*	YAH

[hay]*maker*	YAH
made [hay]	YAH
[went] *haywire*	NEWT
hazard	
hazard [I ran]	RAIN, RANI
hazardous [task]	SKAT
hazel	
Hazel's descendant	AMENT, CATKIN
Hazel's protector	NUTSHELL
hazy	
hazily [recall]	CALLER
hazy [idea]	AIDE
he¹	
he	HE
• he copied	HEAPED
• he exploded, *say*	EPOPT
• he got up, *say*	EROSE
• he *has* a telephone	HEARING
• he is *local*	HEBE
• he licks, *say*	HELIX
• he licks her, *say*	ELIXIR
• he lifted, *say*	ERASED
• he makes tea	HEBREWS
• he spoke to, *say*	HEADREST
• he went on horseback, *say*	ERODE
• he will dance, *say*	HEEL-BALL
• he will ring, *say*	HELLO
he *abandons* . . .	omit HE
• he *abandons* (he)r	R
• he *abandons* t(he) . . .	T
he *escapes from* . . .	omit HE
• he *escapes from* (h)ol(e)	OL
• he *escapes from* t(he) . . .	T
he *leaves* . . .	omit HE
• he *leaves* (he)r . . .	R
• he *leaves* (h)om(e)	OM
• he *leaves* t(he) . . .	T
(h)e *lost his head*	E
he-man	HEART, HELEN
	HEROD, HERON
he *objectively* . . .	HIM
he *quits* . . .	omit HE
• he *quits* (he)ad . . .	AD
• he *quits* t(he) . . .	T
he *turned over*<	EH
he will, *say*	HEEL, HELL
he would, *say*	HED, HEED
he's *put out*	omit HE
he²	
he	MALE
• Effie *and* he, *say*	FEMALE
• he, *say*	MAIL
he	MAN
• he beat it	MANGETOUT
• he gets older	MANAGES
• he is aware, *say*	MANNOSE
• he leaves	MANGOES

Letter replaced \c\at; Omit (a); Pointers *out*; Retain <u>a</u>; Split B_ED; Down (D); Backwards <or ^

• he names . . .	MANHANDLES
• the *French* he . . .	LEMAN
he makes one cross	ELECTOR
he painted (it)	PINXIT, PXT
he sculpted (it)	SC, SCULP(SIT), SCULPT
head¹	
head covering	HAT, SCALP
head garment	CAPE
head measurement	CAPSIZE
head specialist	HAIRDRESSER
	TRICHOLOGIST
headlight	AUREOLE, GLORIA
	HALO, NIMBUS
headlines	CROWS'-FEET, WRINKLES
headlining	BRAIN(S)
headlong	DOLICHOCEPHALIC
headpiece	EAR, NOSE
headroom, *say*	SCULLERY
head's side	OBVERSE
Head's trophy	SCALP
head²	
head	LOAF
• head *has* gin *cocktail*	LOAFING
• head monarch	LOAFER
head	NESS
• hard head	TOUGHNESS
• head of beer	BITTERNESS
• wide head	THICKNESS
head	NUT
• girl *with* head . . .	HAZELNUT
• head girl	NUTMEG
head	PATE
• head *aboard* . . .	SPATES
• head king	PATER
head	RAS
• English head *has* English . . .	ERASE
• head *in* church	CRASH
head	TOP
• head in charge	TOPIC
• head missing	TOPLESS
head *covering*	(in) N–ESS, (in) NU–T
	(in) P–ATE, (in) RA–S
head³	
head East	
• agent *headed* East	ESPY
• man *heading* East	MANE
head North	
• apes *headed* North	NAPES
• girl *heading* North	MAIN
head South	
• sailor *headed* South	STAR
• sailor *heading* South	TARS
head West	
• everyone *headed* West	WALL
• woman *heading* West	SHEW
head⁴	
indicating 1st letter(s):	

deputy *head*	D
head boy	B
head first	F
head of beer	B
Head of Department	D
head of Intelligence	I
head *first*	H
head first	F
head office	O
head *start*	H
head start	S
head teacher	T
head*man*	M
heading ball	B
*head*gear	G
*head*land	L
*head*long *into*	incl L
*head*master	M
heads I win	IW
heads of State *are* gathered . . .	SAG
heads off towards *any* large	
emporium	TALE
heads you lose	YL
*head*ship	S
King's *Head*	K
head⁵	
indicating omission:	
head *away*	omit 1st letter
• head *away* from (S)lough	LOUGH
head *leaves*	omit 1st letter
• head *leaves* study	(d)EN, (c)ON
head *missing*	omit 1st letter
• head *missing from* (f)lower	LOWER
head *not seen*	omit 1st letter
• head *not seen* in (c)lass	LASS
head *not shown*	omit 1st letter
• *head not shown* on (s)nap	NAP
head off (b)ear	EAR
heading from (W)are	ARE
heading *off*	omit 1st letter
• heading *off* (t)he . . .	HE
headless (f)lower	LOWER
headless woman	(m)ARIA, (j)ILL, (w)OMAN etc
head⁶	
other uses:	
head harness, *say*	BRIDAL
head of Intelligence	MISCHIEF
head-over-heels, Eros . . . <	SORE
head pastry-cook, *say*	BUNKING, FLANKING
head race	CROWN DERBY
shook *head to foot*(D)	HOOKS
head-to-tail pins<	SNIP
headlong rush, *say*	CHOREA
headmaster	ARNOLD, HM
headquarters	
headquarters of sect	SE
Police *headquarters*	PEE, PEN, PEW

Anag [cat]; Any *; Begin IGN–; Endings –ING; eg •; Hidden /cat/; Implied add (on); Implied in (in);

<u>S</u>cout *head*quarters	SEE, SEN, SEW	hearing test	TRIAL
<u>Y</u>outh *head*quarters	YEN, YES, YEW	**heart**	
heal		*at heart* s/he w/as . . .	HEW
heal priest	CURE	g<u>ree</u>t *heartily*	REE
healer	DR, GP, MB, MD, MO	heart	H
	(*see* doctor)	heart-*breaking*	(in) CO–RE
health		[heart]-*breaking*	EARTH, HATER, RATHE
good health	TOAST	[heart]-*broken*	EARTH, HATER, RATHE
health authority	WHO	• [heart]-*broken* American	ARETHUSA
hea<u>l</u>th-*centre*	AL	[heart]-*failure*	EARTH, HATER, RATHE
health expert	TOASTMASTER	*heart* of Fren/ch Arm/y	CHARM
health food	TOAST	*heart* of <u>gol</u>d	OL
health official	MO	*Heart* of Mid<u>lo</u>thian	OT
health resort	CLINIC	*heart* of <u>the</u> . . .	H
healthy	omit ILL	*heart of the* ma<u>tt</u>er	TT
• *healthy* PM	CHURCH(ill)	heart recording	TICKER TAPE
• *healthy* hatmaker	M(ill)INER	[heart] *surgery*	EARTH, HATER, RATHE
• *healthy* tree	W(ill)OW	[heart] *transplant*	EARTH, HATER, RATHE
healthy	WELL	*heart transplant for* Be\g\in	BEING
• healthy family, *say*	WELKIN	*heartless* f(emal)e	FE
• healthy man, *say*	WELTED	heart-throb	PULSE
• partner healthy	BRIDEWELL	*heart*-th<u>r</u>ob	R
healthy, *say*	HAIL	hearty	AB, SAILOR, TAR
healthy stock	GOODS TRAIN	h<u>ea</u>rty drink	CORDIAL
heap		Li<u>o</u>n*heart*	IO
heap of fruit	LIMERICK	m/aide/n's *heart*	AIDE
heaps of [soil]	OILS, SILO	* *to heart*	incl *
[slag]-*heap*	GALS, LAGS	• captures *with* blow *to heart*	TRAPS
hear[1]		• sec m–e *take it to heart*	MITE
hear	TRY	**heat**	
• fathers hear . . .	PASTRY	[heat] *exchange*	HATE, THEA
• hear *about*	TR–Y	[heat] *treatment*	HATE, THEA
• hear holy man	TRYST	heated issue	LAVA, STEAM
hear[2]		**heath**	
indicating a homophone:		heath	TED
• *do we hear* rain	REIGN, REIN	heath, *say*	MORE
• hear a loud . . .	ALLOWED	**heavens**	COO, COR, MY, SKY
• *hear* forty . . .	EXCEL, FORTE, XL	**heavy**	
• hear *in conversation*	HERE	heaviness, *say*	WAIT
• hear, *say*	HERE	heavy accent	GRAVE
• *hear* wails	WALES, WHALES	Heavy Artillery	HA
• hear why . . .	WYE, Y	heavy artillery, *say*	CANONRY
• *heard* a noise	ANNOYS	heavy blow CYCLONE, GALE, HURRICANE
• Heard? *Heard!*	HERD		ONER
• *heard* in conversation	HERD	heavy breather	GRAMPUS
• *hearing* a girl	ALAS	heavy going	(in) MU–D
• *hearing* aid	–ADE, AIDE	Heavy Goods Vehicle	HGV
• *hearsay*	HERE	heavy round	DOORSTEP
• *hearsay* cited	SIGHTED, SITED	heavyweight ANTON, BOXER, STONE, TON
• intended *to hear*	–MENT	**Hebrew**	
• more *hearsay*	MOOR	Hebrew	HEB(R)
• Paul *given a hearing*	PALL, PAWL	Hebrew character (=Hebrew letter)
• rumour *that is hearsay*	ROOMER	• first character in	
hear[3]		Hebrew . . .	ALEPH
(he)ar he *left*	AR	• Hebrew character looks	
heard more than ever	CLEVER, TREVOR	crippled	LAMED
hearing aid	EAR	Hebrew	JEW

Letter replaced \c\at; Omit (a); Pointers *out*; Retain <u>a</u>; Split B_ED; Down (D); Backwards <or ^

• Hebrew baby, *say*	JUNIPER
• Hebrew beauty will, *say*	JUDICIAL
• Hebrew is acute	JEW'S-HARP
• Hebrew, *say*	DEW, DUE
Hebrew diet	KNESSET
Hebrew leader	MOSES
Hebrew *leader*	H
hectare	HA
hectic	
hectic [time]	EMIT
[rushes] *hectically*	USHERS
hectolitre	HL
hedge	
hedge	HAW
hedge shrub , *say*	PRIVATE
heed	
heed, *say*	MINED, WRECK
heeds, *say*	REX, WRECKS
height	
height	H
height of fashion(D)	F
held	
held back by man/y	
reve/rent . . . <	EVERY
held by lar/ge ne/w . . .	GENE
held in banks (indicating a river):	
• *held in English banks*	THAMES etc
• *held in French banks*	SEINE etc
• *held in German banks*	RHINE etc
held in *	incl in *
• nitrogen *held in* ba–g	BANG
• nothing *held back in* ba–g	BALING
held Italian capital	HADROME
	(*see also* hold)
Hell	
hell	ABADDON, AVERNUS
hell	DIS
• gangster *in* hell	DIALS
• hell-bent	DISINCLINED
hell	EREBUS, PIT, HADES, TARTARUS
hellhound	CERBERUS, PLUTO
hellish boss	DEVIL, DIS
help	
Help!	SOS
help get o/ver y/our . . .	VERY
help mot/her d/ust . . .	HERD
help out	AI–D
• five help *out*	AVID
help to make aero/plan/es	PLAN
help to make [notes]	ONSET, STONE, TONES
helpful officer	ADC, AIDE
helping of beer	RATIONALE
hem	
hem of skirt	T
hemmed in a . . .	incl A
hemmed in *	incl *
• sea *hemmed* us *in*	MUSED

hemmed in by *	incl in *
• us *hemmed in by* sea	MUSED
hemi-	
*hemi*hedron	HED, RON
hemiolic	OL, IC
hen	
hen	LADYBIRD, LAYER
hen, *say*	FOUL, LAIR
hen's head, *say*	FOULNESS
henna	TONE CONTROL
henry	
Henry	H
• Henry I	HI
• Henry VIII	HEIGHT
Henry	HAL
• Henry Bird, *say*	HALBERD
• Henry *on* the stairs	HALF-LIGHT
Henry	HANK
• Henry went in front	HANKLED
• Second Henry	SHANK
Henry I	H
Henry II	E
her¹	
her fish, *say*	HURLING
her man, *say*	URGENT
her *counterpart*	HIS
her other case	SHE
her view, *say*	URSINE
her²	
Her (Britannic) Majesty	H(B)M
Her Exalted Highness	HEH
Her Grace	HG
Her Imperial Majesty	HIM
Her Majesty's Customs	HMC
Her Majesty's Government	HMG
Her Majesty's Inspectorate	HMI
Her Majesty's Service	HMS
Her Majesty's Ship	HMS
Her (Royal) Highness	H(R)H
Her Serene Highness	HSH
herald	
[Herald] *Extraordinary*	HARELD, HARLED
	–HEDRAL
heraldry	HER
Heralds' College	HC
herb	SIMPLE
herd	
herd of cows	OXGANG
herd, *say*	HEARD
here	
here *in France*	ICI
here *in Rome*	HIC
h*ere in the middle* . . .	ER
here is (laid)	HS
hereafter	
hereafter	HEAVEN
here*after*	

• guard here*after*	HEREWARD
• firm here*after*	COHERE
heretic	ARIAN
hero	
hero	LADYLOVE
Hero worshipper	LEANDER
Hertz	CS, CPS, HZ
hesitate	
hesitation	–ER, UM, UR
• *hesitant* claim	ERMINE
• hesitation *in* time . . .	HUMOUR
• *hesitating in* church	CURE
without hesitation	omit ER, UM, UR
h-hem	HEDGE
hide	
hidden in h/er go/wn	ERGO
hidden in [forest]	FOSTER
hidden in *	incl in *
• fruit *hidden by* divine	DAPPLED
hidden piece of wo/od in/side . . .	ODIN
hide pepper	PELT
hide shield	SCREEN
hiding a . . .	incl A
hiding in cupboar/d un/der . . .	DUN
hiding in [field]	FILED
hiding *	incl *
• divine *hiding* fruit	DAPPLED
hideous	
hideous [face]	CAFE
[Medusa's] *hideous* . . .	ASSUMED
hi-fi	
hi-fi buff	STEREOTYPE
hi-fi *sound*	HYPHAE
Higgins's girl	ELIZA
high	
high	TOP
• high bend	TOPARCH
• high note	TOPE
• high notes	TOPE(E)S
• high speed	TOPKNOTS
high-alumina cement	HAC
high-class	A, AI, U
high-class band	CORONET, TIARA
high diver	OFFENDER
high explosive	HE
high flier	AEROPLANE, AIRSHIP
	BIRD, CONDOR etc
	COMET, ICARUS
	TRAPEZE(-ARTIST)
	WHIZZ-KID
high flier's home	EYRIE, NEST
high flier's home, *say*	EERIE
high frequency	HF
high honour	KING
high jump	OFFSPRING
high-king, *say*	HIKING, TALKING
High Noon	HANDS UP

high place	UP
high point, *say*	PEEK, PIQUE
high-powered firm	STRONG
high priest	AARON, ELI, LAMA etc
high revs	(ARCH)BISHOPS
high-rise building	ANTHILL
high road	FLYOVER
high score	TON
high-*sounding*	HI(E)
• high-*sounding* girl	HYENA
high summer	ADDER, (SENIOR) WRANGLER
High Table	PLATEAU
high tars	SMELLING-SALTS
high tension	HT
high time	NOON
high tower	UPKEEP
high wager	TREBLE
high water	TARN
high water mark	HWM
high wind	JETSTREAM
higher, *say*	HIRE, LEASE, RENT
• higher row, *say*	HYALINE
• higher lamp, *say*	HYALITE
Higher National Certificate	HNC
Higher National Diploma	HND
higher number	NUMERATOR
highest chief	TOPARCH
highest common factor	HCF
highest honour	ACE
highest point, *say*	PEEK, PIQUE
highest speed	C
highlight	MOON, STAR, SUN
highly charged	DEAR, EXPENSIVE
highway, *say*	LAIN, RODE
highball	
highball	LOB
• highball money	LOBLOLLY
• highball specialist	LOBSTER
• second highball	SLOB
Highland	
Highland Light Infantry	HLI
Highland(er) (=Scottish)	
• *Highland* shoemaker	SOUTAR, SOUTER
	SOWTER
• *Highlander's* salutation	BECK
highlight	MOON, STAR, SUN
hill	MT, TOR
Hill 11	TORII
hill-billy	MOUNTAIN GOAT
hill-*climbing*(D)^	ROT
hill-dweller	ANT, TERMITE
hill-guide	TORMENTOR
<u>hill</u>*side*	H
<u>hill</u>*top*(D)	H
Himalayan	SHERPA
hinder	
hinder man	DETERGENT

Letter replaced \c\at; Omit (a); Pointers *out*; Retain <u>a</u>; Split B_ED; Down (D); Backwards <or ^

hindrance	LET	• hit him, *say*	SOCMAN
• hindrance *to ruler, say*	LETTER	• hit it, *say*	SOCKET
hip		hit	SLOG
[hip] *replacement*	PHI	• hit one . . .	SLOGAN
[hip]-*shaking*	PHI	• hit woman, *say*	SLOGGER
hippy	SCIATIC	hit	SMACK
replacement of [hips]	PISH, SHIP	• hit boat	SMACK
his[1]		• hit queen	SMACKER
his	GREETINGS	• hit woman, *say*	SMACKER
his	HIS	hit American, *say*	WAMMUS
• his attempt, *say*	HISTRION	hit and run	BLOWFLY, SLAPDASH
• [his] *characters*	–ISH	*hit for six* [by real] . . .	BARLEY
• [his] *cocktail*	–ISH	hit it, *say*	WAPPET
• [his] *fault*	–ISH	hit number	SCORE
• his knight, *say*	HISSER	[hit] *out*	–ITH
• his teacher, *say*	HISSER	hit a Pole, *say*	LAMP-HOLE
his *counterpart*	HER	hit timekeeper	CLOCK
his eyes, *say*	MAN-SIZE	hit vehicle, *say*	LASHKAR
his *head*(D)	H	hitman	PATRON, PATTED
his[2]		**hitch**	
His (Britannic) Majesty	H(B)M	*hitch in* [part] . . .	RAPT, TRAP
His Catholic Majesty	HCM	hitching-post	GRETNA GREEN
His Eminence	HE		REGISTRY OFFICE
His Exalted Highness	HEH	**Hitler's bodyguard**	SS
His Excellency	HE	**hive**	
His Grace	HG	hive, *say*	BEHOLDER
His Imperial Highness	HIH	**hoard**	
His Imperial Majesty	HIM	hoard, *say*	CASH, HORDE, WHORED
His Majesty's Customs	HMC	*hoarded by* *	incl in *
His Majesty's Government	HMG	• it is *hoarded by* saints	SITS
His Majesty's Inspectorate	HMI	*hoarding* a . . .	incl A
His Majesty's Service	HMS	*hoarding* *	incl *
His Majesty's Ship	HMS	• saints *hoarding* it	SITS
His (Royal) Highness	H(R)H	**hoarse**	
His Serene Highness	HSH	hoarse, *say*	CROQUET, RUPEE
hiss		hoarse sound	CROAK
hiss *at*	incl S	hoarse *sound*	HORSE, MAYOR
• hiss *at* play	SPLAY	*sounding* hoarse	CROQUET, RUPEE
hissing sound	S		HORSE, MAYOR
history		**hogshead**	
historian	ACTON	hogshead	HHD
history teacher	PASTMASTER	hogs*head*	H
hit		**hoist**	
hit	PAT	hoist bird	CRANE
• hit bird	PATTERN	hoist headgear, *say*	WHIN-CHAT
• hit girl	PATELLA, PATINA	*hoist it* . . . (D)^	TI
• hit man	PATRON, PATTED	*hoist* up(D)^	PU
hit	PUNCH	*hoist* sail(D)^	LIAS
• hit horse	PUNCH	**hold**	
• hit *with* wood	PUNCH-BOWL	hold	KEEP
• hit woman, *say*	PUNCHER	• hold *back*<	PEEK
hit	RAP	• hold girl, *say*	KEEPER
• hit double	RAPID	• hold liquor	KEEPSAKE
• hit *in* church	CRAPE	• hold up(D)^	PEEK
• hit the drink	RAPPORT	*hold* firm	incl CO
hit	SOCK	*hold* on	incl ON
• hit girl, *say*	SOCCER	hold stock	STEM

hold-up	DAM	• second hollow	SPAN
hold up	incl UP	**Hollywood**	
• firms *hold* up . . .	COUPS	Hollywood area	CAL, LA
hold-up man	ATLAS, JACK, TURPIN	*in* Hollywood area	C–AL, L–A
hold up paws(D)^	SWAP	**holy**	
holding a . . .	incl A	holy	PI
holding agency	CLAMP, VICE	• holy child	PITOT
	FIXATIVE, GLUE, GUM, PASTE	• Holy City	PILA
holding company	CANOODLING, CUDDLING	• holy man	PINED
	SNOGGING, SMOOCHING	Holy City	JERUSALEM, MEDINA, MECCA,
holding back			ROME ETC
• girl *holding back* about . . . <	LASERS	Holy Communion	HC
holding hose	HASSOCKS	holy day, *say*	SUNDAE
holding on	incl LEG, ON	holy man	S, ST
• drink *holding* on . . .	ALONE	Holy Mother Mary	SMM
• Sally *holding* on	SORTILEGE	holy orders	TEN COMMANDMENTS
holding together t/wo k/inds . . .	WOK	holy river	GANGES
holding up(D)		Holy Roman Empire	SRI
• doctor *held up by* girls	MOLASSES	Holy Virgin	HV
• girl *holding up* a . . .	AMISS	Holy Writ	NT, OT
and		**home**[1]	
• Mo–ses *holding*		home	FLAT
up girl(D)	MOLASSES	• home club	FLAT-IRON
holding *		• home *in* the river	DEFLATE
• pai/r are st/ill *holding*	RAREST	• home trial	FLATTEST
holding *	incl *	home	IN
• ba–g *holding* nitrogen	BANG	• home bird	INTERN
holds		• Home Rule	INLAW
• holds hose	HASSOCKS	• home stretch	INTENSE
• holds *in* church	CHASE	• home team	INSIDE
• holds a row	HASTIER	**home**[2]	
holds bonds	STOCKS	home club	VILLA
holds colour	CLINGSTONE	Home Counties	SE, THESE
	(*see also* held)	home following	CARAVAN
hole		home *front*	H
hole	O	Home Guard	HG, WATCHDOG
hole, *say*	WHOLE	*home-made* soup	BIRDS'-NEST
hole in one	CELLINI	home	
holed	incl O	–of gentlemen	VERONA
holed, *say*	HOLD	–of natives	OYSTER BED
holiday bay	RECESS	–of the brave	HOGAN, TE(E)PEE
hollow			TIPI, WIGWAM
hollow (=nothing inside)		home team	VILLA
• *hollow* s(oun)d	SD	**Homer**	
• *hollow* t(ub)e	TE	Homeric	
• *hollow* v(ictor)y	VY	indicating use of Greek word or character:	
hollow	O	• *Homeric* character	
• cover *hollow* . . .	LIDO	wagered . . .	ALPHABET
• *hollow* sound	ODIN	• *Homeric* character recently . . .	PHILATELY
• *hollow* tree	OPINE	Homer's place	DOVECOT(E)
hollow(ed)	incl O		(PIGEON-)LOFT
• d–ry *hollow*	DORY	**honest**	
• *hollow* ro–d	ROOD	honest footballer	STRAIGHTFORWARD
• sh–e *hollowed* . . .	SHOE	honest member	SQUARE LEG
hollow	PAN	**honeymoon express**	BRIDAL TRAIN
• hollow feature	PANNOSE	**Hong Kong**	HK
• hollow pain	PANACHE	• a river *in* Hong Kong	HARK

Letter replaced \c\at; Omit (a); Pointers *out*; Retain <u>a</u>; Split B_ED; Down (D); Backwards <or ^

honour

honorary	HON
honour	A, ACE, J, JACK
	K, KING, Q, QUEEN
honour	CH
• graduate with honour	MACH
• honour a member	CHAMP
• honour *among* mayors, *say*	MARCHES
honour	OBE
• 50 honour . . .	LOBE
• honour revolutionary	OBECHE
• honourable name	OBERON
• honours, *say*	OBESE, OBIS
honour	OM
• act *with* honour	DOOM
• honour *in* about . . .	COMA
• honour it	OMIT
	(see also award, order)
Honourable	HON
Honourable Artillery Company	HAC
honoured companion	CH
hooded bird	CROW, ROBIN
hook	
hook	PIRATE
• hooklike	ASPIRATE
hoop	
hoop	O
hoop for crinoline	DRESS CIRCLE
	DRESS-RING
hooter	
hooter	NOSE
second feature	SHOOTER
hop	
hopping about [room]	MOOR
hopping [mad]	ADM–, DAM
hope	
Hope's territory	RURITANIA
hopelessly [lost]	LOTS, SLOT
hopin'	ASPIRIN
Horace's work	ODES
horizontal	
horizontal	HOR
horizontal angle	FLATFISH
horizontal equivalent	HE
hormone	
hormone	AUTOCOID
[hormone] *treatment*	MOORHEN
horology	
horology	HOR
horologist	CLOCKWISE
horrible	
horrible [fate]	FEAT
horrible, *say*	VIAL
horribly [made]	DAME, EDAM, MEAD
horrific	
horrific [tale]	LATE, LEAT, TEAL
[it was] *horrifically* . . .	WAIST

horse¹

[horse]-*breaking*	SHORE
[horse]-*racing*	SHORE
[horse]*play*	SHORE

horse²

horse	ARAB
• horse *in* the desert	SARABAND
• horsewoman	ARABELLA
• namely, a horse	SCARAB
horse	ASS
• black horse	BASS
• horse drawing . . .	ASSART
• horse *in* the *French* . . .	LASSES
horse	BARB
• horse one can . . .	BARBICAN
• horse devoured . . .	BARBATE
• horse measures, *say*	BAR-BELLS
horse	BAY
• horseman	BAYED
• mountain horse	TORBAY
• horse, very odd	BAY-RUM
horse	COB
• Horse Artillery	COBRA
• horse-food	COBLOAF, COBNUT
• horse painter	COBRA
horse	G, GEE
• ban horse	BARGEE
• horse-road	GEEST
• horse *without* new . . .	GENE
horse	GG, GEE-GEE
• horse *in* a rage	BAGGIT
• horse *without* an . . .	GANG
• Oriental horse	EGG
horse	H
• horseman	HALF, HANDY
• horse in river	HINDEE
• horse *with* no bit	HOBIT
horse	HACK
• horse joint, *say*	HACKNEY
• horse list	HACKLOG
• second horse	SHACK
horse	NAG
• horse collection	NAGANA
• horse *in* ship	SNAGS
• horse or . . .	NAGOR
• horse*back<*	GAN

horse³

dark horse	NIGHTMARE
horse-drawn carriage	HACKNEY
• horse-drawn carriage, *say*	ACNE
horse disease, *say*	MAL-DE-MER
horse drug	HEROIN
horse-laugh, *say*	NAY
horse pistol	COLT
horse race	HOUYHNHNM
horse-race	DERBY, NATIONAL, OAKS etc
	PLATE

Anag [cat]; Any *; Begin IGN–; Endings –ING; eg •; Hidden /cat/; Implied add (on); Implied in (in);

horse-riding	(in) S–ADDLE, UP	**house²**	
horse-riding, *say*	MANAGE	house	BINGO
horse, *say*	BEY, HOARSE, RHONE	house-boat	HOMECRAFT
horse sound	NEIGH, WHINNY	house builder	JACK
horse *sound*	HOARSE, MAYOR	house buzzer	FLY
horse's foot	TROTTER	house-coat	PLASTER, STUCCO
horse's head	H	house deposit	LODGE
horse trading	STOCK EXCHANGE	house for	
horse*back*<	BOC, GAN	—scientist	LODGE
horse*less*	omit G	—team	VILLA
horseman	CENTAUR	House of Keys	HK
horseplay	EQUUS, RICHARD THE	House of Lords	MANOR
	THIRD, POLO	house-party, *say*	SEA-TROUT
horse's refusal, *say*	NEIGH	house-room	AUDITORIUM
horseshoe	MULE	*housed in* de/relic/t . . .	RELIC
sound horse	HOARSE, MAYOR	*housed in* *	incl in *
steady horses	STABLE	• scholar *housed in* for–t	FORMAT
unhealthy horse	SICK-BAY	housemaid	WENDY
white horse	BREAKER, WAVE	housemaid's knee	BURSITIS
Hosea	HOS	houseman	INTERNE, RESIDENT
hospital			MEMBER OF PARLIAMENT, MP
hospital	H	housemaster	PM, PRIME MINISTER
• hospital *has* changed	HALTERED		SPEAKER
• hospital *has* no use . . .	HOUSE	housework	COTTAGE INDUSTRY
• hospital-planes	HAIRLINE		LEGISLATION
hospital department	ENT	*housing* a . . .	incl A
hospital sign	H	(ho)using *shortage*	USING
hospital wing, *say*	WARDROOM, WARRED	*housing* ol/d art/efacts	DART
hospitalised	INWARD, (in) W–ARD	*housing* *	incl *
hot		• for–t *housing* scholar	FORMAT
hot	H	White House	IGLOO
• hot and *nearly* ful(l)	HANDFUL	**house³**	
• hot *at* church	HATCH	house	HANOVER, STUART
• hot fish	HEEL, HID(E)		WINDSOR etc
• hot oven	HOAST	• house in Holland	ORANGE
hot *and* bothered	RED CROSS	• house plant	TUDOR ROSE
hot-rod driver	RIVETER	• houses sound	YORK STONE
hot tip	FIRE ALARM	houseman	LANCASTRIAN, TUDOR etc
h̲ot *tip*	H	**how**	
hothead	VOLCANO	how	QM
h̲ot*head*	H	*how* [far is a] . . .	SAFARI
hotline	EQUATOR, TROPIC	how fast	MPH
hotplate, *say*	FRIARY	[How] *funny*	WHO
hour	H, HR	how *to follow* teams	SIDESHOW
house¹		**Howard**	
house	CO, COT	Howard's End	D
• a royal house	ARCO	Howard's rhyme	COWARDS
• house *in* the street	SCOT	**hug**	
• houses collections	COSSETS	*hug* a . . .	incl A
house	H, HO	*hug* *	incl *
• house *and* home	HONEST	• Pa–t *hugs* son	PAST
• house in good order	HOOK	*hugged by* *	incl in *
• housework	HOOP	• son *hugged by* Pa–t	PAST
house	SEMI	**huge**	
• house colours	SEMITONES	huge	OS
• house insect, *say*	SEMITIC	huge quarry	OSPREY
• house shakes	SEMIQUAVERS	huge cost	EARTH

Letter replaced \c\at; Omit (a); Pointers *out*; Retain a̲; Split B_ED; Down (D); Backwards <or ^

huge *majority*	HUG	• 150 in s–ly . . .	SILLY
	(*see also* large)	• 150 plus 50	ILL
Hugh		• fast 150	LENTIL
Hugh *said* . . .	HEW, HUE	hundred and sixty	T
Hull transport	BOTTOMRY	hundred and fifty thousand	Y
hum		hundred and sixty thousand	T
hum, *say*	DEMISING	hundred thousand LAC, LAKH, P, R, RHO	
humming-*top*(D)	H	hundred thousand pounds	SEYMOUR
human		hundredth	CENTI–
human	MAN	hundredweight	CWT
• human *meets* alien	MANET	Old Hundred	PSALM
human error	MORTAL SIN	**hung**	(*see* hang)
[human] *error*	NAHUM	**Hungary**	
Humberside	NE	Hungarian capital	FORINT
hundred		Hungarian *capital*	H
hundred	C	Hungarian *leader*	H
• 100 I examine	CIVET	Hungarian steps	CZARDAS
• 100 in church	CINCH	Hungary	H
• 100 girls	CLASSES	**hungry**	
• 100 to one	CAN, CI	hungry (=nothing inside)	incl O
	CLONE, CONE	• *hungry* c–at	COAT
• 100 with nothing on	COON	hungry boy	OLIVER
• a hundred	AC	**hunt**	
• centipede	CLIMBS	hunter ACTAEON, ESAU, ORION	
• hundred pound note	CLA–, CLE	hunters lay about	GUNSLINGER
• hundred pounds	CL	hunting area	SHIRE(S)
• hundreds	CC, CS	hunting leopard, *say*	CHEATER
• one hundred	IC	hunting whales, *say*	WA(I)LING
hundred	CENTUM, CENTURY	huntress ARTEMIS, DIANA	
	P, R, RHO	huntsman's drink	CHASER
hundred	TON	**hurl**	
• hundred directions	TONES	*hurled* [spear] PARES, RAPES, SPARE	
• hundred *in* the Home Counties STONE		*hurling* [stone] NOTES, ONSET	
• one hundred	SINGLETON		SETON, TONES
hundred (county division)	CANTRED	**hurry**	
	CANTREF	hurried	RAN
–hundreds	CHILTERN	• hurried *back*<	NAR
hundred and one	CI	• hurried firing	RANSACKING
• 101 fish	CIGARS	• hurried *up*(D)^	NAR
• 101 grave . . .	CISTERN	• *hurried to* the square	RANT
• 101 surgeons	CIVETS	hurry	DART
hundred and four	CIV	• hurry *back*<	TRAD
• 104 I record	CIVILIST	• hurry *up*(D)^	TRAD
• 104 in charge	CIVIC	• hurry *to* the South	DARTS
• 104 with one learner	CIVIL	hurry	NIP
hundred and twenty GREAT HUNDRED		• hurry back<	PIN
	LONG HUNDRED	• hurry *up*(D)^	PIN
hundred and forty nine	CIL	• hurry *to* the East	PINE
hundred and fifty	CL, Y	hurry	RUN
• 150 deliveries	CLOVER	• hurry back<	NUR
• 150 listeners	CLEARS	• hurry *up*(D)^	NUR
• 150 to one	CLAN, CLONE	• hurry *to* the East	RUNE
and		**hurt**	
• a girl *in* 150	CAVIL	*hurt* [pride]	PRIED
• a graduate *in* 150	CABAL	*hurting* [arm]	MAR, RAM
• or one *in* 150	CORAL	**husband**	
hundred and fifty (one-fifty)	IL	husband	H, MAN

Anag [cat]; Any *; Begin IGN–; Endings –ING; eg •; Hidden /cat/; Implied add (on); Implied in (in);

husband and wife	MATES	**hydrant**	
husband of May Queen, *say*	MAKING	hydrant	H
husbandman	CARL	hydro-electricity	FLOWER POWER
hush	SH, ST	**hymns**	AM
husky food	BRAN	**hypocrite**	PECKSNIFF
hybrid		**hypothesis**	
hybrid [animal]	LAMINA, MANILA	**hypoteneuse**	ALONGSIDE
hybrid bacteria, *say*	GERMULE	**hysteria**	
hybrid [tea rose]	ROSEATE	*hysteria* [in the] . . .	THINE
hybridised [roses]	SORES	[spoke] *hysterically*	POKES
hybridising birds, *say*	CROSS-HATCHING		

I

a, an, ane, ay, aye, beam, che, dotted, electric current, ego, eye, in, inde-pendence, independent, individual, institute, iodine, *iota,* island, isle, Italy, *line, lunchtime,* moment of inertia, one, single, *straight line,* square root of -1, ten, ten thousand, *un,* upright, *yours truly*

I¹		I object	ME
I	A, AN, ANE	I offered	IBID
	EGO	I *omitted . . .*	omit I
	SPEAKER, VOWEL	I owe you	IOU
I *abandon . . .*	omit I	I perform afterwards	IDOLATER
I am	IAM, IM	I possess	–IVE
I am *in . . .*	incl IAM, IM	I postpone	IDOLATER
I *am in*	incl I	I prepare a rota	IDOLIST
I am *standing*(D)^	MAI, MI	I *quit*	omit I
I caught	–IC	I rented, *say*	ISLET
I collapse, *say*	ICE-LUMP	I ride a bike, *say*	ICICLE
I come ashore again	IRELAND	I see	–IC, IV
I come ashore, *say*	ISLAND	I see, *say*	ICY
I deceive	ICON	I shall	ILL, ISLE
I defame	ISLANDER	I shout, *say*	ICE-CREAM
I demonstrated	ISATIN(E)	I spotted, *say*	ICE-SAW
I disembark, *say*	ISLAND	I state	–ICAL
I *don't appear in*	omit I	I *take* on . . .	–ION
I don't know mother, *say*	ADENOMA	I trust	INT–
I *escape from . . .*	omit I	I will, *say*	ILL, ISLE
I *get* about	–IC	I *won't be there*	omit I
I *get* on	–ION	**I²**	
I *get out of . . .*	omit I	I am	
I get smaller, *say*	ICE-RINK	–a Conservative	AMATORY
I *go out*	omit I	–a fish	AMID, AMIDE
I had	–IATE	–an essayist	AMELIA
I had	ID(E)	–a fool	AMASS
• I had been ahead	IDLED	–complete	AMUTTER
• time I had, *say*	TIDE	–dead	AMENDED
I have	IVE	–dying	AMENDING
I have *at heart*	incl IVE	–employing	AMUSING
I have left	omit I	–Lamb	AMELIA
I *have* left	IL	–present, *say*	AMEER, AMERE, AMIR
I inform Scot, *say*	ITALIAN	–working late, *say*	AMMONITES
I *intervene*	incl I	I am	
I *leave*	omit I	–a bird	MEAL-ARK
I *left*	omit I	–a building	MESHED
I look ahead, *say*	PHARISEE	–a child	MESON
I *lost*	omit I	–a detective, *say*	MEDICK
I married . . .	IM–	–a fish	METOPE
I note	–IA, –IC, ID, IE, IF	–a mediaeval noble	METHANE
	IRE, –ITE	–a peg, *say*	MEAT-TEA
I notice	–IAD	–a reviver	METONIC

Anag [cat]; Any *; Begin IGN–; Endings –ING; eg •; Hidden /cat/; Implied add (on); Implied in (in);

–a Welsh girl	MESIAN	**idol**	
–an Indian	MEUTE	idol	MAMMET, MAUMET
–Edward	METED		MAWMET, MOMMET
–fly	MEWING	idol, *say*	IDLE, LAZY
–Kenneth, *say*	MEEKEN	idolatry	MAMMETRY
–Sally	MESAL(LLY)	**if**	
–stern	MEGRIM	if it	∧NT
–timid	MESHY	if *old*	AN
I am	IM	**igloo**	BLOCKHOUSE
–a maiden	IMAM	**ignite**	
–a nuisance	IMPEST	ignite	FIRE
–an animal	IMBRUTE	• girl ignited, *say*	MISFIRED
–an attendant	IMPAGE	• ignites joint	FIRESHIP
–chaste	IMPURE	• sack	FIRE
–debarred, *say*	IMBAND	ignites offal	LIGHTS
–old-fashioned	IMPASSE	**ignore**	
–two	IMPAIR	*ignore* a . . .	omit A
–wan	IMPALE	ignore command	SHUN
I³		ignore feast	PASSOVER
I am told your . . .	YORE	*ignore* the odds	omit alternate letters
I *declared*	AY(E), EYE	• (t)r(i)e(d) t(o) *ignore*	
I (dialect)	CHE	*the odds*	RET
I *hear* news	GNUS	*ignore* the odds	omit SP
I *heard*	AY(E), EYE	• *ignoring* the odds in (sp)ort	ORT
I *say*	AY(E)	• jumped *ignoring* the odds	(sp)RANG
I *say*	EYE	*ignore* *	omit *
• I am clean, *say*	EYE-BATH, EYEWASH	• (ac)tress *ignores* bill	TRESS
• I quote, *say*	EYESIGHT	ignorant alien	THICKET
• I rented, *say*	EYELET	**i-issue**	IDEAL
• I witnessed, *say*	EYESORE	**ill**	
I *say*	OPTIC, VOWEL	*ill-advised* [remark]	MARKER
I say nothing	EGO	ill bird, *say*	ILLEGAL
I say you . . .	EWE, U, YEW	*ill-disposed* [sort]	ORTS, ROTS, TORS
I'd *say*	EYED, IDE	*ill-fated* [ship]	HIPS, PISH
I'll burn them, *say*	ALBURNUM	ill feeling, *say*	AGRIMONY
ice		*ill-fitting* [shoe]	HOES, HOSE
ice	HARD WATER	*ill-organised* [trips]	SPIRT, SPRIT
[ice]-*breaking*	CIE	ill *in* b–ed	BILLED
ice-cream, *say*	SUNDAY	ill temper, *say*	BHYLE
icy greeting	HAIL	[ill]-*treated*	LIL
icy rain, *say*	HALE	*ill-treated* [animal]	LAMINA, MANILA
icy, *say*	–IC	*ill-treatment of* [salt-mine]	AILMENTS
icthyology	ICT(H)	[ill]-*used*	LIL
ideal partner	SOUL MATE	*ill*-[used]	DUES, DUSE, SUED
identify		ill-used vehicle	AMBULANCE
identification	ID		INVALID CHAIR, WHEEL-CHAIR
identified in Fren/ch arm/y	CHARM	*ill-written* [verse]	SERVE, SEVER
identify spirit	NAMESAKE	illness	FLU
idiot		• illness better, *say*	FLUE-CURED
idiot breeds	NUTHATCHES	[it goes] *ill*	EGOIST
idiot's headgear	FOOLSCAP	**illegal**	
idle		illegal army	ETA, IRA, PLO
idle head	LOAF	*illegal* [army]	MARY, MYRA
idle, *say*	IDOL, LAYS	**illegitimate**	
idler	DRONE	*illegitimacy of* [male] . . .	LAME, MEAL
idly [stroll]	TROLLS	*illegitimate* [son can] . . .	CANONS

Letter replaced \c\at; Omit (a); Pointers *out*; Retain <u>a</u>; Split B_ED; Down (D); Backwards <or ∧

illiberal

illiberal	omit L
• *illiberal* (l)out	OUT
• *illiberal* regime	RU(l)E

illicit

act *illicitly*	CAT
illicit [affair]	RAFFIA
illicit diamond buying	IDB

illiterate signature	X
illuminated note	LITRE

illusion

illusion of [speed train] . . .	PEDESTRIAN
[optical] *illusion*	TOPICAL

illustrated

illustrated	ILL
• saint illustrated	STILL
illustration	ILL

image

[formed] *image*	DEFORM
image building	PR
image converter	RETINA
image of [Mary]	ARMY, MYRA
imaginary	INFANCY

imbecile

imbecile [can see] . . .	SEANCE
imbecility of [all the] . . .	LETHAL

imbibing

imbibing a . . .	incl A
imbibing *	incl *
• he–r *imbibing* drink	HEALER
imbibed by *	incl in *
• drink *imbibed by* he–r . . .	HEALER

imitate

imitate tenor	TENNER
imitation of male . . .	MAIL
poor *imitation*	PORE

immediate success	WINNOW

immersed

immerse a . . .	incl A
immerse *	incl *
• king *immersed in* study	DERN
immersed	(in) WA–TER
• one *immersed*	WAITER
immersed in wa/ter, m/y . . .	TERM
**immersing*	incl in *
• study *immersing* king	DERN

impair

impaired [speech]	CHEEPS
impairment of [taste]	STATE, TEATS

impecunious American	NOCENT
imperative	IMP

imperfect

imperfect	IMP
imperfect speech	
• fully	FURRY
• kith	KISS

• tree	TWEE
imperfect [tense]	TEENS

imperial

imperial	IMP
imperial measure	THEFT
Imperial Service Order	ISO

impersonal	IMP

impersonate

impersonate insect	AUNT, BE, NAT
impersonating peer	PIER

impetuous rascal	TEARAWAY

implicate

implicate a . . .	incl A
implicate *	incl *
• Ro–n *implicates* master	ROMAN
implicated by *	incl in *
• master *implicated by* Ro–n	ROMAN
implicated in scanda/lous y/arn	LOUSY

import

import a . . .	incl A
import *	incl *
• ship *imports* drug	SPOTS
imported	FAR-FETCHED
imported by *	incl in *
• drug *imported by* ship	SPOTS
imported, *say*	–MENT
Swe/dish ed/itor's *import*	DISHED

important

important	LARGE
• important letter	LARGESS(E)
• important saint	LARGEST
• measure important . . .	ENLARGE
important	MAJOR
• important officer	MAJOR
• important party method	MAJOR-DOMO
• important prison	MAJORCAN
important connection	EARTH

impose

impose on	
indicating one word written	
above another word or letter:	
• cat *imposed on* by a . . . (D)	ATOM
• he *imposes on* the king(D)	HETHER
imposition, *say*	TACKS
impositions, *say*	TAXIS

imposter

imposter	SHAM
• imposter lost blood	SHAMBLED
• imposter *with* drug	SHAME
imposter's [real] . . .	LEAR
[smart] *imposter*	MARTS, TRAMS

impound

impound a . . .	incl A
impound *	incl *
• German soldiers *impound* cow	SCOWS
impounded by sherif/f in	

Anag [cat]; Any *; Begin IGN–; Endings –ING; eg •; Hidden /cat/; Implied add (on); Implied in (in);

d/efault	FIND	in English	–INE
impounded by *	incl in *	• in English ship	–INESS
• cow *impounded by* German		in *French*	EN
soldiers	SCOWS	• in *French* church	–ENCE
impoverished		in G and S	–INGS
impoverished	(in) NE–ED	in Gateshead	–ING
• a king *impoverished*	NEARED	in German *capital*	–ING
• *impoverished* journalist	NEEDED	in hospital	INWARD(S)
impressive		in imagination	INFANCY
impress city	SHANGHAI	in love	INO
impressive marks	EMBOSSING, ETCHING	in one . . .	INA, INI
imprison		in one quarter	–INE, INN, INS–
A/rab bi/d *to imprison* . . .	RABBI	[in or] out	IRON
imprison gangster	INTERNAL	in order, *say*	INTERN(E)
imprisoned	(in) C–AGE, (in) PE–N	in *retirement*<	NI
imprisoned by Fren/ch Arm/y	CHARM	in *return*<	NI
imprisoned by *	incl in *	in rhyme	INVERSE
• American *imprisoned*		in, *say*	INN, PUB
by German soldiers	SUSS	in *some* cas(es)	INCAS
imprisoned in Al/cat/raz	CAT	in *sound*	INN
imprisoning a . . .	incl A	in Spain	–INE
imprisoning *	incl *	in syrup, *say*	INDUCE
• German soldiers		in *the beginning*	INT–
imprisoning American	SUSS	in *the beginning*	start with IN
impromptu		• obtained in *the beginning*	INGOT
impromptu [remark]	MARKER	in *the centre*	incl IN
[quite] *impromptu*	QUIET	• in *the centre of* the	
improper		London area	SINE
improper [remark]	MARKER	in the East	–INE
improperly [made]	DAME, EDAM, MEAD	in *the end*	–INE
improperly dealt with [much] . . .	CHUM	in *the end*	end with IN
improve		• firm in *the end*	COIN
improved [lamp]	PALM	in the Orient	–INE
improvement in [pay]	YAP	in the papers	INQUIRE
improvise		in the pipeline	INDUCT
improvise [tale]	LATE, LEAT, TEAL, TELA	in time	INT–
improvising [ploy]	POLY–	in *turn*<	NI
improvisation [on a set] . . .	ATONES	in turn, *say*	INTERN(E)
in¹	IN	in wheat, *say*	INKHORN
in a class	INFORM	in*turned*<	NI
in a new way	INANE	**in²**	
[in a] *flap*	AIN, –IAN	implying inclusion:	
[in a] *fury*	AIN, –IAN	in can be used to imply	
[in a] *new way*	AIN, –IAN	the inclusion of one word	
[in a] *panic*	AIN, –IAN	or letter in another word, as in	
[in a] *spin*	AIN, –IAN	• retired	(in) B–ED), (in) C–OT
[in a] *novel*	AIN, –IAN	• under canvas	(in) T–ENT
in a way	–INE, INN, INS	and so on: other examples will be found	
in about . . .	INCA	throughout the book under the appropriate	
in another key	INA, IND, –INE, –ING	headword.	
in apple juice, *say*	INSIDER	**in³**	
in autumn	INFALL	indicating an anagram:	
in *capturing*	I–N	*in* [ascent]	STANCE
• i–n *capturing* firm . . .	ICON	*in a bad way* [after red] . . .	RAFTERED
in church	INCE, INCH	*in a blur* [when I] . . .	WHINE
in company	INFIRM	*in a different order*	

Letter replaced \c\at; Omit (a); Pointers *out*; Retain a̲; Split B_ED; Down (D); Backwards <or ^

[but not] . . .	BUTTON	*in* charge	FE–E
in a flap [over] . . .	ROVE	*in* church	C–E, C–H
in a form [that] . . .	TATH	*in* city	E–C, E–LY
in a mess [for us]	FOURS	*in* communist . . .	RE–D, TRO–T
in a muddle [I went] . . .	TWINE	*in* concert	PRO–M
in a tizzy [about] . . .	U-BOAT	*in* conclusion	EN–D
in a way [mad]	DAM	*in* Cornwall	S–W
in action [St Michael] . . .	ALCHEMIST	*in* credit	C–R
in agony [poisoned] . . .	POSEIDON	*in* crib	BE–D, CO–T
in circulation [in the] . . .	THINE	*in* damp environment	D–AMP, WE–T, MO–IST
in confusion [I ran]	RAIN, RANI	*in* death	EN–D
in disarray [his team]	HAMITES	*in* debt	R–ED
in disorder [when I] . . .	WHINE	*in* deep water	MA–IN
in distress [some lad] . . .	DAMOSEL	*in* Devon	S–W
in error [sent] . . .	NETS, STEN, TENS	*in* dictionary	O–ED
in exchange for [lira]	ARIL, LAIR, LIAR	*in* different ways	N–S, WE–S, etc
in form [player]	REPLAY	*in* dismal *environment*	GRA–Y, GRE–Y, SA–D
in motion [it ran] . . .	TRAIN	*in* document	DE–ED, M–S
in need of repair [shoes] . . .	HOSES	*in* doorway	ENTR–Y
in order to [play she] . . .	SHAPELY	*in* drink	AL–E
in poor shape [I cant] . . .	ANTIC	*in* dry . . .	T–T
in ruins of [Rome]	MORE, OMER	*in* dry grass	T–ED
in smithereens [when it] . . .	WHITEN	*in* expensive coat	FU–R
in the guise of [an old] . . .	NODAL	*in* exploit	DE–ED
in the lurch [when I] . . .	WHINE	*in* exposed situation	BAR–E
in the manner of [a Serb]	BARES,	*in* face of . . .	DI–AL
	BEARS	in fact	DE–ED
	BRAES, SABRE	*in* favour	BO–ON
in turmoil [I ran] . . .	RAIN, RANI	*in* fear	AW–E
in⁴		*in* feat	DE–ED
indicating inclusion:		*in* fixed position	SE–T
in 2000	M–M	*in* flight	W–ING
in a certain situation	S–URE	*in* general	LE–E
in a rush	RE–ED	*in* Gilbert & Sullivan	G–S
in a way	A–RD, AS–T, R–D, S–T	*in* gold	O–R
in act	AC–T, DE–ED	*in* grass	S–ING
in action	AC–T, DE–ED	*in* harmony	TU–NE
in agony	PA–IN	*in* hat	LI–D
in agreement	A–Y	*in* heaven	SK–Y
in America	U–S	*in* Holy Writ	N–T, O–T
in American money	C–ENT	*in* Home Counties	S–E
in an attempt	TRI–AL, TR–Y	*in* hospital	WAR–D
in animal	DE–ER	*in* icy clutches	COL–D
in any case	AN–Y	*in* Ireland	E–IRE
in [bad] *shape*	AB–D	*in* Kent	S–E
in bed	B–ED, CO–T, PA–D, S–ACK	*in* large amounts	C–M, M–C, M–M
in bed in France	LI–T	• unknown *in* large amounts	CYM
in camera	SL–R	• article I *found in* large	
in car	R–R, V–W	amounts	MANIC
in Carlisle	N–W	• first-class, *in* large amounts	MAIM
in case		*in* large measure	ROO–D
• a letter *in* m–y *case*	MESSY	*in* lead	P–B
• gun *in case of* ne–ed	NEGATED	*in* legal document	DE–ED
• it *is in* pastry *case*	PITY	*in* Lincoln	AB–E
• provided *in* briefcase	BIFF	*in* London area	S–E
in character	CAR–D	*in* long grass	RE–ED

Anag [cat]; Any *; Begin IGN–; Endings –ING; eg •; Hidden /cat/; Implied add (on); Implied in (in);

in low *surroundings*	MO–O
in Manhattan area	N–Y
in many ways	SN–ES, N–ESE etc
in midw<u>ee</u>k	E–E
in moist conditions	D- AMP, W–ET, MO–IST
in motorcycle race	T–T
in my *case*	M–Y
in need	NE–ED
in Newcastle	N–E
in newspaper	SU–N
in Norfolk town	DIS–S
in olden days	B–C
in opposition	E–W, N–S, S–N, W–E
in order	C–H, OB–E, O–M
in pain	ST–ING
in <u>p</u>astry *case*	P–Y
in performance	DE–ED
in pipe	RE–ED
in plot	BE–D
in port	DE–AL
in prepaid container	SA–E
in prison	C–AGE, CA–N, GA–OL, P–EN
in pub	BA–R, IN–N, LO–CAL
in question	E–H
in raincoat	MA–C
in residence	N–EST
in retirement	B–ED, C–OT
in retreat	DE–N
in Russian	RE–D
in salt water	SE–A
in Second City	MO–NY
in shape	CON–E
in ship	S–S
in ship's clothing	S–S
in silks	BA–R
in silver	A–G
in Slough	BO–G, FE–N
in some circles	O–O
in some ways	N–ESE, W–E, etc
in tall grass	RE–ED
in temporary home	T–ENT
in the afternoon	P–M
in the air	SK–Y
in the *back* row<	EN–IL
in the Bible	N–T, O–T
in the City	E–C, E–LY
in the Civil Service	C–S
in the clutches of *	incl in *
• I'm *in the clutches of* the *French* . . .	LIME
in the cold	I–CE, I–CY
in the desert	SAN–D
in the drink	AL–E, BE–ER, TO–T
in the end	EN–D
in the face	DI–AL
in the fall	R–AIN

in the Fifties	L–L
in the front	FOR–E
in the garden	B–ED
in the grass	RE–ED
in the grip of *	incl in *
• one *in the grip of* a ca–d	CAID
in the heavens	SK–Y
in the King's name	LEA–R
in the last month	DE–C, UL–T
in the lead	P–B
in the long grass	RE–ED
in the main	DE–EP, SE–A
in the market	E–C
in the match	T–EST
in the middle	COR–E
in the money	CO–IN, C–ENT
in the nude	BAR–E
in the open	OVER–T
in the race	T–T, N–ATION
in the rain	WE–T
in the red	R–ED
in the right	LI–EN, THE–R
in the sea	DE–EP, MA–IN
in the ship	S–S
in the snuggery	N–EST
in the street	AV–E, R–D, S–T
in the vessel	S–S
in the way	AV–E, R–D, S–T N–E,
	N–W, S–E, S–W etc
in this era	A–D
in this *case*	THI–S
in time	AG–E, D–ATE, DA–Y, H–R, MI–N
in traffic	DE–AL
in twenty–four hours	DA–Y
in two hundred . . .	C–C
in two thousand	M–M
in two ways	L–L, L–R, R–L, R–R
	N–S, W–E, etc
	ST–ST
in warm clothing	HO–T
in wet conditions	DA–MP, MO–IST
in wintry conditions	COL–D, IC–Y
in writing	M–S
in * *environment*	incl in *
• king *in* t–ough *environment*	TROUGH

in⁵

meaning:
accepted

• father *accepted* at home	PAIN
• mother *at home*	MAIN

at the wicket

• *batting* after tea, *say*	TIN

batting

• champion *batting*	CHIN

belonging to

Letter replaced \c\at; Omit (a); Pointers *out*; Retain <u>a</u>; Split B_ED; Down (D); Backwards <or ^

• *belonging to* party consisting of	INSECT, INSET
• *consisting of* alloy during	INTERNE
• *during* autumn elected	INFALL
• *elected* to seat esoteric	INSTALL
• *esoteric* class fashionable, etc	INFORM, INSECT, INSET
• *trendy* view favoured	INSIGHT
• *favoured* friend governing	INMATE
• staff *governing* member of	RODIN
• *member of* group planted	INSECT, INSET
• *planted* meadow popular	INFIELD
• good man and *popular* smart	STAND-IN
• *smart* group wearing	INSECT, INSET
• *wearing* undergarments well-favoured	INVESTS
• *well-favoured* position	INSTANCE

in⁶

other uses:

in a jam, *say*	BLOCK-TIN
in a manner of speaking, bare	BEAR
in accordance with	SEC
in agreement	ATONE
in all directions	NEWS
in audition (=homophone)	
• *in audition*, I . . .	AY(E), EYE
• *in audition*, tenor . . .	TENNER
• Perry *in audition* . . .	PERI
in banks (=river)	
• *in English banks*	THAMES
• *in French banks*	SEINE
• *in German banks*	RHINE
in bed (=flower, plant, shrub)	
• girl *in bed*	MYRTLE, VIOLA et al
in capacity of	QUA
• *in the capacity of* a daughter	QUAD
• *in the capacity of* a ruler	QUAKING
in-car music, *say*	CARTOONS
in case	IF
in charge	IC
• Duke in charge	FISTIC
• graduates in charge	BASIC
• scholar *and* saint in charge	MASTIC
in connection with	ON, RE
	(*see* about²)
in conversation (=homophone)	

• *in conversation*, mayor . . .	MARE
• Marie *in conversation* . . .	MARRY
in country style (=dialect)	
• grimace *in country style*	MUMP
• *in country style* lunch . . .	TIFT
in court	UP
in debt	BILLOWED, BILLOWING
in every detail (=to a T)	
• past *in every detail*	OVERT
in extremis take . . .	TE
in favour of	FOR
• in favour of charity	FORGIVING
• in favour of the majority, say	FOREMOST
in favour of	PRO
• in favour of leader	PRODUCE
• in favour of timber, *say*	PROLOGUE
in foreign parts (=foreign language)	
• arrive *in foreign parts*	ANKOMMEN
• live *in foreign parts*	VIVRE
• travel *in foreign parts*	VIAJE
• work *in foreign parts*	LAVORO
in full (=expanded abbreviation)	
• do *in full*	DITTO
• do *fully*	DITTO
• *in full* fig	FIGURE
in Gateshead	–ING
in gear	CLOTHED, DRESSED
in German	–ING
in good condition	ASSENT
in hell	DISPLACED
in-house publication	HANSARD
in imagination	INFANCY
in London (=Cockney)	omit H
• (h)ouse *in London*	OUSE
in my direction	TOME
in opposition	V
in other words	SC
in part di/vide/d	VIDE
in place of (=substitution)	
• l\an\e with one *in place of* an . . .	LIE
in place of	VICE
• in place of boy	VICEROY
• in place of sin	VICE
• refusal in place of . . .	NOVICE
in report, he'd . . .	HEED
in retirement<	NI
in retirement, star . . . <	RATS
in retreat, the *German* . . . <	RED
in return<	NI
in short, cannot	CANT
in some parts (=dialect)	
• go astray *in some parts*	MISGO
• *in some parts* favourable . . .	TOWARD
in speech, told . . .	TOLLED

in splendour	POMPON
in su/ch ef/fort	CHEF
in support of	(see support[3])
in talkies, Hugh . . .	HEW, HUE
in talking, I'd . . .	EYED, IDE
in the Black Watch (=Scottish)	
• man in the Black Watch	MON
in the cast	ACTING, ONSET
in the club	ENCEINTE, PREGNANT
in the country (=dialect)	
• in the country crowd	MONG
• wander in the country	STROAM
in the course of	
goin/g over n/ew . . .	GOVERN
in the first instance, she	
was at pains . . .	SWAP
in the Foreign Legion (=French)	
• man in the Foreign Legion	HOMME
in the glens (=Scottish)	
• home in the glens	HAME
in the last month	ULT(IMO)
in the meantime	AD INT(ERIM)
in the middle of total/ly re/d . . .	LYRE
in the nude (=with nothing on)	add O
	add OON
• father in the nude	DADO
• dance in the nude	BALLOON
	(see also with[2])
in the open	ALFRESCO, OUTDOOR
in the past (=old words)	
• bury in the past	INEARTH
• in the past, boxer . . .	PUGIL
in the pub	(see drunk)
in the role of . . .	AS
• in the role of a bird	ASHEN
• in the role of husband	ASH
• in the role of a Scot	ASIAN
in the saddle	UP
in the same place	IB, IBID
in the sticks (=dialect)	
• farm in the sticks	WICK
• in the sticks, a spider . . .	ATTERCOP
in the style of	ALA
in the time of	TEMP(ORE)
in the wrong direction a rat . . . <	TARA
in the year of . . .	AN, ANNO
–(human) salvation	A(H)S
–the flight	AH
–the king's reign	ARR
–the queen's reign	ARR
–the reign . . .	AR
–the world	AM
in (town) (=foreign language)	
• bridge in Paris	PONT
• house in Milan	CASA
• inn in Madrid	POSEDA

• street in Berlin	STRASSE
in turn, say	INTERN(E)
in waterproof clothing	MACON
in what manner	QM
in woman's clothes	DRAGON
inaccurate	
inaccuracy of [shot]	HOTS, TOSH
inaccurate [report]	PORTER
[wrote] inaccurately	TOWER
inane	
inane [laugh in] . . .	HAULING
inane	AN–E
inapplicable	NA
inaugurate	
inaugurating bursary	B
inauguration of scheme	S
incessant	
incessant (=without end)	
• grumble incessantly	MOA(n)
• sin(g) incessantly	SIN
inch	
inch	IN
[inch]	CHINWAG
incipient	
incipient growth	G
incisive treatment	SURGERY
incite	
incite	CIT–E
incite by speech	INSIGHT
incitement, say	PHILIP
include	
included	INC(L)
included in sho/p lea/se	PLEA
included in *	incl in *
• Herb included in group	SHERBET
including a . . .	incl A
including *	incl *
• group including Herb	SHERBET
incognito	
incognito [prince]	PINCER
[king is] incognito	SKIING
income	
income	COM–E
income tax return	REVENUE
incompetent	NOTABLE
incomplete	
incomplete, say	KNOTHOLE
incomplete boo(k)	BOO
incomplete de/liver/ies	LIVER
incomplete volume	BOO(k)
incomprehensible	
incomprehensible [argot]	GROAT
incomprehensible	
language	DOUBLE DUTCH, GREEK
inconclusive	
discus(s) inconclusively	DISCUS

Letter replaced \c\at; Omit (a); Pointers out; Retain a; Split B_ED; Down (D); Backwards <or ^

inconclusive kin(d)	KIN
inconclusive battle	SALAMI(s)
inconsistent	
inconsistency in [speech]	CHEEPS
inconsistent [views]	WIVES
inconsistently [said] . . .	AIDS, DAIS
inconstant	
inconstant [love]	VOLE
[man is] *inconstant*	MAINS
inconvenience	
inconvenienced by [much] . . .	CHUM
[when I] *inconvenienced* . . .	WHINE
incorporate	
incorporate a . . .	incl A
incorporate *	incl *
• South Africa *incorporates* section	SPARTA
incorporated	INC
incorporated by *	incl in *
• section *incorporated by* South Africa	SPARTA
incorporated in hou/se in E/rith	SEINE
incorrect	
*in*correct	(in) R–T, (in) O–K
incorrect [dates]	SATED, STEAD
incorrectly [laid]	DIAL
increase	
increase	GROW
• increase head, *say*	GROCER
• increase *almost all* th(e) . . .	GROWTH
• increase weight, *say*	GROGRAM
increase labour	WAXWORK
increased by a . . .	incl A
increased by one	incl A or I
increased by 100	incl C
increased by *	incl *
• weight *increased by* king	TORN
incredible	
incredible ascent	INDIAN ROPE TRICK
incredible soak	STEEP
indebted	
indebted	(in) R–ED
• Eli *indebted*	RELIED
• *indebted* following . . .	RAFTERED
indecent	
indecent picture	BLUEPRINT
indecent, *say*	RISKY
[pose] *indecently*	PESO
indeed	
*in*deed	AC–T, DE–ED
• companies *indeed* . . .	ACCOST
• *indeed* allowed . . .	DELETED
indefinite	
*in*definite(ly)	SUR–E
indefinite number	N, NO
	X, Y, Z

indefinite [time]	EMIT, MITE
[remain] *indefinitely*	MARINE
independent	IND
Independent Broadcasting Authority	IBA
Independent Labour Party	ILP
Independent Television Authority	ITV
independent worker	FREE HAND
Indian	
Indian	CREE
• Indian food, *say*	CREEPIE(S)
• Indian friend, *say*	CREMATE
• Indian money	CREED, CREEL, CREEP
• Indian name	CROWN
Indian	CROW
• Indian pub	CROWBAR
• Indian's home	CROW'S NEST
Indian	IND
• Indian *and* one man	INDIGENT
• Indian *with* no alternative	INDOOR
• Indian *with* no fast . . .	INDOLENT
Indian	UTE
• Cape Indian	CUTE
• Indian girl	SALUTE
• Indian *in* credit	CUTER
Indian city, *say*	BOMB–BAY
Indian coin, *say*	ROUPY
Indian fashion	FILE
Indian ox, *say*	BILE
Indian station	CASTE
Indian uncle, *say*	PAWNEE
	(*see also* brave)
indicate	
indicate a number, *say*	SIGNATE
indicated horse power	IHP
indicates [where] . . .	HEWER
indicates where	WARE, WEAR
indicative	IND
indirect	
indirect [route]	OUTER, OUTRE
indirect [speech]	CHEEPS
[speak] *indirectly*	PEAKS, SPAKE
indiscriminate	
indiscriminate [sort] . . .	ROTS, TORS
[throw] *indiscriminately* . . .	WORTH
indispose	
[his] *indisposition*	–ISH
indisposed [when I] . . .	WHINE
indistinct	
indistinct [note]	ETON, TONE
[said] *indistinctly*	AIDS, DAIS
individual	
individual	I, ME, ONE, SOLE
individuality	KA
indoor	
*in*door	DO–OR, ENTR–Y
• caught *indo*–or	DOCTOR

Anag [cat]; Any *; Begin IGN–; Endings –ING; eg •; Hidden /cat/; Implied add (on); Implied in (in);

• eat *in*door	ENTREATY
induce	
induced [trance]	NECTAR
inductance	L
indulge	
indulge in *	incl in *
• lieutenant *indulged in* drink	BELTER
industrialist	BEE
inefficient	
*in*efficient	A–BLE
• *in*efficient artist	ARABLE
inefficient	NOTABLE
inefficient Hoover, *say*	SLOVAK
inefficient person	CHARLEY, CHARLIE
inefficiently	NOTABLY
inept	
inept [player]	REPLAY
ineptly [sung]	GNUS, GUNS, SNUG
[spoke] *ineptly*	POKES
inexperienced	
inexperienced driver	CARL
inexperienced footballers	GREENBACKS
infantry	
infantry	FOOT
• infantry dance	FOOTBALL
• infantry march	FOOTSTEP
• powerful infantry	HOTFOOT
infantry	INF, PBI
infantry instructions	MARCHING ORDERS
infectious disease	ID
inferior	
inferior	B
inferior	BAD
• inferior china	BADMINTON
• inferior drug	BADE
• son in inferior . . .	SINBAD
inferior	POOR
• inferior journalist, *say*	PO(U)RED
• inferior key, *say*	PORKY
• inferior ring, *say*	PO(U)RING
inferior	SUB
• inferior position	SUBSTANCE
• inferior sailor	SUBMARINE
• inferior writer	SUBSCRIBE
inferior	UNDER
• inferior *in* ship	SUNDERS
• inferior novelist	UNDERWRITER
• like inferior . . .	ASUNDER
inferior cow	LOWER
inferior horse	ROSINANTE, TIT
infest	
infested by a . . .	incl A
infested by *	incl *
• Paul *infested by* insect	PANTRY
* *infesting*	incl *
• infested with insects, *say*	MIGHTY

• insect *infesting* Paul	PANTRY
infiltrate	
infiltrate *	incl A
infiltrated by a . . .	incl A
infiltrated by *	incl *
• c–amp *infiltrated by* fifty . . .	CLAMP
infinite	
infinite (=unending)	
• *infinite* tim(e)	TIM
• *infinitely* wealthy	–RIC(h)
infinitive	INF
inflate	
inflated (=containing air)	
• company *after inflation*	CAIRO
• *inflated* afterthought	PAIRS
inflow	
inflow	F–LOW
inform	
inform	GRASS, SQUEAL
inform, *say*	TALON
information	GEN
• information about . . .	GENRE
• information *found in* old	
city square	URGENT
information office	COI
information technology	IT
information unit, *say*	BIGHT, BITE
informer	GRASS, NOSE, SQUEALER
informs, *say*	TELSON
informal shirt	T
infuriate	
infuriated [master]	REMAST, STREAM
infuriating [leer he] . . .	REHEEL
infuriatingly [smug]	GUMS, MUGS
ingest	
ingest a . . .	incl A
ingest *	incl *
• m–an *ingested* drug	MEAN
ingenious	
[act] *ingeniously*	CAT
ingenious [idea]	AIDE
ingredient	
ingredient of s/orb/et	ORB
ingredients of [pie]	EPI–, –IPE
inhabit	
inhabitant of wo/od in/Norway	ODIN
inhabits fla/t in Ge/rmany	TINGE
inhale	
inhale a . . .	incl A
inhale *	incl *
• h–e *inhaled* oxygen	HOE
inharmonious	
inharmonious [airs]	SAIR, SARI
[sung] *inharmoniously*	GUNS, SNUG
inherent	
inherent in mo/st Et/hiopians	STET

Letter replaced \c\at; Omit (a); Pointers *out*; Retain <u>a</u>; Split B_ED; Down (D); Backwards <or ^

inhibit

inhibit a . . .	incl A
inhibit *	incl *
• woman *inhibits* fine . . .	EVOKE
inhibited by t/he r/ules	HER
inhibited by *	incl in *
• chant *inhibited by* h–er	HOMER

inhuman

inhuman	ANIMAL, BEASTLY
in[human]	NAHUM

initial

initial combination	ACRONYM
initial letters	SIGNPOST
Initial Teaching Alphabet	ITA
initially deficient	omit 1st letter
initially they . . .	T
initially they were only . . .	TWO

initiate

commercial *initiate*	C
initiate scheme	S
initiating doctrine	D
initiative to start	S

inject

inject a . . .	incl A
inject *	incl *
• *inject* nitrogen *into* bo–y	BONY
inject drug	incl E
* *injected with*	incl in *
• bo–y *injected with* nitrogen	BONY
injection	JAB, TAB

injure

injured [parties]	PIASTRE
injuring [arm]	MAR, RAM
injury to [horse]	SHORE
ink slinger	OCTOPUS

inland

inland	OFFSHORE
*in*land	LAN–D
Inland Revenue	IR, TAXMAN

inmate

*in*mate	M–ATE
in[mate]	MEAT, TAME, TEAM
inmate of c/ell en/gaged in . . .	ELLEN

innate

innate in so/me Et/thiopians	MEET
innate part of Am/erica/n . . .	ERICA

innards

a/nim/al's *innards*	NIM
innards of com/put/er	PUT

inner

inner chamber, *say*	CELLAR, SELLA, SELLER
Inner Circle	BULL('S-EYE), GOLD, RED
inner circle	incl O
• line *with inner* circle	ROY
• test *inner* circle	MOOT
inner elements of	

reac/tor que/nched	TORQUE
inner part of city	IT
inner parts	ART
inner roof, *say*	SEALING
inner tube	CIRCLE LINE
	ENTERON, INTESTINE
innkeeper	BONIFACE

innovate

[act] *innovatively*	CAT
innovation [made] . . .	DAME, EDAM, MEAD
innovative [idea]	AIDE
inoffensive figures	MILD

inordinate

inordinate [praise]	PERSIA
inordinately [weak]	WAKE

insane

insane [despot]	POSTED
insanely [rages]	GEARS
insanity [plea]	LEAP, PALE, PEAL

inscribe

inscribe a . . .	incl A
inscribe *	incl *
• *inscribe* name *in* 100 ha–ts	CHANTS

insect

insect	ANT
• insect biting	ANTACID
• insect *impersonator*	AUNT
• insect persecution	ANTABUSE
insect	BEE
• insect bites	BEESTINGS
• insect *given* name	BEEN
• insect *impersonator*	B, BE
insect	BUG
• insect damage	BUGLOSS
• insect drinks . . .	BUGGINS
• noise of insect	HUMBUG
insect	GNAT
• insect *impersonator*	NAT
• insect *returns*<	TANG
insect	TICK
• at insect's . . . , *say*	ATTICS
• insect in front	TICKLED
• second insect	STICK
insect breeding establishments, *say*	MOTHERY, NATTERY
insect dances	MOTH-BALLS
insect egg, *say*	KNIT
insect-*free*	omit FLY
• (f)air(ly) insect-*free*	AIR
insect hangover	BEETLE
insect, *say*	AUNT, BE, MIGHT, NAT
insecticide	DDT
insect's mouth parts, *say*	TROPHY

insecure

insecure [door]	ROOD
insecurity of [tenure]	RETUNE

Anag [cat]; Any *; Begin IGN–; Endings –ING; eg •; Hidden /cat/; Implied add (on); Implied in (in);

[tied] *insecurely*	DIET, EDIT, TIDE	• inspect stomach, *say*	CERUMEN
insert		inspect closely, *say*	STAIRWELL
insert in document, *say*	TIE-PIN	inspected dossier	SAWFILE
inserted in docum/ent Eric/ . . .	ENTERIC	inspection chamber	CONSULTING ROOM
inset		inspector	HMI
inset	SE–T	inspects	SEES
in[set]	–EST, TES	• boy inspects	LESSEES
inside		and	
inside	LE–G, L–T, O–N	• inspects drink, *say*	SEA-SWINE
	S–IDE, R–T	• inspects fingertips	SEA-SNAILS
• *inside* left	SLIDE	• inspects fish, *say*	SEASIDE
in[side]	DIES, IDES	**inspiring**	
inside left	L–T, POR–T	inspiring group	MUSES, NINE
• very large *inside*-left	LOST	inspiring passage	BRONCHIOLE, BRONCHUS
• ten *inside* left . . .	PORTENT	**install**	
inside left	incl L	*install* a . . .	incl Λ
• footballer, *inside*-left	BLACK	*install* *	incl *
inside man	PRISONER	• *installed* king *in* state	CARL
inside out	incl in OU–T	*installed in* re/gal a/partment	GALA
• bend *inside* ou–t	OUST	instalment system	HP
inside out	incl OUT	**instant**	
• about *inside* out	ROUTE	instant	INST
inside right	R–T	instant	MO
• holes *inside* right . . .	ROOT	• instant assault	MOONSET
inside right	incl R	• instant tea	MOCHA
• child *inside* right . . .	TROT	instant	SEC
inside t/he Ar/ctic	HEAR	• *after* an instant, worker . . .	SECANT
inside *	incl in *	• equal instant	PARSEC
• measure *inside* crate	CREMATE	instant	TICK
is *inside*	incl IS	• instant credit	TICK
• old fiddle is *inside*	GUISE	• second instant	STICK
insolvent	(in) R–ED	instant assessment	SECOND RATE
inspect		**instead**	
inspect	EYE	*instead*	STEA–D
• inspect ship	EYE-LINER	• me *instea*–d	STEAMED
• inspect molar	EYE-TOOTH	*in*[stead]	DATES, SATED
• inspects mineral	EYESORE	**instinct**	ID
inspect	SCAN	**institute**	
• inspect bonds	SCANTIES	Institute/Institution of	
• inspect junction	SCANT	–Actuaries	IA
• union inspects . . .	TUSCANS	–Advanced Motorists	IAM
inspect	SEE	–Bankers	IB
• inspect corpses, *say*	SEEDED	–Building	IOB
• inspect cut	SEE-SAW	–Civil Engineers	ICE
• inspect porcelain	SEEMING	–Contemporary Artists	ICA
and		–Journalists	IOJ
• inspect coins, *say*	SERIALS	–Linguists	IL
• inspect island, *say*	SECRETE	–Mining and Metallurgy	IMM
• inspect vegetable, *say*	SECALE	–Municipal Engineers	IMUNE
and		–Physics	IP
• inspect drink, *say*	SEAPORT	–Practitioners in Advertising	IPA
• inspect porcelain, *say*	SEAMING	**instruct**	
• inspect telephone, *say*	SEARING	instructed	TAUGHT
and		• instructed a number, *say*	TAUTEN
• inspect corpses, *say*	CEDED	• instructed a woman, *say*	TAUTER
• inspect fish, *say*	CEILING	• instructed, *say*	TAUT

Letter replaced \c\at; Omit (a); Pointers *out*; Retain <u>a</u>; Split B_ED; Down (D); Backwards <or ^

instructing team	COACHWORK	interchangeable	
instructs snooker player	TRAINSPOTTER	indicating substitution:	
insufficient		• *interchangeable* ends	
insufficient money	SHORTBREAD	of \l\eve\r\	REVEL
insufficiently appreciated	UNDERFELT	• \m\ate\s\ *with*	
insure		*interchangeable* ends	SATEM
insurance premium, *say*	PROLIFERATE	**interest**	INT
*in*sure	SUR–E	interest	INT
*in*sure	TAKE COVER	• interest *in* writing	MINTS
*in*sured	SUR–ED	• interest *on* pound	LINT
• horse *in*sured	SURMOUNTED	**interfere**	
intake		interfere, *say*	MEDAL
in[take]	KATE, TEAK	*interfere with* [car]	ARC
intake a . . .	incl A	*interference with* [signal I] . . .	SAILING
intake *	incl *	**interior**	
• he–r beer *intake*	HEALER	interior	INT
• w–e have an *intake*	WANE	*interior of* Am/eric/a	ERIC
integer		*interior* o/f Ame/rica	FAME
integers	Z	*interior of* *	incl in *
integral	INT	• horse *in interior of* be-ar	BEGGAR
integral part of mo/tor c/ar	TORC	interior views	X-RAYS
integrated circuit	IC	**interject**	
intellectual games	MARBLES	*interject* a . . .	incl A
intelligence		*interject* *	incl *
intelligence	MI, NI	• "Pla–n", I *interjected*	PLAIN
intelligence department	ID, MI, NI	**interminable**	
intelligence factor	NEWSAGENT	*interminable* journey	TRI(p)
intelligence group	CID	rod(e) *interminably*	ROD
intelligence operation	COGITATION	**intermittent**	
	THINKING	*intermittent signs of* <u>measles</u>	MALE
intelligence quotient	IQ	<u>painted</u> *intermittently*	ANE
intelligence, *say*	WHIT	**intern**	
intend		*intern* a . . .	incl A
*in*tend	TEN–D	*intern* *	incl *
in[tend]	DENT	• Hu–ns *intern* mother	HUMANS
intended	FIANCE(E), –MENT	*interned by* *	incl in *
*in*tent	T–ENT	• mother *interned by* Hu–ns	HUMANS
in[tent]	NETT	**internal**	
inter		internal combustion engine	ICE
inter	BURY	*internal to* househ/old	
inter	T–ER	est/ablishment	OLDEST
in[ter]	–ERT, RET, TRE	*internally* a . . .	incl A
inter alia	AL–IA	*internally* *	incl *
[*inter*]-*reaction*	NITRE, TRINE	• carrier *with internal* skin	BASKING
inter, *say*	BERRY	**international**	
inter-state	BERRY	International	
inter-state	AVE–R, C–AL, SA–Y,	–Bank	BIS
inter them, *say*	BARIUM	–Development Association	IDA
interred, *say*	BERRIED	–Electrotechnical Commission	IEC
intercept		–Finance Corporation	IFC
intercept a . . .	incl A	–Labour Organisation	ILO
intercept *	incl *	–Monetary Fund	IMF
• sh–ot *intercepted by*		–Olympic Committee	IOC
everyone	SHALLOT	–Organisation for Standardisation	ISO
interchangeable		–Phonetic Alphabet	IPA
[*inter*]*changeable*	INERT, NITRE, TRINE	–Publishers' Association	IPA

Anag [cat]; Any *; Begin IGN–; Endings –ING; eg •; Hidden /cat/; Implied add (on); Implied in (in);

–Publishing Corporation	IPC	• *interview* reserves	SETAE
–Rail Transport	TIF	**interweave**	
–Road Transport	TIR	*interweave* [cane]	–ANCE
–Social Services	ISS	[inter]*woven*	NITRE, TRINE
–Subscriber Dialling	ISD	*interwoven* [mesh]	HEMS, SHEM
–Telecommunications Union	ITU	**into**	
–Trade Organisation	ITO	*into* a mess [I ran]	RAIN, RANI
–Vehicle Registration	IVR	*into* [town]	WONT
international	CAP	*into* hospital	TOWARD(S)
• deceives international . . .	FOOLSCAP	pop *into*	incl PA
• international award	CAP	• pop *into* Pole's . . .	SPAN
• international drug	CAPE	run *into*	incl R
international	INT	• run *into* f–og	FROG
international banker	GNOME	see *into*	incl C
international organisation	UN	• see *into*, s–oon	SCOON
international unit	IU	turn *into*	incl GO
interpolate		• turn *into* a–ny . . .	AGONY
Interpolate a . . .	incl A	**intoxicated**	
interpolate *	incl *	*intoxicated* [by all] . . .	BALLY
• doctor *interpolating*		*intoxication* of [men at] . . .	MANET
figure is . . .	LIMBS		MEANT
interpose		**intricate**	
interpose a . . .	incl A	*intricacy* of [plot I] . . .	PILOT
interpose *	incl *	*intricate* [design]	SIGNED
• *interpose* it *in* directions	SITE(S)	**intrigue**	
interpret		*intriguing* [idea]	AIDE
interpret [Norse] . . .	NOSER, SNORE	[nasty] *intrigue*	TANSY
interpretation of [Pali]	PAIL	**intrinsic**	
interpreter	INT	*intrinsically* hone/st	
interrupt		and s/sane	STANDS
interrupted by a . . .	incl A	s/he w/as *intrinsically* . . .	HEW
interrupted by *	incl *	**introduce**	
• hundreds *interrupted by* shout	CHIC	introduce force	ENTERPRISE
interrupting *	incl in *	*introduced to* *	incl in *
• shout *interrupting* hundreds	CHIC	• man *introduced to* woman	SUEDE
intersect		*introducing* a . . .	incl A
intersect *	incl in *	*introducing* *	incl *
• many *intersect* pat–h	PATCH	• girl *introducing* man	SUEDE
[inter]*section*	INERT, NITRE, TRINE	*introductions* to n̲ew o̲wner	NO
intertwined		introductory letters	INITIALS
intertwined [coil]	–OLIC	**intruding**	
intertwining [arms]	MARS, RAMS	*intruding into* *	incl in *
intervene		• one *intruding into* party	COIN
intervention of a . . .	incl A	**invade**	
intervention of *	incl *	*invaded* by a . . .	incl A
• *intervention* of men		*invaded* by *	incl *
in this *French* . . .	CEMENT	• ship *invaded by* lice	SLICES
• student *intervenes in* b–est . . .	BLEST	*invaded by* fier/ce de/mons	CEDE
interview		*invading* Ameri/can ter/ritory	CANTER
interview	SEE	*invading* *	incl in *
• interview royalty	SEEKING	• lice *invading* ship	SLICES
• interview servant	SEEPAGE	**invalid**	
• interview thousands	SEEMS	*invalid* [claim]	MALIC
interview	(in) SE–E	*invalidly* [claimed]	DECIMAL, DECLAIM
• in *interview*	SEINE		MEDICAL
• *interview* king	SERE	**invariably**	EER

invent		Irish sailors	CORKSCREW
invent plant	MINT	Irish team	DOWNSIDE
invented	INV	Irish warder	CORKSCREW
invented [a thing] . . .	HATING	Irishman, *say*	WRYLY
invention of [plane]	PANEL	**iron**	
inventor	EDISON	iron	DECREASE
invert		iron	CLUB
inversion of part(D)^	TRAP	iron bed	CLUBBED
inversion of [sense]	ESSEN	• ironworker	CLUBMAN
invert parts(D)^	STRAP	iron	FE
inverted cheese(D)^	MADE	• gold *and* iron	ORFE
invest		• iron *in* loa–d	LOAFED
invest a . . .	incl A	• iron lady	FEDORA
invest *	incl *	• iron man	FETED, FEMALE
• mother's *investing* £50	MALLS	iron bird	GOOSE
invested in sha/res t/oday	REST	iron*bound*	(in) F–E
invested in *	incl in *	• iron*bound* curve	FARCE
• £50 *invested in* mother's . . .	MALLS	iron*clad*	(in) F–E
invests at this place, *say*	BANKSIA	• American iron*clad*	FUSE
invisible		iron	PRESS
* *invisible*	omit *	• engineers have iron	REPRESS
• biscuit that is *invisible*	COOK(ie)	• ironworkers	PRESSMEN
• val(is)e is *invisible*	VALE	iron hand	LAUNDRY WORKER
invite		Iron Lady	MAGGIE
invite round	COURT CIRCULAR	iron rations	HARD TACK, STAPLE DIET
invitation	CARD	ironmonger	SCRAP MERCHANT
invitation, *say*	OAKUM	Ironside	EDMUND
invitation to entertain	DOSING	ironside	HARDLINER, HARDSHIP
invoice	INV	ironwork DECREASING, EVENING, PRESSING	
involve		**irregular**	
involved in sc/hem/e	HEM	*irregular* [army]	MARY, MYRA
involved in *	incl in *	*irregular* [verb], English	BREVE
• me *involved in* state	CAMEL	*irregularity of* [line]	LIEN, NEIL, NILE
involved [me in] . . .	MIEN, MINE	*irregularly* [formed]	DEFORM
involving a . . .	incl A	**irreversible letter of credit**	ILC
involving [much] . . .	CHUM	**irritate**	
involving *	incl *	irritability, *say*	BHYLE
• state *involving* me	CAMEL	irritate	PIQUE
inward		• irritate insect, *say*	PIQUANT
inward	HOSPITALISED	• irritate ruler, *say*	PEAKING, PEEKING
in[wards]	DRAWS, SWARD	• irritated, *say*	PEAKED, PEEKED
Iran		irritate(D)^	BUR
[Iran]	RAINMAKER, RAINSTORM	irritate animal	BUGBEAR
Ireland	EIRE, ERIN, EMERALD ISLE	*irritated* [these] . . .	SHEET
	GREEN ISLE, IR, IR(E)L	irritates nose	TROUBLESHOOTER
Irish		*irritation of* [horse's] . . .	SHORES
Irish	IR	**is**	IS
Irish banker	SHANNON	is *about*<	SI
Irish capital	PUNT	is *about*	I–S
Irish *capital*	I	is *absent*	omit IS
Irish capitalist	DUBLINER	is *ahead of* time	–IST
Irish clergyman, *say*	REVERSE	is English	–ISE
Irish *flower*	SHANNON	is *forgotten*	omit IS
Irish house	DAIL	• lift is *forgotten*	HO(is)T
Irish *leader*	I	is *found in* . . .	incl IS
Irish police-chief	RUCKING	• is *found in* poem	EPISODE

Anag [cat]; Any *; Begin IGN–; Endings –ING; eg •; Hidden /cat/; Implied add (on); Implied in (in);

is *French*	EST	Isle of Man	GBM, IOM
is *German*	IST	Isle of Wight	IOW, IW
is *given* Eastern . . .	–ISE	isle, *say*	AISLE, I'LL
is hard	–ISH	islet	LEASED, TENANTED
is hot	–ISH	our islands	GB
is *in France*	EST	this island	UK
is *in Germany*	IST	**isle**	(*see* island)
is *in Spain*	ES	**issue**	
is *in* time	DAISY	issue	CHILD(REN), LITTER, SON
is leased	ISLET	*issue* [shares]	SHEARS
is married	–ISM	**it**	
is no . . .	ISO–	it	SA, T
is nothing	ISO–	*it appears* plain	PLANE
is prosecuted	ISSUED	it is	–ITIS, TIS
is *removed*	omit IS	(i)t is *short*	T
• hagg(is) is *removed* . . .	HAGG	*it might be* great	GRATE
is rented	ISLET	*it might be* [great]	GRATE, TARGE
is *Spanish*	ES	*it sounds like* rain	REIGN, REIN
is square	–IST	*it turns out* [fine]	NIFE
is *taking* time	–IST	[it's] *broken*	–IST, SIT, TIS
is the *first*	–IST	[it's] *free*	–IST, SIT, TIS
is²		[it's] *Greek*	–IST, SIT, TIS
Is he able? *say*	CANNY	it's hot, *say*	SWARM
Is he obliged? *say*	MUSTEE, MUSTY	it's not a bird	SNOWBIRD
is not	AINT, ANT	it's not footwear	SNOWSHOE(S)
is not *commonly* . . .	AINT, ANT	it's not, *say*	SNOT, TAINT
is not [considerate]	DESECRATION	It's [Not] *Unusual*	TON
Is the girl able?	CANADA	it's not your, *say* . . .	TAINTURE
Isaiah	IS(A)	it's nothing, *say*	SNOUT
island		[it's] *rough*	–IST, SIT, TIS
island	AIT, EYOT, I, INCH	*it's said* you . . .	EWE, YEW
	IONA, MONA	[it's] *unusual*	–IST, SIT, TIS
island	CAPRI	[it's] *wrong*	–IST, SIT, TIS
• island crop	CAPRICORN	**Italy**	I
island	COS	**Italian**	
• island group	COSSET	Italian	AUSONIAN, EYETI(E), EYTIE
• island unknown	COSY	Italian	IT
island	CRETE	• Italian *and* English share	ITERATION
• princess's island	DISCRETE	• Italian church	ITCH
• study island	CONCRETE	• Italian letters	ITEMS
island	ELBA	Italian	ROMAN
• island *retreat<*	ABLE	• Italian *and* Scot	ROMANIAN
island	HERM	• Italian church	ROMANCE
• island goddess	HERMAPHRODITE	• Italian capitalist	ROMAN
• island with *German, say*	HERMIT	• Italian insect, *say*	ROMANTIC
island	IS	Italian banker	TIBER etc
• island occupied	ISLET	Italian *capital*	I
• islands	ISIS	Italian capital	EURO, LIRA
island	MAN	Italian *flower*	TIBER etc
• first island	FOREMAN	Italian *leader*	I
• island bird	MANDRAKE	Italian linesman	DANTE
• island *with* unknown . . .	MANY	*Italian-speaking* boy	RAGAZZO
island edge	INCH	Italian way	AUTOSTRADA
island king	SOLOMON	**item**	
islands, *say*	PHARAOHS	item of make-up	CHROMOSOME, GENE
Isle of Dogs	NEWFOUNDLAND	*item in* news/pap/er	PAP

itemise [all the] . . .	LETHAL	**Ivory Coast**	CI
Ivan		**ivy**	
[Ivan] *the Terrible*	VAIN	ivy *maybe* . . .	CREEPER
makes [Ivan] . . .	VAIN	ivy, *say*	IV

J

curve, heat, Jack, Japan, *jay*, *joint*, joule, journal, judge, justice, *knave*, one, pen, spin quantum number, square root of -1

Jack

Jack	J, KITTY, KNAVE
Jack's wedding	UNION
	(*see also* sailor)

jacket

jacket	REEFER
jacket, *say*	REFER
jade	YU
jagged	
jagged [scar]	ARCS, CARS
[made] *jagged*	DAME, EDAM, MEAD
jailed	(in) C–AGE, (in) CA–N,
	(in) PE–N
Jamaica	JA
James	
James	JAS
James	JIM
• James is working	JIMSON
• Jim, can I? *say*	GYMKHANA
jammed cylinder	SWISS ROLL
January	JAN
Japan	J, NIPPON, VARNISH
Japanese	
Japanese	JAP
Japanese capital	YEN
Japanese *capital*	J
Japanese *leader*	J
Japanese palace, *say*	DAIRY
Japanese purchaser	YEN
jaunt	
jaunt [in Wye]	WINEY
[stride] *jauntily*	DIREST, DRIEST
jay	J
jazz	
jazz	TRAD
• jazz queen	TRADER
• jazzman	TRADED
jazz fan	CAT
jazz figure	RIFF
jazzy [coat]	ATOC, TACO
jeer	
jeer leader	BOOKING
jeer *leader*	J
jeers, *say*	BOOZE

jelly

jellied	SET
jellied [eel]	LEE
jelly	GELIGNITE, SHAPE
jenny	
Jennifer, *say*	DONKEY-SKIN
Jenny Hill, *say*	GENITOR
jenny, *say*	ASSESS
jerk	
jerking [rein]	RINE
jerking, *say*	JACKET
jerky [stride]	DIREST, DRIEST
[speak] *jerkily*	PEAKS, SPAKE
[tear]-*jerking*	RATE, TARE
Jerry	
Jerry's (=German)	
• for *Jerry's* . . .	FUR
• *Jerry's* house	HAUS
• with *Jerry's* . . .	MIT
Jersey	
Jersey	GBJ
Jersey, *say*	COW
	PULLOVER
Jesus	IHC, IHS, JC, JHC
	(*see also* Christ)
jet	
jet	BLACK
• jet flier	BLACKBIRD
• jet pilot	BLACK FLY
• jetstream	BLACKBURN
• *see* jet land	BLACK COUNTRY
jet flier	CROW, RAVEN, ROOK
jet set	AIR CREW
jetstream	HIGH WIND
jewelry	
jewelry	PASTE
• jewelry catalogue	PASTELIST
• jewelry lines, *say*	PASTRY
Jewish	(*see* Hebrew)
jilt	
jilted [Delia]	AILED
[she was] *jilted*	WASHES
jittery	
jittery [leader]	DEALER

Letter replaced \c\at; Omit (a); Pointers *out*; Retain <u>a</u>; Split B_ED; Down (D); Backwards <or ^

jittery *leader*	J	**jolly**	
[she was] *jittery*	WASHES	jolly	MARINE, RM
j-jaguar	JOUNCE	• a jolly old fellow	ARMAGEDDON
Joan's friend	DARBY	• in jolly style	ALARM
job		• laugh *and have* jolly . . .	HARM
job description	PATIENT	jolly fellow	ROGER
job-finder	DEVIL, SATAN	**jolt**	
job in the theatre	OPERATING, SURGERY	*jolted* [arm]	MAR, RAM
jockey		*jolting* [blow 'e] . . .	ELBOW, BELOW
jockey's lawyers	SILKS	**Jonathan's bearer**	APPLE-TREE
Joe's double	GIGI	**Jordan**	HKJ
jogging		**jostle**	
jogger	PROMPT(ER)	jostle boat	BARGE
jogging [arm]	MAR, RAM	*jostle* [master]	REMAST, STREAM
[the pony is] *jogging*	HYPNOTISE	*jostling* [elbow]	BELOW
John		**joule**	J
John	JNO	**journalist**	ED
John's place	GAUNT	**journey**	
join		journey after dark, *say*	NITRIDE
join a chief	ACID	journey *by* road	TRIPLANE
join	SEAM	journey shared	GO-BETWEEN
• join an . . .	SEAMAN	journey's end	DESTINATION
• join forces	SEAMSTRESSES	Journey's End	Y
join an orchestra	ALSO	journeyman	GULLIVER, ODYSSEUS
joined forces	INTERPOL	**joy**	
joined in son/g at E/aster	GATE	joyful cry	IO
joined, *say*	TIDE	joyous hoot, *say*	HOOP
joined sect	INCULT	**judge•**	
joiner	AND, HYPHEN	judge	HEAR
	DOWEL, STAPLE	• judge aboard ship	SHEARS
	SNUG	• judge man	HEARKEN
joining in cele/brat/ion	BRAT	• second judge	SHEAR
joining together, *say*	TEEMING	judge	J
joining train	BOARDING SCHOOL	judge	REF
joint	CO–	• judge Indians	REFUTES
–at this point	COHERE	• judge not well	REFILL
–friend	COMATE, COPAL	• judge took advantage	REFUSED
–ruler	COKING	judge instrument	RECORDER
–support	COBRA, COPIER	judge, *say*	GAGE
joint	D!VE, ELBOW	judge's chauffeur	MASTER OF THE ROLLS
joint	KNEE	judge's condition	SOBER, SOBRIETY
• joint fish	KNEELING	Judges	JUD(G)
joint	REEFER	**judo expert**	DAN
joint, *say*	REFER	**juggle**	
joint	SEAM	*juggle* [plates]	PALEST, PETALS, PLEATS,
• joint help	SEA-MAID		STAPLE
• joint, *say*	SEEM	*juggling* [rings, I]	RISING
joint cleaners	KNUCKLEDUSTERS	**July**	JUL
joint guardian	PATELLA	**jumble**	
Joint Matriculation Board	JMB	*jumble* [sale]	ALES, LEAS, SEAL
joke		*jumbled* [letters]	SETTLER
joke mildly	PUNGENTLY	**jumbo pilot**	MAHOUT
joke, *say*	JESSED	**jump**	
joker	RAGMAN	jump aboard, *say*	NIPPON
jokingly ingest . . .	(in) J–EST	*jump* [over]	ROVE
jokingly, *say*	INGEST	*jump over* *	incl *

Anag [cat]; Any *; Begin IGN–; Endings –ING; eg •; Hidden /cat/; Implied add (on); Implied in (in);

• h–e *jumps over* a street	HASTE	junior common room	JCR
jump t̲o̲ *conclusions*	PO	junior minister	CURATE
jump through	HOPPER	**junk food**	TRIPE
jump up		**just**	
• dog *jumps up*(D)^	GOD	*just a bit of* bro/ken t/ableware	KENT
jump well	SPRING	just a piano	UPRIGHT
jumped aboard, *say*	LEPTON	just blond	FAIR
jumper CRICKET, FLEA, KANGAROO,		just characters	FOUR MEN
JERSEY, PULLOVER,		• just characters, *say*	FOREMEN
PARACHUTIST, PARATROOPER		just fine	FAIR
• jumper store	FLEA MARKET	• just line, *say*	PHARAOH
jumper fastener	FROG	• just *the reverse*	UNFAIR
jumping [bean]	BANE	just water	MERE
jumping deer<	REED	just words SENTENCE, VERDICT	
jumpy soldier	PARA(TROOPER)	**justice**	
jumpy [soldier]	SOLIDER	justice	FREEZING
junction			J
junction	T		SHALLOW
junction of a line	ALINE	Justice's clerk	JC
square junction	TT	Justice of the Peace	JP
June	JUN	**Jutes**	SACK RACE
jungle queen	FORESTER	**juvenile**	
junior		juvenile game	KIDNAP
junior	JUN(R), JR	juvenile *lead*	J

K

Boltzmann's constant, carat, conductivity, constant, dissociation constant, kacha, kalium, Kampuchea, kangha, kaon, kappa, kara, karat, kay, *Kay*, kelvin, kesh, Khmer Republic, kilo, kina, king, Kirkpatrick, kirpan, knight, Köchel, krona, krone, kwacha, *monarch*, Mozart's works, potassium, radius of gyration, Scarlatti's works, thousand, twenty (thousand), two-hundred and fifty, velocity constant, vitamin

K9	CANINE
kale	KL
kaleidoscope	
kaleidoscope of [scenes 'e] . . .	ESSENCE
kaleidoscopic [lights]	SLIGHT
kangaroo	
kangaroo	JOEY
kangaroo	ROO
• kangaroo boss, *say*	ROOKING
• kangaroo burrow	ROOPIT
kappa	K
Kay	K
Kayo	LADY-LOVE
keel	
keeling over, Ben . . .<	NEB
sloop *keels over*<	POOLS
keen	
keen cricket side	CRY OFF
keen on	INTO
keen on something, *say*	MADONNA
keen, *say*	EAGRE
keener	NIOBE
keep	
keep burning, *say*	BLAZON
keep commission	RETAIN
keep flying	NEVER-NEVER-LAND
keep healthy	BEFIT
keep in	GATE
• keep in job	GATEPOST
keep playing	ACTON, BATON
keep going	DRAGON
keep notice	OBSERVE
keep quiet	incl P, SH
• Ro–y *keeps* quiet	ROPY
• Mar–y *keeps* quiet	MARSHY
keep quiet, *say*	WIST
keep signalling	FLAGON
keep sovereign	KING OF THE CASTLE
keep tractor	TOWER
keep waving	WAGON

Keeper of the Privy Seal	KPS
Keeper of the Royal Swans	SWANKING
keeping a . . .	incl A
keeping *	incl *
• m–an *keeping* girl	MAIDAN
keeps mum	SAY-SO
kept (in) by t/each/er	EACH
kept (in) by *	incl in *
• girl *kept in by* m–an	MAIDAN
• girl *kept by* parents	PANORAMA
kept quiet	RESERVED
kept waiting (=on ice)	
• *kept waiting with* daughter	ICED
• king *kept waiting*	RICE
• many *kept waiting*	DICE, LICE, MICE
keel	
keeling over, Ben . . . <	NEB
sloop *keels over*<	POOLS
Kelly's eye	I, ONE
kelvin	K
kennel	
kennel fee	CURRENT
kennel club	KC
Kensington district	WEIGHT
Kent	SE
Kenya	EAK
kept	(*see* keep)
kernel	
bro<u>ken</u> *kernel*	OK
b/roke/n *kernel*	ROKE
kernel of p/roble/m	ROBLE
kewpie (doll)	QP
key	
key	A, B, C, D, E, F, G
• key hole	BO, DO, GO
• key note	ATE
• key points	AS, ASS, BE, BEE, EWE etc
• key ring	DO, GO
• key-stone	COPAL
• key *to* room	EDEN
• key *to* the door	GENTRY

Anag [cat]; Any *; Begin IGN–; Endings –ING; eg •; Hidden /cat/; Implied add (on); Implied in (in);

• two keys *with* lock	ACTRESS	• kind helping	MODERATION
key	CAY	kind	TYPE
• key, key, key	DECAY	• kind appearance	TYPEFACE
• key-worker	CAYMAN	• kind author	TYPEWRITER
key batsman	OPENER	kind	NATURE
key feature	WARD	• kind husband	NATURE RESERVE
key figures	EX, EMIL, CIVIC etc	• kind mother	NATURE
key		• kind note	NATURED
–for legumes, *say*	PEAKY	*kind of* [animal]	LAMINA, MANILA
–for vehicle, *say*	KHAKI	**king¹**	
–for relations, *say*	KINKY	king	HM
key personnel	SKELETON STAFF	king	K
key-worker	PIANO TUNER, TYPIST	• king-fish	KEEL
keyboard, *say*	MANUEL	• king in fear, *say*	KINDRED
kick		• The King and I	KI
kick	BOOT	king	KING
• kick sailor	BOOT-JACK	• graduate king	BAKING
• kick son	BOOTS	• island king, *say*	CAKING
• kick the drink, *say*	BOOTLICKER	• king-like	ASKING
kick	HACK	• river-king	POKING
• kick horse	HACK	• royal architect	PLANKING
• kick *on* the knee, *say*	HACKNEY	• royal yacht	KINGSHIP
• son *takes* kick	SHACK	• slim ruler	THINKING
kick-off	KO	king	R
kick *out*	HA–CK	• king is dead	LATER
kick-out [cat]	ACT	• king-bird	REGRET
kicked about [field]	FILED	• The King and I	RI
kickstart	K	king	REX
[unit alive and] *kicking*	ANTEDILUVIAN	• king lives, *say*	RHEXIS
kid		• king, *say*	(W)RECKS
kid brother	BILLY	• model king, *say*	TREKS
kid sister	NANNY	king (Charles)	CR
kids curse	CHILDRENSWEAR	• king *at* work	CROP
kid's father	BILLY, GOAT	• King Charles I	CRONE
kid's mother	GOAT, NANNY	• king has . . .	CROWNS
kidnap		• king I see	CRISPY
kidnap children	TAKE ISSUE	king (Edward)	ER
kidnapped schoolgirl, *say*	MISTAKEN	• king at home, OK	ERINYES
kidnapper	LEATHERHEAD, PARIS	• King-rat with a . . .	ERRATA
kill		• King's English	ERSE
kill	END	king (George)	GR
• kill debtor	ENDOWER	• king and heir	GRANDSON
• kill nettles	ENDANGERS	• King George I	GRIST
• second kill	SEND	• king *with* one son	GRISON
kill	SLAY	kings	
• kill ruler, *say*	SLAKING	• two kings dine at home	KREATIN
• kill Scot, *say*	SLATE-AXE	(*see also* royal¹)	
• kill dog, *say*	SLAP-UP		
• killed, *say*	SLADE	**king²**	
kill mother	DOMAIN	Cockney king	PEARLIE, PEARLY
kill you and me, *say*	CROCUS	King Cole	NAT
killed slug	SHOT	King Edward	LEAR, LEARNED
killer	CAIN	king-emperor	RI
kilo	K	king, *maybe*	CARD, CHESSMAN, PIECE
kind		king of France	ROI, SM
kind	MODE	king of sin	VICEROY
		king watcher	CAT

kingly men	REGAL, ROYAL
king's associate	ANNA
King's Bench	KB
King's College	KC
king's constitution	COLESLAW
King's Counsel	KC
king's downfall	CHECKMATE
King's *Head*	K
king's highway	ROYAL ROAD
king's mistress	NELL
king's rule	COLESLAW
king's weapon	EXCALIBUR
mad king	LEAR
merry king	COLE
old king	COLE, OG
Sun king	LOUIS
king³	
Charles *I*	C
Charles *II*	H
Edward *II*	D
Edward II	SECONDER
Edward *III*	W
George *IV*	R
Henry *V*	Y
Edward *VI*	D
kinky	
kinky [male]	LAME, MEAL
[quite] *kinky*	QUIET
Kipling	
Kipling's character	KIM
Kipling's work	IF
kipper	
kipper	NAPPER
kipper's head	NAPPER
kipper's *head*	K
kipper's *tail*	R
Kirkpatrick	K
kiss	
kiss	BUSS
kiss	PECK
• Kiss me, Hardy	PECKING ORDER
• kiss toes, *say*	PECTOSE
• kissed a number, *say*	PECTATE
• knock-out kiss	KOPECK
kiss	X
• a kiss (English)	AXE
• kiss boy	X-RAY
• the *French* kiss	LAX, LEX
kiss striker	SMACKER
kite	BUS, PLANE
kitten	
kitten's father, *say*	CAT'S-PAW
kitty, *say*	KITE
k-kip	KNAP
KN	CAYENNE
knead	

knead [knead]	NAKED
knead, *say*	WANT
kneaded [clay]	LACY
kneading to [paste]	PATES, PEATS, SPATE
knew	
knew (old)	WIST
knew, *say*	GNU, NEW
	WHIST
knight	
knight	K, KT, N
knight	SIR
• knight copies, *say*	SERAPES
• knight devoured, *say*	SERRATE
• knight *with* Scot, *say*	SERMON
and	
• knight employed . . .	CERUSED
• knight is English	CERISE
• knight was familiar	
with us, *say*	CERNUOUS
and	
• knight *and* a man, *say*	SURGENT
• knight bachelor, *I'm told*	SURCINGLE
• knight *has* a title, *say*	SURNAME
• knight overtakes, *say*	SURPASSES
and	
• knight got up, *say*	CIRROSE
Knight	
–of Labour	KL
–of Malta	KM
–of the Bath	KB
–of the Legion of Honour	KLH
–of the Order of the Garter	KG
–of the Thistle	KT
Knight Bachelor	KB
knight bachelor, *I'm told*	SURCINGLE
Knight Commander	
–of the Bath	KCB
–of the British Empire	KBE
Knight Grand Cross	
–of the Bath	GCB
–of the British Empire	GBE
–of Hanover	GCH
knight, *say*	NIGHT
• Knight E, *say*	NIGHTIE
• Knight Lee, *say*	NIGHTLY
knit	
knit [coat]	ATOC, TACO
knit, *say*	NIT, PEARL, WE'VE
knitted [a scarf]	FRACAS
knitting expert, *say*	PINKING, PINNACE
knitting [pins]	SNIP, SPIN
knock	
knock *back*<	KNOB, PAR, PAT
knock back drink<	REGAL
knock door	CARPENTRY
knock down house	H(O)

Anag [cat]; Any *; Begin IGN–; Endings –ING; eg •; Hidden /cat/; Implied add (on); Implied in (in);

knock down, *say*	RAISE, RAYS	knot in ham, *say*	NOTTINGHAM
knock it back<	TI	*knotted* [ties]	SITE
knock-[knee]	KEEN	*knotty* [timber]	BETRIM, TIMBRE
knock out a . . .	omit A	**know**	
knock out *	*omit* *	know Edward, *say*	KENNED
• *knock out* one of he(i)r's . . .	HERS	*know no bounds*	omit ends
knock over pins<	SNIP	• (g)loo(m) *that knows*	
knock, *say*	WRAP	*no bounds*	LOO
knockabout	PA–T, RA–P, TA–, –P	know, *say*	NO, WATT, WHAT
knockabout<	PAR, PAT, TAP	know-all	CLEVER DICK, SMART ALEC
knockabout [farce]	FACER	knowing	FLY
knockdown [prices]	PRECIS	• knowing baseball player	FLYCATCHER
knocked, *say*	RAPT, WRAPPED	• knowing history	FLY-PAST
• knocked America, *say*	RAPTUS	• knowing sportsman	FLY-FISHER
knocked [into] . . .	–TION	knowledge	–OLOGY
knocked into [shape]	HEAPS, PHASE	knowledge of elves	IMPLORE
knockout	KO	**Köchel**	K
knocks down fish	FELLSIDE	**Korea**	ROK
knee		**kreutzer**	KR
knee-*cap*	K	**krone**	KR
knock-[knee]	KEEN	**Kuala Lumpur**	KL
knot		**Kuwait**	KWT, Q8
knot	KN	**KV**	CAVY

Letter replaced \c\at; Omit (a); Pointers *out*; Retain <u>a</u>; Split B_ED; Down (D); Backwards <or ^

L

angle, angular momentum, apprentice, Avogadro's number, corner, driver, el, elevated railway, ell, fifty (thousand), half century, hand, inductance, Labour, lady, la(e)vo-, l(a)evorotatory, lake, lambda, lambert, latent heat, Latin, latitude, league, learner, learning, lecturer, left, length, Liberal, licentiate, line, libra, library, lira, lire, litre, live, loch, long, longo, lough, lumen, luminance, Luxembourg, many, molar latent heat, new driver, novice, number plate, overhead railway, port, pound, pupil, quantum number, right angle, side, specific latent heat, student, tyro, vitamin

£1	LI	*lacking* *	omit *
£1.51	CLIP	• mot(her)'s *lacking* her . . .	MOTS
£s	LL	**lack**	
label		lack	NEED
label	TAB	• lack at this point, *say*	NEEDIER
• label plot	TABBED	• lack fish	NEEDLING
• label 'Rented'	TABLET	• lack, *say*	KNEAD, KNEED
• label the *French* . . .	TABLE	lacking	NO
label	TAG	• *lacking* direction	NOSE
laboratory	LAB	• *lacking* medicine	NODOSE
labour	LAB	• *lacking* money	NOCENT
labour extremists	WORKAHOLICS	lacking	O
labour *extremists*	LR	• *lacking* people	OMEN
labour leader	FOREMAN	• *lacking* stretch	OGIVE
Labour leader	ATTLEE	• *lacking* trees	OPINES
Labour *leader*	L	lacking, *say*	IN-KNEED
labour movement	CONTRACTION	**ladder**	
labour pains	EFFORT	ladder	RUN
Labour Party	LP	ladderman	JACOB
Labour supporter	MATERNITY BED	**lady**	
Labour [ward]	DRAW	Ladies' Gold Union	LGU
laboured [speech]	CHEEPS	ladies' magazine	POWDER ROOM
Labour's record	BOOK OF JOB	Ladies Only	NOMEN, OMEN
labourer	HAND	lady	DAME, EVE, LUCK
	HERACLES, HERCULES	lady	MISS
lace		• lady gangster	MISSAL
laced [into a] . . .	–ATION	• lady is . . .	MISSIS
[strait]-*laced*	TRAITS	• lady *with* a . . .	MISSA
lack		and	
lack foresight	LOOK AFTER	• Lady Bountiful, *say*	MISGIVING
lacking a . . .	omit A	• lady fly-fisher, *say*	MISCASTING
lacking an alternative	omit OR	• lady magistrate, *say*	MISJUDGE
lacking dash	MINUS	lady	SHE, TRAMP
lacking finish	omit last letter	lady bookmaker	AUTHORESS, RUTH
lacking nothing	omit O	Lady Day	LD
lacking one	omit A, I	lady-in-waiting	EXPECTANT
lacking sex appeal	omit IT, SA		MOTHER
lacking the right . . .	omit R, RT	lady-killer	BLUEBEARD

Anag [cat]; Any *; Begin IGN–; Endings –ING; eg •; Hidden /cat/; Implied add (on); Implied in (in);

lady-love	HERO, KAYO, LASSO, MAYO
Lady of the Lake CONSTANCE, WINDERMERE	
lady *of the* [manor]	NORMA
lady's	HER
• lady's a . . .	HERA
• lady's on trains	HERONRY
• lady's ring	HERO
and	
• lady's clothes, *say*	HIRSUTE
• lady's fish, *say*	HURLING
lady's maid	ABIGAIL
Lady with the lamp	USHERETTE
ladybird	HEN, PEN, SALTERN

laid

laid *back<*	DIAL
laid new grass, *say*	RECEDED
[laid] *out*	DIAL
laid to rest	(in) B–ED, (in) CO–T
• English deserter *laid*	
to rest	BERATED
• son *laid to rest*	COST
laid up	(in) B–ED, (in) CO–T
laid *up*(D)^	DIAL
laid out [wares] . . .	SWEAR, WEARS
	(*see also* lay)

lake

lake	ERIE
• lake*side* dwelling	COTERIE
lake	L, LOCH
	WATER COLOUR

Lamb

lamb	ELIA
• lamb lover	ELIAN
lamb	RAMSON

lambast

lambast [players]	REPLAYS
[master] *lambasting*	REMAST, STREAM

lambda   L

lambert   L

lament

lament, *say*	GREEVE, MOWN
lamented, *say*	SIDE
laments, *say*	SIZE

land

Land Army	TILLER GIRLS
land girls	WLA
land in the water	AIT, EYOT
	ISLAND, ISLE(T)
Land of Hope	RURITANIA
land of rest	BEULAH
land of the wizard	OZ
landed explosive	LITHE
Land's End	WEST POINT
Land's *End*	D
landholder, *say*	FEWER
landing on	
indicating one word written	

above another word or letter:

• flier *landing on*	
prison(D)	BIRDCAGE
• insect *lands on* ring(D)	MOTHBALL
landline	BR, RLY, RY
landlocked	(in) L–AND
	(in) EST–ATE
landlord's job	INNKEEPING
landlord's job, *say*	IN KEEPING
landlords of multi-storey flats BLOCK LETTERS	
landmark	RUT
lampholder	ALADDIN

language

language buff	POLISH
language of love	ROMANCE
language refinement	POLISH

languish   LYDIA

lap

lap a . . .	incl A
[lap]-*dancing*	ALP, PAL
lap speed	LICK
lap *	incl *
• wa–ter *lapping round* one . . .	WAITER
lap *up*(D)^	PAL
lapdog	GREYHOUND
lapped by *	incl in *
• one *being lapped by* wa–ter	WAITER
lap*top*(D)	L

large

large	BIG
• can *in* large *enclosure*	BITING
• large girl	BIGAMY
• large head	BIGNESS
• king *in* large . . .	BRIG
large	GRAND
• large degree	GRANDMA
• large letters	GRANDEE
• large poster, *say*	GRANDDAD
large	MAJOR
• large container	MAJORCAN
• large officer	MAJOR
large	OS
• large duck	OSTEAL
• large flag	OSIRIS
• large tin	OSCAN
• large vehicle	OSCAR
large amount of timber	WOO(d)
large cat, *say*	LINKS
• can *in* large *enclosure*	BITING
large-eyed, *say*	OX-HIDE, OXIDE
large jumper	KANGAROO
large letters	OS
[large] *letters*	ELGAR, LAGER, REGAL
large mouthful, *say*	MEGABYTE
large needle-case	HAYSTACK
large number	ARMY, D, M, NATION
large part of c/once/rt	ONCE

large part of many . . .	MAN, ANY	last vehicle	BIER, HEARSE
large pieces	ARTILLERY	• last vehicle, *say*	BEER, HERS
large scale	EPIC, OS	last war	ARMAGEDDON, RAGNAROK
large stand	GREAT BEAR	last word	AMEN, CUE, GOODBYE
large step	GRANDPAS	last words	PS
large sum	IMPOUNDS	• last words *about*	P–S
large tent, *say*	MARQUIS	• last words *about*<	SP
large tree, *say*	RED-WUD	last words	EPITAPH, OBIT(UARY)
largely wast(ed)	WAST	last words	RIP
larger offer, *say*	MORBID	last worker	COBBLER, SHOEMAKER
larger, *say*	HIRE	[the last] *resort*	STEALTH
lariat	STOCKHOLDER		(*see also* final)
lark		**late**	
larking about [in the] . . .	THINE	late	
[it was] *larking about*	WAIST, WAITS	• late *getting up*(D)^	–ETAL
lasso	LADY-LOVE, STOCKHOLDER	• late *rising*(D)^	–ETAL
last		late	EX
last	END	• late *getting up*(D)^	–XE
• last debtor	ENDOWER	• late *rising*(D)^	–XE
• last man	ENDED	late ball	ATTENDANCE
• way *to* last . . .	SEND, WEND	late fruit	SLOE
last bit of foo<u>d</u>	D	late opening	POST MORTEM
last carrier	BIER, HEARSE	late pressing	EVENING
• last carrier, *say*	BEER, HERS	<u>l</u>ate *starter*	L
last chanc<u>e</u>	E	late shift	NIGHTDRESS, NIGHTGOWN
last characters in A<u>ida</u>	DA		NIGHTIE, NIGHTSHIRT
last couple dan<u>ced</u> lamb<u>ada</u>	EDDA	[late] *shift*	LEAT, TAEL, TALE, TEAL
last drink	HEMLOCK	late worker	BEHINDHAND
last horse in Derby, *say*	ENDORSE	latecomer	JOHNNY
last in, first out	LIFO	later message	PS
last in, last out	LILO	[later] *model*	ALTER, RATEL
last interminably	DRAGON	later postscript	PPS
last laug<u>h</u>	H	*latest* mod<u>el</u>	L
last letter	OMEGA, Z	*latest* information	SP
last man	COBBLER, SHOEMAKER	*latest* informatio<u>n</u>	N
last ma<u>n</u>	N	*latest of* tho<u>se</u> . . .	E
last minut<u>e</u>	E		(*see also* old)
last minute improvement	LATERALLY	**latent**	
last month	DEC	*latent* [heat]	HATE, THEA
• last month I married	DECIMATED	*latent in* yo/ung love/r	UNGLOVE
last month	ULT(IMO)	**Latin**	
last mont<u>h</u>	H	Latin	L
last object	END	• Latin in church	LINCH
last of th<u>e</u> . . .	E	• Latin is part . . .	LISSOME
last of the		• Latin poem	LODE
–beef	OXTAIL	Latin	LAT
–series	OMEGA, Z	• Latin queen	LATER
–wine	GRAVESEND	• Latin *in* the Home Counties	SLATE
Last of the Mohican<u>s</u>	S	• strong Latin . . .	FLAT
last offer	HOLD OUT	Latin	ROMAN
last resort	HOSPICE	• Latin affliction	ROMANTIC
[last] *resort*	ALTS, SALT	• Latin church	ROMANCE
last stop	STAY	• Latin unknown	ROMANY
last stra<u>w</u>	W	**latitude**	L, LAT
last things	BOOTS, SHOES	**laugh**	
last train	CORTEGE	laugh	HA, HAHA, HAWHAW
	FUNERAL PROCESSION		HEHE, HOHO

Anag [cat]; Any *; Begin IGN–; Endings –ING; eg •; Hidden /cat/; Implied add (on); Implied in (in);

laughter, *say*	GESTATION
launch	
launch of ship	S
*launch*pad	P
launching yacht	Y
laundry	
laundering [sheet]	THESE
laundry helper	DETERGENT, SOAP, SODA
	DOLLY, IRON
law	
law	COPS, FUZZ
law agent	LA
[law]-*breaking*	AWL
law lord	LUD
lawman	BL, DA, EARP
lawmen	COPS, POLICE, POSSE
	VIGILANTES
lawgiver	MOSES, SOLON
lawmaker	DRACO, MEDE, MP
lawyer	BL, DA
lawyers	BAR
• international lawyers	UNBAR
• lawyers see . . .	BARELY
• lawyers' stooge	BARSTOOL
lawyers	
indicating use of legal term:	
• bar *for lawyers*	ESTOP
• *lawyer's* house	MESSUAGE
• *lawyers'* right	LIEN
lax [laws]	AWLS, SLAW
Lawn Tennis Association	LTA
lax	
lax [rule]	LURE
[law is] *lax*	WAILS
lay	
lay	AIR
• lay *behind* saint	STAIR
• lay drunk	AIRTIGHT
• quiet lay	PAIR
lay*out*	LA–Y, SE–T
[lay]*out*	–ALY
lay up nuts(D)^	STUN
lay*about*	LA–Y, SE–T
lay*about*<	TES, YAL
layer	E
BIRD, HEN, WYANDOTTE etc	
laying out [cash, Tom] . . .	STOMACH
layout man	PLANGENT
layout of [town]	WONT
[nice] *layout*	CINE
	(*see also* laid)
lazy monk	ABBEY-LUBBER
LC	ELSIE
lead¹	
lead (=1st letter)	
• juvenile *lead*	J
• *lead* off	O
• *lead off* roof	R
• *leads to* better things	BT
lead *off*	omit 1st letter
• *lead off* (t)he . . .	HE
• lead *off* the (c)limb	LIMB
leader (=1st letter)	
• leader *dropped from* (p)arty	ARTY
• Oriental *leader has gone*	(e)ASTERN
• *leader of* flock	F
• *leader of* Marathon	M, MU
• *leaderless* (w)omen	OMEN
• *leaders of* Cyprus	CANDY
• *leaders of* Patagonia	PANDA
• *leaders of* Syria	SANDY
• squadron *leader*	S
• wartime *leader*	W
leading (=1st letter)	
• *leading* article	A
• *leading* character	C
• *leading* character in play	P
• *leading* edges of	
technological advance	TA
• *leading* lady	L
• *leading* light	L
• *leading* man	M
• *leading* seaman	S
led by a . . .	start with A
led by *	start with *
• heir *led by* me	MESON
lead²	
lead	GUIDE
• lead on, *say*	GUIDON
• lead, *say*	GUYED
lead	STAR
• leading directors	STARBOARD
• leading light	STARLIGHT, STARSHINE
• leading performer landed	STARLIT
lead in(to) *	incl in *
• *lead* a king *into* r–ing	RAKING, RARING
lead soldiers	SCOUTS, VANGUARD
leader	A, NOI–
leader	AGA
• leader in the street	AGAINST
• leader lashes, *say*	AGATISE
• leader missed, *say*	AGAMIST
leader	CID
• a leader	ACID
• managed leader	RANCID
• PLA leader	PLACID
leader of	
–flock	BELLWETHER
–queue	HEAD WAITER
leader, *say*	GUYED
leader's address	DOWNING STREET
leading	FRONT
• leading gangster	FRONTAL
• leading journalist	FRONTED

Letter replaced \c\at; Omit (a); Pointers *out*; Retain a; Split B_ED; Down (D); Backwards <or ^

• store leading . . .	SHOP-FRONT	• learn only . . .	CONSOLE
leading	NOI–	• learn *to* dance	CONTANGO
• leading a few . . .	NOISOME	learn *about*	CO–N, REA–D
• leading student	NOIL	learn to swim	MASTERSTROKE
leading	(in) VA–N	[learned] *characters*	LEANDER
• I am *leading*	VAIN	learned man	DR, MAGUS, SAGE
• *leading*, for example . . .	VEGAN	learner	L
leading artist	PRA	• learner finished	LOVER
leading character	A, NOI–	• learner in study	LINDEN
leading characters	INITIALS	• learner *with* spectacles	LOO
leading feature	CHIN	learner's figure	FIFTY, L
leading figure	A, NOI–	learning	LORE
leading firm	UPTIGHT	young learner	BABEL
leading lady	EVE	**lease**	
	USHERETTE	lease it, *say*	WREN-TIT
leading light	POLE STAR	lease more properties	OUTLET
	STAR OF BETHLEHEM	lease*back*<	TEL
leading man	ADAM	leased	ISLET
	GUIDE, USHER	**least common multiple**	LCM
	KING, STAR	**leather**	
leading model	MAINFRAME	leather	KID
leading monk	PRIOR	• leather joint, *say*	KIDNEY
• leading monk, *say*	PRIER, PRYER	• leather *with* woolly surface	KIDNAP
leading player	FIRST VIOLIN	• Leatherhead	KIDNAPPER
	PIED PIPER	leather	LOWER CASE
leading seaman	FIRST HAND	leather	BUFF
[led] *astray*	–DLE, ELD	• concerning leather	REBUFF
lead³		• leather polish	BUFF
lead	PB	• *place* leather *before* queen	BUFFER
• lead-*covered*	P–B	leather dresser, *say*	COURIER
lead-coloured figures	LIVID	leather, *say*	HIED, OXIDE
lead soldiers	SCOUTS, VANGUARD	Leatherhead	L
leaf		**leave¹**	
leaf-eater	BOOKWORM	indicating omission:	
leaf-insect	PAGEANT	he *leaves* t(he) . . .	T
[leaf]-*mould*	FLEA	I *leave* . . .	omit I
	(*see also* leaves)	head *leaves*	omit 1st letter
league		king *left* . . .	omit K or R
league	L	*leave* home	omit in
league match	UNION	*leave* a . . .	omit A
league members	REDHEADS	*leave* it *out*	omit IT
lean		*leave* me *out*	omit ME
lean diet	SLIM	*leave out* a . . .	omit A
lean nurse	TEND	*leave out* *	omit *
leak		• p(l)ayers *leave out*	
leak at this point, *say*	SEPIA	beginner	PAYERS
leak, *say*	LEEK	*leave* quietly	omit P
leaking, *say*	HOLED, HOLY, WHOLLY	*leave* *	omit *
leap		time *to leave*,	omit T
leap over net	CLEAR	**leave²**	
leap over tomb	VAULT	leave	GO
leap shrub	CAPER	• leave drink	GOSLING
leap-year	SPRINGTIME	• leave *in* interior . . .	INGOT
leaping [over] . . .	ROVE	• leave in two directions	GOES, GONE
learn			GOWN
learn	CON	• leave quickly, *say*	GOSSOON
• I learn . . .	ICON	• man *has* leave	MANGO

Anag [cat]; Any *; Begin IGN–; Endings –ING; eg •; Hidden /cat/; Implied add (on); Implied in (in);

leave	PART
• I am *on* leave	IMPART
• leave hilltop	PARTRIDGE
• leave *in* river	SPARTEINE
leave	QUIT
• leave bird *without* ...	REQUITE
• leave the ring	QUITO
• leaves level	QUITS
leave	RAT
• leave church	RATCH
• leave baseball player	RAT-CATCHER
• leave *in* church	CRATE
leave *by* No.1 bus	PARTIBUS
leave harbour	CROSSBAR
leave work	HOLIDAY JOB
leave room for a ...	incl A
leave room for *	incl *
• *leave room for* it in south-east	SITE
leave the North	LEAVEN
leave the South	LEAVES
leaving word	ADIEU, ADIOS, GOODBYE
	(see also left[1])

leaves

leaves	TEA
• leaves directions	TEASE
• leaves *in* tin ...	STEAN
• leaves space	TEA-ROOM
leaves his dinner	HERBIVORE
leaves producer	TREE
leaves supporter	STEM
Lebanon	RL

led

led, *say*	METAL
	(see also lead)

left[1]

left	L
• 100 left	CL
• excessively left	TOOL
• fruit left	PEARL
• left home	LIN–
• left in church	LINCH
• left in debt	LOWING
• left *on* road	LAVE
• left *on* time	LAD, LEON
• left port	LADEN
• left to burn	LIGNITE
• left turn	LU
• left *with* no ship	LOSS
left *behind*	last letter L
• friend left *behind*	PALL
• gangster left *behind*	ALL
• girl left *behind*	NORMAL
left *inside*	incl L
• left *inside* c–ove	CLOVE
• left *ins*–ide	SLIDE
left *out*	omit L

left *right out*	omit L
left-over(D) indicating L written over another word:	
• left-*over* fluid	LINK

left[2]

left	LEFT
left centre	EF
Left? *Left*	L
Left, *Right* ...	T

left[3]

left	LT
• is *in* left ...	LIST
• left *back*<	TL
• left *out* last word	LAMENT
• left *without* spectacles	LOOT
• left *turns*<	TL
left *out*	omit LT
left *right out*	omit LT
left *outside*	(in) L–T

left[4]

left	OFF
• 100 left	COFF
• left side	OFFHAND
• left team	OFFSIDE

left[5]

left	PORT
• I am left	IMPORT
• left one company	PORTICO
• left *in* the act	DEPORTED
left *outside*	(in) POR–T
left-over(D) indicating 'left' written over another word:	
• left-*over* fish	PORTRAY

left[6]

left	RED
• father left	PARED
• left-handed club	REDWOOD
• left, I see	REDIVIDE
• left *in* company	CREDO
• left leg	REDSHANK
left wing	RED
leftist	RED

left[7]

Bolton *left-half*	BOL
left centre	C
left hand	H
left hand of God	G
left of target	T

left[8]

left again	OVER
left at sea	PORT
left boot	SIDEKICK
left centre	LC
left for dead	GONE
left-hand	LH, VERSO, VO

left-hand man	COMMUNIST, SOCIALIST
left hands	LABOUR
left *on road*	NEAR(SIDE)
left *on ship*	PORT
left right *out*	omit R, RT
nothing *left*<	LIN
peek *to left*<	KEEP
	(*see also* leave)

leg

left leg	REDSHANK
leg	LEFT, ON
leg armour, *say*	GRIEVES
leg before (wicket)	LB(W)
[leg]-*break*	GEL, –GLE
leg in front	GAMBLED
leg of lamb/mutton	SHEEPSHANK
leg of mutton, *say*	RAMPART
leg-*over*<	GEL, NO
leg-ring	LIMBO
leg, *say*	ELEGY
leg *up*(D)^	GEL, NO
leg*less*	omit ON
• leg*less* bird	CAP(on)
• R(on) *is* leg*less*	R
legs	ELEVEN

legal

legal	LEG
legal argument	BARROW
legal division	DIVORCE
legal document	DEED
legal exercise	CONSTITUTIONAL
legally	IN-LAW

legate

legate	HE
legatees cried, *say*	AIRSWEPT

legend   FOOT, TOE

legislate

legislating	HOUSEWORK
legislator	DRACO, MEDE, MP
legislature	LEG

legit   RUN

length

fine length	FINCH
length	L
length that is . . .	YARDIE
length in ship	SMILES
length of	
–fish	PERCH
–links	CHAIN
–stick	POLE, ROD
length untied	FOOTLOOSE
lengthy stay	LONGSTOP

Lent

Lent	FAST
• lent a dollar	FAST BUCK
• Lent fare	FAST FOOD
• lent [gin] *cocktail*	FASTING

leopard's weight	OUNCE
Lesotho	LS

less

doe(s) *less*	DOE
less correct, *say*	RONGEUR
less costly, *say*	CHEEPER
less dash	MINUS
less hairy god	BALDER
less important	B
less labour, *say*	MORATORY
less, *say*	FUAR
less smooth, *say*	RUFFER
less than a second	–ATIC(k)
less than al(l) . . .	AL
less than tw/o-pen/ce	OPEN
less than four	THREE
less than (f)our	OUR
less than (t)he *whole* . . .	HE
less than the whole (t)own	OWN
less than their . . .	THE, HEIR
less than twenty	UNDERSCORE
less than (t)went(y)	WENT
lessen	GODOWN

let

let	(in) R–ENT
let down	ABSEIL
[let] *free*	TEL, –TLE
let in a . . .	incl A
let in *	incl *
• sh–e *lets in* a student	SHALE
let loose [all the] . . .	LETHAL
[let] *loose*	TEL, –TLE
[let] *off*	TEL, –TLE
let out a . . .	omit A
let out *	omit *
• t(he)ory he *let out* . . .	TORY
[let] *out*	TEL, –TLE
let us, *say*	LETTUCE
let wine breathe	AIRPORT

letter[1]

letter	CHI
• burnt letter	LITCHI
• letter slopes	CHILEANS
• letter only . . .	CHIMERE
letter	DEE
• letter *in* Indian . . .	INDEED
• letter writer	DEEPEN
• odds on letter . . .	SPONDEE
letter	EFF
• letter employed	EFFUSED
• letter service	EFFACE
• letter *with* a bit . . .	EFFORT
letter	EM
• hard letter	HEM
• letter finished	EMENDED
• letter *in* th–e . . .	THEME
letter	EN

• hard letter	HEN
• letter binder	ENTWINE
• letter *written in* afterthought	PENS
letter	ESS
• letter from Holland, *say*	DUCHESS
• letter *in* m–y . . .	MESSY
• letter *with* directions	ESSENE
letter	MU
• English letter	EMU
• letter *found in* the road	SMUT
• letter-list	MUTABLE
• letter, *say*	MEW
• letter *to* MP	MUMP
letter	O
• lady's letter	HERO
• letter, *say*	OH, OWE
• letter writer	OPEN
letter	PHI
• delete letter	DELPHI
• letter *in* the present day	APHID
• letter *recently* . . .	PHILATELY
• letter, *say*	FIE
letter	PI
• approve a letter	OKAPI
• letter *found in* the road	SPIT
• letter overdue	PILATE
• letter, *say*	PIE
letter	RHO
• letter, *say*	ROE, ROW
• letter *to* boy	RHODES
• letter *to* girl	RHODORA
letter²	
letter-card	CHARACTER
letter from	
–America	REALTOR
–Holland, *say*	DUCHESS
letter *from* [Stell(a)], *maybe*	TELLS
letter *from* Sp(a)in	SPIN
letter of condolence	C
letter of inquiry, *say*	WYE, Y
letter of thanks	COLLINS
letter opener	ADDRESSEE, DEAR PAPER KNIFE
letter *opener*	L
letter *opening* . . .	L
letter or two	BORED, DORIC, HORSE KORAN, LORIS, PORCH SORRY, TORUS, WORTH
letter *out of* li(n)e	LIE
letter *to* a policeman	COPE, COPS COPT, COPY
letter *to* hotel	FRITZ
letters *enclosing* money	MY
letters *from* (Am)erica	ERICA
letters *in* [Times]	ITEMS, MITES, SMITE
letters *for* father	PANDA
letters *from* Spa(in)	SPA
letters *from* (S)tell(a)	TELL
letters of credit	LC, CR
letters of introduction	INITIALS
letters of [love]	VOLE
letters of thanks	TA
letters *said*	AS(E), BEES, SEAS, EASE, GEES, EYES, JAYS, ELLS, EMS, ENS, OHS, PEAS(E), CUES, QUEUES, ARS, TEAS(E), TEES, USE, WISE
letters, *say*	MALE
letters sent	OUTPOST
letters *to*	
–editor	MAILED
–friends	PALSHIP, PALSIED
–queen	MAILER
letters *written in* [haste]	HATES, HEATS
letterhead	L
letterheads	CAPITALS
letterpress	EMPRESS, MUSQUASH
[love] *letters*	VOLE
[send] *letters*	DENS, ENDS
lettuce	
lettuce	COS
• lettuce bag	COSSACK
• lettuce grower, *say*	COSMOLOGIST
• lettuce plants	COSSETS
level head	EVENNESS
levitate	
levitating boy(D)^	YOB
levitation of new . . . (D)^	WEN
Leviticus	LEV
levy	
levy on the obese	CORPORATION TAX
levy, *say*	LEVEE
lexicon	LEX
liable	
liable to tax	DIFFICULT
liability is ours	ONUS
liar	ANANIAS, MATILDA
Liberal	
liberal	BROAD
• liberal clergy	BROADCLOTH
• liberal king	BROADER
• Liberal Party	BROADSIDE
liberal	L
• liberal Emperor	LOTTO
• Liberal loses seat	LOUT
• liberal President	LIKE
Liberal	LIB
• good liberal . . .	GLIB
• Liberal devoured . . .	LIBATE
• liberal share	LIBRATION
liberal	WIDE
• liberal feast	WIDESPREAD
• liberal head	WIDENESS
• liberal king	WIDER
[liberal] *characters*	BRAILLE

liberal [regime]	EMIGRE
liberally [I grant]	GRATIN, RATING
Liberals	LL
liberate	
liberate [slaves]	VALSES
liberation of [Paris]	PAIRS
Liberia	LB
library	
librarian	BOOK-KEEPER
Library Association	LA
Libya	
Libya	LAR
• Libya *and* America	LARUS
• Libya *has* many . . .	LARD
• Libya *has* railway and	LARRY
• Libya *without* iron	FLARE
• live *outside* Libya	BLARE
• talk *about* Libya and	SALARY
• directions *in* Libya	LASER
• grow old *in* Libya	LAAGER
• woman *in* Libya and	LASHER
• doctor *goes to* Libya	MOLAR
• Libya *follows* a . . .	ALAR
• thus Libya . . .	SOLAR
Libyan capital	DINAR
Libyan *capital*	L
Libyan *leader*	L
licence	
[dog] *licence*	GOD
licence [may be] . . .	BEAMY
licentiate	L
Licentiate	
–of Apothecaries' Company	LAC
–of College of Preceptors	LCP
–of Society of Apothecaries	LSA
–in Dental Surgery	LDS
–in Surgery	LCH
–in Theology	LTH, THL
lick	
lick [airmen] *into shape*	REMAIN
[man is] *licked into shape*	MAINS
lie	
lie-abed	OYSTER
lie about	FIBRE
[lie] *about*	ELI
lie in warmth, *say*	BASQUE
Liechtenstein	FL
lief	
[lief]	WILDLIFE
lieutenant	LOOT, LT
life	
[life]-*style*	FILE, LIEF
life symbol	ANKH
lifeboat	ARK

lifeboatman	NOAH
lift	
ban *lifted*(D)^	NAB
lift beams, *say*	RASE, RAYS, RAZE
lift cup	JACKPOT
lift, *say*	RASE, RAYS, RAZE
lifted flower	ROSE
lifting leg(D)^	GEL
light	
light	MATCH
• light entertainment	MATCHPLAY
• light meals	MATCHBOARD
• light staff	MATCHSTICK
light	MOON
• light drink	MOONSHINE
• light *round* king	MORON
light	STAR, SUN, VERY
light a cigarette	FIREWEED
light appearance	DAWN, DAYBREAK
	SUNRISE
light clothing	WINDOW DRESSING
light covering	RAYON
light-emitting diode	LED
light heart	DAY CENTRE
light *heart*	G
Light Infantry	LI
light machine-gun	LMG
light material	CANDLEWICK, TINDER
light music	TORCH-SONG
light of danger	RED
light pastry, *say*	PISOLITE
light sauce	WINDOW DRESSING
light soil	LAND
light spasm	ARCTIC
light symbol	FLOODMARK
light worker	DAY LABOURER
lighter	ARSONIST, FIRESHIP
lighter propeller	BARGE-POLE, SCREW
lighter push	BARGE
lighter stone	FLINT
lighthouse, *say*	FAIR, FARE
lighting offence	ARSON
lightweight	CARAT, CT
	FEATHER G, GRAIN, GRAM(ME)
	OUNCE, OZ
lightweight animal	OUNCE
lightweight monarch	THINKING
like¹	
like	ALA
• black like . . .	BALA
• like a marine	ALARM
• like *in* m–y . . .	MALAY
• like scholars	ALABAMA
like	AS
• like a bird	ASHEN, ASTERN
• like a buccaneer	ASPIRATE
• like a carrier	ASTRAY

Anag [cat]; Any *; Begin IGN–; Endings –ING; eg •; Hidden /cat/; Implied add (on); Implied in (in);

- like a coin   ASCENT
- like a coin, *say*   ASSENT
- like a container, *say*   ASSAPAN
- like a drunkard   ASSOT
- like a fish   ASHAKE, ASIDE
- like a flan   ASTART
- like a loch   ASLAKE
- like a lubricant, *say*   ASSOIL
- like a mariner, *say*   ASSAILER
- like a nun   ASSISTER, ASSAULT
- like a philosopher   ASKANT
- like a relative   ASSISTER
- like a ruler   ASKING
- like a Scot   ASIAN
- like a swan   ASPEN
- like a tar, *say*   ASSAILER, ASSAULT
- like a tree   ASOAK
- like a writer   ASPEN
- like acid   ASCETIC
- like dirt   ASSOIL
- like foreign articles   ASUNDER
- like Henry   ASH
- like the CIA, *say*   ASPIRING
- like a smell, *say*   ASCENT, ASSENT
- like Thomas, *say*   ASTOMOUS
- like wine   ASPORT

and

- as *in* church   CASE
- beetle-like   DORAS

and

- like a detective, *say*   AZTEC
- like a part, *say*   AZAROLE
- like a waste product, *say*   AZURINE

(*see also* as)

like   –ISH

- like a European, *say*   FINISH
- like a bounder, *say*   KADDISH
- like a bridge   SPANISH
- like a cleaner   MOPISH
- like a comb, *say*   RAKISH
- like a couple, *say*   PERISH
- like a cryptogam, *say*   FURNISH
- like a father   POPISH
- like a fish   GARISH
- like a French woman, *say*   FAMISH
- like a friend   PALISH
- like a gala, *say*   FETISH
- like a joke   PUNISH
- like a judo expert   DANISH
- like a lake   TARNISH
- like a rod   POLISH
- like a Russian   SLAVISH
- like a slipper   MULISH
- like a stamp   FRANKISH
- like a stew   HASHISH
- like a vehicle   VANISH
- like a WC, *say*   LAVISH

- like an embargo   BANISH
- like an equal   PARISH
- like anger, *say*   IRISH
- like cereal   CORNISH
- like dough   FLOURISH
- like fruit, *say*   PERISH
- like German writer   MANNISH
- like head, *say*   POLISH
- like motor fuel   DERVISH
- like Norse gods   VANISH
- like part of Yorkshire   MOORISH
- like preserved meat   HAMISH
- like the Air Force, *say*   RAFFISH

(*see also* rather)

like²

like

- –a blender, *say*   WHISKEY
- –a Communist   LOVERED
- –a corsair, *say*   PYRITOUS
- –a detective, *say*   DICKY
- –a hamster, *say*   PETTISH, PETTY
- –a nun   INHABIT
- –a parrot, *say*   PARITY
- –a policeman, *say*   COPPERY
- –a sandwich-filling, *say*   INBRED
- –a soldier   UNCIVIL
- –a vegetable, *say*   PELIKE
- –a young dog   PUPOID
- –an aristocrat   U
- –Cain's brother   LIKABLE
- –Edward   LIKENED
- –fruit   PEARLY
- –kippers   ASLEEP
- –rain   RIGHT
- –Venus   ARMLESS

like³

indicating a homophone:

- *like* meat   MEET
- *like* one . . .   WON
- *like* rain   REIGN, REIN
- *like* some . . .   SUM
- *like* thyme   TIME
- *like* wood   WOULD
- *like* you   EWE, U, YEW

like⁴

likely to appear   (in) OFF–ING
- object *likely to appear*   OFFENDING
- queen *likely to appear*   OFFERING

liken, *say*   COMPERE

likes *to* dine   LOVE-SEAT

lime

lime *peel*   LE

[lime] *squash*   EMIL, MILE

peeled (l)im(e)   IM

limit

limit drink   RATIONALE

limitation of damage   COS(t), HAR(m)

Letter replaced \c\at; Omit (a); Pointers *out*; Retain a̲; Split B_ED; Down (D); Backwards <or ^

limited amount of ca/sh I p/ut	SHIP	*lining* *	incl in *
limited amount	LO(t)	• copper *lining* city . . .	BASCULE
limited are(a)	ARE	**link**	
limited a/rea m/ay . . .	REAM	link-*up*(D)^	EIT
limited by an . . .	incl in A–N	link up *with* Edward	JOIN(T)ED
• state *limited by* an . . .	AMEN	linked characters	SIAMESE TWINS
limited edition	ED	**Linnean Society**	LS
limited liability	LTD, PLC	**lino**	
limited number	N(O)	lino*cut*	LIN(o)
limited subscription	INITIALS	[lino]*cut*	LION
limiting a . . .	incl A	**lion**	
limiting *	incl *	lion family	CATKIN, LEO
• s–un *limiting* power	SPUN		PRIDE
limited by *	incl in *	• lion family, *say*	PRIED
• power *limited by* s–un	SPUN	lion-tamer	ANDROCLES, DANIEL
limits of patience	PE	lioness	ELSA
limousine	OSCAR	*Lion*heart	IO
Lincoln		**lip dressing**	SAUCE
Lincoln	ABE	**liquid**	
• Lincoln Square	ABET	liquid courage	INK BOTTLE, SPIRIT
• Lincoln *with* the *French* . . .	ABELE	*liquidate* [a mob]	BOMA, MOAB
• the morning *after* Lincoln . . .	ABEAM	*liquidation* [by a] . . .	BAY
Lincoln, *say*	BISCUIT	liquefied natural gas	LNG
line		liquefied petroleum gas	LPG
line	I, L	**lira(e)**	L, LR
line across curve, *say*	CORD, CORED	**lisp**	
line manager	SIGNALMAN	lisp	substitute th for s
line of music	CONGA	• *lisp* in song	THONG
line-*out*	omit I	• *lisping* sigh	THIGH
[line]-*out*	LIEN, NEIL, NILE	• sing *lispingly*	THING
line, *say*	RHO, ROE	**list**	
line worker	GENEALOGIST	list at this point, *say*	TABLIER
lined by *	incl *	list of vehicles	CARLIST
• city *lined by* copper	BASCULE	listed building	TOWER OF PISA
lined characters	OG(H)AM	**listen**	
liner	SS	for *listening to*	FORE, FOUR
lines	BR, RLY, RY	I see why *listeners* . . .	ICY
• lines have . . .	BROWN	*listen* to . . .	TOO, TWO
• doctor the lines	MOTHERLY	*listen* to peace . . .	TWO-PIECE
• street *with* no lines	STORY	*listen to* piece	PEACE
lines	ODE	listen to, *say*	HERE
• lines *up*(D)^	EDO	listened to, *say*	HERD
• many lines	LODE, MODE	listener	AUDITOR
• right lines	RODE	listener	EAR
• straight lines	STRODE	• dry *without* listener	DREARY
lines	VERSE	• good listener	GEAR
• fashionable lines	INVERSE	• listener panics	EARFLAPS
• lines *written to* daughter	VERSED	listener	LUG
• study lines	CONVERSE	**lit**	
lines, *say*	ROES, ROSE	lit	DRUNK, LANDED
lines up	DRESSES	lit-*up*(D)^	–TIL
lines *up*(D)^	RB, YR	**literal(ly)**	LIT
linesman	PLIMSOLL	**literature**	
linesman	POET	literacy examiner, *say*	SPELEOLOGIST
• English linesman	KEATS et al	literary giant	DESPAIR
• German linesman	GOETHE	literary hack	ROSINANTE
• Italian linesman	DANTE	literary prop	BOOK-END

literary set	ALPHABET	little by little	ERIC
literature	LIT	little change	D, P, PENNY
litre	L	*little change in* sha\p\e	SHADE
litter		*little change in* [shape]	HEAPS, PHASE
litter container	STY, UTERUS, WOMB	little charge	ION
[papers] *littered about*	SAPPER	little class	TOUCHTYPE
little[1]		little crone, *say*	HAGLET
little	WEE	little cut, *say*	SNIPPET
• little boy	WEENED	*little difference in* board . . .	BEARD
• little for each . . .	WEEPER	little donkey, *say*	ASSET
• little king	WEEK	little fellow, *say*	COVELET
• little Mark	WEEM	little fight	SCRAP
• little tart	WEEPIE	little fish, *say*	BASSET, PIKELET
• shirt *has* little . . .	TWEE	little growth	BUD, LEAFLET
and		little help	MINUTE HAND
• little boy, *say*	WEAKEN, WEANED	little horse, *say*	HACKLET
• little king, *say*	WEAK, WEAR, WEIR	little idiot	ASSET
	(*see also* small[1])	little Indian	PAPOOSE
little	SHORT	little lighter	FIREFLY
• little food	SHORTBREAD	little lower	CALF
• little letter	SHORTEN	little man	MINUTE HAND
• little petticoat	SHORT SLIP	little Mark	SCARLET
• little ring	SHORT CIRCUIT	little marmalade	KITTEN
• little time	SHORTAGE	little Mary	STOMACH, TUM
• little workman	SHORTHAND	little money	D, P, PENNY
little[2]		little mother	MINIMUM
indicating abbreviation:		little music	NOTE
• little Bill	AC	*little* mus*ic*	–IC
• little bounder	ROO	*little of* <u>h</u>is . . .	H
• little Boy Blue	VICTORY	*little of* h/is le/ave	ISLE
• little brother	BRER	little ox, *say*	BULLET
• little brothers	BROS	Little Rock	BOULDER, PEBBLE
• little change	D, –ID, P, –IP	little runner	BROOK, RILL, RIVULET
• little chap	GENT		STREAM(LET)
• little coin	D, –ID, P, –IP	little support	TEE
• little couple	PR	little taxi, *say*	CABLET
• little horse	GEE, GG	little Tommy	SON OF A GUN
• little John	JNO		(*see also* small[3])
• little money	D, –ID, IP, P	**live**	
• little mother	MA	live	BE
• little notice	AD	• live animal	BEHIND
• little response	ANS	• live more violently	BEWILDER
• little river	R	• live *on* fertile land	BEARABLE
• Little Rock	GIB	• live *on* the street	BEST
• little theatre	REP	live teams	BESIDES
• little time	D, H, HR, M, MIN,	[live] *broadcast*	EVIL, VILE
	MO, S, SEC, T	live long, *say*	DILATE
• little way	RD, RY, ST	live round	BEO–
	(*see also* reduce, small[2])	live *round*<	EVIL
little[3]		live teams	BESIDES
other uses:		lived so long	AV
a little of t/he be/ef	HEBE	*lively* [dance]	CANED
little bird, *say*	ROBINET	lively figures	VIVID
Little Boy Blue	PUT TO SEA	<u>l</u>ively *start*	L
little bounder	JOEY	lively voice	ACTIVE
little bread	CRUMB, PETTY CASH	lives	IS
little butter	KID, PAT	• lives *in* about . . .	RISE

Letter replaced \c\at; Omit (a); Pointers *out*; Retain <u>a</u>; Split B_ED; Down (D); Backwards <or ^

• lives in a vessel	ISINGLASS
• lives round city	ISOBATH
• Scot lives . . .	TAXIS
living person	INCUMBENT
living	QUICK
• living space	QUICKSTEP
• living tree	QUICKLIME
one *lives in* . . .	incl A, I
* *lives in* . . .	incl *
• we *live in* he–r . . .	HEWER

lizard

lizard *skin*	LD
lizard's place	CORNWALL

l-letter LEN, LESS

load

load-bearing female, *say*	ASSESS
load, *say*	LAID, LODE
loaded	BULLETIN, DRUNK, RICH

loan

loan records	–IOUS
loan, *say*	LONE, SINGLE

lob HIGHBALL, UPSHOT

lobby correspondent DIETED

local

local	BAR
• local employee	BARMAID, BARMAN
	BARTENDER
• local paper	BARMS
• local profit	BARGAIN
local	INN
• local worker	INNKEEPER
• location for pub, *say*	INCITE, INSIGHT
• pub *in* service	LINNET
local	PH
• local *has* no style	PHOTON
• local one	PHONE
• local one *has almost* al(l) . . .	PHIAL
local	PUB
• local is . . .	PUBIS
• local student in charge	PUBLIC
local	

indicating colloquialism:

• is not *local*	AINT
• *local* (h)aunt	AUNT
• *locally* (h)otter	OTTER
local	

indicating dialect:

• *local* branch	GRAIN, SHROUD
• *locally* caught	CATCHED
• *locally* worse	WUSS
Local Defence Volunteers	HG, LDV
local deliveryman	BREWER, DRAYMAN
Local Education Authority	LEA
local target	DARTBOARD

locate

located in *	incl in *
• I am *located in* Avon	AVION

located in t/he w/oods	HEW
Location of Offices Bureau	LOB
location for pub, *say*	INCITE, INSIGHT
location, *say*	CITE, SIGHT

loch NESS

lock

lock	TRESS
• a lock-*up*(D)^	ASSERT
• girl's locks	DISTRESSES
• the *Camptown* lock-*up*(D)^	DESSERT
lock keeper	HAIR NET, HAIR PIN
	KIRBIGRIP, KIRBY-GRIP
lock, stock and barrel	RIFLE
lock up	INTERN
• lock up drug	INTERNE
• lock up gangster	INTERNAL
• lock up journalist	INTERNED
locked	HAIRY
locker	KEY
locker, *say*	QUAY
locks out	ALOPECIA
locksmith	WIGMAKER

lodge

lodged in *	incl in *
• convict *lodged in* vil–e . . .	VILLAGE
lodger	GUEST
• lodger, *say*	GUESSED
lodger	PG
lodgings	PAD

logarithm LOG

logic

logical *extremes*	LL

London

London	SMOKE, WEN
–and North-Eastern Railway	LNER
–County Council	LCC
–Midland and Scottish	LMS
–Missionary Society	LMS
–Philharmonic Orchestra	LPO
–School of Economics	LSE
–Symphony Orchestra	LSO
London area	SE
• *in* London area, it . . .	SITE
• London area squares	SETS, SETT
• the London area	THESE
London banker	THAMES
London-bound	UP
London landlord	CAPITAL LETTER
London magazine	ARSENAL
London police	MP
London town	DERRY
London train	TRINE
to London	UP

long

long	DIE
• long dead	DIED
• long for Edward	DIETED

• long time	DIET	• look *round*	L–O
long	L	• look round	LOO
• long • one foot	LIFT	• look *up*(D)^	OL
• long round cask	LOVAT	and	
• longboat	LARK	• a look of . . .	ALOOF
long	PINE	• look *in* two directions	SLOW
• circle *has* long . . .	OPINE	• look one way	LOWEST
• long fruit	PINE-APPLE	look	PEEK
• long line	PINERY	• look *back<*	KEEP
• long mallet	PINE BEETLE	• look *up*(D)^	KEEP
• long nettle	PINE NEEDLE	• look, *say*	PEAK, PIQUE
• long stomach	PINETUM	look	SEE
• long tree	PINE	• look *at* five hundred . . .	SEED
• street *without* long . . .	SPINET	• look *out*	SE–E
• second long . . .	SPINE	• look *over<*	–EES
long-awaited man	GODOT	• look *round<*	–EES
long dispute	FARROW	• look *round*	SE–E
long distance runner	AMAZON, NILE etc	• look *up*(D)^	–EES
long metre	LM	• looks *both ways*	SEES
long-playing record	LP	look	V
long range	ALPS, ANDES etc	• look *at* fever	VAGUE
long ruler, *say*	HIKING	• look-*in*	incl V
long runner	THE MOUSETRAP	• look in about . . .	VINCA
long service	OUT OF COURT	• look in square	VINT
long-standing friend	CHRONICALLY	• look-*out*	omit V
Longfellow	SILVER	look	VID(E)
longing *after* god	PANACHE	• look *about* an . . .	VIAND
longing for food	LUSTRATION	• look *round<*	DIV
longitude	LON(G)	• look *round*	VI–D
look¹		• look *round* a soft . . .	VAPID
look	AIR	• look no . . .	VIDEO
• look left	AIRPORT	• look *up*(D)^	DIV
• Look, mister!	AIRMAN	**look²**	
• look unprepossessing,		look ahead, *say*	FARCY, FARSI
say	AIRPLANE	look *around*	PE–ER
• look *up*(D)^	–RIA	look *around<*	KEEP
look	EYE	look at	
• look *both ways*	EYE	–American	GAZEBO
• look lively	EYEBRIGHT	–fish, *say*	PEOPLING
• look *up and down*(D)	EYE	–letter	PEERESS
• looks warm	EYESHOT	–speech	WATCHWORDS
look	LA	look *both ways*	EYE, PEEP
• look *almost* de(a)d	LADED	look equal	PEER
• look *at* the . . .	LATHE	look for	SEEK
• look in	LAIN	• look for ruler	SEEKER
• look-*in*	incl LA	• look for ruler, *say*	SEEKING
• look-*out*	omit LA	and	
• look *round<*	AL	• look for Alf, *say*	SEA-CALF
• look *round*	L–A	• look for argument, *say*	SEA-CROW
• look under	LAUNDER	• look for beer, *say*	SEA-KALE
• look *up*(D)^	AL	• look for wine, *say*	SEA-COCK
look	LO	and	
• look in	LOIN	• look for, *say*	SIKH
• look-*in*	incl LO	and	
• look *on*	LOON	• look for them, *say*	CAECUM
• look-*out*	omit LO	look out	CAVE, FORE
• look *round<*	OL	look *out*	SE–E

lookalike caller	RINGER	*lose* energy	omit E
looked *around*	SE–EN	*lose half* that	TH, AT
looked *back<*	WAS	*lose head*	omit 1st letter
looked *up*(D)^	WAS	• (s)he *loses her head*	HE
looking about	REGARDING	*lose* heart	omit middle
looking *at* cat	PEEPING TOM	• pat(i)ent *loses* heart	PATENT
looking into ne/w ide/as	WIDE	• sc(hol)ar *loses* heart	SCAR
lookout	SE-E	• t(he)y *lose* heart	–TY
• look*out* dog	SECURE	*lose* his shirt	omit T
• Look*out*, Sam!	SESAME	*lose* key	omit A–G
lookout man	EXTRAVERT, EXTROVERT	*lose* king	omit K, R
looks both ways	SEES	*lose* knight	omit N
tots *looking up*(D)^	STOT	*lose* lead	omit 1st letter
loony		*lose* money	omit D, L, P
loony-[bin]	NIB	*lose* nothing	omit O
loony *left*	L	*lose* o*dds* an*d* ends	omit OD
loony [left]	FELT	*lose* one	omit A, I
loop		*lose* one's shirt	omit T
loop	O	*lose* one's shirt	omit IST
loophole, *say*	ISLET	*lose* opener	omit 1st letter
loops in chain, *say*	LYNX	• (M)CC *lose* opener	CC, HUNDREDS
loose		*lose* pawn	omit P
loos*e ends*	LE	*lose* power	omit P
loose [ends]	DENS, SEND	*lose* prisoner	omit CON
loose painter	CAST OFF	*lose* rook	omit R
loosely fastened, *say*	HALF-TIDE	*lose* queen	omit ER, Q
loosely [tied ends]	DESTINED	*lose* silver . . .	omit AG
loosen [ties]	SITE	*lose* tail	omit last letter
loosen up [a bit]	BAIT	• do(g) *loses* tail	DO
loosens part of roof, *say*	FREESTYLE	*lose* the right	omit R
loosens trousers	SLACKS	*lose* the round	omit O
[screw] *loose*	CREWS	*lose* the way	omit N, S, E, W
lop			omit AVE, RD, ST
lop of(f)	OF	*lose* time	omit AGE, MO, SEC, T
lopping (b)ranch	RANCH	*losing* a . . .	omit A
lord	LD	*losing* *	omit *
Lord		• fa(the)r *losing* the . . .	FAR
–Chief Justice	LCJ	*loss of first* . . .	omit 1st letter
–Justice	LJ	• *loss of first* (p)awn	AWN
–Provost	LP	*loss of* ship	omit SS
lord in court	LUD	*loss of* wicket	omit W
Lord North	SIREN	*lost in* . . .	omit IN
Lord's ground	EARLDOM	• *lost in* Spa(in)	SPA
Lordship	LDP, LP	**lose³**	
Los Angeles	LA	lose bottle	COWER, PANIC
lose¹		lose colour	GOWAN
indicating an anagram:		lose girl	MISS
lose [heart]	EARTH, HATER, RATHE	lose *heart*	
[lose] *out*	SLOE, SOLE	• diplomats lose *heart*	CLOSED
lose sequence of [letters]	SETTLER	lose most	WINSOME
lose series of [sets in] . . .	STEINS	loses colour, *say*	GRAZE
lost [a set]	SATE, SEAT, TEAS	lost colour, *say*	GRADE
lose²		lost editor	UNFOUNDED
indicating omission:		**loss**	(*see* lose)
lose all . . .	omit ALL	**lost**	(*see* lose)
• b(all)oon *loses* all . . .	BOON	**lot**	
lose bishop	omit B	a lot of wo/men, tall,	

Anag [cat]; Any *; Begin IGN–; Endings –ING; eg •; Hidden /cat/; Implied add (on); Implied in (in);

y/oung . . .	MENTALLY
lot	C, D, L, M
lot of fruit	ORANG(e), PEA(r)
lot of lines	BR, RY
	ODE, POEM, VERSE
lot of money	IMPOUNDS
lot of <u>seat</u>s	SEA
lots of beer	NINEPINS
lots of ships	FLEET, NAVY, RN
	(*see also* many¹)

loud

loud	F
• a loud anger	AFIRE
• a loud blonde	AFFAIR
• a loud listener	AFEAR
and	
• loud instrument	FLUTE
• loud music	FROCK
• loud yob	FLOUT
loud, *say*	FORTY
loudspeaker	BOANERGES, STENTOR
	PA
very loud	FF
• a very loud blow	AFFRIGHT
• a very loud attack	AFFRAID
• a very loud song	AFFAIR

lousy

lousy [at reading]	TRAGEDIAN
[it was] *lousy*	WAIST, WAITS

love

love	O
• love a little	OBIT
• love china	OPAL
• love divine	ODD
• love letter	O
• love letter	OF, OH, ON, OR, OS
	OMISSIVE
• love letters	OAR, OBE etc
• love offal	OLIVER
• no love	OO
and	
• dog I love	CURIO
• lady's love	HERO
• time for love	MAYO
and	
• accountants in love	CASINO
• love-*in*-a-m–ist	MOIST
• love*less*	omit O
• love*lorn*	omit O
and	
• fifty loves	LOO
• loves old coin	OORIAL
• loves speed	OOMPH
love	ZERO
• earth-love	GROUND-ZERO
• love in a cold climate	ZERO
love	POINTLESS

love-letter	LIKEN
love-sickness	AFFECTION
love *to* search	HONEYCOMB
lovebird	DUCK
lovelight	FLAME
lover	LOTHARIO
lover-boy	CUPID, EROS
lover *of the country*	SWAIN
loving son	TENDERS

low

low	BASE
• low pedestal	BASE
• Low Street	BASEST
• low trap	BASENET
low	MOO
• low church	MOOCH
• low Latin	MOOL
• low point	MOON
• low quarters	MOONS, MOOSE
• low-*rise*(D)^	–OOM
• low river	MOOR
• low stream	MOOR-ILL
• low table	MOOTABLE
• low trap	MOONET
• lowed, *say*	MOOD
Low character	BLIMP
[low] *characters*	OWL
low class, *say*	DEGRADE, FORESEE
[low] *cunning*	OWL
low dance	BASEBALL, LIMBO
low-down	GEN
low fellow	HEAL, HE'LL
low frequency	LF
Low German	LG
low grade	E
• low-grade German . . .	EG
• low grade, *say*	EATEN
• low grades, *say*	EASE
low grade, *say*	DEGRADE, FORESEE
low interest	BOREDOM, ENNUI
Low Latin	LL
low note, *say*	DEEP SEA
low pot	BLUEGRASS
low pressure	LP
low priced	PEACH
low ranker	PAWN, PRIVATE
low *sound*	LO
low swinger	CHARIOT
low tar	SUBMARINER
low tension	LT
lower	COW
• lower class	BOVINE, CATTLE, COWS
• lower fare	CATTLE CAKE, GRASS
• lower fellow	COWMAN
• Lower House	BYRE, COWSHED
• lower in front	COWLED
• lower jumper	JERSEY

Letter replaced \c\at; Omit (a); Pointers *out*; Retain <u>a</u>; Split B_ED; Down (D); Backwards <or ^

• lower sound	MOO
• lower tender	COWHERD, COWMAN
• lower writer	COW-PEN
lower case	LC
lower classes	DE–
lower number	DENOMINATOR
lower percentage	CUT
lowered, *say*	GLAIRED
lowest note	FIVER
loyal friend	ACHATES
lubricate	
lubricate eyes, *say*	GRECISE
lubricate surface, *say*	OILSKIN
lubricates family	OILSKIN
Lucifer's home	MATCHBOX
lucky man	JIM
lumen	L
luminance	L
lump	
lump of bee/f is h/ard	FISH
lump of <u>earth</u>	EAR
lumps of <u>rock</u> <u>are</u> . . .	ROAR
lunatic	
[it was] *lunatic*	WAIST, WAITS
lunatic [king is] . . .	SKIING

lunchtime	ONE, I
lurk	
lurking in hi/din/g	DIN
lurking in [trees]	REEST, RESET, STEER
lurking in *	incl in *
• she is *lurking in* a–n . . .	ASHEN
lux	LX
Luxembourg	L
luxury	
luxurious drinker	LUSH
luxury car	LIMO, RR
lying	
lying around a . . .	incl A
lying around *	incl *
• the–y were *lying* *around* or . . .	THEORY
lying cleric	INCUMBENT
lying in s/un if y/ou . . .	UNIFY
lyrics	AIRLINES
lysergic acid	LSD

M

Bond's boss, em, emma, *Frenchman*, *lot*, Mach number, magnetisation, maiden, male, Malta, *man*, *many*, *mare*, mark, married, masculine, mass, master, medium, medius, member, meridian, meso-, meta-, metre, middle voice, mile, mille, milli-, million, modulus, Monday, monsieur, month, moon, motorway, mu, noon, number, quantum number, roof, *small square*, *spymaster*, thousand, vitamin

£1,000,000	IMPOUNDS	**made**	
M1	MOTORWAY, RIFLE	*freshly* [made]	DAME, EDAM, MEAD
Mac	ASCOT	made better, *say*	HEALD, HEELED
Mac (=Scottish)		made by hand, *say*	HANDMAID
• look warily *for Mac*	GLEDGE	made *comeback<*	EDAM
• Mac *on the wagon*	WAINSCOT	made *for the ear*	MAID
• *Mac's* cottage	BOTHIE, BOTHY	made it	FEC(IT), FF
• *Mac's* laugh	LAUCH	*made it up* [so we] . . .	OWES, WOES
Maccabees	MAC	made late	KILLED, SLEW
machination		*made* [late]	LEAT, TALE, TEAL
[cruel] *machination*	LUCRE, ULCER	made man	ROBOT
machination [that Ed] . . .	HATTED	made notes	COMPOSED, EARNED
machine-gun	MG		PLAYED, SANG
light machine-gun	LMG	*made of* [gin]	–ING
mad		*made of* [steel]	LEETS, STELE
mad character	HATTER	made out [case]	ACES, AESC
[mad] *characters*	ADM–, DAM	made out of p/latin/um	LATIN
mad	BATS	made *over<*	EDAM
• I am *in* mad	BAITS	made *speech*	MAID
• mad creatures	BATS	made tea, *say*	BROOD
• mad individual	BATSMAN	made terrorists, *say*	MADEIRA
• mad strikers	BATS	*made* [to run race]	RACONTEUR
mad [dog]	GOD	made *up*(D)^	EDAM
mad *French* . . .	FOLLE, FOU	made up of [parts]	PRATS, SPRAT, STRAP
mad *German*	VERRUCKT	*made up* [tales]	LEATS, SLATE, STALE, TEALS
Mad [Hatter]	THREAT	*made* [worse]	SWORE
		[made] *worse*	DAME, EDAM, MEAD
mad *Italian*	MATTO	*made worse* [wines]	SINEW, SWINE
mad king	LEAR	made you, *say*	MAY-DEW
• mad king, *say*	LEER		(*see also* make)
mad Leigh, *say*	CRAZILY		
mad Roman	NON COMPOS MENTIS	**magazine**	
mad Scot, *say*	REDWOOD	magazine	GLOSSY, MAG
mad *Spanish* . . .	LOCO		POWDER-ROOM
mad strikers	BATS	magazine	PUNCH
maddened [beast]	BASTE, BATES, BEATS	• magazine editor	PUNCHED
madly [keen]	KNEE	• magazine policy	PUNCH-LINE
madman	HATTER	• poor golfer's magazine	RABBIT
madmen curse . . .	NUTSHELL		PUNCH
Madagascar	RM	magazine	TIME
madam	MDE, MDM	• display magazine	AIRTIME
		• magazine article	TIMEPIECE

Letter replaced \c\at; Omit (a); Pointers *out*; Retain <u>a</u>; Split B_ED; Down (D); Backwards <or ^

• magazine list	TIMETABLE	main battle	TRAFALGAR etc
magazine article	BOMB, BULLET	main course	HARD TACK, SHIP'S BISCUIT
	DYNAMITE, EXPLOSIVE	main event	REGATTA
	GUNPOWDER, SHELL	main force	NAVY
maggot		main robber	PIRATE
maggot	GRUB	main scene	SEASCAPE
• maggot-cutter	GRUB-AXE	main supervisor	NEPTUNE, POSEIDON
• maggot food	GRUB		SEA-GOD
• maggot near	GRUBBY	main support	MAST, YARD(-ARM)
magic		main tower	TUGBOAT
Magic [Circle]	CLERIC	**main²**	
magical flier	FILER	main	COCK
magical flier	CARPET	• main battle	COCKFIGHT
magical [trips]	SPIRT, SPRIT	• main scene	COCKPIT
magician, *say*	TRICKING	• prevent main	STOPCOCK
magician's bird	MERLIN	main aisle, *say*	KNAVE
magistrate		main distributor	AORTA
magistrate	BEAK	*main mass of* her(d)	HER
• magistrate *takes in* money	BLEAK	*main part of* arm(y)	ARM
• magistrate *with* queen	BEAKER	main partner	MIGHT
• magistrate's bill	BEAK	main road	AI, BROADWAY, MI
magistrates note . . .	BENCHMARK	*mainly* woo(d)	WOO
magnetic	MAG	mainstream	RIVER
maiden		**maintain**	
Maid of the Mountains	OREAD	*maintain* a . . .	incl A
maiden	M	maintain tower	KEEP
• maiden in shirt	MINT	• maintain issue	KEEPS ON
• maiden over	MENDED, MOVER	maintain worker	AVOWANT
• Yes, *German* maiden . . .	JAM	*maintain* *	incl *
maiden	GAL	• pi–es *maintain* king	PIKES
• maiden, *after* about . . .	REGAL	*maintained by* m/	
• maiden cut . . .	GALLOP	an ent/irely . . .	ANENT
• maiden *over<*	LAG	*maintained by* *	incl in *
maiden(D)	IO	• king *maintained by* pi–es	PIKES
maiden production	PARTHENOGENESIS	**Majesty**	
	VIRGIN BIRTH	His/Her Majesty	HM
two maidens	MALICE, MANNA, MM	Majesties	MM
mail		Majesty	M
[mail]-*order*	LIAM, MALI	**major**	
mail sent out	OUTPOST	major	BARBARA
[mail]-shot	LIAM	• major film	BARBARA
mailboat	RMS	major	GROWN UP, MAJ
main¹		major sin, *say*	PRIM(A)EVAL
main	DEEP	*majority of* th(e) . . .	TH
• cover main . . .	SKINDEEP	**make**	
• main ruler	DEEPER	make	CREATE
• main note, *say*	DEEP SEA	• make charged particle, *say*	CREATION
main	SEA	• make journalist, *say*	CREATED
• main course	SEA-FOOD	• make mineral, *say*	CREATOR
• main issue	SEASON	• making *say*	CREATIN(E), KREATIN
• main meal	SEAFOOD	make	DO
• main picture	SEASCAPE	• make a bet	DOWAGER
• main road	SEA-LANE	• make fast	DOLENT
• main square	SEAT	• make money	DOCENT, DOYEN
• main support	SEASHORE	• make note	DOB, DOC, DOE, DOG
• main weapon	SEASHELL		DODO, DOME, DOTE

Anag [cat]; Any *; Begin IGN–; Endings –ING; eg •; Hidden /cat/; Implied add (on); Implied in (in);

• make notes	DOFF, DOGE	making waves	CRIMPING, CURLING
make-*up*(D)^	OD		HAIRDRESSING
make	FORM	[she had] *makeover*	HASHED
• make gangster . . .	FORMAL	[shoe]-*making*	HOES, HOSE
• make queen	FORMER		(*see also* made)
• tablet I make, *say*	PILIFORM	**Malachi**	MAL
make a dash	HYPHENATE	**maladjusted**	
make a hash of [it when] . . .	WHITEN	*maladjusted* [boy]	YOB
make a joke of it, *say*	PUNNET	[she was] *maladjusted*	WASHES
make a mess of [things]	NIGHTS	**Malawi**	MW
make a song *about*	S–ING	**Malaysia**	MAL
make an offer	BIDON	**male**	
make changes in [Cremona]	ROMANCE	male	BUCK
make comfortable bed	WELLSPRING	• male artist	BUCKRA
make damp, *say*	WHET	• male sheep	BUCKRAM
ma̲k̲e̲ ends . . .	ME	• noticed male . . .	SAWBUCK
make headlines	FROWN	male	GENT
make her quiet, *say*	USHER	• male fish	GENTEEL
make holes in, *say*	PEERS, PIERS	• male *in* early, *say*	URGENTLY
make it go	WINTRY	• male partner	COGENT
make it safe, *say*	LOCKET	• male Scot	GENTIAN
make it wobble, *say*	ROCKET	• old city male	URGENT
make light of	IGNITE	male	HE
make little difference		• male bird	HEMINA
to design	RESIGN	• male birds	HEAVES
make mention of witch	WHICH	• male cat	HELION
make notes	SING	• male departed, *say*	HEEDED
make notes *about*	S–ING	• male flower	HEAVENS
make of [gin]	–ING	• male group	HELOT
make one	MARRY, UNITE, WED	• male *in* group	SHEET
make people laugh	BEDROLL	• male journalist	HEED
make play	BRAND	• male representative	HEMP
make room	CAUSEWAY	• male sheep	HET-UP
make [tea]	ATE, EAT, ETA	• male students	HELL
make up [a bed]	BADE, BEAD	• male *with* a fellow . . .	HEAD-ON
make-up of [stars]	TSARS	male	HIM
make-up unit	CHROMOSOME, GENE	• male *aboard*	SHIMS
make us		• male *in* church	CHIME
–redundant, *say*	SACCOS, SACCUS	• woman *has* male . . .	WHIM
–sad, *say*	GRIEVOUS	male	M
–stand up, *say*	COCCUS	• male as first-class . . .	MASAI
make wager	BETON	• male in a shirt	MINT
make waves	CRIMP, CURL, PERM	• male tree	MACER, MASH
make way	FASHION	• male *with* nothing on	MOON
*make * heard*		male	MAN
• horse *makes itself heard*	HOARSE	• English male dined . . .	EMANATE
• *make itself heard* by . . .	BUY	• male animal	MANTIGER
*make * redundant*	omit *	• male composer, *say*	MANHANDLE
• fat(her) *makes* her *redundant*	FAT	• male *with* English . . .	MANE
makes [cars]	ARCS, SCAR	male birds, *say*	COX
makes progress	STEPSON	male chauvinist pig	MCP
makes some of t/he Be/lgians . . .	HEBE	male deer, *say*	HEART
making a contribution		male dog	BOBTAIL
to jo/int o/peration	INTO	ma̲l̲e̲ lead	M
making [tarts]	START	male principle	YANG
making of [Mary]	ARMY, MYRA	male reeve, *say*	ROUGH

Letter replaced \c\at; Omit (a); Pointers *out*; Retain a̲; Split B_ED; Down (D); Backwards <or ^

male *said* . . .	MAIL
male twins, *say*	BISONS
males	MEN
• male champions	MENACES
• male pickpockets	MENDIPS
• males curse	MENSWEAR
• without male . . .	OMEN, NOMEN
	(*see also* man)

malform

malformation of [part]	RAPT, TRAP
malformed [arm]	MAR, RAM

malfunction

malfunction of [part]	RAPT, TRAP
malfunctioning [timer]	REMIT
Mali	RMM

malicious

malicious light	ARSON
malicious publisher	LIBELLER

malleable

malleable [as putty]	STAY PUT
[quite] *malleable*	QUIET
Malta	M

maltreat

maltreated [horses]	HOSERS, SHORES
maltreatment of [animal]	LAMINA, MANILA

man¹

commonly used names:

man	AL
• man *carrying* weapon	ALARMED
• man *in* the Home Counties	SALE
• quiet man	PAL
man	BEN
• man *goes to* church	BENCH
• man *on* the square	BENT
• man *with* one child	BENISON
man	DES
• lou–t *set about* man	LOUDEST
• man slays . . .	DESKILLS
• the *French*man	LADES
man	DON
• a number *take* man . . .	TENDON
• man devoured . . .	DONATE
• man *in* shape	CONDONE
man	ED
• he *is with* a man	HEED
• man *has* it or . . .	EDITOR
• man lacking . . .	NEEDED
man	HERB
• man *in* group	SHERBET
• man rented . . .	HERBLET
• shoot man	POT HERB
man	REG
• man *flanked by* daughter and son	DREGS
• man *takes* beer	REGALE
• man without feeling, *say*	REGNUM

man	SID
• a man *takes* drug	ASIDE
• man in front	SIDLED
• *put* hat *on* man	CAPSID
man	TED
• iron man	FETED
• man promises to pay	TEDIOUS
• mother *takes* man	MATED

man²

man	CHAP
• man killed in action	CHAP-FALLEN
• man rented . . .	CHAPLET
• man *without* energy	CHEAP
• man's trousers	CHAPS
• mantrap	CHAPNET
man	CREW
• man aboard	SCREWS
• manned *say*	CRUDE
• second man	SCREW
man	FELLOW
• man, *say*	FELLOE
• man's at home, *say*	FELLAHIN
• plot *with* man	BEDFELLOW
man	IOM, ISLE
man	HE
• man behind	HEARSE
• man speaks to . . .	HEADDRESSES
• man *with* gun	HEROD
• man *with* more than one wife	HEBRIDES
man	M
man *and* boy	GENTLES, JACKSON
	ROBINSON, WILLIAMSON
man *and* woman	EVADES, MANGAL
	REGINA, SALTED, VIAL
man doing housework	BETTY
man from	
−Adelaide	DIGGER
−America	BO
−Am/eric/a	ERIC
−[Ayr]	RAY
−Berlin	MANN
−Glasgow	IAN, MAC, MON
−Madrid	HOMBRE
−New Ze/alan/d	ALAN
−O/reg/on	REG
−Paris	HOMME
−[Roma]	OMAR
−Rome	
ancient	VIR
modern	UOMO
−the river	DON
man *has* one over the eight	LEONINE
man in	
−a tub	DIOGENES
−the . . .	HE
man of	

–determination	WILL
–force	NEWTON
–India	CLIVE
–letters	PAUL, POSTMAN
–magnetism	GAUSS
–might	SMITH
–power	WATT
–pride	LEO
–Savoy	GILBERT, SULLIVAN
–the match	BRIDEGROOM
	LUCIFER
–Verona	GENTLEMAN,PROTEUS,
	VALENTINE
–war	BOER
man on	
–board	DRAUGHT
BISHOP, KING, KNIGHT, PAWN	
–watch	ALBERT
man, *say*	FELLOE, MAIL
man the ring	THEO
man who makes hay	TED
man *with* suit	JUST IN CASE
man's at home, *say*	FELLAHIN
man's drink	PORTER
man's man	VALET
Man's man	DOUGLAS
manservant	FRIDAY, JEEVES
	VALET
manservant, *say*	VALLEY
	(*see also* male)
manage	
manage	COPE
• fairies manage . . .	PERISCOPE
• manage daughter	COPED
• managing jewellery	COPING-STONES
manage	EIGHTEEN
manage	RUN
• manage English . . .	RUNE
• manage *in* exercise	PRUNE
• managing directors	RUNNING-BOARD
manage doctor	TREAT
manage [horse]	HOSER, SHORE
managed	RAN
• 100 managed	CRAN
• managed a few *say*	RANSOM
• managed *without* one . . .	RAIN
management	ADMIN, BOARD
management blunder	OVERSIGHT
management group, *say*	BORED
management [team]	MATE, MEAT, TAME
managing director	MD
managing [director]	CREDITOR
mandarin	
mandarin	DUCK A L'ORANGE
mandarin's coat	ORANGE PEEL
mandari<u>n</u>'s *coat*	MN

mangle	
mangle, *say*	MANGEL, RINGER
mangled [arm]	MAR, RAM
mangling [English]	SHINGLE
manifold divers	MANY
manipulate	
[cruel] *manipulation*	LUCRE, ULCER
manipulate [men as] . . .	MEANS, NAMES
manipulating [pawns]	SPAWN
manipulation of [bone]	EBON
manoeuvre	
manoeuvrable [plane]	PANEL
manoeuvred [his car]	CHAIRS
manoeuvring [ship]	HIPS, PISH
manor	
manor	HOUSE OF LORDS
manor, *say*	GUISE, MANNER
manual	
manual work	BOOKMAKING
manual worker	BOOKMAKER, ORGANIST
manufacture	
manufactured	MFD
manufacturer(s)	MFR(S)
manufacturer of [china]	CHAIN
manufactures [tables]	BLEATS, STABLE
manuscript	
manuscript	MS
• cleaner manuscript	CHARMS
• military manuscript	WARMS
• the lady's manuscript	HERMS
manuscripts	MSS
Manx	
Manx cat	CA(t), PUS(s)
<u>M</u>anx *leader*	M
Manx man	DOUGLAS, KELLY, MA(n)
many	
many	HOST
• good many	GHOST
• many *in* Gilbert &	
Sullivan . . .	GHOSTS
• many times	HOSTAGES
many	LOT
• afterthought *about* many . . .	PLOTS
• many aboard	SLOTS
• many charged particles	LOTIONS
• many not working	LOTUS
many	
indicating Roman	
numerals:	C, CL, D, K, L, M
• many long . . .	CACHE
• many have . . .	CLOWN
• a lot *have* a right . . .	DART
• many sick	KILL
• many articles	LATHE
• fight *with* many . . .	WARM
	(*see also* number)

many ate, *say*	FORTITUDE
many larks	EXALTATION
many mad, *say*	FUSAIN
ma(n)y *nameless* . . .	MAY
many old, *say*	FU YUNG
[many] *parts*	MYNA
many sane, *say*	FUSILLI
many welcome, *say*	FUSION
m(an)y *won't have* an . . .	MY
mapmakers	OS
marathon runner	(THE) MOUSETRAP
marble	
[marble] *bust*	RAMBLE
marbles champion	ELGIN
march	
March	MAR
• army *on the* march	TAMAR
• March 10	MARIO
• March *with* 1000 . . .	MARK
march	TRAMP
• fish *after* March	TRAMPLING
• march in front	TRAMPLED
march	YOMP
March Militaire	FROG MARCH
	MARSEILLAISE
marching order	L–R
	BEAT IT, SCRAM
marching together	INSTEP
mare	
mare	DAM
• a mare	ADAM
• English mare	EDAM
• mare got old	DAMAGED
mare, *say*	MAYOR
marginal advantage	EDGE
marijuana	
marijuana	POT
• marijuana *found in* vessel	SPOTS
• marijuana refuse	POTASH
• son *has* marijuana	SPOT
marine	
Marine	JOLLY
marine animal, *say*	SELION, WAIL, WALE
Marine band	CREW
marine biologist, *say*	SEA-LACE
marine detachment	ISLAND, ISLE(T)
marine, *say*	NAVEL
Marines	RM
• a jolly girl	ARMADA
• company of Marines	CORM
• he *joined* the Marines	HERM
[Marines] *at sea*	REMAINS, SEMINAR
mark¹	
mark	DM
mark	M
• Mark I	MI

• Mark is tired	MISSPENT
• Mark *wearing* a tie	TIME
• *see* Mark *after* tea	TEAM
mark	MK
mark *out*	omit M
• mark *omitted by* (m)ale . . .	ALE
• (m)aster *omits* Mark	ASTER
mark²	
mark	ANTONY
mark	BRAND
• Mark will, *say*	BRANDLE
• the revolutionary *in* Mark	BRANCHED
mark	SCAR
• mark church	SCARCE
• mark sailor	SCARAB
• the *French* mark . . .	LASCAR
Mark I	MI
Mark II	(MARK) TWAIN
mark butterfly	COMMA
Mark of the Beast	MB
mark, *say*	MINED
mark time	DOTAGE, LINEAGE
marksman, *say*	CHICO, GROUCHO
	HARPO, KARL
market	
market	CM, E(E)C
market square	FAIR
maroon thread	STRAND
marriage	(*see* marry)
marry	
marriage-bowl	MATCHWOOD
marriage	UNION
• marriage declines	UNION FLAGS
• second-rate marriage	BUNION
• marriages	UNITED STATES
married	M
• a married woman	AMERICA
• married man	MART
• married quarters	MESE, MESS, MEW(S)
• married woman	MALICE, MANNA,
	MINA
married	WED
• American married . . .	BOWED
• father married . . .	PAWED
• married girl	UNAWED
• name *in* married . . .	WEND
married couple	H–W
married people	THEWED
marry again	REPAIR
marry many	MATELOT
marry, *say*	TAKE AMISS
marrying man	PRIEST, REGISTRAR,
	VICAR
Mars	
[Mars]	ORDER ARMS
order [mars] . . .	ARMS, RAMS

Marshal	
marshal	FOCH, NEY
Marshal [Ney]	YEN
[race] *marshal*	ACER, ACRE, CARE
martyr	
martyr	M
martyrs	MM
marvellous	
marvellous	FAB
• page about marvellous . . .	PREFAB
• marvellous girl	FABELLA
• marvellous man	FABIAN
Marxist drug	OPIUM
Mary's follower	LAMB
masculine	M, MAS(C)
mash	
[bran]-*mash*	BARN
mashed [peas]	APSE
mashing [tea]	ATE, EAT, ETA
Masonic chief	MASTER BUILDER
masquerade	
masquerade as [Oriental]	RELATION
masquerading [in gown]	OWNING
mass	
mass	M
mass producer	LITURGIST, PRIEST
mass production	EUCHARIST
Massachusetts Institute	
of Technology	MIT
massacre	
[Herod's] *massacre*	HORDES
massacre of [babes]	ABBES
massage	
massage	RUB
• daughters massages . . .	DRUBS
• massage donkey, *say*	RUBASSE
• massage girl	RUBELLA
massage [arm]	MAR, RAM
massaging [leg]	GEL
master	
master	AM
• 150 masters	CLAMS
• master *has* afterthought	AMPS
• master *in the French* . . .	LAMA, LAME(S)
master	DAN
• directions *to* master	SEDAN
• master is hard	DANISH
• master *at* church	DANCE
master	M
• master *and* emperor	MOTTO
• master in America	MINUS
• master *with* a girl	MALICE
master	MA
• master *has* one study	MAIDEN
• master-key	MAB, MAC, MAD,
	MAE, MAG

• masterly figure	MAC, MAD, MAL,
	MAM, MAX
master	SIR
• master approves, *say*	SURPASSES
• master *has* awful . . . *say*	SERVILE
• raise master, *say*	GROCER
[master]-*builder*	REMAST, STREAM
master key for . . .	HEADLOCK
Master of	
–Arts	MA
–Dental Surgery	MDS
–Foxhounds	MOF
–Laws	LLM
–Science	MSC
–Surgery	MCH, MS, CHM, CM
–the Rolls	MR, CHAUFFEUR
–Theology	MTH
Master of Ceremonies	MC
Master of Ceremonies, *say*	COMPARE
[master] *switch*	REMAST, STREAM
masterpiece	MAS, TER
masterstroke	COUP, HOLE IN ONE
maths master	EUCLID
mat	
mat *finish*	T
matted [fibre]	BRIEF
match	
match	LIGHT, VESTA
match	TEST
• match-box	TEST CASE
match goddess	VESTA
match colour	TIERED
match level	SET ASIDE
match points	COMPARE
matches [none]	NEON
matchmaker	WOOD
matchmaker, *say*	PARER, WOULD
mate	
mate	CHINA, PAL, WIFE
mating of bears	BARES
mating of pairs	PEARS
material	
material	REP
• material consumer	REPEATER
• material *in* church	CREPE
• sit *on* material	SITREP
material	SERGE
• material on, *say*	SURGEON
• Russian material	SERGE
material [part]	PRAT, TRAP
material for [book]	BOKO
material used in [a cheap] . . .	APACHE
maths	
maths function	COS, LOG, SINE, TAN
• function put . . .	COSSET
• function in charge	LOGIC

Letter replaced \c\at; Omit (a); Pointers *out*; Retain a̲; Split B_ED; Down (D); Backwards <or ^

• function makes better . . .	SINECURES
• function with grand . . .	TANG
maths master	EUCLID
Mauretania	RIM
Mauritius	MS
maximum	
maxim*um*	MAX
maximum speed	C
may	
May 8th	V-DAY
may appear [later]	ALTER
may be [sent]	NETS, STEN, TENS
may become [weak]	WAKE
may he/she rest well	BQ
May's follower	JUNE
maybe	
indicating anagram:	
• *maybe* [Manet]	MEANT
• [I can] *maybe* . . .	CAIN
indicating homophone:	
• *maybe* right	WRITE
• nose, *maybe*	KNOWS
indicating one of a class:	
• *maybe* setter	DOG
• dog, *maybe*	SETTER
Mayday	SOS
Mayfair	WI
mayhem	
mayhem [in the] . . .	THINE
[or cause] *mayhem*	CAROUSE
Mayo	LADY-LOVE, TREE RING
mayor	
mayor, *say*	MARE
mayor's allowance, *say*	MACERATE
maze	
[Hampton] *maze*	PHANTOM
maze in [garden]	DANGER, RANGED
me	
me and the girl, *say*	MEANDER
me *following* the *French* . . .	LAME
me *in* France	MOI
me *in* Germany	MICH
me *in* Italy	MI
me *in* Spain	MI
meadow	
meadow	LEA
• exercise *around* meadow	PLEAT
• fine meadow	FLEA
• meadow grass	LEASING
meal	
meal	TEA
• meal *in* tin	STEAN
• meal *with* king	TEAK, TEAR
• meals will, *say*	TEASEL, TEASLE, TEAZEL
meal, *say*	FLOWER
meal ticket	LV

meal times	LUNCHEONS
meals on wheels	MOVEABLE FEASTS
mean	
mean	POOR
• mean, *say*	PORE, POUR
• mean city, *say*	PAUCITY
• mean old city, *say*	POROSITY
mean business	USURY
mean monarch	NEARER
mean person	AVERAGE MAN
mean, *say*	MIEN
mean sea-level	MSL
mean time	MT
means of	
–identification	PIN
–travel	BR
meant, *say*	–MENT
meantime	PARAGE
meander	
meander [about]	U-BOAT
meandering [stream]	MASTER, REMAST
measure	
measure	EL(L)
• good measure	GEL
• measure *in* king's . . .	HELMS
• measure part of fish	ELFIN
and	
• fine measure	FELL
• measure *in* grass	SELLING
• measure edges, *say*	ELLIPSE
measure	EM
• hard measures	HEMS
• measure corpse	EMBODY
• measure vehicle	EMBUS
measure	EN
• hard measures	HENS
• measure coin	ENNOBLE
• measure *in* doctor's . . .	MENDS
measure	FT
• a measure	AFT
• measure *about* a . . .	FAT
• the *French* measure	LEFT
measure	Y(D)
• measure *about* the *Spanish* . . .	YELD
• measure a street	YARD
• reasonable measure	FAIRY
measure	M
measure	PINT
• measure *about* a . . .	PAINT
• measure can . . .	PIN-TABLE
• measure nothing	PINTO
measure depth, *say*	PLUM
measure of a/le d/runk	LED
measure ribbon	TAPE
measure, *say*	GAGE, MEAT, MEET, WAY
measure stick	ROD

measure union	LEAGUE
measured, *say*	GAGED, WADE
meat	
meat sandwich	(in) MEA–T
meat *to* scoff	HAMMOCK
meat was bleeding	HAMBLED
meat *with* pickle, *say*	LAMPLIGHT
mechanical	
mechanical engineer	ME
mechanical transport	MT
medal	
medal	GONG
• king *wearing* medal	GORING
• one *wearing* medal	GOING
medal	MC, MM, TD
medal, *say*	MEDDLE
mediaeval	MED
medical	
[medical] *disorder*	CLAIMED, DECIMAL
	DECLAIM
medical graduate	MB
medical man	DR, GP, MB, MO
Medical Officer (of Health)	MO(H)
Medical Research Council	MRC
medical social worker	MSW
medical speciality	ENT
[medical] *treatment*	CLAIMED, DECIMAL,
	DECLAIM
medicine	
medicine	MED
medicinal group	WHO
medicine ball	PILL
medicine-man	DR, GP, MB, MO
medicine-men	DRAUGHT
Mediterranean	MED
medium	
medium	MED
medium-sized jumper	CRICKET, KANGAROO
medium standard frequency	MSF
medium wave	MW
medley	
medley [in A Flat]	FANTAIL
medley [race]	ACER, CARE
medley of [tunes]	UNSET
meet	
meet	SEE
• meet daughter	SEED
• meet finest girl, *say*	SEBESTAN
• meet girl-friend, *say*	SEDATE
and	
• meet Arab, *say*	SEA-HORSE
• meet prostitutes, *say*	SEA-HORSE
• meets prostitute, *say*	SEA-SHORE
meet people	HUNTSMEN
meeting	AGM
meeting-house	AUDIENCE

meeting place for merry men	ROUND ROBIN
meeting-points	AGENDA
	(*see also* met)
mega-	(*see* million)
mélange	
mélange of [cream]	CRAME, MACER
[taste] *mélange*	TEATS, STATE
mêlée	
mêlée [in street]	INTEREST
[recent] *melee*	CENTRE
melt	
melt [fat]	AFT
melt, *say*	THOR
melting point	MP
melting [snow]	OWNS, SOWN
molten [steel]	LEETS, STELE
member	
member	ARM, LEG, M, MP, TOE
• church member	CHARM
• member makes a mistake	LEG-SLIPS
• member *takes* cereal	MOATS
• member *of* Dail	EMPIRE
• member *takes in* new . . .	TONE
member	MEM
Member of	
• Congress	MC
• Council	MC
• County Council	MCC
• House of Representatives	MHR
• Institute of Journalists	MJI
• Legislative Assembly	MLA
• Council	MLC
• Order of the British Empire	MBE
• Parliament	MP
• Pharmaceutical Society	MPS
• Philological Society	MPS
• Royal Victorian Order	MVO
member of fir/m an/d . . .	MAN
member's movement	STEP
members of [SAS]	ASS
memorial service	OBIT
men	
men jump	PAWNSHOP
men of intelligence	AGENTS, CIA, SPIES
men, *say*	GUISE
men with guns	RA
	(*see also* man)
mend	
mend [plate]	PETAL
mending [china]	CHAIN
mental	
mental case	CRANIUM, SKULL
[mental] *case*	LAMENT
[mental] *defective*	LAMENT
mention	
make mention of a juice	ADDUCE

Letter replaced \c\at; Omit (a); Pointers *out*; Retain <u>a</u>; Split B_ED; Down (D); Backwards <or ^

mention their . . .	THERE	metal oxide silicon	MOS
mentioned new . . .	GNU, KNEW	metal, *say*	METTLE, LED, STEAL
mentioning some . . .	SUM	metal van	LEAD
merchant		metal washer	COPPER
Merchant Navy	MN	**metamorphosis**	
Merchant of Venice	ANTONIO, POLO	*metamorphose* [into a] . . .	–ATION
merchant vessel	MV	*metamorphosis*	
mercy		of [an insect's] . . .	INCESSSANT
mercy	QUARTER	**metaphorical**	MET
• mercy returned	QUARTERBACK	**metaphysics**	MET
mere		**meteorology**	MET
mere colour	LAKE	**mete**	
mere existence	POND-LIFE	[mete] *out*	MEET, TEEM
mere reserve	JUSTICE	**meter**	(*see* metre)
merry		**Methodist Episcopal**	ME
[a small] *merry-go-round*	LLAMAS	**metre**	
Merry Christmas (=[Noel])	LONE	metre	M
merry fellow	ANDREW	metre*less*	omit M
merry-go-round	GA-Y	metrically rendered	INVERSE
merry minute	TIDDLY	**metrical**	INVERSE
Merry [Wives]	VIEWS	**Metropolitan Police**	MET, MP
Merseyside	NW	**Mexico**	MEX
mess		M̲exican capital	M
in a mess [it ran] . . .	TRAIN	M̲exican *flower*	RIO GRANDE
make a mess of [things]	NIGHTS	M̲exican *leader*	M
mess *about*	M–ESS	**mezzo**	
mess-box	CANTEEN	mezza-voce	MV
messed up [a paper] . . .	APPEAR	mezzo-forte	MF
messing about in [boats]	BOAST	mezzo-piano	MP
messy [eaters]	RESEAT, TEASER	**Micah**	MIC
met		**mickey-taker**	CAT, MOUSER
met her again, *say*	REJOINDER	**mid-**	
Met line	ISOBAR	*mid*-a̲i̲r̲	I
Met office	(NEW) SCOTLAND YARD	mid-morning	ATTEN–
met *on the way back*<	TEM	*mid*-mo̲r̲ning	N
met *up*(D)^	TEM	*mid*-st̲r̲e̲a̲m	RE
	(*see also* meet)	*mid*-su̲m̲mer	MM, THOUSANDS
		mid-W̲e̲s̲t	ES
metal		*mid*-W̲estern	T
metal	IRON	midday	N, NOON
• iron man	IRONED	midd̲a̲y	A
• metal club	IRON	midday *break*	NO–ON
• "Metal", I state	IRONICAL	*Mid*la̲n̲ds	N
• metal unknown	IRONY	*mid*night	G
metal	LEAD	*mid*o̲f̲f̲	F
• metal guide	LEAD	*mid*r̲i̲f̲f̲	IF
• metal ruler	LEADER	midriff, *say*	WASTE
• soft metal	PLEAD	midshipman	EASY, SNOTTY
metal	TIN	*mid*shipman	P
• metal cover	TIN-HAT	midwe̲e̲k	EE
• metal *found in* the road	STINT	midwe̲e̲k, *say*	EASE
• metal key	TINE, TING	*mid*wi̲f̲e̲	IF
• metal ruler	TINKING	midwife's fee	CASH ON DELIVERY
• metal trophy	TINPOT	**middle**	
metal container	ORE, TIN	*middle* age	G
metal *in* s/cu/lpture	COPPER, CU	Middle America	CENTER
metal money	BRASS		

Middle America	R	military (personnel)	REME
middle class	BOURGEOIS	• former square *with*	
middle class	A	military . . .	EXTREME
Middle East	CENTRE POINT	• military clock	REMEDIAL
Middle East	AS	• three military . . .	TRIREME
Middle English	ME	Military Police	(R)MP
Middle English	L	military rations	WARFARE
middle gear	LOINCLOTH	military study	WARDEN
middle of the . . .	H	military uniform	WARDRESS
middle of the road	OA	military unit, *say*	TROUP(E)
middle, *say*	CENTAUR, COLONEL	**milk**	
Middle School	HO	milk of magnesia	WINDCHEATER
middle way	MIDST	milky eyes, *say*	OPALISE
middleman	MEDAL	**mill**	
middleman	A	[grist] *to the mill*	GRITS, STRIG, TRIGS
midst		miller	DUSTY
in the midst of lif/e we/ are . . .	EWE	miller's corn	GRIST
we a/re in/ *the midst*	REIN	*milling* [oats]	STOA
might		**milli-**	
might appear [that Ed] . . .	HATTED	millibar	MB
might be [a pet]	PATE, PEAT, TAPE	milligram(me)	MG
might he, *say*	MIGHTY	millilitre	ML
mighty king	STRONGER	millimetre	MM
mighty man	SMITH	millisecond	MS
mighty queen	STRONGER	**million**	
mild		million	M, MEGA
mild case	PATIENT	million cycles per second	MPS
mild man	CLEMENT	million electron-volts	MEV
mild temper	MODERATE	million joules	MJ
mile	M	million pounds	IMPOUNDS
miles *away*	omit M	**mimic**	
• miles *away from* ho(m)e	HOE	*mimic* nun	NONE
• Pa(m) *was miles away*	PA	*mimicry of* male . . .	MAIL
miles per gallon	MPG	**mince**	
miles per hour	MPH	*minced* [lamb]	BALM
milestone	MS	*mince*[meat]	MATE, TAME, TEAM
military		**mine**	
military	MIL	mine	PIT
military agent	TEAR GAS	• mine collapses	PITFALLS
military band	GUERRILLAS	• mine *in* the Home Counties	SPITE
	PLATOON, TROOP	• mine working	PITON
military bands	CHEVRONS, SASHES	mine entrance	ADIT
	STRIPES	*mine entrance*	M
military briefing	PRIVATE LESSONS	mine expired, *say*	MINDED
Military Cross	MC	mine had, *say*	MAENAD
military exercise	OP	mine, *say*	WEAL, WE'LL, WHEEL
Military Intelligence	MI	miner, *say*	MINOR
Military Medal	MM	miners	NUM
military (personnel)	RA	mining engineer	ME
• horse *with* military . . .	COBRA	**mineral**	
• *military exercises*	RAPE, RAPT	mineral water	EVIAN, PERRIER
• *military victory is hard*	RAVISH		SERPENTINE
military (personnel)	RE	mineralogy	MIN
• military district	REWARD	**minimal**	
• military intelligence	RENEWS	minimal amount	D, P, ID, IP
• military vehicle	REHEARSE	*minimal amount of* drug	D

Letter replaced \c\at; Omit (a); Pointers *out*; Retain a; Split B_ED; Down (D); Backwards <or ^

minimal change	D, P, ID, IP
minimal ta(x)	TA
minimum lending rate	MLR
minister	
minister	DD
minister's assistant	CURATE, PPS
ministerial box	CABINET
ministry	D(O)E, FO, MIN
Ministry of Defence	MOD
Ministry of Transport	MOT
minor	
minor	WARD
• concerning minor . . .	REWARD
• minor aboard	SWARDS
• minor opportunity	WARDROOM
• minor, *say*	WARRED
minor	WEE
• minor coin	WEED, WEEP
• minor note	WEED
• shirt *has* minor . . .	TWEE
minor burn	BROOK(LET), RILL
	STREAM(LET)
minor county	OXON, YORKS etc
minor cut	SLIGHT
minor *disagreement*	MAJOR
minor highway	BROAD
minor key	AIT, AYOT, INCH, ISLET
minor points	LESSEE(S)
minor railway	INFANTRY
minor road	B
minor road	RD
minor work	COTTAGE INDUSTRY
minor work	OP
Minority Rights Group	MRG
minor, *say*	MINER
minor street	ST
mint	
mint centre	BULL'S-EYE
mi<u>nt</u> *centre*	IN
mint money	NEW GUINEA
minted [coins]	ICONS, SONIC
minus	
minus a . . .	omit A
minus five	omit V
• se(v)en minus five	SEEN
minus *	omit *
• song *minus* all . . .	B(all)AD
minute	
minute	M, MIN
minute	MO
• a pair of minute . . .	DUOMO
• minute flower	MOROSE
• minute boy	MODES, MORON
minute	SMALL
mis-	
many words beginning with	

mis-, some of which follow,	
are used to indicate anagrams	
misadventure	
misadventure [in great] . . .	TEARING
[recent] *misadventure*	CENTRE
misaligned	
[gears] *misaligned*	RAGES
misalign [stream]	MASTER, REMAST
misalliance	
[German] *misalliance*	MANGER
misalliance of [Norse] . . .	SNORE
misanthrope	TIMON
misbehave	
misbehaving [with] . . .	WHIT
misbehaviour of [boys]	YOBS
miscast	
mis[cast]	CATS, SCAT
[mis]*cast*	–ISM
miscast [role]	LORE
miscellaneous	
miscellaneous [items]	METIS, MITES
	SMITE, TIMES
miscellany of [tunes]	UNSET
mischief	
mischief [done]	NODE
mischievious [kids]	SKID
misconceive	
misconceived [idea]	AIDE
misconception [that Ed] . . .	HATTED
misconstrue	
misconstrue [words]	SWORD
misconstrued [what] . . .	THAW
miscreant	
mis[creant]	RECANT
miscreant [gave ear]	AVERAGE
miscreant, *say*	RETCH
[vile] *miscreant*	EVIL, LIVE
miscue	
miscue on [break]	BRAKE
mis[cued]	DUCE
miscued [on red]	DRONE
misdirect	
mis[directed]	CREDITED
misdirected [players]	PARSLEY
misdirection of [throw]	WORTH
miser	HARPAGON, SCROOGE
miserable	
[made] *miserable*	DAME, EDAM, MEAD
miserable	BLUE
• miserable china, *say*	BLOOMING
• miserable daughter	BLUED
• miserable scum	BLUE FILM
miserable	DOWN
• display miserable . . .	SHOWDOWN
• miserable *about* king	DROWN
• miserable team	DOWNSIDE

miserable	SAD	misprinted [page]	GAPE
• miserable *about* the *French* . . .	SALAD	[name] *misprinted*	MANE, MEAN
• miserable girl	SADINA	**misquote**	
• miserable lair	SADDEN	*misquotation* from [bard]	BRAD, DRAB
miserable outlook, *say*	PORCINE	*misquote* [poem]	MOPE
miserable [sinner]	INNERS	*misquoting* [verse]	SERVE
miserably [cried]	DICER	**misread**	
misfire		*mis*[read]	DARE, DEAR
mis[fire]	RIFE	*misread* [words]	SWORD
mis[fired]	FRIED	*misreading* of [text or] . . .	EXTORT
misfired, *say*	BLUE-BACK	**misrepresent**	
misfiring [car]	ARC	*misrepresent* [case]	ACES, AESC
misfortune		*misrepresented* [a lot in] . . .	TALION
[great] *misfortune*	GRATE	**misrule**	
misfortune to [meet] . . .	TEEM	*mis*[rule]	LURE
misguide		*mis*[ruling]	LURING
misguided [souls]	SOLUS	[Tsar's] *misrule*	STARS
misguidedly [said] . . .	AIDS, DAIS	**miss**	
[more] *misguided*	OMER, ROME	miss	GAL, GIRL
mishandle		Miss America	MISSUS
mis[handle]	HANDEL	*miss* [bus]	SUB
mishandled [case]	AESC	miss girl, *say*	LACUNA
mishap		miss lady	SPINSTER
[large] *mishap* ELGAR, GLARE, LAGER, REGAL		*miss* nothing	omit O
mishap [in game]	GAMINE	Miss Sybil, *say*	MISCIBLE
mishmash		missed a number, *say*	LACTATE
[mish]*mash*	SHIM	missed, *say*	MIST
mishmash of [all the] . . .	LETHAL	missed *speech*	MIST
misinform		missing	AWOL
misinform *in speech*	SCHOOLGIRL	*missing* a . . .	omit A
misinformed [editor]	RIOTED	missing journalist	UNFOUNDED
misinterpret		*missing* journalist	omit ED
misinterpret [false] . . .	FLEAS	missing husband	omit H
misinterpretation of [words]	SWORD	missing mark	CARET
mislay		*missing* mark	omit M
mis[laid]	DAIL, DALI, DIAL	*missing* money	omit L
mislaid [ring]	GRIN	*missing* motorway	omit M, MI
mislay a . . .	omit A	*missing* out	omit OUT
mislay card	LOSE HEART	*missing out part of* st(or)y	STY
mislay [coin]	ICON	missing person	BUTTER FINGERS
mislay head	omit 1st letter	*missing start of* (r)ace	ACE
mislay one	omit I	*missing* student	omit L
mislay *	omit *	*missing* *	omit *
• *mislay* her rat(her) . . .	RAT	• th(row) *missing* tier	TH
mislead		[near] *miss*	EARN
mislead [solver]	LOVERS	misstate, *say*	MISSISSIPPI
misleading [clue]	LUCE	**misshape**	
mis[led a] . . . DALE, DEAL, LADE, LEAD		*misshape* [form]	FROM
mismanage		*misshapen* [arm]	MAR, RAM
mismanaged [much] . . .	CHUM	**missile**	
mismanagement of [team] MATE, MEAT, TAME		missile	ARROW
misplace		• many missiles	MARROWS
misplaced [letters]	SETTLER	• missile base	ARROWROOT
misplacing [words]	SWORD	missile	BULLET
misprint		• missile enters . . .	BULLETIN
misprint	LITERAL, TYPO	• snap missile	BITE THE BULLET

Letter replaced \c\at; Omit (a); Pointers *out*; Retain <u>a</u>; Split B_ED; Down (D); Backwards <or ^

missile	IBM, SAM, VI	• model city	POSEUR
missile plant	ROCKET	• model question	POSER
missiles	AMMO, DARTS	model	STANDARD
missionaries	CMS	• model colours	STANDARD
misspell		• model servant	STANDARD-BEARER
misspelled [words]	SWORD	Model Army	PLANTA
misspelt [a notice]	ACONITE	*Model* [Army]	MARY, MYRA
mist		model car	T
mist, say	HAYS, MISSED	*model* [cars]	ARCS, SCAR
misty [start]	TARTS	*model* [models]	SELDOM
mistake		model support	CATWALK
mistake in [line ten]	LENIENT	**moderate**	
mistake problem	SLIP-KNOT	moderate	MOD
mistaken [for the] . . .	FOTHER	moderate means	MEDIUM
mistakenly [said] . . .	AIDS, DAIS	moderate mood	TEMPER
mistakes underwear	BLOOMERS	*moderate* [views]	WIVES
mister	MR	moderate weight, *say*	KERBSTONE
mistreat		moderations	MODS
mistreat [horse]	HOSER, SHORE	**modern**	
mistreating [cat]	ACT	Modern Language Associaton	MLA
misuse		modern miss	MS
misuse [mails]	ISLAM	modern power	US(A)
misused [cutlery]	CRUELTY	modern *sound*	GNU, KNEW
mix		modern-*sounding* race	NUMEN
mix, *say*	(K)NEED	modern times	AD, ADAGE
mix-up of [dates]	SATED		NEWT
mix up, *say*	JUMBAL	modern ways	NEW(S)
mixed drinks	SHANDY	**modify**	
mixed [blessing]	GLIBNESS	*modification of* [rules]	LURES
mixed-[up Mel] . . .	PLUME	*modified* [brakes]	BAKERS, BASKER
mixed-up type	PI		BREAKS
mixed-up [type I] . . .	PIETY	**modulate**	
mixture [of beer]	BEFORE	*modulate* [note]	ETON, TONE
Mk II	(MARK) TWAIN	*modulation of* [tone]	ETON, NOTE
mm!	EMS	**modulus**	M
m-mokes	MASSES	**moist**	
mob		moist, *say*	WHET
mob's sponsor	GODFATHER	moisten her, *say*	W(H)ETHER
mobster	OCHLOCRAT	**mole**	
mobile		mole	ADRIAN, MOL
mobile [crane]	CANER, NACRE	mole	PIER
mobile home	CARAPACE, SHELL, TENT	• mole, *say*	PEER
Mobile state	ALABAMA	• power *in* mole	PIPER
mobile workers	SHIFT	mole	SPY
[the] *mobile*	ETH, HET	**molten**	(*see* melt)
mock		**mon**	ASCOT
[man I] *mocked*	MAIN	**Monaco**	MC
mock battle	COD WAR	**monarch**	
mock [duel Ed] . . .	ELUDED	monarch	ER, K, R
mock food	SCOFF	Monarch of the Glen	CLANKING
mock-*up*(D)^	DOC	monarch's chair, *say*	THROWN
mocked, *say*	GUIDE		(*see also* king)
mocking sheep, *say*	WRITE-UP	**monastic custom**	HABIT
model		**Monday**	
model	POSE(R)	Monday	M, MON
• girl's model	DISPOSE(R)	[Monday] *off*	DYNAMO

Anag [cat]; Any *; Begin IGN–; Endings –ING; eg •; Hidden /cat/; Implied add (on); Implied in (in);

money

money	BRASS
• money-belt	BRASS BAND
• money collapses	BRASSFOUNDERS
money	BREAD
• little money	SHORTBREAD
• money policy	BREADLINE
• money *to* directors	BREADBOARD
money	CASH
• king *in* the money	CRASH
• only *after* money	CASHMERE
money	CENT
• about money	RECENT
• make money	DOCENT
money	COIN
• money present	COINHERE
• money safe	CO-INSURE
money	DOUGH
• bad money	SOURDOUGH
• son *after* money	DOUGHBOY
• money, *say*	DOE, DOH
money	L
• money I have	LIVE
• p–ot *with* money *in*	PLOT
money	OOF(TISH)
• hard money	HOOF
• woman *has* money	WOOF
money	P
• money *has* much . . .	PLOT
• money to every . . .	PEACH
money	READY
• money earned	READY-MADE
money	SHEKELS
money	SUM
• money raised	SUM UP
• money *with* German . . .	SUMMIT
money	TIN
• money-box	TINPOT
• money less restricted	TIN-OPENER
money belt	POUND
money maker	MINT, FORGER
money, *say*	CACHE, COIGN, CAPITOL, DOE, DOH, QUOIN

monk

monk in possession	FROWNING
monk *with* unknown . . .	PRIORY

monkey

monkey, *say*	LANGOUR
monkey's brother	CAPUCHIN

monkshood COWL
monseigneur MGR
monsieur M
monstrous regiment WOMEN

month

month	JAN, FEB etc M, MO, MOON, MTH

month after sight	MS
Moon River	RILL(E)

moor

Moor	SARACEN
moor *about . . . <*	ROOM
moor, *say*	GREATER, HIGHER, MORE
moor space	HEATHEN
moored (=alongside)	
• vessel *moored by* firm beach	HARDSHIP
Moorish cover	HEATH(ER), MOROCCO

mop

mop *up*(D)^	POM
mop up a . . .	incl A
mop up [ink]	KIN
mop up *	incl *
• ra–g *mops up French* wine	RAVING
mopped up by *	incl in *
• *French* wine mopped up by r–ag	RAVING
Moral Rearmament	MRA

more

more	MORE
• more cereal, *say*	MORRICE
• more cleaners, *say*	MORMOPS
• more fiddles, *say*	MORGUES
• more fools, *say*	MORASSES
• more or less, *say*	MORPHEW
[more] *complicated*	OMER, ROME
more cross	PLUS
more daughters, *say*	LESSONS
more discomfort, *say*	LESSEES
more equitable method, *say*	WAYFARER
more free	RIDDER
more frivolous period	LIGHTERAGE
more frozen	EVEN NUMBER
more *hearsay*	MOOR
More ideal	UTOPIA
more ill, *say*	SICCAR
more impressive, *say*	GRATER
more incorrect, *say*	RONGEUR
more offensive soldier	RANKER
more perforated, *say*	HOLIER
more polluted, *say*	FOWLER
more than 500	DI–
more than enough for mo/st ar/mies	STAR
more than one	BONE, CONE, DONE, GONE, HONE, LONE, NONE, ONER, PONE, TONE
more than one, *say*	PLEURAL
more tinny, *say*	CANNIER
[more] *stirring*	OMER, ROME
More work	UTOPIA
o/ne pal/ace *is more than enough*	NEPAL

Letter replaced \c\at; Omit (a); Pointers *out*; Retain <u>a</u>; Split B_ED; Down (D); Backwards <or ^

morning	
mid-mor<u>n</u>ing	N
morning	AM
• many mornings	CAMS, DAMS, LAMS, MAMS
• morning in the East	AMINE
• morning *in the French* . . .	LAME
• morning service	AMUSE
morning air	AUBADE
morning off	omit AM
• entertain with *morning* off	(am)USE
• S(am) *has* morning *off*	S
Morocco	MA, MOR
Morris garage	MG
mosaic	
[marble] *mosaic*	RAMBLE
mosaic of [pieces]	SPECIE
most	
most *disagreeable*	LEAST
Most Excellent	ME
most of	
–all	AL, LL
–<u>the</u> . . .	TH
–the <u>time</u>	TIM
most parts	PAR, ARTS
most perforated, *say*	HOLIEST
most severe person	GRAVESTONE
most stupid	LEASTWISE
most tinny, *say*	CANNIEST
most w/omen s/ay	OMENS
mostly fashionable	ALAMO, CHICK
mostly tall	ALL, THIGH
mother	
mother	DAM
• mother *and* son	DAMSON
• mother country	DAMNATION
• mother swan	DAMPEN
mother	MA
• mother *and* child	MASON
• mother at home	MAIN
• Mother Earth	MAGE
• mother in court	MAINYARD
• mother's double	MAMA
• mother's picture	MAINFRAME
• mother-ship	MASS
• mother wearing blouse	MAINTOP
• mother *with* robe	MAKIMONO
• motherlessness	NOMA
mother	MAM
• mother *and* friend	MAMMATE
• mother encountered . . .	MAMMET
• mother *with* Scotsman	MAMMON
mother	MUM
• little mother	MINIMUM
• mother *has* directions on . . .	MU-MESON
• mother *has* power	MUMP
motherless	omit MA
• mother*less* wo(ma)n	WON
Mothers' Union	MADAM, MAMA, MAMMA
two mothers	MADAM, MAMA, MAMMA
motion	
motion of [moon]	MONO–
[tram] *in motion*	MART
[tram in] *motion*	MARTIN
motley	
motley [garb]	BRAG, GRAB
[robed] *in motley* . . .	BORED
motor	
motor	CAR
• bird *follows* motor	CARGOOSE, CAROUSEL
• motor race	CARNATION
• motor travels . . .	CARGOES
motor fleet vessel	MFV
motor sport improving	RALLYING
motor torpedo boat	MTB
motor vessel	MV
motoring	(in) CA–R
motoring friend	CARPAL
motoring organisation	AA, RAC
motoring people	CARNATION
motorists	AA, RAC
motorist's club	DRIVER
motorway	M, MI
• motorway building	MISTY
• motorway in Germany	MING
• motorway madness	MIRAGE
• motorway restaurant	MIDINETTE
• motorway *turn*<	IM–
• motorways merge	MIMI
• posts *on* the motorway	MISTAKES
mould	
moulded [clay]	LACY
moulded, *say*	DICAST, DIKAST
moulding [vase]	AVES, SAVE
mouldy, *say*	MUSTEE
moult	
moult(ed)	CAST DOWN
	DOWNCAST, DOWNFALL
mount	
mount	MT
mount drama	HORSEPLAY
mounted	UP
• mounted coach	UPSTAGE
• mounted players	UPCAST
• mounted team	UPSIDE
mounted artillery(D)^	SNUG
mounted huntsman's . . . (D)^	SLEEP
mounted police	MP, RCMP
mounted police(D)^	PM
mounted soldiers(D)^	AR, AT, ER, SIG–
mounting disorder	RIOT, UPRISING
mounting step(D)^	PETS

mounts stairs	TAKES FLIGHT
mountain	
a Scandinavian *mountaineer*(D)^	APPAL
mountain	ALP
• eastern mountain	ALPINE
• mountain-*climbing*(D)^	PLA
• mountain *retreat*<	PLA
mountain	ETNA
• mountain-*climbing*(D)^	ANTE
• mountain *retreat*<	ANTE
mountain	TOR
• mountain-*climbing*(D)^	ROT
• mountain guide	TORMENTOR
• mountain *retreat*<	ROT
• mountain split	TORRENT
mountain goat	HILL-BILLY
mountain in	
−France	MONTAGNE
−Germany	BERG
−Italy	MONTAGNA, MONTE
−Scotland	BEN, MUNRO
−Spain	MONTANA
Mountain Standard Time	MST
mountaineer	SHERPA
mountaineer, *say*	CLIMATOLOGIST
mourn	
mourn, *say*	GREAVE, MORN, W(H)ALE
mourned, *say*	SIDE
mourner, *say*	SIRE, W(H)ALER
mourns,say	GREAVES, SIZE, W(H)ALES
mouse	
mouse	MICKEY
mousey female	MINNIE
mousse	
[orange] *mousse*	ONAGER
mousse [made] . . .	DAME, EDAM, MEAD
mouth	
big-*mouth*	B
foul-*mouthed*	F
mouth of river	R
mouth ointment	BALMORAL
mouthpiece	GUM, LIP, MOLAR
	TONGUE, TOOTH
mouth*piece*	M
move¹	
indicating an anagram:	
• [counter]-*move*	RECOUNT, TROUNCE
• [epic] *movie*	PICE
• *move out of* [range]	ANGER
• *move* [castle]	CLEATS
• *moved* [it to] . . .	TITO
• *movement of* [tide]	DIET, EDIT, TIED
• *movie* [actor]	CROAT
• *moving* [parts]	PRATS, SPRAT, STRAP
• *movingly* [depict an] . . .	PEDANTIC
• [slow] *movement*	LOWS, OWLS

move²	
indicating changed position	
of some letter(s):	
move *	
• c\l\am *moves* left	CALM
• fou\r\ thousand *move* right	FORUM
• *move* East of L\e\ith	LITHE
• *move* south *in* \s\cow	COWS
move³	
indicating omission:	
move in	omit IN
move on	omit ON
move out	omit OUT
• *move out*, p(out)ing	PING
move * *from*	omit *
• *move* North *from* Bar(n)es	BARES
• *move* South *from* (S)lough	LOUGH
• *move* pawn *from* s(p)ot	SOT
moving a . . .	omit A
moving *	omit *
• *moving* animal from c(rat)e	CE
move⁴	
move	GO
• move *after* god . . .	LARGO
• move away from the south-west	GONE
• move *into* the interior	INGOT
• move sheep	GOT-UP
• move *to* the back, *say*	GORIER
move *round*<	OG
move⁴	
other uses:	
move quickly	HARE
• move quickly, *say*	HAIR
move right *round*<	TR
move round on< . . .	NO
move something, *say*	BUDGET
move to North	LEAVES
move to South	LEAVEN
moveable feasts	MEALS ON WHEELS
moved camp	AFFECTED
moved into *	incl in *
• animal *moved into* church	CRATE
moving about	TOUCHING
moving ceremony	FLY-PAST, MARCH-PAST
moving picture	DRAWING
moving proposal	MOTION
moving spirit	PETROL
Mozart's works	K
MP	HOUSEMAN
Mr	
Mr, *say*	MISSED HER
Mr *Turner*<	RM
mu	M
much	
much	BAGS, LOTS
much-liked	IN

Letter replaced \c\at; Omit (a); Pointers *out*; Retain a̲; Split B_ED; Down (D); Backwards <or ^

much money	IMPOUNDS	music directors	SCOREBOARD
much of September	EMBER	Music of the Muses	NONET
much time	TIM	music school	RAM
much-used	(see Old)	musical	CATS
much-v/aunt/ed	AUNT	• musical animals	CATS
mud		• musical mounted	CATSUP
muddied [pool]	LOOP, POLO	• tolerate musical . . .	BEARCAT
muddy [waters 'e] . . .	SWEATER	musical	HAIR
muddle		• fewer *following* musical . . .	HAIRLESS
muddle [things]	NIGHTS	• musical party	HAIR-DO
muddled [men eat a] . . .	EMANATE	• musical season	HAIRSPRING
muff		musical cleric	CANON
muffed [shot]	HOST, HOTS	musical girl	ANNIE, BOHEMIAN
muffing [every]	VEERY	musical number	SCORE
mug		musical prince	IGOR
mug(D)^	GUM UP	musical show, *say*	REVIEW
[mug]-*shot*	GUM	musical tempo	AIRSPACE
mug up	SWOT	musical whim	CAPRICE, CROTCHET
mug *up*(D)^	GUM, TOWS	musicians	RAM, MCM
mulch		musician's character	FLAT, NATURAL
mulch	BEDSPREAD		NOTE, SHARP
mulch of [dead] . . .	EDDA	musicians cried	WINDSWEPT
mulched [petals]	PLATES, PLEATS	musician's house	FLAT
	STAPLE	**muster**	
mull		*muster* [army]	MARY, MYRA
mulled [ales]	LEAS, SALE, SEAL	*mustering* [regiment]	METERING
mulling [over] . . .	ROVE	**mutate**	
multiple sclerosis	MS	*mutant* [ape]	PEA
multiplication stable	STUD	*mutated* [trees]	RESET, STEER, STERE
mum		*mutation of* [flies]	FILES
mum	MA	**mutiny**	
	(*see* mother)	*mutinous* [sepoy]	POESY
mum	SH	*mutiny in* [army]	MARY, MYRA
• mum *at* work	SHOP	[regiment] *mutinied*	METERING
• turn mum	GOSH	**mutton**	RAMPART
mum	ST	**mutual friend**	COPAL
• father *has* Mum . . .	PAST	**muzzle velocity**	MV
• mum always . . .	STAY	**my**	
munch		my	MY
munched [grain in] . . .	RAINING	• my lamp is, *say*	MYELITIS
munch grass, *say*	BROWS, GRAYS, GREYS	• my scythe, *say*	MYTHICAL
munching [oats]	STOA	• my stick will, *say*	MYSTICAL
Municipal Police	MP	and	
murder		• my anger, *say*	MIRAGE
murder mother	DOMAIN	• my bet, *say*	MISTAKE
murder *on the rebound*<	RED RUM	• my porcelain,say	MIMING
murder [sister]	RESIST	• my tea, *say*	MIGHTY
murder victim	ABEL	• my wife, *say*	MIMESIS
murderer	CAIN	My!	COO
museum	BM, MUS, VA, VANDA	• my fish	COOLING
mush		• my money	COOL
mushed up [snow]	OWNS, SOWN	• my shirt	COOT
mushy [peas]	APES, APSE	My!	COR
music		• my boy	CORDON, CORED
music	MUS	• my name	CORN
music *centre*	S	• my soldier	CORGI

Anag [cat]; Any *; Begin IGN–; Endings –ING; eg •; Hidden /cat/; Implied add (on); Implied in (in);

My!	GEE	my name is	
• my daughter	GEED	–Kenneth, *say*	MEEKEN
• My, my!	GEE-GEE	–Sally	MESAL(LY)
• my son	GEES	–Sian	MESIAN
My!	O, OH	My, *no*!	omit MY
• my fast . . .	OLENT	• Fa(m)il(y)? My, *no*!	FAIL
• My, my!	OGEE	**mystery**	
• my tree	OPINE	*mystery of* [death]	HATED
my bet, *say*	MISTAKE	*mysterious* [tribe]	BITER
My measurements	GO SHARES		

N

Avogadro's number, born, bridge player, en, half an em, indefinite number, knight, name, nano-, natural numbers, natus, neper, neuter, neutral, neutron number, new, newton, ninety, ninety thousand, nitrogen, no, noon, normal, north, northern, Norway, note, noun, nu, number, quantum number, unknown number, unlimited number, viscosity

1984	YEAR BOOK	**name³**	
1986 car	DREG	name	
Nahum	NAH	indicating origins:	
nail		• *Emilio's* city	CIUDAD
nail in front	TACKLED	• *Fritz's* farm	BAUERNHOF
nail policeman	PINCOP	• *Pierre's* town	VILLE
nail, *say*	TINGAL	• *Dante's* house	CASA
naked			(*see also* from⁴)
naked	OUT OF GEAR	**name⁴**	
naked (=with nothing on)		named	DIT
• dance naked	BALLOON	named, *say*	HEIGHT, SIGHTED, SITED
• naked girl	SALOON	name*less* (di)ve	VE
• naked light	LAMPOON	namely	SC, SCIL, SCIZ, VIZ
	(*see also* bare, nothing)	**nanny goat**	BUTTRESS
naked	BARE	**nanosecond**	NS
• naked musical, *say*	BEARCATS	**Napoleon**	
• naked saint	BAREST	Napoleon's child	PIGLET
naked, *say*	WORN-OUT	Napoleon's foot	TROTTER
name¹		Napoleon's supporters	TROTTERS
name	CALL	**narrow**	
• concerning names	RECALLS	narrow road	BROAD
• name in Germany	CALLING	narrow ruler	THINK(ING)
• naming vocation	CALLING	**nasal**	(*see* nose)
and		**nasty**	
• name her, *say*	COLLAR	nasty attack	OFFENSIVE
• name it, *say*	COLLET	na<u>sty</u> *end*	STY
and		*nasty* [end]	DEN, NED
• name, *say*	CAUL	**nation**	
name	CITE	nation	RACE
• former name	EXCITE	• black nation	BRACE
• name, *say*	SIGHT, SITE	• hand *in* nation's . . .	RACHES
• popular name	INCITE	• nation state	RACEME
name	TERM	**national¹**	
• abbreviated name	SHORT TERM	national	NAT
• name I note	TERMITE	national composer	GERMAN
• name ruler	TERMER	national extremists	ETA, IRA, PLO
name²		<u>national</u> *extremists*	NL
name	N	National *Front*	N
• name unknown	NU, NY	national *flower*	THAMES
• new name	NN	National Hunt jockey	OVER-RIDER
• write name *in* re–d . . .	REND	national issue	SUBJECT
name-*dropping*	omit N	national register	SWISS ROLL
name*less*	omit N	national roll	SWISS

Anag [cat]; Any *; Begin IGN–; Endings –ING; eg •; Hidden /cat/; Implied add (on); Implied in (in);

National runner	RED RUM
national *runner*	THAMES etc
national tax	SCOT
national writer	FRANCE
nationalists	SDP

national²
National

–Board for Prices and Incomes	PIB
–Book League	NBL
–Broadcasting Company	NBC
–Bureau of Standards	NBS
–Cash Register Company	NCR
–Coal Board	NCB
–Enterprise Board	NEB
–Exhibition Centre	NEC
–Farmers' Union	NFU
–Fire Service	NFS
–Front	NF
–Graphical Association	NGA
–Health	
Insurance	NHI
Service	NHS
–Incomes Commission	NIC, NICKY
–Insurance	NI
–Opinion Poll	NOP
–Physical Laboratory	NPL
–Portrait Gallery	NPG
–Rifle Association	NRA
–Trust (for Scotland)	NT(S)
–Union of	
Journalists	NUJ
Mineworkers	NUM
Railwaymen	NUR
Seamen	NUS
Students	NUS
Teachers	NUT
–University of Ireland	NUI
–Youth Orchestra	NYO

native

native	ABO(RIGINAL)
native chief	BLACKHEAD
native's home	OYSTER BED
Nativity of the Virgin Mary	NVM

natural

natural base	E
natural *base*(D)	L
natural cover	FIG LEAF
natural drawing	MAGNETISM
natural order	NO
natural topic	SUBJECT

naught

naught	O
• came to naught	CAMEO
• naughty, *say*	OE

naughty

naughtily [trips] . . .	SPIRT, SPRIT
naughty	BLUE
• naughty girl	BLUEBIRD
• Naughty Nineties	BLUE PERIOD
• naughty pictures	BLUEPRINTS
naughty age	NINETIES
naughty [boys]	YOBS
naughty girl	BAD FAITH, BLUEBIRD
	(*see also* naught)
naval	(*see* Navy)

navigate

| navigation | NAV |
| navigator | HENRY |

Navy

naval	NAV
naval architect	WREN
naval assistance, *say*	MARINADE
naval commander	CORN
naval directors HELMS, RUDDERS, SEABOARD
naval port	LARBOARD, LEFT
Naval Reserve Decoration	NRD
naval, *say*	NAVEL
navy	BLUE
• Navy flier	BLUEBIRD
• Navy officer	BLUE ENSIGN
Navy	RN

NE

| NE | NORTH-EAST |
| NE, *say* | ANY |

near

factory *nearly complete*	PLAN(t)
near average	MEAN
near (old)	NIE
[near] *disaster*	ARNE, ANER, EARN
Near East	EAS, AST
near London	(THE)SE
near mealtime, *say*	NIGHTIE
near miss	OUTER
near redundant	NEEDLES(s)
[near]-*riot*	ARNE, ANER, EARN
nearside of road	R
near the drier, *say*	NIGHT-OWL
nearest figure	MISER
nearly al(l)	AL
nearly all gon(e)	GON
nearly all skin	KIN, SKEIN
	SKINK, SKINT
nearly all th(e) . . .	TH
nearly complete volume	BOO(k)
nearly finished	DON(e), MAD(e)
nearly finished drink	BEE(r), BRAND(y)
	WIN(e), WHISK(y)
nearly naked	INVEST
nearly (n)ew	EW
nearly read(y)	READ
nearly there	HERE, THER
ver(y) *nearly*	VER

neat¹

| [neat] | ALTERNATE |

Letter replaced \c\at; Omit (a); Pointers *out*; Retain <u>a</u>; Split B_ED; Down (D); Backwards <or ^

neat *ending*	T	needlewoman	CLEOPATRA
neat *start*	N		GOAD HER
neat²		needle worker	ACUPUNCTURIST
neat	CATTLE		TATTOOIST
• neat building	CATTLE SHED	**negative**	
• neat diagram	CATTLE GRID	negative	NEG, NONPLUS
• neat writer	CATTLE PEN	negative principle	YIN
neat	COW	negative, *say*	KNOT
• neat accommodation	BYRE	negatives, *say*	NAZE, NEIGHS, NOSE
	COWHOUSE, COWSHED	**neglect**	
• neat mistake	COWSLIP	*neglect* a . . .	omit A
• neat underwear	COWSLIP	*neglect* *	omit *
• son *has* neat . . .	SCOW	• per(son) *neglected* child	PER
neat	KINE	**negotiate**	
neat	OX	*negotiable* [terms at] . . .	MATTERS
• 100 neat . . .	COX	negotiate *with* monarch	TREATER
• neat ending	OXTAIL	*negotiation of* [lease]	EASEL
• neat look(er)	OX-EYE	*negotiated* [truce]	CUTER, RECUT
• neat mistake, *say*	OXLIP	**Nehemiah**	NEH
• neat ornament	OX-BOW	**neither**	
neat control	STEER	neither	NOR
neat couple	YOKE	• mother *has* neither . . .	MANOR
neat description	BEEFY	• neither *found in* the road	SNORT
neat drive	ROUND-UP	• neither person	NORMAN, NORROY
neat leg	CALF	**Nelson**	
neat little animals	CALVES	Nelson's employer	WRESTLER
neat pullover	GUERNSEY, JERSEY	Nelson's ship	VICTORY
neat *Scotch*	KY(E), SNOD	Nelson's woman	EMMA
neat sound	LOWING, MOO	**neper**	N
neat theft	RUSTLING	**Neptune**	NEP
neat³		**nerve**	
neat	TRIM	nerve, *say*	STEAL
• a neat . . .	ANTRIM	[nerve]-*shattering*	NEVER
• neat compound	TRIMESTER	*nervous* [friend]	FINDER
• neat eater, *say*	TRIMETER	nervous twitch, *say*	CAREER
Neath river	UNDERWEAR	**nest**	
necessary		a nest of agents, *say*	ASPIRING
necessary [part]	PRAT, TRAP	bird *nesting in* ship	SPIES
necessary part of		*nesting in* li/me tre/e	METRE
ste/am en/gine	AMEN	**net**	
necessary to ass/emble		net	CLEAR, GAIN
m/any . . .	EMBLEM	[net] *result*	ENT, TEN
[no tips] *necessary*	POINTS	*netting* a . . .	incl a
neck		*netting* *	incl *
neck hair, *say*	MAIN	• prisoner *netting* fish	CRAYON
neckband, *say*	CALLER, CHOLER	**Netherlands**	NL
neckline	LANYARD, NOOSE	Netherlands Antilles	NT
	TIDEMARK, V	**network**	
need		network	BR, RY, RLY
needed for mo/st aff/airs	STAFF	[net]*work*	ENT-, TEN
needed in man/y ear/ly . . .	YEAR	**neuralgia**	TIC
needing kicks, [take] . . .	KATE, TEAK	**neuter**	N
needing repair, [shoe]	HOES, HOSE	**neutral**	
needs [a set] . . .	SATE, SEAT, TEAS	neutral	(in) L–R
		• woman *is neutral*	LEVER
needle		neutral	N
needle*point*	N	• neutral area	NACRE

never

[never]-*changing*	NERVE
never-*ending*	WHENEVER
neve<u>r</u>-*ending*	R
never-ending	omit last letter
• *never-ending* night	NIGH
• *never-ending* journey	TRI(p)
never leaves off	EVERGREEN
nevertheless	EVER MORE
never*theless*	omit O

new¹

new	FRESH
• concerning new . . .	REFRESH
• new layer, *say*	FRESHEN
• new novel	FRESH
• new ruler	FRESHER
	(*see also* fresh)
new	N
• New Age	NEON
• new member	NEAR
• new safety-measure	NEAR-THING

new²

indicating anagram:

new-born [lamb]	BALM
new course of [action]	CATION
new development in [Neath]	THANE
new edition of [Wells]	SWELL
[*new*]-*fangled*	WEN
new-fangled [tools]	LOOTS, STOOL
new form [master]	STREAM
new form of [words]	SWORD
New [Forest]	FOSTER
new formula [oils]	SILO
new layout of [E Street]	TEETERS
new order for [shoes]	HOES, HOSE
New [Orleans]	SALERNO
new position of [table]	BLEAT
new production of [Tosca]	ATOCS, COATS
new regulation [made in] . . .	MAIDEN
new role for [director]	CREDITOR
new setting for [garnets]	STRANGE
new [shoes]	HOSES
new sort of [medical]	CLAIMED, DECIMAL, DECLAIM
new style of [shoe]	HOES, HOSE
New [Testament]	STATEMENT
new use for [tool]	LOOT
new version of [stage] . . .	GATES
new way to [run] . . .	NUR, URN
New [Year]	YARE
newly-built [town]	WONT
newly-coined [words]	SWORD
newly-gathered [flower]	FOWLER, REFLOW
newly-planted [forest]	FOSTER
newly-[wed]	DEW
New[town]	WONT
New[castle]	CLEATS

new²

indicating homophone:

new capital, *say*	NEUROMA
new flower, *say*	NEUROSE
new *rhyme*	GNU, KNEW
new river, *say*	NEURONE
new, *say*	GNU, KNEW
new *sound*	GNU, KNEW
new sound of waves	WAIVES
new spell of weather	W(H)ETHER

new³

New Church	NC
New England	NE
New English	
–Bible	NEB
–Dictionary	NED
New Jersey	CALF, NJ
New Orleans	NO
New Providence	NP
New South Wales	NSW
New Testament	NT
New York	BIG APPLE, GOTHAM, NY
–City	NYC
–district	BOWERY, BRONX
	HARLEM, MANHATTAN, QUEENS
–opera	MET
–Times	NYX
New Version	NV
New Zealand	(*see separate entry*)

new⁴

other uses:

new coat	WET PAINT
new driver	L
New Forest	GREENWOOD
new girl	DEB(UTANTE)
• a right new girl	ARDEB
• new girl scoffed	DEBATE
New Left	UNUSED
new lines	AD LIBS
new look	NOVELLO
new partner	BRIDE(GROOM)
new start for felon	MELON
new suit	GEAR CHANGE
new tip on \p\ike	BIKE, LIKE, MIKE
New World (=American)	
• criticise New World . . .	PAN-AMERICAN
• New World clergy	AMERICAN CLOTH
new writing	NOVEL
New Year's Day(=Jan 1st)	J
newly arrived	JUSTIN

New Zealand

New Zealand	NZ
New Zealand *flower*	CLUTHA
<u>New</u> <u>Z</u>ealand *leaders*	NZ

newcomer

newcomer	DEB
new[comer]	CROME

Letter replaced \c\at; Omit (a); Pointers *out*; Retain <u>a</u>; Split B_ED; Down (D); Backwards <or ^

Newry	DOWNTOWN
news	
news	GEN
• News at Eleven	GENII
• news that is . . .	GENIE
• newsboy	GENERIC
news, *say*	GNUS, WHIRRED
newspaper	
newspaper	RAG
• 100 newspapers	CRAGS
• newspaper *in* the river	DRAGEE, DRAGON
• newspaper magazine	RAGTIME
• newspaper published	RAGOUT
newspaper	FT, SUN, TIMES
newspaper column	STANDARD
newspaper boss	ED, EXPRESSED
	PRESS STUD, PRESSED
newspaper leader	ED, EXPRESSED, PRESSED
newspaper *leader*	N
newton	
newton	N
new[ton]	NOT
next	
next county	CLOSE DOWN
next month	PROX(IMO)
next to nothing	add O
• room <u>next to nothing</u>	CELLO
	(*see also* nothing³)
Nicaragua	NIC
nice	
Nice chap	FRENCHMAN
nice man	KINDLES
Nice people	FRENCH
Nice policeman	GENDARME
Nice surroundings	RIVIERA
nickname	DARTMOOR, PARKHURST, etc
	PRISON
	DEVIL
Nigel	
[Nigel] *Twist*	ELGIN
Nigella (=Love-in-a-mist)	MOIST
Niger	RN
Nigeria	WAN
niggard	CARL
night	
night air	NOCTURNE, SERENADE
night-light	MOON, STAR
[night]-*out*	THING
night, *say*	ENNOBLE
[night]-*shift*	THING
night-time, *say*	DAGON
night watchman	CHARLEY, CHARLIE
	STARGAZER
nigh(t) *without end*	NIGH
nightmare	BLACK BEAUTY, DARK HORSE
nil	
nil	LOVE

nil	O
nil-nil	OO
	(*see also* no)
nine	
nine	IX, THETA
nine Christmas presents	LADIES
nine dancers	MORRIS MEN
nine days' . . .	WONDER
nine days of devotion	NOVENA
nine eyes	LAMPREY
nine hundred	CM, SAMPI
[nine] *letters*	NEIN
nine letters *returned<*	IOTA
nine lives of . . .	CAT
nine nil	NINETY
nine points of . . .	LAW
nineteen	
1984	YEARBOOK
1986 cars	DREGS
nineteenth (hole)	BAR, CLUBHOUSE
ninety	
Nineties	NAUGHTY
ninety	N, Q, XC
ninety-nine	IC
ninety thousand	N, Q
nip	
nip(D)^	PIN-UP
nipped *round*	BI–T
NME	
NME, *say*	ENEMY
no¹	
no	LOVE
• 100 love	CLOVE
• no fruit	LOVE-APPLE
• no home	LOVE-NEST
	(*see also* love)
no	NIL
• greeting *in* no . . .	NIHIL
• no point	NILE
	(*see also* nil)
no²	
no	NO
• no directions	NOSE
• no good	NOOK
• no medicine	NODOSE
• no-one	NOI–
• no right	NOR(T)
• no spare key	NOTHING
n<u>o</u> *beginning*	N
n<u>o</u> *end*	O
no *entry*	incl NO
• there is no *entry in* a–n . . .	ANON
no French . . .	NON
no *going back<*	LIN, ON
n<u>o</u> *head*	start with NO
n<u>o</u> *head*	N
no *heart*	incl NO

Anag [cat]; Any *; Begin IGN–; Endings –ING; eg •; Hidden /cat/; Implied add (on); Implied in (in);

• knight *has no heart*	KNOT
No, no!	omit NO
• Learner? *No, no!*	(no)VICE
no *return<*	LIN, ON
no Scot, *say*	GNOMON
no *Scotch*	NA, NAE
no *turning back<*	LIN, ON
no way	NOE, NON, NOS, NOW

no³

no	O
• no co-ordinates	OXY–
• no cover	OLID
• no employment	OUSE
• no food	ORATIONS
• no friends	OPALS
• no love	OO
• no noise	OBANG, ODIN
• no people	OMEN
• no part	OBIT, OE, ON, OS, OW
• no right	OR(T)
• no share	ORATION
• no space	OVOID
• no theologian	ODD
• no trees	OPINES
• no VAT	ORATED
• no-way	OE, ON, OS, OW
	ORD, OST

and

• company *has no* . . .	COO
• cover *with no* . . .	LIDO
• girl *with no* . . .	MAYO
• father *has no* . . .	DADO
• no credit	LENTO
• no *support for* leg(D)	LIMBO
no *entry*	incl O
no love	omit O
no score	incl O
no score draw	O–O

no⁴

indicating omission:

no account	omit AC
• *no*-account performer	(ac)TRESS
no alternative	omit OR
• st(or)y *with no* alternative	STY
no aspiration	omit H
• (h)as *no* aspiration	AS
• (h)e *has no* aspiration	E
• *no* aspiration to (h)arm . . .	ARM
no bounds	omit ends
• (c)it(y) *has no bounds*	IT
no claim	omit AM, IAM, IM
no conclusion	omit last letter
• ha(s) *no conclusion*	HA
no end	omit END
no end of th(e) . . .	TH
no entrance to (p)ort	ORT
no go	omit GO

no good	omit G
no head	omit 1st letter
no heart	omit H
no heart	omit centre
• M(ar)y *has no heart*	MY
no initial . . .	omit 1st letter
no limits to (w)eight(s)	EIGHT
no love	omit O
no money	omit L
no need for a . . .	omit A
no need for *	omit *
• do(l)t *has no need for* money	DOT
no novice	omit L
no-one	omit I
no opening	omit 1st letter
no parking	omit P
no point *in* . . .	omit N, S, E, W
no power	omit P
no publicity	omit AD
no resistance	omit R
no right	omit R, RT
no ring	omit O
no roof on(D)	omit 1st letter
no saint	omit S, ST
no sign of a . . .	omit A
no sign of *	omit *
• moth(er) *shows no sign*	
of hesitation	MOTH
no start for . . .	omit 1st letter
no stomach for ba(tt)le	BALE
no thanks	omit TA
no time	omit AGE, T
• men(age) *has no* time . . .	MEN
• (t)hey *have no* time	HEY
no way	omit N, S, E, W
• *no* way pa(s)t	PAT
no way	omit RD, ST
• *no* way ha(rd)y . . .	HAY
• *no* way pa(st)	PA

no⁵

indicating opposite:

no admission	DENIAL
no expert	L, LEARNER
no handicap	SCRATCH
no high-flier	LOWLANDER
no inclination	FLAT, LEVEL
no mistake	CORRECT, R, RT, RIGHT

no⁶

other uses:

no bloody good	NBG
no charges	FREE FOR ALL
no commercial value	NCV
no date	ND
no drink	TT
no film	NEGATIVE
no good	NG, US
no-good [liar]	ARIL, LIRA, RAIL

Letter replaced \c\at; Omit (a); Pointers *out*; Retain a̲; Split B_ED; Down (D); Backwards <or ^

no longer	LATE	*noisy* band	BANNED
no longer (=old word)		noisy preacher	BOANERGES
• song *no longer*	FIT(T), FITTE, FYTTE	noisy unit	(DECI)BEL
no *meaning*	REFUSAL	• noiseless	NOBEL
no (place of publication)	NP	rumour *noised abroad*	ROOMER
no proper [cures]	CURSE	**nomadic**	
no rain *about*	(in) DR–Y	[Is Arab] *nomadic*?	ARABIS
no trumps	NT	*nomadic* [tribe]	BITER
no value declared	NVD	**nominal**	
Noah		nominal subscription	SIGNATURE
Noah ANCIENT MARINER, ARKWRIGHT		nominal winner	VICTOR
Noah's lamp, *say* ARCLIGHT, FLOODLIGHT		**nominative**	NOM
Noah's wife, *say*	JOAN OF ARC	**non-**[1]	NON–
nob	JACK, KNAVE	non-*extreme members*	NN
noble		non-*finisher*	N
noble churchman	DUKEDOM, EARLDOM	[non]-*runner*	ONN
noble friend, *say*	DUCALLY	non-*starter*	N
noble journalist	COUNTED	**non-**[2]	
noble queen	COUNTER	indicating omission:	
noble, *say*	MARQUEE, PIER	*non*-British	omit B
noble vessel	LORDSHIP	*non*-English	omit E
noble's joint	COUNTSHIP, DUKESHIP	*non*-European	omit E
nobles, *say* MARQUEES, PIERCE, PIERS		*non*-extreme (m)ember(s)	EMBER
nobility, *say*	PIERAGE	*non*-U	omit U
nobody		• *non*-U ho(u)se	HOSE
nobody	ALL SOULS, POOTER	*non*-union	omit TU, U
nobody called	ORANG	• *non*-union (tu)tor	TOR
nod		• *non*-union to(u)r	TOR
nod *back<*	DON	*non*-university . . .	omit U
[nod] *off*	DON, –OND	**non-**[3]	
noise		other uses:	
noise	DIN	non-commissioned officer CPL, CQMS, CSM	
• noise abates	DINGOES		NCO, RQMS, RSM
• noiseless	ODIN		SGT, SM
noise	RACKET	*non-conformist* [priest] RIPEST, STRIPE	
• noise in court	RACKET		TRIPES
• noise of showjumping BADMINTO RACKET		non-drinker	TT
• *noise, say*	RACQUET	non-medal-winner	FOURTH
• *noisy dance, say*	RACQUET BALL	non-military numbers	CIVIL
noise and number index	NNI	non-professional	LAY
noise of rain	REIGN, REIN	non-specific urethritis	NSU
noiseless NOBEL, OBANG, ODIN		non-striker	SCAB
	QUIETER	non-U	NAFF
noiseless ty(ping)	TY	**none**	
noisily opening	DOR, GAIT	none	NOTARY
noisy (very noisy)	F(FF)	none left	ALL RIGHT
• a noisy attack	AFRAID	none oversleep	ON A PLATE
• a noisy carnival	AFFAIR	none*theless*	omit O
• a noisy company	AFFIRM	• *nonetheless* s(o)lid	SLID
and		• s(o)ap *nonetheless* . . .	SAP
• noisy cow	FLOWER	**nonsense**	
• noisy way	FEAST	*nonsense* [verses]	SERVES
• noisy work	FOP	nonsensical fellow	LEAR
and		**noon** AMENDS, HANDS UP, M, N	
• a very noisy listener	AFFEAR	**Norfolk town**	
• a very noisy tune	AFFAIR	Norfolk town	DISS
(see also loud, strong)		*in* Norfolk town	DIS–S

Anag [cat]; Any *; Begin IGN–; Endings –ING; eg •; Hidden /cat/; Implied add (on); Implied in (in);

• wine *in* Norfolk town	DISPORTS

normal

normal	PAR
• I am *in* normal . . .	PAIR
• normal family	PARKIN
• ship *outside* normal . . .	SPARS
normal colour	STANDARD
normal soldier	REGULAR
normal temperature and pressure	NTP

Norman

Norman (=French)	
• *Norman's* residence	CHATEAU, MAISON
• present *for Norman*	CADEAU
Norman French	NF

north

north	N
North Africa	NA
• North African girl	NASAL
• North African perfume	NASCENT
• North African tree	NAPALM
North America	NA, US, USA
North American (=Red Indian)	
• North American wife	SQUAW
	(see also brave, Indian)
North British	NB
North Circular (Line)	NO
North-east	NE, PREMIERE
north-facing door(D)^	ROOD
north-north-east	NNE
north-north-west	NNW
north of the Border (=Scottish)	
• go *north of the Border*	GANG
• man *north of the Border*	MON
• town *north of the Border*	TOON, TOUN
North Pole	NP
north-west	NW
northern	N
Northern French	NF
Northern Ireland	NI
• Northern Ireland apprentice	NIL
• Northern Ireland church	NICE
• Northern Ireland tre(e) *cut*	NITRE
Northern Territory	NT
northwards	TON

Norway   N

nose

nasal drip	DEWDROP
nose	HOOTER
nose of rocket	R
nose *off* (f)ace	ACE
[nose] *put out*	EONS, NOES
nosey client	PARSON
Nosey Parker, *say*	PRIOR
noseless, *say*	NONOSE

not[1]

not	NOT
• not a child	NOTCH
• not any *local* . . .	NOTARY
• not church	NOTCH
• not decorated	NOTICED
• not English	NOTE
• not frozen	NOTICE
• not if I, *say*	NOTIFY
• not in key	NOTING
• not well	NOTABLY
[not](D)^	TON-UP
not a sign	NOTARIES
not *as before*	NE
not *back*<	TON
[not] *bad*	TON
not *backward-looking*<	TON
not *beginning*	start with NOT
• not *beginning* sweet . . .	NOTICE
n̲o̲t *beginning*	N
no̲t *central*	O
no̲t *closing*	T
not *coming back*<	TON
[not] *converted*	TON
n(o)t *disheartened*	NT
n(o)t *emptied*	NT
not *ending*	T
n̲o̲t *extremely* . . .	−NT
no̲t *finally* . . .	T
not *French*	NON
n̲o̲t *head* . . .	N
not *heard*	KNOT
not *hurried*	NT
not *known before*	NE
not *lacking*	omit NOT
• (not)ably not *lacking*	ABLY
not *listened to*	KNOT
not *long ago*	NE
not *missing*	omit NOT
• not *missing* s(not)ty . . .	STY
[not] *moving*	TON
not *old*	NE
not *once*	NE
not *one*, twice	NENE
no̲t *opening*	N
not *opening*	start with NOT
• not *opening* sweets	NOTICES
[not] *out*	TON
n(o)t *out* nought	NT
[not] *out of place*	TON
not *raised*(D)^	TON
not *reduced*	NO, NT
not *round*	NO–T
not, *say*	KNOT
• not all, *say*	KNOT-HOLE
• not that man, *say*	KNOTTY
not *Scottish* . . .	NA, NAE
not *seen on the Continent*	NON
not *starting*	start with NOT
• not *starting* directions	NOTES

Letter replaced \c\at; Omit (a); Pointers *out*; Retain a̲; Split B_ED; Down (D); Backwards <or ^

not *starting*	N	• grip *not* constant	(c)LAMP
not *up*(D)^ . . .	TON	*not* dead	omit D
not *using* a . . .	NOTA	*not entirely* (c)lear	LEAR
not *very old*	NE	*not entirely* cle(ar)	–CLE
not *without*	NO–T	*not equal to* teacher	(m)ASTER
n(o)t *without* love	NT	*not exactly* (w)hat . . .	HAT
not²		*not* fifty	omit L
not	O	*not finally* sen(t)	SEN
• not at all	–OWAY	*not finishing*	omit last letter
• not empty	OVOID	*not finished* wit(h)	WIT
• not marked	OSCAR	• *not finishing* of(f) . . .	OF
• not married	OWED	*not* following	omit F
• not pleasant	ON ICE	• (F)red *not* following	RED
• not taxed	ORATED	*not full* co(mpany)	CO
not³		*not full* stoma(ch)	STOMA
indicating anagram:		*not fully* (o)pen	PEN
[it was] *not true*	WAIST	*not* good	omit G
not normally [made]	DAME, EDAM, MEAD	• sharp pain *not* good	TWIN(g)E
not really [new]	WEN	*not got* *	omit *
not right [in the] . . .	THINE	• mot(her)'s *not got* her . . .	MOT
not true [by her] . . .	HERBY	*not* half!	omit half of word
not usual [in an] . . .	NAIN	• Hun(gry)? *Not half!*	HUN
not usually [said]	AIDS, DAIS	• (Sca)red? *Not half!*	RED
not⁴		*not* hard	omit H
indicating hidden word:		*not having* it	omit IT
not all tha/t in t/he . . .	TINT	*not having* money	omit L
not all of t/he ar/tist's . . .	HEAR	*not head* of (p)arty	ARTY
not altogether c/lear n/ow . . .	LEARN	*not* in	omit IN
not complete in/stall/ation	STALL	*not keeping* a . . .	omit A
not entirely c/lea/r	LEA	*not keeping* quiet	omit P
not full s/tom/ach	TOM	*not keeping* time	omit T
not fully a/war/e	WAR	*not keeping* *	omit *
not much of t/he m/oney	HEM	• r(up)ee *not keeping* up	REE
not the whole tru/th in/side	THIN	*not* long	omit L
not wholly finish/ed, it/ was . . .	EDIT	*not long enough* for the(m)	THE
not⁵		*not* male	omit M
indicating omission:		*not* married	omit M
not a co(a)t	CAT	*not* me	omit ME
not about	omit C, CA, RE	*not much* t(ime)	T
not accepted	omit U	*not* new	omit N
not al(l)	–AL	*not* noisy	omit F
not all that . . .	THA, HAT	*not* OK	omit OK
not altogether (c)lear	LEAR	*not* old	omit O
not America	omit US	• c(o)at *not* old	CAT
• A(us)tria *not* America	ATRIA	*not* on	omit ON
not approved	omit OK	*not* one	omit I
not available	·(see unavailable)	*not* opening	omit 1st letter
not beginning	omit 1st letter	• (p)lay *not opening*	LAY
• *not beginning* (r)ace	ACE	• pub *not opening*	(i)NN
not big enough for (m)any	ANY	*not* popular	omit IN
not charged	omit ION	*not* posh	omit U
• rat(ion) *not charged*	RAT	*not* quiet	omit P
not complete	FUL(l)	*not* quit(e)	QUIT
not completely done	DON, ONE	*not quite* 50%	HAL(f)
not completely finished	DON(e), MAD(e)	*not quite* al(l)	–AL
not constant	omit C	*not quite* certain	SUR(e)
• (c)over *not* constant	OVER	*not quite* the finest	THEBES(t)

Anag [cat]; Any *; Begin IGN–; Endings –ING; eg •; Hidden /cat/; Implied add (on); Implied in (in);

not right	omit R, RT	*not* good	BAD, OFF
not round	omit O	*not* grand	UPRIGHT
not so	omit SO	*not* here	THERE
• *not* so (so)on	ON	*not* I	CONSONANT, YOU
not soft	omit P	*not in* employment	OUTWORK
not square	omit T	*not* in form	OUTCLASS
not starting	omit first letter	*not* left	R, RT, RIGHT
• (t)rain *not* starting	RAIN	*not* long	SHORT
not the capital	omit 1st letter	*not* natural	FLAT, SHARP
• *not the capital of* (C)had	HAD	*not* one, *say*	MOOR, NUN, TOO
not the doctor . . .	omit DR or MO	*not* ordained	LAY
not the *first*	omit T	*not* out	IN
not the *first* one	omit first I	*not* partial	TOTAL
• *not the first* one wa(i)ling	WALING	*not* positive	NAY, NEGATIVE, NO
not th(e) *whole* . . .	TH	*not* qualified	ABSOLUTE, AMATEUR, LAY
not the whole thin(g)	THIN	*not* reacting	INERT, NEUTRAL, NOBLE
not there *	omit *	*not* recorded	LIVE
• *not there*, we (we)ren't . . .	RENT	*not* right	L, LEFT, LT, WRONG
not trendy	omit IN	*not* singular, *say*	PLEURAL
not unknown	omit X, Y, Z	*not* so good, *say*	PORER, POURER
• point *not* unknown	APE(x)	*not* spliced	SINGLE
• pixie *not* unknown	FAIR(y)	*not* tart, *say*	SUITE
• Jerusalem *not* unknown	(z)ION	*not* the main . . .	LAND
not upper class	omit U	*not* that	THIS
not using head	omit 1st letter	*not* those	THESE
not using motorway	omit M(I)	*not* tired BARE, NAKED, NUDE, UNDRESSED	
not using *	omit *	*not* top quality	B
not very	omit V	*not* upright	GRAND
not wearing tails	omit last letters	*not* 'urtful	ARMLESS
• ne(w) on(e) *not wearing tails*	NEON	*not* vacant	ISLET
not wholly manufactured . . .	MAD(e)	*not* watered	NEAT
* *not seen*	omit *	*not* worn out	UNDERWEAR
• king *not seen in* Dove(r)	DOVE	*not* written	ORAL

not[6]

not[7]

indicating opposite:		other uses:	
not a man	FEMALE, WOMAN	not at all	NO–WAY
not acting	OFFSET	not clear	NL
not all	APART, SOME	not crazy	NOMAD
not all black, *say*	JETSAM, JETSOM	not dated	ND
not at home	OUT	not decimal	UNTENABLE
not automatic	MANUAL	*not exactly* weak	TEAK, WEAN, WEEK
not bad	FAIR, GOOD	not fine enough	UNDERGROUND
not batting	FIELDING, OUTSIDE	*not full* stomach	TUM(MY)
not big-*hearted*	SWEET, TWEED	not identified	X, Y
not bound	FREE	*not just* hot	SHOT, HOTEL
not bulls	INNERS	*not many* vocalise, *say*	FUSING
not exactly	ROUGHLY	*not often* if I, *say*	RAREFY
not even	ODD	*not on* purpose	OFFEND
not fair	DARK	not otherwise provided	NOP
not far	NEAR	not out	NO
not fast	ADRIFT, SLOW	not paid	AMATEUR, HON
not favouring	ANTI, CON–	not permitted	NL
not fielding	BATTING, INSIDE	*not quite* beautiful	DUTIFUL
not first class	B	*not so much* chicken, *say*	LESSEN
not for	ANTI, CON–	*not so much* comfort, *say*	LESSEES
not full	STILLROOM	*not* so bright	MATTER
not fully dressed, *say*	BEARER, LESSON	not specific	NS

not suited	BARE, NAKED, NUDE
	UNDRESSED
not *to get* left in . . .	incl R, RT
• f–ight *not to get* left *in*	FRIGHT
• ma–y *not get* left *in*	MARTY
not *to get* right into	incl L, LT
• f–ight *not to get* right *in*	FLIGHT
• ma–y *not get* right *in*	MALTY
not upper class	NON-U
not 'urt	UNARMED
not willing	INTESTATE
not working	DOWN
• not working properly	DOWNRIGHT

notable

notable	CANNOT, CANT
notably (=in music)	
• *notably* fast	ALLEGRO
• *notably* slow	LENTO
	(*see also* note)

Notary Public	NP
notch	V

note¹

group of notes	ABE(D), ACE
	BAD(E), BAG, BEAD, BEE, BEG
	CAB, CAD, CAFE
	DAB, DEB, DEAD, DEAF
	EBB
	FAD(E), FEE(D)
	GAD, GAFF, GEE
note	A, B, C, D, E, F, G, N
• cover note	CACHED
• love-notes	ODD, OFF
• notebooks	ENT–
• pound notes	LADE, LEE, LEG
note	DO, DOH, UT, RE
	ME, MI, FA, FAH
	SO, SOH, SOL, LA
	LAH, SI, TE, TI
• note most . . .	UTMOST
• note, *say*	DOE, DOUGH
• notebook	SOB
• two notes	FARE, FATE
note	FLAT, NATURAL, SHARP
• note *to* Times	FLATTEN
• note *to* first . . .	NATURALIST
• notes owl	SHARPSHOOTER
note	BREVE, MINIM etc
• note shirt	BREVET
• note viewers, *say*	MINIMISE
note *from* . . .	omit A, B, C etc
	omit DO(H) etc
noted	incl A,B, etc
	incl DO(H) etc
noted	COMPOSED
noted (=in music)	
• *noted* boy	DANNY
• *noted* man from Seville	BARBER

• *noted* waltzer	MATILDA
noted group	CHORD
	OCTET, QUARTET etc
	(*see also* notable)

note²

note well	NB
note landlord	LETTER
notebook	MARK noted,
	say SCENE
notes	–IOUS
printed notes	FIVER, TENNER
written notes	PS, PPS

nothing¹

nothing	LOVE
• fifty *to* nothing	CLOVE
• nothing right	LOVER
• nothing's right	LOVE-STORY
	(*see also* love, no)

nothing²

nothing	NIL
• nothing *back* in s.a.e	SALINE
• nothing English	NILE
• nothing *in* bishop's office	SENILE
	(*see also* love, no)

nothing³

nothing	O
• nothing American	–OUS
• nothing changes	OVARIES
• nothing left	OL
• nothing pleasant	ON ICE
• nothing right	OR, ORT
• nothing the matter	OPUS
• nothing *to* America	–OUS
• nothing to eat	OATMEAL, ORATIONS and
• advanced nothing	LENTO
• came *to* nothing	CAMEO
• cover *with* nothing . . .	LIDO
• order nothing	COMMANDO
• surgeon *has* nothing . . .	VETO
nothing *forgotten*	omit O
nothing *in* it	incl O
nothing *is lacking*	omit O
nothing *less*	omit O
nothing *lost*	omit O
nothing *missing*	omit O
nothing *more*	add O
• father *has nothing more*	DADO
• girl *has nothing more*	MAYO
• record *with nothing more* . . .	DISCO
nothing *on*	–O
• father *with* nothing *on*	DADO
• man *with* nothing *on*	HALO
• sailor *with* nothing *on*	TARO
nothing on	–OON
• dance *with* nothing on	BALLOON
• girl *with* nothing on	SALOON

• many *with* nothing on	MOON
	(see also with)
nothing *short*	omit O
nothing *to lose*	omit O
• b(o)y has nothing *to lose*	BY
nothing⁴	
nothing but	PURE
nothing on the clock	BAREFACED
nothing, *say*	KNOUT
nothing to declare	DUMB, MUTE
notice	
notice	AD
• distant notice	FARAD
• notice *in* m–e . . .	MADE
• notice the mud	ADMIRE
notice	D
• notice dog	DROVER
• notice *to* paper	DREAM
• notice perused	DREAD
notice	SEE
• notice article	SEETHE
• notice Frenchman, *say*	SERENE
• notice many . . .	SEED, SEEL, SEEM
and	
• notice child, *say*	SEASON
• notice him, *say*	SEAMAN
• on notice, *say*	OVERSEA
notice	SPY
• notice feature, *say*	SPINOSE
• notice joint, *say*	SPINODE, SPINY
• notice woman, *say*	SPIRE
notice keep	OBSERVE
noticed	SAW
• dance noticed	JIGSAW
• noticed magistrates	SAW-BENCH
• noticed poster	SAWBILL
and	
• noticed a wise man, *say*	SAUSAGE
• noticed you and me, *say*	SAURUS
noticed *in* Dai/ly Re/cord	LYRE
notices	SEES
• notices, *say*	SEAS, SEIZE
• notices boy, *say*	SEISMAL, SEISTAN
noticing, *say*	CITING, SITING
short notice	AD(VERT)
notorious kisser	JUDAS
notwithstanding	LOW CLASS
nought	LOVE, NIL, NO, O
	(see also naught, nothing)
noun	N
novel	
novel	NEW
• concerning novel . . .	RENEW
• novel race	NEWSPRINT
• novel shirt	NEWT
• novel style	NEWTON
and	

• novel, *say*	GNU, KNEW
novel	SHE
• novel articles	SHEATHE
• novel many . . .	SHED
• novel record	SHEEP
• novel report	SHEBANG
novel headgear	TRILBY
novel place	UTOPIA, WESTWARD HO etc
novel [present]	SERPENT
novelist	MANN, STERNE et al
novel[ist]	SIT
[Proust] *novel*	SPROUT, STUPOR
[wrote] *novel*	TOWER
November	NOV
novice	
novice	L
• novice *has* current . . .	LAMP
• novice priest	LLAMA
• *place* horn *before* a novice	CORAL
	(see also learner)
now	
now	AD, ANON
nowadays	AD(AGE)
noxious	
[it was] *noxious*	WAIST, WAITS
noxious [weeds]	SEWED, SWEDE
n-number	NONE
NTT	
NTT, *say*	ENTITY
nu	N
nucleus	
nuclear	(in) COR–E
• five nuclear . . .	CORVE
• nuclear rod	CORRODE
• nuclear sheep	CORTEGE
[nuclear] *fallout*	UNCLEAR
[nuclear] *fusion*	UNCLEAR
nucleus of a<u>tom</u>	TO
nude	OUT OF GEAR
	(see also bare, naked)
number¹	
number	C, CL, D, L, M, N, V
• a number of coins	ACCENTS
• number one	CLONE
• number in Queen's . . .	DINERS
• number *in* c–are	CLARE
• number in America	MINUS
• number at church	NATCH
• number one *German*	VEIN
number	EIGHT
• number unknown	EIGHTY
• French number	FREIGHT
• women number . . .	WEIGHT
number	NINE
• firm number	CONINE
• number of matches	NINETIES
• write nine . . .	PENNINE

number	NO	number of French . . .	MARSEILLAISE
• live *with* a number	BEANO	number of Germans	LIED
• number play badly	NOSTRUM	number of Hungarians	CSARDAS
• round number	ONO	number of Spaniards	PASA DOBLE
and		**number one**	
• *back* number<	ON	number one	ADAM, I, ME, NOI
number	ONE	number one craze	EGOMANIA
• number *following* saint	STONE	*number one from* London	L
• number *in* trains	BONER	number one *French*	UN, UNE
• square number	TONE	number one *German*	EIN
number	TEN	number one *Italian*	UNA, UNO
• number expert	TENACE	number one man	ADAM
• number he intended, *say*	TENEMENT	number one mother	EVE
• number of workers	TENANTS	number one on ship	MATE
• numbered apartment	FLATTEN	number one *on* ship	S
• round a number	OATEN	number one *returning*<	–ION
number her feet, *say*	COUNTERFEIT	number one wife	EVE
number of Romans	C, CL, D, L, M, V	number one woman	EVE
number chooser	ERNIE	**numerical control**	NC
number cruncher	COMPUTER	**nurse**	
number eight, *say*	FORTITUDE	nurse	EDITH (CAVELL)
number, *say*	WON		FLORENCE (NIGHTINGALE)
	TO, TOO		SCN, SEN, SRN, VAD
	FOR, FORE	nurse	SHARK
	AIT, ATE, EYOT	nurse	TEND
	FOR TEA, FORTE	• nurse working	TENDON
numbers	NOS	• popular nurse	INTEND
Numbers	NUM(B)	nurse goat	NANNY
		nurse, *say*	MISTREATING
number²		nursemaid	ALICE
number	ANAESTHETIC, LOCAL	nursery gardener	MARY
	OPIATE	nursery *rhyme*	BURSARY, CURSORY
back number	EPIDURAL, SPINAL	*nursing* a . . .	incl A
number [three], *say*	ETHER	*nursing* *	incl *
number³		• a *French* female *nursing* boy	UNDONE
number	SONG, TUNE	**nut**	
number of Argentinians	TANGO	[I am] *nuts*	AIM, MAI
number of Brazilians	SAMBA	[nut]*cracker*	TUN, UNT–
number of Cubans	R(H)UMBA	nuts	BANANAS, MAD

O

all-rounder, **anthem**, *around*, **aught**, *bald patch, ball, band, blob*, **blood group**, *cavity*, **cipher**, *circle, circuit, circular letter, descendant of, dial, disc, duck, egg*, **eleven (thousand)**, *empty*, **examination**, *full moon, globe, grade, gulf, hole, hollow, hoop, level, loop*, **love**, **meditation**, **naught**, **nil**, **nothing**, **ought**, **Ohio**, **old**, **omega**, **omicron**, **on**, *opening*, **ordinary**, *ortho-*, **ought**, *oval*, **oxygen**, *pellet, pill, rotund, round, ring, spangle, vacancy*

O	
O	CIRCLE, CIRCULAR LETTER
	LOVE LETTER
O	RING
• garbo	DRESS RING
• Mayo	TREE-RING
• Soho	KEY-RING
O	ROUND
• good round	GROUND
• fine round, *say*	FROWNED
• OUP	ROUND-UP
O, *certainly*	OXYGEN
oatmeal	BRANDISH
Obadiah	OB(AD)
obese	
obese	FAT
• obese friend	FATALLY
• obese man	FATAL, FATED
• obese woman	FATHER
• test for obesity	FATTEST
object	
object	IT, OBJ
objection	BUT
• objection *following* looting	SACKBUT
• objection *to* hair	BUTTRESS
• objection *to* weight	BUTTON
objection to [prices]	SPICER
objective	OBJ
objective, *say*	GHOUL
objector	CO
oblige	
obligation, *say*	DHOOTIE
obliged to jump	BOUND
oblique	
oblique	OBL
oblique [angle]	GLEAN
[laid] *obliquely*	DIAL
obliterate	
obliterate a . . .	omit A
obliterate *	omit *

• uproar *eliminates* us	RUCK(us), RUMP(us)
oblong	OBL
obscure	
obscure book	BLURB
obscure note	DIME
obscure [views]	WIVES
obscured by mu/ch ar/gument	CHAR
obscuring [a scene]	SENECA
obsequious man	FUNERAL DIRECTOR UNDERTAKER
observe	
observation	OBS
observe	SEE
• observe mortals, *say*	SEMEN
• observe ruler	SEEK, SEER
• observe square, *say*	SEAT
• observe vehicle, *say*	CEBUS
observe branch	TWIG
observed	SAW
• observed deer	SAWBUCK
• observed skeleton	SAWBONES
• worker observed . . .	HANDSAW
observed in [Leith]	LITHE
observed in Lei/th en/tirely . . .	THEN
observed, *say*	SCENE
Observer Magazine	SPECTATOR
observes retinue	EYE-STRAIN
	(*see also* notice, see)
obsolete	(*see* old[3])
obstacle	
obstacle *on* journey	TRIPLET
obstacle race	HANDICAP
obstacle, *say*	ITCH
obstreperous	
[he acted] *obstreperously*	CHEATED
obstreperous [men are] . . .	RENAME
obtain	
obtainable from [large] . . .	LAGER, REGAL
obtainable from lar/ge an/imals	GEAN
obtainable in b/ig, loos/e packets	IGLOOS

Letter replaced \c\at; Omit (a); Pointers *out*; Retain <u>a</u>; Split B_ED; Down (D); Backwards <or ^

obtained from [lime]	EMIL, MILE
obtained from li/me tre/es	METRE
obtains support	GAINSAID
obvious disagreement	PLAINTIFF
occupy	
occupational therapy	OT
occupied by a	incl A
occupied by *	incl *
• sh–ed *occupied by* a king	SHARED
occupied this place, *say*	STADIA
occupying position	INSTANCE
occupying Russi/an vil/lages	ANVIL
occupying *	incl in A
• a king *occupying* sh–ed	SHARED
ocean	
ocean	MAIN
• about the ocean	REMAIN
• ocean-drilling rig	MAINBRACE
• ocean race	MAIN COURSE
• ocean, *say*	MANE
ocean-going junk	FLOTSAM
	(*see also* sea)
ochlocrat	MOBSTER
octavo	OCT
October	OCT
odd	
odd	RUM
• many odd . . .	DRUM
• odd coin	RUMP
• odd family	RUMKIN
• odd matter	RUMPUS
• Oddfellow	RUMAL
odd bits of fo͟od	FO
odd character	CARD, ECCENTRIC
odd characters in p͟lay	PA
odd [shape]	HEAPS, PHASE
oddball [actor]	CROAT
oddfellow	OF
oddfe͟llo͟w	FLO
oddity of [Norse] . . .	SNORE
oddly deficient (s)t(o)r(e) (w)e (s)e(t) . . .	TREE
oddly neglected (o)p(e)r(a) (b)y . . .	PRY
oddly [shaped]	PHASED
odds	SP
sho͟rt *odds*	SOT
of¹	
of *French*	DE
• of *French* fathers	DESIRES
• of *French* money	DECENT
• of *French* wine	DEPORT
of *German*	VON
of *French* and *German*	DEVON
of the *French*	DELA, DES, DU
• of the *French* hill	DELATOR
• of the *French* note	DELATE
• of *the French* unknown	DELAY
and	

• of the *French* city	DESTROY
• of the *French* couple	DESPAIR
• of the *French* hypocrisy	DESCANT
and	
• of the *French* affliction	DUG-OUT
• of the *French* share	DURATION
• of the *French* sportsman	DUSKIER
of the *Italian*	DEL
• of the *Italian* measurement	DELFT
• of the *Italian* river	DELOUSE
• of the *Italian* sweet	DELICE
of the *Spanish*	DEL
• doctor of the *Spanish*	MODEL
• of the *Spanish* army	DELTA
• of the *Spanish* victory	DELVE
of²	
indicating origins:	
• half *of France*	DEMI
• lady *of Madrid*	SENORA
• leader *of Italy*	DUCE
• soldiers *of Germany*	SOLDATEN
of³	
other uses:	
of course	(*see* course)
of some c/once/rn	ONCE
of ten, *say*	DEANERY
of the lungs, *say*	PLURAL
of them, *say*	THERE
of th/in mate/rial	INMATE
of use [in the] . . .	THINE
of use in [the war]	WREATH
* of	
–a boy	BROTH
–a gun	SON
–cake	PIECE
–my eye	APPLE
–the month	FLAVOUR
–the walk	COCK
–the world	MAN
off¹	
off	BAD
• *put* off *after* error	SINBAD
• off English . . .	BADE
off	OUT
• 150 off	CLOUT
• off the team	OUTSIDE
• road off . . .	STOUT
off	R, RT, RIGHT
off²	
indicating an anagram:	
[I went] *off the rails*	TWINE
[let] *off*	–TLE
[Monday] *off*	DYNAMO
off course [in a golf] . . .	FOALING
off-[drive]	DIVER, VERDI
off [hooks]	SHOOK
off the rails [a train]	ANITRA

Anag [cat]; Any *; Begin IGN–; Endings –ING; eg •; Hidden /cat/; Implied add (on); Implied in (in);

off[beat]	BATE
offbeat [march]	CHARM
off[cuts]	SCUT
off-key [note]	ETON, TONE
off[side]	DIES, IDES
[take]-*off*	KATE, TEAK
[trade]-*off*	DATED, TREAD
[write]-*off*	TWIER
[wrote]-*off*	TOWER

off³

meaning:

away

• away result	OFFEND

bad

• that is bad	SCOFF

right

• daughter with right . . .	DOFF

stale

• stale buffet	OFFBEAT

off⁴

other uses:

off Cowes	(in) SO–LENT, INSOLENT
off cricket	R, RT, RIGHT
off its food	
(=taking nothing in)	incl O
• c–at *is off its food*	COAT
off-key	omit A, B, C, D, E, F, G
• *off*-key (b)ass	ASS
• *off*-key son(g)	SON
off-peak call	YODEL
off them	ONUS
offhand impression	FINGERPRINT
offensive striker	BATTLE-AXE, CLUB
	COSH, SWORD

offer

offer	BID
• artist *takes* offer	RABID
• four offer study, *say*	FORBIDDEN
• offer English . . .	BIDE
offer sweet, *say*	SERVICE
offer *up*(D)^	DIB
offer up a jar(D)^	RAJA
offer vessel	TENDER
offered in so/me sh/ops	MESH
wom/an des/iring *offers*	ANDES

office

office	MASS
• office provided . . .	MASSIF
• soldiers *in* office	MORASS
• state office	MASS
office girl	TEMP
Office of Fair Trading	OFT

officer

officer	COL
• officer in charge	COLIC
• officer *in* service dress	SCOLD
• officer *with* daughter	COLD
officer	LT
• commander *with* lieutenant	COLT
• lieutenant *outside* the ring	LOT
officer-commanding	CO
• ban officer-commanding	BANCO
• officer-commanding engineers	CORE
• officer-commanding in prison, *say*	COINCIDE
• officer-commanding, married	COWED
officer-commanding	OC
• officer-commanding (Mediterranean)	MEDOC
• officer-commanding sect	OCCULT
officer-in-charge	OIC
officer is able	MAJORCAN
officer of the crown	MAJOR
Officer of the Order of the British Empire	OBE
officer, *say*	KERNEL
Officer Training Corps	OTC

official

official	MARSHAL
• display official . . .	AIR-MARSHAL
• official, *say*	MARTIAL
official	OFF
official	REF
• jerk official	CANTREF
• official purposes	REFUSES
• official *without* English . . .	REEF
Official Chaplain to the Forces	OCF
official language	MANDARIN
official *opening*	O
official receiver	ADDRESSEE
officinal	OFF

offspring

offspring	HEIR
• offspring, *say*	AIR
offspring	LITTER
• fine offspring	FLITTER
• offspring scoffed, *say*	LITERATE

often

often	DECIMAL
often *reduced*	OF, TEN

ogee

ogee	RING-HORSE
ogee, *say*	OG

oh

oh	O
oh, why, *say*	OY
ohs	OO, OS

oil

change [oil]	OLI–
oil container	PICTURE FRAME
[oil] *rig*	OLI–
oil sellers	OPEC
[oil]-*spill*	OLI–
OK	ROGER

old¹

old	OLD
• *late* queen	OLDER
• *much-used* letter	OLDEN
• *retired* head	OLDNESS
[old]-*fashioned*	DOL, LOD
[old]-*fiddler*	DOL, LOD
old *French*	VIEILLE, VIEUX
old *Scottish*	AULD
<u>o</u>ld *leader*	O
older tree	ELDER

old²

old	AGED
• old cards	PACKAGED
• old fellow	MANAGED
• Old English	ENGAGED
• old fish	GARAGED
• old fruit	PLUMAGED
• old hounds	PACKAGED
• old mare	DAMAGED
• old medication	PILLAGED
• old orchestra	BANDAGED
• old players	BANDAGED
• old spirit, *say*	RUMMAGED
• old swindle	RAMPAGED
• old weir	DAMAGED
• old woman	DAMAGED
old	EX
• *former* deed	EXACT
• *late* claim	EXCLAIM
• *no longer* clear	EXPLAIN
• old *and* ugly	EXPLAIN
• old nurse	EXTEND(ER)
• *once* stood	EXPOSED
• *one-time* shelter	EXTENT
• *outdated* tax	EXCESS
• *past* it	EXIT
• *previous* pamphlet	EXTRACT
• *retired* player	EXACTOR
• *stale* wine	EXPORT
• *used to be* the thing	EXIT
old	LATE
• *Old and* New Testament	LATENT
• *old* cross	LATEX
• *old* king	LATER
old	O
• Old Age Pension(er)	OAP
• old boy	OB
• Old English	OE
• Old Etonian	OE
• Old French	OF(R)
• Old Irish	OIR
• Old Measurement	OM
• old newspaper	OFT
• Old Norse	ON
• Old Style	OS
• Old Testament	OT

old	PAST
• *old* gold	PASTOR
• *old, old* use	PASTURE
• *old* one, *German*	PASTE-IN
• old soldiers	PASTOR
old	STALE
• old friend	STALEMATE
• old saint	STALEST

old³

indicating ancient, archaic,
obsolete, previously expressed,
out of fashion, superannuated:
etc:

old bag	RETICULE
old does . . .	DOTH
old enough	ENOW
old measure	HAY, MINUET etc
old writer	STYLE
	(*see also* ancient)

old⁴

other uses:

old banger	MUSKET
old boy	ALUMNUS
old coppers	PENNYFARTHING
old crocks	MING
old digger	ABORIGINE
old Dutch	WIFE
old Englishman	ANGLE
old-fashioned corsets	OUTSTAYS
old-fashioned medium	STEAM RADIO
old fellow	STALEMATE
old fiddler	COLE, NERO
old flame	LOVER, SWEETHEART
old girl	ALUMNA
	(*see also* old woman *below*)
old hat	DATED
old king	COLE, LUD, OG
old lady	(*see* old woman *below*)
old man	DAD, PA, POP
old man of Paris	PRIAM, VIEUX
old master	CHIPS, PAINTER
	TOP DRAWER
old model	T
Old Nick	MARSHALSEA
old player	HARPSICHORD, SPINET
	KEAN, TREE
old port	LARBOARD, SANDWICH
old Prime Minister	EDEN, PEEL, PITT *et al*
old queen	BESS
old scholar	ERASMUS
old ship	ARGO
old sloth	MEGATHERIUM
old stager	KEAN, TREE
old timer	CLEPSYDRA, HOUR-GLASS
	SUNDIAL, WATER-CLOCK
old woman	BETTER HALF, DUTCH
	EVE, GRAN, HAG, MA, WIFE

Anag [cat]; Any *; Begin IGN–; Endings –ING; eg •; Hidden /cat/; Implied add (on); Implied in (in);

Olympic

O̲lympics *entrants*	OL
Olymp<u>ic</u> *finalists*	IC

omega   Z

omelette

[made] *omelette*	DAME, EDAM, MEAD
omelette of [eggs or] . . .	GORGES

omicron   O

omit

omit captain	SKIP
omit nothing	incl ALL
• sh–ow *omits nothing*	SHALLOW

on¹

on	ON
on *ending*	end in ON
o<u>n</u> *ending*	N
on *entering*	incl ON
• on *entering* ship	SONS
o̲n *entering*	O
on finishing	end in ON
o<u>n</u> *finishing*	N
on *leaving*	omit ON
on */off*	omit ON
• on */off* bat(on)	BAT
• on */off* butt(on)	BUTT
on *opening*	start with ON
• on *opening* hospital wing	ONWARD
o̲n *opening*	O
on points	ONES
on *reflection<*	NO
o̲n *starting*	O
on *the inside*	incl ON
• painter on *the inside*	LONELY
on time	ONT–

on²

on	LEG
• four on, *say*	FORELEG
• on a peg	LEGATEE
• on a rota	LEGALIST
• on *about* an error	LEASING

on³

implying inclusion:
on can be used to imply the addition
of one word to another word,
as in

flying	(on) PLANE, (on) WING
• father *flying*	PAWING
• test *flying, say*	TRIPLANE
sailing	(on) SHIP
• teacher *sailing*	HEADSHIP
walking	(on) LAND
• bird *walking*	CROWFOOT

and so on: other examples will be
found throughout the book under the
appropriate headword

on⁴

indicating addition:

about *on* time	CAGE, CAT, RET–
company *on* the way	CORD, COST
look *on* board	LOSS
put *on* about . . .	CAPUT

on⁵

indicating origins:
on Clydeside (=Scottish)

• man *on Clydeside*	MON

on Fujiyama (=in Japan)

• temple gateway *on Fujiyama*	TORII

on Mont Blanc (=French)

• man *on Mont Blanc*	HOMME

on⁶

meaning:
aboard

• islander *aboard*	MINOR CANON

above

• pass *above*	COLON

acceptable

• *acceptable to* you and me	ONUS

acting

• *acting* group	ONSET

advanced

• John's *more advanced*	JACKSON

ahead

• right *ahead*	RON

appearing

• Greek letter *appearing*	MUON

attached

• orb *with* ring *attached*	BALLOON

available

• cricketer *available*	BATON

bowling

• bat *before bowling*	BATON

charged to

• *charged to* group	ONSET

continue

• *continue to* signal	FLAGON

forward

• haul *forward*	DRAGON

functioning

• officer *functioning*	COLON

further

• weaken further	WILTON

further forward

• bed-time *further forward*	COTTON

in

• *in* the reeds	ONRUSHES

lit

• lamp *lit*	TORCHON

operational

• 100 *operational* types	CONSORTS

over

• *overprice*	ONCOST

performing

• *performing* one on . . .	ONION

playing

• *playing* before church	ONCE
re	
• *re* Advent	ONCOMING
running	
• go running	GOON
supported by	
• vehicle *supported by* . . .	CARTON
working	
• Marx *working*	HARPOON
worn by	
• hat *worn by* . . .	CAPON

on⁷

other uses:

on a ramble [in the] . . .	THINE
on account of . . .	OA
on active service	OAS
on behalf of	FOR, PP
• exist on behalf of, *say*	BEFORE
• on behalf of	
some . . .	FOUR-PART, FOURSOME
• on behalf of Sybil, *say*	FORCIBLE
• on behalf of the	
majority, *say*	FOREMOST
on board	(in) BOA–T, (in) LIN–ER,
	(in) S–S
• son *on board*	BOAST
• king *on board*	LINKER
• a prince *on board*	SAPS
* *on board*	incl *
• king *on board* galle–y	GALLERY
on either side	
• *on either side of* the . . .	TE
• *on either side of* the road	RD
on head	
• Ron *standing on* his head(D)^	NOR
• pat *on head*(D)^	TAP
on holiday	OFFBREAK
on horseback	UP
on it	ONT
on purpose	–MENT
on set	ACTING
on side	L, LEG, LT, LEFT
on side, *say*	RITE, WRIGHT, WRITE
on target earnings	OTE
on top(D)	
• parking sign *on top*	RAMP
• parking *on top* of sign . . .	PRAM
on tour [in the] . . .	THINE
on the conservative side	RIGHT
on the Continent	(see abroad)
on the contrary, parts . . . <	STRAP
on the fire	INGRATE
on the go [nurse] . . .	RUNES
on the loose [in Greek] . . .	REEKING
on the move [when I] . . .	WHINE
on the panel	INJURY
on the prowl, [animal] . . .	LAMINA

on the radio, news . . .	GNUS, NOOSE
on the rampage, [Huns] . . .	SHUN
on the run [in Glos]	LOSING
on the ship	(in) S–S
on the way	incl N, S, E, W
• he's *on* the way	HEN, HEW
• it *is on* the way	NIT, SIT, WIT
• stop *on* the way	BARE, BARN BARS
on the way North, walker . . . (D)^	RECAP
on the wing	UP
on this very spot, *say*	WRIGHTIA
on trial	UP

once

once	EX
• flourished once	FLEX
• once clear	EXPLAIN
• once working	EXACTING
	(*see also* old²)

once

indicating old word:

• host *once*	HARBINGER
• *once* in spite of . . .	MA(U)LGRE
• *once* more	MO(E)
	(*see also* old³)

one¹

one	A, AN
• one *and* one	AI
• one daughter	AD, AND
• one-fifteen	ASIDE
• one-fifty	–AL
• one gets up	ARISES
• one in Poplar, *perhaps*	AINTREE
• one *in* a tree, *perhaps*	FAIR
• one son	AS
• one-time	ANT, AT–
one *inside*	incl A, AN
one *leaving*	omit A, AN
one *less (than)* . . .	omit A, AN
ones	AA, AI, ANA, AS

one²

one	I
• one about . . .	–IC
• one account	–IAC
• one *after* another	ELEVEN
• one against	ICON
• one *and* one	–AI, –IAN, II
	ELEVEN
• one answer	IANS–
• one boy	IDES
• one *by* one	–IA, –IAN, II
	ELEVEN
• one cold . . .	–IC
• one cross	IX
• one daughter	ID
• one-fifty	IL
• one-five	IV
• one gets up	IRISES

Anag [cat]; Any *; Begin IGN–; Endings –ING; eg •; Hidden /cat/; Implied add (on); Implied in (in);

• one *has a* point	–INESS	• one twitch	ACETIC
• one head	–INESS	one	AN
• one hundred	–IC	• one *and* one	ANA–, ANI–
• one *in* a hundred	–TION	• one *in* the French . . .	LANE
• one *in* 100,000	LAIC	• one man	ANDES
• one *in* record-book	EPITOME	one	EA
• one kiss	IX	• one church	EACH
• one leg	–ION	• one *in* transport	BEAR
• one man	IRON(SMITH)	• square one	TEA
• one measure	–ICT, –IFT, ILB	one	EACH
• one member	IMP–	• copper one	PEACH
• one member in the cast	IMPACTING	• learner *has* one . . .	LEACH
• one metre stake	IMPALE	• square one	TEACH
• one mile	IM–	one	ONE
• one name	IN, IRON(SMITH)	• 101	CONE
• one name is suitable	INAPT	• [one] *broken* . . .	NEO–
• one-nil	IO	• (o)ne *loses* nothing	NE
• one no-good . . .	–ING	• one *might say*	WON
• one on	–ION	• *one might say* we've . . .	WEAVE
• one *on* the road	–IRD, –IST	• [one] *wrongly* . . .	NEO–
• one *performing*	–ION	one	UN
• one politician	IMP–	• one *local* local	UNBAR
• one quarter	IE, IN, IS	• one *locally* bred	UNBORN
• one race	–INATION	• one *rustic* hat	UNCAP
• one right	IR	one	UNIT
• one saint	IS–, –IST	• one devoured . . .	UNITATE
• one silver ring	IAGO	• one *in* one	UNIAT
• one son	IS	• one particle	UNITION
• one son *has* nothing	ISO–	• one *short*	UNI–
• one state	–ICAL, –IME	**one⁴**	
• one thousand	IM	other uses:	
• one thousand *and* two	IMPAIR	¹/₁₀₀	ONCE
• one thousand pounds	IMPOUNDS	one	EVERYBODY
• one-time	IT		LUNCH-TIME
• one way	–IE, IN, IS	MONAD, SINGULAR, SOLO, UNIT(Y)	
	–IRD, –IST	one after another, *say*	INTERN(E)
• one *with* a . . .	–IA	one *and* two	TWELVE
and		one capable	PERSONABLE
• hard ones	HIS	one Christmas present	PARTRIDGE
• one's	–IA, II, IS		PEAR-TREE
• one's girl	ISSUE	one cross	IX, NINE
• one's *in* the sea	MISER	one desiring, *say*	LUSTRE
• one's ruler	–ISER	one *divided by* 100	ONCE
one-eyed	incl one I	one drawing	TOWER
• *one-eyed* man	MAIN	one Dutch state	MONOGAMY
• *one-eyed* painter	TIT(i)AN	one each	PER
one *inside*	incl I	• about one each	CAPER
one *leaving*	omit I	• one each child	PERCH
one *less (than)*	omit I	• one each *in* support	SPERLING
one *missing*	omit I	one expert	ACE
one *out of* . . .	omit I	one French	UN, UNE
ones	ELEVEN, IS	• one *French* prison	UNCAGE
one's *double*	ELEVEN, IS	• North *with* one *French* . . .	NUN
one³		• king *with* one *French* . . .	RUNE
one	ACE	one German	EIN
• one flower	ACEROSE	one in	
• one king	ACER	–a quarter	NUMERATOR

Letter replaced \c\at; Omit (a); Pointers *out*; Retain a; Split B_ED; Down (D); Backwards <or ^

–bed	FLOWER, ROSE, SHRUB etc
–bingo	KELLY'S EYE
–cast	FERRET
–colony	ANT, BADGER, PENGUIN
–eight	OAR, STROKE
–exaltation	LARK
–flight	SWALLOW
–mob	KANGAROO
–parliament	MP, OWL
–pod	DOLPHIN, WHALE
–school	FISH, PORPOISE, WHALE
–sounder . . .	BOAR, PIG
–swarm	BEE, LOCUST
–ten	NEXT TO NOTHING
–the pack	ACE etc, CARD
	DOG, WOLF
	SCOUT, WOLF-CUB
one *Italian*	UNA, UNO
one lamenting, *say*	W(H)ALER
one left money	COINHERITOR
one letter	SINGLET
one *local*	UN
one missing, *say*	LACQUER
one nil	TEN
one not identified	X, Y
one (number one)	FIRST MATE
	LIEUTENANT
one of 9	MUSE
one of 27	BOOK
one of 39	BOOK, STEP
one of these	THIS
one of those	THAT
one of us	ME, YOU
	ISLANDER
one *old*	J
one on the staff	BREVE, MINIM
	NOTE, FLAT
	NATURAL, SHARP
one or the other, *say*	ETHER
one out for a duck	(WILD)FOWLER
one over the eight	COX(SWAIN)
	DRUNK
	NINE
one round *short*	'omit O
one *Scotsman*	SOLOMON
one *Scottish* . . .	AE, ANE
one *short* of team	TEN
one sided	BIAS(S)ED
one-sided	incl L, R
• *one-sided* recess	LAPSE
• *one-sided* tree	LASH, RASH
one spot	ACE
one taking	
–over	BOWLER
–the pledge	PAWNBROKER
one thousand	LAC
–pounds	GRAND

one time	SINGLET
	(*see also* old, one-time)
one under par	BIRDIE
one up	RIDER
one way and another	STANDARD
one way or another	LR, RL
one who	
–can	PERSONABLE
–conceals, *say*	EIDER
–eats pigmeat, *say*	AMMETER
one's performance	SOLO
one's pixie	ONESELF
one's successor	TWO
one-time	
one-time	
indicating old word:	
• *one-time* British soldier	LOBSTER
• *one-time* feat	POINT
• *one-time* lover	PARAMOUR, SWAIN
only	
only	BUT
• loot only . . .	SACKBUT
• only a note	BUTTE
• only hair	BUTTRESS(ES)
only	JUST
• only fish, *say*	JOSTLING
• only sweet	JUSTICE
• only the queen	JUSTER
only	SOLE
• at home only . . .	INSOLE
• only daughter	SOLED
• only fish	SOLE
• only son	SOLES
• only you and me	SOLEUS
only	NO
• only bread	NOCAKE
• only East	NOW
• only NW	NOSE
• only SW	NONE
• only a boundary	MERE
only a small lake	MERE
only *half*	ON, LY
only one *	omit the other *
• dul(l)y *with only one* pound	DULY
onset	
gradual *onset*	G
onset	ACTING
onset of <u>w</u>inter	W
onward	
onward	FORTH
• onward, *say*	FOURTH
• onward together	FORTHWITH
o-ort	OBIT
open	
<u>e</u>ye *opener*	E
open	FRANK
• open anger	FRANKINCENSE

Anag [cat]; Any *; Begin IGN–; Endings –ING; eg •; Hidden /cat/; Implied add (on); Implied in (in);

• open commitment	FRANKPLEDGE		KICK-OFF, SERV(IC)E
• open ravine	FRANKLIN	*opening of* play	P
open	OVERT	*opening stages of* tennis	
• open parliament	OVERTRUMP	tournament	TT
• open vessel	OVERTURN	*opening* time	T
• open works	OVERTOPS	*Opening* Today!	T
open (=start with)		opening *up*(D)^	ROOD
• ally *opens with* spades	SALLY	*opening* word	SESAME
• man *to open* road	HERD	*opening* word	W
open accounts	PUBLIC RELATIONS	openwork	OVERTOP
open air	CANDOUR	tin-*opener*	T
open air	A	**opera**	
open-air actors	OUTCAST	opera	OP
open [arms]	MARS, RAMS	opera girl	AIDA, CARMEN, LOUISE
open arms	A		MARTHA, MIMI, NORMA
open country, *say*	WIELD		TOSCA
open house	NEST	opera house	MET
open house	H	opera wives	SERAGLIO
open order	DIRECT, SESAME	operatic drivers	CARMEN
open order	O	operatic game	PATIENCE
open plain	TRANSPARENT	operatic part	ACT, SCENA
open safe	CRACK	operatic ruler	THE MIKADO
open safe	S	**operate**	
open season	FREE FALL	operating	ON
open season	S	*operating* [on her] . . .	HERON
Open University	OU	operating system	(D)OS
Open University	U	operation(s)	OP(S)
open up [crate]	CATER, TRACE	*operation of* [levers]	REVELS
open vault	CLEAR	operational research	OR
opener	KEY	Operations Officer	OPS
opening	ACTI–	Operations Room	OPS
opening	GATE	**opiate**	NUMBER
• an opening	AGATE	**oppose**	
• opening fall	GATECRASH	opponents	(*see* bridge)
• opening, *say*	GAIT	*opponents of* them	US
opening	HOLE	*opponents of* us	THEM
• daughter *has* opening	DHOLE	oppose(d)	CON, OPP, V
• opening a few, *say*	WHOLESOME	*opposing* them	US
• opening *in front of* son	HOLES	*opposing* us	THEM
opening	PORE	**opposite**	
• opening *in* vessel	SPORES	opposite	COUNTER
• opening, *say*	POOR, POUR	• opposite direction	COUNTERPOINT
• son *has* opening	SPORE	• opposite table	COUNTER
opening	O	• space opposite	ENCOUNTER
opening batsman	B	opposite	OP(P)
opening gambit	PLOY	opposite directions	EW, NS, SN, WE
opening gambit	G	*opposite ends of* the . . .	TE
opening loss	UNDOING	*opposite ends of the* field	FD
opening of Parliament	P	*opposite* number<	ON
opening out [ends]	DENS, SEND	*opposite of* new	OLD
opening pair	ADAM AND EVE	*opposite of* new<	WEN
	HINGES	opposite prompt	OP
opening pair	P	*opposition to* tall . . .	SHORT
opening part	DOOR, WINDOW etc	**oppress**	
opening part	P	indicating one word written	
opening [part]	RAPT, TRAP	above another word or letter(D):	
opening of play	ACTI–, BREAK, FACE-OFF,	as *oppressed by* ruler	KINGLIKE

Letter replaced \c\at; Omit (a); Pointers *out*; Retain a̲; Split B_ED; Down (D); Backwards <or ^

man *oppressed by* weight	TONAL
opt	
[easy] *option*	AYES, YEAS
[opt] *out*	POT, TOP
optative	OPT
optional [extra]	TAXER
optional music	VOLUNTARY
optional score	VOLUNTARY
optic	
optical character reading	OCR
optical character recognition	OCR
[optical] *illusion*	TOPICAL
optical learner	PUPIL
optical solution	EYEWASH
optician, *say*	CYTOLOGIST, SEEKING
optician's fee, *say*	IRATE
option	(*see* opt)
opus	OP
or	
or nearest offer	ONO
or ox, *say*	AUROCHS
or verbal, *say*	AURORAL
	(*see also* alternative, gold)
oral	
oral examiner	DENTIST
oral, *say*	AURAL
oral tale	TAIL
orally I'd . . .	EYED, IDE
orange	
[Orange] *Free State*	ONAGER
orange *peel*	OE
orange spot	JAFFA, SEVILLE
[orange] *squash*	ONAGER
Orangeman	MANDARIN
orator	CICERO, LOUDSPEAKER
orb	O
orchestra	
orchestra	BAND
• orchestra sash	BAND
• orchestra noticed . . .	BANDSAW
• orchestra, *say*	BANNED
• state orchestra	RIBAND
orchestra	LSO
orchestra *leader*	O
ordained	ORD
order	
order	CH, OBE, OM
	(*see also* award, honour)
order	ORD
order alteration	ANAGRAM, (MATISE)
order cooker	RANGE
order duck	COMMANDO
order fish	RANKLING
order form	CLASS
order [form]	FROM
order house	FRIARY, MONASTERY
	NUNNERY, PRIORY

order it, *say*	WILLET
order member	FRIAR, MONK, NUN,
	PRIOR
order member, *say*	FRYER, NONE
Order of	
–British Empire	OBE
–Merit	OM
order tub	BATH
ordered [wines]	SINEW, SWINE
orderly-[room]	MOOR
[rest is] *ordered*	RESIST, SISTER
ordinary	
ordinary	ORD
Ordinary National	
–Certificate	ONC
–Diploma	OND
ordinary pedestrian	PROSAIC
ordinary seaman	AB, OS
ordnance	
ordnance	ORD
ordnance datum	OD
Ordnance Survey	OS
organ	
organ cover	EARWIG
[organ]-*grinding*	GROAN
organists	RCO
organ stop	COLON, EAR PLUG
	HEART ATTACK
organisation	
Organisation of African Unity	OAU
Organisation of American States	OAS
organisation of [women is] . . .	WINSOME
organise	
organise	RUN
• organise English . . .	RUNE
• organise *in* fast car	GRUNT
organise [seminar]	REMAINS
organised	RAN
• 100 organised . . .	CRAN
• organised detectives	RANCID
• organised *in* church	CRANE
organised [demo]	MODE
orient	E, ELAND, FARE
oriental	
oriental	E
• man *has* Oriental . . .	MANE
• Oriental network	–ERY
oriental	INE
• Oriental right . . .	INERT
• swindle Oriental	CONINE
oriental	SHAN
oriental meal	FARE
	(*see also* eastern)
origami figure	PAPER BOY
origin	
Origin of Species	S
origin, *say*	DECENT

Anag [cat]; Any *; Begin IGN–; Endings –ING; eg •; Hidden /cat/; Implied add (on); Implied in (in);

original address	MAIDEN SPEECH	*ousted* [leader]	DEALER, REDEAL
original clothes	FIG-LEAVES	*ousts* a . . .	omit A
original manuscript	AUTOGRAPH, MS	*ousts* *	omit *
	SIGNATURE	• s(imp)ly *ousts* the little devil	SLY
original odds	SP	**out¹**	
original plot	EDEN	out and many words beginning	
original [plot]	POLT	with out, some of which follow,	
original story	AVERSION	are used to indicate anagrams,	
originally [lived] . . .	DEVIL	inclusion or omission	
originally <u>s</u>een <u>i</u>n <u>N</u>ewark	SIN	**out²**	
originally seen in Ne/war/k	WAR	indicating an anagram:	
originates from A/sia M/inor	SIAM	[bail] *out*	BALI
originating from [Rome]	MORE	[bale] *out*	ABLE
originator of <u>p</u>lan	P	[chickened] *out*	CHECKED IN
origins of <u>the</u> <u>U</u>niverse	TU	[make] *out*	KAME
ornate		*out* [in the] . . .	THINE
ornate [garb]	BRAG, GRAB	*out*[take]	KATE, TEAK
ornately [tooled]	LOOTED	(*see also* out of³)	
orphan	ANNIE	**out³**	
oscillate		indicating inclusion:	
oscillating [wires]	SWIRE	call *out*	CITE, CIT-E
oscillation of [A string]	STARING	day *out*	DA–Y
other		dry *out*	DR–Y
other people	THEM	last *out*	LAS–T
other people's	OPS	*out*-date	D–ATE
other [times]	ITEMS, MITES, SMITE	*out* East	incl E
others *from Rome*	ET CETERA, ETC	• f–ast *out* East	FEAST
others relax	REST	out West	incl W
otherwise		*out* West	W–EST
otherwise	OR	• is *out* W–est	WISEST
otherwise [it was] . . .	WAIST, WAITS	sit *out*	SI–T
otherwise used [by a] . . .	BAY	time *out*	A–GE
otorhinolaryngology	ENT	tire *out*	T–IRE
ought	O	way *out*	WA–Y
I ought	IO	wear *out*	WEA–R
ought he, *say*	OE	**out⁴**	
(*see* no², nothing, zero)		indicating omission:	
ounce	CAT, SNOW LEOPARD	*out* East	omit E
	OZ	• fin(e) *out* East	FIN
OUP	ROUND-UP	*out* West	omit W
our		• (w)omen *out* West	OMEN
our era	AD	*out*line	omit I
our leader	ER	• ma(i)n *out*line	MAN
our leader		• sing(l)e *out*line	SINGE
indicating a word written		**out⁵**	
in front of our:	OUR	meaning:	
• officer is our *leader*	COLOUR	abroad	
<u>o</u>ur *leader*	O	• girl *abroad*	MISS OUT
our man	HE	asleep	
our opponents	THEM	• king *asleep*	ROUT
our ships	NAVY, RN	away	
our time	AD	• start <u>s</u>cratching *away*	SCOUT
ours	ONUS	beyond bounds	
oust		• 150 *beyond bounds*	CLOUT
ousted leader	omit 1st letter	blooming	
• (p)arty *ousted* leader	ARTY	• *blooming after a* time	TOUT

Letter replaced \c\at; Omit (a); Pointers *out*; Retain <u>a</u>; Split B_ED; Down (D); Backwards <or ^

bowled	
• Guiana *opener bowled*	GOUT
caught	
• learner *caught*	LOUT
considering verdict	
• *considering verdict* suitable . . .	OUTFIT
dismissed	
• Black *dismissed*	BOUT
exceeding	
• *exceeding* the call	OUTCRY
excluded	
• *excluded* group	OUTSET
fielding	
• *fielding* players	OUTCAST
fired	
• quietly *fired*	POUT
flowering	
• *flowering* head	OUTNESS
in error	
• *in error with* offer	OUTBID
in the field	
• run *in the field*	ROUT
not acceptable	
• odds *not acceptable*	SPOUT
not allowed	
• Rod *not allowed* . . .	STICK OUT
not in	
• *not in* key	BOUT, GOUT
old hat	
• *old-hat* group	OUTSET
on strike	
• actors *on strike*	OUTCAST
published	
• paper *published*	RAGOUT
square	
• T-*square*	TOUT
strike	
• *strike* actors	OUTCAST
• *striking* clothes	OUTWEAR
unacceptable	
• *unacceptable* timber	OUTBOARD
unconscious	
• 150 *unconscious* . . .	CLOUT
unfashionable	
• *unfashionable* fashion	OUTRAGE
out⁶	
other uses:	
out and about	
• [he's] *out* and *about* in . . .	SHINE
out *and* about	OUTRE
out least	INMOST
out West	–INE
outer cover of ₐirship	AP
outer covers of ᵦook	BK
out of¹	
out of	EX–

• out of beer	EXPORTER
• out of breath	(in) WIN–D
• out of money	EXPOUNDS
• out of sight, *say*	EXCITE
out of²	
implying inclusion:	
out of action	(in) B–ED
out of water	(in) DR–Y
out of³	
indicating an anagram:	
[letters] *out of* sequence	SETTLER
out of [breath]	BATHER, BERTHA
out of *control* [I ran] . . .	RAIN, RANI
out of *form* [player]	REPLAY
out of *kilter* [after he'd] . . .	FATHERED
out of *line* [steps] . . .	PESTS
out of *order* [today]	TOADY
out of *place* [in the] . . .	THINE
out of *sequence* [when I] . . .	WHINE
out of [step]	PEST, PETS
out of *the ordinary* [sort] . . .	ORTS, ROTS, TORS
out of *the way* [town]	WONT
out of [time]	EMIT, MITE
out of *tune* [in song]	NOSING
out of *turn* [he is] . . .	HIES
out of⁴	
indicating inclusion:	
out of line	incl I, L
out of money	incl L
out of the race	incl TT
out of the way	incl N, S, E, W
• ge–t *out of* the way	GENT
• *out-of*-the-way h-at	HEAT
out of the way	incl RD, ST
• *out-of*-the-way river	TARDY, TASTY
out of time	incl T
out of turn	incl U
out of work	incl OP
out of *	incl *
• w–e *are out of* an . . .	WANE
out of⁵	
indicating omission:	
out of date	omit D
• (d)ye *is out of date*	YE
• *out of date* fat	LAR(d)
out of time	omit T
• despatched *out of* time	POS(t)ED
• sen(t) *out of* time	SEN
out of *	omit *
• he *is out of* t(he) . . .	T
• I am *out of* ra(i)n	RAN
• I'm *out of* sl(im)y . . .	SLY
• Jack *out of* (j)ob	OB–
• one *out of* m(one)y	MY
• ran *out of* cur(ran)t . . .	CURT
• (r)an right *out of* sight	AN

Anag [cat]; Any *; Begin IGN–; Endings –ING; eg •; Hidden /cat/; Implied add (on); Implied in (in);

• run *out of* b(r)ead	BEAD
• run *out of* (ru)i(n)ous . . .	–IOUS

out of⁶
other uses:

out of breath, *say*	PUFFIN
out of court	LONG SERVICE
out of date	(*see* old)
out of date medication	PILLAGED
out of gear	BARE, NAKED, NUDE
	UNDRESSED
out of gear, *say*	BEAR
out of key	NOTING
out of order	FORMER MONK, LAY
out of or/der at E/nglish,	DERATE
out of print	OP
out of sight, *say*	PASTEURISE
out of the sun here, *say*	SHADIER
out-of-t/he-w/ay	HEW

outbreak

outbreak	BOIL, RASH
[out]*break*	TOU–
out[break]	BAKER, BRAKE
outbreak of [flu]	–FUL
outbreak of herpes	H

outburst

[nasty] *outburst*	TANSY
[out]*burst*	TOU–
outburst [in night]	HINTING

outcast

outcast	ISHMAEL, LEPER, PARIAH
out[cast]	CATS

outcome

[bad] *outcome*	ABD–, DAB
outcome of [a new] . . .	WANE, WEAN
outcome of te/st on e/engine	STONE

outcry

outcry	C–RY
out[cry]	–RCY

outdated   (*see* old)

outdo

outdo	BARBECUE, PICNIC
*out*do	D–O

outdoor

outdoor	EGRESS, EXIT
*out*door	DO–OR
out[door]	ROOD
outdoor meal, *say*	FIELDFARE, PYKNIC
outdoor seat	SHOOTING STICK

outlandish
outlandish (=foreign)

• *outlandish* course	PASTA etc
• *outlandish* tongue	FRENCH etc
• *outlandish* way	RUE, STRASSE etc
outlandish [garb]	BRAG, GRAB
outlandish place	ISLAND, ISLE(T)

outlaw

out[law]	AWL

outlaw	incl LAW
• f–ed *outlaw*	FLAWED
outlaw gangster	BANAL
out[lawed]	WALED, WEALD
outlaws' meeting place	ROUND ROBIN

outlay

outlay	LA–Y
out[lay]	–ALY

outlie

mineral *outliers*	ML
outlie	LI–E
outlying parts of town	TN

outline

outline	LIN–E
out[line]	LIEN, NILE
outline a . . .	incl A
outline *	incl *
• r–ed *outlining* ear	REARED
outlined in *	incl in *
• ear *outlined in* r–ed	REARED

output

output	PU–T
out[put]	TUP
output of [men she] . . .	ENMESH
out of sewers	EMBROIDERY, TAPESTRY

outrace

outrace	T–T
outrace	incl TT
out[race]	ACER, ACRE

outrage

outrage	R–AGE
out[rage]	GARE, GEAR
outrage in [Iran]	RAIN, RANI
outraged [mother]	THERMO–
outrageous	OTT
outrageous [plot on a] . . .	PLATOON

outré

[it was] *outré*	WAIST, WAITS
outré [garb]	BRAG, GRAB

outright

outright	incl R, RT
• *outright* li–e	LIRE
• pa–y *outright*	PARTY
outright	R–T
• I have *outright* . . .	RIVET
outright	omit R, RT
• *outright* fa(r)ce	FACE
• *outright* pa(rt)y . . .	PAY

outset

at the *outset* she told youth . . .	STY
outset	SE–T
out[set]	–EST
outset of expedition	E
unpromising *outset*	U

outside

is *outside*	I–S
• member i–s *outside*	IMPS

outside	PEEL, SKIN
out[side]	DIES, IDES
[outside] *broadcast*	TEDIOUS
outside a . . .	incl A
outside right	incl R, RT
• *outside* right ha–d . . .	HARD
• *outside* right ma–y . . .	MARTY
outside <u>Torbay</u>	TAY
outside *	incl *
• fa–r *outside* the . . .	FATHER
outsides of <u>house</u>	HE
<u>rank</u> *outsiders*	RK

outsize

outsize	OS
• h–e *goes round* outsize . . .	HOSE
• king *in* outsize . . .	OHMS
• outsize vehicle	OSCAR
• tub *has* outsize . . .	BATHOS

outskirts

outskirts of	
–<u>Bombay</u>	BANDY, BY
–<u>city</u>	CANDY, CY
–<u>Holloway</u>	HANDY, HY
–<u>Mandalay</u>	MANDY, MY

outspoken

he'll *outspokenly* . . .	HEAL, HEEL
outspoken	FOURTH
outspoken leader	LIEDER
outspoken male	MAIL
outspoken Pete	PEAT

outspread

out[spread]	RASPED, SPARED
[*out*]*spread*	TOU–
outspread [arms]	MARS, RAMS

outstanding

outstanding	OS
outstanding account	BILLOWING, BILLOWED
outstanding characters	BRAILLE
outstanding colour	ACETONE
outstanding item	CHIN, PARTICULAR
outstanding man	SENTRY
outstanding message	SIGNAL
outstanding rota, *say*	DUELLIST
outstanding vocalist	CAROL SINGER
outstanding work	CAMEO, RELIEF
outstanding *	incl in *
• th–e *outstanding* queen	THERE
• som–e *outstanding* British . . .	SOMBRE

outward

*out*ward	W–ARD
out[ward]	DRAW
outward bound	TI–ED
outwardly <u>nice</u>	NE
outwardly *	incl in *
• hard, *outwardly* nic–e	NICHE
• *outwardly* courageous god	BOLLARD

oval

	EGG, O

oven-ready

oven-ready, *say*	FRIABLE

over[1]

[over]*cooked*	ROVE
[over] *excited*	ROVE
over *half*	OV, ER

over[2]

indicating inclusion:	
• c–ry *over* old city	CURRY
• pass *over* ring	COOL
• ru–n *over* one . . .	RUIN

over[3]

indicating one word written	
above another word or letter(D):	
• engineers *with* one *over*due	RESIDUE
• girl *over*age	TESSERA
• girl *over*worked	KATYDID
• he *is going over* the road	HERD
• he is *over*bearing	HEN, HEW
• in lieu of *over*time	FORAGE, FORT
• large *over*head	BIGNESS
• live *over*night	BENIGHT
• no *over*charge	ORATE
• no *over*dose	NODOSE
• numbers *over*see	TENSELY
• skill is *over*t	ARTIST

over[4]

indicating reversal:	
• *over* ten<	NET
• *over*laid<	DIAL
• *over*pay<	YAP
• war *over*<	RAW

over[5]

meaning:	
about, anent, concerning,	
in connection with, on,	
regarding	RE
• about over	CARE
• over the bar	REPUBLIC
• overseas	REMAINS
above	
• above the table	ON BOARD
• animal above . . .	CATSUP
completed, done, ended,	
finished	
• fifty *completed*	LOVER
• *done to a* turn	OVERTURN
• *ended with* highest . . .	OVERTOP
• doctor *finished* . . .	DROVER

over[6]

other uses:	
over half mad(e)	MAD
over matey	BIGAMOUS, POLYGAMOUS
over ten	ELEVEN, TENT
over [ten]	ENT, NET

overbearing

indicates a word written	

Anag [cat]; Any *; Begin IGN–; Endings –ING; eg •; Hidden /cat/; Implied add (on); Implied in (in);

above a compass point(D):

• be *over*bearing	BEE, BEN
• found *over*bearing	CASTE, CASTS
• the *over*bearing . . .	THEE, THEN, THEW

overcast

overcast but . . . <	TUB
was *overcast*<	SAW

overcoat   BENJAMIN

overcome

indicating one word written
above another word or letter(D):

• boy *overcomes* the *French* . . .	LADLE
• I *overcome* Bible queen	INTER
• we *overcome* the backs	WESTERNS
• woman *overcomes* 500 . . .	SHED

overcook

overcook<	WETS
[over]*cook*	ROVE
overcooked, *say*	CHARD

overdose   OD

overdrawn

overdrawn	OD
overdrawn	(in) R–ED
• *overdrawn* account	RACED

overdue

overdue	LATE
• overdue books	LATENT
• overdue improvement	LATERALLY
• overdue *Times*	LATEX
over[due]	–UDE

overhaul

overhaul [car]	ARC
overhauled dray<	YARD

overhead

*over*head	O
*over*head<	POT
*over*head	(*see* over³)
overhead cover	CAUL, HAT, SKY
overhead light	AURORA, GLORIA HALO, MOON, STAR, SUN
overhead lines	AIRWAYS
overheads	ANTLERS, HATS, HORNS
over[heads]	HADES, SHADE

overlong

overlong	TOOL
*over*long	

indicating a word
written over L(D):

• ditch–digger *has* *over*long . . .	OFFAL
• *over*long charge	FEEL

overlook

overlook a . . .	omit A
overlook nothing	omit O
overlook *	omit *
• ba(n)ker *overlooks* new . . .	BAKER

overnight

over[night]	THING
overnight cover	BLANKET, DUVET etc, NIGHTDRESS, PYJAMAS etc
overnight trip, *say*	NITRIDE

overrun

overrun

indicating one word written
above another word or letter(D):

• one animal *overruns* another	WOLFRAM
• vehicle *overruns* soldiers	CARMEN

overrun

indicating a word written
above run (cricket)(D):

• planet *over*run	WORLDWIDE
• site *over*run	PLACER
• well *over*run	GOODBYE
overrun	EXTRA
*over*run<	NUR
over[run]	NUR, URN
*over*run a . . .	incl A
*over*run *	incl *
• soldiers *overrun* Georgia	MEGAN
*over*run by * . . .	incl in *
• Georgia is *overrun by* soldiers	MEGAN

overseas

overseas

indicating a word written
above seas or main(D):

• not closed *over*seas on . . .	OPEN SEASON
• make *over*seas	DOMAIN

overseas

indicating a foreign
language:

	(*see* abroad)
overseas, *say*	SUPERVISES

overshoot

over[shoot]	HOOTS
overshot the airport	PASTORLY

overtake

overtake, *say*	CATCHUP, KETCHUP
overtake worker	PASSANT
*over*take son(D)	STAKE

overthrow

[emir] *over*thrown	MIRE, RIME
*over*throw tsar<	RAST

overtime¹

*over*time<	EMIT
*over*time	(*see* over³)
over[time]	EMIT, MITE
overtime, *say*	NITRATE

overtime²

indicating a word written above
a word or letter for time(D):

• double *over*time	BIT
• hard *over*time	HERE

• single *over*time	SAGE
• work *over*time	OPERA
	(see also over³*)*

overture

overture to Aida	A
William Tell *overtures*	WT

overturn

overturn it	TI–
overturn it, *say*	TIPPET
[over]*turning*	ROVE
overturning dray<	YARD
overturning [dray]	–ARDY, YARD

overweight

overweight	EXTRACT
overweight	
indicating a word written	
over weight(D):	
• Black *is over*weight	BOUNCE
• fruit *is over*weight	LIMESTONE
• vehicle *is over*weight	CARTON
overweight ladies	FATHERS

overwhelm

overwhelm a . . .	incl A
overwhelm *	incl *
• weight *overwhelms* a student	TALON
overwhelmed by *	incl in *
• a student *overwhelmed*	
by weight	TALON

overworked

[over]*worked*	ROVE
overworked *rhymes*	BURKED, IRKED etc

overwrought

overwrought [man is] . . .	MAINS
[she is] *overwrought*	SHIES

owe

owe(s)	O, (OO, OS)
owing knight, *say*	OWENITE
owing money	(in) DEB–T, (in) R–ED
	–IOUS

own

own goal	OG
own jewelry	HAVERINGS
own *Scottish*	AIN
owned	HAD
• doctors owned . . .	MOSHAD
• owned *in* the Home Counties	SHADE
• owned quays	HADDOCKS
owned by *	incl in *
• company *owned by* drunkard	SCOOT
owned by com/pan/y	PAN
owner	CONFESSOR
owner *with* wine	HAVERSACK
owner's claim	LANDMINE
owning a . . .	incl A
owning *	incl *
• drunkard *owning* company	SCOOT
owns	HAS
• owns a number . . .	HASTEN
• owns a vegetable, *say*	HASBEEN
• owns vehicle	HASSLED

Oxford

lower part of Oxford	SOLE, WELT
Oxford accent	BROGUE
Oxford dreamer	SPIRE
Oxford English Dictionary	OED
Oxford manufacturer	SHOEMAKER
Oxford Street	BROAD, HIGH
upper part of Oxford	TONGUE

ox

oxhide	LOWER CASE
slaughter ox, *say*	KILLOCKS

oxygen

oxygen	O
oxygenate	incl O
• *oxygenated* drink	ALOE, POINT

oyster

oyster	BEDMAKER
oysters, *say*	AUSTRIA

P

Angola, Cape Verde Islands, Celt, *copper*, four hundred (thousand), Kelt, momentum, Mozambique, page, parity, park, parking, participle, Pastor, pawn, *pea*, pedal, *pee*, *peg*, penny, peseta, peso, peta-, phosphorus, pi, piano, pico-, poise, Portugal, Portuguese Guinea, Portuguese Timor, positive, power, president, pressure, priest, prince, Principe Islands, pula, quiet, rho, Sao Tome, semi-conductor type, soft, vitamin

Pa	PANDA
pace	
pace stage	STEP
pacer, *say*	STRIDOR
pacify	
pacifist	CO, DOVE
• pacifist *goes to* New York	CONY
• pacifist conclusion	DOVETAIL
pacifist *conclusion*	T
pacify journalist	CALMED
pack	
pack dress	DECK
pack of hounds	CRY
pack *up*(D)^	MAR(C)
package of [papers]	SAPPER
packaged [crate]	CATER, TRACE
packed with *	incl in *
• ship *packed with* relatives	SKINS
packer, *say*	STOA
packing a . . .	incl A
packing *	incl *
• relatives *packing* ship	SKINS
packing [extra] . . .	TAXER
paddy	
Paddy (=Irish)	
• flattery *for Paddy*	BLARNEY
• *Paddy's* accent	BROGUE
	(*see also* Pat)
page	P
page *in front of* book	PRESERVE
pages	PP
page(s) *missing*	omit P(PP)
paid	
paid	PD
paid model	PROPOSER
pain	
pain *in France*	BREAD
pained expression	OUCH, OW
painful, *say*	SOAR
paint	
paint distributor	ARTIST, BRUSH

[paint] *mixing*	INAPT, PINTA
painted	PXT
painter	ARA, PRA, RA
	ETTY, TURNER et al
	(*see also* artist)
painter	ROPE
painterman	RADON, RALES, RAMON, RATED
painter's jacket	SPENCER
painting and drawing, *say*	ARTERY
painting book	PRIMER
painting, *say*	CANVASS
painting with rollers	SEASCAPE
paints family	OILSKIN
pair	
pair	OO, PR
pair of	
–braces	FOUR
–clubs	CC
–diamonds	DD
–ducks	OO
–hearts	HH
–slippers	SKIS
–spades	SS
–students	LL
pair, *say*	TO, TOO, TOU, TU
• fashionable pair, *say*	INTO
• pair in front, *say*	TOOLED
• pair is able, *say*	TOUCAN
• pairs, *say*	TUTU
	(*see also* two)
Pakistan	PAK
pale	
pale	WAN
• become pale	GOWAN
• pale fashion	WANTON
• pale man	WANTED
pale yellow alien	BUFFET
Palestine	
Palestine	PAL
Palestine Liberation Organisation	PLO

Letter replaced \c\at; Omit (a); Pointers *out*; Retain a; Split B_ED; Down (D); Backwards <or ^

palm		**paragon**	S, SAINT, ST
palm-house, *say*	DATARY	**paragraph**	
palm oil	BRIBE(RY)	paragraph	PAR(A)
pamphlet	PAM	paragraph, *say*	CLAWS
Panama	PA(N)	**Paraguay**	PY
panda	PA	**parallel**	PAR
Pan's pipes	SYRINX	**paramount cover**	OVERALL
panic		**paranormal**	
panic [over]	ROVE	[heard] *paranormally* . . .	HARED
panicking [over] . . .	ROVE	*paranormal* [views]	WIVES
panicky [fear]	FARE	**parasite**	
pant		parasite	(in) HO–ST
panting *say*	PUFFIN	• one *parasite*	HOAST, HOIST
pants advertisements	PUFFS	• right *parasite*	HORST
paper		**parcel**	
paper	COMIC	parcel	LOT
• paper-boy	COMICAL	parcel it up, *say*	PACKET
paper	MAIL	*parcel of* [food let] . . .	FOOTLED
• links paper . . .	CHAIN-MAIL	*parcel* [post]	OPTS, POTS, STOP, TOPS
• paper, *say*	MALE	parcelled, *say*	RAPT
• paper*back*<	LIAM	**parent**	
paper	MS	parent	DAD
• a royal paper	ARMS	• parent expires	DADDIES
• daily paper	CHARMS	• parent *goes round* English . . .	DEAD
• is *in* the paper	MISS	parent	MA, MUM
• paper*back*<	SM	• follow parent	DOGMA
• papers	MSS	• parent *has* an afterthought	MUMPS
paper	RAG	parent	PA, POP
• paper published	RAGOUT	• parent *is after* money, *say*	LOLLIPOP
• paper seller	RAG MERCHANT	• son *with* parent	SPA
• paper*back*<	GAR	Parent Teachers Association	PTA
paper	SUN	**Paris**	
• American *with* paper	BOSUN	*Paris-style* hat	CHAPEAU
• paper flower	SUNBURN		(*see also* foreign)
• paper*back*<	NUS	**parish priest**	PP
paper	TIMES	**park**	
paper*back*<	SEMIT–	park	P
paper carrier	BRIEF CASE	• park at ten	PATIO, PATTEN
paper cupboard	PRESS	• park in a street	PINARD
paper headgear	FOOLSCAP	• park in New York	PINNY
paper maker	CELLULOSE, ESPARTO	• vehicle park	TRAMP
	PAPYRUS, (WOOD) PULP	parked in s/tree/t	TREE
	EDITOR	parking	P
papers, *say*	CHOIR	• parking *beyond* the edge	HEMP
parachute		• parking *in* South America	SPA
parachutist	JUMPER	• parking in the square	PINT
parachutist	PARA	• parking space	PLATITUDE, PLOT
• parachutist's headgear, *say*	PARABOLA	parking space	CARLOT
• parachutist's height		**parliament**	
gauge, *say*	PARAMETER	parliament	DIET
		Parliamentary Labour Party	PLP
parade		parliamentary opponents	CAVALIERS
parade ground	DRILLING SITE	Parliamentary Private Secretary	PPS
parade ground, *say*	MAIDEN	**parrot**	
parade time	EASTER	parrot	ECHO(IST), POLLY
paradise	EDEN	parrot, *say*	POLI–, POLY

Anag [cat]; Any *; Begin IGN–; Endings –ING; eg •; Hidden /cat/; Implied add (on); Implied in (in);

• parrot-fish, *say*	POLIGAR
• parrot *has* fleas, *say*	POLITICS
• parrot *has* the right mark and	POLITIC
• parrot-fish, *say*	POLYCARP
• parrot has escaped *say*	POLYGON
• parrot *with* cat, *say*	POLYPUS

part

[many] *parts*	MYNA
part	PT
Part I	CHARACTER
part company	DIVORCE
part company	PLATOON
part company	CO, PAN, ANY
[part]-*exchange*	PRAT, TRAP
part of . . .	incl in *
• it *is part of* m–e	MITE
part of Ayrshire	UDDER
part of Ayrshire	A
part of Ayrs/hire d/airy	HIRED
part of bird	PARSON'S NOSE
part of bird	BITTERN, HAWKBIT, HENBIT
part of bird	B
part of bir/d I sh/ot	DISH
part of chestnut	FETLOCK
part of chestnut	C
part of collar	S, ESS
part of collar	COL, LAR
part of collar	C
part of col/lar ge/ts . . .	LARGE
part of county	HUNDRED, RIDING
part of foot, *say*	HEAL, HE'LL, TOW
part of leg	L
part of leg	THEFT
part of leg, *say*	THY
part of mercy	QUARTER
part of Oxford	SOLE, UPPER, WELT
part of school	GAMBIT
part of the . . .	T
part of yard	THEFT
part in dra/ma p/layed . . .	MAP
part-pierced	EAR-LOBE
part, *say*	PEACE
part-tim(e)	TIM
part-time doctor	JEKYLL
partial s/hade s/should . . .	HADES
partially demoli/sh a pe/rgola	SHAPE
partly close, *say*	PUSHTU
partly-grown snake	AS(p)
partly Ic/eland/ic	ELAND
partly mad(e)	MAD
partly reveal . . .	SHOWPIECE
partly spirit(ual)	SOMEBODY
parts of coffee ta<u>ble</u>	FEEBLE
parts of cof/fee t/able	FEET
parts of police force	CANDID

parts of [speech]	CHEEPS
Parts 1 & 3 of th<u>e</u>saurus	TE
[remote] *parts*	METEOR

partake

partake of ho/spit/ality	SPIT
partaking of fo/od in/side . . .	ODIN
partial	(*see* part)

participate

participants in the mat/ch I p/layed	CHIP
participate in t/he re/vels	HERE
participate in *	incl in *
• me *participating in* a–n . . .	AMEN
participle	P
participial adjective	PA

particle

[grit] *particles*	GIRT
particle, *say*	MOAT, WIT
particles [or waves]	OVERSAW

particular

particularly nice	PEDANTIC
particularly well(=to a T)	
• live *particularly well*	BET
• ran *particularly well*	RANT
partnership	EW, NS, SN, US, WE

party

party	BAND
• girl *at* a party, *say*	SARABAND(E)
• party girl	BANDANNA
• party-time	BANDAGE
• party, *say*	BANNED
party	CON
• one party	ICON
• party in charge	CONIC
• party outing	CONTOUR
party	DO
• one party *after* another	DODO, LIBIDO
• party *cancelled*	omit DO
• party member	DOM
• party workers	DOMINIONS
party	LAB
• party *at which* I ate . . .	LABIATE
• party speeches	LABORATORY
• second party	SLAB
• strong party	FLAB
party	LIB
• grand party	GLIB
• party I do . . .	LIBIDO
• party *with* the *Spanish* . . .	LIBEL
party	TORY
• declare party	AMATORY
• not her party	HISTORY
• second party	STORY
party-giver	MAD HATTER
party habit	BALL GOWN, COCKTAIL DRESS
	DINNER JACKET, GLAD RAGS

Letter replaced \c\at; Omit (a); Pointers *out*; Retain <u>a</u>; Split B_ED; Down (D); Backwards <or ^

party *leader*	P
party line	CONGA
party *piece*	P
part(y) *piece*	PART
p/art/y *piece*	ART
par̲t̲y *pieces*	PRY
party whip	THRASH
pascal	PA
pass¹	
come *to* pass, *say*	COMPASS
[pass] *muster*	ASPS, SAPS, SPAS
pass *out*	PAS–S
• Hill's pass-out	PASTORS
[pass] *out*	ASPS, SAPS, SPAS
pass time	PASSAGE
pass²	
pass	COL
• pass 500	COLD
• pass on	COLON
• pass our . . .	COLOUR
and	
• find artist *in* pass	CORAL
• find nothing *in* pass	COOL
and	
• Passover<	LOC
pass *out*	CO–L
• gunners pass out	CORAL
pass³	
pass	HAND
• back pass	SECOND HAND
• pass a few	HANDSOME
• passes the fish	HANDSHAKE
• passing nothing	HAND IN GLOVE
pass girl	VERONICA
pass out cube	DIE
pass round a . . .	incl A
pass, *say*	GOBY
• pass rat, *say*	GOBI DESERT
• pass the fish	GOBY
pass time, *say*	WILE
passed out, *say*	FEINTED
passed round *	incl *
• prince *passed round* beer	PALER
passed round by *	incl in *
• beer *passed round by* prince	PALER
passed, *say*	PAST
• passed exam, *say*	PASTORAL
passed staff college	PSC
passenger-carrying flight	ESCALATOR
passion	
passion-fruit drink	CRUSH
passionate love	FLAMINGO
past	
past	EX
• past alteration	EXCHANGE
• past terrorists *with* it	EXPLOIT

• past wrong	EXTORT
	(*see also* old)
past	OVER
• 150 past . . .	CLOVER
• past directors	OVERBOARD
• run past	ROVER
past	PA
• past *in* error	SPAIN
• past tense	PAT
past Grandmaster	PGM
past Master	PM
past participle	P(A)P
past president	PP
past, *say*	PASSED
pastmaster	HISTORIAN
	HISTORY TEACHER
paste	
paste diamond	SHAMROCK
paste equipment	CLOBBER
paste [papers]	SAPPER
paste table	PLASTERBOARD
[spread] *paste*	SPARED
pastry	
pas̲t̲ry *case*	PY
short past(ry)	PAST
pat	
Pat (=Irish)	
• judge *Pat's* . . .	BREHON
• *Pat's old* doctor	OLLA(H)M, OLLAV
	(*see also* Paddy)
pat *on* the head	PATNESS
patch	
patch [over an] . . .	VERONA
patched [sleeve]	LEVEES
paté	
[meat] *paté*	MATE, TAME, TEAM
paté of [game] . . .	MEGA–
patent	
patent agent	CPA
patent in nav/al ar/chitecture	ALAR
patent in [steam] . . .	MATES, MEATS
	TAMES, TEAMS
pathetic	
pathetic meeting	TOUCHING
pathetic [meeting]	TEEMING
patient	
patient	CASE
patient attention	NURSING, TREATMENT
patient helper	DOCTOR, MATRON
	NURSE, SISTER
patient man	JOB
patient sewer	SURGEON
patient woman	GRISELDA
pawn	
pawn	P
pawn *opening*	P

pawnbroker's daughter	NIECE	pees, *say*	PEACE, PIECE
pawnbroker's son	NEPHEW	**peel**	
pawnee	UNCLE	<u>o</u>range *peel*	OE
pawn's complaint	AMUSED	*peeled* (o)rang(e)	RANG
pay		peeler	BOBBY, POLICEMAN, ROBERT
pay *back*<	YAP	peeler, *say*	PAIRER
pay on delivery	POD	peeling, *say*	BARKHAN
pay *out*	PA–Y	**peep**	
[pay]-*out*	YAP	peeped, *say*	PRIDE
pay-phone	WAGERING	peeper	TOM
pay soldiers	FOOTMEN	peephole, *say*	PEOPLE
pay *up*(D)^	YAP	**peg**	P, T, TEE, TOT
paying guest	PG	**pellet**	O
paymaster	PMR	pellets	OO, OS
Paymaster General	PMG	**pen**	
payment order, *say*	CHECK, CZECH	pen	PEN
pea		• pen friend	PENALLY
pea	P	• pen-name	PENAL
pea-jacket	POD	• penman	PENAL
[pea] *soup*	APE	pen	SWAN
peas, *say*	PEACE, PIECE, PP, PS	• I am *in* the pen	SWAIN
peace		• pen-pusher	SWAN-HERD
peace, *say*	PACKS, PIECE, PP, PS	pen	WRITE
peacekeeper	UNMAN	• finished pen	OVERWRITE
peacekeepers	UN	• write *say*	RIGHT, RITE
peacemakers	ACAS	*penned in by* *	incl in *
peak		• woman *penned in by* youngster	LASHED
peak	BEN, TOR	**penal**	
peak of <u>R</u>ockies(D)	R	[penal] *reform*	NEPAL, PANEL, PLANE
peak performance	MOUNTAINEERING	[penal] *settlement*	NEPAL, PANEL, PLANE
	YODELLING	**penetrate**	
Pearl's mother	NACRE	*penetrate* *	incl in *
peculiar		• hard *to penetrate* t–in	THIN
peculiar	ODD	penetrate log	ENTER
• peculiar child	ODDS-ON	peninsula	PEN
• peculiar head	ODDNESS	**penny**	
• throw *round* peculiar . . .	SHODDY	penniless	NOCENT
peculiar	RUM	penni*less*	omit D, P
• 500 peculiar . . .	DRUM	penny	D
• footpath *round* peculiar . . .	FRUMP	• penny a go	DAGO
• peculiar stomach	RUM-TUM	• penny fine	DWELL
peculiar [ways]	SWAY, YAWS	• penny paper	DRAG
peculiarly [placed S]	SCALPED	penny	P
pedagogue	BED	• penny and a . . .	PANDA
pedal		• penny each	PEACH
pedal	P	• penny fine	POKE
pedal appendages, *say*	TOWS, TOZE	• pennyweight	POUNCE
pedal, *say*	PEDDLE	penny off	omit D, P
peddle		pennyweight	DWT, PWT
peddle bird	HAWK	**Pentateuch**	T(H)ORAH
peddle, *say*	PEDAL	**penthouse**	LEAN-TO
peddled, *say*	SOLED	**penultimate**	
pedestrian	FOOTMAN, PED	penultimate letter	Y
pee		*penultimate* lett<u>e</u>r	E
pee	P	**people**	
pees	PP, PS	people	MEN

• a people	AMEN	• of cat, *say*	TABESCENT
• people expired, *say*	MENDED	• of *French* perfume	DESCENT
• people *in* high places	TORMENTOR	• perfume, *say*	CENT, SENT
• people *start* talking	–MENT	**perfunctory goodbye**	SHORT WAVE
people	NATION	**perhaps**	
• mother *has* people . . .	DAMNATION	indicating anagram:	
• people *have* a friend	NATIONALLY	• [maybe], *perhaps* . . .	BEAMY
• transport people	CARNATION	• *perhaps* [not]	TON
people	RACE	indicating homophone:	
• black people	BRACE	• might, *perhaps*	MITE
• people *found in* Eliot	TRACES	• *perhaps* not	KNOT
• people *taking* drug	RACEHORSE	indicating one of	
people get older	MASSAGE	a class:	
people inside	MORTAL SIN	• *perhaps* private . . .	SOLDIER
people, *say*	PEEPHOLE	• soldier, *perhaps*	PRIVATE
people say "When!"	WEN	**perilous**	
per		*perilous* [trips]	SPIRT, STRIP
per	PR	[totters] *perilously*	STRETTO
per annum	PA	**period**	
perambulate		period	AD
perambulating [Pole]	LOPE	• hard period	HAD
perambulation of [master]	REMAST, STREAM	• period *in* novel . . .	SHADE
perceive		• period with the *German* . . .	ADMIT
perceived in ti/me to l/end . . .	METOL	• two periods	ADAGE
perceived, say	SCENE	period	AGE
perceptible in ol/d art/icles	DART	• period books	AGENT
percentage		• period aboard	SAGES
percentage of t/urn/over	URN	• Second Period	SAGE
small percentage of profit	P	• two periods	ADAGE
perch on		period	BC, EPOCH, ERA
indicating one word written			FULL STOP
above another word or letter(D):			PER
• bird *perching on* an . . .	TITAN	period charm	SPELL
• monkey *perching on* line	APERY	period drama	TIMEPIECE
perfect		period of	
perfect	NOVICES	–play, *say*	CHUCKER
perfect	UTTER	–revolution	DAY, MONTH, YEAR
• perfect fit	UTTERABLE	*period piece*	PER
• perfect son	UTTERS	pe/rio/d *piece*	RIO
• saint *has* perfect . . .	STUTTER	period *piece*	ER(a), TIM(e)
perfect letter	T	periodical	MAG
perfect order	APPLE PIE	periodical row	PUNCH-LINE
perfect state	UTOPIA, UTTER	**peripatetic**	
perfect weapon	SPEARMINT	*peripatetic* [dealer]	LEADER
perfection	NOVICES	*peripatetical* [priest]	STRIPE
perform		**permanent position**	STANDING
performing	(in) A–CT, (in) DE–ED	**permit**	
performing	ON	permission to depart	LEAVE
• cricketer performing	BATON	permissive	
• the lady's performing	HERON	–missive	LETTER
performing [bear]	BARE, BRAE	–occupation	LETTING
perfume		permit Henry . . .	LETHAL
perfume	ESSENCE	**perpetuate**	
• perfume from fuel, *say*	COALESCENCE	perpetuate driving area	COMMITTEE
perfume	SCENT	*perpetuating* [evil]	LIVE, VILE
• inapplicable perfume	NASCENT	*perpetuation of* [line]	LIEN, NILE

Anag [cat]; Any *; Begin IGN–; Endings –ING; eg •; Hidden /cat/; Implied add (on); Implied in (in);

perplex
perplexed [by a] . . .   BAY
perplexing [poser]   ROPES, PORES, SPORE
Persian   PERS
person
   person   BOD, BLOKE, CHAP
     MAN, ONE, PER(S)
   person of note   COMPOSER
     VERDI et al
   person speaking   I
   personal ambition   OWN GOAL
   personal assistant   PA
   personal column   BACKBONE, SPINE
   personal computer   BRAIN, PC
   personal cover   SKIN
   personal donation   BLOOD
   personal hint   INTIMATE
   personal letters   INITIALS,
     SIGNATURE
   personal subscription   SIGNATURE
     YOURS SINCERELY
     YOURS TRULY
   personal to Benjamin, *say*   BENZOIN
   personal transport   FEET, LEGS
   personal voucher   GODPARENT, REFEREE,
     SPONSOR
   personnel carrier   (SEDAN-)CHAIR
     STRETCHER
pertain
   pertaining to
   –a number   OFTEN
   –cavity lining, *say*   PLURAL
   –cheek, *say*   BUCKLE
   –Christmas, *say*   OVULE
   –focus, *say*   PHOCAL
   –food, *say*   ELEMENTARY
   –seals *say*   FOCAL
   –the ear, *say*   ORAL
   –the mouth, *say*   AURAL
perturb
perturbation of [N orbit]   BRITON
perturbed [by a] . . .   BAY
Peru
   Peru   PE
   Peruvian parentage   INCANDESCENT
pervade
*pervade**   incl *
   • colour *pervading* vessel   STONES
*pervaded by**   incl in *
   • lines *pervaded by* one . . .   BONER
perverse
[act] *perversely*   CAT
perverse boy<   YOB
perversion of [desire]   RESIDE
perverted [love]   VOLE
peso   P

pet
   pet   CAT
   • pet boy   CATALAN
   • pet name   CATCALL
   • strike pet   WHIPCAT
   pet   DOG
   • execute pet   HANGDOG
   • pet lost   DOGGONE
   • pet that is . . .   DOGIE
   pet food   LIGHTS
petition
   petition, *say*   PREY
   petition *to* queen   PRAYER
   petitions, *say*   PRAISE, PREYS
petrol engine   ICE
petty
   petty cash   P
   • officer *takes* petty cash   COP
   • petty cash book   PRESERVE
   • petty cash *hidden in* bed   COPT
   Petty Officer   PO
pewter toy   TRIFLE
Pharmaceutical Society   PS
phase
phase of [moon]   MONO–
[phase] *out*   HEAPS, SHAPE
   phase, *say*   FAZE
Philological Society   PS
philosopher
   philosopher   BACON, ERASMUS
     HUME, PLATO et al
   philosopher   LOCKE
   • philosopher-king   LOCKER
   • philosopher *has* many . . .   LOCKED
   philosopher   PHB, PHD
   Philosophy, Politics
     and Economics   PPE
phobia   THING
phone
   phone *about*   R–ING
   phone, *say*   FOEN, FO(E)HN, FONE
phoney
phoney tale   TAIL
   phoney, *say*   SUED
phoney [tale]   LATE, LEAT, TEAL
photo-electric cell   PEC
phrase   PHR
physical
   physical education   PE
   physical training   PT
physician
   physician   BM, DR, GP, MB, MD, MO
     LUKE
   physicians   RCP
     (*see also* doctor)
physiologists   CSP

Letter replaced \c\at; Omit (a); Pointers *out*; Retain a; Split B_ED; Down (D); Backwards <or ^

pi	P
piano	
piano	GRAND
• piano keys	GRANDEE
• piano scholar	GRANDMA
• pianos playing	GRANDSON
piano	P
• girl *at* piano	PALMA
• piano keys	PAD, PEA, PED, PEE
	PEACE, PEG
• piano music	PAIR
piano	UPRIGHT
piano piece	KEY(BOARD), IVORY
	PEDAL, STRING
piano *piece*	P
pianissimo	PP
pianoforte	PF
pick	
pick horse	HACK
pick *over<*	LOOT
pick-up	PU
pick up a . . .	incl A
pick up *	incl *
• ma–n *picks up* one . . .	MAIN
pick-up notes(D)^	SETON
picked up by *	incl in *
• one *picked up by* ma–n	MAIN
pickle	
pickle factory	TANNERY
pickled [cauli]flower *head*	AULIC
[quite] *pickled*	QUIET
pickpocket	
pickpocket	DIP
• pickpocket *takes* each	DIPPER
• pickpockets *get* right mark	DIPSTICK
picnic	
picnic	OUTDO, OUTSPREAD
picnic food	FIELDFARE
picture	
picture	SHOT, SNAP
picture-house, *say*	SYNEMA
picture only	SOUND OFF
picture postcard	PPC
pictured	
indicating character in	
film or painting:	
• *pictured* deer	BAMBI
• *pictured* dog	LADY, LASSIE
	PLUTO, TRAMP
• *pictured* mouse	MICKEY, MINNIE
• *pictured* sad lad	BLUE BOY
• two soldiers *pictured*	GIGI
pie	
pie [is hot]	HOIST
[pie]-*throwing*	EPI–
[steak] *pie*	SKATE, STAKE, TAKES

piece	
party piece	P
piece	MAN, PAWN etc
piece of bread	SLICE
piece of bread	B
piece of cake	EASY
piece of cake	C
piece of fencing	EPEE, FOIL, SABRE
	PANEL, POST
piece of music	BAR, NOTE etc
piece of music	MU, SIC
piece of p/arch/ment	ARCH
piece of the cloth	BISHOP
piece of toast	CHEER(s)
pieces of eight	OCTET
pieces of eight	EI, GHT
pieces of [stone]	NOTES, ONSET, TONES
pieces of stone	ST, ONE
*piece*meal	M
piecemeal [way]	YAW
piecework	MOSAIC
piecework	WOR
pierce	
pierce alien	PRICKET
pierce fish	STABLING
pierce flower	PINK
pierce it, *say*	PRICKET
pierce, *say*	PEERS, PIERS
pig	
pig devoured, *say*	BORATE
pig feed	MAST
pig*headed*	P
pighouse rented	STYLET
pig*tail*	G
pile	
pile	NAP
pile-*up*(D)^	PAN
pile up [earth]	HATER, HEART, RATHE
pile up maps(D)^	SPAM
pilfer	
pilfer, *say*	STEEL, STEIL, STELE
pilfered scarf	STOLE
pilgrim's token	ABBEY-COUNTER
	ABBEY-PIECE
pill	MEDICINE-BALL, O
pilot	
pilot	GEORGE
Pilot-Officer	PO
pin	
case of pins and needles	ETUI
pin-*up*(D)^	–LIAN, NIP
pincer	
[pincer] *movement*	PRINCE
pincer operator	CRAB
pinch	
pinch(D)^	PIN-UP

Anag [cat]; Any *; Begin IGN–; Endings –ING; eg •; Hidden /cat/; Implied add (on); Implied in (in);

pinch a . . .	incl A	pixie, *say*	PERRY
pinch *	incl *	**pizzicato**	UNBOWED
• bo–y *pinches* books	BOOTY	**place**	
pinched by *	incl in *	place	PUT
• books *pinched by* bo–y	BOOTY	• fashionable place	INPUT
pine		• place at this spot	PUTTIER
chop down pin(e)	PIN	• place bonds	PUTTIES
pine	LONG	place	SET
• live pine	BELONG	• fashionable place	INSET
• pine building	LONGHOUSE	• he *is in* place . . .	SHEET
• pine marten, *say*	LONGFELLOW	• place peg	SETTEE
[pines] *away*	SNIPE, SPINE	place	SITE
Ping's other half	PONG	• fashionable place, *say*	INCITE, INSIGHT
pink		• place, *say*	CITE, SIGHT
pink haze, *say*	PIN-CASE	• soft *in* places	SPITES
pink jumper	SALMON	place	LIEU
pint		• motorway place	MILIEU
pint	P, PT	• place occupier	LIEUTENANT
pint of beer, *say*	PINTAIL	place for	
pip		–animals	INSTALL
pip	ACE	–blow-out	ETNA, VOLCANO
• many pips	LACES, MACES	–hanging	GALLERY, TATE
• Pip got up	ACEROSE	–napkin	OVERLAP
pipe		–players	ONSET
piped music	PIBROCH	–putting club	GREENWOOD
pipeline, *say*	HOES	–soldiers	TOAST-RACK
piper's child	TOM	place of service	BASELINE, COURT
pirate			CHURCH
pirate	CORSAIR, PRIVATEER		OMEGA
	MORGAN, SILVER et al	*placed in* *	incl in *
pirate flag	(JOLLY) ROGER	• silver *placed in* r–ing	RAGING
pirate treasure	SILVER	*placed round* *	incl *
pirate's place	PENZANCE	• r–ing *placed round* silver	RAGING
pirouette		placeholder	LIEUTENANT
[neat] *pirouette*	ANTE, ETNA	**plagiarise**	
pirouetting [dancer]	CRANED	*plagiarise* [article]	RECITAL
pit		plagiarise musical	COPYCATS
pi<u>t</u> *closure*	T	**plain**	
pit men	NUM	plain bicycle	ORDINARY
pit stratum	MINELAYER	plain chant	EVENSONG
pit workers	NUM	plain colour	PRAIRIE-OYSTER
pithead	BROW	plain creature	PRAIRIE-DOG
<u>p</u>it*head*	P		PRAIRIE-OYSTER
pit-stop	MINEFIELD	plain glass	PRAIRIE SCHOONER
pitch		plain *speaking*	PLANE
pitch	TAR	plain words	PROSE
• pitch container	TARPAN	**plan**	
• pitch sticks	TARGUMS	plan garden	PLOT
• second pitch	STAR	Plan Position Indicator	PPI
pity		plan table	IDEALIST
[cried] *piteously*	DICER	plans of action, *say*	POLLICES
piteous [pleas]	PALES	**Planck's constant**	H
pity girl	RUTH	**plane**	
pity Herb	RUE	*accident to* [plane]	NEPAL, PANEL
pixie		plane	SMOOTHER
pixie is warm	ELF-SHOT	[plane] *crash*	NEPAL, PANEL

placed in s/ome ga/rdens — OMEGA

[plane] *disaster*	NEPAL, PANEL	play part	ROLE
plane driver, *say*	PILATE	*play part in* t/he m/atch	HEM
plane, *say*	PLAIN	play patience	TOLERANCE
plank		play-school	RADA, RUGBY, SCANDAL
a plank	ABOARD	play-time	TEMPO
plank *say*	BORED	play-*up*(D)^	HON, ON
planking, *say*	WAILING, WHALING	played first in rubber	WHISTLED
plant		player sacked	BACKFIRED
plant	INTER	players	CAST
• plant seed, *say*	INTERCEDE	• 501 players	DICAST
• second plant	SINTER	• players service . . .	CASTLET
• wide plants	WINTERS	• players went ahead	CASTLED
plant	SOW	players	SIDE
• plant in good . . .	SOWING	• players *have* true . . .	SIDEREAL
• plant *in* rows	DISOWNS	• players in pavilion	OFFSIDE
plant banner	FLAG	• reserve players, *say*	BESIDES
plant cut back	DOCK	players	TEAM
plant fertiliser	STAMEN	• players aboard	STEAMS
plant goddess	HEBE, KALI	• players *follow* second . . .	STEAM
planted *	incl *	• players in good . . .	TEAMING
• the *Spanish planted*		players	BRASS, STRINGS
in row–s	ROWELS	• players *have* a way . . .	BRASSARD
planted round a . . .	incl A	• central players	HEARTSTRINGS
planted round *	incl *	player's	
• row–s *planted round*		indicating words relating	
the Spanish . . .	ROWELS	to music:	
planter's dog	SETTER	• *player's* slow . . .	LENTO
planting period	BEDTIME	• *player's* softly . . .	PIANO
plasma injection	BLOODSHOT	• quickly *for the players* . . .	ALLEGRO
plaster			PRESTO
plaster jacket	RENDER(ING),ROUGHCAST	players' style	CAST
plastered [niche]	CHINE	playful chief	ARCH
plastering [over]	ROVE	playground	REC
plastic		playhouse	CAPULET, MONTAGUE
plastic [bag]	GAB	playing	IN, INSIDE, ON
[thermo]*plastic*	MOTHER	*playing about* [with Alf]	HALFWIT
plate		playing-field	REC
plate	L	*playing*-[field]	FILED
plate, *say*	PLAITER	playing-field, *say*	POLOCYTE
play		*playing* [Hamlet]	THELMA
[nine-act] *play*	ANCIENT [parts] *in*	*playing* [role]	LORE
	play PRATS, STRAP, TRAPS	playpen, *say*	DRAMATIST
play	TOY	**plea**	
• play-boy	TOYED	plea	O
play *around*	PLA–Y, TO–Y	• plea for organ	OLIVER
play-boy	BRANDED, WINSLOW	• plea to allow some, *say*	OMASUM
	TOYED	• plea to congregate	ORALLY
play-group	BRASS, STRINGS	(*see also* PLEASE)	
	CAST, SIDE, TEAM	plea, *say*	PREYER
	(*see also* players *below*)	pleas, *say*	PLEASE
play-group, *say*	MINISCULE	**plead**	
play (Japanese)	NO(H)	plead	BEG
play of [T S Eliot]	LITOTES	• continue pleading, *say*	BEGONE
play on	ACTON, BATON	• plead for island, *say*	BEGUILE
	GAME LEG	• plead strongly	BEGHARD
play on [words]	SWORD	• plead *with* alien	BEGET

pleasant

pleasant *at first*	P
pleasant associations	NICETIES
pleasant Sunday afternoon	PSA
pleasant pasture, *say*	FAIRLY, NICELY
pleasant, *say*	GNEISS

please

please	
–be Ronald	OBERON
–be revolutionary	OBECHE
–change	OVARY
–dance, *say*	OGIVE
–don't die	OLIVE
–fly	OWING
–line up	ORANGE
–scrap	OPHITE
–snap her, *say*	OBITER
–stay, *say*	OTARY
	(*see also* plea)
please make notes	DOSING
please, *say*	PLEAS

pledge

pledge, *say*	GAUGE
pledge taker	TT, UNCLE
pledges	–IOUS

plenty

plenty of remedies, *say*	MANICURES
plenty of scope	A–Z

plough

plough [field]	FILED
ploughed up [earth]	HATER, HEART, RATHE
ploughman	SHAREHOLDER
ploughman, *say*	MANTILLA
ploughman's position	ATTRACTOR

plucky

plucky attempt	PIZZICATO
plucky player	HARPIST

plug

	AD(VERT)

plumbers' association

	SOUNDING BOARD

plump

plump friend	FATALLY
plump man	FATAL

plunder

plunder a . . .	omit a
plunder gold	omit AU, OR
plunder money	omit L
plunder, *say*	LUTE
plunder *	omit *
• *plunder* silver *from* vill(ag)e	VILLE

plural

	PLU(R)

Pluto

	DIS

Plymouth Brethren

	PB

PM's address

	TEN, X

pneumatic drill

	AEROBICS

poacher

	COOKER

pocket

pocket a . . .	incl A
pocket *	incl *
• Ma–e *pockets* a penny	MADE
pocketed by *	incl in *
• penny *pocketed by* Ma–e	MADE

Poe

letter *to* Poe	POEM, POET
[Poe's] *characters*	POSE

poem

	IF, ODE, VERSE

poet

poet	AE, DANTE, DUNNE, ELIOT EZRA, HOOD et al BARD, SWAN
poet laureate	PL
poet *with* economist	MILTON KEYNES
poet's flower	CAMPION
poet's inspiration	ERATO
poet's pen	POUND
poet's weight	POUND
poets	PEN

poetic

poetic	INVERSE
poetic	
indicating old words	
used by various poets	
by phrases such as	
• *according to Spenser*, bent	CORBE
• *as the poet said* again	AGEN
• often *used in poetry*	OFT
• *poetic* peasant	SWAIN
• *poetically* gloomy	DARKSOME
• *Shakespeare's* child	COLLOP

point¹

point	PT
• a point	APT
• point *behind* painter	RAPT
• princess *has* point . . .	INAPT
point	HEAD
• girl *has a* point	MAIDENHEAD
• point *to* vessel	HEADSHIP
• *put* point *to* teacher	HEADMASTER
point	NESS
• good point	FAIRNESS
• invalid point	ILLNESS
• tapering point	SHARPNESS

point²

point	N, S, E, W
• game point	NAPE
• point *to* point	EN, WE
• point to point	ETON, STOW
and	
• he points *out*	SHEW
• points out	SNOUT
• points *out* a woman	SEVEN
point behind	EASTERN

Letter replaced \c\at; Omit (a); Pointers *out*; Retain <u>a</u>; Split B_ED; Down (D); Backwards <or ^

point *out*	omit N, S, E, W	• police truncheon	YARDSTICK
point *taken*	incl N, S, E, W	• police weapon	YARDARM
pointed	incl N, S, E, W	• support the police	BACKYARD
• *pointed* ears	NEARS, SEARS	police artist	CONSTABLE
	SWEARS, WEARS	police car	BLACK MARIA, PANDA
• *pointed* gun	WARMS		STATION WAGON
• *pointed* heels	SCADS	Police Constable	BOBBY, PC
pointed stake, *say*	PICQUET	Police Corps	RMP
pointer *to* worker, *say*	NORTHERNER etc	police district	MANOR
pointless	LOVE, TIP-OFF	police power	FORCE
pointless	omit N, S, E, W	policeman	BIZZY, BLUEBOTTLE
• *pointless* li(e)	LI		BOG(E)Y, BUSY, MP
• *pointless* (s)ort . . .	ORT		MR PLOD, PC, ROZZER
points against	ENCOUNTER	policeman	COP
points *out*	N, S, E, W at each end	• policeman *standing in*	
• he points *out* . . .	WHEN	*front of* queen	COPER
poise	P	• policemen *with* one lot . . .	CO-PILOT
poisoner		• policeman *with* unknown	
poisoner	ASP, SNAKE	animal	COPYCAT
poisonous [snake]	SKEAN, SNEAK	policemen, *say*	COPSE
Poland	PL	policewoman	FAIR COP
pole		**polish**[1]	
in polar regions	(in) N–S	polish	RUB
• *French* one *in* polar regions	NUNS	• good polish	GRUB
polar regions	NS	• polish statue	RUBICON
• he *goes to* polar regions	HENS	and	
pole	N, S	• polish (=rub-up)(D)^	BUR
• he *is leading* Poles	HENS	polish	SHINE
• pointer *between* poles	NARROWS	**Polish**[2]	
• Poles *in* characteristic . . .	TRANSIT	Polish capital	ZLOTY
pole	NP, PO, SP	Polish *capital*	P
	PERCH, ROD, STAFF	Polish *flower*	VISTULA
pole-axed [beast]	BASTE, BATES, BEATS	Polish expert	BUFF
pole position	POST	Polish *leader*	P
Pole Star	POLARIS	Polish translation	GLOSS
Pole-star gazer	COPERNICUS	Reverse Polish Notation	RPN
poles *apart*	omit N, S	**politic**	
polesquatter's home	PERSONAL COLUMN	Political and Economic Planning	PEP
police		political leader	PM
police	CID	political *leader*	P
• managed police	RANCID	political opponents	CLEFT
• police *with* queen	CIDER	politician	CON
• port authority police	PLACID	• become a politician	BEACON
police	FORCE	• politician punished	CONFINED
• character *has* police . . .	AIRFORCE	politician	LAB
• county police	DOWNFORCE	• fine politician	FLAB
• police *nearly* complete . . .	FORCEFUL	• politician's speech	LABORATORY
police	MET	politician	LIB
• police have English . . .	METE	• good politician	GLIB
• police in charge	METIC	• politician *has* the *Spanish* . . .	LIBEL
• policeman	METAL, METED	politician	MP
police	RUC	• a politician *in* the study	DAMPEN
• police *break* [into] . . .	RUCTION	• lawyer *with* politician	DAMP
• police *in* live . . .	BRUCE	politician	TORY
• police *return*<	CUR	• politician's claim	AMATORY
police	YARD	• *put* list *in front of*	

politician	ROTATORY	pop	PA
politicians do . . .	PARTY	• pop *back*<	AP
poll		• pop in	PAIN
poll tree	(l)ARCH	• pop *up*(D)^	AP
poll (t)ree	REE	pop *in*	incl PA
polling (d)ay	AY	• the others pop *in*	REPAST
pollute		pop *into*	incl PA
[oil] *pollution*	–OLI	• pop *into* a–rt . . .	APART
polluted [air]	RIA	pop	DAD
pollution of [stream]	MASTER, REMAST	• pop *back again*	DAD
polo	MERCHANT OF VENICE	• pop *up* again(D)^	DAD
pond	ATLANTIC (OCEAN)	pop song	INLAY
ponder		*pop up* again(D)^	ER
ponder it, *say*	MULLET	rat *pops up* (D)^	TAR
ponder, *say*	MEWS, WAY (UP)		*(see also* popular)
pondered, *say*	WADE		
pontifical	AARONIC	**pope**	
Pooh		pope	ALEXANDER, CLEMENT, PAUL et al
Pooh	BEAR	pope	PAPA
• on behalf of Pooh	FOR(E)BEAR	• pope *takes* a diocese, *say*	PAPACY
• Pooh can . . .	BEARABLE	• pope *with* . . .	PAPAW
• Pooh's relatives	BEARSKIN	• pope's rota	PAPALIST
poor			SSD
poor	BAD	**popular**	
• learner *in* poor . . .	BALD	popular	LAIC, LAY
• poor china	BADMINTON	popular	IN
poor	BROKE	• popular *and* cosy, *say*	INKOSI
poor	OFF	• popular demand	INEXACT
• 100 poor . . .	COFF	• popular dog	INCUR
• poor finish	OFFEND(ING)	• popular food, *say*	INBRED
poor, *say*	PORE, POUR	• popular form of writing	INCURSIVE
poor	(in) NE–ED	• popular group	INSET
• *poor* race	NETTED	• popular leader	INDUCE
• *poor* saint	NESTED	• popular monarch	INKING
• poor meal, *say*	POORT	• popular officer	IN GENERAL, INMATE
• son *has* poor . . .	SPOOR	• popular nurse	INSISTER
and		• popular place	INPUT
• poor *and* thin, *say*	PAULINE	• popular present	INHERE
• poor Kate, *say*	PORCATE	• popular team	INSIDE
• poor solution, *say*	PORKY	popular	HOT
poor	STONY	• popular song	HOT AIR
poor	WEAK	• son *has* popular . . .	SHOT
• junction *with* poor . . .	TWEAK	• son *in* popular . . .	HOST
• poor fish	WEAKLING	popular	POP
poor builder	JERRY	• pop song	INLAY
poor golfer	RABBIT	**pork-pie wrapper**	HATBAND
poor grades	DE–	**pornographic**	
poor horse	JADE, ROSINANTE, TIT	pornographic publication	BLUEPRINT
poor [relation]	ORIENTAL	pornographic writer	BLUE PENCIL
poor service	FAULT, LET	**porridge**	
poorly	ILL, SICK	porridge	PRISON
poorly [made]	DAME, EDAM, MEAD	porridge-maker	OATMEAL
poorly made [table]	BLEAT, BLATE	**port**	
poorly qualified, *say*	DEGRADE(D)	port	ADEN, DOVER, ORAN, RIO etc
pop		• student *has* port	LADEN
pop	FATHER	• port only	DOVER SOLE
		• port *surrounded by* iron . . .	FORANE

Letter replaced \c\at; Omit (a); Pointers *out*; Retain a̲; Split B_ED; Down (D); Backwards <or ^

• port *with* square . . .	RIOT
port	L, LEFT, LT
• port in debt	LOWING
• sea port	SEAL
and	
• port deliveries	LEFT-OVERS
• port that is . . .	LEFTIE
• port worker	LEFT HAND
and	
• exist *before* port . . .	BELT
• space *in* port	LENT
port	WINE
• port authority	OENOPHILE
• second port	SWINE
port authority	PLA
• port authority building	PLASHED
• port authority fiddle	PLAGUE
• port authority leader	PLACID
port wine	BORDEAUX, MALAGA
portable lamp	LIGHT
portion	
portion of cake	CA, KE
portion of h/is sue/t . . .	ISSUE
portion of lobster	CLAW
portion, *say*	PEACE, PEAS, PEES
portly porter	STOUT
portmanteau	GEAR-BOX
portray	
portrayed in Gothi/c art on/ show	CARTON
portrayed in [oils]	SILO, SOIL
Portugal	LUSITANIA, P
posh	
posh	U
• posh fur	USABLE
• posh knight, *say*	USER
• posh party	UDO
posh car	LIMO, RR
position	
position of	
–actor	ONSET
–Americans, *say*	OVERHEAR
–school governor	OVERHEADS
–sleeper	UNDERLINES
position, *say*	CITE, SIGHT
positive	
positive negative	NEVER
positive principle	YANG
possess	
possess *	incl *
• w–e *possess* an . . .	WANE
possessed by mo/st ag/es	STAG
possessed by *	incl in *
• mineral *possessed by* the–m	THEOREM
possible	
indicating an anagram:	
• *possibility of* [rain]	IRAN, RANI

• *possibly* [an erg]	RANGE
indicating a homophone:	
• made *possibly* . . .	MAID
• *possibly* grown	GROAN
indicating one of a class:	
• Rover, *possibly*	SCOUT
• scout, *possibly*	ROVER
post	
post card	PC
post-chaise	MAIL COACH
post-date	APPOINTMENT
post-graduate	BA, MA
post-holder	LETTER BOX
post-impressionism	FRANKING, STAMPING
post office	PO
• post office advanced a,	POLENTA
• post office is over . . .	POISON
• post office work	POOP
post-office order	POO
post, *say*	MALE, STEAK
post town	PT
postal order	PO
postman, *say*	MAIL
postmaster	PM
Postmaster-General	PMG
postscript	PS
poster	
poster	AD
• 50 posters	LADS
• poster at this point	ADHERE
• poster *placed by* Liberal	AD LIB
poster	BILL
pot	
pot-bellied, *say*	TUBIFORM
pot-plant	GRASS
pot-thrower	PITCHER
potman's jacket, *say*	REEFER
potted bird, *say*	SHOTTEN
potter's achievement	BREAK, CLEARANCE
potter's ball	WHITE
potter's craft	GAMESMANSHIP
	ONE-UPMANSHIP
potter's colours	BLACK, BLUE, BROWN,
	GREEN, PINK, YELLOW
potato	
potato	MURPHY, SPUD
	TATER, TAT(T)IE
potato disease, *say*	TUBERCULOSIS
potato king	EDWARD
potato *peel*	PO
potential	
[great] *potential*	GRATE
[it was] *potentially* . . .	WAIST
potential [in postman]	POINTSMAN
potential queen	PAWN
potentially [a choir man]	HARMONICA

poultry		and	
poultry country	TURKEY	• praises, *say*	LORDS
poultry-maid, *say*	ENCOUNTER	praise, *say*	PRAYS, PREYS
pound		**prance**	
£1.05	NEW GUINEA	*prance* [about]	U-BOAT
five hundred pounds	MONKEY	*prancing* [horse]	SHORE
pound	L, LB	**precede**	
• each one pound	PERIL	*following* precedent	T
• fifty pounds	LL	*precedence of* king	K
• one pound	AL, ALB, IL, ILB, L, LB	preceding MP	LO
• pound *and* a quarter	LE, LEAST	**preceptors**	CP
• pound *and* three quarters	LEES, LENS	**precious**	
• pound note	LA, LB, LC, LD, LE, LF, LG	precious fish	TWEELING
• pound notes	LAC(E), LAD(E), LAG	precious girl	PEARL, RUBY
	LE(A)D, LEAF, LEE, LEG	**precise**	
pound	QUID	precise time	PRIMAGE
• pound will, *say*	QUIDDLE	precise particle	EXACTION
• *put a pound on by* morning	QUIDAM	precisely (=to a T)	
• second pound	SQUID	• everything *precisely* . . .	TALL
pound for poet	EZRA	• *Pale? Precisely*	WANT
pound notes	STRUM	• *precisely* because . . .	FORT
pound sign	LIBRA	**preferred girl**	BLONDE
pounded [table]	BLEAT, BLATE	**pregnant woman**	LADY-IN-WAITING
twenty-five pounds	PONY	**prelate**	DD
pour		**prelude**	
poured into *	incl in *	*prelude to* Act I	A
• drink *poured into* jug–s	JUGGINS	spirited *prelude*	S
poured out [gins]	–INGS, SING	**premature**	
powder		premature *end*	E
powder-room	MAGAZINE	*premature end* to tri(p)	TRI–
powdered [face]	CAFE	**premiere**	
powdered head	GROUNDNUT	film *premiere*	F
powdery [snow]	OWNS, SOWN	*premiere of* play	P
power	HP, P, VIS	**pre-pack**	
power bloc	E, W	pre-packed	(in) BA–G
powerboat	STEAMSHIP	• *pre-packed* tin	BATING
powerful dives	PLUTOCRAT	pre-*packed*	(in) PR–E
powerful influence	STRONGHOLD	• *pre-packed* at . . .	PRATE
powerful man	QUEEN	**prepare**	
powerful tug	TOWER OF STRENGTH	*preparation of* [team and] . . .	MANDATE
powerhouse	MOD, PENTAGON	prepare(D)^	WARD
powerless	omit P	prepare for execution	ENGROSS
• powerless (p)resident	RESIDENT	*prepare* [meal]	LAME, MALE
p-piece	PARTICLE, PENNY-WHISTLE	prepared	ALA
p-pole	PROD	prepared letter	SAE
practice	–ISM	*prepared* [tea]	ATE, EAT
practice costume	HABIT		prepared to
praise		–play about, *say*	WOODLARK
praise	CLAP	–stand up, *say*	WOODCOCK
• praise gin	CLAPTRAP	–take a job, *say*	WOODWORK
• praise woman, *say*	CLAPPER	–talk, *say*	WOODCHAT
• shout praise	THUNDERCLAP	**preposterous**	
praise	LAUD	*preposterous* [idea]	AIDE
• a very quiet praise	APPLAUD	*preposterously* [garbed]	BADGER, BARGED
• praise a politician	LAUDATORY	**present**	
• praise ruler	LAUDER	present	AD

Letter replaced \c\at; Omit (a); Pointers *out*; Retain <u>a</u>; Split B_ED; Down (D); Backwards <or ^

• many present	MAD
• present with *German* . . .	ADMIT
present	GIVE
• no present	OGIVE
• present name	GIVEN
present	HERE
• fashionable present	INHERE
• present company	COHERE
• present for daughter	HEREFORD
• present song, *say*	HEREDITY
and	
• present, *say*	HEAR
• second present, *say*	SHEAR
present	PR
• I'm present above . . .	IMPROVER
• present at . . .	PRAT
present at robbery	ATHEIST
present day	AD
• people *in the present day*	AMEND
• present day period	ADAGE
• *present day* clothes	ADDRESSES
present day	BIRTHDAY, CHRISTMAS
present day animals	REINDEER
present day visitor	FATHER
	CHRISTMAS
	SANTA CLAUS
present pupil	PP
present stream	CURRENT
present time	AD, BIRTHDAY, CHRISTMAS
present writer	I, ME
preserve	
preservationists	NT
preserve	BOTTLE
• athlete preserves . . .	BLUEBOTTLES
• preserve nerve	BOTTLENECK
preserve	CAN
• German preserves, *say*	JERRICANS
• preserve *aboard*	SCANS
• preserve city	CANNY
preserve	TIN
• preserve city	TINNY
• preserve *in* very *Spanish* . . .	MUTINY
• the *French* preserve . . .	LATIN
preserve cat	MARMALADE
preserve jam	PICKLE
preserve tar	SALT
preserved	(in) CA–N, (in) TI–N
preserved in bri/ne ver/y . . .	NEVER
president	
president	ABE, IKE et al
	CHAIR
	P, PR, PRES
presidential address	WHITE HOUSE
president's position	OVERSTATES
press	
press	DECREASE

press	IRON
• press agent	IRON
• Press Club	IRON(WOOD)
• press teams	IRONSIDES
• pressing	IRONWORK
• press function	IRONWORK
press agent	(STEAM) ROLLER
press ahead	SURGEON
Press Association	PA
press cutting	PAPER CLIP
press gang	CROWD
press game	SQUASH
press notice	NEW-SAD
pretend	
pretend, *say*	FAIN, FANE
pretend to look	SEEM
pretending to be [dead]	EDDA
pretty	
pretty	DISHY
pretty	FAIR
• a quiet, pretty . . .	AFFAIR
• pretty road	FAIRWAY
and	
• pretty line, *say*	PHARAOH
pretty clever	CUTE
pretty *conclusive*	TY
pretty girl	BELLE, CUTIE, DISH
	DOLLY, PEACH, STUNNER
prevent	
prevent profit	BARGAIN
prevent *revolutionary*< . . .	POTS
previous	
previous	EX
• previous wrong	EXTORT
• previously first	EXIST
• previously played	EXACTED
	(*see also* old)
previous address	
indicating title used	
in front of name:	
• ambassador's	
address	EXCELLENCY, HE
• king's address	MAJESTY
• vicar's address	REV
	(*see also* address)
price	
price	PR
(p)rice *cut*	RICE
price-earnings ratio	PE
price I have . . .	COSTIVE
price index	CPI, RPI
price maintenance	RPM
price of beer, *say*	ALECOST
price per page, *say*	PERFORATE
Prices and Incomes Board	PIB
pride	GANGLIONS

priest	
French priest	ABBE, CURE
priest	AARON
priest	ELI
• priest dead, *say*	ELIDED
• priest quoted	ELICITED
• priest *takes* note	ELIDE
priest	ENOCH
priest	PR
• priest *and* philosopher	PRAYER
• priest *has* no dossier	PROFILE
• priest *with* order	PROBE
priest	REV(D)
• priest *by* lake	REVERIE
• priest is fine	REVOKE
• priest is Irish	REVERSE
priest *with* friend	PASTORALLY
priestess	HERO, PYTHIA
priesthood	COWL
Priestley	
characters in [Priestley]...	PERISTYLE
[Priestley] *novel*	PERISTYLE
primary	
primary colour	CARDINAL
primary colour	C
primary school	S
primarily about the . . .	AT
primarily seen in very young . . .	IVY
prime	
prime example of the . . .	T
prime example of the style	S
prime item in collection	C
prime material	GUNPOWDER
Prime Minister	CABINET MAKER, PM
Prime Minister	M
prime mover	M
prime mover in revolt	R
prime piece (=first letter)	
• *prime piece of* beef	B
prime requirement in politician	P
prime sheep	START-UP
primitive	
primitive	UR
primitive man	URGENT
primitive instinct	ID
primitive, *say*	ALIMENTARY
Primrose League	PL
prince	
prince	P, PR, RAS
Prince Albert	ELECTORAL
Prince Edward Island	PEI
princess	ANNE, DI, IDA
	INA, REGAN
principal	
principal	HEAD
• power in principal . . .	PINHEAD

• principal country	HEADLAND
• principal method	HEADWAY
principal	TOP
• bend principal . . .	STOP
• principal problem	TOPKNOT
• principal spinner	TOP
principal charge	PRIME
Principal Clerk of Sessions	PCS
principal directors	STARBOARD
Principal Medical Officer	PMO
principal assistant	A
principally made of wood	MOW
print	
print supplier	FINGER(TIP)
printed material	BATIK
printer's measure	EL, EM, EN
printers	CUP, OUP
	NGA, SOGAT
prison	
prison	BIRD
prison	CAN
• prison area	CANZONE
• prison *has* so . . .	CANTHUS
• prison work	CANOPUS
prison	CLINK, COOLER
prison	HOCK
• prison in Greek . . .	HOCKING
• second prison	SHOCK
prison	JUG
prison	NICK
• ancient prison	OLD NICK
• prison *with* the Spanish . . .	NICKEL
• second prison	SNICK
prison	NICKNAME
prison	PEN
• prison monster	PENDRAGON
• prison *near* New York	PENNY
• second prison exactly	SPENT
prison	QUAD
• prison animal	QUADRAT
• prison square	QUAD
• second prison	SQUAD
prison	STIR
• live *with* prison . . .	BESTIR
• prison breakfast	STIR-FRY
• prison circle	STIRRING
prison camp	OFFLAG, STALAG
• prison-camp child, *say*	STALAGMITE
prison food	PORRIDGE
prison labour	CONFINEMENT
prisoner	BIRDMAN
prisoner	CON
• educated prisoner	MACON
• prisoner in Eastern . . .	CONINE
• prisoner's rights	CONSTRUES
prisoner	LAG

• escaped prisoner	OFFLAG
• strong prisoner	FLAG
• prisoner *with* nothing on	LAGOON
prisoner of war	POW

private

private	GI
• private member	GIMP
• private road	GIST
• private transport	GIBUS
private	GUNNER
• private article	GUNNERA
private	INNER
• 500 private . . .	DINNER
• private chapel	INNER TEMPLE
• private circle	INNER RING
• private soldier	INNER MAN
private	TOMMY (ATKINS)
• private bunk	TOMMY ROT
• private saloon	TOMMY BAR
• private weapon	TOMMY GUN
private automatic exchange	PAX
private branch exchange	PBX
private carrier	TROOPSHIP
private *entrance*	P
private *French* . . .	ENTRE NOUS
private home	BARRACKS, DUGOUT
	FOXHOLE, TENT,
	TRENCH
private hope	STRIPE(S)
private soldier	PTE
private soldier, *say*	RANCOUR
private soldiers	OR
private transport	TROOPSHIP
Privy Councillor	PC

prize

prize animal	MEDALLION, START-UP
prize-ring	PR
prize, *say*	PRIES, TROPHI
probationary	PRO

probe

probe *	incl in *
• one *probing* scheme	PILOT

problem

[great] *problem*	GRATE
problem	SUM
problem children	ISSUE
problem	RUB
• 500 problems	DRUBS
• namely, a problem	SCRUB
• problem I leave	RUBIGO
problem putter	POSER
problem [solved is] . . .	DISSOLVE
problematical, [the gain] . . .	HEATING

proceed

proceed	GOAT, GOON
proceeds of [sale]	ALES, LEAS, SEAL

process

[nuclear] *process*	UNCLEAR
process of [law]	AWL
processed [peas]	APSE
processing [past] . . .	PATS, TAPS
processor	CPU

proclaim

proclaim birth	BERTH
proclaiming great . . .	GRATE
procrastinator's declaration	IDOLATER

produce

[counter]-*productive*	RECOUNT, TROUNCE
[garden] *produce*	DANGER, RANGED
produce air	COMPOSE, PLAY, SING
produce animal	BEAR
produce notes	PLAY, SING
produced by goats	MOHAIR
produced by [goats]	TOGAS
produced in mo/st are/as	STARE
producer of [fir cone]	CONIFER
producer of turnips	WATCHMAKER
produces eggs, *say*	LAZE
producing [notes]	ONSET, STONE
	TONES
product [I sent]	INSET, TINES
product of [Iran]	RAIN, RANI
product of I/ran, Ge/rmany . . .	RANGE
production of [stage] . . .	GATES

profess

profession, *say*	CHOREA, KOREA
professional	ACE
• many professionals	LACES, MACES
• professional *follows*	
the sun	SOLACE
• quiet professional	PACE
professional	DAB-(HAND)
• acceptable *in* a professional	DAUB
• professional lost some blood	DABBLED
• professional plot	DABBED
professional	PRO
• professional criminal	PROROGUE
• professional *in* service dress	SPROD
• professional model	PROPOSER, PROSIT
Professional Golfers'	
Association	PGA
Professor of Theology	STP
professor's address	LECTURE
	(*see also* expert)

profit

ban profit	BARGAIN
profit continues	PROCEEDS
profit, *say*	PROPHET, SEER
profit *to* the people	DIVINATION

prohibit

prohibit	BAN
• prohibit 500 . . .	BAND

Anag [cat]; Any *; Begin IGN–; Endings –ING; eg •; Hidden /cat/; Implied add (on); Implied in (in);

• prohibit fruit, *say*	BANBURY	• proper, *say*	MEAT, METE
• prohibit ruler	BANK(ING)	proper	PRIM
and		• one *in* proper . . .	PRIAM
• bone prohibited, *say*	RIBBAND	• proper ruler	PRIMER
• prohibited mineral, *say*	BANDORE	• proper sign	PRIMARIES
prohibit	BAR	proper	REAL
• prohibit cartel	BARRING	• proper amount	REALLOT
• prohibit fruit, *say*	BARBARY	• proper eyes, *say*	REALISE
• prohibit profit-making	BARGAIN	• proper place	REALLOCATION
and		*properly built* [theatre]	THEREAT
• prohibited obstruction, *say*	BARDLET	**property**	
• reserves prohibited, *say*	TABARD	property	PTY
prohibitionist placard	BANNER	property charge	ATTRIBUTE
project		property conveyance	ESTATE CAR
project players	CAST	Property Services Agency	PSA
projected, *say*	THRONE, THROUGH	**prophet**	
projecting place	CINEMA	prophet	AMOS, ELI, ELISHA
projection	EAR		MOSES et al
projectionist	MERCATOR	prophetess	CASSANDRA, DEBORAH
prominent			SIBYL, SYBYL
prominence	TOR	prophetic article	VATICAN
prominently-featured Communist	STARRED	prophet's grandmother	MOSES
promiscuous		**proportion**	
[a bit] *promiscuous*	BAIT	*proportion of* e/lector/ate	LECTOR
promiscuous [roués]	ROUSE	proportional representation	PR
promise		**proprietary**	PTY
promise peg	COMMITTEE	**prosecute**	
promises to pay	–IOUS	prosecute	SUE
promissory note	IOU, PN	• is prosecuted	ISSUED
promote		• prosecute Edward, *say*	SUITED
promote ruler	RAISER	• prosecute it, *say*	SUET
promote ruler, *say*	RAZOR	• prosecute Scotsman, *say*	SUMACH
promote star(D)^	RATS	and	
promote worker, *say*	RASANT	• prosecuted a politician,	
promoting, *say*	RAISIN	*say*	SUDATORY
promotion of tiler(D)^	RELIT	• prosecuted, *say*	PSEUD
prompt service	AUTOCUE	**prosperous**	
prone to perjury	LYING	prosperous part	SE
pronounce		pros/per/ous *part*	PER
pronounce complete	UTTER	**prostitute**	
pronounced gait	GATE	prostitute	HOOKER
pronouncement is not . . .	KNOT	• prostitute, *say*	HOOKA(H)
proof	GALLEY	prostitute	PRO
prop		• prostitute's clientele	PROFILE
prop up bar(D)^	REVEL	• prostitute's weight . . .	PROGRAM(ME)
prop, *say*	SURE		PROTON
propagate		prostitute	TART
propagate [roses]	SORES	• prostitute *in* ship	STARTS
propagate, *say*	SEW, SO, SOUGH	• prostitute *has* a run . . .	TARTAR
propagation of [tubers]	BRUTES, BUSTER	• prostitute's fee	TARTRATE
proper		prostitute	WHORE
proper	MEET	• prostitute laments, *say*	HORMONES
• assist proper . . .	HELPMEET	• prostitute, *say*	HOAR
• proper encounter	MEET	**protect**	
and		*protected by* *	incl in *
• proper *and* good, *say*	MEAT-PIE	• a king *protected by* c–at	CARAT

Letter replaced \c\at; Omit (a); Pointers *out*; Retain <u>a</u>; Split B_ED; Down (D); Backwards <or ^

protecting a . . .	incl A
protecting *	incl *
• c–at *protecting* a king	CARAT
protector	CROMWELL, NOLL
	GLOVE, OVERALL, HELMET
Protestant Episcopal	PE
proton number	Z
Proust	
[Proust] *novel*	SPROUT, STUPOR
prove	
prove of use [in the] . . .	THINE
proves to be [wrong]	GROWN
Provencal	PR
proverb	
proverbially	
–bald	COOT
–black	DEVIL, INK, SOOT, YOUR HAT
–blind	BAT
–bright	BUTTON
–brown	BERRY
–clean	WHISTLE
–clear	BELL
–cold	CHARITY, ICE
–cool	CUCUMBER
–cunning	FOX
–daft	BRUSH
–dead	DODO, DOORNAIL, MUTTON
–deaf	POST
–deep	OCEAN
–drunk	LORD
–dull	DITCHWATER
–fast	LIGHTNING
–fat	PIG
–flat	PANCAKE
–fresh	PAINT
–happy	LARK, SANDBOY
–high	KITE
–hot	HELL
–mad	HATTER, MARCH HARE
–miserable	SIN
–nice	PIE
–old	HILLS
–patient	SAINT
–plain	PIKESTAFF
–poor	CHURCH MOUSE
–pretty	PICTURE
–pure	SNOW
–quick	FLASH, LIGHTNING
–red	BLOOD
–rich	CROESUS
–right	NINEPENCE, RAIN, TRIVET
–rough	BADGER
–sick	DOG, PARROT
–slow	SNAIL, TORTOISE
–sly	FOX
–smooth	SILK

–snug	BUG (IN A RUG)
–soft	BUTTER, PUTTY
–strong	BULL, LION, OX
–sweet	HONEY, SUGAR
–thick	(TWO) PLANK(S), THIEVES
–thin	LATH, RAKE
–tight	DRUM, NEWT
–ugly	DEVIL, SIN
–weak	KITTEN, WATER
–white	GHOST, LILY, SHEET, SNOW
–wide	BARN DOOR
provide	
provide a seat	ELECT
provide material for [a new]	WANE, WEAN
provide refuge for a . . .	incl A
provide refuge for *	incl *
• *provide refuge for*	
sheep *in* time	HEWER
provide shelter for a . . .	incl A
provide shelter for *	incl *
• w–e *provide shelter for* an . . .	WANE
provided	IF, LENT, SO
provided by [friends]	FINDERS
provided in lar/ge ar/eas	GEAR
providing	IF
providing [arms]	MARS, RAMS
provision-merchant, *say*	GROSSER
province	
some Canadian provinces:	
Alberta	ALBA, ALTA
British Columbia	BC
Manitoba	MAN
New Brunswick	NB
Newfoundland	NF(D)
Nova Scotia	NS
Ontario	ONT
Quebec	PQ, Q, QUE
provincial	
provincial (=dialect)	
• *provincial* girl	GAL
• *provincial* man	MUN
• *provincial* partner	BUTTY
• *provincial* worker	EMMET
provision	
provisional accommodation	DEEP FREEZE
	FREEZER, FRIDGE, LARDER
	PANTRY, REFRIGERATOR
provoke	
provoke	NEEDLE
• provoke lady	NEEDLEWOMAN
• provoke saints	NEEDLESS
provoke	STIR (UP)
• provoke *following* live . . .	BESTIR
• provoke king	STIRK
• provoke, *say*	STIRRUP
Provost Marshal	PM

Anag [cat]; Any *; Begin IGN–; Endings –ING; eg •; Hidden /cat/; Implied add (on); Implied in (in);

prowl		[rice] *pudding*	CIRE, ERIC
prowling [lion]	LINO	**Puerto Rico**	PR
[wolf] *on the prowl*	FLOW, FOWL	**puff**	
Prudential	PRU	puff	AD
prune		puff oxygen	GUSTO
prune (b)us(h)	US	puff will, *say*	TOOTLE
prune plan(t)	PLAN	puffy nose	SNOUT
prune spruce	TRIM	**pull**	
psalm		pull	DRAW
psalm	PS(A)	• having pull	WITHDRAW
psalmist	DAVID	• pull in front	DRAWLED
Psalms	PSA(A)	• pull spanner	DRAWBRIDGE
psychokinesis	PK	pull	LUG
psychotic state	DT	• pull *aboard*	SLUGS
public		• pull fruit	LUGGAGE
public	OVERT	• quietly pull	PLUG
• many public . . .	COVERT	pull	TOW
• public ballot-box	OVERTURN	• pull *aboard*	STOWS
• public individual	OVERTONE	• pull knight, *say*	TOWSER
• public works	OVERTOPS	pull	TUG
public address (system)	PA	• pull *in front of* artist	TUGRA
public building	PO	• pull *round* king	TRUG
public good	PB	pull American	YANK
pub(lic house)	BAR	pull *back*<	GARD, GUL, GUT, WARD
• bird *in front of* pub	CROWBAR	*pull out of* dangerou/s	
• pub brawl	BARROW	ent/erprise	SENT
• pub storage	BARRACKS	*pull out* [stops]	SPOTS
pub(lic house)	INN	pull punch	CLOUT
• local queen	INNER	pull sail	LUG
• pub ghost, *say*	INSPECTOR	pull, *say*	HALL, TOE
pub(lic house)	LOCAL	pull *up*(D)^	GARD, GUL, GUT, WARD
• pub *has* English . . .	LOCALE	*pull up* robe(D)^	EBOR
• pub is English	LOCALISE	*pull up round* bend(D)^	GUARD
pub(lic house)	PH	*pull * from*	omit *
• ducks *in* local . . .	POOH	• king *pulled from* T(r)ent	TENT
• pub *has* nothing to . . .	PHOTO	• *pull* wife *from* (w)aves	AVES
public lending right	PLR	*pulled out of* t/he p/lace	HEP
public library	PL	pulling punches	CARTHORSES
public record office	PRO	*pulling* [rank]	KNAR
public relations (officer)	PR(O)	pull*over*<	GARD, GUL, GUT, WARD
Public Service Vehicle	PSV	**pulse code modulation**	PCM
Public Services Authority	PSA	**pulverise**	
publicise		[it was] *pulverised*	WAIST, WAITS
publicise	AIR	*pulverisation of* [oats]	STOA
• publicise *after* many . . .	LAIR	*pulverise* [bran]	BARN
• publicise skill	AIRCRAFT	*pulverise* [pulverise]	REPULSIVE
• publicise wine	AIRPORT	*pulverised* [ash]	HAS
publicity	AD, PR, PUFF	pulverised earth	GROUND
• he *gets* publicity	HEAD	*pulverised* [earth]	HATER, HEART, RATHE
• publicity is over . . .	PRISON	**punch**	
• publicity *in* second . . .	PUFFINS	punch drunk	WALLOP
publishers	CUP, OUP	punch-*up*(D)^	MAL, PAR
pudding		**punish**	
pudding inside	SAGOIN	*punish* [evil]	LIVE, VILE
pudding [made in] . . .	MAIDEN	*punishing* [sinner]	INNERS
pudding, *say*	SUITE	punishment tires . . .	FATIGUES

Letter replaced \c\at; Omit (a); Pointers *out*; Retain <u>a</u>; Split B_ED; Down (D); Backwards <or ^

pupil		**pussyfoot**	(CAT'S) PAW
pupil	APPLE, L	**put¹**	
pupil teacher	PT	put *down*(D)^	TUP
pupil's cover	EYELID	put *back*<	TUP
pupil's environment	EYE, IRIS	[put] *out*	TUP, UPT–
purchase		put *over*<	TUP
purchase	BUY	**put²**	
• purchase *round* ring	BUOY	indicating inclusion:	
• purchase ruler	BUYER	*put in* a . . .	incl A
• purchase cable, *say*	BIFLEX	*put in* *	incl *
• purchase cereal, *say*	BICORN	• Greek *put in* cha–ins	CHAGRINS
• purchase paper, *say*	BIREME	*put round* a . . .	incl A
• purchase ruler, *say*	BIKING	*put round* *	incl *
purchase tax	PT	• cha–ins *put round*	
pure		Greek . . .	CHAGRINS
pure	NOVICES	*put through* *	incl in *
[pure] *chaos*	PUER	• tyro *put through* p–aces	PLACES
pure lake	MERE	**put³**	
pure, *say*	CHASED	indicating omission:	
pure *sound*	CHASED	*put aside* a . . .	omit A
pure water	MERE	*put aside* money	omit D, L, P
purify insects	DISINFECTANTS	*put aside* *	omit *
purée		• c(are)s are *put aside*	CS
[orange] *purée*	ONAGER	*put away* a . . .	omit A
purée of [leeks]	KEELS, SLEEK	*put away* *	omit *
purgatory		• ha(sten) to *put away* gun	HA
purgatory for misers	CLAMSHELL	*put out* a . . .	omit A
purgatory for the crazy	NUTSHELL	*put out* *	omit *
purify	(*see* pure)	• s(cat)ty to *put out* cat	STY
purloin		**put⁴**	
purloin painting	ABSTRACT	other uses:	
purloined, *say*	STOLON	[nose] *put out*	EONS, NOES
pursue		put across	VOTE, X
indicating one word after or		put an end to	
below another word or letter:		• Con/stable/ *puts an end to* . . .	STABLE
• award *pursued* by VIP	MEDALLION	• *put an end to* man	MANY
• mother *pursues* the *French* . . . (D)	LAMA	• time *puts an end to* man	MANAGE
push		put an end to Edward	CLOSETED
push Black	RAMJET	put away	EAT
push forward	SURGEON	*put back* part<	TRAP
push in a . . .	incl A	*put clock back*<	REMIT
push in *	incl *	put down	BURY, INTER
• fish *pushed in* the . . .	GATHER	put down again, *say*	RELAYED
push in *	incl in *	put down ramps	SQUASH RACKETS
• *push* penny *into* s–lit	SPLIT	put 'em *up*(D)^	ME
push lighter	BARGE	*put heads together*	
push over [stool]	LOOTS, TOOLS	• makers of pens should *put*	
push over stool<	LOOTS	*heads together*	MOPS
push up part . . . (D)^	TRAP	*put out* [cat]	ACT
pushover [for a] . . .	FARO		
pushover was<	SAW		

Anag [cat]; Any *; Begin IGN–; Endings –ING; eg •; Hidden /cat/; Implied add (on); Implied in (in);

boat, Celt, cue, electric charge, factor, farthing, fever, five hundred (thousand), heat energy unit, Kelt, koppa, ninety, ninety thousand, Qatar, quadrans, quality, quark, quart, quarter, *quarto*, quartz, Quebec, queen, Queensland, query, question, quetzal, *queue*, quintal, quintus, rational number, ship, sort, train, trichosanthin

Q8	KUWAIT	*quarter*-deck	D, E, C, K
QE	ER	*quarter*-deck	C, CLUBS, D, DIAMONDS
QEII	SECONDER		H, HEARTS, S, SPADES
quail	COLIN		SUIT
quake		*quarter of* loaf	L, O, A, F
[aspen] *quaking*	NAPES, PANES, PEANS	quarter of Paris	LATIN
[earth]*quake*	HATER, HEART, RATHE	quarter of tongue	LATIN
quaking [in the] . . .	THINE	quarter-sessions	QS
Quaker City	PHILADELPHIA	quartermaster(-general)	QM(G)
qualified		quartermaster(-sergeant	QM(S)
qualified	BA, MA	**quartet**	
qualification of [terms as] . . .	MASTER	quartet	IV
	REMAST, STREAM	quartet *from* Beethoven	BEET, HOVE, OVEN
qualified mother	MAMBA	**quarto**	QTO
qualified teacher	BED	**quash**	
qualified [teacher]	CHEATER, RETEACH	*quash* [riots]	TIROS, TRIOS
quality		['e soon] *quashed* . . .	NOOSE
quality	Q	**quasi-stellar object**	QSO, QUASAR
quality improved	STANDARD ROSE	**quay**	
quantity		quay, *say*	KEY
quantity of gold	GO	quay(side)	PORTEND
quantity of g/old en/closed	OLDEN	**queasy**	
quantity, *say*	WAIT	*queasy* [when I] . . .	WHINE
quarry		[quite] *queasy*	QUIET, –TIQUE
quarry manager	GAME WARDEN	**Quebec**	Q
quarry, *say*	PRAY	**queen¹**	
quart	QT, QU(AR)	queen	BESS
quarter		queen	ER
quarter	N, S, E, W, NE, NW, SE, SW	• queen's circle	ERRING
• quarter horse	SHACK, WHACK	• queen in charge	ERIC
• quarter *to* one	EA, NA, SA, WA	• Queen Street	ERST
	EI, NI, SI, WI	and	
	NAN, SAN, SWAN, WAN	• composer *to* Queen	HOLSTER
	NONE	• kneel *to* Queen	BENDER
• quarter *to* five	EV, VE	• me and the Queen	MEANDER
• quarter *to* six	EVI--, VIE, VIN, VIS	• Queen Elizabeth II	SECONDER
• quarter to nine	SIX	• Queen's hotel	INNER
• quarter *to* ten	EX–	queen	HM, Q, QU, R
• quarterly	ELY, SLY	Queen Anne	AR
quarter	FRACTION, MERCY, QR, QU(AR)	Queen Elizabeth	ER

Letter replaced \c\at; Omit (a); Pointers *out*; Retain a̲; Split B_ED; Down (D); Backwards <or ^

Queen Mary	MR	question of place	WHERE
Queen Victoria	VIR, VR(I)	question of time	WHEN
queen's letters	ER	question, *say*	GRILLE
queen²		*questionable* [deal]	DALE, LADE
Queen of			LEAD, LEDA
–Carthage	DIDO	questionnaire	FORM
–Cockneys	PEARLIE, PEARLY	**queue**	
–Douglas	MANX CAT	queue	CUE, Q, TAIL
–France	REINE	queue, *say*	CUE, KEW, TALE
–Germany	KONIGIN	**quick**	
–heaven	ASHTORETH	quick	ALIVE
–Italy	REGINA	quick century	C
–Navarre	MARGUERITE	quick cleaner	NAIL FILE
–Sheba	AAZIZ, BALKIS	quick diet	FAST
–spades	BASTA	quick digest	SUMMARY
–Spain	REINA	quick dip	PICKPOCKET, SNEAK THIEF
–the dead	HEL	quick hundred	C
–the fairies	MAB, TITANIA, UNA	quick trim	SMART
–the Nile	CLEO(PATRA)	quick way	FLEET STREET
queen³		quick writer	SWIFT
queen	CAT	quickly (=careless speech)	
• queen of Douglas	MANX CAT	• *quickly* I would . . .	ID(E)
• queen's admirer	TOM(-CAT)	• we will *quickly* . . .	WEAL, WE'LL, WHEEL
• queen's children	KITTENS	quickest way	BEELINE
• queen's mate	TOM(-CAT)	**quid**	
queen city	CINCINATTI	quids *in*	incl LL, LS
queen, *maybe*	CARD, PIECE	• 'e's quids *in*	ELSE
Queen Anne's Bounty	QAB	• she's quids *in*	SHELLS
Queen Elizabeth Hall	QEH	**quiet¹**	
Queen's Bench	QB	fairly quiet	MP
Queen's College	QC	• one fairly quiet . . .	AMP, IMP
Queen's Counsel	QC	• one *in* fairly quiet *surroundings*	MAP
queen's carriage	VICTORIA	• soldier *has* fairly quiet . . .	GIMP
Queen's pudding	CHARLOTTE	quiet	EASE
Queensland	Q	• many quiet . . .	LEASE, MEASE
queer		• quiet, quiet . . .	PEASE
queer	RUM(MY)	• quiet sovereign	EASEL
• queer animal, *say*	RUMBLE	quiet	ODIN
• queer game	RUMMY	quiet	P
• queer graduate	RUMBA	• a quiet bit, ,	APORT
• queer period, *say*	RUMMAGE	• a quiet friend	APPAL
queer practices	CAMPUSES	• a quiet man	APRON
Queer [Street]	RETEST, TESTER	• a quiet square	APT
queerly [spelt]	PELTS	and	P
query	EH	• quiet drink	PALE
question		• quiet road	PLANE
question	EH	• quiet woman	PROSE
• pictures *in* question	EARTH	• quiet worker	PARTISAN
question	PUMP	and	
• energy question	FORCE-PUMP	• insect *has* quiet . . .	BEEP
• question family	PUMPKIN	• little quiet . . .	WEEP
• question MPs	PUMPHOUSE	• motor quietly	CARP
question	Q	quietly *drop off*	omit P
question cook	GRILL	• (p)lumber quietly *drops off*	LUMBER
question of identity	WHO	quietly *left*	omit P
question of motive	WHY	• aircraft quietly *left*	(p)LANE

Anag [cat]; Any *; Begin IGN–; Endings –ING; eg •; Hidden /cat/; Implied add (on); Implied in (in);

very quiet	PP
• a very quiet dog	APPROVER
• a very quiet fish	APPROACH
• a very quiet man	APPAL, APPLES
and	
• very quiet *in* the valley	DAPPLE
• very quiet *round* a . . .	PAP
	(*see also* gentle, soft)

quiet²

quiet	QT
• you and I, *say, in* quiet . . .	QUIT
quiet	SH
• quiet listener	SHEAR
• quiet person	SHONE
• quiet stream	SHRILL
and	
• I *am in* quiet *surroundings*	SHIP

quiet³

quiet dinner, *say*	PIECEMEAL
quiet in here, *say*	MUTINEER
quiet thief	RUSTLER
quiet words	ASIDE, WHISPER
quietener	KO, SH
quieter road	TAMERLANE
quietly *converse*	LOUDLY

quintal   Q

quintet

quintet	V
quintet *from* St/ravin/sky	RAVIN

quirk

quirk of [fate]	FEAT
quirky [sort]	ROTS, TORS

quip

quip	SALLY
quip, *say*	SALLIE

quit

quit	LEFT
• 100 quit	CLEFT
• quit hospital	LEFTWARD
quit twice	DESERT RAT

quite

quite fair	JUST
quite heavy, *say*	TONISH
quite high	SOUP
quite likely	ON
quite sane	NOMAD
[quite] *wrong*	QUIET, –TIQUE
quite wrongly [wrote] . . .	TOWER

quiver

quivering [lump]	PLUM
quiveringly [take]	KATE, TEAK

quote

I *quote*	AYE, EYE
not *quoted*	KNOT
quote news	GNUS
quote [Shaw]	HAWS, WASH

R

are, arithmetic, canine letter, castle, eighty, eighty thousand, gas constant, hand, *king, monarch, month, queen,* radius, *rain,* rand, *ray, reading,* real numbers, Réaumur, received, recipe, rector, regina, registered trademark, Republican, resistance, respond, rex, rho, right, river, *road, Roger,* Romania, röntgen unit, rook, *rotund character, r(o)uble, royal,* run, rupee, Russia, Ryberg's constant, side, *writing*

rabbit	
rabbit	BRER, POOR GOLFER
tailless rabbi(t)	RABBI
rabid	
[acts] *rabidly*	CATS, SCAT
rabid [animal]	LAMINA
race¹	
race	NATION
• change race	ALTERNATION
• motor race	CARNATION
• race *with* friend	NATIONALLY
race	TT
• race *in* circles	OTTO
• race *round* circuits	TOOT
• race *round* Westminster	TWIT
• road race	MITT
race	DERBY, (GRAND) NATIONAL
	OAKS
• racehorse	DERBYSHIRE
• gamble *on* race	NATIONAL
	LOTTERY
• southern race	SOAKS
race²	
[horse]*racing*	SHORE
race broadcast	RELAY
race commentator	ETHNOGRAPHER
race description	BLOOD RELATION
race leader	ADAM
race *leader*	R
race starter	ADAM
race *starter*	R
racehorse, *say*	COARSER
races	HEATS
Racing Club	FLAT IRON
racing [start]	TARTS
racing start	R
racket skills	RAMPARTS
radian	RAD
radical	RAD, RED
radical [Tory]	TROY

radiation protection adviser	RPA
radio	
radio frequency	RF
radio receiver	ELECTRIC FENCE
radio technique	AIRCRAFT
radio telephone	RT
radiological safety officer	RSO
radius	R, RAD
ragged	
ragged [edges]	SEDGE
[robes] *ragged . . .*	BORES, SOBER
Ragnarok	GODSEND
Raffles port	SINGAPORE
rage	
[depart] *in a rage*	PARTED, PRATED
raging [gale]	GAEL
railway	
rail connection	FISH-PLATE
[rail] *trip*	LIAR, LIRA, RIAL
railway	BR
• railway in Greece	BRING
• railway not working	BRIDLE
• railway points	BREW
railway	MET
• company railway	COMET
• put railway *round* a . . .	MEAT
• railwayman	METAL, METED
railway	RLY
• lay railway *round* east . . .	RELY
• mother *on* the railway	MARLY
• railway *without* record . . .	REPLY
railway	RY
• and *in* railway . . .	RANDY
• put railway *round* a . . .	RAY
• spoil railway . . .	MARRY
railway region	GWR, LMS, LNER, SR
railway sorting office	RSO
railway sub-office	RSO
railway *termini*	RY
railway *terminus*	Y

Anag [cat]; Any *; Begin IGN–; Endings –ING; eg •; Hidden /cat/; Implied add (on); Implied in (in);

Railway Traffic Officer	RTO	**ramshackle**	
railwayman	(in) B–R	[quite] ramshackle	QUIET, –TIQUE
railwaymen	NUR, RUNABOUT	*ramshackle* [huts]	SHUT, THUS
railwaymen(D)^	RUN-UP	**ran**	
rain		ran	RAN
rain	R, WATERFALL	• ran *around*	RA–N
rain fell	PELT	• ran *out*	RA–N
rain indicator	SHOWER	• [ran] *out*	ARN
[rain] *squall*	IRAN, RANI	• [ran] *riot*	ARN
[rain]*fall*	IRAN, RANI	• ran *round<*	NAR
[rain]*maker*	IRAN, RANI	• ran *round*	RA–N
[rain]*storm*	IRAN, RANI	ran	SMUGGLED
raise		• many smuggled . . .	CRAN
raise		• smuggled diamonds	RAND
indicating reversal in		• smuggled king *and* queen . . .	RANKER
Down clue(D)^:		ran all the time	RACE DAY
• *raise* boy	YOB	ran daily	EDITED
• *raise* money	NEY, NIT, RENNET	*ran riot* [in Gath]	HATING
• *raise* mug	GUM	ran weekly	EDITED
• *raise* note	RENNET		*(see also* **run***)*
• *raise* objection	STUB, TUB	**rand**	R
• *raised* edge	MIR, PIL	**random**	
• *raised* highway	DR, EVA–, –IM, –TS	*random* [shot]	HOST, HOTS
• *raised* objection	STUB, TUB	*randomly* [cast] . . .	CATS, SCAT
raise back	REAR	**range**	
raise capital	REALISE	*free* [range]	ANGER
raise garret	LOFT	*range* [free]	REEF
[raise] *rent*	AESIR, SERAI	Rangers	QPR
raise your, *say*	RASURE, RAZURE	*ranging* [in on a] . . .	ANION
raised by . . .	UPPER	**rank**	
raised anchor, *say*	WADE	*first* rank	R
raised capital	QUITO	rank *outsiders*	RK
raised family, *say*	BREADLINE	rank, *say*	GREYED
raised flag	KERB(STONE)	ranker, *say*	RANCOUR
raised streak, *say*	WAIL, WHALE	**ransack**	
	WHEAL, WHEEL	*ransack* [drawers]	REDRAWS, REWARDS
raises family	BEARSKIN	[room] *ransacked*	MOOR
rake		**rapid**	
rake	LOTHARIO, RIP	rapid eye movement	REM
rake's epitaph	RIP	rapidly dissipated	FAST
rallying ground	TENNIS COURT	**rare**	
ram		rare bird	RARA AVIS
female ram, *say*	BUTTRESS	*rare* [bird]	DRIB
ram	BUTTER	[rare] *disorder*	REAR
• ram vessel	BUTTERCUP	rare meat	HAMBLED
ramble		*rarely* [read]	DARE, DEAR
ramble in [field]	FILED	**rash**	
rambling [roses]	SORES	rash investigation	SPOT CHECK
rampage		*rash* [step]	PEST, PETS
rampaging [Norse] . . .	SNORE	rasher	BACON
[Huns] *on the rampage*	SHUN	**rate**	
rampant		rate	MPH
rampant [lion]	LINO	rate	SPEED
[spread] *rampantly*	DRAPES, SPARED	• rate-capping	SPEED LIMIT
rampart	LAMB, MUTTON	• rate highly	SPEEDWELL
	SHEEPSHANK	• wife *included in* rate	SPEWED

Letter replaced \c\at; Omit (a); Pointers *out*; Retain a̲; Split B_ED; Down (D); Backwards <or ^

rate increase	ACCELERATION, TEMPORISE	*read in* T/he St/rand	HEST
rate of progress	MPH	read it, *say*	RE-EDIT
rate of tax, *say*	LEVIRATE	[read] *out*	DARE, DEAR
[rate] *reform*	TARE, TEAR	*read out* banns	BANS
rating	AB	read, *say*	RED, SCARLET
	(*see also* sailor)	[reading a] *novel*	GARDENIA
rather		*reading of* [letters]	SETTLER
rather	–ISH	*reading* review	REVUE
• rather dull	BLANDISH	reads list	CONSTABLE
	(*see also* like)	[reads] *novel*	DARES, DEARS, RASED
rational number	Q	**readjust**	
rattle		*readjust* [ladies'] . . .	SAILED
rattled [dice]	DECI–, ICED	*readjustment of* [centre]	RECENT
rattle [snake]	SNEAK	**ready**	
rattling [plates]	PETALS, STAPLE	ready	CASH
raucous dog	HUSKY	• ready at this point, *say*	CASHIER
ravage		• ready *to* fight	CASH-BOX
ravage, *say*	PRAY	ready	MONEY
ravager, *say*	PRAYER	• ready *for* sea	DRINK-MONEY
ravaged [by a] . . .	BAY	• ready *to* fight	MONEY-BOX
ravaging [town]	WONT	ready to play	INSTANCE, ONSET
raw		**real**	
raw *beginner*	R	real numbers	R
raw [deal]	DALE, LADE, LEAD	[real] *potential*	EARL, LEAR, RALE
raw (l)am(b)	AM	real, *say*	PUCKER, REEL
raw, *say*	CREWED, SOAR	[real son]	NEW ORLEANS
ray	X	[real] *trouble*	EARL, LEAR, RALE
razor-man	OCCAM	re(ally) *friendless*	RE
re		**realign**	
re	ABOUT	*realign* [stream]	MASTER, REMAST
• about time	RET	*realigning* [rail]	LAIR, LIAR
• ca–t *goes round* about . . .	CARET		LIRA, RIAL
• landed about . . .	LITRE	*realignment of* [lane]	LEAN
re	AGAIN	**reallocate**	
• felt pain again	REACHED	*reallocate* [letters]	SETTLER
• landed again	RELIT	*reallocation of* [grant I] . . .	GRATIN
• make further mistake	RESIN		RATING
re-		**reappear**	
many words prefixed with re-, some		*reappearance of* [players]	REPLAYS
of which follow, are used to indicate		*reappearing* [later]	ALTER, RATEL
anagrams or reversal		**reapply**	
re-arrange		*reapplication* [to let]	LOTTE
re-arrange [diary]	DAIRY	*reapplied* [his] . . .	–ISH
re-arrange [kingpin]	PINKING	**rear**	
reach		Rear Admiral	RA
reach end	DIE	*Rear* Admira<u>l</u>	L
[reach] *out*	RACHE	rear animal	BUM STEER
react		rear garden	BACKGROUND
[nuclear] *reaction*	UNCLEAR	rear of ship	STERN
react fast	REDOLENT	*rear of* ship	P
reacting to [news]	SEWN, WENS	rear post, *say*	RUMPSTEAK
reaction [to the] . . .	THINE	rear, *say*	RHEA
reactionary wets<	STEW	rear sheep	BUCKRAM
read		rear view	HINDSIGHT
read aloud	ALLOWED	reared *say*	BREAD
read *aloud*	RED, REDE, REED	rearing, *say*	RAISIN

rears tree	RUMPSTEAK
rearrange	
[game] *rearranged*	MEGA–
rearrange [chairs]	CHARIS
rearrangement of [parts]	PRATS, STRAP, TRAPS
reason	
reason, *say*	CAWS
reasonable	FAIR
• king *in* reasonable . . .	FAKIR
• reasonable argument	FAIRGROUND
• reasonable method	FAIRWAY
reasonable, *say*	DESCENT
reassemble	
[Class E] *reassembled*	SCALES
reassemble [warders]	DRAWERS, REWARDS
reassure	
reassuring report	AMOK
Réaumur	R
rebel	
rebel	CADE, TYLER
rebel group	CONTRABAND
rebellious [race]	ACER, ACRE, CARE
rebels	ETA, IRA, PLO
rebuild	
rebuild most of [town]	WON, NOT, TON
rebuild [town]	WONT
rebuilding hospital	REWARDING
rebuff	
moderates *rebuffed*<	STEW
rebuff Enid<	DINE
rebut	
rebut DA's . . . <	SAD
rebut his . . .	HER
rebuttal of large . . .	SMALL
recall	
recall time<	ARE, EMIT
recalled dog<	GOD
recast	
recast [lure]	RULE
recasting [Tosca]	ASCOT, ATOCS, COATS, TACOS
recede	
receding gums<	SMUG
tide *recedes*<	EDIT
receipts	–IOUS
receive	
receive approval	incl OK
• w–e *receive* approval	WOKE
receive grant	ACCEPT
receive title, *say*	BENIGHTED
received by *	incl in *
• car *received by* Ma–y	MARRY
receiver	FENCE
• receiver's crime	OFFENCE
receiver of wreck	ABANDONEE
receives a . . .	incl A

receives *	incl *
• Ma–y *receives* car	MARRY
receiving attention	(in) H–AND
receiving deliveries	BATTING, NOT OUT
recent	
recent delivery	NEONATE, NEW YORKER
[recent] *disturbance*	CENTRE
recent friend	LATERALLY
recent graduate, *say*	PNEUMA
recent history	
–English	YESTERDAY
–French	HIER
–German	GESTRIGE TAG
–Italian	IERI
–Spanish	AYER
[recent] *novel*	CENTRE
recent race	NEWSPRINT
receptive	
receptive to a . . .	incl A
receptive to *	incl *
• w–ere *receptive to* hot . . .	WHERE
	(*see also* receive)
Rechabite	TT
recipe	
recipe	R, REC
recipe book	RB
recipe for [stew]	WEST, WETS
reciprocate	
reciprocal action	DEED
reciprocate Ben's . . . <	SNEB
reciprocating sound	TOOT
recite	
maid *reciting* . . .	MADE
recitation of ode	OWED
reckless	
reckless [action]	CATION
[throw] *recklessly*	WORTH
reclaim	
reclaimed [lost] . . .	LOTS
reclamation of [land, ie] . . .	NAILED
reclassify	
reclassification of [animal]	LAMINA, MANILA
reclassified [general] . . .	ENLARGE
reclassify [owls]	LOWS, SLOW
recollect	
[I can't] *recollect*	ANTIC
recollected [tale]	LATE, LEAT TAEL, TELA
recommend	
recommend lawyer	ADVOCATE
recommended retail price	RRP
recondition	
recondition [frayed] . . .	DEFRAY
reconditioned [or new]	OWNER
reconditioning of [furs]	SURF
reconfigure	

reconfiguration of [plane]	PANEL		TURNTABLE
reconfigure [shape]	HEAPS, PHASE	record-*holder*	incl EP, LOG, LP
reconstitute		• she is hot record-*holder*	SHEEPISH
reconstitute [meat]	MATE, TAME, TEAM	• ship is record–*holder*	SLOGS
reconstituted [soup]	OPUS	• one in first is	
reconstitution of [side]	DIES, IDES	record-*holder*	ALPINIST
reconstruct		record-maker	ACETATE, STYLUS, VINYL
[dome] *reconstructed*	MODE		EMI
reconstruction of [Rome]	MORE	record number	FORTY-FIVE
recopied	REAPED		SEVENTY-EIGHT, THIRTY-THREE
record			SCORE
record	CD	record-player	DISC JOCKEY
• look *in* the record	CLOD		NEEDLE, STYLUS
• nothing *in* the record	COD		TURNTABLE
record	DIARY	record rebellion	FORTY-FIVE
record	DISC	record time	DISCAGE, MINUTE
• record finished	DISCOVER	record turnover	FLIPSIDE
• record producing		*recorded in* Bib/le st/ory	LEST
royalties, *say*	DISCERNING	recording band	TRACK
• record time	DISCAGE	recording head	ARCHANGEL
record	ENTER, ENTRY	**recover**	
• record it is . . .	ENTERITIS	*recover from* gra/ve il/ness	VEIL
• second record	SENTRY	*recovered by* *	incl RE
record	EP	• *recovered by* th–e . . .	THREE
• record-carrier	EPHOD	*recovering* *	incl in R–E
• saint records . . .	STEPS	• *recovering* fish	RIDE
• we record	WEEP	recovery ship	ARGO
record	FORTY-FIVE	**recreate**	
record	LOG	[later] *recreated*	ALTER, RATEL
• loud record	FLOG	*recreate* [theatre]	THEREAT
• record a beat, *say*	LOGARITHM	**rectify**	
• record *in* ship	SLOGS	*rectification of* [AC to] . . . ATOC, COAT, TACO	
record	LP	*rectify* [slip]	LIPS
• a record in Eastern . . .	ALPINE	rector	REV(D)
• he records	HELPS	**recur**	
record	MONO	*recurrent* moan< I . . .	NAOMI
• record container	MONOPOD	*recurrent* note<	ETON
• record weight	MONOGRAM	recurring decimal	OFTEN
• record the first . . .	MONOTHEIST	**recycle**	
record	SEVENTY-EIGHT	*recycled* rag<	GAR
record	SINGLE, STEREO	*recycled* [rags in] . . .	GRAINS
record	TAPE	*recycling* [centre]	RECENT
• English record	ETAPE	**red**[1]	
• king *on* record	TAPER	meaning:	
• record *in* ship	STAPES	angry	
record	THIRTY-THREE	• angry *carrying* silver . . .	RAGED
record book	ALBUM	bloody	
record-*breaking*	incl EP, LOG, LP	• short time *in* bloody . . .	REMIND
• record-*breaking* ste–le	STEEPLE	communist, left, etc	
• record-*breaking* gas . . .	CLOGS	• anarchist deed	REDACT
• a–s record-*breaking* . . .	ALPS	• communist landlord	RED LETTER
record-*breaking*	incl in EP, LOG, LP	• left study	REDDEN
• Who? *French* record-*breaking* . . .	EQUIP	• Russian sailor	RED ADMIRAL
• win record-*breaking* . . .	LOWING	flushed	
• each record-*breaking* . . .	LEAP	• flushed *in* company	CREDO
record-holder	ALBUM, SLEEVE	Inner Circle	

Anag [cat]; Any *; Begin IGN–; Endings –ING; eg •; Hidden /cat/; Implied add (on); Implied in (in);

• like sanctimonious Inner Circle	ASPIRED
owing etc	(in) R–ED
• dismissed, owing . . .	ROUTED
• rower in debt	ROARED
radical	
• radical water transport	REDRAFT
stop	
• bet *on* red	BACK-STOP
• stop English scheme	REDEPLOY
red²	
red *and* green	RED RAW
Red Army man	FLAMENCO
red *cover*	(in) R–ED
• red *cover for* organ	REARED
Red Cross	RC
red *flower*	DON, VOLGA
Red Norseman	ERIC
Red Queen	CZARINA, TSARINA
red rag	PRAVDA
Red Rum	COMMUNIST SPIRIT
Red Rum *turns back<*	MURDER
red, *say*	READ, STUDIED
red setter	SUN
red suit	D, H
redbreast, *say*	ROBBIN, ROBBING
redcap	(R)MP
red*cap*	R
redhead	GINGERNUT
	MAO, STALIN
	POPPY
	REDNESS
red*head*(D)	R
redheaded Australian	BLUE
reddish beer	GINGER ALE
reddish, *say*	RHONE
red*start*	R
redecorate	
[recent] *redecoration*	CENTRE
redecorate [room]	MOOR
redeploy	
redeploy [army]	MARY, MYRA
redeployment of [regiment]	METERING
redesignate	
redesignate [keys]	SKYE
redesignation of [place]	CAPEL, CAPLE
redevelop	
redevelop [town]	WONT
redeveloping [skill]	KILLS
redevelopment of [region]	IGNORE
redirect	
redirect [trains]	STRAIN
redirecting [fire]	RIFE
redirection of [mail]	LIAM, MALI
redistribute	
redistribute [wares]	SWEAR, WEARS

redistribution of [seats]	SATES, TESSA
redraft	
[much] *redrafting*	CHUM
redraft [letters]	SETTLER
redraw	
[face] *redrawn*	CAFE
redraw [plans Tim] . . .	IMPLANTS
reduce	
reduce	GODOWN
reduce agreement	CONTRACT
reduce agreement	YE(s)
reduce by a pound	omit L
reduce by a quarter	omit N, S, E, W
reduce fare	DIET
reduce friction	OIL-WELL
reduce light	TAPER
reduced by *	
• len(gth) *reduced by* half	LEN
• (of)ten *reduced by* 40%	TEN
reduced cos(t)	COS
reduced [cost]	COTS, SCOT
reduced field	GROUND
reduced price	RP
reduced price	COS(t), (p)RICE
reduced responsibility	(o)NUS
reduced state	(*see* state²)
reduced ta(x)	TA
reduced t/o the r/anks	OTHER
reduces credit	CHOPSTICK
reducing velocity	V
reduction of energy	omit E
reduction of	
–height	H, HT
–power	P
–weight	WT
reduction of (h)eight	EIGHT
reduction of rat(es)	RAT
	(*see also* little², small²)
redundant	
a *redundant*	omit A
• a *redundant* man(a)ger	MANGER
redundant *	omit *
• peas(ant), *redundant* worker	PEAS
re-edit	
re-edited [Verne]	NEVER
[tome] *re-edited*	MOTE
reel	
reel, *say*	REAL, ROLE
reeling [in a line]	ANILINE
[sent] *reeling*	NETS, STEN, TENS
refashion	
refashion [bust]	BUTS, STUB
[robes] *refashioned*	BORES, SOBER
refer	
refer to drawer	RD
referee	REF

Letter replaced \c\at; Omit (a); Pointers *out*; Retain <u>a</u>; Split B_ED; Down (D); Backwards <or ^

reference REF
reference book OED
refine
refine [ore] ROE
refined [oils] SILO, SOIL
refinement of [taste] STATE, TEATS
refit
refit [large] . . . ELGAR, GLARE
LAGER, REGAL
refitted [tyre] TREY
refix
[parts] *refixed* PRATS, STRAP, TRAPS
refix [hinge] NEIGH
reflect
reflected Don's . . . < SNOD
reflection of room< MOOR
reflective type ECHO, NARCISSUS
reflex expert PAVLOV
reform
reform [railmen] MINERAL
reform of [penal] . . . PANEL, PLANE
Reformation [artist] TRAITS
reformation of [sinner] INNERS
reformat
[later] *reformatted* ALTER, RATEL
reformats [pages] GAPES
reformulate
reformulating [recipe] PIERCE
reformulation of [rules] LURES
reframe
reframe [Lely] . . . YELL
reframed [oils] SILO, SOIL
refreshment interval ELEVENSES
refuge
refugee DP
* *is refuge for* incl in *
• church *is refuge for* prince CRASH
refurbish
refurbish [snug] GNUS, GUNS
refurbishing hospital REWARDING
refurbishment of [loos] OSLO, SOLO
refuse
refusal, *say* KNOW, NEIGH
refuse, *say* WAIST
refuse to declare BATON
refuse to *return*< ON
refuse young . . . LITTER
refusing *to rise*(D)^ ON
regal
regal coin PENNY ROYAL
regally ASKING
regard
regard drink SAKE
regard, *say* WRECK
Regency
Regency man BEAU (NASH)

Regency man, *say* BONE-ASH
regenerate
regenerate [Ulster's] . . . LUSTRES, RESULTS
regeneration of [life] FILE, LIEF
regiment
regiment R(E)GT
Regimental Court-Martial RCM
Regimental Sergeant-Major RSM
regina R
regional
regional (=dialect)
• regional farm WICK
• regional network KELL
• regional quarrel FRATCH, WHID
Regional Seat of Government RSG
register
dog register TERRIER
register fighter TERRIER
Registered General Nurse RGN
regrade
regrade [slope] LOPES, POLES
regraded [pupils] SLIP UP
regress
regression of time< ARE, EMIT
regressive way< DR, EVA, TS, YAW
regret
regrets, *say* RUSE
regretted, *say* ROOD, RUDE
regroup
regroup [army] MARY, MYRA
regrouping [in there] NEITHER
regular
regular EVEN
• building *about*
regular . . . SEVENTY
• regular number EVENSONG
• second regular . . . SEVEN
regular absences of f(o)u(r) r(a)s(h) FURS
regular habit UNIFORM
regular ingredients of lo<u>a</u>f
of . . . OFF
regular soldier ORDERLY
regularly viewed ho<u>use</u> US
tr<u>oop sh</u>e *regularly reviewed* ROSE
regulate
regulate [flow] FOWL, WOLF
regulation of [credit] TRICED
rehabilitate
[recent] *rehabilitation* CENTRE
rehabilitated [slum] LUMS
rehash
rehash [meal] LAME, MALE
rehashed [lamb] BALM
rehearsal SHOW-TRIAL
reincarnate
reincarnating [dead] . . . EDDA

Anag [cat]; Any *; Begin IGN–; Endings –ING; eg •; Hidden /cat/; Implied add (on); Implied in (in);

reincarnation of [king is] . . .	SKIING
reinstate	
reinstate [teacher]	CHEATER, RETEACH
reinstated [master]	REMAST, STREAM
reinstatement order	STET
reissue	
[plays] *reissued*	SPLAY
reissue of [novels]	SLOVEN
reject	
reject a . . .	omit A
reject devil<	LIVED
reject rubbish	REFUSE
reject the article	omit A, AN, IT, THE
reject *	omit *
• fat(her) *rejects* her . . .	FAT
rejoin	
rejoin [Marines]	REMAINS, SEMINAR
[wires] *rejoined*	SWIRE
relate	
relating	REL
relating to	OF
• 500 relating to fine . . .	DOFF
• relating to iron circle	OFFERING
• relating to receiver	OFFENCE
relation	SIB
relationship	COS, PI, SINE, TAN
relative	BRER, BRO, REL, SIS
relative arrived, *say*	ANTICUM
relative article	UNCLEAN
relative atomic mass	RAM
relative, *say*	ANTI, COZEN
relative speed	GRANNY KNOT
relatively favourable	NEPOTIC
relatively *small*	BRER, BRO, REL, SIS
relatives	MASON
relatives fear, *say*	KINDRED
relative's friend	AUNT SALLY
relevant stuff	MATERIAL
relax	
relaxation of [strain]	TRAINS
relaxed (=laid *back*<)	DIAL
relaxed [rules]	LURES
relay	
relay [races]	CARES, SCARE
[tale] *relayed*	LATE, LEAT, TEAL
release	
after release [it was] . . .	WAIST, WAITS
[birds] *released*	DRIBS
release a . . .	omit a
release knight, *say*	FREEZER
release money	omit L
release *	omit *
• soldiers *released from* tor(men)t	TORT
releasing [tension]	INTONES
reliable	
reliable	SURE

• reliable cashier	SURE-FIRE
• reliable man, *say*	SHORTED
• reliable number, *say*	SHORTEN
reliable dog	SOUNDTRACK
reliable piano	UPRIGHT
reliable sort of cricketer	BRICKBAT
relief work	CAMEO, CARVING, EMBOSSING
religious	
religious	PI
• approve a religious . . .	OKAPI
• religious character	PICARD
• religious ceremony	PIRITE
• religious code	PILAW
• religious group	PILOT
• way *round* religious . . .	SPIT
religious ceremony, *say*	RIGHT, WRIGHT
religious house	CE, CH(URCH)
religious *leader*	R
religious point	SPIRE, STEEPLE
religious setting	(in) HO–LY
religious work	ALTAR PIECE
relish difficulty	PICKLE
relocate	
relocate [shop]	HOPS, POSH
relocation of [route]	OUTER, OUTRE
reluctant	
reluctant	LOTH
• 100 reluctant . . .	CLOTH
• reluctant Scot	LOTHIAN
• reluctant *to go aboard*	SLOTHS
remain	
remain at the wicket	BATON
remain indoors, *say*	STATOHM
remain unruffled	BECALM
remained at this spot, *say*	STADIA
remains	ASH
• many remains	CASH
• remains *in* the sea	MASHED
• remains *of* ghost, *say*	GOULASH
remains silent	SAY-SO
remake	
remake [coat]	ATOC, TACO
[when] *remade* . . .	HEWN
remarkable	
remarkable	TALL
• remarkable child	TALLBOY
• remarkable ruler	TALLER
remarkable man	COMMENTATOR
remarkable [pearl]	PALER
remarkably [paler]	PEARL
remedy	
remedial [phase]	HEAPS, SHAPE
remedied [all the] . . .	LETHAL
remedy [made]	DAME, MEAD
reminders	–IOUS

Letter replaced \c\at; Omit (a); Pointers *out*; Retain <u>a</u>; Split B_ED; Down (D); Backwards <or ^

remit		• with *René's* . . .	AVEC
[remit]	ORDER OF MERIT		*(see also* abroad, cross[4], continental)
remit *by return*<	TIMER	**renegade**	
[remit] *maybe* . . .	MERIT, MITRE, TIMER	[he was] *renegade* . . .	HAWSE
remix		*renegade* [priest]	RIPEST, STRIPE
[it was] *remixed*	WAIST, WAITS	**renegotiate**	
remix [paté]	PEAT, TAPE	*renegotiate* [terms I] . . .	MISTER
remodel		*renegotiation of* [truce]	CRUET
[face] *remodelled*	CAFE	**renew**	
remodel [gown in] . . .	OWNING	*renew* [fears]	FARES, SAFER
remote		*renewal of* [sub]	BUS
remot<u>e</u> *ending*	E	**renounce**	
[remote] *parts*	METEOR, –OMETER	renounce *	omit *
remove		• ri(sin)g to *renounce* sin	RIG
I'd *removed* . . .	omit ID	**renovate**	
• I'd *removed from* state	FLOR(id)A	*renovate* [sofa]	OAFS
remove a . . .	omit A	*renovation of* [table]	BLATE, BLEAT
remove core of a(ppl)e	AE	**rent**	
remove date	TAKE OUT	[raise] *rent*	AESIR, SERAI
remove from gr/asp en/closing . . .	ASPEN	rent	LET
remove leader of (g)roup	ROUP	• rent increase	LET-UP
remove lid from . . .	omit 1st letter	• rented	ISLET
• *remove lid from* (b)ox	OX	• rented *in* friends' . . .	PALLETS
• *remove lid from* chest	(c)RATE	rent	TEAR
remove lock	(D)EPILATE	• rent completely	TEARFULLY
remove packing of pa/int		• rent reduction	TEARDROP
ro/ller	INTRO	• second rent . . .	STEAR
remove ring	omit O	rent	HIRE
remove [stain]	SAINT, SATIN	• rent fish . . .	HIRELING
remove tail of kit(e)	KIT	• rent an ox, *say*	HIREABLE
remove wrinkles	DECREASE	• rent in ship	SHIRES
remove *	omit *	rent-a-party	TORNADO
• (bar)ely *remove* obstruction	ELY	ren(t) *reduction*	REN
remove * *from*	omit *	rent [rise]	SIRE
• *remove* child *from* class	LES(son)S	rent, *say*	HIGHER, TARE
removed centre, *say*	C(H)ORD		*(see also* rend)
removed [van I] . . .	IVAN, VAIN	**reorder**	
removing veins	MINING	*reorder* [parts] PRATS, SPRAT, STRAP, TRAPS	
remuster		*reordering of* [words]	SWORD
[army] *remustered*	MARY, MYRA	**reorganise**	
remuster [cadres]	SACRED	*reorganisation of* [life]	FILE, LIEF
rend		*reorganise* [stores]	SOREST
rend [open]	NOPE, PEON, PONE	**repack**	
rend, *say*	TARE	[case] *repacked*	ACES, AESC
rending [noises]	ESSOIN	*repack for* [trips], ,	SPIRT, STRIP
	(see also rent)	*repackaged* [parts]	PRATS, SPRAT
render			STRAP, TRAPS
render almost [secur(e)]	CURSE	**repair**	
render first aid	PLASTER	repair	DOUP
rendered intoxicated	PLASTERED	repair	MEND
rendering [dues]	SUED	• repair ruler	MENDER
rendition of [song]	NOGS, SNOG	• repair *to* a large town	MENDACITY
[Satchmo's] *rendition*	STOMACH	repair porcelain, *say*	GLOOMING
René		repaired shoes, *say*	HEALED, SOLD
René's (=French)		*repairing* [hose]	HOES, SHOE
• *René's* house	MAISON	[shoe] *repair*	HOES, HOSE

Anag [cat]; Any *; Begin IGN–; Endings –ING; eg •; Hidden /cat/; Implied add (on); Implied in (in);

repeat
repeat performance	ECHO, ENCORE
repeat performance	DODO
repeatedly volunteers	TATA
repeating decimal	OFTEN
repetition, *say*	WROTE
	(*see also* double, two)

repel
repel a . . .	omit A
repel one . . .	omit A, I
repel king	omit K, R
repel queen	omit ER, Q, R
repel *	omit *
• wh(it)en *to repel* it	WHEN
repellent one	GRIMACE
repellent tang<	GNAT
repelling Satan<	LIVED

repetition   (*see* repeat)

replace
drink *replaces* one *in* th\i\s . . .	THRUMS
replace cover	REINSURE
replace [old Rover]	OVERLORD
replace contents of c\as\k	CORK
replace New Deal	OLD HAND
replace [R with A]	WRAITH
replace weak link	REFUSE
replacement [hip]	PHI
replacement of [parts]	PRATS, SPRAT, STRAP,
	TRAPS
replacing locks	FORTRESSES, WIG
replacing rubber bands	RETIRING

replan
replan [estate]	TEA SET
[town] *replanned*	WONT

replant
replant [shrub]	BRUSH
[trees] *replanted*	ESTER, REEST, RESET

reply
reply	ANS
replying, *say*	ANSERINE

report
report	BANG, POP, REP(T)
report, *say*	BHANG
reported	DIT
reported you're . . .	URE
reportedly knew	GNU, NEW
reporter	GUN, REP
reporter's paper	CARTRIDGE

repose
reposing in *	incl in *
• a king *reposing in* b–ed	BARED

reposition
[castle] *repositioned*	CLEATS
reposition [lamps]	PALMS

represent
representation of [flowers]	FOWLER

representative
representative	MP
• about a representative	CAMP
• business representative	COMP
• nothing *in* representative's . . .	MOPS
representative	REP
• representative *in* church	CREPE
• representative Indian	REPUTE
• seat representative	SITREP

representative of
–England	LION, ROSE
–Ireland	SHAMROCK
–Scotland	THISTLE, UNICORN
–Wales	DRAGON, DAFFODIL, LEEK
representative of [tribe]	BITER
representative from [Neath]	THANE
represented by [seven] . . .	EVENS
represented in [art]	RAT, TAR
represented [in art]	INTRA–, TRAIN
represented in P/aris ta/lks	ARISTA
representing [Wells]	SWELL
represents [Esher]	SHEER

reprobate expires   CADDIES

reprocess
[meat] *reprocessed*	MATE, TAME, TEAM
reprocess [oils]	SILO, SOIL

reproduce
is *reproduced*	ISIS
reproduce [much] . . .	CHUM
reproduced by [seed Vi] . . .	DEVISE
reproduced in [garden]	DANGER
reproducing dog	POMPOM
reproduction of cat	TOM-TOM
reproduction [sideboard]	BROADSIDE
reproduction of [files]	FLIES
	(*see also* double, two)

reprogram
reprogram [timer]	MERIT, REMIT
reprogrammed [IBM at] . . .	IMBAT

republic   REP

repulse
may *be repulsed*<	YAM
repulsed Devil<	LIVED

require
[I am] *required* . . .	AIM, MIA
requires [me to] . . .	MOTE, TOME
requiring a synonym	NEEDING

reroute
reroute [stream]	REMAST, MASTER
[road] *rerouted*	DORA

rerun
rerun [heat]	HATE, THEA
rerun time<	ARE, EMIT
rerunning [tape]	PATE, PEAT

reschedule
reschedule [planes]	PANELS
rescheduling of [tour]	ROUT

rescue	
rescue	SAVE
• novice *in* rescue . . .	SLAVE
• rescue husband	SAVE
• rescue king	SAVER
and	
• rescue girl, *say*	SAVANNA(H)
• rescue ox, *say*	SAVEABLE
rescue from [yacht]	CATHY
rescue ship	(NOAH'S) ARK
rescuer	NOAH, WHITE KNIGHT
resemble	
resembles \G\erald	HERALD
resembles [parents]	PASTERN
reserve	
Reserve Decoration	RD
reserve	BOOK
• reserve currency	BOOKMARKS
• reserve seat	BOOKSTALL
• reserves dance	BOOKSHOP
reserve wife	SPARE RIB
reserves	TA, THETA
• reserve member	TAMP
• reserve team	TAXI
• reserves jeered	TABOOED
	(*see also* army)
reset	
[not] *reset*	TON
reset [field in] . . .	INFIDEL
resettle	
resettle [a tribe]	BAITER
resettled in [Paris]	PAIRS
reshuffle	
reshuffle [cards as] . . .	CSARDAS
[team] *reshuffled*	MATE, MEAT, TAME
resident	
Resident Medical Officer	RMO
Resident Surgical Officer	RSO
resident magistrate	RM
residue	
residue	ASH
• residue of end, *say*	ASHEN
• residue of reefer	POTASH
• with residue	WASH
resistance	R
resolution	
[new] *resolution*	WEN
resolution of [tough] . . .	OUGHT
resolve	
resolve [in game]	ENIGMA
resolved [to send]	STONED
resort	
[Alpine] *resort*	NEPALI
[cheap] *resort*	PEACH
resort	SPA
• English resort bores, *say*	ESPADRILLES

• resort finished	SPADONE
• resort fish	SPALING
resort [to a] . . .	OAT
[the last] *resort*	STEALTH
responsible	
responsible for	–IC
responsibilities, one	
at a time	CARESSINGLY
rest	
r*est* *centre*	ES
rest finished	BREAKTHROUGH
rest in peace	RIP
rest of the paintings	EASEL
rested, *say*	LADE, LANE
resting	(in) B–ED, (in) CO–T
resting place	BED, COT, DORM
	DEN, LAIR
restaurant	
restaurant bill	MENU
restaurant cutlery box	CANTEEN
restore	
restoration of [garden]	DANGER
restore [law] . . .	AWL
restore revs	REORDAIN
restored [stool] . . .	LOOTS
restoring [much] . . .	CHUM
restrain	
restrain a . . .	incl A
restrain *	incl *
• lead *restraining* dog	PROVERB
restrained by *	incl in *
• dog *restrained by* lead	PROVERB
restrict	
restrict (i)t	T
restrict stream	PINCHBECK
restricted by t/he ar/my	HEAR
restricted by *	incl in *
• learner *restricted by* p–ay	PLAY
restricted road	RD
restricted (s)cope	COPE
restricting a . . .	incl a
restricting vie(w)	VIE
restricting *	incl *
• p–ay *restricting* learner	PLAY
restrictive practice	GAROTTING
	STRANGULATION
restructure	
restructure [chapter]	PATCHER, REPATCH
[side] *restructured*	DIES, IDES
restyle	
restyle [acts]	CATS, SCAT
[wigs] *restyled*	SWIG
result	
result of [foresight]	GIFT HORSE
resulting from [state] . . .	TASTE, TEATS
resume play	ACTON, BATON

retail

retail (=change last letter(s))	
• *retail* brea\d\	BREATH
• *retail* stor\e\	STORM
• *retailing* mea\t\	MEAD, MEAL, MEAN
retail fish, *say*	SELFISH
retail price	RP
retail price index	RPI
retail price maintenance	RPM
retailer, *say*	CELLAR

retain

retain fort	KEEP
retain the right	incl R
• state *retains* the right	CARL
retained by *	incl in *
• agent *retained by* men	MALEFACTORS
retaining a . . .	incl A
retaining *	incl *
• men *retaining* agent	MALEFACTORS
retaliate	PAY BACK, YAP

retire

retire to . . . <	OT
retired	(in) B–ED, (in) C–OT
retired	EX, RETD
retired head	omit 1st letter
• *retired* headmaster	(m)ASTER
retired lady<	ASSET
retired leader	omit 1st letter
• *retired* leader of (p)arty	ARTY
retired nurse<	DAV, NES
retired salesman<	PER
retirement cover	BLANKET, DUVET
	SHEET etc
retirement of sailor<	BA, RAT
retiring at ten<	NETTA
retiring member<	GEL, PM
retiring premier<	MP

retouch

[it was] *retouched*	WAIST, WAITS
retouch [snap]	NAPS, PANS

retract

not *retracted*<	TON
retract	DRAWBACK, WARD
retract No 1 tale<	ELATION

retrain

[guns] *retrained*	GNUS, SNUG
retrain [dogs]	GODS
retraining [all the] . . .	LETHAL

retreat

retreat (=go *back*<)	–OG
retreated tidily	EBBED
retreating object<	TI
retreating waters<	SLOOP

retrograde

retrograde step<	PETS
was *retrograde*<	SAW

retrospective

put *retrospective* . . . <	TUP
retrospective look<	–AL, OL

return

return flight	BACK STAIRS
return from work	INCOME, PROFIT
return game<	FLOG
return of service<	FAR
return reward<	DRAWER
return thanks<	AT
return ticket	OUTBACK
return ticket<	GAT
return to . . . <	OT
returned	RETD
Returned Letter Office	RLO
returned sweets<	STRESSED
returning learners<	SLIP-UP
returning missile	BOOMERANG
returning missile<	TRAD
returning nomad<	DAMON
returning traveller<	PER

reunion

[army] *reunion*	MARY, MYRA
reunion of [former] . . .	REFORM

rev

rev counter	ALTAR
rev indicator	DOG-COLLAR
rev up	HIGH PRIEST, SKY PILOT
rev *up*(D)^	VER

revamp

revamp [room]	MOOR
revamped [gown in] . . .	OWNING

reveal

revealed by Fren/ch art/ist	CHART
revealed in de/noumen/t	NOUMEN
revealing [hand is] . . .	DANISH
revealing performance	FAN DANCE
	STRIP-TEASE
reveals [a new] . . .	WANE, WEAN
revelation, *say*	AURICLE
Revelations	REV

revel

revel [at Lent]	LATENT, TALENT
revelling [in night]	HINTING

reverberate

[noises] *reverberating*	ESSOIN
reverberates [tin] . . .	INT–, NIT
reverberation of [steel] . . .	LEETS, STELE

revere

revere, *say*	WARSHIP
Reverend	REV(D)
	(*see also* rev)

reverse

Reverse Arms!<	SNUG
reverse bureaucracy	TAPERED

Letter replaced \c\at; Omit (a); Pointers *out*; Retain <u>a</u>; Split B_ED; Down (D); Backwards <or ^

reverse gear<	BRAG
reverse mail chain	ARMOUR
	CHAIN-MAIL
reverse support	BACK(ING)
reverse tide<	EDIT
reversible notices	SEES
reversible parts<	STRAP
reversible revolver	ROTOR
reversible uniform	LEVEL
review	
[army] *review*	MARY, MYRA
review [all the] . . .	LETHAL
reviewing [novels]	SLOVEN
revise	
revised	REV
revised [ice act]	ACETIC
Revised (Standard) Version	R(S)V
revision of [chapter]	PATCHER, REPATCH
revive	
revived [sister]	RESIST
revival of [play]	PALY
[slow] *revival*	LOWS, OWLS
revolt	
revolting	UP
• 100 revolting . . .	CUP
• revolting drunk	UPTIGHT
• revolting players	UPCAST
revolution	
[counter]-*revolutionary*	RECOUNT
	TROUNCE
prevent *revolutionary*<	POTS
revolution	REV
revolution [in art]	TRAIN
revolution in [art]	RAT, TAR
revolutionary	CHE
• artist *and* revolutionary . . .	RACHE
• revolutionary directions	CHEESE
• revolutionary English	
radical	CHEERED
revolutionary	RED
• about revolutionary . . .	CARED
• revolutionary action	REDACT
• revolutionary movement	RED SHIFT
revolutionary	
–command	ABOUT FACE, ABOUT TURN
–landlord	CIRCULAR LETTER
–movement	ABOUT FACE, ABOUT TURN
–music	INTERNATIONALE
–painter	TURNER
–period	DAY, MONTH, YEAR
–piece of equipment	LATHE
revolutionary [design]	SIGNED
revolutionary part<	TRAP
revolutionary period<	ARE, EMIT
revolutionise [all the] . . .	LETHAL
revolutions per minute	RPM

revolve	
revolve, *say*	TERN(E), WE'LL, W(H)EAL
revolver	CATHERINE WHEEL
	IRON, PIECE, ROD,
	LATHE
revolver, *say*	PISTIL, SPINSTER
revolving door<	ROOD
revolving [fast]	FATS
reward	
reward, *say*	PRISE, TROPHI
reward workers	TIPSTAFF
rework	
rework [sums]	MUSS
reworking of [timber]	TIMBRE
rewrite	
rewrite [section]	NOTICES
rewriting [note]	ETON, TONE
rewritten [page]	GAPE
Rhodesia	RSR
ribonucleic acid	RNA
rice	
rice	ARCHIE
[rice] *pudding*	CIRE, ERIC
rich	
rich	ROLLING
• rich gravy	ROLLING STOCK
• rich Irishman	PATROLLING
• self-contained and rich	SCROLLING
rich, American-style, *say*	DOLOROUS
rich entertainer	COMIC
rich man	DIVES, MIDAS
rickety	
[it was] *rickety*	WAIST, WAITS
rickety [ladder]	RADDLE
riddle	
riddle [cinders]	DISCERN, RESCIND
riddled, *say*	HOLY, WHOLLY
riddling [soil]	OILS, SILO
ride	
rider	AFTERTHOUGHT, PS
	GILPIN, REVERE
riding	UP
• *riding* engagement	UPDATE
• *riding* school	UPSET
• *riding* well	UPRIGHT
riding	(in) S–ADDLE, (on) HORSE
riding	(*see* astride)
riding master	RM
[rode]	WRONG-DOER
ridicule	
[it was] *ridiculous*	WAIST, WAITS
ridicule	BOO
• reserves ridicule . . .	TABOO
• ridicule *and then* celebrate	BOOSING
• ridicule ruler	BOOK(ING)
ridicule man	GUY

Anag [cat]; Any *; Begin IGN–; Endings –ING; eg •; Hidden /cat/; Implied add (on); Implied in (in);

ridiculed, *say*	GUIDE
ridiculous [shape]	HEAPS, PHASE
ridiculous shape, *say*	SILICONE
ridiculous position, *say*	SILICITE
rife	
[rife]	WILDFIRE
rifle	
Rifle Brigade	RB
rifle drill	GUNCOTTON, SACKCLOTH
rifle fire	SACK
rifle school	WINCHESTER
rift	
[cause] *rift*	SAUCE
rift in [lute or] . . .	ELUTOR
rig	
rig [up a net]	PEANUT
rigged [race]	ACER, ACRE, CARE
[rig]-*out*	GIR, GRI
right¹	
right	LIEN
• a right . . .	ALIEN
• right *back*	NEIL
• right *in* court	CLIENT
• right, *say*	LEAN
right	OFF
• 100 right . . .	COFF
• right result	OFFEND
• right *in* the peg	TOFFEE
right	OK(E)
• 100 right . . .	COKE
• not right	NOOK
• right *in* church	COKE
right	R
• right *and* wrong	RILL
• right *at the end of* road	AVER
• right *at the start of* row	ROAR
• right *behind* you, *say*	UR
• right exit	REGRESS
• right *from the start of* (r)ace	ACE
• right in Kent, *say*	RINSE
• right lines	–RRY
• right on	ROVER
• right round	RO–
• right time	RAGE, RT
• right turn	RU
right	RT
• about right	CART
• one *in* the right	RAT
• right *at the end of* revolutionary . . .	CHERT
• right *round* an . . .	RANT
• right *turn*<	TR
• turn *in* right . . .	RUT
right	TORY
• bird right . . .	MINATORY
• second right	STORY
• telephone right, *say*	DILATORY
right *at the end* . . .	end with R, RT
right *away*	omit R, RT
right *back*<	TR
right boot	SIDEKICK
right fish, *say*	BLUE-EYED
right *from the start*	omit initial R
• (r)ash, right *from the start*	ASH
right *ingredient*	incl R, RT
right *inside*	incl R, RT
right *out of it*	omit R, RT
right *outside*	(in) R–T
right²	
meaning:	
off	
• again to off	RETORT
OK, oke	
• OK *behind* the Post Office	PORT
lien	
• has a lien *on* first . . .	ARTIST
title	
• right attendant	TITLE PAGE
Tory	
• born Tory	BRIGHT
right³	
right amount	NINEPENCE
right angle	L
right away	OFF
right-half for Bol<u>ton</u>	TON
right half of ro<u>ad</u>	AD
right-hand	RECTO, RH, RO
right-hand man	CONSERVATIVE, TORY
right mark	TICK
right name	TITLE
right of way	ROW
right of wa<u>y</u>	Y
Right Reverend	RR
right side of road	AD, D
right sign	TICK
right-thinking person	CONSERVATIVE, TORY
right way	CONSERVATIVE, TORY, EAST
Right Worthy	RW
[right] *wrong*	GIRTH
ring¹	
ring	DISC
• ring, ring . . .	DISCO
• ring gone	DISCOVER
• ring rider	DISC JOCKEY
ring²	
ring	O
• ring Mark . . .	OSCAR
• ring twice	OO
• Ringway	–OPATH, ORD, OST
and	

• dress ring	GARBO
• key-ring	BO, GO, SOHO, SOLO
• smoke-ring	RE-ECHO
• tree-ring	MAYO
• vice-ring	SINO–
ring *in*	incl O
• ring *in* bo–th . . .	BOOTH
ring *for* a . . .	substitute O for A
• *ring for* a d\a\te	DOTE
ring *from* . . .	omit O
• ring *from* bo(o)th	BOTH
ring *off*	omit O
ring *out*	omit O
ringleader	start with O
• mark ring*leader*	OSCAR
ring³	
ring a . . .	incl A
ring about a . . .	incl A
ring about *	incl *
• w–ear *ring about* the . . .	WEATHER
ring *back<*	LAID, POOH
ring bird	MAGPIE
ring container	PHONE-BOX
ring engineer	CHIMERE
ring fence	TELEPHONE RECEIVER
ring journalist	BANDED
ring laundryman	WASHER
ring-*leader*	R
ring lightly, *say*	TINCAL
ring off	CLOSE CALL, HANG-UP
ring painter	CHIMERA
ring round bull	INNER
ring, *say*	CYGNET, PEEL, SURCLE
ring-*side*	G
ring the pub	TOLLBAR
ring the queen	CALLER
ring *up*(D)^	LAID, POOH
ring *	incl *
• m–e *ringing* at . . .	MATE
ringless	NOTING
riot	
riot of [slaves]	SALVES, VALSES
rioting [tribe]	BITER, TIBER
riotous [ways]	SWAY, YAWS
riotous characters [in street]	INTEREST
riots	GORDON, REBECCA
rip	
rip	TEAR
• rip off	TEARAWAY
• rip sack	TEARBAG
• second rip	STEAR
[rip]-*off*	PRI–
rip-off [client]	LENTIC
rip, *say*	TARE
rip [vest]	VETS

ripped bird, *say*	TORMINA
ripped us, *say*	TAURUS
rise	
pay *rise*(D)^	YAP
rise, *say*	SORE
rising crime(D)^	–NIS
rising fury(D)^	ERI
rising man	INSURGENT, REBEL, RIOTER
rising star(D)^	AVON, RATS
river¹	
mythical river	ACHERON, STYX
poetic river	ALPH
river	AIRE
• river *in* quiet delta	PAIRED
• river valley	AIREDALE
river	ALPH
• river helps . . .	ALPHABETS
• river *joins* another	RALPH
river	CAM
• insect *covering* river	BECAME
• *rising* river(D)^	MAC
• river-*side* tower	CAMSHAFT
river	DART
• river authority	DARTBOARD
• *throw* record *in* the river	DEPART
river	DEE
• River Dee	DEED
• river *has* vermin	DEEPEST
• river *in* India	INDEED
river	DON
• artist *on* the river	RADON
• River Wear	DON
• river-goddess	DONATE
river	DOVE
• river bird	DOVE
• river bed	DOVECOT
river	EXE
• river *has* attractive . . .	EXECUTE
• river *has* the right . . .	EXERT
• river inspector, *say*	EXCHEQUER
river	FAL
• one *in* river	FAIL
• pertaining to the river	OFFAL
river	FORTH
• river appearing . . .	FORTHCOMING
• river ceremony, *say*	FORTHRIGHT
river	INDUS
• River Test	INDUSTRIAL
• tree *by* river, *say*	INDUSTRY
river	ISIS
• creditor on river	CRISIS
• river goddess	ISIS
• river islands	ISIS
river	OUSE
• learner *on* the river	LOUSE
• river-*side* (bird)	OUSEL

Anag [cat]; Any *; Begin IGN–; Endings –ING; eg •; Hidden /cat/; Implied add (on); Implied in (in);

river	PO	• road rage	MIRAGE
• river board	POTABLE	• road *up*(D)^	IM–
• river boards	POSTAGE	• road vehicle	MISLED
• river god	POLAR	road	R
• river insects	POLICE	• road *back* to<	ROT
river	TAY	• road in London area	RINSE
• car *falls in* river	TARRY	• road is quiet	RISP
• ship *goes round* river	STAYS	road	RD
• South African river	SATAY	• directions *on* a road	SWARD
river	TEES	• nothing *in* the road	ROD
• place *on* river	PUTTEES	• ring road	ORD
• rain *swells* river	TRAINEES	• road *round* an . . .	RAND
river	TEST	• road *up*(D)^	DR
• boiling river	HOTTEST	road	ROAD
• city *on a* river	LATEST	• road, *say*	R(H)ODE
• river *on* a mountain	TESTATOR	• road to home	ROADHOUSE
river	TWEED	• second-class road	BROAD
• a king *in* the river	TWEAKED	road	ST
• river in front	TWEEDLED	• nothing *in* the road	SOT
river	URE	• private road	GIST
• quiet river	PURE	• ring road	OST
• river-insect, *say*	URETIC	• road *round* his . . .	SHIST
river	WEAR	• road *up*(D)^	–TS
• River Don	WEAR	road	VIA
• river erosion	WEAR	• learner *on* the road	VIAL
• river bed	UNDERWEAR	• road opening	VIADUCT
river, *say*	HEIR, OOZE, ROAN	• test the road, *say*	TRIVIA
	TEAS(E), WARE, WHY	road block	FLAGSTONE, SETT
river²		[road]-*builder*	DORA
river	FLOWER	[road] *construction*	DORA
• bottom of river	FLOWERBED	Road Haulage Association	RHA
• river engineer	FLOWER ARRANGER	road-hog	JEHU, TOAD
• river vessel	FLOWERPOT	road maker	TAR(MACADAM)
river	R	road, *say*	RODE, WEIGH
• East River	ER	Road *Up!*(D)^	DR, EVA, IM–, –TS
• river animal	ROTTER	roadman	MACADAM
• river currents	RAMPS	roadside *verges*	RE
• river fish	REEL, RID, RIDE	road*sides*	RD
• walk *by* river	RAMBLE	[road]*works*	DORA
river crossing, *say*	FAIRY	Roman road	VIA
river king	STREAMER		(*see also* street, way)
	(*see also* banker, flower²)	**roam**	
RKII	ARCHAISE	*roaming about* [in gown]	OWNING
road		*roaming* [free]	REEF
road	AVE	**roast goat**	BUTTER DISH
• hard road	HAVE	**robin's home**	SHERWOOD (FOREST)
• road *and* river	AVER	**robots**	RUR
• road *to the* right	AVERT	**rock**	
• road *up*(D)^	EVA	rock	DIAMOND
road	M	rock	GEM
• road directions	MEWS	• rock-*climbing*(D)^	MEG
• road in America	MINUS	rock	GIB
• road *with* no directions	MOSES	• rock-*climbing*(D)^	BIG
road	MI	rock-adder	TOTTER
• road *leading to* another	MIST	rock band(s)	STRATUM (STRATA)
• road-race	MISPRINT, MITT	rock climber	BARBARY APE

rock fracture	TORRENT	room *on* vessel	SPACECRAFT
rock [garden]	DANGER, GANDER, RANGED	**roost**	
rock group	MASSIF	*roosting in* *	incl in *
rock-music	CRADLE SONG, SWING	• bird *roosting in* h–er . . .	HOWLER
rock, *say*	BOLDER	**root**	
rock show	OUTCROP	root	RAD
rock singer	LORELEI, SIREN	root-mean-square	RMS
rock [singer]	RESIGN	*root of* evil(D)	L
rocking-[horse]	SHORE	*rootless* plan(t)(D)	PLAN
Rocky Mountain area	BC	**rope**	
rocky [shore]	HORSE	rope-dance, *say*	GUIDANCE
rocket		rope decorator	PAINTER
rocket	ARIANE, BLUE STREAK	rope, *say*	CHORD, CORED
	SATURN, VI	ropemaker	COIR, NYLON, SISAL
rocket designer	STEPHENSON	**rose**	
rocket-launcher	STEPHENSON	rose-lover	APHIS
Rod		rose, *say*	GELDER
Rod	PERCH, POLE	**Rossetti's group**	PRB
Rod in the saddle	STICK-UP	**Rossini**	
rode	(*see* ride)	Rossini *trio*	SIN
Röntgen unit	R	**rot**	
rogue		[goes] *rotten*	EGOS
rogue [male]	LAME, MEAL	rotten	OFF
rogue, *say*	NAVE	• rotten beef	BULLY OFF
roguish chief	ARCH	• rotten cargo	OFFLOAD
role		• rotten finale	OFFEND(ING)
role	HAMLET, LEAR, PART	rotten	BAD
role in T/he M/ousetrap	HEM	• man's rotten . . .	CARLSBAD
[role]-*playing*	LORE	• rotten food	BADDISH
roll		• rotten in time	BADINAGE
dog *rolling over*<	GOD	Rotten Row	RANK
rolled umbrella	BROLLY	rotten, *say*	VIAL
rolling-[pins]	NIPS, SNIP	*rotten* [tread]	RATED, TRADE
rolling ruler	PLUTOCRAT	rotting flesh, *say*	CARRY ON
rolling [stone]	NOTES, ONSET, SETON	*rotting* [meat]	MATE, TAME, TEAM
Rolling [Stones]	ONSETS, SETONS	**rotate**	
rollick		rotate flap	SPIN
[gave a] *rollicking* . . .	AGAVE	*rotate* [orb]	ROB
rollicking [song]	NOGS, SNOG	rotate lever<	REVEL
Roman		*rotating* [spit]	PITS, TIPS
Roman couple	II	*rotating* spit<	TIPS
• legislator *hemmed in by*		rotor arm	REVOLVER
Roman couple	IMPI	**rotund**	
Roman figures	EXCEL, VIVID, XL	rotund	O
Roman governor, *say*	PILOT	rotund character	O
Roman invasion	CAESAREAN OPERATION	[we rotund] *characters*	UNDERTOW
Roman peace, *say*	PACKS	**rough**	
Roman road	VIA	*rough and ready* [sort I] . . .	RIOTS, ROSTI
Romans	ROM	rough	COARSE
Romania	R	• rough appearance, *say*	CORSAIR
roof		• rough service, *say*	CORS(E)LET
church *roof*(D)	C	• rough times, *say*	CORSAGE
roof of house(D)	H	rough, *say*	COURSE, CREWED, RUFF
rook	R	rough-*sounding*	RUFF
room		rough-*spoken*	RUFF
room for improvement	WARD	*rough-spoken* male	MALE

Anag [cat]; Any *; Begin IGN–; Endings –ING; eg •; Hidden /cat/; Implied add (on); Implied in (in);

rough stuff	SACKCLOTH
rough [terrain]	RETRAIN, TRAINER
roughed up [a bit]	BAIT
roughened, *say*	BIRD, BURD
roughly	C, CA, CIRC, CIRCA
	(see about¹)
roughly speaking, eight	AIT, ATE, EYOT
roughly [ten]	ENT, NET
roughly treated [cats]	ACTS, SCAT
round¹	
round	CATCH
• learner *in* round . . .	CLATCH
• round coin	CATCHPENNY
• round rod	CATCHPOLE
round	LAP
• many round . . .	CLAP
• round on horseback	LAP UP
• round*about*<	PAL
	(see also roundabout)
round	O
• bread round	ROLLO
• girl *with* round . . .	MAYO
• round ball	–OO–
• whip-round	CATO
and	
• round America	–OUS
• round enclosure	OPEN
• round number	ONO, OTEN
• round tree	OPINE
• round-up	OUP
round *off*	omit O
round the ring	incl O
round²	
put *round*<	TUP
round a . . .	incl A
round a nut<	TUNA
round about	incl C, CA, RE
• particle *round* about . . .	ICON
• se–nt *round* about . . .	SECANT
• si–n *round* about . . .	SIREN
round *about*	RO–UND
• ro–und *about* the *start* . . .	ROTUND
round house<	–IMES, –OH
round mollusc	SLUG
round [table]	BLATE, BLEAT
round the bend	MAD
round the bend	incl U
round up ducks	incl OO
• doctor *rounded up* ducks	DOOR
round-up<	PU
• *round* up< father	PUPA
round-up of [cows]	SCOW
round up [lost] . . .	LOTS, SLOT
round up rats(D)^	STAR
round *	incl *
• wat–er *round* church	WATCHER

rounded peak<	PLA–
with * *round*	incl in *
• church with wat–er	
round	WATCHER
roundabout	
roundabout	OC, OCA, ORE
• kings *go round* round	
about . . .	ROCK
• learners *circling* roundabout	LOCAL
• quiet roundabout	PORE, SHORE
round*about*	RO–UND
• square roundabout	ROTUND
*round*about	incl C, CA, RE
• lan–e *round*about	LANCE
• Poles' *round*about	SCAN
• hi–s *round*about	HIRES
*round*about<	AC, ER
roundabout route	ORBIT
roundabout [route]	OUTER, OUTRE
rouse	
rouse prison	STIR
rouse [prison]	PRIONS
rout	
[army] *routed*	MARY, MYRA
rout [hordes]	RESHOD
rove	
rove [about]	U-BOAT
[went] *roving*	NEWT
row	
Rotten Row	RANK
row	ADO
row	OAR
• row a circuit	OARLAP
• row *in* ship	SOARS
• second-class row	BOAR
row	PULL
• circular row	RING-PULL
• row about . . .	PULLOVER
• row *with* alien	PULLET
row	RANK
• loud row	FRANK
• quiet row	SHRANK
• row in front	RANKLED
row	TIER
• mark row	DOTTIER
• row *about* note	TIGER
• row *with* journalist	TIERED
row *about*	LIN–E, RO–W, TI–ER
row of vehicles	CARLINE
row, *say*	ORE, SKULL
rower	BOW
• angry rower	CROSSBOW
• rower in front	BOWLED
• tall rower	LONGBOW
rower	STROKE
• rower dead	STROKED

• rowing expert	MASTER-STROKE	Highness	RH
• support rower	BACKSTROKE	Historical Society	RHS
rowing boat	EIGHT, FOUR	Horse	
rowing team, *say*	AIT, ATE, EYOT	–Artillery	RHA
	FORE	–Guards	RHG
		Horticultural Society	RHS
royal¹		Humane Society	RHS
royal	R	Institute	RI
• royal assent	RAY	–of Chemistry	RIC
• royal bird	REGRET	Institution of Painters	RI
• royal worker	RANT	Irish	
royal badge/insignia	ER	–Academy	RIA
royal chairperson	REGIUS PROFESSOR	–Constabulary	RIC
royal fashion	PRINCETON	Mail	RM
royal governess	ANNA	–Steamer	RMS
royal horse artist	KING COBRA	Marines	RM
royal needlewoman	CLEOPATRA	Microscopical Society	RMS
royal neighbour	BISHOP	Military	
royal supporter	LION, UNICORN	–Academy	RMA
royal town	CAMELOT	–Police	RMP
royal yacht	BRITANNIA	Naval Reserve	RNR
	COURTSHIP, KINGSHIP	Navy	RN
royalty	ER	Observer Corps	ROC
	(*see also* king²)	Order of Victoria and Albert	VA
		Philharmonic Orchestra	RPO
royal²		Photographic Society	RPS
Academician/Academy	RA	Radar Establishment	RRE
Academy of Music	RAM	School of Music	RSM
Air Force	RAF	Scottish	
Artillery	RA	–Academician/Academy	RSA
Australian Navy	RAN	–Water Colour Society	RSW
Automobile Club	RAC	Society of	
Arch Charter	RAC	–Antiquaries	RSA
Armoured Corps	RAC	–Arts	
Asiatic Society	RAS	–British Artists	RBA
Astronomical Society	RAS	–British Sculptors	RBS
Canadian Academy	RCA	–Edinburgh	RSE
College of		–Etchers and Engravers	RE
–Art	RC, RCA	–Literature	RSL
–Music	RCM	–Medicine	RSM
–Organists	RCO	–Painters in Water Colours	RWS
–Physicians	RCP	–Portrait Painters	RP
–Preceptors	RCP	Statistical Society	RSS
–Science	RCS	Ulster Constabulary	RUC
–Sculptors	RCS	Yacht Squadron	RYS
Corps of		Yachting Association	RYA
–Signals	RCS	Zoological Society	RZS
–Transport	RCT	**r-rower**	ROAR
Dublin Society	RDS	**rub**	
Engineers	RE	rub *up the wrong way*(D)^	BUR
Exchange	RE	rubber	TOWEL, ULE
Flying Corps	RFC	rubber bands	TYRES
Geographical Society	RGS	rubber pipe, *say*	HOES
Grenadier Guards	RGG	**rubbish**	
Hibernian Academy	RHA	rubbish devoured	ROTATE
Highland		*rubbish* [in hedge]	HEEDING
–Fusiliers	RHF		
–Show	RHS		

rubbished [his] . . .	–ISH	run *off*	omit R
rubbishy [sort]	ORTS, ROTS, TORS	run out	RO
rude		run *out (of)*	omit R
rude *noise*	ROOD	run *over*(D)	start with R
rude [Roman]	MANOR, NORMA	• run *over* a pretty girl	RADISH
rude song, *say*	CORSAIR	run round	RO
rudely [shaped]	PHASED	run rings . . .	ROO
rudimentary	ABCEDARIAN	run *short*	omit R
ruffle		runs *round*	R–R
ruffled [lake]	KALE, LEAK	**run²**	
ruffling [calm I] . . .	MALIC	run	RUN
rugby		run *about*	RU–N
Rugby	RU	[run] *away*	NUR, URN
• rugby building	RUSHED	[run]-off	NUR, URN
• rugby craze	RUMANIA	[run] *out*	NUR, URN
• rugby forward	RUPERT	run *over*<	NUR
• rugby match	RUB-OUT	run *round*	RU–N
Rugby bully	FLASHMAN	run *round*<	NUR
Rugby Football Club	RFC	run *the wrong way*<	NUR
rugby player	LION	run-*up*(D)^	NUR
rugby player, *say*	HOOKA(H)	run*about*	RU–N
ruin		run*about*<	NUR
[ancestral] *ruins*	LANCASTER	[run]*about*	NUR, URN
mother's ruin	GIN	**run³**	
[mother's] *ruin*	SMOTHER, THERMOS	run	BYE
ruin [meal]	LAME, MALE	• two runs	BYE-BYE
ruin, *say*	RECK	run	DESERT
ruination of [much] . . .	CHUM	• second *in* run	DESSERT
ruined girl, *say*	RECTOR	• run away twice	DESERT RAT
ruined [life]	FILE, LIEF	run	EXTRA
ruins drink	SPOILSPORT	• run over	EXTRA
ruins of [Troy]	TORY	run	FLEE
ruins, *say*	RECKS, REX	• run from anarchist	FLEERED
rule		• run from teacher, *say*	FLEECER
rule	LAW	• run, *say*	FLEA
• fine rule	FLAW	run	LEGIT
• king's rule	COLESLAW	• run *with* one friend	LEGITIMATE
• rule ceremony, *say*	LAURITE	run	MANAGE
[rule] *out*	LURE	• run, *say*	MANEGE
rule, *say*	RAIN, REIN	• run soldiers exactly . . .	MANAGEMENT
ruler	ER	run	RAT
ruler	KING	• quiet run	PRAT
• ruler is quite with it	KINGSHIP	• run *during* exercise	PRATE
• ruler manufacturer	KINGMAKER	• run away twice	DESERT RAT
• ruler of the oceans, *say*	SEEKING	run	SINGLE
rum		• knight *takes* a run, *say*	SURCINGLE
rum[baba]	ABBA	• run *with* shirt	SINGLET
rum [affair]	RAFFIA	• run *with* weight	SINGLETON
rum chaps	ODDFELLOWS	run	TROT
rum child	ODDS-ON	• animal runs	FOXTROTS
run¹		• run *about*	TRO–T
run	R	• run *about*<	TORT
• run over	ROVER	• run *back*<	TORT
• run round	RO	**run⁴**	
run *away*	omit R	[done a] *runner*	ANODE
run *into*	incl R	run	CRESTA, LADDER

Letter replaced \c\at; Omit (a); Pointers *out*; Retain a̲; Split B_ED; Down (D); Backwards <or ^

run amok [in the] . . .	THINE	• g–ut ruptured by duck	GOUT
run-of-the-mill	RACE	rupturing *	incl in *
run in front	ANTELOPE	• duck rupturing g–ut	GOUT
run rings round	O–O	**rural**	
run riot [in the] . . .	THINE	rural automatic exchange	RAX
run straight	DIRECT	Rural Dean	RD
run twice	DOUBLE	Rural District Council	RDC
* run into	incl *	rural sub-office	RSO
• everyone runs into		**rush**	
good fortune	BALLOON	rush around	FLA–G, RE–ED
run[about]	U-BOAT	rush forward	SURGEON
runabout [can go] . . .	CONGA	rush job	BASKETRY, THATCHING
runaway	DISH, SPOON	rush up(D)^	DEER
runaway [trains]	STRAIN	rushing [stream]	MASTER, REMAST
runner	BEAN	**Russia**	SU, USSR
• runners speak	BEANSTALK	**Russian**	
runner	COE	Russian	BEAR
• runner takes in five . . .	COVE	• Russian dead, say	BEARDED
runner	EMU	Russian	IVAN
• strong runner-up(D)^	FUME	• dead Russian	DIVAN
runner	MANAGER	• many Russian . . .	DIVAN
• home runner	HOUSE MANAGER	• Russian weedkiller	IVANHOE
runner	RILL, RIVER, STREAM	Russian	RED
	(see river)	• Russian food	REDDISH
runner	SKI	• Russian grabbed by commander	CREDO
• runner has quiet . . .	SKIP	• Russian's family	REDSKIN
runner	SMUGGLER	Russian	RUSS
runner, say	STOLEN	• Russian alien	RUSSET
runner unsuited	STREAKER	Russian	SERGE
runner-up	B	• Russian cloth	SERGE
runner-up in race	A	• Russian soldier	SERGEANT
runners neverending . . .	RACEME(n)	Russian capital	ROUBLE
running	ADMIN, DIRECTION	Russian capital	R
running	(in) HAS–TE	Russian flower	VOLGA etc
running amok, [IRA men] . . .	MARINE	Russian leader	R
running out of stock	STAMPEDE	Russian measure, say	VERSED
running [race]	ACER, ACRE, CARE	**rust**	
running [shoes]	HOSES	rust colour	RUSTRED
running total	CRICKET SCORE	rust on weapon, say	PIE-CRUST
running water	EA	rusty [blade]	BALED
running wild in [Penarth]	PANTHER	[sword] rusts	WORDS
runny [nose]	NOES, ONES	**rustic**	
runway	TRIPLANE	rustic	HIND, HOB
	(see also ran)	• rustic accommodation	HINDQUARTERS
runt	ANTHONY, TANTONY	• rustic skill	HOBART
rupee	R	**rustling**	STOCKTAKING, TAKING STOCK
rupture		**rut**	LANDMARK
rupture [vein]	VINE	**rutherford**	RD
ruptured by a . . .	incl0 A	**Rwanda**	RWA
ruptured by *	incl *		

S

as, Bach's works, *bend*, *bob*, bridge player, dollar, entropy, es, ess, God's, has, his, *hiss*, is, *largesse*, *Old Bob*, paragon, *part of collar*, Sabbath, saint, Saturday, schilling, Schmieder, second, segno, seven, seventy (thousand), several, shilling, ship, side, siemens, sigma, singular, *sinistra*, *sister*, *snow*, society, soh, son, soprano, south, southern, spade, special, square, stokes, strangeness, succeeded, sulphur, sun, Sweden, two hundred (thousand), us

Sabbath	S
sabotage	
sabotage [plane]	PANEL
[secret] *sabotage*	RESECT
sack	
sack	FIRE
• girl sacked, *say*	MISFIRED
• sack race	FIREFLY
• sacked a representative	FIREDAMP
sack journalist	OUSTED
sack race	GOTHS, JUTES, VANDALS
sacrifice	
[lamb] *sacrificed*	BALM
sacrificed [all the] . . .	LETHAL
sad	
sad	BLUE
• sad fish, *say*	BLUE-EYED
• sad time	BLUEBIRD
• sailors *have* sad . . .	NAVY BLUE
sad	DOWN
• bird *with* sad . . .	EIDERDOWN
• lives *in* sad . . .	DISOWN
• sad team	DOWNSIDE
sad *end*	D
sad [end]	DEN, NED
sad outlook, *say*	SORICENE
sadden worker	DEPRESSANT
sadly [spoke]	POKES
safe	
safe	PETER
• safe-blower	PETER PIPER
• safe *to* criticise	PETER PAN
• sailor *has* safe, *say*	SALTPETRE
safe conduct	EARTH
safe passage	SOUND
safety catch	SHOOTING BRAKE
safety *first*	F
safety wire	EARTH
°**said**	
said he intended, *say*	SEDIMENT
said, *perhaps*	TOLLED
(*see also* say)	
sail	
sail again, *say*	RESALE
sail, *say*	SALE
sailed	SLD
sailing	(in) S–HIP
• sailors *sailing*	STARSHIP
sailing	(in) S–S
• sailor *sailing*	STARS
sailing	(on) SHIP
• master *sailing*	HEADSHIP
sailing	(on) SS
• scholar *sailing*	MASS
sailing [along]	LOGAN
sailor	
sailor	AB
• 100 sailors	CABS
• ordinary sailor	ABNORMAL
• sailor employs . . .	ABUSES
• sailors in the . . .	ABSINTHE
sailor	HAND
• sailor *has* a few . . .	HANDSOME
• sailor's drink	HAND-SALE
• support sailor	BACKHAND
sailor	HEARTY
sailor	JACK
• sailor *on* vessel	JACKPOT
• sailor's greeting	HIJACK
• sailors working	JACKSON
sailor	MATELOT, MATLO(W)
sailor	OS
• Henry the sailor	HALOS
• sailor *has* a bird	OSTEAL
• sailor is able . . .	OSCAN
sailor	SALT
• city sailors	BATH SALTS
• sailor, English Navy	SALTERN

Letter replaced \c\at; Omit (a); Pointers *out*; Retain <u>a</u>; Split B_ED; Down (D); Backwards <or ^

• unwashed sailors	SMELLING SALTS	• salesman *with* fish	REPROACH
sailor	TAR	**sally**	
• black sailor	COALTAR	Sally is efficient	SALABLE
• sailor Brown	TARTAN	Sally's introduction	MESAL(LY)
• sailors	TARTAR	**saloon**	
• sailor's *double*	TARTAR	saloon body	CARCASE
• sailors on their knees	TARSPRAYING	saloon brawl	BARROW
• sailor's *return<*	RAT	saloon keeper	GARAGE
sailor-boy	ABED, JACKSON, SALTED	**salt**	
sailor-boy, *say*	SALTPETRE, SEASON	salt	AB
sailor *has* much . . .	MATELOT	• salt only . . .	ABALONE
sailor-king	MARINER	• salt fish	ABIDE, ABROACH
sailors	CREW	• salt-mark	ABSTAIN
• sailors notice, *say*	CRUCITE	• salt on road	ABROAD
• sailors *take* girl, *say*	CRUCIBLE	• salt solution	ABSOLUTION
sailors	NUS	salt box	SEA-CHEST
sailors	RN	salt container	OCEAN, SEA
• officer *with* sailors	CORN		SHIP
• you and I, *say*, *in* sailors' . . .	RUIN	salt *in it*	incl AB, TAR
sailor's daughter	POP-EYED	• M–el *puts* salt *in* . . .	MABEL
sailor's hat	BOATER	• saint *takes* salt *in* . . .	START
sailor's turn	ABOUT FACE	*(see also* sailor, tar)	
(see also salt, tar)		**Salvation Army**	SA
saint		**same**	
saint	S	same	DO
• one saint	IS–	• same entrance	DOGATE
• saint is ill	SAILING	• same little vessel	DOMINICAN
• saint will . . .	SWILL	• same money	DOCENT, DOYEN
• saints, *without* hesitation, . . .	SUMS	same	ID, IDEM
saint	ST	• dress the same	RIGID
• 51 saints	LISTS	• same fish	IDLING
• one saint	–IST	• same island	IDIOM
• saint getting old	STAGED, STAGING	same place	IB
• saint *takes in* city . . .	SECT	**sample**	
saint	PETER	qui/te a l/arge *sample*	TEAL
• concerning a saint, *say*	REPEATER	*sample of* chee/se w/ith . . .	SEW
• saint *has* false . . .	PETERSHAM	**sanctimonious**	
• saint *takes in* another	PESTER	sanctimonious	PI
saintly	NOVICES	• approve a sanctimonious . . .	OKAPI
saints	SS, STS	• sanctimonious people	PILOT
salacious mariner	SALT	• saint *without* sanctimonious . . .	SPIT
salad		**sandalwood**	SHOE TREE
[green] *salad*	GENRE, NEGRE	**Sandhurst**	RMA
salad of [greens and] . . .	ENDANGERS	**sandwich**	
salary		meat *sandwich*	(in) MEA–T
salary	SCREW	• directions *found in* meat	
• international salary	UNSCREW	sandwich	MEANEST
• salary limit	SCREW TOP	*sandwiched in* *	incl in *
sale		• small piece	
sale in May, *say*	MACE–ALE	*sandwiched in* p–ly	PORTLY
sale of		sandwiched, *say*	INBRED
–partitioning, *say*	STUDDINGSAIL	**sane**	NOMAD
–wives	DUTCH AUCTION	**sap**	
salesman	REP	sap	TRENCH
• salesman *and* consumer	REPEATER	sap, *say*	DEUCE
• salesman *in* church	CREPE	sapling, *say*	TREASON

Anag [cat]; Any *; Begin IGN–; Endings –ING; eg •; Hidden /cat/; Implied add (on); Implied in (in);

sapper	RE
sat	
sat *out*	SA–T
[sat] *out*	AST, ATS
Satan	(*see* devil)
satisfy	
satisfied constituents	CONTENT
satisfying encounter	MEETING
Saturday	S, SAT
sauce	
sauce	CHEEK, LIP
sauce [is hot]	HOIST
saucer	PLATELET
saucier, *say*	BOULDER
saucy novel	FRESH
sauna for vagrants	TRAMP STEAMER
sausage	
contents of sa/usage/s	USAGE
sausage crate	BANGER
sausage *skin*	SE
savage	
[leader] *savaged*	DEALER, REDEAL
savage [beast]	BASTE, BEATS
savaged [lambs]	BALMS
save	
save	BUT
• save money	BUTT IN
• save *up*(D)^	TUB
save a . . .	omit A
save a Conservative, *say*	CONSERVATORY
save chopper, *say*	STORAX
save more	USELESS
save, say	CASH, HORDE, WHORED
save time	omit T
save *	omit *
• (k)night *saves* king	NIGHT
saving Grace	DARLING
saving weight	BUTTON
saw	
saw gun	MAXIM
saw Herb, *say*	SAUSAGE
saw joint, *say*	SAWNEY
saw off end of timber	BOAR(d), PLAN(k)
sawn-off gu(n)	GU
	(*see also* see)
say¹	
say	EG
• say nothing	EGO
• square, say	TEG
• student, say	LEG
say	SPEAK
say	SAY
• say *about* the wife	SWAY
• says nothing	SAY-SO
and	
• say "Fish", *say*	SAILING
• say "Light", *say*	SALITE
• say "Row", *say*	SALINE
• say "shells", *say*	SEYCHELLES
say	UTTER
• many say	CUTTER, MUTTER
• say in paper	MUTTERS
• say more than the others	UTTERMOST
say²	
indicating an anagram:	
• [Germans] *say*	MANGERS
• *say* "[Quiet!]"	QUITE
• [some] *say*	MOES
indicating homophone:	
• nose, *say*	KNOWS
• *said to be* you	EWE, YEW
• *said we ten* . . .	WHEATEN
• *say* no	KNOW
• *say* Sir	NIGHT
• *saying* aloud	ALLOWED
• *some say*	SUM
indicating one of a class:	
• cat, *say*	PERSIAN
• Persian, *say*	CAT
say³	
said *in French*	DIT
say French . . .	DIT
say "No rubbish!"	REFUSE
say quickly	EXPRESS
says the prophet, *say*	SESELI
	(*see also* said)
scale railway	LIBRARY
scalene triangle	ALONGSIDE
scalp	
scalp	omit 1st letter
• *scalp* actor	(p)LAYER
• *scalp* (d)rummer	RUMMER
scan	
scan	PORE
• scan opening	PORE
• second scan	SPORE
• silver *found in* scan	PORAGE
scan, *say*	POOR, POUR
Scandinavian vegetable	SWEDE
scare	
scare	SHOO
• scare model	SHOOT
scare, *say*	SHOE
• scare boy off	SHOE-BOY
Scarface	AL
Scarlatti's works	K
scatter	
scatter bedding	LITTER
scatter children	LITTER
scatter[brain]	BAIRN, BRIAN
scattered [remains]	MARINES, SEMINAR
scattered around [seaport]	ESPARTO

Letter replaced \c\at; Omit (a); Pointers *out*; Retain a̲; Split B_ED; Down (D); Backwards <or ^

scatty	
scatty [boss]	SOBS
[she is] *scatty*	SHIES
scene	
scene of action	ONSET
scene, *say*	CITE, SIGHT
scenes	ACT
scholar	
scholar	BA
• scholar *and* Marine	BARM
• scholars in charge	BASIC
• scholar's quickly . . .	BASSOON
scholar	MA
• scholar in court	MAIN-YARD
• scholars deceive	MASCON
• tidier *after* scholar . . .	MAN-EATER
(*see also* graduate)	
school¹	
school	ETON
• British school	BRETON
• master in charge	
around school	METONIC
• school *returns<*	NOTE
school, *say*	EATEN
school	GAM
• school book	GAMB
• school *has* scholar	GAMBA, GAMMA
• school, see	GAMELY
school	SCH
• nothing *in* British school	BORSCH
• school in America	SCHINUS
• school not in	SCHOUT
school, *say*	INFORM
• Communist school	COMINFORM
• school friend	INFORMALLY
• schoolgirl, *say*	MISINFORM
school²	
school [bus]	SUB–
school [horses]	SHORES
school member	FISH, PORPOISE, WHALE
School Mathematics Project	SMP
school procession	TRAIN
school stage	COACH
school subject	DISCIPLINE
school teachers	NUT
school transport	COACH, TRAIN
schoolboy overdue, *say*	PUPILATE
Schubert's works	D
sciatic	HIPPY
science	
science	–OLOGY
science centre	LAB
science *centre*	E
science fiction	SCIFI, SF
science institution	RS
Science Research Council	SRC

scientist	FRS
scoff	
scoff	BOO
• box *enclosing* scoff	CABOOSE
• reserves scoff	TABOO
• scoff *at* monarch	BOOK(ING), BOOR
scoff	WOLF
• scoff *at* monarch	WOLFER
scoffed	–ATE
scoffed, *say*	AIT, EIGHT, EYOT
scorch	
scorch	SEAR
• scorch, *say*	CERE
• scorch them, *say*	SERUM
• scorched earth policy	SEA-ROVER
scorched earth	BURNT SIENNA
	BURNT UMBER
scorched [earth]	HATER, HEART, RATHE
score	
score	TWENTY, XX
score a goal	NETBALL
score adjuster	ARRANGER
score less than 100	EIGHTY
score *quickly*	ALLEGRO, PRESTO
score *slowly*	LENTO
score twice	FORTY
scoreless draw	O–O
scorer	COMPOSER
Scot/Scotsman	
scot	TAX
• a Scot *returns* first-class< . . .	ATAXIA
• Scot lives . . .	TAXIS
• Scotsman	TAXMAN
scot, *say*	TACKS
Scotsman	IAN
• equal with Scot	PARIAN
• Flying Scot	SWIFTIAN
• well-mannered Scot	CIVILIAN
Scotsman	JOCK
• Scot *has cut* ey(e)	JOCKEY
• Scotsman *has* a ring	JOCKO
• Scotsman's gin	JOCKSTRAP
Scotsman	MAC
• Scot in front	MACLED
• Scotsman *with a* heretic	MACARIAN
• Scottish sailor	TARMAC
Scotsman	MON
• Scotsman looked . . .	MONEYED
• Scotsman that is dead	MONIED
• Scotsman's battle	MONS
Scotsman	SANDY
Scottish	
Scottish border	SCOTIA
Scottish capital	S
Scottish chieftain	CLANKING
Scottish *flower*	TAY etc

Anag [cat]; Any *; Begin IGN–; Endings –ING; eg •; Hidden /cat/; Implied add (on); Implied in (in);

Scottish *leader*	S	scruple	SC
	(see also Caledonian)	scuffle	
scoundrel		*scuffle* [in the] . . .	THINE
scoundrel, *say*	NAVE	*scuffling* [over] . . .	ROVE
scoundrel's honour	KNAVE	**sculpture**	
scrag		*sculpted* [torso]	ROOTS, STOOR
scrag-*end*	G	sculpture class	FORM
scraggy [lamb]	BALM	sculptured	SC, SCULP(SIT)
scramble		*sculptured* [bust]	BUTS, STUB
[much] *scrambling*	CHUM	**scuttle**	
scrambled [eggs]	SEGG	*scuttled* [ship]	HIPS, PISH
scrambling [nets]	STEN, TENS	*scuttling* [along]	LOGAN, LONGA
scrap		**sea¹**	
scrap dismissed . . .	RAGOUT	sea	SEA
scrap [iron]	ROIN	• sea fish	SEALING
scrap merchant	BOXER, PUGILIST	• sea king	SEAR
scrap [paper as] . . .	APPEARS	[sea]-*change*	ASE
scrap vessel	JUNK	sea, *say*	SEE
scrappy [tale]	LATE, LEAT, TEAL	• sea king, *say*	SEEK(ING), SEER
scratch		• seas, *say*	SEES, SEIZE
scratch	PAR	[sea]-*trip*	ASE
• scratch golfer	PARTAKER	*seafront*	S
scratch *head*	S	[sea]*sick*	ASE
scratch head	omit 1st letter	seaside	S, A
• parent *scratched* head	(m)OTHER	*storm at* [sea]	ASE
• (s)on *scratches* head	ON	**sea²**	
scratch, *say*	GREYS	sea	DEEP
scratch starter	ITCH	• sea-bed	DEEP LITTER
scratch *starter*	S	• sea directions	DEEPENS
scratch starter	omit 1st letter	• sea-ice	DEEP FREEZE
scratched record	PALIMPSEST	sea	DRINK
scrawl		• ready for sea	DRINK-MONEY
scrawling [line]	LIEN, NILE	• sea-room	DRINK-HALL
[weird] *scrawl*	WIDER, WIRED	• sea-king	DRINKER
screecher	SWIFT	sea	MAIN
screen		• shirt *in* sea	MATIN
screen guide	CURSOR	• the same sea	DOMAIN
[screen] *production*	CENSER	• the sea remains . . .	MAINSTAYS
top of screen(D)^	S	sea	MED
screw steamer	SS	• sea, I see	MEDIC
scribble		• sea *touching* America	MEDUSA
scribble [note]	ETON, TONE	• seaman	MEDAL
scribbled [verse]	SERVE	and	
scribbling [in the] . . .	THINE	• sea-fish, *say*	MEDDLING
scrimmage		sea	MER
[I made] *scrimmage*	AIMED	• sea-lines	MERRY
scrimmage [near the] . . .	EARTHEN	• sea-song	MERCHANT
scripture		• the sea I hold back	MERISTEM
Scripture Union	SU	**sea³**	
scriptures	NT, OT	*at sea* [all the] . . .	LETHAL
scruffy		sea, *say*	C
[quite] *scruffy*	QUIET, –TIQUE		DIOCESE, ELY
scruffy [nurse]	RUNES	sea-air	SHANTY
scrum		sea-bird	WREN
scrum in [field]	FILED	sea-bird, *say*	PUFFING
scrummage [for the] . . .	FOTHER	sea-dog	OCEAN GREYHOUND

Letter replaced \c\at; Omit (a); Pointers *out*; Retain a̲; Split B_ED; Down (D); Backwards <or ^

sea-green	WATER COLOUR
sea power	MAIN
sea room	CABIN
Seabee	CB
seafood	BISCUIT, HARD TACK
seafront	BOW, PROM(ENADE)
seaman	(*see* sailor)
seamen	NUS
seaport	SPT
seas	CC, CS
seaside	LARBOARD, LEE, PORT
	STARBOARD, WINDWARD
seaside branch	DRIFTWOOD
seaweed, *say*	RACK
seal	
sealed in [amber]	BREAM
sealed in am/berg/ris	BERG
sealed in *	incl in *
• god *sealed in* bo–x	BORAX
seam	
seam, *say*	SEEM
	VAIN, VANE
seamstress	(*see* sempstress)
search	
search	COMB
• search one country	COMBINATION
• search round	COMBO
season	
season	FALL
season	SALT
• graduate season	BASALT
• horse *in* season	SHALT
• we *follow* the season	SALTUS
season	SPRING
• season food	SPRINGBOARD
• season well	SPRING
• well season	WELLSPRING
seasoned	
–banger	PEPPERONI
–worker, *say*	MATURANT
seat	
seat material	CARLISLE, SATIN
seat of Empire	OTTOMAN
secant	SEC
second¹	
second	B
• name a second	NAB
• second eleven	BIX
• second line	BRANK, BROW
second	BACK
• pull second ...	DRAWBACK
• second drink	BACKDROP
• second team	BACKSIDE
second	MO
• second lake	MOLOCH
• second little dog	MOP UP
• second man	MORON, MOTED
second	S
• Second Avenue	SMALL
• second best	SCREAM, STOP
• second class	SILK
• second edition	SPRINT
• second eleven	STEAM
• second gear	SKIT
• second hand	SL, SR
	STAR
• second organ	SLIVER
• second row	STIFF
• second ship	SKETCH
• seconds *out*	omit SS
and	
• three seconds	MOSS
second	SEC
• equal second	PARSEC
• second beer	SECALE
• *broken* [into] *after*	
second ...	SECTION
second²	
Charles *II*	H
second b*e*st	B
second bit of c*l*oth	L
second character in p*l*ay	L
second c*l*ass	L
second dose of m*e*dicine	E
second e*l*even	L
second h*a*lf	A
second half of ga*me*	ME
second-h*a*nd	A
second-in-c*o*mmand	O
second of A*u*gust	U
second o*p*inion	P
second part of p*l*ay	L
second piece of c*a*ke	A
second q*u*ality	U
second r*a*te	A
Second T*e*st	E
second w*i*nd	I
second³	
second best	B
second character	B, EVE
second child	ABEL
second class	B
• copper *has* second-class ...	CUB
• second-class highway	BROAD
• second-class marriage	BUNION
and	
• second-class playground	
equipment, *say*	BEESWING
• second-class team, *say*	BESIDE
second-hand	PREPOSSESSED, USED
second-hand *addition*	PAWPAW
second-hand item	CLOCK, WATCH

Anag [cat]; Any *; Begin IGN–; Endings –ING; eg •; Hidden /cat/; Implied add (on); Implied in (in);

second helping	DOUBLE TAKE	secure	SAFE
second in importance	MOMENT	• secure street	SAFEST
second mover	BLACK	• trustee *in* secure . . .	STRAFE
second person	EVE, YOU	secure locker	CHASTITY BELT
second quality	B	secure post	CHAIN MAIL
second-rate	B	secured by *	incl in *
Second Test	RESIT, RETRIAL	• organ *secured by* sh–ed	SHEARED
second thoughts	PS	*secured in* stron/g room/s	GROOM
second wedding	REMATCH	secures objective	LANDS END
secondary		*securing* a . . .	incl A
secondary	B	*securing* *	incl *
• company *has* secondary . . .	COB	• sh–ed *securing* an organ	SHEARED
• secondary road	BROAD	**see**	
• secondary school	BETON	see	C
secret		• see about	CC, CRE
secret agent	MOLE	• see girl	CLASS
• secret agent defects	MOLE-RATS	• see one	CONE
• secret agent *surrounds* artist	MORALE	• see one rear . . .	CISTERN
• secret agent's family	MOLESKIN	and	
secret drinkers	AA	• see *into* far–e	FARCE
Secret Intelligence Service	SIS	• see why, *say*	CY
secret service	CIA	• see you, *say*	COPPER, CU
secret service *leaders*	SS	sec	DIOCESE
secretary		see	ELY
secretaries	CIS	• king *takes* see	RELY
secretary	SECY	• see *about* a king	EARLY
secretary	TEMP	• see water-parsnip	ELYSIUM
• secretary *to* the queen	TEMPER	see	EYE
• secretary overdue	TEMPLATE	• animal sees . . .	OX-EYES
• secretary's hair-do	TEMPTRESSES	• see ship	EYE-LINER
secrete		• see small coin	EYED
secrete	HIDE	and	
• Green secretes . . .	RAWHIDES	• sees Hell	EYE-SHADES
• secrete, *say*	HIED	• sees mineral	EYESORE
• secrete spring	HIDEBOUND	• sees retinue	EYE-STRAIN
secreting a . . .	incl A	see	LA
secreting *	incl *	• see *into* last . . .	ELAND
• ma–n *secreting* one . . .	MAIN	• see representative	LAMP
secreted by *	incl in *	• see the doctor	LAMB
• one *secreted by* ma–n	MAIN	and	
section		• see about	LAC
[inter]*section*	NITRE, TRINE	• see *about*<	AL
section of the . . .	T, H, E	see	LO
section of th/e lates/t	ELATES	• see female laugh	LOHENGRIN
secure		• see fruit	LOP-EAR
secure	BAG	• see fur	LOSABLE
• secure duct	BAGPIPE	• see nothing	LOO
• secure fruit	BAGGAGE	and	
• worker secures . . .	HANDBAGS	• see about	LOC–
secure	LOCK	• see *about*<	OL
• fine *and* secure . . .	FLOCK	see	LOOK
• gas *surrounds* secure . . .	CLOCKS	• father, see as . . .	PALOOKAS
• secures mine	LOCKSPIT	• see child	LOOKS ON
secure	NAIL	• see the queen	LOOKER
• second secure . . .	SNAIL	and	
• secure dossier	NAIL-FILE	• see twice	LOOKSEE

Letter replaced \c\at; Omit (a); Pointers *out*; Retain a̲; Split B_ED; Down (D); Backwards <or ^

see	NOTICE	*seen in* [China]	CHAIN
see	SEE	*seen in* French town	VILLE
• the *French* see . . .	LESSEE	*seen in* German book	BUCH
• see many . . .	SEEM	*seen in* Italian hotel	ALBERGO
• see quiet . . .	SEEP	*seen in* Phi/lad/elphia	LAD
and		*seen in* Roman road	VIA
• see *about*	SE–E	*seen in* Spanish house	CASA
• [see] *differently*	–ESE	*seen in* *	incl in *
and		• German *seen in* ship	SHUNS
• see friends, *say*	SEPALS	*seen primarily* in very young	IVY
• see gentleman, *say*	SET-OFF	*seen talking*	CITED, SCENE, SITED
• see girl, *say*	SENORA	(*see also* see, saw)	
and		**seer**	
• see animal, *say*	SEA-DOG	seer	EYE, OPTIC
• see fish, *say*	SEALING	seer, *say*	AUGER, PROFIT
• see ring, *say*	SEATING		CERE, SEAR
and		**seize**	
• see fish, *say*	CEILING	seize claw	POUNCE
• see insect, *say*	CETIC	seize eggs	CLUTCH
and		seize her, *say*	CAESAR
• see Nicholas, *say*	SCENIC	seize journalist	GRIPED
and		seize one, *say*	CHOLERA
• see twice	LOOKSEE	seize, *say*	SEAS, SEES
see	SIGHT	seize space	GRABEN
• see *about* money	SLIGHT	*seized by* *	incl in *
• see *after* animal	HINDSIGHT	• king *seized by* b–east	BREAST
• see prophet	SIGHTSEER	seizer, *say*	CAESAR
see	SPOT	seizing a . . .	incl A
• see *about* one good . . .	SPIGOT	*seizing* *	incl *
• see fewer . . .	SPOTLESS	• b–east *seizing* king	BREAST
• warm sea, *say*	HOTSPOT	**select**	
see	SPY	select	PICK
• English see . . .	ESPY	• select a defender	PICKABACK
• see knight, *say*	SPICER	• select chopper	PICKAXE
• see state, *say*	SPICAL	• select fish	PICKLING
and		and	
• saw her, *say*	SPIDER	• select a bag, *say*	PICCADILLY
see	V	• select ceremony, *say*	PICRITE
• see flowers	VLEI	• select speed, *say*	PICRATE
• see no married . . .	VOWED	select group	IMPANEL
• see one vehicle	VICAR	selected	INSIDE
see	VID, VIDE	*selected from* t/he be/st . . .	HEBE
• see last one	VIDENDA	*selection from* gran/d ope/ra	DOPE
• see nothing	VIDEO	*selection* [panel]	PLANE
see below	ASUNDER	Selective Employment Tax	SET
(*see also* saw)		selector	ERNIE
seedy		**self**	
[seem] *seedy*	MESE	self-assured, *say*	CONFIDANT(E)
seedy, *say*	CD	self-banking aircraft	AUTOGIRO
seem		se**l**f-*centred*	EL
seems like new . . .	GNU, KNEW	self-confessed	AM, IAM, IM
seems right	RITE, WRITE	• *self-confessed* essayist	AMELIA
seems to be fur	FIR	• *self-confessed* fool	AMASS
seen		• *self-confessed* Scotsman	AMMON
[seen] *around*	–ENSE, –NESE	and	
seen close at hand, *say*	NICENE	• *self-confessed* adult	IMMATURE

• self-confessed beauty	IMPEACH	sent, *say*	NOSE, SCENT
• *self-confessed* pretender	IMPOSER		TRAIL
	(*see also* admit)		(*see also* send)
self-contained	SC	**separate**	
self-description	AM, IAM, IM	separate quickly	BREAKFAST
self help	DIY	*separate parts of* h<u>ouse</u>	HUE
<u>s</u>elf-*starter*	S	*separate parts of* [Spain]	PAINS
sell		separate way	SEVERE
sell cosh, *say*	CELL-SAP	*separated by* a . . .	incl A
sell	VEND	*separated by* *	incl *
• sell fish, *say*	VENDACE	• Poles *separated by* father	SPAN
• sell one . . .	VENDACE	*separating* *	incl in *
• sell *without* note	VENTED	• father *separating* Poles	SPAN
sell hawk	RETAIL	**September**	SEP(T)
sell-off, *say*	SAIL	**sequence**	
sell, *say*	PEDAL	*sequence from* Bib/le st/ories	LEST
seller's option	SO	*sequence in* music/al so/lo	ALSO
semester	TERMINUS	*sequence of* head/s or t/ails	SORT
seminary	SEM	**sergeant**	
semi-		*drill* [sergeant]	ESTRANGE
semi-molten	MOL, TEN	sergeant	NCO, SERG(T), SGT
[semi]-*molten*	–IMES	sergeant-at-law	SL
semi-tone	TO, NE	sergeant-major	SM
semitone	FLAT, SHARP	[sergeant's] *mess*	ESTRANGES, GREATNESS
sempstress		**series**	
sempstress	MIMI	serially, *say*	INTERN(E)
• sempstress *has* a hundred . . .	MIMIC	series	SER
• sempstress *has* to weep	MIMICRY	series, *say*	SWEET
senator	SEN	**serious matter**	GRAVEDO
send		**sermon**	SER
send car	TRANSPORT	**serve**	
[send] *letters*	DENS, ENDS	serve	
send notes to . . .	SERENADE	• former pupil serves	OBSERVES
[send] *off*	DENS, ENDS	and	
[send] *out*	DENS, ENDS	• serve many, *say*	CERVELAT
send to bed	SCUTTLE, SINK	• serve one state, *say*	CERVICAL
	(*see also* sent)	serve sentence	BEHELD
Senegal	SN	serve singer	WAIT
senior		*served up* in . . . (D)^	NI
senior	SENR, SR	*served up* [stew]	WEST, WETS
senior common room	SCR	*served up* stew(D)^	WETS
Senior Deacon	SD	**service**	
Senior Medical Officer	SMO	service	ACE
sense		• document *about* service	MACES
sense	NOUS	• service *to* king	ACER
sense of worry, *say*	GILT	• strong service	FACE
sense*less*	omit NOUS	service	LET
sensitive		• second service	BLET
sensitive	TENDER	• service he . . .	LETHE
• ban sensitive . . .	BARTENDER	• service *without* normal . . .	LENT
• sensitive back	TENDERLOIN	service	MASS
• sensitive support	TENDERFOOT	• service area	MASSACRE
sent		• service provided	MASSIF
sent boy to the bottom	SUNCLAD	• service vehicles	MASS MEDIA
sent *by* rail	SENTRY	• serviceman	MASSED
sent man, *say*	CENTRON PERFUMIER	service	RAF

Letter replaced \c\at; Omit (a); Pointers *out*; Retain <u>a</u>; Split B_ED; Down (D); Backwards <or ^

• service at this point, *say*	RAFFIA
• service charge	RAFFEE
• service *in* court	CRAFT
service	RN
• acceptable *in* service	RUN
• against church service	CONCERN
• graduate *takes* service	BARN
service area	CATHEDRAL, CHURCH
service book, *say*	MISSEL, MISTLE
service-charge	COURT MARTIAL
service dress	CASSOCK, SURPLICE
	SD
service *return*<	FAR
service tree	SORB
serviceman	AIRMAN, GI
	SAILOR, SOLDIER
	PRIEST
	WAITER
serviceman's cap	BIRETTA, MITRE
servicewoman	AIRWOMAN, ATS
	WAAF, WREN
	WAITRESS
serving as	QUA
• serving as a building	QUASHED
• serving as a light	QUAVERY
serving girl	AIRWOMAN, ATS
	TENNIS PLAYER
	WAAF, WREN
	WAITRESS
serving man	AIRMAN, GI
	SAILOR, SOLDIER
	TENNIS PLAYER
	WAITER
set¹	
set	SET
set *about* . . . <	TES
set *about*	S–ET
• s–et *about* man	SHERBET
[set] *free*	–EST, STE, TES
[set] *off*	–EST, STE, TES
set *out*	SE–T
• se–t *out* new . . .	SENT
[set] *out*	–EST, TES, STE
se–t *outside* a . . .	SEAT
setback<	TES
[set]*off*	–EST, STE, TES
[sets] *free*	TESS
set*up*(D)^	TES
set²	
set	PUT
• set about group	PUTREFACTION
• set point	PUTS
and	
• set *about*<	TUP
• set *up*(D)^	TUP
• setback<	TUP

set	GEL
• *back* in< set	NIGEL
• set fire	GELIGNITE
and	
• set *about*<	LEG
• set *up*(D)^	LEG
• setback<	LEG
set	LAID
• about *in* a set	LAIRED
• quiet set	PLAID
• *take* one *out of* set	LA(i)D
and	
• set *about*<	DIAL
• set *up*(D)^	DIAL
• setback<	DIAL
set³	
set a *precedent*	start with A
• leader *sets* a *precedent*	ACID
set [a test]	TASTE, TEATS
set *about* a	incl A
set *about* it	incl IT
• w–e set *about* it	WITE
set *about* it<	TI
set *about* *	incl *
• w–e set *about* her	WHERE
set *aside* a . . .	omit A
set *free* [slave]	LAVES, VALES, VALSE
set *aside* money	omit D, L, P
set *aside* *	omit *
• (p)arish *sets aside* park	ARISH
set *in* a sil/ver se/a	VERSE
set *in* s/ton/e	TON
set *in* * . . .	incl in *
• one set *in* he–r . . .	HEAR
set of books	NT, OT
set *off* quietly	1st letter(s) P, SH
• I led *and set off* quietly	PILED
• journalist *set off* quietly	SHED
set *off with* a . . .	1st letter A
set *off with* king	1st letter K, R
set *off with* student	1st letter L
set out (=start)	
• *train sets out* . . .	T
set *out in* [bedroom]	BOREDOM
set *out in* pla/in ter/ms	INTER
set *up* pins(D)^	SNIP
setter	DOG, PECTIN
setting for a . . .	incl A
setting for *	incl *
• h–e *provides setting for* queen	HERE
[setting] *out*	TESTING
setting [sun I'm] . . .	MINUS
setback	
new *setback*	WEN
setback<	TES
setback Ben's . . .	SNEB

Anag [cat]; Any *; Begin IGN–; Endings –ING; eg •; Hidden /cat/; Implied add (on); Implied in (in);

setback for Cupid<	SORE
setback ten<	NET
settle	
settle	SAG
• settle *up*(D)^	GAS
settle down	PREEN
settle in German currency	LANDMARKS
settle on(D)	
• bird *settles on* the *French*	TITLE
settle score	BENCHMARK, COMPOSE
settle [score]	CORES
settled for [ever]	VEER
settled matter	SEDIMENT
settlement of [case]	ACES, AESC
seven	
seven	VII, S
seven Christmas presents	SWANS
seven days, *say*	WEAK
[seven] *letters*	EVENS
seven-nil	SEVENTY
seventy	
70% of hall	AUDITOR(ium)
seventy	O, OMICRON, S
seventy-eight	DISC, RECORD
seventy miles per hour	LIMIT
seventy thousand	O, OMICRON, S
seventy years	LIFESPAN
several	
several	VI, V, VI, S, TEN, X
several birds	DIVERS
several weapons, *say*	FOREARMS
several working, *say*	SUMMON
	(*see also* some[1])
severance pay	ALIMONY
sew	
sew, *say*	SO, SOW
sewer	MIMI
	SEAMSTRESS, SEMPSTRESS
	NEEDLE
sewer cover	ETUI, THIMBLE
sews, *say*	SOSO, SOWS
sex	
sex appeal	IT, SA
[sex]-*change*	EXS
sex drive, *say*	LUSTRATE
sextet	VI
Seychelles	SY
shack	QUARTER-HORSE
shade	
[acts] *shadily*	CATS, SCAT
shade doorway	HATCH
shady [deal]	DALE, LADE, LEAD
shake	
shake	ROCK
• shake sailor	ROCK-TAR
• shakes fish, *say*	ROCK-SEAL
• shakes pensioner	ROCK-SOAP
[no great] *shakes*	ETON RAG
shake [dice]	ICED
shake head	omit 1st letter
• (g)oat *shakes head*	OAT
• parent *shakes head*	(m)OTHER
• *shakes* (h)is *head*	IS
shake off a . . .	omit A
shake off *	omit *
• (M)other *shakes off* Frenchman	OTHER
shake up [bolster]	LOBSTER
shaken [by a] . . .	BAY
shaking [rattle]	TATLER
shaky condition	AGUE, PALSY
shaky notes	QUAVERS
shaky [notes]	ONSET, SETON
	STONE, TONES
sham	
[it was] *sham*	WAIST, WAITS
sham fabric	PETER
sham [satin]	STAIN
shamrock	ARTIFICIAL DIAMOND
shameful	
[acts] *shamefully*	CATS, SCAT
shameful [action]	CATION
shape	
shape insect	FORMANT
shape [of a] . . .	OAF
shape of [vase]	AVES, SAVE
shaping [ends]	DENS, SEND
share	
share allotment	ALLOWANCE
share beds	ALLOTMENT
share bill	CO-STAR
share dessert	SPLIT
share issue	SOLOMON'S JUDGEMENT
share of champ/agne s/upper	AGNES
share of m<u>one</u>y	ONE
share of profit	PR, OF, IT
share pusher	PLOUGHMAN
share, *say*	QUOTER
shared china, *say*	COMING
shared out [loot]	TOOL
[share]*out*	HARES, HEARS
	RHEAS, SHEAR
sharp	
sharp	UNNATURAL
sharp alien	BRISKET
sharp fall	ACID DROP, ACID RAIN
Sharp girl	BECKY
sharp lament	KEEN
sharp stone	BRILLIANT
sharpen, *say*	WET
sharper port	TANGIER
sharpshooter	ANNIE (OAKLEY)
	CUPID, EROS

Letter replaced \c\at; Omit (a); Pointers *out*; Retain <u>a</u>; Split B_ED; Down (D); Backwards <or ^

shatter

shatter	WRECK
• second joint shattered	SHIPWRECKED
• shatter ruler, *say*	WRECKING
• shatters, *say*	RECKS, REX
and	
• shatter Conservative, *say*	RECTORY
• shattered America, *say*	RECTUS
• shattered them, *say*	RECTUM
shatter a number, *say*	RUINATE
shatter, *say*	BRAKE, RECK
shattered a street	BUSTARD
shattered [vase]	SAVE
shattering [blow]	BOWL
shatters, *say*	BRAKES

Shaw

Shaw	GBS
[Shaw] *play*	HAWS, WASH
Shaw's girl	ELIZA

she

she drowned, *say*	SEA-ADDER
She, *for one*	NOVEL
she is in debt, *say*	HEROES
she, *objectively*	HER
she will	SHE'LL
she will, *say*	SHEAL, SHEEL, SHIEL
she would	SHE'D

shed

(o)ran(g) *shed its skin*	RAN
shed a . . .	omit A
shed leaves	omit FF
shed weight	omit TON
shed will, *say*	SHACKLE
shed *	omit *
• ba(skin)g, *shedding* skin	BAG
shed [tears]	ASTER, RATES
	STARE, STEAR, TARES

sheep

sheep	RAM
• sheep and fish, *say*	RAMEAL
• sheep attendant	RAMPAGE
• sheep sheared	RAMOON, RAMSHORN
• sheep stealer	RAM RAIDER
• sheep's hobble	RAMSHACKLE
sheep-dog's kennel, *say*	COLLIERY
sheep noises	BAAS
sheep, *say*	USE, YEW(S), YOU
	WEATHER, WHETHER
sheep's family	LAMBSKIN, RAMSKIN

sheepshank

sheepshank	LEG OF LAMB
	LEG OF MUTTON
sheepshank, *say*	RAMPART

sheet

sheet	P
• sheet *missing*	omit P

sheet music	NOTEPAPER

shell

(n)ut(s) *shelled*	UT
say "shells"	SEYCHELLES
shell-(c)as(e)	AS
shell (f)ire(d)	IRE
shell of nuts	NS
shell from mortar	MR
shellfish, *say*	MUSCLE

shelter

shelter	LEE
• shelter minor	LEEWARD
• sheltered circle	LEERING
• sheltered hospital unit	LEEWARD
shelter squirrel	SKUG
sheltered by li/me tre/e	METRE
sheltered by *	incl in *
• bird *sheltered by* l–and	LOWLAND
sheltering a . . .	incl A
sheltering in c/aver/n	AVER
sheltering king	incl R
sheltering *	incl *
• l–and *sheltering* bird	LOWLAND

shenanigans

[loud] *shenanigans*	LUDO
shenanigans [in the] . . .	THINE

shield

shielded by sm/all ow/l	ALLOW
shielded by *	incl in *
• girl *shielded by* metal . . .	TANNIN
shielding a . . .	incl A
shielding *	incl *
• metal *shielding* girl	TANNIN
youn/g ash/ *shielding* . . .	GASH

shift

[gear]-*shift*	RAGE
shift [soil]	OILS, SILO
shift worker	FURNITURE REMOVER
shiftily [take] . . .	KATE, TEAK
shifting [the car]	THRACE
shifty person	NOMAD
[late] *shift*	LEAT, TALE, TEAL

shilling

shilling	BOB
• shilling animal	BOBCAT
• shilling duck	BOB
• sound shilling	PLUMB-BOB
shilling	S
• shilling *on* a horse	SHACK
• shilling *off*	omit S
shilling canopy	TESTER

shimmer

shimmering [silk 'e] . . .	LIKES
[star] *shimmers*	RATS, TARS

shine

shine	GLOW

Anag [cat]; Any *; Begin IGN–; Endings –ING; eg •; Hidden /cat/; Implied add (on); Implied in (in);

• shine a light	GLOW LAMP	shir̲t-*tail*	T
and		shirtmaker	SHIFTWORKER
• shine *on* porcelain, *say*	GLOAMING	**shiver**	
• shine perfectly, *say*	GLOAT	[quite] *shivery*	QUIET, –TIQUE
shiny, *say*	GLACIS	*shivering* [fits are] . . .	FAIREST
ship		**shock**	
ship	CRAFT	shock, *say*	HARE
• house-boat	HOMECRAFT	shock treatment	HAIRCUT, HAIRDRESSING
• ship *with* unknown . . .	CRAFTY	*shocking* [case]	ACES, AESC
• shipping trade	CRAFT	shocking drink	JAR
• which ship, *I ask*	WITCHCRAFT	*shockingly* [bad]	ABD–, DAB
ship	HOY	**shoe**	
• a king *in* ship	HOARY	shoe	LAST THING
• ship study	HOYDEN	shoe tree	SANDALWOOD
ship	KETCH	shoemaker	CRISPIN, SUTOR
• second ship	SKETCH		LEATHER
• ship to windward	KETCHUP	shoemaker, *say*	SUITOR
ship	SS	shoemaker's drink	COBBLER
• big ship	LARGESS	[shoe]*making*	HOES, HOSE
• mother-ship	MASS	**shoot**	
• ship *carrying* hot . . .	SHOTS	shoot	FIRE
• the *French* ship	LESS	• girl shooting, *say*	MISFIRING
and		• shoot a bullet	FIREBALL
• ship *has left*	omit SS	• shoot a soldier	FIREMAN
ship	LINER	and	
• been *on* ship, *say*	BIN-LINER	• shoot *after* uncle, *say*	SAMPHIRE
• display ship	AIRLINER	shoot	POT
• most important ship	MAINLINER	• second shoot	SPOT
ship	MV	• shoot *at* can	POTABLE
ship-breaker	DESTROYER	• shoot old hen	POT-BOILER
[ship]-*breaking*	HIPS, PISH	• shoots *at* mare	POTSDAM
ship *docked*	LINE(r)	shoot	SNIPE
ship launcher	HELEN	• shoot a woman, *say*	SNIPER
shipboard games, *say*	DECATHLON	• shoot bird	SNIPE
ship's . . .	HER	*shoot* dog *up* . . . (D)^	GOD
ship's name	HERN	[shoot]-*out*	HOOTS
ship's working	HERON	shooting	(in) BU–D
ship's bar	TAFFRAIL	*shooting all over* [Wales]	SWALE
ship's barber	CLIPPER, CUTTER	*shooting all over*	
ship's bell, *say*	LUTEIN	the place, [we hit], ,	WHITE
ships' companies, *say*	CRU(I)SE	shooting box	CAMERA
ship's company, *say*	KROO	shooting brake	SAFETY-CATCH
ship's glasses	SCHOONERS	shooting break	TRUCE
ship's orchestra	WAVEBAND	shooting equipment	CAMERA
ship's side beams	PORTRAYS	shooting-men	GUNNERS, RA
ship's timber	FLEETWOOD	shooting star	ANNIE (OAKLEY)
shipping company	LINE	shoots animals	POTSHERD
shipping line	CABLE, PLIMSOLL	shoots sailors	FILM STARS
shipshape	SCAPHOID		(*see also* shot)
[ship]*shape*	HIPS, PISH	**shop**	
shipworker, *say*	DECANT	[shop] *around*	HOPS, POSH
[ship]*wreck*	HIPS, PISH	shop laws	COUNTERACTS
shirker	CUTHBERT	shop-lifting	RUSTLING, STOCKTAKING,
shirt			TAKING STOCK
shirt	T	sho̲pping *centre*	PP
s̲hirt-*front*	S	shopworker	COUNTERMARCHER

Letter replaced \c\at; Omit (a); Pointers *out*; Retain a̲; Split B_ED; Down (D); Backwards <or ^

shorn	DISTRESSED, UNLOCKED
short[1]	
indicating abbreviation:	
short answer	A, ANS
short break	HOL(S), VAC, WE
short contest	COMP
short course	PUD
short day	D, MON etc
short drink	METHS
short holiday	HOL(S), VAC, WE
short measure	FT, IMM–, IN, MM, YD
Short Metre	SM
short notice	AD(VERT)
short publication	MAG
short question	Q
short regulation	REG
short spell (=abbreviation)	
• always *has short spell*	EER
• *short spell of* work	OP
• *short spell* will not . . .	WON'T
short time	HR, MIN, MO, SEC, T, YR
short vacation	HOL(S), VAC, WE
short walk	PROM
short wave	SW
short work	OP
shortly I will . . .	I'LL
shortly release	DEMOB
	(see also contract)
short[2]	
indicating omission:	
a *short* . . .	omit A
quit(e) *shortly*	QUIT
run *short*	omit R
short cut	CU(t), (l)OP, AX(e)
short *cut*	SHOR(t)
short-le(g)	LE
short-list	INVENTOR(y)
short measure	PIN(t)
short of a . . .	omit A
short of a bob	omit S
short of a bit of sugar	CUB(e)
short of energy	omit E
short of a hundred . . .	omit C
short of money	omit L, P
short of oxygen	omit O
short of space	SPA, ACE
short of time	omit AGE, T
short of *	omit *
• b(all)et *short of* all . . .	BET
short story	(s)TORY, TAL(e)
short term	HILAR(y)
short time	(h)OUR, TIM(e)
short wal(k)	WAL
shortage of cash	CAS, ASH
shorten skir(t)	SKIR
shorter (st)ride	RIDE

shorter than you(r) . . .	YOU
shortfall in remuneration	PA(y), (s)CREW
	WAG(e)
short[3]	
other uses:	
short break	COMMA
short dance	ONE-STEP, TWO-STEP
short holiday	OFFBREAK
short illness	CURTAILMENT
short jacket, *say*	BASK
short measure	INCH, LOWELL
short of	LACK
• second short of . . .	SLACK
• short of a number, *say*	LACCATE
• short of time	LACK-A-DAY
short of funds	(in) R–ED
short race	DASH, SPRINT
	LILLIPUTIANS
	PIGMIES, PYGMIES
short sentence, *say*	FRAISE, FRAYS
short skirt, *say*	MINNIE
short stop	COMMA
short suit	BRIEFCASE, SINGLETON
short telephone call	RINGLET
shorten	DOCK
• shorten *after* son had . . .	SHADDOCK
• shorten it, *say*	DOCKET
• shortened airport, *say*	DOCTORLY
shorten bridge	CONTRACT
shorten crossing	CONTRACT BRIDGE
shorten item	DETAIL
shortfall	SHOWER, UNDERGROWTH
shot	
[moon]*shot*	MONO
shot [daring spy]	DAYSPRING
shot-wound	STAB
should	
should, *say*	AUTO
• should criticise, *say*	AUTOCARP
• should eat, *say*	AUTODYNE
• should marry, *say*	AUTOMATE
shout	
a loud *shout*	ALLOWED, ALOUD
shout	CRY
• shout *before* exercise	CRYPT
• shout louder	OUTCRY
• shout *to* child	CRY-BABY
and	
• shout "Hooter", *say*	CRINOSE
• shout "Porcelain" *say*	CRIMING
• shout *to knight, say*	CRINITE
shout in pain	CALLOW, YELLOW
[shout] out	SOUTH, THOUS
shouted, *say*	BALE, HALLOWED
shouting for meals, *say*	ROARING FORTIES
shove	

Anag [cat]; Any *; Begin IGN–; Endings –ING; eg •; Hidden /cat/; Implied add (on); Implied in (in);

shove [under a] . . .	UNREAD	**shy**	
shoving [past]	STAP, TAPS	shy bear, *say*	COYPU
show		shy writer	LOBELIA
show	AIR	**Sibyl's job**	PROPHECY
• quiet shows	PAIRS	**sick**	
• show people	AIRMEN	sick	AILING
• showboat	AIRCRAFT, AIRSHIP	• a very sick . . .	AVAILING
show a . . .	incl A	• sick king	RAILING
show *	incl *	• sick *on* a ship	ASSAILING
• lea–rn *to show* the . . .	LEATHERN	sick	ILL
show embarrassment	GORED	• saint *has* sick . . .	SILL, STILL
show-girl	EVITA	• sick head	ILLNESS
show hospitality	ENTERTAINMENT	• sick joke	ILL-HUMOUR
show-house	THEATRE	and	
show jumper	VAULTING HORSE	• sick bird, *say*	ILLEGAL
show over	CATSUP	sick person	O'NEILL
s/how/-*piece*	HOW	*sick*-[note]	ETON, TONE
show-[pieces]	SPECIE	*sick* [to her] . . .	OTHER
show-ring	MANIFESTO	*sickly* [baby 'e] . . .	ABBEY
show, *say*	SEEN	sickly child	PALETOT
show tolerance	PLAY	sickly, *say*	PICQUET
show-trial	REHEARSAL	**side**	
showboat	STAGECRAFT	side	L, R
shower	SHORTFALL	• side-*splitting* one . . .	ACRE
showing as [it was]	WAIST, WAITS	• side-*splitting* girl	LEVER, REVEL
showing in cine/ma ne/ar you	MANE	side	TEAM
shown in t/heat/re	HEAT	• second side	STEAM
shred		• side *with* journalist	TEAMED
[rag]-*shredding*	GAR	side	XI, XV
shred [papers]	SAPPER	side at sea	LARBOARD, PORT, STARBOARD
shredded [nerves]	SEVERN	[side] *at sea*	DIES, IDES
shrew	KATE, XANTIPPE	[side]-*splitting*	DIES, IDES
shrink		side to side movement	TRANSFER
shrink	omit 1st and last letters	side of	
• *shrink* (c)lot(h)	LOT	–field	LEG, OFF
• *shrunken* (c)otto(n) . . .	OTTO	–road	NEAR, OFF
shrinking violet	LET, VET, VI, VIOL	–ship	LARBOARD, PORT
shudder			STARBOARD
shuddering [when I] . . .	WHINE	side plank, *say*	WAILER, WHALER
[stop] *shuddering*	OPTS, POTS, SPOT, TOPS	side promises . . .	FACETIOUS
shuffle		side *with* friend	LEGALLY
shuffle [teams]	MATES, MEATS, STEAM	*sides of* bacon	BN
shuffling [along]	GOLAN	sides of stage	OPPOSITE PROMPT
shuffling around [town]	WONT		PROMPT SIDE
shunt		*sides of* stage	SE
shunt [engine D]	NEEDING	sidesman	BISHOP, CASTLE, ROOK
shunting [train as] . . .	ARTISAN	West *Side*	W
shut		**siemens**	S
shut in *	incl in *	**Sierra Leone**	WAL
• man *shut in* food store	PEDANTRY	**sift**	
[shut] *off*	HUTS, THUS, TUSH	[clues I] *sift* . . .	SLUICE
[shut] *out*	HUTS, THUS, TUSH	*sifting* [soil]	OILS, SILO
shut *up*(D)^	NEP	**sight**	
* *shut in*	incl *	sight, *say*	CITE, EIFFEL, SEEN, SITE
• I am *shut in* study	COIN	sight-screen	EYELID
shutter	EYELID	**sigma**	S

sign
right sign	TICK
sign	ARIES, RAM etc
sign	MINUS, PLUS, V
sign of error	(A)CROSS, X
sign of summer	PLUS
sign of take-away	MINUS
sign of the times	DATE STAMP, X
sign, *say*	CYMBAL
sign-writing	CRYPTOGRAPHY, SHORTHAND
[sign]-*writing*	GINS, –INGS, SING
signing-on place	DOTTED LINE
signs of hesitation	ER(ER), UM
wrong sign	CROSS

signal
signal "Abandon"	MAROON
signal frequency	SF
Signal Officer	SO
signal *to* workers	FLAGSTAFF

signature   SIG, SUBSCRIPTION
Sikorski's tomb   POLE VAULT
silent
silence	GAG, SQUASH RACKET, TACE
silencer, *say*	USHER
silent	MUM, SH, ST
silent cast	DUMBFOUND
silent god	ODIN
silent picture	STILL

silks   BAR
silly
silly	LOOPY
• silly knight, *say*	LUPINITE
• silly number, *say*	LUPININE
• silly shape, *say*	LUPIFORM
silly girl	ASSESS
silly [girl in] . . .	RILING
silly [part]	PRAT, TRAP
silly way [to put] . . .	PUTTO
silly way to put [things]	NIGHTS

silver¹
silver	AG
• silver grass	AGREED
• silver *and* blue	AGLOW
• silver ring and	AGO, AGROUND
• British silver	BRAG
• hard silver	HAG
• royal silver and	RAG
• silver *in* hair	MANAGE
• silver *in* river	DAGON
• silver *in* warehouse	STORAGE
silver	ARGENTUM
silver-*covered*	(in) A–G
silver-*edged*	(in) A–G

silver-*lined*	incl AG
silver-*mounted*	(in) A–G
silver-*mounted*(D)^	GA
silver-*plated*	(in) A–G

silver²
silver	PIRATE
silver pin	PEG-LEG, WOODEN LEG
silver underwear	LONG JOHNS

simple
simple	HERB
• simple list	HERBAL
• simple man	HERB(AL)
• simple plot	HERB-GARDEN
• simple retailer	HERBALIST
• simple song	HERBARIA
simple	PLAIN
• formerly simple	EXPLAIN
• simple argument	PLAINTIFF
simple feline, *say*	MEERKAT
simple man	SIMON
simple victory	BALDWIN
simpleton	ABDERITE, GOTHAMIST GOTHAMITE, JOHN, SIMON
simply marsh	MERE

sin
sin-bin, *say*	SINKAGE
sin king	VICEROY
sinning, *say*	HERRING

sincere
sincere flatterer	IMITATOR
sincere pledge	EARNEST

sine   SIN
sing
sing	BETRAY, GRASS, SQUEAL, TELL, CAROL, YODEL
sing softly, *say*	DEMISING
singer	LAYMAN
singer, *say*	BASE, TENNER
singers, *say*	QUIRE
sings [tenor]	NOTER, TRONE
singing well	INVOICE

Singapore   SGP
single
single	A
• lady's single . . .	HERA
• single carat	ACT
single	ACE
• fine single	FACE
• paper *without* a single	MACES
• single flower	ACEROSE
single	I
• sea *has* single . . .	MERI
• single transaction	IDEAL
single	LONE
• ba–y *running round* single . . .	BALONEY
• single sailor	ABALONE

• single single	ALONE	site of industry	HIVE
and		site of storm	TEACUP
• single fish, *say*	LOAN SHARK	site, *say*	CITE, PLAICE, SIGHT,
• single word, *say*	LOAN WORD		SEEN
single	MONO	**six**	
• single fish, *say*	MONOCARP	six	VI
• single college	MONOPOLY	• 6.50	VIL
• single man	MONODON	• six die	VIPERISH
• single round	MONOCYCLE	• six each	VIPER
single	RUN	• six rulers	VIKINGS
• exercise *outside* single . . .	PRUNE	• six *to* one	VIA
• single ply	RUN	• six vehicles	VICARS
single	SOLE	• six wise men	VISAGES
• 500 *on* a single	DOVER SOLE	• sixpence	VID, VIP
• single.artist	SOLERA	and	
• single fish	SOLE	• 66 groups	VIVISECTS
• time *in* a single . . .	STOLE	six balls completed, *say*	OVERBOLD
single data converter	SDC	six-footer	ANT, BEE, INSECT
singular German	HAN(s)		HEXAMETER
singular poet	GRAVE(s)		TALLBOY
singular Scotsman	SOLOMON	six-nil	SIXTY
singular spirit	ONEGIN	six pounds, *say*	SICK SQUID
singular trade	IDEAL	six-thirty	HANDS DOWN
singularly crazy	BANANA(s)	sixpence	SICE, TANNER
Sinhalese	SINH	**sixteen**	
sinister		sixteen inches	HAND AND FOOT
sinister	LEFT	sixteenth note	SEMIQUAVER
sinister fighter	SOUTHPAW	**sixth**	
sinister trait	LEFTHANDEDNESS	sixth (music)	SEXT
sink originator	FOUNDER	sixth former	UPPER-CLASS
Sinn Fein	SF	sixth of circle	C, I, R, C, L, E,
sinuous			SEXTANT
sinuous [snake]	SNEAK	sixth-sense	ESP
sinuously [glide in]	ELIDING	**sixty**	
sir		60% of <u>crude</u>	CRU
sir	KNIGHT, SR, TEACHER	sixty	LX
Sir Ian, *say*	SERIAN, SYRIAN	sixty grains	DRAM
sister		sixty seconds	MINUTE
sister	NUN	sixty-one seconds	MINUTES
• sister, *say*	NONE	sixty-six	VIVI
• sister's hat	NUNHOOD	• sixty-six cults	VIVISECTS
sister	NURSE, S, SIS	**skate**	
sit		skating (=on ice)	
sit in *	incl in *	• pair-*skating*	PRICE
• he *sits in* s–et . . .	SHEET	• playwright *skating*	COWARDICE
[sit] *out*	–IST, ITS, TIS	**sketch**	
sit *up*(D)^	TIS	sketch	DRAW
sitter-in	PERCHERON	• accompanying sketch	WITHDRAW
sitting-bower	CELLIST	• sketch fish	DRAWLING
sitting in sha/de ne/ar . . .	DENE	• sketch game	DRAWBRIDGE
sitting, *perhaps*	NOTWITHSTANDING	**skid**	
sitting-room	COURT	[car] *skidded*	ARC
sitting, *say*	CESSION	*skid* [in road]	DORIAN
sitting tenant	SQUATTER	*skidding* [bus]	SUB
site		**skill**	
site for lavatory, *say*	LEUCITE	skilful international, *say*	HANDICAP

Letter replaced \c\at; Omit (a); Pointers *out*; Retain <u>a</u>; Split B_ED; Down (D); Backwards <or ^

skill *on* the river	FEATURE	skylight	MOON, STARS, SUN
skilled, *say*	VERST	**slack**	
skilled man	PRO	*slack* [rule]	LURE
skim		*slacken off* [ropes]	PORES, SPORE
skimmed (m)ilk	ILK	**slap**	
(t)op *skimmed*	OP	*slap-happy* [sort]	ORTS, ROTS, TORS
skin		slap-*up*(D)^	PALS
lizar<u>d</u> *skin*	LD	slapdash	SMACK
skin	HIDE	*slapdash* [sort]	ORTS, ROTS, TORS
• skin valued, *say*	HYDRATED	**slash**	
skin	PEEL	slash girl	CUTLASS
• second skin, *say*	SPIEL	*slashed* [wrist]	WRITS
• skin say	PEAL	*slashing* [rain]	IRAN, RANI
skin	PELT	**slate vessel**	PAN
• second skin	SPELT	**slattern**	
• skin a saint	PELTAST	slattern	BAG
• skin devoured	PELTATE	• betraying slattern	SHOPPING BAG
skin disease, *say*	HACKNEY	• slattern cries	BAGPIPES
skin fish	STRIPLING	• slattern killed	BAGSHOT
skin of <u>his</u> . . .	HS	**slaughter**	
skin of <u>orange</u>	OE	[animal] *slaughtered*	LAMINA, MANILA
skin off (o)rang(e)	RANG	*slaughter* [deer]	REDE, REED
skin opening	PORE	slaughter game	KILLDEER
• skin opening, *say*	POOR, POUR	**slave**	
skin <u>tight</u>	TT	slave	SERF
skin<u>head</u>	S	• I *have* slaves *around*	SERIFS
skinny	DERMIC, EPIDERMAL	• slave devoured, *say*	SURFEIT
skinny monarch	THINKING	slave girl	AIDA
skins pickles	SCRAPES	**sleep**	
skip		sleep	NAP
skip a . . .	omit A	• child sleeps	KIDNAPS
skip it!	omit IT	• sleep aboard	SNAPS
skip *	omit *	• sleep *with* family	NAPKIN
skipper	LAMB	• sleep *around*<	PAN
skipping	OMITTING	sleeper	EARRING
skipping [rope]	PORE	sleeper's position	UNDERLINES
skirmish		sleeping	(in) B–ED
[men are] *skirmishing*	RENAME	• a king *sleeping*	BAKED, BARED
skirmish [in glade]	LEADING	sleeping partner	BEDFELLOW, BEDMATE
skirt		sleepyhead	NAPPER
skirt	MINI	sleepy*head*	S
skirted by *	incl in *	slept around	OUTLAY
• bend *skirted by* la–ne	LASAGNE	**slice**	
skirting <u>Southampton</u>	SOON	*slice* [loaf]	OLAF
skirting a . . .	incl A	slice of bread	TRANCHE
skirting *	incl *	*slice of* bre/ad I t/ook . . .	ADIT
• la–ne *skirting* bend	LASAGNE	*sliced* [beans]	BANES
skirts of <u>satin</u>	SN	*sliced by* *	incl in *
skit		• c–ake *sliced by* essayist	CLAMBAKE
skit on [medical] . . .	CLAIMED, DECIMAL	**slide**	
	DECLAIM	*slide back* door<	ROOD
[smart] *skit*	MARTS, TRAMS	*sliding* [panel]	PLANE
skull	HARDTOP	sliding scale	GLISSANDO
sky		**slight**	
sky	LIMIT	*slight change of* hear\t\	HEARD, HEARS
skyscrapers	TALL STORIES	*slight change of* [heart]	EARTH, HATER

Anag [cat]; Any *; Begin IGN–; Endings –ING; eg •; Hidden /cat/; Implied add (on); Implied in (in);

	RATHE
slight change of pace	PICE, PACT
slight change of [pace]	CAPE
slight fall	RAINDROP, SHOWER
slight mist, *say*	PETTIFOG
slightly mistimed	SECONDS OUT
slim	
slim (t)high(s)	HIGH
slimmers' conference	DIET
slip	
slip in front	MUFFLED
slip into *	incl in *
• I *slip into* wa–ter	WAITER
slip, *say*	LAPS
slip-*up*(D)^	RRE, PILS
slip-up when *climbing*(D)^	PUPILS
slipped [over]	ROVE
slipper	EEL
slippery one, *say*	GRECIAN
slippery, *say*	GLACIS
slippery [slope]	LOPES, POLES
slipping [into]	–TION
[slip]*knots*	LIPS
slip[knots]	STONK
slips *	omit *
• lin(net) *slips the* net	LIN
slip[stream]	MASTER, REMAST
slipshod	
slip[shod]	HODS
slipshod [sort]	ORTS, ROTS, TORS
sloppy	
sloppy [date]	–ATED
sloppy [thing]	NIGHT
sloth	AI
slough	
slough	BOG
slough skin	omit 1st and last
• (h)yen(a) *sloughs its skin*	YEN
slovenly	
slovenly, [untidy] . . .	NUDITY
[Tom is] *slovenly*	MOIST
slow	
slow deliveryman	SPIN BOWLER
slow down, *say*	BREAK
slow movement	SNAIL'S PACE
[slow] *movement*	LOWS, OWLS
slow-*spoken*	SLOE, SLOUGH
slow *start*	S
slow vehicle	BRAKE, HEARSE
slug	
slug killer	BULLET
sluggish vehicle	SLOWCOACH
slur	
slur [she 'ad]	HADES, HEADS
slurred [speech]	CHEEPS
sly	CHRISTOPHER

small¹	
small	TINY
small	WEE
• shirt (small)	TWEE
• small chessman	WEEK NIGHT
• small daughter	WEED
• small letters	WEEKS, WEEPS
• small mark	WEEM
• small points	WEENS
• small type	WEEPIE
	(*see also* little¹)
small²	
indicating abbreviation:	
small arms ammunition	SAA
small book	B, BK, VOL
small bottle	BOT
small box	B
small branch	DEPT
small business	BIZ, CO(Y)
small capitals	SC
small change	D, –ID, IP, P
small coin	D, –ID, IP, P
small firm	CO
small girl	DI, G
small house	H, HO, COT
small illustration	FIG
small investment	P
small man	GENT, M
small marsupial	ROO
small measure	CC, EL, EM, EN
	FT, IN, MM, YD
small number	NO
small party	CON, LAB, LIB
small photograph	PIC
small point	PT
small quantity	CC
small relative	BRER, BRO, SIS
small research establishment	LAB
small section	DEPT
small volume	CC, VOL
small weight	CT, GR, OZ, WT
	(*see also* little², reduce)
small³	
other uses:	
small account	BILLET
small amount of fish	CARPORT
small amount of gold	CARAT, CT
small amount of gold	G
small amount off (p)rice	RICE
small audience	POORHOUSE
small beer	HALF-PINT
small blow	COUPLET
small bottle, *say*	CREWS, CRUISE, VILE
small burn	BROOK(LET), RILL
	STREAM(LET)
small car, *say*	MINNIE

small carriage, *say*	GIGLET	• smart fisherman	DAPPER
small cat, *say*	GIBLET	• smart girl	DIDAPPER
small catch	FRY, MINNOW, SARDINE	smart	HIP
	TIDDLER	• leads smart . . .	HEADSHIP
small circle	RINGLET	• smart joint	HIP
small coat	MATINEE	• woman *has* smart . . .	WHIP
small Dickensian	(LITTLE) NELL	smart Alec	CLEVER DICK, KNOW-ALL
	(TINY) TIM	smart boy	STING-RAY
small digger	TROWEL	smart deal	SPRUCE
small family	MINIKIN	smart man	ALEC
small fly, *say*	WINGLET	smart *riposte*<	TRAMS
small fruit, *say*	BURY	smartypants	ALEC
small footballer	HALF, THREE-QUARTER	**smash**	
small hooter	OWLET	*smash*-[hit]	ITH
small island, *say*	EYELET	smash, *say*	BRAKE
small jacket, *say*	PETTICOAT	*smash-up of* [cars]	ARCS, SCAR
small journalist	SHORTED	smashing opportunity	LOB
small jumper	CRICKET, FLEA	*smashing* [vases]	SAVES
	JOEY, LEVERET	**smell**	
small letter	MINIM, MUTINY	smell	BO
small letters	MINUTE HAND	smell alien	WHIFFET
small loophole	EYELET	smell insect	ODORANT
small luggage compartment	BOOTEE	smell your, *say*	RECURE
small m	MINIM	smelling salts	HIGH TARS
small man	CHAPLET, MINIMAL, SHORTED	**smile**	
small margin	CANVAS, HEAD, NECK, NOSE	smile	GRIN
small model	BABYSITTER	• smile *about* a . . .	GRAIN
small mother	MINIMA, MINIMUM	• smile *after* tea	CHAGRIN
small moustache	CHARLEY, CHARLIE	• smile fades, *say*	GRINGOS
small nails, *say*	TAX	**smithereens**	(*see* in³)
small, neat . . .	CALF	**smitten**	
small part	WALK-ON	[love]*smitten*	VOLE
small party	DWARF, MIDGET	*smitten* [by a] . . .	BAY
small piece of timber, *say*	LOGGET	**smoke**	
small record	MINUTE	smoke-ring	RE-ECHO
small road, *say*	LAIN	smoke screen	FILTER-TIP
small space	EM, EN, M, N	smoke, *say*	WREAK
small square	EM, EN, M, N	smoker	CHIMNEY, LUM
small-time collector	GLEANER	smoking hat	STOVEPIPE
small turnover	CUFF, LAPEL	smoking jacket	REEFER
small witch, *say*	HAGLET	smoky city	HAVANA
small wood, *say*	COPS	**smooth**	
small worker	MINUTE HAND	smooth	DECREASE
small world	LILLIPUT	smooth current	EVENTIDE
small wound	CUTLET	smooth foil	IRON CROSS
smaller boat	LIGHTER	smooth metal	IRON
smaller girl	RUTHLESS	smooth operator	LAUNDRYMAN
smaller, *say*	T(A)ENIA	smooth tree	PLANE
smallest roads	LEASTWAYS	smoother	IRON, PLANE
	(*see also* little³)	smoother praise	FLATTER
smart		smoother, *say*	PLAIN
smart	CHIC	**smother**	
• alternative in smart . . .	CHORIC	*smother* a . . .	incl A
• smart man	CHICKEN	*smother* *	incl *
• smart one	CHICANE	• s—ores *smother* husband	SHORES
smart	DAPPER	*smothered in* *	incl in *

Anag [cat]; Any *; Begin IGN–; Endings –ING; eg •; Hidden /cat/; Implied add (on); Implied in (in);

• husband *smothered in*		snooper	(PAUL) PRY
s–ores	SHORES	**snow**	
smug		snow	S
smug	PI	• snowman	SHE
• smug group	PILOT	• snowplough	STILL
• smug king (English)	PIKE	• snows *cover* car	SCARS
• smug novices	PILL	[snow] *clearing*	OWNS, SOWN
smuggle		snow shifter	ADDICT
smuggle	RUN	snowball	INCREASE
smuggle bird	OWL	[snow]*drift*	OWNS, SOWN
smuggled	RAN	snowdrop	AVALANCHE
• smuggled *in* ar–t	ARRANT	snowfall	AVALANCHE
• smuggled *in* church	CRANE	[snow]*fall*	OWNS, SOWN
• smuggled wine	RANSACK	[snow]*flakes*	OWNS, SOWN
smuggler in court	RUNNER-UP	*snowing* [in the] . . .	THINE
snake		snowman	YETI
snake	ASP	**so**	
• 150 snakes	CLASPS	so	AS
• angry snake	ASPIRATE	• so say . . .	ASSAY
• royal snake	RASP	• so sure	ASCERTAIN
• snake I call . . .	ASPIRING	• so *to* bed	ASCOT
snake	BOA	so	ERGO
• snake *and* dog	BOAT-RACE	• so *round*<	OGRE
• snake-bite	BOASTING	• so square	ERGOT
• snake *on* the road	BOARD	so	SIC
• snake tracks	BOAT-RACES	• graduate so . . .	BASIC
snake	SEPS	• so the man . . .	SICKEN
• snake inside	SEPSIN	so	SO
• snake lives	SEPSIS	• *maybe* so	SEW, SOW
• snake, *say*	CEPS	• so-*called*	SEW, SOW
snake	RATTLER	• so *it's said*	SEW, SOW
snake, *say*	CRATE	• so *they say*	SOMITE
snap		• so *they say*	SEW, SOW
snap, *say*	BIGHT, BYTE	• so *to speak*	SEW, SOW
snap *up*(D)^	PANS	• so *upset*(D)^	OS
snapped	BIT	so	THUS
• bird snapped	TITBIT	• preserve *so*	CANTHUS
• snapped bird	BITTERN	so *as to* [startle] . . .	RATTLES
• snapped you soldiers, *say*	BITUMEN	so-*called* manor	MANNER
snapper	ALLIGATOR, CROCODILE	so *to speak*, a dew	ADIEU
	PHOTOGRAPHER	**soak**	
snare pirate	HOOK	soak	RET
snarl		• about to soak	CARET
[quite] *snarled up*	QUIET, –TIQUE	• soak container	RETURN
snarl up [nets]	STEN, TENS	• soak *up*(D)^	TER
sneak		**soap**	
sneakily [slid] . . .	LIDS	soap	OPERA, SITCOM
sneaking [past]	PATS, STAP, TAPS	soap works	OPERA
sneaky [dealer]	LEADER, REDEAL	soft soap	FLANNEL
snooker		**soar**	
snooker-ball	RED	[plane] *soared* . . .	PANEL
snooker fee, *say*	CURATE	*soaring* [notes]	ONSET, SETON
snooker manual	POCKETBOOK		STONE, TONES
snooker match, *say*	CUTEST	**soccer**	
snoop		soccer blunder	OG
snoop *around*	PR–Y	soccer suit	HEARTS

Letter replaced \c\at; Omit (a); Pointers *out*; Retain a̲; Split B_ED; Down (D); Backwards <or ^

social	
social crawler	ANT
social, domestic and pleasure	SDP
social *ends*	SL
social gathering	BEE
social worker	ANT, BEE
socialist	LAB, RED
socialist *backing<*	BAL, DER
socially acceptable	U

society	
society	S, SOC
Society for Psychical Research	SPR
Society member	FRIEND
Society of	
–Antiquaries	SA
–Arts	SA
–Engineers	SE
–Incorporated Accountants	SAA
–the Holy Cross	SSC

sock	
socks	LOW GEAR
socks, *say*	HOES

soft[1]	
soft	P
• a soft fruit	APPEAR
• a soft one	APACE
• a soft spot	APPOINT
and	
• soft drink	PALE, PIT
• soft stratum	PLAYER
• soft touch	PREACH
• soft toy	PRATTLE
• softwood	PASH, PLUMBER
and	
• softwood, *say*	POKE
soft centre(d)	incl P
• *soft-centred* ro–e	ROPE
soft-*hearted*	incl P
• soft-*hearted* fellow	MAPLE
very soft	PP
• a very soft fish	APPROACH
• a very soft lotion	APPOINTMENT
• learner *has* a very soft . . .	LAPP
(*see also* gentle, quiet)	

soft[2]	
soft	GENTLE
• soft fellow	GENTLEMAN
• soft maggot	GENTLE
• soft point	GENTLENESS
soft *centre*	OF
soft colour	MILDRED
soft drug	MELTING-POT
soft offer	TENDER

sold	
sold, *I hear*	SOLED
sol(d) *short*	SOL

solder	
solder [parts]	PRATS, SPRAT, STRAP
soldering-[iron]	NOIR

soldier	
airborne soldier	PARA
American soldier	GI, GRUNT, JOE
• American infantry vehicle	GIBUS
• American officer	GILT
• soldier's double	GIGI
• soldier's *return<*	IG–
French soldiers	SOLDATS
German soldiers	SOLDATEN, SS
soldier	ANT
• 10 soldiers	TENANTS
• 100 soldiers	CANTS
• woman soldier	WANT
soldier	MAN
• measure soldier	FOOTMAN
• soldier *has* unknown . . .	MANX
• soldier takes exercise	MANDRILLS
soldier	PRIVATE
• soldier-king	PRIVATEER
soldier	PARA
• soldier has left, *say*	PARAGON
• soldier of the *French* . . .	PARADE
• soldier *on* horse	PARAMOUNT
soldier	TOMMY
• soldier *goes to* the pub	TOMMY-BAR
• soldier *takes* a weapon	TOMMY-GUN
soldier-surgeon	LANCER
soldiers	IMPI
soldiers	MEN
• Home Counties' soldiers	SEMEN
• soldiers take the oath	MENSWEAR
• soldiers the *German* . . .	MENDER
soldiers	OR
• *put* kit in front of soldiers	RIGOR
• soldiers *in* Maine	MORE
• soldiers rebuked	ORCHID
soldiers	RA
• soldiers in East End	RAINBOW
• soldiers offer	RABID
• soldiers watch	RASPY
soldiers	RE
• soldiers do duty	RESERVE
• soldiers in certain . . .	REINSURE
• soldiers jumped	REBOUNDED
and	
• soldiers guard, *I hear*	REGARD
soldiers	SAS
• immerse soldiers	DIPSAS
• soldiers *have* hard . . .	SASH
• soldiers in the East	SASINE
soldiers	TA
• goodbye *to* soldiers	VALETA
• soldiers *at* exercise	TAPE

Anag [cat]; Any *; Begin IGN–; Endings –ING; eg •; Hidden /cat/; Implied add (on); Implied in (in);

• soldiers know . . .	TAKEN
soldiers dance	LANCERS
soldier's father	CHAPLAIN, PADRE
soldiers in France	AEF, BEF
soldiers *in France*	SOLDATS
soldiers *on*	add –OR, –RE
• fellow soldiers *on*	DONOR
• man soldiers *on*	HERE
soldier's salute	PRESENT
	(*see also* army)

sole

sole accompaniment	HEEL, UPPER, WELT
sole expert	CHIROPODIST
sole impression	FOOTPRINT
sole of foot(D)	T
sole protector	HOBNAIL, SOCK
sole supplier	FISHERMAN, FISHMONGER
	FISHWIFE
sole supporter	FOOT-REST
sole tender	CHIROPODIST

solemn tomb	GRAVE

solicit

solicit support, *say*	CANVAS
solicitor	SOL(R)
Solicitor at Law	SL
solicitor before superior court	SSC
Solicitor General	SG
solicitor's dress	BRIEF ATTIRE
	LAW-SUIT

Solomon's judgement	SHARE ISSUE

solution

[saline] *solution*	LIANES
solution	SOL
solution of [clue]	LUCE
solution of [weak] . . .	WAKE

solve

[not] *solved*	TON
solved [clue]	LUCE

some[1]

indicating numbers:

some	IV, V, VI
• some unknown	IVY
• some in square . . .	VINT
• some New Testament . . .	VINT
some	PART
• some allowed	PARTLET
• some unknown	PARTY
• someone	PARTI
some	TEN, X
• some can . . .	TENABLE
• some church . . .	TENCH
• some workers	TENANTS

some[2]

other uses:

some ba/d apple/s	DAPPLE
some degree of hope	HOP

some *French*	DES
some idea	ID
some money	ONE
some of the . . . !	TH
some of the men	ME
some of t/he m/en	HEM
some on, *say*	SUMMON
some [quite] . . .	QUIET, –TIQUE
some poetry	AVERSE
some *rhymes*	BUM, COME, CRUMB,
	DRUM, DUMB, GUM, HUM,
	LUM, MUM, SUM, TUM

some say (=colloquial speech)

• "Cannot", *some say*	CANT
• *some say* folks will . . .	FORECASTLE

some say (=dialect)

• friendly, *some say*	CADGY
• *some say* fine	GRADELY, GRAITHLY
some *say*	SUM
some time	TIM
to some extent hap/py	
re/garding . . .	PYRE

somebody

somebody	ARM, LEG
• somebody rented	ARMLET
• somebody scoffed	LEGATE
somebody	CHEST, TORSO etc

somehow

[felt] *somehow* . . .	LEFT
somehow [tried] . . .	TIRED

somersault

somersault [done at] . . .	ATONED, DONATE
somersault made . . . <	EDAM

something

not *something* like . . .	KNOT, NOTE, NOWT
something from comi/c ope/ra	COPE
something like a cow	CHOW, COWL, SCOW

sometimes	TEMPI

somewhat

somewhat	–ISH
• cereal somewhat . . .	CORNISH
• part of fish somewhat . . .	FINISH
• somewhat masculine, *say*	ISHMAEL
*somew*hat	HAT
somewhat hackn/eye/d	EYE
somewhat minor . . .	MI
somewhat sooner	RATHER

somewhere

somewhere else, *say*	KNOTTIER

son

son	S
• son *and* parent	SMOTHER
• son in church	SINCE
• son *in* ho–t . . .	HOST
• twin sons	SS
son of	

Letter replaced \c\at; Omit (a); Pointers *out*; Retain a̲; Split B_ED; Down (D); Backwards <or ^

		sort	
–a bitch	SOB	sort	
–a prostitute, *say*	HORSE-BOY	sort of bone	T
–Englishman	FITZ	sort of boy, *say*	BELL, BREECHES
–Scotsman	MAC		LIFE
–Welshman	AP	sort of fish	KINDLING
song		sort of heather	KINDLING
song		sort of horse	ARAB
–French song	CHANSON	*sort of* [horse]	SHORE
–German song	LIED	sort of shirt	T
–Italian song	CANZONE	sort of square	T
–Spanish song	CANCION	[sort] *out*	ORTS, ROTS, TORS
song	AIR	*sort* [out R's]	TOURS
• loud song	FAIR	*sorted* [letters]	SETTLER
• quiet song	PAIR	*sorted out* [main date]	ANIMATED
• song *in* company	CAIRO	*sorting out* [papers]	SAPPER
and		**soufflé**	
• songman, *say*	AIRMAIL	[lemon] *soufflé*	MELON
song	ARIA	*soufflé* [dishes]	HISSED
• song *in* Merchant Navy	MARIAN	*soufflé of* [date, cream] . . .	MACERATED
• song *in* test	PARIAH	**soul mate**	HEART
• song *with* new . . .	ARIAN	**sound**	
song	LAY	click *sound*	CLIQUE
• loud song	FLAY	great-*sounding*	GRATE
• quiet song	PLAY	sound as a bell	DING, RING, TING
• song relating to . . .	LAYABOUT	*sound as a* bell	BEL, BELLE
Song of Solomon	SOLARIA	*sound* broadcast	SEW, SO(W)
song, *say*	HIM, LEAD	*sound* heart	CORPS, HART
song tour	ROUND	*sound* men	GUISE
song-writer	SOLOMON	*sound* money	CACHE
song-writer's friend	MILKMAN	sound of bird	CHEEP, TWEET
song-writer's performing	FOSTER-SON	*sound of* bird	BURD, BURRED
songs, *say*	LEADER	sound of Davis	MILESTONE
songster, *say*	BURD, BURRED	sound of dumb-bell	NOTING
sophisticated	IN	*sound of* gong	MEDDLE
soprano	S, SOP	sound of horse	NEIGH, WHINNY
sorceress		*sound of* horse	HOARSE
sorceress	SIBYL	*Sound of* Music	HEIR
• sorceress devoured, *say*	SIBILATE	sound of pain	OUCH, OW
• sorceress *with* worker, *say*	SIBILANT	*sound of* pain	PANE
sorceress	WITCH	sound of rain	PATTER
• live sorceress	BEWITCH	*sound of* rain	REIGN, REIN
• second sorceress	SWITCH	sound of sleep	Z
and		*sound of* sleep	DOES, KNAP, WREST
• sorceress, *say*	WHICH	*sound of* the sea	C, CEE, SEE
sore		sound pleased	PURR
sore	RAW	sound properties	ACOUSTICS
• saint *with* sore . . .	STRAW	sound reproducer	GRANDFATHER
• sore head	RAWNESS		GRANDMOTHER
• sore skin	RAWHIDE	sound reproducer, *say*	HYPHAE
sore *back<*	EROS	sound sleeper	TOP
[sore] *distress*	EROS, ROES, ROSE	*sound* waves	WAIVES
sore *head*	S	*sound* way . . .	WEIGH
sorry		*sound* wood	TIMBRE, WOULD
sorry expression	APOLOGY	*sounded* a chord	ACCORD
sorry outfit	SACKCLOTH (AND ASHES)	*sounding*-board	BORED
sorry performance	PENANCE	*soundly* based	BASTE

---

soundly designed	–MENT
soundly educated	TAUT
soundness of limb	LIMN
sounds as if I . . .	AYE, EYE
sounds like rain	REIGN, REIN
sounds weak	WEEK
soup	
[pea] *soup*	APE
soup	DAMPCOURSE
soup [made] . . .	DAME, EDAM, MEAD
sour	
sour beer	BITTER
[sour] *disposition*	OURS
sweet-and-sour	TART
source	
source	PARENT
source of dates	PALM
source of [dates]	SATED
source of <u>d</u>ates	D
source of draughts	DISPENSARY, PHARMACY
source of <u>d</u>raughts	D
source of evidence	GRASS, WITNESS BOX
source of <u>e</u>vidence	E
source of quarrel	FLETCHER, QUIVER
source of <u>q</u>uarrel	Q
source of [stream]	MASTER, REMAST
source of <u>s</u>tream	S
south	
south	S
south-east	SE
south *of France*	SUD
south-south-east	SSE
south-west	SW
south-south-west	SSW
South Africa	
South Africa	RSA
South Africa	SA
• South African climber	SAVINE
• South African footballer	SAPELE
• South African women	SASHES
• young Boer and	SALAD
• girl *goes to* South Africa	SALSA
• South Africans and	MENSA
• South African insect, *say*	SAMITE
• south African sheep, *say*	SALAAM
• South African ship, *say*	SALINA
South Africa	ZA
South African Airways	SAA
South African capital	RAND
<u>S</u>outh <u>A</u>frican *leaders*	SA
South African runner	ORANGE, OSTRICH
South African wine	CAPERED
South America	
South America	SA

• South American boy	SALAD
• South American gin	SATRAP
• South American girl	SABELLA
• South American shipping company	SALINE
South America	SUS, SUSA
South American girl	PERUSAL
South American runner	AMAZON, NANDOO, N(H)ANDU, RHEA
South Australia	SA
South Island	SI
South Latitude	SL, SLAT
South Pole	SP
southern	
southern	S
• southern bit	SORT
• southern cape	SHORN
• southern state	SAVER
Southern Railway	SR
Southern Region	SR
sovereign	
sovereign	ER, EMPEROR, IMP K, KING, R, REX Q, QUEEN, REGINA L, POUND
sovereigns	DYNASTY, ROYALTY LL, LS, POUNDS
Soviet Union	
Soviet Union	SU, USSR
Soviet Union, *say*	RUSHER
space	
space	EM
• space complete	EMENDED
• space encountered . . .	EMMET
• space in manuscript	MENS
space	EN
• spaceship	ENS
• space shots	ENTRIES
• space suit	ENCASE
space in Fleet Street	EM, EN
space in the roof, *say*	RHEUMATIC
space traveller	ASTEROID, COMET METEOR(ITE), PLANET
spacecraft working	LEMON
spacemen	NASA
spacious, *say*	RHEUMY
spacious ship	LARGESS
spade	S
spaghetti	STRING COURSE
Spain	E
span	
span 3ft, *say*	SPANIARD
span a . . .	incl A
spanned by *	incl in *
• river *spanned by* boy	LARD
spanner	BRIDGE
spanning *	incl *

• boy *spanning* river	LARD
Spanish	
Spaniard, *say*	MANUAL
Spanish capital	EURO, PESETA
Spanish *flower*	TAGUS
Spanish fly	MOSCA
Spanish football team	SIDEREAL
Spanish leader	CID
Spanish *leader*	S
Spanish-speaking man	HOMBRE
Spanish steps	FLAMENCO, SARABANDE
spare	
spare	THIN
• spare key	THINE, THING
• spare sovereign	THINKING
spare locker	DUPLICATE KEY
spare *part*	SPAR, ARE
[spare] *parts*	PARES, PEARS, RAPES
	REAPS, SPEAR
spare ribs	HAREM
spare room	CLEARANCE, TOLERANCE
sparkle	
sparkling girl	BERYL, RUBY
sparkling [lights]	SLIGHT
sparkling plan	STARMAP
spatter	
[rain] *spattered*	IRAN, RANI
spattering [drops]	PRODS
speak	
French-speaking waiter	GARCON
German-speaking wife	FRAU
Italian-speaking girl	RAGAZZA
right *in speech*	RITE
so to speak, red	READ
Spanish-speaking teacher	MAESTRO
speak longer	UTTERMOST
speak fast	EXPRESS
speak, *say*	TORQUE
speaker	I, MOUTH
Speaker's wig	WHIG
speakers	LIPS
speaking part	LARYNX, LIPS, TONGUE
speaking to the . . .	TOOTHY
speech in chapel	ORATORY
	(*see also* spoke, spoken)
spear	
broken [spear]	PARES, PEARS
	RAPES, REAPS, SPARE
point of spear	S
spearhead	S
[spear]*cast*	PARES, PEARS
	RAPES, REAPS, SPARE
special	
Special Air Service	SAS
Special Constable	SC
special delivery	CHINAMAN

	GOOGLY, YORKER
special drawing right(s)	SDR
special order	SO
special [care]	ACER, ACRE, RACE
special sort of [plane]	PANEL
special treatment of [steel]	LEETS
	STELE
specially-arranged [tables]	BLEATS
	STABLE
specially-shaped [canoe]	OCEAN
species	SP(P)
specify	
specific demand	EXACT
specific gravity	SG
specifically	AS
specification of [stone]	NOTES, ONSET
	SETON, TONES
specifies [whiter] . . .	WRITHE
specifying [older] . . .	DROLE
specimen	
anot/her pes/t *as specimen*	HERPES
specimen of pl/ant I c/ollected	ANTIC
spectacle	
spectacle case	FRAME
spectacle, *say*	CITE, SEEN, SITE
spectacles	OO
spectacular	incl OO
• *spectacular* mountain	MOOT
• *spectacular* woman	MOORS
	(*see also* bespectacled)
speculate	
speculated, *say*	GUEST
speculator	THEORIST
speculator	BEAR, STAG
• speculator's relative	BEARSKIN
• speculator (German)	STAGGER
speech	(*see* speak)
speed	
speed	MPH
• circles *at* speed	OOMPH
speed	RATE
• *quietly* speed . . .	PRATE
• speed of bowling	OVERRATE
• speed of delivery	BIRTHRATE
speed	TEMPO
• speed increase	TEMPORISE
• speed *to* meeting	TEMPORALLY
speed merchant	DRUG DEALER
speed of light	C, RUSH
speeded *up*(D)^	NAR
speedy	RAPID
• speedy ship	RAPIDS
• speedy, *say*	RABID
spell	
spell [cast] . . .	ACTS, SCAT
spell of [cool] . . .	LOCO

Anag [cat]; Any *; Begin IGN–; Endings –ING; eg •; Hidden /cat/; Implied add (on); Implied in (in);

spelling	SP	• split *in* ship	STORES
spelling [danger]	GANDER, GARDEN	• split twice, *say*	TORRENT
	RANGED	*split* [atoms]	MOATS, STOMA
spelling expert	WARLOCK, WITCH, WIZARD	*split by* a . . .	incl A
spelling work	SORCERY, WITCHCRAFT	*split by* *	incl *
sphere		• lo–g *split by* pin	LOPING
sphere of vision	EYEBALL	*split from* big/ger m/ass	GERM
spherical bullet	ROUND	split fruit	BANANA
spice ship	SMACK	split pasture	GRASS
spider		Split personality	CROAT, SERB, YUGOSLAV
spider	WEBSTER		DIVORCEE
spiderman	BRUCE	Split tongue	SERBO-CROAT
spies	CIA	split spice	CLOVE
spill		*splitting* *	incl in *
[Aintree] *spill*	TRAINEE	• pin *splitting* lo–g	LOPING
spill [gin]	IGN–, –ING	**spoil**	
spilled [over]	ROVE	spoil	MAR
spilt [ale on] . . .	ALONE	• spoil a fight	MARABOUT
spin		• spoil drink	MARGIN
spin a record	ROLL	• spoil fish	MARID, MARLING
spin [drier]	RIDER	• spoils of war	MARS
spinner	JENNY	and	
spinner's delivery	SPIDER'S WEB	• soldiers spoil . . .	TAMAR
spinning [tops]	POTS, SPOT, STOP	*spoil* [meal]	LAME, MALE
spinning tops<	SPOT	spoil plans, *say*	RECTRIX
spun [yarn]	NARY	*spoiled* [brat]	BART
spirit		*spoiling* [all the] . . .	LETHAL
spirit	RUM	*spoils of* [war]	RAW
• 500 spirits	DRUMS	**spoke**	
• spirit-man	RUMAL, RUMBO	spoke from memory, *say*	RESITED
• spirits dance	RUM-SHOP	spokesman	VOICE, WHEELWRIGHT
• spirited scholar	RUMBA	*spokesman's* time	THYME
• spirited game	RUMMY		(*see also* speak)
Spirit of America	GASOLINE, RYE	**spoken**	
Spirit of St Louis	APPLEJACK, BOURBON	*spoken* aloud	ALLOWED
spirit photograph	BRANDY SNAP	*spoken* rites	RIGHTS
spirit, *say*	(D)JINN, RHUMB	*spoken word* which it . . .	WITCHES
	SOLE	**sponsor film**	GODFATHER
splash		**sport**	
[mud she] *splashed*	MUSHED	[field] *sport*	FILED
splashing [scent]	CENTS	sport	FA, FL, RL, RU
splatter		• sport-shirt	FAT
[drops] *splattering*	PRODS	• first-class *in* sport	FAIL
splattered [mud on] . . .	MOUND	• for example, one *in* sport	REGAL
splendid		• sports group	RUSSET
splendid	BULLY	*sporting* a . . .	incl A
• splendid start	BULLY-OFF	*sporting* [a new] . . .	WANE, WEAN
splendid	DANDY	sporting animal	LION, SPRINGBOK, WALLABY
• splendid star, *say*	DANDELION	sporting bird	KIWI
split		sporting headgear	CAPON
split	RENT	sporting side	LEG, OFF, ON
• shirt split	TRENT	sporting situation	ARENA, COURT, PITCH,
• split gangster's . . .	RENTALS		RINK etc
• split twice, *say*	TORRENT		LORDS, TWICKENHAM
split	TORE		WEMBLEY etc
• second split	STORE	*sporting* *	incl *

Letter replaced \c\at; Omit (a); Pointers *out*; Retain a̲; Split B_ED; Down (D); Backwards <or ^

• di–ed *sporting* medal	DIMMED	
sports car	GT, ROD	
sports [car]	ARC	
sports-*centre*	OR	
sports club	BAT	
• *put* nothing *into* sports club	BOAT	
sportsman, *say*	FUNGI, FUNGUS	
sportsman's column	CORINTHIAN	

spot

spot	ACE
spot	DOT
• small spot	MICRODOT
• spot Henry	DOTH
• spot worker	DOTANT
spot	SEE
• spot attendant	SEEPAGE
• spot gnomes	SEE-SAWS
• spot many . . .	SEED
and	
• spot animal, *say*	SEA-BEAR
• spot insect, *say*	SEMITE
spot marked	X
spotless instrument	VIRGINAL
spots	SEES
• the *French* spots . . .	LESSEES
and	
• spots fish, *say*	SEASIDE
• spots insect, *say*	SEA-STICK
spots, *say*	FLEX
spotted	SAW
• spotted animal	SAWBUCK, SAW-HORSE
• spotted deer	SAWBUCK
spotted insect	SAWFLY
and	
• spotted Scot, *say*	SAURIAN
• spotted seabird(s), *say*	SAUTERNE(S)
spotted bananas	DOTTY
spotted bats	DOTTY
spotted cube	DI(C)E
spotted in Lon/don s/hop	DONS
spotted in *	incl in *
• dress *spotted in* Dis–s	DISROBES
spotted *outside*	SE–EN

sprawl

sprawled about [on bed]	BONED
sprawling [town]	WONT

spray

spray of flowers	HOSE, ROSE
	WATERING-CAN
spray-[tested]	DETEST
sprayed [into a] . . .	–ATION
spraying [trees]	REEST, RESET
	STERE, STEER

spread

spread *about*<	GRAM
spread [about]	U-BOAT

[spread] *about*		DRAPES, RASPED, SPARED
spread about [field]		FILED
spread container		CORSETS, CUMMERBUND
		GIRDLE, GREEN BELT
		JAR
spread [fear]		FARE
[spread] *out*		DRAPES, RASPED, SPARED
spread out [in the] . . .		THINE
spread [yarns]		SNARY
spreading [the slurs]		RUTHLESS
spreads news of fall		AIRSTRIP
spread[sheet]		THESE

spree

[go on crime] *spree*	ERGONOMIC
[A river], *Spree*	ARRIVE

spring

spring	CEE
spring	SPA
• spring about	SPARE
• spring the . . .	SPATHE
• springtime	SPAT
spring examination	MAYORAL
spring over	WELL DONE
spring publication	ISSUE
spring shrub	CAPER
spring vegetable	SPROUT
springs from [soil]	OILS, SILO
springtime	LEAP YEAR

sprinkle

sprinkle [salt]	LAST
sprinkled [over] . . .	ROVE
sprinkling of [snow]	OWNS, SOWN

sprout

sprouting	(in) BU–D
sprouting [bean]	BANE

spun	(see spin)
spur road	DRIVE

spurn

spurn a . . .	omit A
spurn *	omit *
• (O)liver *spurns* love	LIVER

spurious

[deal] *spuriously*	DALE, LADE, LEAD
spurious [art in] . . .	TRAIN

spy

spy	AGENT, BOND, SNOOP
[spy] *out*	PSY–
spy-ring, *say*	SPIRING
spymaster	M

squadron

squadron	SQN
squadron-*leader*	S

squall

[line] *squall*	NEIL, NILE
squall [coming]	GNOMIC
squally [weather[	WREATHE

Anag [cat]; Any *; Begin IGN–; Endings –ING; eg •; Hidden /cat/; Implied add (on); Implied in (in);

squander

squander savings	BLUESTOCKING
squandered [much] . . .	CHUM
squander[mania]	ANIMA

square

square	FOUR, NINE, SIXTEEN
square	S
• all square	TOTALS
• square head	STOP
• square playing-field	SPARK
square	SQ
square	T
• main square	SEAT
• set square	PUTT, SETT
• square one	TI–
• square pipe	THOSE
square cape	TRAFALGAR
square garden	MADISON
square meal	RAVIOLI
square-root of –1	I
square seat	SETTLE

squash

[lemon] *squash*	MELON
[lime] *squash*	EMIL, MILE
[orange] *squash*	ONAGER
squash fruit	GOURD
squash racket	SILENCE
squash [racket]	RETACK, TACKER
squashed [finger]	FRINGE
squashes relative	STEPSON

squeeze

squeeze from [oranges]	ONAGERS
squeeze in a . . .	incl A
squeeze in *	incl *
• fish squeezed in pres–s	PRESIDES
squeezing *	incl in *
• pres–s *squeezing* fish	PRESIDES

squelch

squelch [about]	U-BOAT
[quite] *squelchy*	QUIET, –TIQUE

squiffy

[quite] *squiffy*	QUIET
squiffy [Scot]	COTS

squiggle

squiggle [in the] . . .	THINE
squiggly [letters]	SETTLER
[words] *squiggled*	SWORD

squirm

squirm [in anger]	EARNING, NEARING
squirming [eel]	LEE

Sri Lanka	CL
s-shed	SHUT

St Paul's

St Paul's, *for example*	WRENCH

stable

stable	STOCKHOLDER
stable at this place, *say*	STUDIER
stable closed, *say*	STUDDED
stable company	FIRM
stables, *say*	MUSE

stack wood	RICKSHAW

staff

staff appointment	MANDATE
staff character	FLAT, NATURAL, SHARP
staff claim	POST BAG
Staff College	SC
Staff Corps	SC
staff criticism	STICK
Staff Officer	SO
staff whip	POLECAT

stag party	MALEFACTION

stage

[in stage] *production*	SEATING
stage school	COACH
[stage] *make-up*	GATES
[stage] *production*	GATES

stagger

[it was] *staggering*	WAIST, WAITS
stagger *about*<	LEER
stagger [along]	LOGAN, LONGA
stagger around	RE–EL
stagger, *say*	REAL, ROLE
staggered [into] . . .	–TION
staggering [feat]	FATE

stain

causing [stains]	SAINTS
[stain] *remover*	SAINT
stain, *say*	DAI, DIE
stain timber, *say*	DIALOGUE

stale

stale	OFF
• 100 stale . . .	COFF
• Peg *puts* stale *in* . . .	TOFFEE
• stale buffet	OFFBEAT
stale	OLD
• 100 stale . . .	COLD
• finest *includes* stale . . .	BOLDEST
• stale fish	OLD SCHOOL
stale	
indicating old word:	
• *stale* cabbage	WORT
• *stale* jibe	BOB, GIRD
• *stale* taste	GUST
stale loaf	FLATHEAD

stamp

stamp	FRANK
stamp card	CHARACTER
stamped addressed envelope	SAE

stampede

stampede of [steers]	RESETS
stampede, *say*	BULRUSH
stampeding [herds]	SHERD, SHRED

Letter replaced \c\at; Omit (a); Pointers *out*; Retain <u>a</u>; Split B_ED; Down (D); Backwards <or ^

stand

stand	TEE
• stand *astride* as . . .	TEASE
stand bats . . . (D)^	STAB
stand-in	LOCUM, REGENT
stand in church	LECTERN
stand in court	DOCK
stand-_off_ half	DOFF
stand straighter	LISTLESS
standing order	SO
standing order(D)^	EBO, MO
standing up(D)^	PU
standing up as Sam . . . (D)^	MASSA
stands up, *say*	COX

standard¹

standard	FLAG
• standard length	FLAGPOLE
• Standard Time	FLAG DAY
• standard weight	FLAGSTONE
standard	NORM
• friend *follows* standard . . .	NORMALLY
• standard article	NORMA(N)
• standard man	NORMAL
standard	PAR
• standard English	PARE
• standard operation	PARENT
• standard quantity	PARAMOUNT
• standard tim(e), *almost*	PARTIM
• standard weapon	PARLANCE
standard	STOCK
• standard measure	STOCKYARD
• standard table	STOCKLIST
• standard vehicle	STOCK CAR
Standard Book Number	SBN
standard deviation	SD
Standard Serial Number	SSN
standard setter	JONES
standard temperature and pressure	STP
standard tools	HAMMER AND SICKLE

staple

staple diet	IRON RATIONS
staple food, *say*	BRED
stapling machine, *say*	TACHOMETER

star

shooting star	ANNIE OAKLEY
	ARCHER, SAGITTARIUS
star	LEAD
star	SUN
• former pupil *returns*< to star	BOSUN
• star goes for a swim	SUNBATHES
• starling	SUNFISH
star-gazer	NIGHTWATCHMAN
[star] *potential*	ARTS, RATS, TARS, TSAR
star professional	SOLACE

star-rating	MAGNITUDE
star *turn*<	RATS
[star] *turn*	ARTS, RATS, TARS, TSAR
starfish	PISCES
twinkling [star]	ARTS, RATS, TARS, TSAR

start

kick*start*	K
red*start*	R
start	ENTERON, GOAT
start *and* finish	OFFEND(ING)
start attack	ONSET
start _a_ttack	A
start coaching	EMBUS
start _c_oaching	C
start of match	KICK-OFF, KO
start of _m_atch	M
start of play	ACTI
start of _p_lay	P
start of winter	FALL OVER
start of _w_inter	W
start _o_ff . . .	O
start off (t)he . . .	HE
start off the (r)ace	ACE
start on _M_onday	M
start race	FOUND
start _r_ace	R
start race, *say*	SAGO
start _r_ising up(D)^	SIR
start school	INSTITUTE
start _s_chool	S
start _t_o . . .	T
start to cheer	HIP
start to _c_heer	C
start to disappear	omit 1st letter
• (m)any *start* to disappear	ANY
start to _d_isappear	D
start to rain	TRAIN
start to _r_ain	R
start to serve	WIND UP
start to _s_erve	S
start-_u_p	U
start up factory	FIREWORKS
start working	SETON
start _w_orking	W
starters for The Oaks	ACORNS
starters for _T_he _O_aks	TO
starting-_g_ate	G
starting point	LINE
starting _p_oint	P
starting price	SP
starting _p_rice	P
starting price, *say*	COMMENSURATE
starting speed	FIRST RATE
starting speed	S
starts off (i)n (E)ast (b)y . . .	NASTY
starts off _t_he _r_ace _o_n _t_ime	TROT

Anag [cat]; Any *; Begin IGN–; Endings –ING; eg •; Hidden /cat/; Implied add (on); Implied in (in);

starts to <u>c</u>limb	CL	• South American state	SAGA
starts work	TITLE PAGE	• state highway	–GARD, GAST
starts <u>w</u>ork(ing)	W	• state railway	GARY
starvation	FAST WORK	• two states	GAGA, GALA
state¹		Illinois	ILL
inter-*state*	BERRY	• quiet state	PILL, SHILL
state	AVER	Indiana	IND
• many state number	CAVERN	• Western state	WIND
• Royal states	RAVERS	Kansas	KAN, KS
• state the time	AVERAGE	• state *with* a . . .	KANA
and		• managed state	RANKS
• states "Charged particle . . . "	AVERSION	• two states	KANGA
• states "Diocese . . . "	AVERSELY	Kentucky	KEN, KY
• States worker	AVERSANT	• works *returned*< *to* state	SPOKEN
state	SAY, UTTER	• spirit *returns*< *to* state	MURKY
state *briefly*	ARK, CAL, GA etc	Louisiana	LA
	(see state²)	• state highway	LARD, LAST
State Certificated Midwife	SCM	• state representative	LAMP
State Enrolled Nurse	SEN	• two states	LAME
state of collapse of [Red Inn]	DINNER	Maine	ME
state of [the art]	HATTER, THREAT	• state publication	MEAD
state of vehicle	CARNATION	• two states	GAME, LAME
<u>s</u>tate *opening*	S	Massachusetts	MASS
state ownership	CLAIM	• state service	MASS
State Registered Nurse	SRN	Mississippi	MI, MISS
state support	MAINTAIN	• about *to* state . . .	REMISS
state train	EXPRESS	• state *found in* alien . . .	EMIT
state where . . .	WARE, WEAR	• two states	MIME
stately home	PILE	Missouri	MO
statement	AC	• state god	MOLAR
statement of identity	AM, IAM, IM	New York	NY
	(see admit, confess, declare)	• imitator in state . . .	NAPERY
states	US	North Dakota	ND
• second-class states	BUS	• priest in state	NABBED
• states *in* about . . .	RUSE	• two states	LAND, MEND
• states time	USAGE	Ohio	O
statesman	AMERICAN, TEXAN, YANK	Rhode Island	RI
	EDEN, PEEL et al	• state vehicle	RIMINI
stating all . . .	AWL	South Carolina	SC
state²		• state current . . .	SCAMPS
commonly used names:		South Dakota	SD
Alabama	AL, ALA	• dined *in* state	SATED
• good state	GAL, GALA	Tennessee	TEN(N)
Arkansas	ARK	• state workers	TENANTS
• quiet state	PARK, SHARK	• state is . . .	TENNIS
California	CAL	Texas	TEX
• gold *in* state	CORAL	• state *exactly*	TEXT
Colorado	COL(O)	Utah	U(T)
• state *has* 500 . . .	COLD	• quiet state	PUT, SHUT
Columbia (District)	DC	Vermont	VT
Connecticut	CT	• so far *into* the state	VAST
• terrible state	DIRECT	Virginia	VA
Florida	FLA	• state permit	VALET
• state *has* quiet . . .	FLAP, FLASH	**station**	
• two states	FLAME	station	ST
Georgia	GA	station battle	WATERLOO

Letter replaced \c\at; Omit (a); Pointers *out*; Retain <u>a</u>; Split B_ED; Down (D); Backwards <or ^

station wagon	POLICE CAR
statuette	EMMY, OSCAR
staunch	
staunch ally	TROOPER
staunch supporter	STEM
stay	
"Stay hidden", *they said*	LILO
stay in	BATON
stay out (too long)	OVERSLEEP
stay put	SHIFTLESS
stay, *say*	WEIGHT
stay true	STAUNCH
stayed here, *say*	STADIA
stays silent	SAY-SO
steady	
steady business	FIRM
steady habit	UNIFORM
steal	
she *steals some* epic . . .	SHEEP
steal a bit	SNAFFLE
steal cat	WHIP
steal cattle, *say*	RUSSEL
steal cook	POACH
steal cot	NABBED
steal cutlery	POCKET KNIVES
steal money	TAKE NOTE
steal painting	ABSTRACT
steal weapon	RIFLE
stealer of tarts, *say*	PITAKA
stealing, *say*	ROB(B)IN
• stealing at this place, *say*	ROBINIA
• stealing cowl, *say*	ROBIN HOOD
• stealing it, *say*	ROBINET
stole drink	WRAPS UP
stole, *say*	RAP
stolen	HOT
• stolen animals	HOT-DOGS
• stolen silver	HOTPLATE
• stolen vessel	HOTPOT
steam	
steamer	STR
steaming [hot so] . . .	HOOTS, SHOOT
steamship	SS
steel drawers	MAGNETS
steeplechasers	OVERRIDERS
steer	
steer	CON
• become a steer	BEACON
• steer boat	CONTENDER
• steer *with* stick	CON-ROD
steer	OX
• second-class steer	BOX
• steer gets down, *say*	OXALITES
• steer round . . . and	OXO
• steer I placed, *say*	OCCIPUT

steering group	DRIVERS, PILOTS
step	
step on ladder, *say*	WRUNG
[step] *out*	PEST, PETS
step *out*	ST–EP
• ste–p *out of* the way	STEEP
step *out*	P–ACE
• step *out of* the way	PEACE
step-*up*(D)^	PETS
steradian	SR
sterling	STER, STG
stern	
stern	BACK
• sternpart	BACKBIT
• stern punishment	BACKLASH
• stern talk	BACKCHAT
stern	GRAVE
• friend *has* stern . . .	PALGRAVE
• stern *at the finish*	ENGRAVE
• stern saint	GRAVEST
stern	GRIM
• speaker *has* stern . . .	MEGRIM
• stern expert	GRIMACE
• stern man	GRIMED
stern accommodation	CHAIR, SEAT
stern appearance	HINDSIGHT
stern Athenian	DRACO
stern leader	STROKE
stern *leader*	S
stern of dinghy	Y
stern nurse	REAR
stern warning	REAR-LIGHT
Stevenson	RLS
stew	
in a stew about [seven]	EVENS
[stew]	WILD WEST
stew [recipe]	PIERCE
stewed [eels]	ELSE, SEEL
stewing-[steak]	KEATS, SKATE
	STAKE, TAKES
stick	
stick	GLUE
• stick my, *say*	GLOOMY
• stick ten, *say*	GLUTEN
• stick together, *say*	GLUON
stick	GUM
• stick my, *say*	GUMMY
• stick to second-class painting	GUMBOIL
• stick *up*(D)^	MUG
• *sticks* to tool	GUMSHOE
stick	ROD
• stick *around*<	DOR
• stick *around* a . . .	ROAD
• stick-*up*(D)^	DOR
• saint *takes* stick	

to English . . .	STRODE
stick-figure	PASTEL
stick out	CAN–E, RO–D
[stick] *out*	TICKS
sticker	CEMENT, GLUE, GUM
sticky *end*	Y
sticky food	CELERY, RHUBARB
sticky hand	TAR
sticky sweets	ICE-LOLLY
	TOFFEE-APPLE
sticky tin, *say*	JAMAICAN
sticky wicket	PITCH
stuck in mu/d at e/bb tide	DATE

stiff

stiff	BODY, CORPSE
stiff back	STERN
stiff examination	AUTOPSY, POST-MORTEM
stiff examiner	CORONER
stiff fabric, *say*	CANVASS
stiff paper	HARD TIMES
stiff suit	ARMOUR
stiff support(er)	BIER
stiffen signal	STAR CHAMBER

stifle

stifled by lar/ge m/uffler	GEM
stifled by *	incl in *
• is *stifled by* ho–t . . .	HOIST
stifling a . . .	incl Λ
stifling *	incl *
• male *stifling* one . . .	MAIN

still

still	PHOTO(GRAPH), SNAP(SHOT)
still employed	INFIRM
still flying	HOVERING
still single	YETI
still there	INACTIVE

stir

stir food	BREAD AND WATER, PORRIDGE
stir-fryer, *say*	PANMIXIA
stir [soup]	OPUS
stir up [anger]	RANGE
stirred [tea]	ATE, EAT, ETA
stirring article	(TEA) SPOON
stirring [march]	CHARM

stitch

stitch	SEW
• stitch in . . .	SEWIN
• stitch *round* shirt	STEW
and	
• stitch, *say*	SO, SOW
stitch	TACK
• second stitch	STACK
• stitch it, *say*	TACKET
• stitch *round* right	TRACK

stoa

[stoa]	WILD OATS

stock

stock book	RESERVE
stock car	CATTLE TRUCK
stock exchange	CATTLE MARKET
stock heroin	RACEHORSE
stocked by wi/ne st/ore	NEST
stocked by *	incl in *
• sulphur *stocked by* de–pot	DESPOT
stocked in *	incl in *
• silver *stocked in* shop	STORAGE
stockholder	CATTLEMAN, RANCHER
stocking shoe/s and s/ocks	SANDS
stocking *	incl *
• de–pot *stocking* sulphur	DESPOT
stocks drink	KEEPSAKE
stocking *	incl *
• shop *stocking* silver	STORAGE
stocktaking	RUSTLING, SHOPLIFTING

stocking

stocking filler	(FATTED) CALF
	LEG, THIGH
stockings, *say*	HOES

stoke

stoker	BRAM
stokes	S(T)

stolen (*see* steal)

stomach

be(a)st has *no stomach*	BEST
losing stomach, patient	PANT, PATENT

stone

stone	OPAL etc
stone	PIT
• smooth stone	SANDPIT
• stone church	PITCH
• stone *found in* Home Counties	SPITE
stone	ST
• about stone	REST
• stone *found in* river	TASTY
• stone road	STAVE
stone	ROCK
• 100 stones	CROCKS
• fine stone	FROCK
• stone a goat	ROCKABILLY
and	
• stone at this place, *say*	ROCKIER
• stone it, *say*	ROCKET, ROCQUET
stone circle	ETERNITY RING
stone club	BRICKBAT
stone dam	NIOBE
stone figure	DIAMOND
stone type	EMERALD, RUBY
stone worker	LAPIDARY
stony-*hearted*	O
stony-hearted girl	OLIVE, PEACH

stop

stop	BLOCK

Letter replaced \c\at; Omit (a); Pointers *out*; Retain a̲; Split B_ED; Down (D); Backwards <or ^

• stop in Greece	BLOCKING
• stop time	BLOCKAGE
stop	COLON
stop	HO
• a total number stop . . .	TALLY-HO
• stop exercises	HOPE
• stop work	HOOP
stop	POINT
• dance *comes to* a stop	BALLPOINT
• stop *before* journalist . . .	POINTED
stop	PT
stop	STAY
• stop *after* player . . .	BACKSTAY
• stop *without* a car	STARRY
and	
• stop soldiers, *say*	STAMEN, STARE
stop advertisement	PLUG
stop *and* listen	ENDEAR
stop *at sea*	AVAST, BELAY
stop cheating	SQUASH RACKETS
stop growth	BARGAIN
stop in America	PERIOD
stop looking	PEERLESS
stop master	STEMMA
stop music	REFRAIN
stop, *say*	CHEQUE, FINNISH, SEAS, SEES, SEIZE
stop searching	CLOSE
stop short	COMMA
stop short of tow(n)	TOW
stop *talking*	SEAS, SEES, SEIZE
stopped instrument . . .	ORGAN
stopped skating	OFFICE
stopped work, *say*	WRESTED
store	
store, *say*	HORDE, WHORED
stored in *	incl in *
• one car *stored in* sh–ed	SHIRRED
storing a . . .	incl A
storing fence	HOARDING
storing *	incl *
• sh–ed *storing* one car	SHIRRED
storm	
[Desert] *Storm*	RESTED
storm damage	CHARGE
storm lantern	BLOWLAMP, BLOWTORCH
storm location	TEACUP
storm [rages]	GEARS
stormed, *say*	REI(G)NED
stormy [waters]	WASTER
story	
story	TALE
• second story	STALE
• story *about* mother	TAMALE
• story books	TALENT
and	

• story, *say*	TAIL
story in parts, *say*	CEREAL
stout	
stout carrier	PORTER
stout leader	FATHEAD
stout *leader*	S
stout man	FATAL, PLUMPED
stout spar	STRONGBOX
straddle	
straddled by *	incl in A
• a horse *straddled by* J–ean	JACOBEAN
straddling a . . .	incl A
straddling river	incl R
straddling *	incl *
• J–ean *straddling* a horse	JACOBEAN
straggle	
[conifers] *straggling*	FORENSIC
straggling [line]	LIEN, NEIL, NILE
straight line	I
strain	
strain, *say*	WRETCH
strained [soup]	OPUS
straining [all the] . . .	LETHAL
strait	ST
Strand entrance	PLYMOUTH
strange	
strange	ODD
• strange child	ODDS-ON
• strange dance	ODDBALL
• strange men	ODDFELLOWS
strange	RUM
• saint *has* strange . . .	STRUM
• strange *and* quiet	RUMP
• strange manager	RUM RUNNER
and	
• strange cat, *say*	RUMPUS
strange [bird]	DRIB
strange *end*	E
strange individual	PECULIAR
strange origins	ST
strange [thing]	NIGHT
strange [to relate]	TOLERATE
strange turn of [phrase]	SERAPH
strange way to [act]	CAT
strangely [silent]	ENLIST
stranger [saw her] . . .	HAWSER
Stravinsky	
Stravinsky *quintet*	RAVIN
straw	
straw	BOATER
straw cable	HAYWIRE
stray	
stray [dogs in] . . .	DOINGS
straying [over] . . .	ROVE
stream	
stream	BANKER, FLOWER

Anag [cat]; Any *; Begin IGN–; Endings –ING; eg •; Hidden /cat/; Implied add (on); Implied in (in);

stream serving mill, *say*	MILREIS
streamlining, *say*	FARING
street	
street	ST
• street light	STRAY
• street needs repair	STRUTTED
• streetwarden	STRANGER
and	
• Meadow Street	LEAST
• Virginia Street	VAST
• West Fish Street	WIDEST
and	
• house *in* the street	SHOT
street *in Berlin*	STRASSE
street *in Madrid*	CALLE
street *in Paris*	RUE
street *in Rome*	STRADA
street, *say*	LAIN, RODE
streetwise bosses	LEADERSHIP
strengthen	
strengthen coast	SHORE
strengthen coast, *say*	SURE
strenuous	
[I tried] *strenuously*	TIDIER
strenuously [tries]	RITES, TIRES
stretch	
stretch	PORRIDGE, SENTENCE
stretch	
indicating abbreviation	
to be expanded:	
• can't *stretch*	CANNOT
• *stretch* arm	ARMENIAN, ARMORIC
stretch bird	CRANE
stretch [PC30]	TRIPTYCH
stretcher	BRICK, PROCRUSTES
stretcher-bearer	HOD
stricken	
stricken [by a] . . .	BAY
[it was] *stricken*	WAIST, WAITS
strict	
strict	STERN
• strict follower	STERN-CHASER
• strict parent	PASTERN
• strict treatment rooms	STERNWARDS
strict *limitations*	ST
strike	
strike	BEAT
• strike on the head	BROWBEAT
• strike queen	BEATER
strike	BELT
• inexperienced *before*	
strike	GREEN BELT
• strike one . . .	BELTANE
strike	BLOW
• strike *about* English . . .	BELOW
• strike insect	BLOWFLY

strike	BUMP
• strike family	BUMPKIN
• strike Henry	BUMPH
• strike monarch	BUMPER
strike	COSH
• strike queen	COSHER
and	
• strike woman, *say*	COSHER, KOSHER
strike	HIT
• 100 strikes	CHITS
• strike woman	HITHER
• woman *on* strike	WHIT
strike	LAM
• strike a . . .	LAMA
• strike a difficulty	LAMPLIGHT
• strike girl	LAMELLA
• strike victim	LAMPREY
strike	PAT
• second strike	SPAT
• strike *and* uprising	PATRIOT
• strike *in* the Home Counties	SPATE
strike	PELT
• second strike	SPELT
• strike a number, *say*	PELTATE
• strike a saint	PELTAST
strike	PUNCH
• strike a horse	PUNCH
• strike journalist	PUNCHED
• strike the ball	PUNCHBOWL
strike	RAM
• 100 *on* strike	CRAM
• strike attendant	RAMPAGE
• strike *in* iron . . .	FRAME
and	
• strike *over<*	MAR
strike	RAP
• strike fish	RAPID
• strike *in* church	CRAPE
• time *to* strike	TRAP
and	
• strike *over<*	PAR
strike	SLAP
• strike rod	SLAPSTICK
• strike sailor	SLAPJACK
• strikes insect	SLAPSTICK
and	
• strike dog, *say*	SLAP-UP
• strike *over<*	PALS
strike	SOCK
• players *on* strike	WINDSOCK
• strike son	SOCKS
• strike *without* Henry	SHOCK
and	
• strike it, *say*	SOCKET
• strike woman, *say*	SOCCER
strike	TAP

Letter replaced \c\at; Omit (a); Pointers *out*; Retain a̲; Split B_ED; Down (D); Backwards <or ^

• end strike	STOP-TAP		OAR, ROWER
• strike in ship	STAPS	**strong**[1]	
• strike it, *say*	TAPPET, TAPPIT	strong	F
and		• strong arm	FARM
• strike *over*	PAT	• strong back	FRUMP
strike	WHIP	• strong jug	FEWER
• animal *on* strike	HORSEWHIP, WHIPCAT	and	
• strike favourite	WHIPPET	• a strong anger	AFIRE
• striking the best . . .	WHIPPING CREAM	• a strong company	AFFIRM
and		• a strong flow	AFFLUX
• strike it, *say*	WHIPPET	very strong	FF
strike	TEST MATCH	• a very strong light	AFFLUX, AFFRAY
strike *about* . . . <	MAR, PALS, PAR, PAT	• a very strong melody	AFFAIR
strike coins	MAKE READY	• a very strong No. 9	AFFIX
strike off doctor	omit DR, MO	strong	IRON
strike pest	SLUG	• drunk *in* iron . . .	ISOTRON
strike rhythm	BEAT	• strong hand	IRON DUKE
strikes fly, *say*	WAXWING	• strong slaves	IRONWORKS
striking	OUT	strong	STR
• 50 striking . . .	LOUT	**strong**[2]	
• afterthought *about* striking . . .	POUTS	strong-arm man	SAMSON
• striking mechanic	OUTFITTER	strong binding	STRAPPING
• striking *on* the head	OUTNESS	strong bird, *say*	TOUGHEN
• striking players	OUTCAST	strong dog	HUSKY
• striking *with* whip	OUTCROP	strong catkin	FIRMAMENT
strikebreaker	RAT, SCAB	strong current	CAMPS
strikers	MATCHES, LUCIFERS, VESTAS	strong drink	STOUT
striking redhead	MATCH, LUCIFER, VESTA	strong man	HERCULES, SAMSON, TITAN
struck on the head	BROWBEATEN	strong man, *say*	TIGHTEN, TUFTED
struck with knee, *say*	KNEAD, NEED	strong noise	SOUND
string		strong point	FORTE
string course	SPAGHETTI	• strong point, *say*	FOR TEA, FORTY
string worn	G	strong porter	STOUT
stringed instrument, *say*	LIAR, LIER	strong stem	STAUNCH
	LOOT	strong suit	ARMOUR, TRUMPS
	VIAL, VILE	strong team, *say*	MITICIDE
strings (violin)	A, D, E, G	**strontium unit**	SU
stringy bird, *say*	TOUGHEN	**struck**	(*see* strike)
strip		**structure**	
strip copy	TAKE-OFF	[plane's] *structure*	PANELS
strip off	omit ends	*structure of* [chapter]	PATCHER, REPATCH
• (a)skin(g) *to strip off*	SKIN	**struggle**	
• *strip off* (p)ain(t)	AIN	struggle forward	VIEWING
strip off	omit OFF	*struggle* to [rise]	SIRE
• *strip* off t(off)ee . . .	TEE	*struggled* [like] . . .	KIEL
strip weapon	RIFLE	struggled *with* mineral	BATTLEDORE
stripper	LOCUST, SALOME	*struggling* [up an] . . .	PUNA
stroke		**stub**	
stroke	COUP	*stub out* [a cigar]	AGARIC
stroke fawn	CRAWL	[stub] *out*	BUST, BUTS, TUBS
• stroke fish	COUPLING	stubby tail	DOG-END
stroke gander	GLANCE	**stuck**	(*see* stick)
• stroke leg	COUPON	**stud manager**	BOSS
stroke-maker	ARTIST, DECORATOR	**student**	
	PAINTBRUSH	student	L
	BATSMAN	• student in church	LINCH

• student *in* rear . . .	BLACK
• student quarters	LEE, LEN, LES, LEW
• student *takes* port	LADEN
Student Christian Movement	SCM
Student of Civil Law	SCL
Student Representative Council	SRC
students	NUS
	(*see also* learner)

study

study	CON
• study dance	CONTANGO
• study music	CONSTRAIN
• study poetry	CONVERSE
and	
• studies birds	
family, *say*	CONSTERNATION
• studies particles	CONSORTS
study	DEN
• study gallery	DENTATE
• study weight	DENOUNCE
• the *French* study . . .	LADEN
and	
• study conurbation, *say*	DENSITY
study	READ
• study only . . .	READJUST
• study *with* one journalist	READIED
• study with *German* . . .	READMIT
study	PORE
• second study	SPORE
• study aboard	SPORES
and	
• study food, *say*	PORTABLE
• study, *say*	POOR, POUR
study	SCAN
• king *in* study	SCRAN
• study row	SCANTIER
• study square	SCANT
study *French* . . .	ETUDE
study of	
–chains, *say*	OROLOGY
–fish, *say*	IDEOLOGY
–Romans, *say*	VIROLOGY
–tarts, *say*	HOROLOGY
studied *speech*	RED
studies	COURSE

stuff

stuff young bird	SQUAB
stuffed into *	incl in *
• fruit *stuffed into* cleric	DAPPLED
stuffed with a . . .	incl A
stuffed with *	incl *
• cleric *stuffed with* fruit	DAPPLED

stumble

stumble[bum]	UMB–
stumbles *about*<	SPIRT
stumbles [over] . . .	ROVE

stumbles over [step]	PEST, PETS
stumbling [words]	SWORD
stumped	ST
stun	
stun, *say*	DAYS
stunner	DISH, KO
stunning finale	KNOCK-OUT, KO
stunt	
quit(e) *stunted*	QUIT
[quite] *stunted*	QUIET, –TIQUE
stunted tree	(l)ARCH, (t)REE
stupefy	
stupefy	NUMB
• stupefy man	NUMBLES
and	
• stupefy girl, *say*	NUMMARY
• stupefy man, *say*	NUMERIC
stupid	
stupid compact	DENSE
stupid team, *say*	SILICIDE
stupidly [dared]	ADDER, DREAD
[tried] *stupidly*	TIRED
sty	LITTER CONTAINER
style	
style	
indicating mode of	
address:	
• bishop's style	GRACE
• style of prince	HIGHNESS
	(*see also* address)
style [in art]	TRAIN
stylish nightclub	HIP-JOINT
stylish [robe]	BOER, BORE, EBOR
stylite	
stylite	POLE-SQUATTER
stylite's home	PERSONAL COLUMN
sub-	
indicating one word written	
below another word or letter(D):	
• *sub*marine ruler	SEAR
• *sub*-standard colour	PARTAN
• *sub*terranean gold	LANDAU
sub-group	WOLF-PACK
subject	
subject	SUB(J)
subject me . . .	I
subject of autobiography	I, ME
subject them . . .	THEY
subject to	UNDER
• subject to friction	UNDERWEAR
• subject to theft	UNDERTAKING
and	
• subject to delay, *say*	UNDERWEIGHT
• subject to proper, *say*	UNDERWRITE
subject to	
indicating one word	

written below another(D):	
• circle *subject to* queen	ERRING
• head *subject to* Russian . . .	REDPOLL
subject to error [in gold]	DOLING
subject us . . .	WE
subjunctive	SUB(J)
submarine	
submariner	LOW TAR, NEMO
submariner's gear	UNDERWEAR
submit	
submit account	RELATE, RETAIL
submit return	YIELD
subscriber trunk dialling	STD
subsequent	
subsequent	LATER
• *find* time *in* subsequent . . .	LATTER
• second *and* subsequent . . .	SLATER
• subsequent article	LATERAN
substitute	
substitute for [actor]	CROAT
substitute husband	RESERVE
substitute stableman	STANDING-ROOM
substitute train	STANDING-ROOM
subtle punishment	FINE
subtract	
subtract a . . .	omit A
subtract *	omit *
• *subtract* five *from* se(v)en	SEEN
succeed	
succeed	FAREWELL
succeed	WIN
• succeed *in* the Home Counties	SWINE
• succeed occasionally	WINSOME
• succeed *with* effort	WINTRY
• time *to* succeed	TWIN
succeed, *say*	DOWEL, WHIN
succeeded	S
succeeded	WON
• succeeded Edward	WONTED
• succeeded the *German* . . .	WONDER
• succeeded *without* the king	WORN
successful day	VE
successful dieter	LIGHTERMAN
successful singer	INVOICE
successful songwriter	HITMAN
succession, *say*	CERES
successor	HEIR
• successor appears	HEIRLOOMS
• successor *to* Portuguese noble	HEIRDOM
successor to Brand X	BRANDY
sucker	ACID DROP, STRAW
sudden stroke	SNAPSHOT
suffer	
suffer perforation, *say*	BEHOLD
suffering	(in) PA–IN
suffering [badly]	BALDY

suffering breakdown [I went] . . .	TWINE
suffering relative	AGONY AUNT
sufficient	QS
suffix	SUF(F)
sugar	
sugar beet	CUBE ROOT
sugar container	BEET, CANE
sugar daddy	TATE
sugarloaf	SWEETBREAD
sugar soap	FLATTERY
suggest	
he'll *suggest* . . .	HEAL, HEEL
suggested you will . . .	YULE
suit	
suit	C, D, H, S
suit	QUARTERDECK
suitable dance, *say*	MEATBALL
suitable for [use]	SUE
suitable head	FITNESS
suitably dressed	INVESTMENT
suitably [sited]	EDITS, TIDES
suitably prepared [meal]	LAME, MALE
suitcase	GEARBOX
sultanate	OMAN
sum of money	IMPOUNDS
summary hearing	BRIEFCASE
summer	
summer	ADDER
• many summer . . .	LADDER, MADDER
• second-rate summer	BADDER
• summer's shade	ADDERSTONE
summer	COUNTER
• summer month	COUNTERMARCH
• summer role	COUNTERPART
• summer wind	COUNTERBLAST
	COUNTERBLOW
summer job	ADDITION, ARITHMETIC
summer time	BST
summit	
international *summit*(D)	I
summit coverage	CAP, HAT, HEADGEAR
	SNOWCAP
summit of Everest(D)	E
sun[1]	
sun	S
• sunbird	SCOOT, SKITE, SOWL
	STEAL, STERN
• sun dance	SHOP
• sundown	SLOW, SNOWDROPS
• sundress	SWEAR
• sunfish	SEEL, SHAKE, SIDE
	SLING, SPIKE, STENCH
• sunflower	SLILY
• sunhat	STOPPER
• sunrise	SUP
sun *comes out*	omit S

sun*less*	omit S
sun²	
sun	SOL
• Indian sun, *say*	CRESOL
• sun *has* 500 . . .	SOLD
• sun *on* English . . .	SOLE
and	
sun-*up*(D)^	LOS
sun*rise*(D)^	LOS
sun³	
sun	SUN
sun*dancing*	NUS, UNS–
sunbathing	(in) SU–N
• father sunbathing	SUPAWN
sun*rise*(D)^	NUS
[ɒun]*oot*	NUS, UNS
sun*up*(D)^	NUS
sun⁴	
sun	STAR
• sun king	STARER
• sunfish	STARLING
• sun *goes round* one . . .	SITAR
sun*rise*(D)^	RATS
sun*up*(D)^	RATS
sun⁵	
sun-god	RA, SOL
sun king	LOUIS
sunbathed, *topless*(D)	(b)ASKED
sunbather	BAKER
sunny chap	RAY
sunny, *say*	SUMMARY
sunshade	CLOUD
Sunday	S, SUN
Sunday *opening*	S
sundry	
[sent] *sundry* . . .	NETS, STEN
sundry divers	MANY
sundry [items]	EMITS, MITES, TIMES
supercilious soldier	CAVALIER
superb icing	TOPPING
superconductor	MAESTRO
superfine	SUP
superintending	–IC
superior	
superior	ARCH, OVER, U, UP
• superior head	ARCHNESS
• many superior . . .	COVER, LOVER, MOVER
• superior philosopher	USAGE
• superior group	UPSET
superior	
indicating word written	
above another (D):	
• man *is superior to* many	HELOT
• staff *with* man *in superior*	
position	HEROD
superior *American*	SWELL
Superior companion	ERIE, HURON etc
superior example	UPPER CASE
superior, *say*	HIRE
superior standing	DAIS, PLATFORM
	SOAPBOX, STAGE
superlative	SUP
supersonic transport	SST
supine	SUP
supplement	PS, SUP
supply	
supplied by hospi/tal c/linic	TALC
supplier of dope	GRASS, INFORMANT
supplies flowers	STOCKS
supply lines	PROMPT
supply material for [shop]	HOPS, POSH
support	
support	
–claim	MAINTAIN
–evil	BASE
–ruler	BOOSTER, BRAKING
–others	REST
–robbery	HOLD-UP
support	
indicating one word written	
below another word or letter(D):	
• child *supporting* mother	MASON
• mother *supported by* child	MASON
support	BACK
• boot-support	KICK-BACK
• proper support	RIGHT BACK
• support Bacon	BACKGAMMON
• support clergy	BACKCLOTH
• support team	BACKSIDE
and	
• support composer, *say*	BACH
• support relative, *say*	BACCHANTE
• support you and me, *say*	BACCHUS
support	BEAR
• miserable support	GRIZZLY BEAR
• note *in* support	BEATER
• supports family	BEARSKIN
and	
• several supports, *say*	FOR(E)BEARS
support	BRA
• county supporter	COBRA
• support church	BRACE, BRACH
• support-ship	BRASS
support	BRACE
• support *after* space . . .	EMBRACE
• support allowed . . .	BRACELET
• support son	BRACES
and	
• support woman, *say*	BRACER
support	LEG
• support friend	LEGALLY

Letter replaced \c\at; Omit (a); Pointers *out*; Retain <u>a</u>; Split B_ED; Down (D); Backwards <or ^

• support one on . . .	LEGION	sure-fire	CRACK SHOT
• support queen	LEGER	sure, *say*	SHORE
support	PROP	sur(e)ly *not all* . . .	SURLY
• support no girls	PROPOSALS	**surface**	
• support queen	PROPER	*slippery surface*(D)	S
• support railway	PROPEL	*surface of* the . . . (D)	T
support	SECOND	*surface of the* <u>m</u>oon(D)	M
• support a transport system	SECONDARY	surface-to-air missile	SAM
• support worker	SECOND-HAND	surface-to-surface missile	SSM
• supporter's gear	SECOND	**surgeon**	
support, *say*	BEFORE	surgeon	VET
supporter	FAN	• son *in* surgeons' . . .	VESTS
• supporter *has* brown . . .	FAN-TAN	• state surgeons	RIVETS
• supporter *takes* note	FAND, FANE, FANG	• surgeon in debt, *say*	VETOING
and		surgeons	RCS
• supporter notices, *say*	FANCIES	**surgery**	
• supporter has a cat, *say*	PHANTOM	[heart] *surgery*	EARTH, HATER, RATHE
supporter	BRA, BRACE, GUY, PROP,	*surgery on* [spine]	PINES
	STAY	**Suriname**	SME
supporting	PRO–	**surmount**	
• supporting position	PROPOSE	indicating one word	
• supporting the originator	PROFOUNDER	written above another	
• supporting timber	PROPINE	word or letter (D)	
supporting		• dog *surmounting* a height	CURATOR
–actress	MAE WEST	• dog *surmounting* 500 . . .	CURD
–Bill, *say*	FOUR POSTER	**surplus**	
–stocking	CARRYING, HOLDING	surplus	EXTRA
–strut, *say*	SURE	• surplus account	EXTRAVERSION
supportive		• surplus parties	EXTRADOS
–couple	BRACE	• surplus weight	EXTRACT
–member	LEG	surplus	OVER
supports	PIERS	• 500 surplus . . .	DOVER
• supports, *say*	PEERS, PIERCE	• surplus *in* credit	COVER
suppose		• surplus garment	OVERCOAT
supposed, *say*	GUEST	**surprise**	
supposing	IF	*surprising* [result]	LUSTRE
suppress		*surprisingly* [weak]	WAKE
suppress a . . .	omit A	**surrender**	
suppress *	omit *	*surrender a* . . .	omit A
• de(s)pot *suppresses* son	DEPOT	*surrender* king	omit R
suppress a	incl A	surrender profit	YIELD
suppress *	incl *	surrender, *say*	SESSION
• k–ing *suppresses* sick . . .	KILLING	*surrender* *	omit *
suppressed by m/ad dict/ator	ADDICT	• bar(ely) *surrenders* city	BAR
supra	SUP	**Surrey feature**	FRINGE
supreme		**surround**	
supreme	SUP	*surrounded by* animals	DE–ER
supreme champion	STARCH	• not *surrounded by* animals	DENOTER
supreme directors	OVERBOARD	*surrounding a* . . .	incl A
Supreme Court	SC	*surrounding* *	incl *
supreme head	ARCHNESS	• drunks *surrounding* house	SHOOTS
supreme ruler, *say*	HIKING	*surrounded by* *	incl in *
surcingle		• house *surrounded by* drunks	SHOOTS
surcingle, *say*	KNIGHT BACHELOR	**survey**	
sure		surveillance error	OVERSIGHT
sure	BOUND	survey, *say*	REVUE

Anag [cat]; Any *; Begin IGN–; Endings –ING; eg •; Hidden /cat/; Implied add (on); Implied in (in);

surveyor	LANDSEER
survive test	WEATHERPROOF
suspend	
suspend	HANG
• suspend deliveries	HANGOVER
• suspend *in* church	CHANGE
• suspend sack	HANG FIRE
and	
• suspended sentence	HANGING
• suspended	
work	HANGING GARDENS OF BABYLON
suspender	HANGMAN, JACK KETCH
suspicious	
[acts] *suspiciously*	CATS, SCAT
suspicious [action]	CATION
sustain	
indicating one word written	
below another word or letter(D):	
• alien *sustaining* bird	MARTINET
• bird *sustained by* alien	MARTINET
swagger	
swaggering boaster	BOBADIL
swaggering [boaster]	BOATERS
swallow	
swallowed up *	incl *
• it *is swallowed up in* t–he . . .	TITHE
swallowing a . . .	incl A
swallowing *	incl *
• s–age *swallowing* tablet	SPILLAGE
swallowed by *	incl in *
• tablet *swallowed by* s–age	SPILLAGE
swamp	
swamp a . . .	incl A
swamp *	incl *
• wat–er *swamping* church	WATCHER
swamped by *	incl in *
• church *swamped by* wat–er	WATCHER
swan	
swan	COB
• swan *has* a high tone	COBALT
• swan painter	COBRA
swan	PEN
• swan expired, *say*	PENDED
• swan *on* the river	DEEPEN
• swan-song	PENCHANT
swanning around [in fine	
car]	FINANCIER
young swan	CYGNET
young swan, *say*	SIGNET
swap	
swap defenders	SWITCHBACKS
swap [coins]	ICONS, SONIC
swap components of [cars]	ARCS, SCAR
swap leaders	
• party *swaps leader*	GORY
• *swap leaders* \la\ter	ALTER
• *swap* \lu\nar *leaders*	ULNAR
swarm	
[gnats] *swarming*	ANGST, STANG, TANGS
swarm, *say*	TEAM
swarming [flies]	FILES
sway	
swaying [hips]	PISH, SHIP
swaying around [a lido]	IDOLA
swear	
swearer, *say*	CURSOR
swearword	TETRAGRAM
Sweden	S
Swedish	
Swedish	SW
Swedish capital	KR, KRONA
Swedish *capital*	S
Swedish *leader*	S
sweep	
sweep	GRIMES
swept-up hair styles(D)^	SNUB
sweet	
sweet-and-sour	TART
sweet centre	BULL'S-EYE
sweet factory	ROCK PLANT
sweet Fanny Adams	SFA
sweet fool	GOOSEBERRY
sweet money	LOLLY
sweet store	HIVE, HONEYCOMB
sweet toy	TRIFLE
sweetbread	SUGARLOAF
sweetheart	JO(E)
swe*etheart*	E
sweets finished	DROPS OFF
sweets *returned*<	STRESSED
swell meal	SPREAD
swift	
swift	SCREECHER
swift father	PAPACY
swift horse	HOUYHNHNM
swift race	LAPUTAN
swift traveller	GULLIVER
swill	
[beer]-*swilling*	BREE
swilled [over]	ROVE
swim	
swimmer	COD, EEL, LING etc
swimmer	LEANDER
• swimmer's plea	OLEANDER
swimming club	ASA
swimming in [Lido]	IDOL
swimming [pool]	LOOP, POLO
swindle	
swindle	(BEA)CON
swindle	DO
• 51 swindles	LIDOS
• swindle money	DOCENT, DOYEN

Letter replaced \c\at; Omit (a); Pointers *out*; Retain a̲; Split B_ED; Down (D); Backwards <or ^

• swindle people	DONATION
• swindle twice	DODO
swindle man	ROOK
swindler, *say*	CHEETAH
swindles *on* credit	FIDDLESTICK
swine	
swine draw, *say*	PIGSTY
swine family	HOGSKIN, PIGSKIN
swine underfed	PIGNORATION
swinish boss	HOGSHEAD, NAPOLEON
swing	
swing	ROCK
• loud swing	FROCK
• swing at this place, *say*	ROCKIER
• swing it, *say*	ROCKET
• swing sailor	ROCK-TAR
and	
swing [door]	ODOR, ROOD
swing door<	ROOD
swing music	CRADLE SONG, ROCK
swirl	
swirl of [a skirt]	AT RISK
swirled [along]	LOGAN, LONGA
swirling [waters]	WASTER
swish	
swish [cane]	–ANCE
swishing [cane isn't] . . .	INSTANCE
switch	
switch *back*<	DOR
switch ends of \l\eve\r\	REVEL
switch [on light]	THOLING
switch on<	NO
switch[blade]	BALED
switched [over]	ROVE
switched over to . . . <	OT
Switzerland	
Switzerland	CH
• Egypt and Switzerland . . .	ETCH
• old city *in*	
Switzerland's . . .	CHURCH

• Switzerland *has* no way	CHORD
swivel	
swivel [gun]	GNU
swivel seat	WHEELCHAIR
swivelling [seat]	EATS, SATE, TEAS
sword	
sword bearer	FROG, SCABBARD
[sword] *dance*	WORDS
sword swallower	SCABBARD
swore	
swore vehemently, *say*	CUSTARD
	(*see also* swear)
swot	
start <u>s</u>wotting	S
swot *up*(D)^	MARC, GUM, TOWS
swung	
swung, *say*	SUEDE
	(*see also* swing)
Sydney's box	CARTON
symbol	
symbol	SIGN, SYM
symbol, *say*	CYMBAL, SINE
symbol	LOGO
• symbol *and* name	LOG-ON
• symbol *with* very loud . . .	LOG-OFF
sympathetic lady	AGONY AUNT
synonym	SYN
synthesise	
synthesise [ester]	REEST, RESET
	STEER, STERE, TREES
synthetic	
–spirit	LABRUM
–stone	SHAMROCK
syrup	SYR
system	
system [made in] . . .	MAIDEN
system for [taxes]	TEXAS
system of [gears]	RAGES
Systéme Internationale	SI
SX	ESSEX

Anag [cat]; Any *; Begin IGN–; Endings –ING; eg •; Hidden /cat/; Implied add (on); Implied in (in);

T

bandage, bar, bone, cart, cell, cloth, commence, cross(ed), group, *half-dry*, hundred and sixty (thousand), isotopic spin, it, junction, kinetic energy, model, *perfect letter*, lymphocyte, period of function, plate, rail, shirt, square, strap, surface tension, tare, tasto, tau, *te*, *tea*, *tee*, temperature, tenor, tense, tension, tera-, tesla, Thailand, the, theta, time, to, tonic, ton(ne), transitive, transmittance, trill, tritium, troy, Tuesday

3.1416	PIRATE
£1,000	IMPOUNDS
tab	BILL
little tab, *say*	BILLET
table	
table	TIMES
ta*ble-centre*	B
table opposite	COUNTER
table, *say*	ALTER
*t*able-*top*(D)	T
tail	
shirt *tail*	T
tail	BACKBIT
tail *at an* angle	DOGFISH
tai*l-back*	L
Tail-end Charli*e*	E
tai*l-ender*	L
tail-ende*r*	R
tail *first*	
• cat'\s\ *tail first*	SCAT
*t*ail *first*	T
tailless insect	LOCUS(t), MOT(h)
	WAS(p)
tailless rabbi(t)	RABBI
tail of queu*e*	E
tail of th*e* . . .	E
tail *off* th(e) . . .	TH
[tail]*spin*	–ITAL, –TIAL
[tail]*wagging*	–ITAL, –TIAL
tailing ma(n)	MA
tails I̲ wi̲n	IN
tails yo̲u los*e*	–UE
top and tail (b)ean(s)	EAN
wag*tail*	G
whit*e tail*	E
tailor	
tailored [to his] . . .	HOIST
tailoring	HABIT-FORMING
[trews] *tailored* . . .	STREW, WREST
Taiwan	RC

take[1]	
indicating inclusion:	
take about . . .	incl RE
• mother *takes* about . . .	MARE
take in	incl IN
• support *takes* in . . .	BRAIN
take in a . . .	incl A
take in *	incl *
• w–e *take in* oars, *say*	WORSE
take it from /me, sh/e . . .	MESH
take it to heart	incl IT
take nothing *in*	incl O
take notice	incl AD
take on	incl ON
take part in ga/me al/though . . .	MEAL
take shelter in cast/le af/ter . . .	LEAF
take some of o/ur ge/nes	URGE
take to . . .	incl TO
• good men *take to* . . .	PIMENTO
take to heart a . . .	incl A
take to heart *	incl *
• doctors *take boy to heart*	MOBS
take your pick of t/he ap/ples	HEAP
taken from Lon/don s/hop	DONS
taken in by fal/se w/oman	SEW
taken in by *	incl in *
• men *taken in by* editor	EMEND
taken out of cont/ext in E/ast	EXTINE
taken to heart by *	incl in *
• boy *taken to heart by*	
doctors	MOBS
taking in *	incl *
• editor *taking in* men	EMEND
taking part in h/ome ga/mes	OMEGA
take[2]	
indicating omission:	
I *take leave*	omit I
head takes leave	omit 1st letter
take a day off	omit AD, D
• *Take a day off*, l(ad)	L

Letter replaced \c\at; Omit (a); Pointers *out*; Retain a̲; Split B_ED; Down (D); Backwards <or ^

• *Take* day *off*, (D)on	ON
take a day *off*	omit MON, etc
• *Take* day *off*, (fri)end	END
take away a . . .	omit A
take away *	omit *
• m(ind)ing Indian *takeaway*	MING
• the *Spanish takeaway*	omit EL
take head off	omit 1st letter
take heart from re(lat)ed . . .	REED
take heart out of c(it)y	CY
take lead from	omit 1st letter
take money *from*	omit D, L, P
• *take* money *from* the b(l)ind	BIND
take morning *off*	omit AM
take name *from*	omit N
take no notice	omit AD
take off a . . .	omit A
take off first quarter	omit Q
take off (first) quarter	omit N, S, E, W
• *take off first*	
quarter of (s)wing	WING
• *take off* second	
quarter of s(w)ing	SING
• *take off* third	
quarter of swi(n)g	SWIG
take off head	omit 1st letter
take off *	omit *
• fat(al) *to take off* a pound	FAT
take out a . . .	omit A
take out *	omit *
• rat(her) *take out* her . . .	RAT
take time *off*	omit AGE, T
• man(age) *to take* time *off*	MAN
• (t)hey *take* time *off*	HEY
take top off (c)ream	REAM
take * *from*	omit *
• *take* a hundred *from* (ac)count	COUNT
take³	
other uses:	
[ship] *taken apart*	HIPS, PISH
[take] *a break*	KATE, TEAK
take [a count]	TOUCAN
take a course	DINE, EAT
take a lease here, *say*	RENTIER
take a toss [riding]	INGRID
take a turn \on\ her . . .	HERON
take ages	BELONG
take amiss, *say*	MARRY
take apart	ACT
take apart [all the] . . .	LETHAL
take back from r/ecip/ient<	PICE
take back note<	ETON
take command	BEHEAD
take down	EAT
take Ecstasy	TRANSPORT
take exercise	DOPE

take flight	SKYJACK
take her in, *say*	SUCCOUR, SUCKER
take in	EAT
take in	COD, CON, DO
	(*see also* swindle)
take issue	incl SON
• mother *takes* issue	MASON
take it easy, *say*	WREST
take it easy in this way	SOREST
take liberty	ENSLAVE
take money from account	DRAWL
take notice	NB
take off	APE, COPY
take off	
indicating a homophone	
• plane *takes off*	PLAIN
• *take off* for . . .	FORE, FOUR
[take] *off*	KATE, TEAK
take off years	DOCKAGE
take on a . . .	end with A
take on [a new] . . .	WANE, WEAN
take out a . . .	omit A
take over	BOWL
take part of Anto/nio	
be/fore . . .	NIOBE
take part in h/ome ga/mes	OMEGA
take second opinion, *say*	CROSS CHEQUE
take sides, *say*	BEFORE
take some	
• he *takes some* <u>ar</u>tificial . . .	HEART
• *take some* litt/le the/atre	LETHE
take [steps]	PESTS
take turns	ROTATE
take up golf(D)^	FLOG
takeaway counter	ABACUS
takeaway sign	MINUS
takeaway worker	DUSTMAN
taken aback, Liam . . . <	MAIL
taken from P/rover/bs	ROVER
taken in, *say*	ETON
taken orally, spirit . . .	(D)JINN, RHUMB
takeover operator	FERRYMAN
takes	X
• rocket *takes* measure	VIXEN
• chesspiece *takes* another	MANXMAN
takes a part, *say*	AZAROLE
takes [blame]	AMBLE, MABEL
taking a drink, *say*	WHINING
taking heart *from* . . .	AKIN
taking heart *from* Ge(rm)an . . .	GEAN
taking issue	ADOPTING, ADOPTION
taking offence	RECEIVING, RUSTLING,
	STEALING, SHOPLIFTING
	THEFT
taking part in nov/el even/ts	ELEVEN
taking stock	RUSTLING, SHOPLIFTING

Anag [cat]; Any *; Begin IGN–; Endings –ING; eg •; Hidden /cat/; Implied add (on); Implied in (in);

taking thought	ABSTRACTION	**Tanzania**	EAT, EAZ
	(*see also* took)	**tap**	
tale		[tap]-*dancing*	APT, PAT
tale of a foot	LEGEND	**tar**	
tale, *say*	STOREY, TAIL	tar	AB
tale *told*	STOREY, TAIL	• tar compound	ABSOLUTION
tales	ANA	• tar marks	ABSTAINS
talent	NOUS	• tar *on* the highway	ABROAD
talk		tar assessment	RATING
talk fast	EXPRESS	[tar]-*spraying*	ART, RAT
talk of Bonn	GERMAN	tarry rope	STAY
talk of Paris	FRENCH	tarry, *say*	WEIGHT
talk of rain	REI(G)N	(*see also* sailor, tar)	
talk of Sidney	STRINE	**taste**	
talk of the Costa del Sol	SPANISH	taste	TANG
talk of the East End	COCKNEY	• taste butter	TANGRAM
talk sense	CENTS, SCENTS	• taste fish	TANGLING
talking a lot	FETE	• taste nothing	TANGO
talking bird	BUDGERIGAR, MINA,	**tatter**	
	MYNA, PARROT, MYNAH	*in tatters* [I'd made]	DIADEM
talking bird	CHAT	*tattered* [rags]	GARS
talking bird	BURD, BURRED	*tatty* denim	MINED
	MINER, MINOR	**tau**	T
talking forbidden	BAND	**taught**	
talking parrot, *perhaps*	POLYGLOT	taught, *say*	TAUT
talking pictures	PICKS, PYX	taught ten, *say*	TAUTEN
tall		taught bird, *say*	TAUTEN
tall	HIGH	**tax**	
• tall man	HIGHJACK	tax	IMPOST
• tall stories	HIGH-RISE (FLATS)	• tax *on* gold	IMPOSTOR
• tall window	HIGHLIGHT	• tax queen	IMPOSTER
and		tax	PAYE
• tall chimney, *say*	HILUM	tax	SCOT
• tall detective, *say*	HI-TEC,	• tax capital *return<*	SCOTIA
	HIGH-TECH	• tax *on* property	SCOTLAND
• tall posters, *say*	HYADS	• tax *cut*	(s)COT
• tall ruler, *say*	HIKING	tax	TRY
tall, skinny person, *say*	GANGLION	• tax-*free*	omit TRY
tall worker	LONGHAND	tax	VAT
taller and skinnier, *say*	GANGLIA	• tax *cut*	(v)AT
taller insect, *say*	TOLERANT	• tax *in* Old English . . .	OVATE
taller loft, *say*	HIERATIC	• tax *return<*	TAV
taller, *say*	HIRE	tax cut	EXCISE
tallboy	SIX-FOOTER	tax cut	AX, TA
Tamil	TAM	tax-free	ORATED
Tanganyika	EAK	tax *haven*	R–ATE, VA–T
tangent	TAN, TOUCHLINE	• the *Spanish* tax *haven*	RELATE
tangle		• the *French* tax *haven*	VALET
[roots] *tangled*	ROOST, TORSO	tax inspector	SUPERCHARGER
tangled [webs or] . . .	BROWSE	taxmen	IR
tanner		**taxi**	
tanner	NATURIST, NUDIST,	taxi	CAB
	SUNBATHER, SOLARIUM,	taxi(D)	BACUP
	SUNBED, SUNLAMP	**Tchaikovsky**	
tanner	SIXPENCE, VID, VIP	T<u>chai</u>kovsky *trio*	CHA
Tantalus's prisoner	DECANTER	T<u>chai</u>kovsky *quartet*	CHAI

Letter replaced \c\at; Omit (a); Pointers *out*; Retain <u>a</u>; Split B_ED; Down (D); Backwards <or ^

te	T
tea	
tea	CHA
• tea-boy	CHARON
• tea brewed	CHAMADE
• tea-money	CHAL
and	
• tea-dance	CHA-CHA
• tea for two	CHA-CHA
tea	CHAR
• tea *in* free . . .	RICHARD
• tea-lady	CHARLOTTE, CHARWOMAN
• tea *with* jam	CHARLOCK
tea	TEA
• tea *at* the fête	GALATEA
• tea *with* queen	TEAR
and	
• [tea] *blend*	ATE, EAT
• [tea] *break*	ATE, EAT
• [tea] *in mess*	ATE, EAT
• [tea] *mixture*	ATE, EAT
tea, *say*	T, TEE
teas, *say*	TEASE, TS, TT
teapot	BILLY
teatime	IV
teach	
teacher	MISS, SIR
teachers	NUT, STAFF
teaches clayworker	TRAINSPOTTER
team	
team	SIDE
• left team	OFFSIDE
• novice *in* team	SLIDE
• support team	BACKSIDE
and	
• team, *say*	SIGHED
team	XI, XV
team *leader*	T
team's quarters	ELEVENSES
[team]*work*	MATE, MEAT, TAME
tear	
tear	RIP
• tear *about<*	PIR
• tear container	RIPSACK
• tearaway	RIP-OFF
• tearproof	CANTRIP
tear [a T-shirt]	ATHIRST
tear *about*	RE–NT
tear [about]	U-BOAT
tear *round*	RE–NT
tear to pieces	
[in ring at] . . .	TRAINING
[tear]*about*	RATE, TARE
[tear]*away*	RATE, TARE
tearing [about]	U-BOAT
[tearing] *about*	TANGIER

tear²	*(see also* tore)
[mothers] *in tears*	SMOTHER, THERMOS
tear-jerker	ONION
[tear]-*jerking*	RATE, TARE
tease	
tease animal	BADGER
tease boy	CHAFFRON
tease [listeners]	RE-ENLISTS
tease, *say*	TEAS, TEES, TS, TT
teasing [dogs]	GODS
technology	
alternative technology	AT
information technology	IT
technology school	CAT
technology institute	MIT
tedious	
tedious	LONG
• tedious dance	LONG HOP
• tedious farewell	SO LONG
• tedious musical	LONG HAIR
tedious	SLOW
• Henry *is in* tedious . . .	SHALLOW
• tedious contest	SLOW MATCH
• tedious trainer	SLOWCOACH
tee	
tee	AFTERS, PEG
tee *off*	omit T
[tee] *off*	–EET, –ETE
tee, *say*	T, TEA
[teed] *off*	–ETED
tees, *say*	TEAS(E), TS, TT
	(see also teetotal)
teenager	UNDERSCORE
teepee	TP
teeter	
teeter [on her] . . .	HERON
teetering [near the] . . .	EARTHEN, HEARTEN
teetotal	
teetotal	TT
teetotal	EIGHTEEN, NINE
telegraph	
telegram	TEL
telegram, *say*	KABUL
telegraph	TEL
telegraph office	TO
telepathy	ESP
telephone	
telephone	BLOWER
telephone	CALL
• about *to* telephone	RECALL
• telephone you and me	CALLUS
telephone	PHONE
• telephone a number, *say*	PHONATE
• telephone nothing, *say*	PHONICS
telephone	RING

Anag [cat]; Any *; Begin IGN–; Endings –ING; eg •; Hidden /cat/; Implied add (on); Implied in (in);

• second telephone	BRING	• 10SE	TENNESSEE
• telephone *about* a race	RATTING	• [ten] *letters*	ENT, NET
• telephone circuit	RING	ten	X
• telephone receiver	RING FENCE	• monkey *has* ten . . .	APEX
• telephone rent	RINGLET	• ten *behind* the Post Office	POX
telephone	TEL	• ten *drunk*	AXLE
telephone kiosk	CHATTERBOX	• ten pence	–XP–
telephone man	BELL	Ten Commandments	HOLY ORDERS
telephone, *say*	CAUL, FO(E)HN, WRING	ten days	SEP, TEM, BER
teleprinter	TPR	ten-nil	HUNDRED
television		ten-nil *reversed<*	LINNET
television	TV	**tenanted**	ISLET
television disconnected	OFFSET	**tend**	
tell		tend	NURSE
Tell	BOWMAN	tender	NURSE
tell	INFORM	• tender shark	NURSE
• tell friend	INFORMALLY	tender	OFFER
• tell workers	INFORMANTS	• 100 tender . . .	COFFER
tell lies	FIB	• tender monarch	OFFERER
• tell lies about	FIBRE	• tender politician	OFFERTORY
• tell lies *to* Returning Officer	FIBRO	tender	SHEPHERD
tell tales	SING	tender words	OFFER, QUOTATION
• tell tales *about*	S–ING	**Tennessee**	
telling tales	TAILS	Tennessee	TEN(N)
tell target	APPLE	Tennessee transport	DESIRE, STREETCAR
temper		Tennessee Valley Authority	TVA
[lose] *temper*	SLOE, SOLE	**tenor**	T, TEN
temperance group	AA	**tense**	
temperate area	CONTINENT	tenor, *say*	TENNER
tempered [steel]	LEETS, SLEET, STELE	tense	T
temporary		tense finish	PERFECT
temporary		tense, *say*	QUAYED, TAUGHT
accommodation	BRIDGING LOAN	tense over . . .	PAST
temporary accommodation	TENT	**tent**	
• king *in* temporary		*in* tent	TEN–T, T–ENT
accommodation	TRENT	• English men *in* ten–t	TENEMENT
• in temporary accommodation	INTENT	• gangster *in* t–ent	TALENT
• temporary accommodation		tent-maker	PAUL
in the river	DETENTE	tent, *say*	TP
temporary darn	STOPGAP	(*see also* temporary accommodation)
temporary site *by* a river	CAMPANILE	**tentative**	
ten		[smile] *tentatively*	LIMES, MILES
pertaining to ten	OFTEN	*tentative* [plan I] . . .	PLAIN
ten	CHI	**terminal**	
• ten about . . .	CHIC	terminal	POLE
• ten quiet . . .	CHIP	*terminal* illness	S
• ten-ten	CHICHI	*terminally* ill	L
ten	CROSS	**terminate**	
• doublecross	TWENTY	*terminate* lease	E
• ten above . . .	CROSSOVER	*termination of* tenancy	Y
• ten land . . .	CROSS COUNTRY	*termini* of railway	RY
ten	IO	**terrace**	TER(R)
• spoil ten . . .	MARIO	**terrible**	
• stroke ten . . .	PATIO	[Ivan] *the Terrible*	VAIN
• ten reserves	IOTA	*terrible* [heat]	HATE, THEA
ten	TEN	terrible man	IVAN

Letter replaced \c\at; Omit (a); Pointers *out*; Retain a; Split B_ED; Down (D); Backwards <or ^

terrible skin	FELL
terrible way	DIREST
terribly [cruel]	LUCRE
t(erribl)y *heartless*	TY
terriers	
terriers	TA
• crossed terriers	TAX
• Terriers gave blood	TABLED
• Terriers I led	TAILED
(*see also* army, reserve, territorials)	
terrify	
[quite] *terrified*	QUIET, –TIQUE
terrifying [ascent]	SECANT
territorials	
Territorials	TA
Territorial Decoration	TD
Territorial Force (Reserve)	TF(R)
(*see also* army, reserve, terriers)	
territory	TER(R)
terrorist	
terrorists	ETA
• *almost all of* th(e)	
terrorists . . .	THETA
• *return, for example<, after*	
terrorists . . .	ETAGE
• terrorist exercise	ETAPE
terrorists	IRA
• terrorists *found in* <u>pira</u>te . . .	IRA
• terrorists *in* five long . . .	VIRAL
• terrorists, note	IRATE
terrorists	PLO
• terrorist branch	PLOWING
• terrorists *have* 500 . . .	PLOD
• terrorists *take* square	PLOT
terrorists	PROVOS
tesla	T
test	
test	MOT
• nothing *in* test	MOOT
• test I have . . .	MOTIVE
• test *in* the Home Counties	SMOTE
test	ORAL
• 100 tests	CORALS
• Spring test	MAYORAL
• test finished	PASTORAL
test	TRY
• cars test . . .	MINISTRY
• test the road	TRYST
and	
• test fish, *say*	TRIANGLE
• test-paper, *say*	TRIREME
test case	MATCHBOX
test centre	LORDS, OVAL
te<u>st</u> *centre*	ES
<u>test</u> match	CHECKMATE
	STRIKE A LIGHT

	TRIAL MARRIAGE
test playing	AUDITION
[test] *playing*	SETT, STET
testy fellow	EXAMINER
tethers donkey	CHAINSMOKE
text	MS
texturised vegetable protein	TVP
Thailand	T
Thames boatman	HARRIS
thank	
thank you letter	COLLINS
thanks	TA
• thanks, man	TAMALE
• thanks members	TAMPS
• thanks the *French* . . .	TALE(S)
thank*less*	omit TA
that	
that church	THATCH
that *French* . . .	CELA
that is	IE
• swamp that is . . .	BOGIE
• that's *about* right	IRE
• that's right	–IER
that is	SC
• that is current . . .	SCAMP
• that is *in* the e–ar	ESCAR
• that is torn, *I hear*	SCRIPT
that man	HIM
that man, *say*	HYMN
that old . . .	YT
that place	THERE
that place, *say*	THEIR
that Roman . . .	ID
that woman	HER
that you cause to know	SCI FA
	SCIRE FACIAS
that's *been stolen*	omit IE, SC
that's *missing*	omit IE, SC
that's not right	LEFT, LARBOARD, PORT
that's *not* right	omit R
• F(r)ee? That's *not* right!	FEE
that's right	STARBOARD
that's *the end*	end with IE
• measure that's *the end* . . .	GILLIE
• *That's the end of*	
<u>it</u>, That's *the end*	TIE
the¹	THE
he *leaves* t(he)	T
part of the . . .	T, TH, H, HE, E
some of the . . .	T, TH, H, HE, E
the bar	THEBAN
<u>the</u> *beginning*	T
<u>the</u> *border* of . . .	T
<u>the</u> *borders of* . . .	TE
<u>the</u> *boundaries* . . .	TE
th(e) *detailed* . . .	TH

the *edges*	TE
the embargo	THEBAN
the *central* . . .	H
the *central* . . .	incl THE
• use the *Central* fo–r . . .	FOTHER
the *centre*	H
the check	THEREIN
the Circle Line	THEORY
the *climbing* . . . (D)^	EHT
the *contents*	incl THE
• wea–r the *contents* . . .	WEATHER
the *contents*	incl in TH–E
• about th–e *contents* . . .	THREE
the *core*	H
the course	THEE, THEN, THEW
the *directions*	THESE, THEWS
[the] *drunk(en)*	ETH, HET
the *end*	E
the *entrant*	incl THE
• see–s the *entrant*	SEETHES
the *entrant*	T
the *extremes*	TE
the *finish*	E
the first	THEIST
the *first* . . .	T
the *first slice of* apple	TAP
th(e) *footloose*(D) . . .	TH
the *front end*	T
the Globe Circle	THEORBO
(t)he *headless* . . .	HE
t(h)e *heartless* . . .	TE
• t(h)e *heartless* man	TEAL
• t(h)e *heartless* woman	TENANCY
• t(h)e *heartless* US agent	TEGMAN
the *initial* . . .	T
the *initiative*	T
"The *Insider*"	H
the *last* . . .	E
the *last comes first*	start with E
the *latter*	E
the *leader*	T
[the] *mixture*	ETH, HET
[the] *mobile* . . .	ETH, HET
the *most*	TH
t(he) *non-male*	T
the *Northern(er's)* . . .	T
• the *northern* end	TEND
• the *Northern* Line	TROW
• the *northerner's* drink	TALE
[the] *novel* . . .	ETH, HET
the offender	THERAPIST
the old	YE
• the old shirt	YET
• the old soldiers	YEMEN
the others	REST
• graduate *with* the others	BAREST
• the others scoffed	RESTATE
the others, *say*	WREST
• the others went in front, *say*	WRESTLED
the *outside*	TH–E
• queen *with* th–e *outside* . . .	THERE
"The *Outsiders*"	TE
the *penultimate* . . .	H
the place in question	WHERE
the place in question, *say*	WARE, WEAR
the *point*	THEE, THEN, THEW
the *point*	T
th(e) *pointless* . . .	TH
the reserves	THETA
the *second* . . .	H
th(e) *short* . . .	TH
the *summit*(D)	T
the ten of us, *say*	WHEATEN
the thing in question	WHICH
the thing in question, *say*	WITCH
the *third* . . .	E
[the] *Twist*	ETH, HET
th(e) *Unfinished* . . .	TH
the woman	HER
• the woman has expired, *say*	HERDED
• the woman spoke, *say*	HERSED
• the woman was in front, *say*	HURLED
[the] *wrong* . . .	ETH, HET
[the] *wrong way*	ETH, HET

the²
alien (=foreign)

the *alien* . . .	AL, DAS, DER, DIE, EL, IL
	LE, LA, LAS, LES, LOS
the *Arabic* . . .	AL
• drink *with* the *Arabic* . . .	TOTAL
• the *Arabic* in m–e	MALE
• the *Arabic* lily	ALARUM
the *Camptown* . . .	DE
• the *Camptown* drink	DECIDER, DEPORT
• the *Camptown* money	DECENT
• the *Camptown* trail	DESCENT
the *foreign* . . .	(*see* alien *above*)
the *French (style)* . . .	LA, LE, LES
• circle the *French* . . .	HOOPLA
• the *French-style* bird	LAMINA
• the *French in* F–red and	FLARED
• require the *French* . . .	NEEDLE
• the *French* gentleman	LET-OFF
• the *French in* need, *say* and	KNEELED
• bird *without* the *French* . . .	COOLEST
• hit the *French* . . .	COUPLES
• the *French* boy	LESSON
the *French/English* . . .	LATHE, LETHE
the *French/German* . . .	UNDER

Letter replaced \c\at; Omit (a); Pointers *out*; Retain a; Split B_ED; Down (D); Backwards <or ^

the *German* . . .	DAS, DER, DIE
• Russian king with the *German*	CZARDAS
• the *German with* horse	DASH
• unknown *in the German* . . . and	DAYS
• gained the *German* . . .	WONDER
• state *in the German* . . .	DRIER
• the *German* near . . . and	DERBY
• the *German caught in* a mist	HARDIER
• the *German* died	DIED
• king *in the German* . . .	DIRE
the *Italian* . . .	IL, LA, LE, LO
• the *Italian* has one bill	ILIAC
• the *Italian* street	LAST
• master the *Italian* . . .	MALE
• the *Italian* honour	LOOM
the *old (style)* . . .	YE
• the *old* people	YEMEN
• the *old* record-editor	YELPED
• the *old-style* students	YELL
the *Spanish* . . .	EL, LA, LAS, LOS
• drink the *Spanish* . . .	LAPEL
• the *Spanish* alcove	ELAPSE
• the *Spanish in* transport and	RELY
• firm *with* the Spanish . . .	COLA
• the *Spanish* hut	LASHED
• the *Spanish in* Cyprus and	CLAY
• knock out the *Spanish* . . .	KOLAS
• the *Spanish in* Communist Party	CLASP
• the *Spanish* vehicles and	LASCARS
• guns the *Spanish* . . .	HALOS
• the *Spanish* can . . .	LOSABLE
• the *Spanish in* church	CLOSE
the *Spanish/French* . . .	ELLA
the *Spanish/German* . . .	ELDER

the³

the beginning of l̲ife	L
the bitter̲ end	R
the borders of F̲ranc̲e	FE
the centre of Pa̲r̲is	R
the end of i̲t	T
the final stra̲w̲	W
the finish of pla̲y̲	Y
the first b̲all	B
the first slice of a̲p̲ple	AP
the footloose tram(p)(D)	TRAM
the initial g̲esture	G
the last of winter̲	R
the leader of R̲ussian . . .	R
The L̲ion's *Head*	L

the⁴

the boy's . . .	HIS

the girl's . . .	HER
the lady's . . .	HER
[the last] *resort*	STEALTH
the man's . . .	HIS
the old	AGED
the others	EM, DEM, THEIR, THEM
[the rate] *of exchange*	THEATRE, THEREAT
the same	DITTO, DO
the subject	IT
the writer	I, ME

theatre

theatre company	PLAYGROUP
theatre company	REP
• Oriental theatre	REPINE
• theatre atmosphere	REPAIR
• theatre is not . . .	REPAINT
• theatre royal	REPR–
• theatre scoffer	REPEATER
• theatre *with* Indian . . .	REPUTE
theatre director	STAGECOACH SURGEON
theatre designer	PLASTIC SURGEON
theatre-goer	GLOBETROTTER
theatre in the round	GLOBE
[theatre] *movement*	THEREAT
theatre part	SHOWPIECE
theatre performer	SURGEON
theatre producer	EMPIRE-BUILDER
theatre strike	CAST OUT, OUTCAST
theatre tour	CASTAWAY
theatrical number	ANAESTHETIC, ETHER
theatrical part	BOX, GODS, PART PROSCENIUM STAGE, WINGS
theatrical [part]	PRAT, RAPT, TRAP
theatrical performance	OPERATION SURGERY

their

Their Majesties	MM
their opponents	US
Their Royal Highnesses	TRH
their, *say*	THERE
them	EM, NOTUS
theme	EGO, I
theologian	ANSELM, BEDE, ORIGEN et al BD, DD

there

there *in France*	LA
there, *say*	THEIR

these

[these] *characters*	SHEET
these days	AD
these *in France*	CES

they

t̲hey *initially*	T
they object	THEM

they say	
indicating a homophone:	
• "No", *they say*	KNOW
• *they say* not	KNOT
• *they say* we'll . . .	WEAL, WHEEL
thick	
thick	FAT
• learner *in* thick . . .	FLAT
• thick head	FATNESS
• thick soup	FATSTOCK
thick slice, *say*	STAKE
thief	AUTOLYCUS, MAGPIE
thin	
thin	LEAN
• 100 thin . . .	CLEAN
• thin ruler	LEANER
• thin shirt	LEANT
thin	SPARE
• key *found in* thin . . .	SPARGE
• thin bone	SPARE RIB
• thin tycoon	SPARE WHEEL
thin copy	FLIMSY
thin letter	MUSLIM
thin metal sword	FOIL
thin note	SHARP
thin porcelain	SLIMMING
thin shirt	LEANT
thinner	ACETONE, TURPENTINE
think	
think *about*	MUS–E
thin(k) king *is lost*	THIN
third	
third	C
third half	SIXTH
third man	ABEL, LIME
third of August	AU, GU, ST
third of August	G
third out of four	U
third party	R
third place in race	C
third-rate	C
thirteen	
thirteen	BAKER'S DOZEN
	TEAM
	UNLUCKY (NUMBER)
thirteen witches	COVEN
thirteenth loaf	MAKEWEIGHT
thirty	
thirty	L, LA(M)BDA
thirty seconds,	MIN, UTE
thirty-three	DISC, LP, RECORD
thirty-nine	BOOKS, STEPS
this	
this bird, *say*	DISPARATE
this country	UK
this era	AD

this evening, *say*	TONITE
this *foreign* . . .	CE, CET, CETTE
this *French* . . .	CE, CET, CETTE
this *in France*	CE, CET, CETTE
this *in Rome*	HIC
th(is) *is missing*	TH
this month	INST(ANT)
• queen *in* this month's . . .	INSERT
• this month's record	INSTEP
• this month's worker	INSTANT
this *Roman* . . .	HIC
this time	AD
this way	SO
• mountain this way	TORSO
• this way is legal	SOLICIT
• this way over	SOON
this way	THUS
this year	HA
this way [leads]	DALES, DEALS
	LADES, SLADE
Thomas	THO(S)
T(h)orah	PENTATEUCH
those	
those killed in combat	WARDED
[those] *parts*	ETHOS
though	
though *brief* . . .	THO
th–ough *run in* . . .	THROUGH
though square . . .	THOUGHT
thoroughfare	COMPLETE MEAL
thousand	
one *and* a half thousand	ID
thousand	CHILIAD
thousand(s)	G(G)
• a thousand English . . .	AGE
• one in a thousand	UNITING
• silver *in* thousands	GAGS
thousand	K
• managed a thousand . . .	RANK
• thousand English records	KELPS
• thousand *in* cash	MONKEY
thousand(s)	M(M)
• a thousand drill	AMBIT
• one *in* thousands	MAM
• thousand refuse	MASH
and	
• thousand *and* one	MA, MACE, MAN, MI
• thousand *and* two	IMPAIR
• thousand pounds	IMPOUNDS
thousand	THOU
thousand	X
thousandth	THOU
thrash	
thrash idler	LAYABOUT
thrash worker	WHIPHAND
thrashed out ['is ideas]	DAISIES

Letter replaced \c\at; Omit (a); Pointers *out*; Retain a̲; Split B_ED; Down (D); Backwards <or ^

thread of story	YARN
threat	
[threat]	MAD HATTER
three	
three	CROWD, GAMMA
three articles	ANTHEA, LAUNDER
three blind mic(e)	MIC
three boys	PATERNAL, PATRONAL
[three-card] *trick*	CHARTERED
three Christmas presents	FRENCH HENS
three drinks	CHA-CHA-CHA
three figures	LID
three-foot coppers	YARD
three foreign articles	LAUNDER
three girls	VIVALDI
three-handed murderer	CUT-THROAT
three keys	DECAY
three-legged race	MANX
three-man	TRIAL
three men	PATERNAL, PATRONAL
Three Men in a Boat	COXED PAIR
three-nil	THIRTY
three notes	ABE, BEG etc
	DOTED, MIMIC etc
three of <u>hea</u>rts	HEA
three parts <u>win</u>e	WIN
three people	BETRAYAL
three points	ESCAPE, NEEDLESS
	NEW, SEN, SEW, WEN
three rings	OOSPHERE
threefold voice	TREBLE
thresh	
thresh grain	BEATRICE
threshing [grain in] ...	RAINING
threw	
threw, *say*	THROUGH
threw [stones]	ONSETS, SETONS
	(*see also* throw)
throb	
[heart]*throb*	EARTH, HATER, RATHE
throbbing [beat]	BATE
throe	
[death] *throes*	HATED
throe, *say*	THROW
through	
through	PER
• about through	CAPER
• through one building	PERISHED
• through the tower	PERSPIRE
through	VIA
• sun *gets in* through ...	VISA
• through *in* a–n ...	AVIAN
• through passage	VIADUCT
through, *say*	THREW
through *	incl in *
• run *through* exercises	PRUNE
through the agency of	PP
throughout	PE–R
*through*out	OU–T
throughout *	incl in *
• sleep *throughout* ship	SNAPS
*through*put	PU–T
throw	
throw	CAST
• girl *takes* a throw	DICAST
• throw a fight	CAST ABOUT
• throw *over* ring	COAST
throw	LOB
• second throw	SLOB
• throw *into* ship	SLOBS
• throw *to* essayist	LOBELIA
throw	PITCH
• throw *at* queen	PITCHER
• throw tar	PITCH
• throw tool	PITCHFORK
throw	SHY
• spoil throw	MARSHY
• throw *around* in ...	SHINY
• throw joint, *say*	SHINY
throw around on< ...	NO
throw around [on her] ...	HERON
throw away a ...	omit A
throw away money	omit D, L, P
throw away *	omit *
• h(old)er *threw away* old ...	HER
throw [caution] *to the winds*	AUCTION
throw drink	SLING
throw [grenade]	DERANGE
throw in a ...	incl A
throw in *	incl *
• two hundred *thrown* into o–ur ...	OCCUR
throw out a ...	omit A
throw out beetle	PROJECT
throw out [man or] ...	ROMAN
throw out * ...	omit *
• *throw* fool *out of* cl(ass)	CL
throw over [regime]	EMIGRE
throw over bows<	SWOB
throw over *	incl *
• *throw* h–er *over* high ...	HALTER
throw [pie]	EPI–
throw [rope]	PORE
throw *up*(D)^	BOL
throw up bat(D)^	TAB
throwback<	BOL
throwback part<	TRAP
thrower, *say*	CHUKKA, CHUKKUR
throwing disc, *say*	DISCUSS
throwing [darts]	STRAD
thrown [at me]	MATE, MEAT, TAME, TEAM
thrust ahead	(see also throw)
	RAMON

thunder		timber *frame*	TR
Thunderer	THOR, TIMES	timber measure	STERE
thundering [past]	PATS, STAP, TAPS	timber measure, *say*	STEARE, STEER
Thursday	TH(UR)	timber-merchant	ALDERMAN
thus		timber, *say*	TIMBRE, WOULD
thus	SIC	**time[1]**	
• the graduate thus . . .	BASIC	time	AGE
• thus the king . . .	SICK	• quiet time	PAGE
thus	SO	• time away from work	OUTAGE
• thus copied	SOAPED	• time *in* ship	SAGES
• thus the painter . . .	SOLELY	time	EON
tickertape	CARDIOGRAM	• model *in* time	ETON
tide		• student *has* time . . .	LEON
tide	EBB, FLOW	• swelling *before* time	GALLEON
tide *over<*	EDIT, WOLF	time	ERA
tidy		• time *in* fine library	FERAL
tidy	NEAT	• time *to* celebrate	ERASING
• tidy cattle	NEAT	• victory time	VERA
• tidy sum	NEAT FIGURE	and	
tidy up [a mess]	MESAS	• time *after* time	ERAT
tidying [a tress]	ASSERT	• time *and* time *again*	ERAT
tie		time	HR
tie	X	• time *in* t–ough . . .	THROUGH
[tie]-*break*	–ITE	time	MO
tie-breaker	DIVORCEE	• soldiers *take* time . . .	GISMO
tie design	DRAW	• time *in* a–n . . .	AMON
[tie] *design*	–ITE	• time *flying*	MOWING
tie fastener, *say*	TYPE IN	and	
tie game	DRAWBRIDGE, TIEPOLO	• time *after* time	MOT
tie-*up*(D)^	FIT, ROOM, WARD	• time *and* time *again*	MOT
tie up, *say*	MORE	• time to run	MOTOR
tie up Moroccan	MOOR	time	SEC
[tied] *in* knots	DIET, EDIT, TIDE	• equal time	PARSEC
tied [ropes]	PORES, SPORE	• time *in* part . . .	BISECT
tied, *say*	TIDE	• worker *behind* time	SECANT
tied [Tory] *in knots*	RYOT, TROY	and	
tying again	RECORDING	• time *after* time	SECT
tight		• time *and* time *again*	SECT
tight	DRUNK, INEBRIATED	and	
tight finish	CLOSE	• time to support	SECOND
tight, *say*	TAUGHT	time	T
tight space	TAUTEN	• leave *before* time	GOT
Tiller girls	LAND ARMY	• time *after* time	TT
tilting object	WINDMILL	• time *and* time *again*	TT
timber		• time *to* die	TEND
replace end of timbe\r\	TIMBRE	• time *to* leave	GOT
rotten [timber]	TIMBRE	and	
split [timber]	TIMBRE	• time *off*	omit T
timber	DEAL	• time *to leave*	omit T
• 100 *in* timber . . .	DECAL	• time *out*	omit T
• *put* timber *before* ruler	DEALER	• time-*wasting*	omit T
• timber trade	DEAL	• time*less*	omit T
timber	LOG	time	TIME
• timber in ship	SLOGS	• time *of backwardness<*	EMIT
• timber record	LOG	• [time] *off*	EMIT, MITE
• timber reserve	LOGBOOK	• [time]-*out*	EMIT, MITE

Letter replaced \c\at; Omit (a); Pointers *out*; Retain <u>a</u>; Split B_ED; Down (D); Backwards <or ^

• <u>time</u>*piece*	TIM	tint	CANT
• time's *up*(D)^	EMIT	**tip**	
• time-*sharing*	EM–IT, IM–TE, M–ITE	<u>a</u>sparagus *tip*	A
• time *to get up*(D)^	EMIT	good *tip*	G
• [time] *warp*	EMIT, MITE	*new tip on* \c\ue	HUE, RUE, SUE
• tim(e) *without end*	TIM	tip *backwards*<	PIT
• [times] *change*	EMITS, MITES, SMITE	*tip backward*<	DRAW
time	YR	*tip from* (t)out	OUT
• time's *up*(D)^	–RY	*tip of* <u>i</u>ceberg	I
time	TEMPO	tip of foil	BUTTON
• time to get up	TEMPORISE	*tip of* <u>f</u>oil	F
• The Times	TEMPI	tip-off	POINTLESS
time	(THE) ENEMY	tip *off* (s)pike	PIKE
<u>time</u> *limits*	TE	tip out of bed	DEBUNK
time²		*tip* [over]	ROVE
time *and* money	TIDEMARK	*tip over* jar<	RAJ
time of arrival	ETA	*tip over* [vase]	SAVE
time-server	CONVICT	tip *up*(D)^	PIT
timely strike	CHIME	*tip up* pots(D)^	STOP
times	X	*tip stew*<	WETS
Times factor	NEWSAGENT	*tip* <u>w</u>inner	W
<u>T</u>imes *leader*	T	*tips off* (s)pie(s)	PIE
Times Educational Supplement	TES	tiptop	PEAK
Times Literary Supplement	TLS	*tip*[top]	OPT, POT
Times past	THUNDERER	<u>ti</u>p*top*(D)	T
Timothy		*tip*top<	POT
Timothy	TIM	tiptop accommodation	ATTIC,
<u>T</u>imothy's *origin*	T		GARRET, LOFT
<u>T</u>imothy's origin	GRASS ROOTS	tiptop wear	(C)OVERALL
tin		<u>v</u>aluable *tip*	V
tin	CAN	**tipsy**	
• large tin	MAJORCAN	[leer] *tipsily*	REEL
• tin man	CANAL, CANED, CANTED	*tipsy* [state]	TASTE, TEATS
• tin monkey	CANAPE	**tire**	
tin	MONEY	[tired]	TRIED OUT
• potassium *in* tin	MONKEY	tired fellow	STALEMATE
• tin container	MONEY-BAG, MONEY-BELT	[tired] *out*	DETRI–, TRIED
	MONEY-BOX, WALLET	tired period	BEAT TIME
tin	SN	[tires] *out*	RESIT, RITES, TRIES
• nothing *in* tin	SON	tiresome child	SMALL BORE
• tin fish	SNIDE	**tissue**	
• tin mineral	SNORE	*tissue of* [lies]	LEIS, SILE
and		*tissue* [papers]	SAPPER
• tin-*plated*	(in) S–N	**Titus**	TIT
tin fish	TORPEDO	**to¹**	TO
<u>ti</u>n-*opener*	T	to east	TOE
tin plate	TERNE	to flower	TOASTER
tin plate, *say*	TERN, TURN	to left	TOL, TOLT
tinned	(in) CA–N, (in) TI–N	to north	TON
• no *canned* . . .	CANON	to one side	TOL(T), TOR(T), TOWING
• *tinned* beef	TOXIN	to plant	TOASTER
tinker		to right	TOR(T)
tinker	SLY	to the Home Counties	TOSE
• tinker *about*	S–LY	to *turn* to<	OTTO
tinker *about*<	REKNIT	to Tyneside	TONE
tinker *with* Rod's . . .	FIDDLESTICKS	to understand	TOKEN

Anag [cat]; Any *; Begin IGN–; Endings –ING; eg •; Hidden /cat/; Implied add (on); Implied in (in);

to west	TOW	toe	LEGEND
to your, *say*	TOOTHY	[toe]-*tapping*	OTE
to²		*twiddling* [toes]	TOSE
indicating foreign language:		**Togo**	TG
• give *to* Italian	DARE	**toilet**	
• road *to* German . . .	STRASSE	toilet	LOO
• say *to* Spaniard	DECIR, RECITAR	• soldier *returns*< *to* toilet	IGLOO
• walk *to* French . . .	MARCHER	• toilet *has* directions . . .	LOOSE
and		• toilet-master	LOOKING
• send *to* Jose	ENVIAR, REMITIR	and	
• sing *to* Luciano	CANTARE	• toilet training, *say*	LUCENCE
• speak *to* Pierre	PARLER	**told**	
• write *to* Hans	SCHREIBEN	*perhaps* told	TOLLED
to the French . . .	ALA, AU, AUX	[told] *off*	DOLT
• to the French doctor	ALAMO	**Toledo housing**	SCABBARD
• o the French spirit	AURUM	**Tom**	
• to the French in . . .	AUXIN	Tom's tongue	CLAPPER
to the Italian . . .	AL	tom-tom	CATS
• add lard to the Italian . . .	FATAL	Tommy	SOLDIER
• to the Italian group	ALLOT	Tommy's father	CHAPLAIN, PADRE
• to the Italian in b–ed	BALED	**tome**	TOM(US)
to³		**ton**	
look *to-and-fro*	PEEP	ton	T, TONNE
to a large extent th(e) . . .	TH	ton-*up*(D)^	NOT
to-and-fro action	DEED	**too**	
to be heard		too	
• intended *to be heard*	–MENT	indicating palindrome:	
• *to be heard* when . . .	WEN	• served *up, too*(D)	DID
to do with	RE	• send *back, too*	REFER
	(*see* about²)	too fat	OS
to infinity	AD INF(INITUM)	too fine	OVERGROUND
to London	UP	t(o)o heartless	TO
to no purpose	(in) VA–IN	*too long for* man	MANE, MANY
to some degree	(in) PAR–T	too much	OTT
• quarters, *to some degree*	PARENT	*too much* m/one/y	ONE
to some extent go/od in/side, ,	ODIN	*too short to* spa(n)	SPA
to start with, <u>c</u>heese <u>on</u> <u>t</u>oast	COT	*too small for* arm(y)	ARM
to take leave	PPC, TTL	too unprofessional	OVERLAY
to the beginning	AD INIT(IUM)	**took**	
to the end	AD FINEM	took advantage, *say*	MAYDAY
to the ear, airs . . .	HEIRS	took afternoon meal, *say*	EIGHTY
to the fore in <u>n</u>early <u>e</u>very <u>way</u>	NEW	took amiss	MARRIED
to windward	UP	took courses	ATE, DINED
toady	JENKINS	took it easy, *say*	WRESTED
toast			(*see also* take)
British toast	CHEERS	**tool**	
French toast	BON SANTE	[garden] *tool*	DANGER, GANDER
German toast	GESUNDHEIT	tool, *say*	ADDS, SPAYED
Irish toast	SLAINTE	tool thief, *say*	PICNICKER
Roman toast	BENE VOBIS	*tooled* [letters]	SETTLER
Scandinavian toast	SKO(A)L	**tooth**	
very thin toast	MELBA	tooth	FANG
tobacco-bird	SHAG	• tooth in front	FANGLED
today	AD	**top**	
toe		<u>B</u>ig *Top*(D)	B
broken [toe]	–OTE	top	APEX

Letter replaced \c\at; Omit (a); Pointers *out*; Retain <u>a</u>; Split B_ED; Down (D); Backwards <or ^

top	BEST	top man	CO, KING
• learner *in* top . . .	BLEST	*top* *m*an(D)	M
• top Irish . . .	BESTIR	*top* (m)an	AN
• top mount	BESTRIDE	top mark	A, ALPHA
top	CAP	*top* *m*ark	M
• top cereal	CAPRICE	*top* (m)ark(D)	ARK
• top *in* London area	SCAPE	top musician	SUPERCONDUCTOR
• top mount	CAPTOR	*top* *m*usician(D)	M
top	HEAD	*top* musician	(d)RUMMER
• top branch	HEAD OFFICE	top needle manufacturer, *say*	PINKING
• top brands	HEADLINES	*top*-*n*otch(D)	N
• top orchestra	HEADBAND	top note	G
top(D)	omit 1st letter	*top* *n*ote(D)	N
• *top* (t)ab'‹	ABLE	*top* note(D)	start with A, B, C, D, E, F, G
• *top* table	(l)IST		start with DO, RE etc
top and bottom of the . . . (D)	TE	• hundred *top* notes	MIMIC
top and bottom of the matter(D)	MR	• man *takes top* note	REAL
top and tail (t)wi(g)	WI	• *top* note is not . . .	FAINT
top artist	PRA, RAKING	top notes, *say*	HIGH SEAS
top *a*rtist(D)	A	top of head	VERTEX
top artist	(l)ELY	*top of* head(D)	H
top barman	QC, SILK	*top of* the . . . (D)	T
top cat	CHIEF WHIP	*top of* the chart(D)	C
top *c*at(D)	C	top of the chart	(TRUE) NORTH
top (c)at	AT	*top off* (t)he . . .	HE
top class	U	*top off* the (c)hart	HART
top *c*lass(D)	C	top of the hill	CAPTOR
top (c)lass	LASS	*top of* the hill(D)	H
top company man	MD	*top off* the (h)ill	ILL
top confectioner, *say*	BUNKING	top players	HEADBAND
top dog	WINNER	*top* *p*layers(D)	P
top *d*og(D)	D	*top* (p)layers	LAYERS
top (d)og	OG	*top* *r*ace(D)	CROWN DERBY
top drawer	FAST GUN, GUNSLINGER	*top* *r*ace	R
	DEGAS, LEONARDO et al	*top* (r)ace	ACE
	PRA	top specialist	HAIRDRESSER
	U		TRICHOLOGIST
top *d*rawer(D)	D	top trophy	GOLD, SCALP
top (d)rawer	RAWER	top *up*(D)^	POT
top dressing	BRILLIANTINE,	topless dress	SHOW JUMPERS
	SHAMPOO, WIG	*topless* (g)own(D)	OWN
	OVERCOAT	topper	EXECUTIONER
	LIME, MULCH	topping place	GIBBET, SCAFFOLD
top *d*ressing(D)	D	*topping* (p)lan(D)	LAN
top figure	NUMERATOR	**topple**	
top floor	ATTIC	dog *topples over*<	GOD
top *f*loor(D)	F	topple mountain	FELL
top (f)loor	LOOR	*toppling over* step<	PETS
top floor, *say*	GAROTTE	**topsy-turvy**	
top gear	HAT	[it was] *topsy-turvy*	WAIST, WAITS
top *g*ear(D)	G	*topsy-turvy* [reasons]	SENORAS
top (g)ear	EAR	**tore**	
top grade	A	tore	RIPPED
top-*h*eavy(D)	H	• 100 tore, *say*	CRYPT
top honours	A, ACE, K, KING	• tore fish, *say*	RIPTIDE
top lawyer, *say*	BARKING		(*see also* tear)

Anag [cat]; Any *; Begin IGN–; Endings –ING; eg •; Hidden /cat/; Implied add (on); Implied in (in);

tore up [papers]	SAPPER
torn	RENT
• shirt torn	TRENT
• torn at this point, *say*	RENTIER
• torn volume	RENT BOOK
torn [towel]	OWLET
torn up [papers]	SAPPER
	(*see also* tear)
torment	
[devil] *tormented* . . .	LIVED
torment animal	BADGER
torment *say*	PANE
tormented [animal]	LAMINA, MANILA
torn	
torn	RENT
• shirt torn	TRENT
• torn at this point, *say*	RENTIER
	(*see also* tear, tore)
torpedo-boat	
torpedo-boat	MTB, TB
torpedo-boat destroyer	TBD
tortuous	
tortuous [lane]	LEAN
[writhe] *tortuously*	WITHER
torture	
torture machine, *say*	WRACK
tortured by [fire]	RIFE
torturing [slave]	SALVE, VALSE
Tory	
Tory	BLUE
• sad Tory	BLUE
• Tory high-flier	BLUEBIRD
Tory	C
• it *is back*< to Tory . . .	TIC
• Tory *has* many	CLOT
Tory	CON
• Tory *backing*<	NOC
• Tory in charge	CONIC
Tory	RIGHT
• second-class Tory	BRIGHT
• strong Tory . . .	FRIGHT
Tory, *say*	WIG
toss	
[ship] *tossed about*	HIPS, PISH
toss head	SHYNESS
toss tool	PITCHFORK
toss up(D)^	NIPS
toss up Ben's . . . (D)^	SNEB
toss up [coin]	ICON
tossed [caber]	ACERB, BRACE
tossed about [in the] . . .	THINE
tossed out [into an] . . .	NATION
Tosti's song	TATA
total	
total	ALL
• 100 total . . .	CALL

• b–et *about* total . . .	BALLET
• total disrepute	ALLODIUM
• totally dependent and	ALLOWING
• credit total, *say*	CRAWL
total	SUM
• total account	SUMAC
• total, *say*	SOME
• total with *German* . . .	SUMMIT
total	WHOLE
• total *and* more	WHOLESOME
• total, *say*	HOLE
• totally *say*	HOL(E)Y
total number	GENERAL
	ANAESTHETIC
	GROSS
total *speaking*	SOME
totter	
tottered [into] . . .	–TION
tottered, *say*	SUEDE
tottering [steps]	PESTS
touch	
touch	FEEL
• touch fish, *say*	FEELING
• touching sympathy	FEELING
touch	PAT
• second touch	SPAT
• touch a number	PATTEN
• touch bird	PATTERN
touch coin	FINGERMARK
touch fish	DAB
touch lightly, *say*	GRAYS, GREYS
touch of garlic	G
touched	FELT
• touched cloth	FELT
• touched journalist	FELTED
touching	ANENT
touching	RE
• touching song	RELIED
• try touching . . .	GORE
touchingly written	TYPED
touchline	TANGENT
tough	
tough	HARD
• tough course	HARD TACK
• tough defender	HARDBACK
• tough guy, *say*	HARD-WON
• tough joint	HARD SHOULDER
• tough ship	HARDLINER
tough bird, *say*	TOUGHEN
tough blades	ESPARTO
tough lawman	DRACO
tough Scot, *say*	RUFFIAN
tough worker	NUTANT
toughen	ANNEAL
toughen, *say*	ANNELE

Letter replaced \c\at; Omit (a); Pointers *out*; Retain <u>a</u>; Split B_ED; Down (D); Backwards <or ^

tour		**trade**	
on tour [in the] . . .	THINE	trade centre	MALL, MART
Tour de France	EIFFEL (TOWER)	tr<u>a</u>de *centre*	A
tour of [Rome}	MORE	trade name	TN
toured by *	incl in *	trade union	TU
• north *toured by* bu–s	BUNS	trademark	TM
touring car	GT	trader	INDIAMAN, MERCHANTMAN
touring [car]	ARC	Trades Union Congress	TUC
touring a . . .	incl A	• Trade Unionists	CUTBACK
touring *	incl *	tradesmen	TU
• bu–s *touring* north	BUNS	tradesmen's *entrance*	T
tou<u>ri</u>st *centre*	R	*trading* [coins]	ICONS, SONIC
Tourist Trophy	TT	**traditional**	
towards		indicating old words:	
towards boy	TOKEN	• *traditional* hero	EORL
towards dog	TOP-UP	• *traditionally* excellent	EXIMIOUS
towards Sussex	DOWNWARDS	**traffic**	
tower		traffic light	CAT'S-EYE
tower block(s)	TALL STORIES		AMBER, GREEN, RED
tower in Paris, *say*	EYEFUL, TOUR	traffic sign	TRADEMARK
tower maintenance	KEEP	traffic signal	GO, STOP
Tower of London	BARBICAN, CENTRE POINT	**tragic**	
tower (of strength)	CARTHORSE, SHIRE	*tragic* [Latin hero]	LIONHEART
	TRACTOR, TUG	tragic woman	ELECTRA, HECUBA,
town			MEROPE et al
town		*tragically* [dead]	EDDA
indicating origins:		**train**	
• car *in Boston*	AUTO	train	APT
• house *in Essen*	HAUS	train fish	SCHOOL
• *Paris-style* hat	CHAPEAU	train line	REARRANGE
• *Roman* boy	RAGAZZO	train reserves	EXERCISE BOOKS
	(*see also* from[3])	train, *say*	SWEET
town	TN	*train* [seals]	SALES
• I am *in* town	TIN	*trained as* [nurse]	RUNES
• nothing *in* town	TON	*trained* [guns]	GNUS, SNUG, SUNG
town ahead	BURGLED	trainee	L
town *centre*	(l)OUT(h), (n)EAT(h) etc	training	PE, PT
tow<u>n</u>-*centre*	OW	training centre	STATION
town crier, *say*	BAULKING		WATERLOO etc
town house	HANOVER, LANCASTER	tra<u>ini</u>ng *centre*	IN
	WINDSOR, YORK etc	*training* [centre]	RECENT
Town Planning Institute	TPI	training manual	EXERCISE BOOK
town sub-office	TSO	*training* [ship]	HIPS, PISH
townsman, *say*	BURGER	Training within Industry	TWI
toy		trains	BR, RY
toy	DOLL	*train*[spotter]	POTTERS
• toy instruments, *say*	DOLDRUMS	**tramp**	
• toy *with* unknown . . .	DOLLY	tramp	HOBO, STEAMER
• toyboy, *say*	DOLMAN	tramp steamer	DRIFTER
toy revolver	CAROUSEL, (PEG-)TOP	**tramples**	STEPSON
	ROUNDABOUT, WHIRLIGIG	**transactions**	
toy sweet	TRIFLE	transactions	TR
toyed with [soup]	OPUS	*transactions* [in grain]	RAINING
track		**transatlantic**	US
tracked vehicle	CAT, TANK		(*see also* America)
tracks	R(L)Y	**transcendental meditation**	TM

transcribe

transcribe [older] . . .	DROLE
transcribing nearly	
all [Chines(e)]	INCHES
transcription of [trio]	RIOT

transfer

transfer	PASS
• reserves *involved in* transfer	PASTAS
• transfer help, *say*	PASSADE
• transfer I have . . .	PASSIVE
transfer [a winger]	WEARING
transference of [coins]	ICONS, SONIC

transfigure

transfigured [sinner]	INNERS
transfiguration of [devil]	LIVED

transform

transform [my pet]	EMPTY
transformation of [stage] . . .	GATES
transforming [into] . . .	–TION

transfuse

transfusion of [saline] . . .	LIANES
[weak] *transfusion*	WAKE

transgress

transgress again	RESIN
transgress before nine, *say*	SCINTILLATE
transgress [laws]	AWLS, SLAW
transgression of [rules]	LURES

translate

translate	
–*French* word	MOT
–*German* word	WORT
–*Italian* word	PAROLA
–*Latin* word	VERBUM
–*Spanish* word	PALABRA
translate	
–*French* book	LIVRE
–*German* book	BUCH
–*Italian* book	LIBRO
–*Latin* book	LIBER
–*Spanish* book	LIBRO
translate	
–from *French*	DE
–from *German*	VON
–from *Italian*	DA
–from *Latin*	AB
–from *Spanish*	DE
–from the *French*	DELA, DES, DU
translate	
–into *French*	EN, ENTRE
–into *Italian*	DENTRO
–into *Latin*	INTRO
–into *Spanish*	EN, ENTRE
translate	
–the *French* . . .	LA, LE, LES
–the *German* . . .	DAS, DER, DIE
–the *Italian* . . .	GLI, IL, LA, LO, LE
–the *Spanish* . . .	EL, LA, LAS, LOS
translated [verse]	SERVE, SEVER
translation	CRIB, TR
translation of [Norse]	SENOR, SNORE
translator	TR

transmute

[may be] *transmuted*	BEAMY
transmutation of [silver]	LIVERS, SLIVER
transmute [lead]	DALE, DEAL, LADE

transplant

transplant [shrub]	BRUSH
transplantation of [tree]	RETE
transplanted [heart]	EARTH, HATER
	RATHE
transplanted heart of m\a\in . . .	MINA

transport

transport	BR
• transport expert	BRACE
• transport school	BRETON
• transport worker	BRANT
transport	BUS
• about transport	REBUS
• transport army *by* road	BUSTARD
• transport sheep	BUST-UP
transport	CAB
• transport fish	CABLING
• transport *in* front	CABLED
• transport *on* the *French*	
road	CABLEWAY
transport	CAR
• six transport . . .	VICAR
• transport *in* ship	SCARS
• transport *to* harbour	CARPORT
transport	ENTRANCE
transport	RLY
• man *in* transport	RALLY
• mother *has* transport	MARLY
transport	RY
• everybody *in* transport	RALLY
• mother *has* transport	MARY
transport	TRAM
• transport a man . . .	TRAMMEL
• transport *has* quiet . . .	TRAMP
Transport Officer	TO
transport opening	ENTRANCE
transport worker	SHIRE (HORSE)
transported [in car]	CAIRN

transpose

transpose [result]	LUSTRE, ULSTER
transpose reviled . . . <	DELIVER

transvestite

transvestite, *say*	DRAGSTER
transvestites	DRAG-RACE

Transworld Airlines — TWA

trap

trap	GIN

Letter replaced \c\at; Omit (a); Pointers *out*; Retain <u>a</u>; Split B_ED; Down (D); Backwards <or ^

• a trap *has* good . . .	AGING	*travelling* [crane]	NACRE
• live trap	BEGIN	travelling light	HEADLAMP
• trapnet	GINNET	travelling players, *say*	ROADSIDE, TROOP
and		**treacherous**	
• trap dog, *say*	JINKER	[act] *treacherously*	CAT
• trap, *say*	(D)JINN	treacherous guy	BURGESS
trap	MOUTH	*treacherous* [reef]	FEER, FERE, FREE
trap	NET	**treacle**	
• 50 in a trap	LINNET	[treacle] *pudding*	ELECTRA
• trap a spirit	NETRUM	spread [treacle]	ELECTRA
• trap a woman	NETHER	**treasury**	
trap European	CATCHPOLE	treasury keeper	DRAGON
trapped by Fren/ch arm/y	CHARM	treasury note, *say*	TENOR
trapped by *	incl in *	**treat**	
• one *trapped by* m–en	MIEN	[hormone] *treatment*	MOORHEN
trapped in ca/ve al/l . . .	VEAL	[painless] *treatment*	SPANIELS
trapped spirit	SNARE DRUM	[medical] *treatment*	CLAIMED, DECIMAL,
trapping a . . .	incl A		DECLAIM
trapping *	incl *	treat timber	DEAL
• m–en *trapping* one	MIEN	*treated* [timber]	TIMBRE
trash		*treating* [flu]	–FUL
[it was] *trashed*	WAIST, WAITS	*treatment of* [yaws]	SWAY, WAYS
trashed [all the] . . .	LETHAL	**tree**	
travel		tree	ALDER
travel	GO	• black tree	BALDER
• travel *by* rail	GORY	• tree joint, *say*	ALDERNEY
• travel *in* al–l . . .	ALGOL	• tree *on* island	ALDERMAN
• travel *with* wife	GO DUTCH	tree	ASH
and		• hard tree	HASH
• travel east *and* south	GOES	• tree-god	ASHLAR
• travel north-east	GONE	• tree *in* China	MASHING
• travel west *and* north	GOWN	tree	FIR
travel	TO	• king *has* a tree	KAFIR
• travel north	TON	• saint *hid behind* tree	FIRST
• travel north-east	TONE	• tree-ring	FIRRING
• travel west	TOW	tree	MAY
travel agency	CARRIAGE	• girl's tree	DISMAY
travel guide	SIGNPOST	• king *hidden in* tree	MARY
travel [in car]	CAIRN	• tree-ring	MAYO
travel West		tree	OAK
• dog *travels West*<	GOD	• second tree	SOAK
travelled	RODE	• tree unknown	OAKY
• travelled *by* Circle	RODEO	• tree *used in* ship	SOAKS
• travelled on pig, *say*	ROAD-HOG	tree	PALM
• travelled to this place, *say*	ROE-DEER	• goat *behind* tree	PALM-BUTTER
traveller	REP	• North American tree	NAPALM
• traveller in the East	REPINE	• tree in Greece	PALMING
• traveller isn't . . .	REPAINT	tree *climbing*(D)^	EMIL, YAM
• traveller wandered	REPROVED	tree expert	GENEALOGIST
• traveller's *return*<	PER	tree-house	ORANGE
• traveller's tales	REPLIES	tree list, *say*	TREATABLE
traveller's fare	PASSENGER	tree maintenance	SERVICE
travelling bag	CARCASE	Tree, *perhaps*	ACTOR, TRAGEDIAN
travelling-case	OUT-PATIENT	tree, *say*	BEACH, EWE, FUR, OKE
travelling-[case]	ACES, AESC		PLAIN, SEEDER, YOU
travelling companion	CARPET	tree, *say*	–TERY, –TRY

• criticise tree	PANTRY
• half-standard tree	CEMETERY
• osier	BASKETRY
• river tree	INDUSTRY
• saucepan rack	PANTRY
• smelly tree	MUSKETRY
• twisted tree	BANDITRY
tree worship	SERVICE
treeless	OPINES
trees *with* everything	FORESTALL
treetops, *say*	BEACHHEADS
tremble	
[leaf] *trembling*	FLEA
trembling [lips]	PILS, SLIP
tremulous	
[speak] *tremulously*	PEAKS, SPAKE
tremolo [notes]	ONSET, SETON
	STONE, TONES
tremulous [speech]	CHEEPS
trench digger	JCB, RE, SAPPER
trendy	
trendy	IN
• ask trendy . . .	BEGIN
• trendy *in* ways	NINE, SINE, SINS
	WINE, WINS
• trendy people	INSET
Trent Bridge	NE
trial	
trial	TEST
• large trial	FATTEST
• trial marriage	TEST MATCH
• trial TV	TEST-TUBE
trial marriage	PRACTICE MATCH
trial shot, *say*	CITER
triangular	DELTA
tribe	
tribe	DAN, GAD
tribe	SEPT
• beyond the tribe	TRANSEPT
• tribe *has* a . . .	SEPTA
• tribe in charge	SEPTIC
tribute	CAIN
trick	
[quite] *tricky*	QUIET, –TIQUE
trick	CON
• one trick	ICON
• trick *in* the Home Counties	SCONE
• trick questions	CONTESTS
trick of [fate]	FEAT
trick, *say*	FAINT, RUES, WHILE
tricky achievement	GRAND SLAM
tricky command	ABRACADABRA
	HEY PASS, HEY PRESTO
	OPEN SESAME
tricky contest	BRIDGE, WHIST
tricky [part]	PRAT, RAPT, TRAP

tried	
[tried]	TIRED OUT
[tried] *out*	TIRED
	(*see also* try)
trifle	
a trifle depressed	WHITLOW
trifling with [meal]	LAME, MALE
trim	
trim [ends]	DENS, SEND
trim (h)air	AIR
trim t/he len/gth	HELEN
trim tree	SPRUCE
trimmed both ends of (s)car(f)	CAR
trimmer ship	CLIPPER, CUTTER
trinity	
Trinity College, Dublin	TCD
Trinity College of Music	TCM
trio	
Beethoven's *first trio*	BEE
Mozart's *second trio*	ART
trio from Rossini	SIN
trip	
trip over	JOURNEY'S END
trip [over]	ROVE
trip over [step]	PEST, PETS
trip over step<	PETS
trip [to Mars]	STROMA
triumph	
triumph	V
triumphant cry	IO
trivial sum	ID, IP
troop	
troop	TP
troops *on* jetty	RAPIER
tropic disease	CANCER
trot	
trot [past]	PATS, SPAT, STAP, TAPS
trotting [race]	ACER, ACRE, CARE
trouble	
[real] *trouble*	LEAR
[take] *trouble*	KATE, TEAK
trouble	ADO, AIL
trouble afoot	BUNION, CORN, VERRUCA
trouble (and strife)	WIFE
trouble in [Iran]	RAIN, RANI
trouble maker	GREMLIN
troubled [times]	ITEMS, MITES, SMITE
[trouble]*maker*	BOULTER
troublesome [priest]	RIPEST, STRIPE
	TRIPES
trounce	
trounced [team]	MATE, MEAT, META–, TAME
trouncing [best] . . .	BETS
true	
true blue	RIGHT
true height	REALTOR

Letter replaced \c\at; Omit (a); Pointers *out*; Retain <u>a</u>; Split B_ED; Down (D); Backwards <or ^

[true or] *false*	ROUTER, TOURER
[true] *to form*	–TURE
true, *say*	REEL, STRAIT
trumpeter	ARMSTRONG, JAMES
	ELEPHANT
	JOSHUA
trunk	
trunk, *say*	BOWL
trunk service	STD
trust	
trusted friend	ACHATES
trustee	TR
trustee *said* . . .	TRUSTY
Trustee Savings Bank	TSB
trusty pilot	SAFE CONDUCT
truth	
truth-drug, *say*	LIGHTEST
try	
try	GO
• to go *after* graduate	TOBAGO
• try *covered by* wager	BEGOT
• try publicity	GOAD
try	HEAR
• second try	SHEAR
• try the Home Counties	HEARSE
• try *to capture* note	HEATER
and	
• try and try again	HEAR-HEAR
and	
• try excessively, *say*	HERETO
• try, *say*	HERE
try	TEST
• city tries . . .	LATESTS
• try a peg	TESTATEE
• try *about* everything	TALLEST
and	
• try at this place, *say*	TESTIER
try-*out*	T–EST, TR–Y
[try]-*out*	TYR
try *to contain* . . .	T–EST, TR–Y
try to fish	CASTANET
TT	
TT	DOUBLET
TT	DRY
• old *and* dry	OTT
TT	RACE
• one *in* race	TAT, TIT
t-take in	TEAT
tub	
tub	BATH, BOAT
tubby fellow	DIOGENES
tubby trio	BAKER, BUTCHER
	CANDLESTICK MAKER
tube	UNDERLINE
French tube	METRO
tube fare	MACARONI

Tube Investments	TI
tube traveller	TORPEDO
tuber	MURPHY, POTATO, SPUD
tuberculosis	TB
TUC	
TUC(D)	CUT UP, NOTCH UP
TUC *rises*(D)^	CUT
tuck	
tuck, *say*	FRIAR
tucked in *	incl in *
• tyro *tucked in* s–acks	SLACKS
tucked into	ATE
tucked into mea/l at e/ight	LATE
tucked into sin/gle be/d	GLEBE
tucked into *	incl in *
• airman *tucked into* me–at	MEERKAT
tucked round a . . .	incl A
tucked round *	incl *
• s–acks *tucked round* tyro	SLACKS
Tuesday	T, TU, TUES
tumble	
tumble [drier]	DIRER
tumble [dryer]	DERRY
tumbled [into Po]	OPTION, POTION
tumbled over step<	PETS
tumbled over [step]	PEST, PETS
tumbledown [shack]	HACKS
tumbler	JILL
tumbler-maker	ACROBAT, LOCKSMITH
tumult	
tumult [in the] . . .	THINE
tumultuous [riot]	TRIO
tune	
[fine]-*tuning*	NIFE
tune, *say*	HEIR, REAL
tuned [a sitar]	TIARAS
Tunisia	TN
tuppence	DD, PP
turbulent	
[act] *turbulently*	CAT
[air] *turbulence*	RIA
turbulent [priest]	RIPEST, STRIPE
	TRIPES
turf	
turf out	DIVOT
turf study	SODDEN
Turkey	TR
turmoil	
[much] *turmoil*	CHUM
turmoil [in great] . . .	INGRATE, TEARING
turn[1]	
turn	ACT
• space *to* turn	ENACT
• transport turns . . .	BRACTS
• turn gold	ACTOR
• turns book	ACTS

Anag [cat]; Any *; Begin IGN–; Endings –ING; eg •; Hidden /cat/; Implied add (on); Implied in (in);

turn	GO
• a turn *to* the north	AGON
• turn *and* throw	GOSLING
• turn sheep	GOT UP
• turn *to* latest . . .	GONE WEST
• turn *to* publicity	GOAD
and	
• turn *back*<	OG
• turn *over*<	OG
• turn *up*(D)^	OG
turn	S
• turn *in*	incl S
• turn *into*	incl S
• turn *out*	omit S
turn	SPIN
• one *in* a turn	SPAIN
• turn a number	SPINAL
• turn alien . . .	SPINET
and	
• turn *back*<	NIPS
• turn *over*<	NIPS
• turn *up*(D)^	NIPS
turn	U
• turn about	URE
• turn *in* church	CUE
• turn round	UO
• turn ship	U-BOAT
and	
• turn *in*	incl U
• turn *into*	incl U
• turn *out*	omit U
turn	·WHEEL
• turn a hair	WHEEL LOCK
• turn *behind* the vehicle	CARTWHEEL
• turning circle	STEERING WHEEL
and	
• turn, *say*	WEAL, WE'LL, WHEAL
turn	WIND
• turn girl	WINDLASS
• turn *to* hospital wing	WINDWARDS
• turn *round* English . . .	WINED
• turn here, *say*	WINDIER
turn²	
turn	
indicating anagram:	
• *turn* [into] . . .	–TION
• *turn* [into a] . . .	–ATION
• *turn* into [street]	SETTER, TESTER
• *turn* [it on]	INTO, –TION
• *turn* of [phrase]	SERAPH, SHERPA
• [*turn*] out	RUNT
• *turn* out [the guard]	DAUGHTER
• *turn* over [a bit]	BAIT
• *turn* [over a bit]	ABORTIVE
• *turn* [sour]	OURS
• *turn* [tables]	BLEATS, STABLE

• *turned out* [fine]	NIFE
• *turned out to be* [a dry] . . .	DRAY, YARD
• *turn*[coats]	ASCOT, ATOCS, COAST, TOSCA
turn	
indicating reversal:	
• *turn* about<	ER, AC
• *turn* again<	ER
• *turn* back<	NIPS
• *turn* Communist<	DER
• *turn* green<	WAR
• *turn* in<	NI
• *turn* it< on	–TION
• *turn* it over<	TI
• *turn* it *up*(D)^	TI
• *turn* on<	NO
• *turn* over to< . . .	OT
• *turn* red<	DER
• *turn* round but . . . <	TUB
• *turn* to . . . <	OT
• *turn* up<	PU
• *turn* up parts(D)^	STRAP
• *turning* tide<	EDIT
• *turnover* made . . . <	EDAM
• *turn*spit<	TIPS
turn³	
turn again	ENCORE
turn left	BEND SINISTER
turn on	SWITCH
turn out fine	omit F
turn over	TO
turn quickly	VS
turn ring	ROLLCALL
turn round	SCREWBALL, UO
turn *tail*	
• Boe\r\ *turns tail*	BORE
• *turn tail of* lin\e\	LIEN
turncoat feature	LAPEL
turned out fine	omit F
turner	LATHE, SPIT, WHEEL
	PAINTER
turning force, *say*	TALK, TORC
	(*see also* twist)
Turnberry	
Turnberry *they say* . . .	SINTER
Turnberry's first	T, TEE
tweak	
tweak [ear]	ARE, ERA
tweaked [nose]	NOES, ONES
twelve	
Glorious Twelfth	AUGUST
twelve	DOZ(EN), HANDS UP, XII
twelve Christmas presents	DRUMMERS
twelve hours	AM, PM
twelve houses	ZODIAC
twelve hundred	MCC
twelve inches	AFOOT

Letter replaced \c\at; Omit (a); Pointers *out*; Retain <u>a</u>; Split B_ED; Down (D); Backwards <or ^

twelve jobs	LABOURS OF HERCULES
twelve men	JURY
twelve tribes	ISRAELITES
twenty	
20	DOUBLE CROSS, XX
21	KEY OF THE DOOR, MAJORITY
22	CATCH, TWO-BY-TWO
24	BLACKBIRDS
25 pounds (£25)	PONY
25% *off* bee(f)	BEE
25% price *cut*	COS(t)
27 books	NT
28 grams	OZONE
Twentieth Century Dictionary	TCD
twenty	SCORE
• twenty directors	SCOREBOARD
• twenty *plus* 500	SCORED
• twenty ties	SCORE DRAWS
twenty thousand	K
twenty-twenty	VISION
twice	
twice blessed	BB
	(*see also* double, doubly, two³)
Twickenham game	RU, RUGBY
twiddle	
[stop] *twiddling*!	OPTS, POST, POTS, SPOT
twiddle [toes]	TOSE
twin	
twin	CASTOR, POLLUX
twin daughters	DD
twin sons	SS
	(*see also* two³)
twine	
[liane] *twined* . . .	ANILE
twining [arms]	MARS, RAMS
twinkle	
[in a] *twinkling*	AIN, IAN
twinkling [star]	ARTS, RATS, TARS, TSAR
twirl	
twirl knob<	BONK
twirling [stick]	TICKS
twist	
twist a number, *say*	TERNATE
twist alien	CRICKET
twist road	WARPLANE
twist-ring	SCREWBALL
twist, *say*	REST, RING, TERN
twist verse	SPINODE
twisted [a leg]	GALE, GAEL
twisted injury	WOUND
twisted, *say*	RESTED, RUNG, RYE
twisted sheep, *say*	WRITE-UP
twisted you and me, *say*	RICTUS
twisting [client]	LENTIC
twists nut	RICKSHAW
	(*see also* turn)

twitch	
twitch [nose]	NOES, ONES
twitching [nerves]	SEVERN
two¹	
two	COMPANY
two	COUPLE
• one *French with* two . . .	UNCOUPLE
• two *plus* 500	COUPLED
• two shirts	COUPLETS
two	II
two	PAIR, PR
• 1000 couples	IMPAIRS
• about two	REPAIR
• I am two . . .	IMPAIR
• two soldiers	REPAIR
two-by-two	FOUR
two-*by*-two	TWENTY-TWO
two Christmas presents	TURTLEDOVES
two-dimensional figure	FLATTEN
two holding hands	EN, NS, WE etc
two hundred	CC
two hundred thousand	S, SIGMA
two in song	LILLYWHITE BOYS
two-nil	TWENTY
two spades	SP
two, *say*	BRAYS, PARE, PEAR
two, *say*	TO, TOO, TOU, TU
• two names	TONS
• two shirts	TOOTS
• two tins	TOUCANS
• two extra	TUMOUR
two score, *say*	FOR TEA, FORTE
two thousand	MM, Z
two-way names	LEON, NOEL
two-way transport	KAYAK
writer or two	TWAIN
	(*see also* pair)
two²	
actions	SUITCASE
advertisements	BILLPOSTER
animals	BUCKRAM, BULL-PUP,
	BULLDOG, FOXHOUND
	RAMCAT, SHEEPDOG
	WOLFRAM
animals, *say*	RAMBLE
arguments	SPARROW
articles	AIL, ALA, LATHE
	LETHE, THEA, UNDER
bases	BEDEVIL
beds	CRIBBED
Biblical characters	JOB LOT
birds	COCKCROW, RAVENDUCK
	TITLARK, TITREE
black things	NIGHTCLUB
blows	SMASH HIT
blues	ROYAL NAVY

Anag [cat]; Any *; Begin IGN–; Endings –ING; eg •; Hidden /cat/; Implied add (on); Implied in (in);

boys	ALBERT, ALFRED, ARTHURIAN	finals	TAIL-END
	BASILDON, BASILIAN, BENTHOS	fish	CODLING, IDLING
	DONJON, DENTED, EDWARDIAN,		NURSELING, RUDDLING
	FRANKED, GLENGARRY, GREGORIAN	fish, *say*	DABBLING
	GUYED, HALBERT, HALTED,	flavours	PEPPERMINT
	HERBAL	foods	BREADFRUIT, CHEESECAKE
	JACKAL, JACKED, MALTED,		JELLYBEAN, JELLYFISH
	MARKED		PEANUT, SWEETMEAT
	NICKED, NORMAL, NORMANDY,	forms of transport	CARRY
	PATRON,	friends	PALMATE
	PATTED, PETERED, REGAL,ROYAL,	fruits, *say*	PLUMBERY
	RUSSIAN, SAMIAN, SIDED, SIDLES,	games	PONTOON BRIDGE
	TOMBOY, TIMED, VICTIM,	garments	BRAVEST
	VICTORIAN	generations	DAMSON, MASON
boys and a girl	BETRAYAL	Germans	HUNGER
buildings	HUTCH	girls	BELLADONNA, CLARABELLA
cans	POTABLE		DISALLY, DIVI, GALENA
card games	PONTOON BRIDGE		MILLIGAL, PATELLA, PATINA
cards	TENACE		ROSEMARY, SALINA, TESSELLA
cats	TOMALLEY	girls *with* a Scotsman	SALMONELLA
celestial bodies	EARTHSTAR	glances	LOOK-SEE
characters	(*see* letters)	goddesses	DEVIATE
chiefs	HEADFIRST	graves	STERN-CHASE
children	–DS	Greek letters	PIETA
churches	ROMANCE	groups of officers	COSMOS
circles	DISCO	hands	–RL
cities	ROMANY	headdresses	CROWN DERBY
clubs	IRONWOOD	heads	BLUFFNESS, ONION DOME
colours	OLIVETAN	homes	HONEST
containers	BASKET CASE, CHAMBERTIN	in family	DAMSON, MASON
	PAN-JUG, POT BOILER	insects, *say*	NATANT
	TINPOT, TUNDISH	inspections	LOOK-SEE
coppers	CUD, CUP, DD, DP, PD, PP	instruments	HORNPIPE
	PENNYFARTHING	journalists	CUBED
cots	CRIBBED	keys	BORA, CORA, DORA
courses	JELLYFISH, SWEETMEAT		BORD, CORD, FORD
court calls	LET OUT		BORE, CORE, FORE, GORE
creatures	CLAMANT	kings	EDWARD LEAR, GRANDER, GROG
cuts	HACK-SAW	languages	FRENCH POLISH
dances	FOOTBALL, FOOTSTEP	lashers	WHIPCAT
defects	DESERT RAT	learners	TYROL
dioceses	ELYSEE	letter girl	ELLA, ELLEN, EMMA
directions	EN, WE etc	letters	BANDY, CANDY, DANDY
	WANDS		MANDY, PANDA, RANDY
disputes	SPARROW		SANDY, TANDEM
doctors, *say*	PARADOX	letters, *say*	TEPEE
dogs	CURTAIL	lots of coins	BITS AND PIECES
dots	COLON	maidens	MALICE, MANNA
drinks	ALEVIN, SUPPORTER	means of transport	CARAVAN, MOTORBOAT,
drugs	CRACKPOT, TEAPOT		TRAMCAR
enclosures	DAMPEN, HEMPEN	measures	FOOTSTEP, ELLEN
expressions of surprise	HOOCH	men	ALBERT, CHAPMAN, DESMAN
fabrics	REPLACE		GENTLES, GILBERTIAN
fathers	PAPAW		HE-MAN, HEAL, HELEN, HEROD
favourites	PUPPET		HERON, LANCE-JACK, MACRON
fells	DOWNHILL		MANAL, MELTED

Letter replaced \c\at; Omit (a); Pointers *out*; Retain <u>a</u>; Split B_ED; Down (D); Backwards <or ^

	(see also boys *above)*
men and a woman	BETRAYAL, HELEN
months	DECOCT
mothers	DAMPEN, MADAM, MAMMA
movements	SPRING ROLL
natural products	FURORE
negatives	NONARY
notes	DOME, DOTE, LATE, MERE
	METE, MIRE, REDO, SOFA
	REME, SITE, SOLE, SOME, TIME
novices	TYROL
numbers, *say*	TOFORE
odd fellows	CRANKCASE
old elements	FIREWATER
paces	JOG-TROT
paper sizes	CROWN IMPERIAL
parts of goal	BARNET
people	DAWNED, DIAL, DIED, VIAL, VIED
periods	ADAGE
pieces	BIT PART
–of timber	LOGWOOD
pins	PEG-LEG
pints, *say*	QUARTZ
placards	BILLPOSTER
poets, *say*	HARDIHOOD
points	NIBS, SNIB,
	NEEDLESS
	PEAKS, SPEAK
	TINES
political parties	CLEFT
politicians, *say*	LABORATORY
pounds	LIQUID
presents	NOWHERE
pronouns	USHER
records	LOGBOOK
reduced	LOWDOWN
regiments	RARE
relations	MASON, SISKIN
remarks in court	OUTLET
resins	GUMLAC
rings	DINGO, DISCO
rivers	AIRER, DEER, RALPH
	ROUSE, RURAL
roads	AVER, MIST
	PATHWAY, RAILROAD
	STANDARD, STAVE
rows	RANK AND FILE
Scots	CAMERONIAN
scraps	SPARROW
seamen	MERCHANTABLE
seas	SEAMED
seater bicycle (tandem)	TM
sentences	LIFE AND DEATH
sets of cards	DECKHAND
short periods	MOHR
sides	OFF AND ON, ON AND OFF

sleeping places	CRIBBED
sources of water	WELLSPRING
spoons	NECK AND NECK
states	FLAME, GALA, LAVA, MEMO
	NYALA, PENNILL, RIME
streets	*(see* roads *above)*
sticky things	TARGUM
strikes	SMASH HIT
surprised reactions	JUMP-START
tennis shots	SMASH HIT
things	
–naturally produced	FURORE
–to eat	*(see* courses, foods *above)*
timepieces	WATCH (THE) CLOCK
torches	LAMPLIGHT
traps	GINNET
trees	BOX ELDER, BOXTHORN
	OAK APPLE, PINEAPPLE
undergarments	BRAVEST
vehicles	CARAVAN, TRAMCAR
violent people	GO THROUGH
water sources	WELLSPRING
ways	EN, WE, etc
	MODEST
–to go	*(see* roads *above)*
weapons	BOMBSHELL
whiskies	PAIR OF SHORTS
wines	RED ROSE, WHITE ROSE
women	LADYBIRD, MADAM
	MADONNA, MALADY
	VIDAME
two³	
adverts	PUFF-PUFF
agreements	DADA
animals in…	ASSASSIN
armies	TATA
army men	GIGI
basic subjects	RR
bears	POOH-POOH
berries	HAW-HAW
black queens	BERBER
blows	CHOP-CHOP
boys	TOM-TOM, WILLY-WILLY
cats	TOM-TOM
chants	SING-SING
cheers	HEAR-HEAR
coats	FURFUR
coins	DD, PP, SS
companies	COCO
containers	JUG-JUG
cuts	CHOP-CHOP
daughters	DD
days	DD
detectives, *say*	DIK-DIK
digits	TOETOE
discounts	DIVI-DIVI

Anag [cat]; Any *; Begin IGN–; Endings –ING; eg •; Hidden /cat/; Implied add (on); Implied in (in);

dogs	POMPOM	pounds	LL
drinks	CHA-CHA	presents, *say*	HEAR-HEAR, NOW-NOW
essays	GOGO	prisons	CAN-CAN
extras	BYE-BYE	quiet . . .	HUSH-HUSH
fathers	PAPA	ravines	NULLANULLA
features	CHIN-CHIN	refusals	NEVER-NEVER
feet	PAWPAW	roads	MIMI, MM
firms	COCO	Romany women	CHICHI
French words	MOT-MOT	runs	BYE-BYE
friends	PALPAL	sailors	TARTAR
fruits	HAW-HAW, HIP-HIP	seconds	SS
fruits, *say*	BERI-BERI	shillings	SS
girls	LILLIL	soldiers	GIGI
girls, *say*	SOOSOO	sounds	HUMHUM
graduates	BABA, MAMA	starting points	TEE-TEE
grasses	SING SING	starting points, *say*	TITI
halves of <u>mi</u>ld	MIMI	states	GAGA
hands	PAWPAW	stomachs	TUM-TUM
hats	TAM-TAM	supports	TEE-TEE
hundred	CC	supports, *say*	TITI
Israelites, *say*	JU-JU	teas	CHA-CHA
jeers	BOOBOO	tests	MOT-MOT
kicks	TOETOE	thousand	MM
learners	LL	tins	CAN-CAN
letters	CHICHI	tree trunks	LOG-LOG
lots of		tries	GOGO, HEAR-HEAR
−hair	FURFUR	volcanic rocks	LAVA-LAVA
−salt	TARTAR	votes for	AYE-AYE
male birds	TOM-TOM	water sources	WELL WELL
meals, *say*	TEE-TEE, TITI	(*see also* double[2])	
men	PP, TOMTOM	**Tyneside**	
mothers	MAMA	Tyneside	NE
motorways	MIMI, MM	• about Tyneside	CANE
noises	DIN-DIN	• arrive *in* Tyneside	NARRE
notes	DODO, MIMI, SO-SO	• Tyneside entrance	NEGATE
oaths, *say*	C(O)USC(O)US, KHUSKHUS	Tynesider	GEORDIE
officers	COCO	**tying**	(*see* tie)
parents	MAMA, PAPA	**type**	
parties	DODO	type	KIND
pawns	PP	• type in front	KINDLED
peers	SEESEE	• type queen's letters	KINDER
pegs	TEE-TEE	• type "Red"	KINDRED
pegs, *say*	TITI	typical measure	ELITE, PICA
pence	DD, PP		EM, EN, POINT
pieces	PP	typical traveller	REPRESENTATIVE
pieces of		**tyro**	L
−meat	CHOP-CHOP	(*see also* learner)	
−timber	LOG-LOG		

U

acceptable, *aristocratic*, bend, boat, bolt, *educational establishment*, ewe, *film*, *high-class*, *posh*, *superior*, title of respect, trap, tube, turn, union, Unionist, united, universal, universe, university, upper-class, upsilon, uranium, Uruguay, Utah

U-boat	SUB	umpire's announcement	OUTCRY
U-turn		**un**[1]	A, AN, I
U-turn was . . . <	SAW	**un-**[2]	
new *U-turn*<	WEN	many words with the prefix	
Uganda	EAU	un-, some of which follow,	
ugly		are used to indicate anagrams	
ugly	PLAIN	**un-English**	omit E
• Penny *has* ugly, *say*	PENEPLAIN	**unable**	
• ugly quarrel	PLAINTIFF	unable	CANT
• ugly queen	PLAINER	unable (=having no . . .)	O
ugly, *say*	PLAIN	• unable to fly	OWING
ugly [mug]	GUM	• unable to stretch	OGIVE
ugly sister	GORGON	• unable to write	OPEN
ugly truth	PLAIN FACTS	**unacceptable**	
Ulster		unacceptable	NON-U
Ulster	NI	unacceptable	OUT
Ulster		• unacceptable habit, *say*	OUTWEIGH
–Defence Association	UDA	• unacceptable job	OUTPOST
–Defence Regiment	UDR	• unacceptable players	OUTCAST
–Freedom Fighters	UFF	**unaccompanied**	ALLA BREVE
–Unionists	UU		A(LLA) CAPELLA
–Volunteer Force	UVF	**unaffected by reversal**	
ultimate		indicating a palindrome:	
the *ultimate* . . .	E	• boat *unaffected by reversal*	KAYAK
the ultimate deterrent	T	• woman *unaffected by reversal*	AVA, EVE
ultimate letter	OMEGA, Z, ZED, ZEE		MADAM
ultimate outcome	E	**unauthorised**	NOOK
ultimately	(in) EN–D	**unavailable**	
• can *ultimately* . . .	ENABLED	money *unavailable*	omit D, L, P
• prison *ultimately* . . .	ENCAGED	father *unavailable*	omit PA
• *ultimately* prosecute	ENSUED	* *unavailable*	omit *
ultimately went *to* Germany	TOY	unavailing, *say*	VANE, VEIN
ultra		**unbalanced**	
ultra high frequency	UHF	[quite] *unbalanced*	QUIET, –TIQUE
ultrashort wave	USW	*unbalanced* [German I] . . .	REAMING
ultrasonic waves	USW	*unbalanced* [scale]	LACES
ultra-violet	UV	**unbelievable female**	CASSANDRA
umbrella	BROLLY, MUSH	**unbounded**	
umpire		(j)o(y) *unbounded*	O
umpire	REF	*unbounded* (p)lain(s)	LAIN
• umpire allowed	REFLET	**unbowed**	PIZZICATO
• umpire has hurt his leg	REFLAME	**unbridled**	
• umpire not well	REFILL	[horse] *unbridled*	HOERS, SHORE

Anag [cat]; Any *; Begin IGN–; Endings –ING; eg •; Hidden /cat/; Implied add (on); Implied in (in);

unbridled [greed]	EDGER
unbroken past	SOLIDAGO
unceasing	FORAY
uncertain	
uncertain [sort]	ORTS, ROTS, TORS
uncertainty [as to] . . .	OATS
unchanged	
unchanged	SIC
[un]*changed*	NU
uncharged particle	NOTION
uncle	
uncle	PAWNBROKER
• uncle's place	PAWNSHOP
uncle	SAM
Uncle Sam (=America)	
• *Uncle Sam's* braces	SUSPENDERS
• *Uncle Sam's* lift	ELEVATOR
• *Uncle Sam's* marines	LEATHERNECKS
uncle	BOB, TOM
unclosed	
back-(d)oor< *unclosed*	ROO
unclosed cove(r)	COVE
unclothed	
unclothed	OUT OF GEAR
unclothed (=with nothing on)	
• father *unclothed*	DADO
• *unclothed* drivers	RACOON
	(*see also* nothing³)
uncomfortable	
uncomfortable [seat]	EATS, SATE, TEAS
uncomfortably [seated]	TEASED
uncommon	
uncommon coin	NOBLE
uncommon person	NOBLE
uncommonly [silent]	ENLIST, LISTEN
uncompleted	
stag(e) *uncompleted* . . .	STAG
uncompleted book	LEDGE(r), TOM(e)
uncompleted bus(t)	BUS
unconscious	
unconscious	COLD
• son unconscious	SCOLD
• unconscious queen	COLDER
unconscious	OUT
• 150 unconscious . . .	CLOUT
• unconscious players	OUTCAST
unconscious	UNDER
• second unconscious . . .	SUNDER
• unconscious boxer	UNDERDOG
unconstrained	
unconstrained [by a] . . .	BAY
[it was] *unconstrained*	WAIST, WAITS
uncontrolled	
[quite] *uncontrolled*	QUIET, –TIQUE
uncontrollable [rage]	GARE, GEAR
uncontrolled [anger]	RANGE

unconventional	
[acted] *unconventionally*	CADET
unconventional [ways]	SWAY, YAWS
uncoordinated	
[a bit] *uncoordinated*	BAIT
uncoordinated [action]	CATION
uncouth	
[spoke] *uncouthly*	POKES
uncouth actors	ROUGHCAST
uncouth [Huns]	SHUN
uncover	
un*cover*	incl UN
• *uncovered by* note	TUNE
un*cover* *	U–N
• *uncovering* right . , ,	URN
uncovered	OLID
uncovered (c)ache(D)	ACHE
uncurl	
[rope] *uncurls*	PORE
uncurl [coil C]	COLIC
undecided	
[he is] *undecided*	HIES
undecided [voter]	TROVE
undecorated	NOTICED
under¹	
many words beginning with under,	
some of which follow, are used	
to indicate a word or letter written	
underneath another in Down clues	
under²	
indicating implied inclusion:	
under canvas	(in) TEN–T
under control	(in) H–AND
under cover	(in) HA–T
	(in) TEN–T
under the blankets	(in) BE–D
	(in) CO–T
under³	
indicating a word or letter	
written under another(D):	
• exercise *under*lines	RYPE
• free *under*current	ACRID
• good *under*study	CONFINE
• I am *under*study	DENIM
• I have some *under*wear	WEARISOME
• or *under*sea . . .	MAINOR
• piece *under* 1 metre	IMPART
• row *under*way	STRANGE
• Scot *under*cooks	FRIESIAN
• son is *under*graduate	MASON
• space *under* the table	BOARD ROOM
• the French *under*garment	GARBLE
• *under* five beers	VALES
• *under*go a(n) . . .	GOA(N)
• *under*write church	PENCE
	(*see also* underwater, underwrite)

under⁴
other uses:

under consideration	SUBJUDICE
under cover	INSURED, INTENT
under forty	FOR, FORT
under-secretary	US
under seven	SIX
under (s)even	EVEN
under stress [arch] . . .	CHAR
under tension [rope] . . .	PORE
under that heading	VV
under the rose	SUB ROSA
under the table	DRUNK
under the word	SV
under this word	SH

underarm bowler   LOBSTER
underclothes   LOW GEAR
undercooked

undercook, *say*	BAKELITE
undercooked	RARE
[under]*cooked*	RUNED

undercurrent   ACHERON, LETHE, STYX etc
undercut

undercut side of stream	BAN(k)
[under]*cut*	RUNED

underdone

bee(f) *underdone*	BEE
underdone	RARE
underdone lam(b)	LAM

undergarment

undergarment	BRA
• undergarment at the laundry	BRAINWASH
• undergarment in wash-basin	BRAINPAN
• undergarments *and* hose and	BRASSOCK
• firm undergarment	COBRA
• undergarments	BRAVEST

undergo

undergoing instruction	INTUITION

undergraduate   ONE UP
underground

underground	METRO, SUBSOIL
underground	TUBE
• underground plant	TUBEROSE
• underground ruler	TUBER
underground spring	VAULT
underground stem, *say*	ROUTE
underground vault	LANDGRAVE
underground worker	(EARTH)WORM, MINER
underground worker, *say*	MINOR

underlined   UL
underneath   (see under³)
underpinned   ONE-LEGGED
underscore   TEENAGER

undersea   IN THE MAIN
understand

understand	DIG
• understand it	DIGIT
understand, *say*	NO
understand trick	TAKE IN
understands measures	FATHOMS
understands, *say*	NOES, NOSE
understood	–MENT, ROGER
understood by foreigners (=foreign language)	
• language *understood by foreigners*	LANGUE
• verse *understood by foreigners*	STANZA
• word *understood by foreigners*	PALABRA
understood, *say*	GNU, NEW
understood vessel	TACITURN

understood   (see understand)
understudy
undertaker

undertakers' business	GRAVE CONCERN
undertakers' magazine	GRAVE NEWS
undertaking, *say*	DYE-WORK

underwater
indicating one word or letter
written underneath the name of
a river, lake, etc(D):

• boy *under*water	MEDIAN
• child *under*water	SEASON
• clever *under*water	EXECUTE
• *under*water *and* [into a] . . .	TARNATION
• *under*water fleas	POLICE
• *under*water object	TEETHING

underwear

underwear	LOW GEAR
underwear, *say*	NICKERS

     (see also undergarment)
underworld

underworld	ABADDON
underworld	DIS
• underworld class	DISORDER
• underworld character	DISCARD
• underworld makes . . .	DISUSES
underworld	EREBUS, HADES, HELL PIT, TARTARUS

underwrite
underwrite
indicating one word or letter
written below another(D):

• church *has underwritten* it	ITCH
• reserves *used to underwrite* the . . .	THETA
• Times *underwriting* bond	BONDAGES

underwriter	SUBSCRIBER
	(*see also* under³)
undeveloped country	GREENLAND
undisciplined	
undisciplined [form]	FROM
undisciplined career	WILDLIFE
undivided	ONE
undo	
[I am] *undone*	AIM
undoing [clasp]	CLAPS
un[done]	NODE
undressed	OUT OF GEAR
	(*see also* unclothed)
uneasy	
[toss] *uneasily*	SOTS
uneasy [sleep]	PEELS
unemployed	
unemployed	OUSE
unemployed man	FREE-HAND
unending	
unending journey	TRI(p)
unending rout(e)	ROUT
uneven	
uneven [road]	DORA
unevenly [laid]	DIAL
unexpected	
[quite] *unexpected*	QUIET, –TIQUE
unexpected [snag]	NAGS, SANG
unfair	BRUNETTE, DARK
unfamiliar	
unfamiliar [taste]	ETATS, STATE, TEATS
unfamiliarity of [route]	OUTER, OUTRE
unfashionable	
unfashionable	OUT
• afterthought *about*	
unfashionable . . .	POUTS
• road *has* unfashionable . . .	STOUT
• unfashionable clothes	OUTWEAR
unfashionable	SQUARE
• model *has* unfashionable . . .	T-SQUARE
• unfashionable food	SQUARE MEAL
	SQUARE ROOTS
unfashionable	omit IN
• *unfashionable* material	SAT(in)
unfashionable	omit U
• *unfashionable* ca(u)se	CASE
unfavourable aspect	N
unfinished	
unfinished business	FIR(m)
unfinished tas(k)	TAS
unfeeling	
unfeeling	NUMB
unfeeling, *say*	NUM–
• unfeeling girl, *say*	NUMMARY
• unfeeling man, *say*	NUMBLES, NUMERIC
	REGNUM

unfit	
['e felt] *unfit*	FLEET
unfit [to plead]	TADPOLE
unfixed	
[rates] *unfixed*	ASTER, STARE, TARES
	TEARS,
unfixed [latches]	SATCHEL
unfold	
unfold [a tale]	ALATE
unfolding [arms]	MARS, RAMS
unfortunate	
unfortunate [end]	DEN, NED
unfortunately [not her] . . .	THRONE
unfrozen	NOTICE(D)
unfulfilled	
MP *unfulfilled*	TOR(y)
unfulfilled need	NEE(d), LAC(k), WAN(t)
unfurl	
[tops'l] *unfu.rled*	PLOTS
unfurl [sails]	SILAS
ungainly	
[Len is] *ungainly*	LIENS, LINES
ungainly [stride]	DIREST
ungrammatical	
ungrammatical introduction	SMEE
ungrammatical refusal	WONT
unhappy	
unhappily [married]	ADMIRER
unhappy [feeling]	FLEEING
unhealthy	
unhealthy	SICK
• unhealthy horse	SICK-BAY
• unhealthy man	SICKLES
unhesitating	
unhesitating(ly)	omit ER, UM, UR
• moth(er) *unhesitating* . . .	MOTH
• s(um)s *unhesitatingly* . . .	SS
• *unhesitating* co(ur)se	COSE
unidentified	
unidentified	NU
unidentified flying object	UFO
unilateral	
unilateral (=one-sided)	
• *unilateral* help	LAID, RAID
• *unilateral* states	RUSA
Unilateral Declaration of Independence	UDI
unimaginative	NON-FICTION
uninhibited	
uninhibited (p)layer(s)	LAYER
uninhibited [when it] . . .	WHITEN
uninspired footman	PEDESTRIAN
union	
union	MARRIAGE
• union charter	MARRIAGE LICENCE
• union convenor	MARRIAGE BROKER
• union meeting	MARRIAGE, WEDDING

Letter replaced \c\at; Omit (a); Pointers *out*; Retain <u>a</u>; Split B_ED; Down (D); Backwards <or ^

union	NUS, NUT etc	Universal Postal Union	UPU
• number *in* union	NUNS	universal set	E
• union row	NUTTIER	Universal Time	UT
union	RUSSIA	**university**	U, UNIV
union	TU	at university	UP
• union *has* second-class . . .	TUB	combined universities	OXBRIDGE
• union inspection	TUSCAN	Open University	OU
union	U	• Open University man	OUTED
• union representative	–UMP	university drop-out	omit U
union agreement	BETHROTHAL	University Grants Committee	UGC
	ENGAGEMENT	university man	BA, MA
union attendant	BEST MAN, BRIDESMAID		DON, PROF
	MATRON OF HONOUR	university press	CUP, OUP
union colleague	BRO	university sinecure	EASY CHAIR
	JOINER, WELDER	university student	UL
union issue	CHILD(REN)	university study	READING
union leader	SHERMAN	university teachers	UAT
Union *leader*	U	**unkempt**	
union measure	LEAGUE	[man is] *unkempt*	MAINS
union member	BRIDE, GROOM	*unkempt* [beard]	BARED, BREAD
	HUSBAND, WIFE	**unknown**	
union negotiator	MARRIAGE BROKER	unknown	X, Y, Z
	MATCHMAKER	• unknown man	X-RAY
union of man or . . .	MANOR	• unknown quarter	YEAST
union trouble	DIVORCE	• unknown river	ZAIRE
	SEVEN YEAR ITCH	unknown number	N
Unionist	U	unknown private	SECRET
unique		**unladen**	
unique	ONE, SOLE	unladen (=with nothing on)	
unique fish	SOLE	• *unladen* tree	MAYO
unique *sound*	SOUL, WON	• *unladen* wagon	CARTOON
unit		(*see also* unload)	
unit	A, I	**unlikely**	TALL
unit of the Marines	THERM	[not] *unlikely*	TON
units	SI	*unlikely* [tale]	LATE, LEAT, TEAL
united[1]		**unlimited**	
united you and me, *say*	LINCTUS	(c)rim(e) *unlimited*	RIM
united, *say*	TIDE	*unlimited* liability	(r)IS(k)
united[2]		*unlimited* (m)one(y)	ONE
United Arab Republic	UAR	**unlined**	
United Dominions Trust	UDT	*unlined*	omit BR
United Free Church	UF	• *unlined* (b)owe(r)	OWE
United Kingdom	UK	*unlined*	omit centre
United Nations Association	UNA	• t(h)e *unlined* . . .	TE
United Nations (Organisation)	UNO	• *unlined* s(kir)t	ST
United Presbyterian	UP	*unlined*	omit L
United Press	UP	• *unlined* ki(l)t	KIT
United States	US, USA	*unlined*	omit RY
–Army	USA	• *unlined* fine(ry)	FINE
–(Army) Air Force	US(A)AF	**unload**	
–Navy	USN	*unload contents*	omit middle
–Ship	USS	• *unload contents of* l(orr)y	–LY
universal		unload fish	DUMPLING
universal	U	(*see also* unladen)	
Universal Decimal Classification	UDC	**unlock**	
universal organisation	UN	unlock	DISTRESS

Anag [cat]; Any *; Begin IGN–; Endings –ING; eg •; Hidden /cat/; Implied add (on); Implied in (in);

unlocked	BALD, DISTRESSED, SHORN
unlocking	HAIRCUT
unloved	
unloved	omit O
• b(o)re *unloved by* journalist	BREED
• *unloved* t(o)y	–TY
unmanned	
unmanned	omit HE
• *unmanned* Jew	(he)BREW
unmanned	omit MAN
• smuggled *unmanned* Ger(man)	RANGER
unmarried	
unmarried	MATCHLESS
unmarried	omit M
• *unmarried* (m)other	OTHER
unmarried heavyweight	SINGLETON
unmasked	
unmasked [US spy]	PUSSY
unmasking [German] . . .	MANGER
unnamed	
unnamed	omit N
• Germ(an) *without* a name	GERM
• *unnamed* male	MA(n)
• *unnamed* ma(n)	MA
unnatural	
unnatural	FLAT, SHARP
unnatural [desire]	RESIDE
unnaturally [created]	REACTED
unnumbered	
unnumbered	omit C, D, L, M, V etc
• *unnumbered* (c)hair	HAIR
• *unnumbered* car(d)	CAR
• *unnumbered* p(layer)	PAYER
• *unnumbered* roo(m)	ROO
• *unnumbered* (v)erse	ERSE
unoccupied	
o(fte)n *unoccupied*	ON
unoccupied h(ous)e	HE
unofficial	
unofficial [rule]	LURE
unofficially [agreed]	GEARED
unopened	
(c)rate *unopened*	RATE
unopened (c)ask	ASK
unorthodox	
[most] *unorthodox*	MOTS
unorthodox [means]	MANES, NAMES
unpaid	
unpaid	HON
• unpaid *in* Kent	SHONE
• unpaid monarch	HONKING
unpaid account	BILLOWED, BILLOWING
unplaced	
unplaced	FOURTH
unplaced, *say*	FORTH
unpopular doctor	FELL
unpredictable	
unpredictable [weather]	WREATHE
unpredictably [threw a] . . .	WREATH
unpreferred girl	BRUNETTE
unqualified	
unqualified	LAY
• mother *takes* unqualified . . .	MALAY
• unknown *in* qualified . . .	LAZY
and	
• unqualified fellow, *say*	LAID-ON
unqualified	TOTAL(LY)
unqualified person	L, NOTABLE
unravel	
[test case] *unravelled*	CASSETTE
unravelled [a scarf]	FRACAS
unravels, say	FRAISE, PHRASE
unreasonable	
unreasonable [fear]	FARE
unreasonably [demand] . . .	DAMNED
unrecognised	
unrecognised [danger]	GANDER
	GARDEN, RANGED
unrecognisable [faces]	CAFES
unrefined actors	ROUGHCAST
unreliable	
[he is] *unreliably* . . .	HIES
unreliable [man is] . . .	MAINS
unrest	
[much] *unrest*	CHUM
unrest in [Yemen]	ENEMY
unrestrained	
unrestrained [anger]	RANGE
[Australian]	
unrestrained	SATURNALIA
unruly	
[she was] *unruly*	WASHES
unruly [kids]	SKID
unsafe	
[plane] *is unsafe*	PANEL
unsafe [car]	ARC
unscramble	
unscramble [atom's cipher]	ATMOSPHERIC
unscrambling [data man] . . .	ADAMANT
unseen companion	GUIDE DOG
unsettled	
[score] *unsettled*	CORES
unsettled	NOMADIC
	OWED, OWING
unsettled [weather]	WREATHE
unskilled	NOTABLE
unsnarl	
unsnarled [ropes]	PORES, SPORE
unsnarling [tape]	PATE, PEAT
unsound	
[parts] *unsound*	PRATS, STRAP, SPRAT
unsound [wares]	SWEAR, WEARS

Letter replaced \c\at; Omit (a); Pointers *out*; Retain <u>a</u>; Split B_ED; Down (D); Backwards <or ^

unstable

[land is] *unstable*	ISLAND
unstable [site]	–ITES, TIES

unsteady

unsteady [steps]	PESTS
unsteadily [rise]	SIRE

unstuck

[came] *unstuck*	MACE
[tape] *came unstuck*	PATE, PEAT
unstuck [when I] . . .	WHINE

unsuccessful

unsuccessful fisherman	NONET(S)
unsuccessful oilman	NOWELL
unsuccessful suitor	NOWED
unsuccessful vocalist	NOSING

unsuited

unsuited	BARE, NAKED, NUDE
unsuited runner	STREAKER

untangle

untangle [threads]	HARDEST
untangling [nets]	TENS, SENT, STEN

untaxed   ORATED

untearable   CANTRIP

untidy

untidy [heaps]	PHASE, SHAPE
[wraps] *untidily*	WARPS

untied

untie [knots]	STONK
untied [rope]	PORE

untimed

untimed	omit AGE, T
• *untimed* communication	MESS(age)
• *untimed* (t)rip	RIP

untreated wood   RAW DEAL

untrue

[it was] *untrue*	WAIST, WAITS
untrue [tales]	LEATS, STEAL
	SLATE, TEALS

untutored saint   RUDEST

unusual

unusual	ODD
• *unusual in* bashful . . .	SHODDY
• *unusual* man	ODDFELLOW
• *unusual* people	ODDFELLOWS
unusual	RARE
• copper *with* unusual . . .	CURARE
• unusual choice	RARE
• unusual coin	RAREBIT
unusual athlete	RUM RUNNER
unusual [fate]	FEAT
unusual production of [Tosca]	ASCOT, ATOCS
	COATS
unusually [fat]	AFT

unused

unused *	omit *
• *entrance to* (t)own *unused*	OWN

• *unused* money in b(l)ack . . .	BACK

unwanted

unwanted fruit	GOOSEBERRY
unwanted *	omit *
• man *unwanted in* t(he)re	TRE–
• (was)her was *unwanted*	HER

unwieldy

unwieldy [tool]	LOOT
[it was] *unwieldy*	WAIST, WAITS

unwilling   INTESTATE

unwind

unwind [hose]	HOES, SHOE
unwinding [yarn]	NARY
unwound [reel]	LEER

unwrap

unwrap (g)if(t)	IF
unwrap [parcel]	PLACER
unwrapping (s)hoe(s)	HOE
unwrapping [T-shirt]	THIRST

up¹

many words beginning with up, some of which follow, are used to indicate words written backwards in Down clues

up²

indicating words written
backwards in down clues (D)^:

• *up*-beat	NAT, PAR
• *up*-country	MAIS, MASSA
• *up* late	MANET
• *up*-market	TRAM
• *up* the mountain	ANTE, ROT
• *upped* the ante	ETNA

up³

meaning:
ahead

• *leading* firm	UPTIGHT
• time *ahead*	TUP

at university

• 100 *at university*	CUP

in court

• in court *with* a group	UPSET

riding

• child *riding*	TOT UP

to windward

• ship *to windward*	KETCHUP

up⁴

up *front*	start with UP
• actors up *front*	UPCAST
• hurry up *front*	UPRUSH
• wild animal up *front*	UPBEAR

up North
indicating use of
Scottish words:

• go *up North*	GANG
• *up North*, only . . .	ANERLY
• useful *up North*	WAKERIFE

up⁵

up in arms	RAMPANT
up the creek [in an] . . .	NAIN
up with the lark	(in) S–KY
upper	AMPHETAMINE, SPEED
upper case	CAPS, CAPITALS
upper class	A, SIXTH FORM, U
upper classes	AB–
upper house	ATTIC, GARRET, LOFT
Upper House	LORDS
Upper House, *say*	LAUDS
upper limit	CEILING
upper limit, *say*	SEALING
upper set	DENTURE, TEETH

upbringing

poor *upbringing*(D)^	ROOP
upbringing of Eros(D)^	SORE

upcoming

upcoming supporter(D)^	ARB–, GEL
was *upcoming*(D)^	SAW

upfront

money *upfront*	M
upfront	U

upheaval

[great] *upheaval*	GRATE
upheaval [in her] . . .	RHINE

uphill

uphill(D)^	ROT
trot *uphill*(D)^	TORT

upholding

up-*holding*	U–P
upholding indicating reversal and inclusion in Down clues:	
• l–aw *upholding* learner(D)^	WALL

uplift

uplift	BUST-UP
uplift spirits(D)^	SNIG
uplifting art (D)^	TRA–

upon

indicating one word written above another word or letter(D):	
• live *upon* state	BEAVER
• look *upon* American	GAZEBO
• man *is upon* the *Spanish* . . .	HEEL
indicating one word written backwards above another(D):	
• act *upon* our . . .	ODOUR
• live *upon* on(e) *almost* . . .	EBON
• sit *upon* girl	TISSUE
indicating one word written backwards above 'on'(D):	
• honour *upon* . . .	MOON
• man *upon* . . .	LEMON
• works *upon* . . .	SPOON

upper	(*see* up⁵)

uppity

[act] *uppity*	CAT
uppity boy(D)^	YOB

upright¹

upright	I
• upright board	IDEAL
• *upright* man	IRON
• *upright* one	IAN
upright	PI
• *upright* attendant	PIPAGE
• *upright* friend	PIPAL
• *upright* girl	PIANINA
upright	POST
• upright character	POSTCARD
• upright monarch	POSTER
• upright person	POSTAL, POSTMAN
upright player	PIANO
upright reputation	STANDING
upright type	ROMAN

upright²

upright(D)^	TR
upright bat(D)^	TAB

uprising

some con/tinu/ous *uprising*(D)^	UNIT
uprising(D)^	PU
uprising at . . . (D)^	TA

upriver

indicating name of river written backwards, usually in Down clues:	
• look *upriver*	LOOP
• *upriver with* man	MACRON
• run *upriver*	REED
• sun unknown *upriver*	SYNOD

uproot

uproot yew(D)^	WEY
uprooting [yew]	WEY, WYE

upset

upset(D)^	TES
upset class(D)^	SLIP-UP
upset gin	RATTLETRAP
upset [master]	REMAST, STREAM
upset no-one(D)^	–ION
upset revel<	LEVER
upset shed	SPILL
upset [timer]	MITRE, REMIT
upset timer(D)^	REMIT
upset Tom	TIPCAT

upshot	CHIP, LOB

upside

upside down(D)^	
• draw *upside down*	WARD
• put *upside down*	TUP
• was *upside down*	SAW

upstairs lighting	LANDING

upstanding

be *upstanding* on . . .(D)^	EBON
upstanding part(D)^	TRAP
upstart	
*up*start	U
up*start*	start with UP
• killed up*start*	UPSHOT
• up*start* making loud noises	UPROARS
• when up*starts* . . .	UPAS
upstream	
*up*stream(D)^	EDIT
upsurge	
upsurge of sap(D)^	PAS
up-to-date business	NEWMARKET
upturn	
up*turn*<	PU
• up*turn*< about . . .	PURE
• up*turn*< *for* animals	PUMICE
• up*turn*< *for* friend	PUPAL
upturn of . . . (D)^	FO
upward	
*up*ward(D)^	DRAW
*up*ward step(D)^	PETS
upwardly mobile way . . . (D)^	YAW
Urban District Council	UDC
urge	
urge	SPUR
• violent urge	HOTSPUR
• urge Communist . . .	SPURRED
• urge Edward	SPURTED
urge crowd	PRESS
urges insects	EGG-SLICE
urgent	
urgent	BABYLONIAN
urgent mood	IMPERATIVE
ursine group	BEARSKIN
Uruguay	
Uruguay	ROU, U, URU
capital of Uruguay	PESO
capital of U̲ruguay	U
US(A)	(*see* America)
use	
buil/d ark/ *using* . . .	DARK
[not] *used*	TON
usable as [a bed]	BADE, BEAD
use [a pen]	NAPE, NEAP, PANE, PEAN
use drill	DOPE, EXERCISE
[use] *guile*	SUE
use, *say*	EWES, US, UU
	YOUSE, YEWS
used abroad (=foreign language)	
• cup *used abroad*	TAZZA
• hat *used abroad*	CHAPEAU
• shawl *used abroad*	MANTILLA
	(*see also* abroad)
used as [part] . . .	PRAT, TRAP
used by man/y es/timators	YES
used car dealer	AUTO-CHANGER
used in pa/in k/illers	INK
used in poetry	(*see* poetic)
used to be	EX
	(*see also* old²)
useful card	PRACTICAL JOKER
useful headgear	HANDICAP
useless	DUFF
• fruit *has* useless . . .	PLUM DUFF
• useless journalist	DUFFED
• useless ruler	DUFFER
useless	US
use*less*	omit USE
• use*less* ho(use)	HO
useless [tool]	LOOT
using part of h/er go/od . . .	ERGO
using some ne/w ide/eas	WIDE
using [tools]	LOOTS, STOOL
usher	
usher in a . . .	incl A
usher in *	incl *
• bu–tler *ushers in* son	BUSTLER
usher, *say*	GUYED, SILENCER
ushered in by *	incl in *
• son *ushered in by* bu–tler	BUSTLER
usherette	GIRL GUIDE
usual	
usual colour	STANDARD
usual flag	STANDARD
usually	USU
usurp	OUSTER
utilise	
[other] *characters utilised*	THROE
utilised [tool]	LOOT
utmost	
utmost ends of t̲h̲e̲ eart̲h̲	EH
utmost urgenc̲y̲	Y
utter	
utter	
indicating a homophone:	
• not *utterly*	KNOT
• *utter* rot	WROUGHT
• *utter* some . . .	SUM
• *utterance of* boy	BUOY
• *utterance of* a girl	ALAS
• *uttered* word	WHIRRED
• *uttering* rhyme	RIME
• *utterly* cruel	CREWEL
utter cry	CALLOW, YELLOW
uttermost ends of t̲h̲e̲ eart̲h̲	EH
uttermost parts of C̲h̲ina	CA
u-upset	URILE

Anag [cat]; Any *; Begin IGN–; Endings –ING; eg •; Hidden /cat/; Implied add (on); Implied in (in);

V

against, **agent, bomb, chevron, chip, day, electric potential difference, five, five thousand, frequency, thousand,** *look,* **neck,** *neckline, notch, nu, see,* **shape, sign, valve, vanadium, Vatican, vatu, vee, velocity, verb, verse(d),** *verso, versus,* **very, victory,** *vide,* **violin, voice, volt, volume, win**

vacant		**vandal**	
vacancy	O	[louts] *vandalise* . . .	LOTUS
vacant	VAC	*vandalised* [parks]	SPARK
vacant h(ous)e	HE	**vanguard**	
vacant job	FREE POST	fleet *vanguard*	F
vacant (=nothing in it)	incl O	*vanguard* of army	A
• co–t *is vacant*	COOT	**vanity case**	EGO(T)IST
• *vacant* lo–t	LOOT	**vapour**	
• *vacant* church	COE	vapour caused corrosion	MISTRUSTED
vacation	VAC	vapour density	VD
vacillate		vapour pressure	VP
vacillating [priest]	STRIPE, TRIPES	**variable**	(*see* vary)
vacillation [by a] . . .	BAY	**varsity**	U
vacillated [when I] . . .	WHINE	**vary**	
vacuous		*variable* [gear]	RAGE
t(otall)y *vacuous*	TY	variant	VAR
vacuous i(dio)t	IT	*variations of* Elgar . . .	GLARE, LAGER
vagrant			LARGE, REGAL
vagrant	TRAMP	*varies* in [shape]	HEAPS, PHASE
• vagrant in front	TRAMPLED	*variegated* [tints]	STINT
• vagrant in Germany	TRAMPING	varietal	VAR
vagrant [airs]	SAIR, SARI	*varieties of* [meat]	TEAM-MATE
vagrant *American*	HOBO	variety	VAR
vague		variety	
vague [noises]	ESSOIN	indicating origins:	
vaguely [hears] . . .	HARES, SHARE, SHEAR	• *German variety* with . . .	MIT
vale		• *Italian variety* of wine	VINO
vale (=goodbye)		• one *Scottish variety*	ANE
vale *in England*	FAREWELL, GOODBYE	• the *French variety*	LA, LE, LES
vale *in France*	A BIENTOT, ADIEU	• this *Latin variety*	HAEC, HIC, HOC
vale *in Germany*	AUF WIEDERSEHEN	*variety* [show]	HOWS, WHOS
vale *in Italy*	ADDIO, ARRIVEDERCI	*variety* of [crocus]	OCCURS
vale *in Spain*	ADIOS, HASTA LA VISTA	various dates	VD
valiant Indian	BRAVE	various years	VY
value		*various* [items]	EMITS, SMITE, TIMES
valuable coat	GOLDEN FLEECE	*variously prescribed*	
value	PH, RATE, VAL	[doses a] . . .	ODESSA
Value-added Tax	VAT	*vary* [rate]	TARE, TEAR
value of function	PIRATE	vary, *say*	ALTAR
value of soil	PH	*varying* [all the] . . .	LETHAL
value*less*	ORATED, OVAL	**vast**	
valuer's statement	IRATE	*not really* [vast]	VATS
valuing at 3.14	PIRATING	*vast majority*	VAS

Letter replaced \c\at; Omit (a); Pointers *out*; Retain a̲; Split B_ED; Down (D); Backwards <or ^

VAT-free	ORATED	Venerable	VEN
Vatican	V, VAT	venereal disease	VD
vault		**Venetian**	
vault, *say*	CELLA, SELLA, SELLER	Venetian	OTHELLO
vault working	CRYPTON	Venetian leader	DOGE
vaulting horse	SHOW JUMPER	Venetian *leader*	V
vaulting [horse]	SHORE	Venetian merchant	ANTONIO, POLO
vee	V	**Venezuela**	YV
vegetable		**ventilate**	
vegetable	BEET	ventilate	AIR
• run *in* vegetable . . .	BERET	• ventilates *inside* saint's . . .	STAIRS
• vegetable first	BEETLED	• ventilate liner	AIRSHIP
vegetable	PEA	• ventilates *after* Henry . . .	HAIRS
• vegetable competes	PEAVIES	ventilate	SUNDRY
• vegetables *with* fish	PEALING, PEASCOD	**verb**	
• vegetables *have* worker . . .	PEASANT	verb	V, VB
and		verb intransitive	VI
• vegetable *with* fish, *say*	PEELING	verb transitive	VT
vegetable	VEG	verbal	
vegetables, *say*	CHARRED, LEAK, SALARY	indicating a homophone:	
vegetarian		• *verbal* refusal	KNOW, NEIGH
indicates word 'eating'		• *verbally* made an . . .	MAIDEN
a vegetable:		• *verbally* not . . .	KNOT
• vegetarian animal(AP–E)	APPEASE	verbal reasoning quotient	VRQ
vehicle		verbally	BY-WORD
vehicle	CAB	verbally, *say*	AURALLY
• run-*in* vehicle	CRAB	**verge**	
• vehicle container	CABURN	highway *verges*	HY
• vehicle *in front of*		*verges* of road	RD
obstruction	CABLET	**vermouth**	IT
vehicle	CAR	**Verne**	
• vehicle number	CARD, CARL	[Verne] *work*	NEVER
• vehicle speeding	CARAPACE	*rehash* [Verne's] . . .	SEVERN
• vehicle weight	CARTON	**versatile**	
vehicle	CART	[quite] *versatile*	QUIET, –TIQUE
• vehicle *on* high ground	CARTRIDGE	*versatile* [actor]	CROAT
• vehicle working	CARTON	**version**	
vehicle	TRAM	[new] *version*	WEN
• vehicle goes inside	TRAMLINES	*version* [of a] . . .	OAF
• vehicle park	TRAMP	*version of* [Tuscan's] . . .	SANCTUS
vehicle application	DILIGENCE	**versus**	V
vehicle corrosion	CARROT	**vertical**	
vehicle cover	BONNET	vertical, *say*	PLUM
	CARPORT, GARAGE	vertical take-off	VTO
	INSURANCE	vertical take-off and landing	VTOL
	VANGUARD	**very**	
vehicle entrance	TRANSPORT	very	V
vehicle for a . . .	incl A	• very close	VEND
vehicle for *	incl *	• very offhand	VAIRY
• rotten *vehicle for* learner	BALD	• very spry	VAGILE
vehicle traffic	TRUCK	very black	BB
vehicle was blue	MOPED	very cheerful	JOLLY
vein		very *French*	TRES
vein joint	SEAM	very good	VG
vein, *say*	LAIR, LOAD, SEEM, VAIN, VANE	very green	EXTRAVERT
velocity	MPH, MV, V, VEL	very hesitant	–ERER

Anag [cat]; Any *; Begin IGN–; Endings –ING; eg •; Hidden /cat/; Implied add (on); Implied in (in);

very high frequency	VHF	**vibrate**	
very large	OS	[rich, deep] *vibrato*	DECIPHER
very low frequency	VLF	*vibrating* [noises]	ESSOIN
very hard	HH	*vibration of* [plane]	PANEL
very late	STONE DEAD	**vicar**	
very little	WEE	vicar	REV(D), VIC
very loud	FF	Vicar Apostolic	VA
very *much like* Leeds	LEADS	Vicar-General	VG
very *musical*	ASSAI, MOLTO	vicarage	VIC
very *nearly*	ERY, VER	**vice**	
very quiet	PP	Vice-Chancellor	VC
very *Scottish*	UNCO	Vice-Consul	VC
very short	INSTALL	Vice-President	VP
very *short*	V, VER(y)	**Vichy water**	EAU
very short distance	IMM–	**vicious**	
very small European	TADPOLE	[snap] *viciously*	PANS, SPAN
very soft	PP	*vicious* [circle]	CLERIC
very soft *centre*	incl PP	**Victoria**	
• apple *with* very soft *centre*	PIPPIN	Victoria Cross	VC
• co–in *with* very soft *centre*	COPPIN	Victoria Medal of Honour	VMH
very sore	REDRAW	**victory**	
very strong	FF	victory	V
very young	ONE OR TWO	• victory in Asia	VINE
vessel		• victory shout	VOUCH
vessel	MV, SHIP, SS, SUB	• victory sign	VINDICATION
vessel	EWER	victory	VE
• fine vessel	FEWER	• 51 *victories*	LIVES
• second king *has* a vessel	SKEWER	• victory in . . .	VEIN
vessel	POT	• victory *to the Italian* . . .	VEIL
• one vessel *inside* another	SPOTS	victory	VJ
• second vessel	SPOT	victory day	VE, VJ
• vessel is warm	POTSHOT	victory race	MARATHON
vessel	URN	**vide**	V
• graduate *in* vessel	URBAN	**video**	
• second-class vessel	BURN	video cassette recorder	VCR
• vessel *in* garden	BURNED	video frequency	VF
vessel	VASE	video tape recorder	VTR
• 51 *in* vessel	VALISE	**Vietnam**	
• vessel *has* pedigree	VASELINE	Vietnam	VN
	(*see also* ship)	Vietnamese	BOAT RACE
Vesta's home	MATCHBOX	**view**	
veteran		view	SCAPE
veteran		view	SEE
indicating old words:		• normal view	PARSEE
• *veteran's* friend	INGLE	• view Parliament	SEETHING
	(*see also* old [3])	• view *round* royal . . .	SERE
veteran actor	OLDHAM	• view twice	LOOK-SEE
veteran car	CHARIOT	and	
veterinary		• view fifty, *say*	SEAL
veterinary	VET	view America	PROSPECTUS
veterinary surgeon	VET, VS	view the king of	
vex		beasts, *say*	SEA-LION, SELION
[act] *vexatiously*	CAT	view, *say*	CITE, SEEN, SITE
[most] *vexing*	MOTS, TOMS	viewed, *say*	SCENE
vexation, *say*	PEAK	viewer	EYE
vexed [teacher]	CHEATER, RECHEAT	views always . . .	SIGHTSEER

Letter replaced \c\at; Omit (a); Pointers *out*; Retain <u>a</u>; Split B_ED; Down (D); Backwards <or ^

vigorous

vigorous fight	STRONG-BOX
vigorously [defend]	FENDED

vile

[acted] *vilely*	CADET
vile [deed Tom] . . .	DEMOTED
vi<u>le</u> *outsiders*	VE

village

village	HAMLET, VIL(L)
village drama	HAMLET
village hero	HAMLET

vintage

vintage car	OLD BEAN
vintage poet	GRAVES

violate

violate at this spot, *say*	RAPIER
violated [rules]	LURES
violation of [code I get] . . .	GEODETIC

violent

[shove] *violently*	HOVES
violent players	ROUGHCAST
violent [push to] . . .	UPSHOT

violin

old violin	GJO, GJU, GU(E)
violin	AMATI, STRAD, V
violin lessons	STRING COURSE
violin strings	A, D, E, G
violin swindle	FIDDLE

virtual

virtual [space]	CAPES
virtually al(l)	AL
virtually identical	SAM(e)
virtually [real]	LEAR, RALE

virtuous

virtuous	NOVICES
virtuous amateur	NOVICE

viscount

viscount	VIS
viscount's son	HON

visible

visible	INSIGHT
visible in h/er e/yes	ERE
visible inside t/he ro/om	HERO
visible, *say*	INSIGHT

visit

visit	SEE
• visit many . . .	SEED
• the *French* visit and	LESSEE
• visit boy, *say*	SEASON
• visit Egypt, *say*	SENILE
• visit the sea, *say*	SEAMED, SEAMER
visited by a . . .	incl A
visited by *	incl *
• county *visited by* queen	YORKERS
visited frequently	CAMELOT

visitor, *say*	CHOLER, COLLAR GUESSED
visits *	incl in *
• queen *visits* county	YORKERS

visual

visual aid	CONTACT LENS, MICROSCOPE MONOCLE, SPECTACLES TELESCOPE
visual display unit	VDU

vital

vital ingredient of fre/sh e/ggs	SHE
vital part of en/gin/e	GIN
vital part perishes	ORGANDIES
vital timber	KEYBOARD
vital to Briti/sh in/terests	SHIN
vital to Britis/h int/erests	HINT

vitamin A, B, C, D, E, F, G, H
K, I, M, P, X

vivisection

[detest] *vivisection*	TESTED
vivisection of [rat]	ART, TAR

vocal

plain *vocal* style	PLANE
vocal number	AIT, ATE, EYOT FOR(E), TO(O), WON
vocal style of tenor	TENNER
vocal turn	TERN(E)
vocalising all . . .	AWL
vocalist's statement, *say*	ICING
vocally rough	RUFF
vocally, *say*	ALLOWED

vocative VOC

voguish IN

voice

[it was] *voiced*	WAIST, WAITS
voice-box	BOCKS
voice frequency	VF
voiced [all the] . . .	LETHAL

volatile

volatile [oils]	SILO, SOIL
volatility of [gas]	SAG

volcanic

volcanic rock	LAVA
• two lumps of volcanic rock	LAVA-LAVA
• volcanic rock, right?	LAVATORY
• volcanic rock, time and time again . . .	LAVATERA
volcanic rock	MOYA
volcanic rock	TUFF
• son *has* volcanic rock	STUFF
• volcanic rock, *say*	TOUGH
volcanic [tremors]	STORMER

volt V

volt-amp	VA
volt-ampere-reactive	VAR

Anag [cat]; Any *; Begin IGN–; Endings –ING; eg •; Hidden /cat/; Implied add (on); Implied in (in);

volume

volume	BOOK
• volume of income	PAYBOOK
• volume of money	CASHBOOK
• volume of small . . .	MINUTE BOOK
volume	TOM, TOME, TOMUS V, VOL

volunteer

Voluntary Aid Detachment	VAD
Voluntary Defence Corps	VDC
Volunteer (Officers') Decoration	VD
Volunteer Reserve Decoration	VRD
Voluntary Service Overseas	VSO
voluntary work	ORGAN RECITAL
volunteer	VOL
volunteers	TA, THETA
• volunteers 49 . . .	TAIL
• volunteers blood	TAGORE
• volunteers *to* a man	TAKEN, TALES

(*see also* army, reserve, terrier)

vote

vote	CROSS
• vote on . . .	CROSS OVER
• vote twice	DOUBLE CROSS
• vote *with* lawyers	CROSS-BAR
vote	PUT ACROSS
vote	X
• a vote the *French* . . .	AXLE
• copy vote	APEX
• vote counter, *say*	EXCHEQUER
vote against	BEANO

voyage

voyage, *say*	CREWS, CRUSE
voyaging [in the] . . .	THINE
[went] *voyaging*	NEWT

vulgar

are not *vulgarly* . . .	AINT
vulgar	VUL(G)
vulgur (lı)at	AT
Vulgate	VUL(G)
v-ventilated	VAIRY

W

boson, bridge player, complex cube root, particle, tungsten, watt, weak, Wednesday, week, weight, Welsh, west, western, whole numbers, wicket, wide, width, wife, William, winter, with, wolfram, woman, women, won

W8	WEIGHT	walking	(on) FOOT
wacky		• bird *walking*	CROWFOOT, GOOSEFOOT
wackiness [of a] . . .	OAF	• Negro *walking*	BLACKFOOT
wacky [ideas]	AIDES, ASIDE, SADIE	• *walking* to dance	FOOTBALL
Wacky [Races]	ACERS, CARES, SCARE	*walking* [along]	GOLAN
wader	HERON	walking-on part	FOOT, HEEL, SOLE
wag		**wall**	
wag [finger]	FRINGE	wall builder	HADRIAN
wagging [dog]	GOD	wall *in France*	MUR
*wag*tail	G	(w)all *with no opening*	ALL
wag[tail in a] . . .	ITALIAN	wall's make-up	ROUGHCAST
wager		walled city	BERLIN, JERICHO
wager	BET, BETON	**Walloon**	WAL
• wager *on Cockney* horse	BETOSS	**walrus**	MORSE
• wager *on* fish	BETIDE, BETRAY	**wan**	
• wager on unknown . . .	BETONY	wan	PALE
wager, *say*	STEAK	• claim to be wan	IMPALE
waggle		• wan child	PALETOT
waggle [rear]	RARE	• wan race, English	PALETTE
waggling [hips]	PISH, SHIP	wan, *say*	PAIL
Wagner's work	RING	**wander**	
wait		[Ezra] *the wanderer*	RAZE
waiters	QUEUE	*wander about* [in the] . . .	THINE
waiters, *say*	CUE, KEW	wander around	MOON
waitress, *say*	MADE	[wander] *around*	WARNED
Wales	CYMRU	wander round the	
walk		hospital, *say*	ROMEWARDS
walk	FOOT	wandering eyes, *say*	ROMANISE
• walk *to* dance	FOOTBALL	*wandering* [stream]	MASTER, REMAST
• walks the plank	FOOTSLOG	**want**	
• warm walk	HOTFOOT	want fish	NEEDLING
walk	LEGIT	want, *say*	KNEAD, KNEED
walk *about*	TREA–D	want spinster	MISS
walk *about*<	MAOR	*wants* a . . .	incl A
walk in front	TRAMPLED	*wants* *	incl *
walk [on beside]	EBONISED	• *wants* everything *in* p–et	PALLET
walk over	WO	wanted	(in) NE–ED
walk *over*<	MAOR	• saint *wanted*	NESTED
walk, *say*	GATE	*wanting* a . . .	omit a
walk straight	LEGIT	*wanting* *	omit *
walk *then* run	MARCH HARE	• ma(n) *wanting* new . . .	MA
walk through water, *say*	WEIGHED	• (p)arty *wanting* leader	ARTY
walked	RODEO	**wanton**	
walker	JAY, PED	[act] *wantonly*	CAT

Anag [cat]; Any *; Begin IGN–; Endings –ING; eg •; Hidden /cat/; Implied add (on); Implied in (in);

wanton [waste]	SWEAT, TAWSE	warmly dressed	(in) FU–R
wantonly [drive] . . .	DIVER	warmly dressed, *say*	INFER
war		**warning**	
at war [over] . . .	ROVE	warning	AMBER
spoils of war	MARS	• 51 warnings	CLAMBERS
spoils of [war]	RAW	warning	FORE
[total class] *war*	AT ALL COSTS	• warning *to* man	FORECASTLE
war	WAR	• warning *to* prop	FORESHORE
• war at sea	WARMED, WARMER	warning card	CAUTION
• wartime	WART	warning cry	CAVE, FORE
and		warning light	AMBER, RED
• [war] *dance*	RAW	**warp**	
• war *over<*	RAW	*warp* [into an] . . .	NATION
• *spoils of* [war]	RAW	*warped* [door]	ODOR, ROOD
war artist	ACTION PAINTER	**Warrant Officer**	WO
war *at* sea	WARMED, WARMER	**Warsaw Pact**	WP
war club	WADDY	**was**	
war club, *say*	WADI	was not loud	WASP
war criminal	HESS	was painful	DIDACHE
war of [words]	SWORD	was *raised*(D)^	DEVIL, SAW
War Office	WO	[was] *wrong*	SAW
war record	LILI MARLENE, SCRAPBOOK	**wash**	
war, *say*	WORE	wash comb	SCOUR
*war*head	W	[wash]-*out*	HAWS, SHAW
warhorse, *say*	HORS DE COMBAT	**Washington**	DC
warlike poet	MARTIAL	**waste**	
warlike, *say*	MARSHAL	[waste] *disposal*	SWEAT, TAWSE
warlord	KITCHENER	waste food	FRITTER
warmonger	SCRAP MERCHANT	waste nothing	USEFULLY
warring [tribes]	BITERS	waste of water	OCEAN
warship *returns<*	POOLS	waste of time	SPILLAGE
wartime act	DORA	waste-paper basket	WPB
*war*time *leader*	W	*waste* [time]	EMIT
ward		*waste* time	omit T
ward<	DRAWBACK, PULLOVER	waste wool, *say*	PHLOX
warder returns<	REDRAW	*wasted* [life]	FILE, LIEF
warder's salary	SCREW	*wasting* [asset]	TASSE, TESSA
warm		*wasting away*	omit *
warm	HEAT	• b(adl)y *wasting away*	BY
• sun *has* warm, hard . . .	SHEATH	• ca(usi)ng *wasting away*	CANG
• warm bird	HEATHEN	**watch**	
• warms kettle	HEATSPOT	watch	BEHOLD
warm	HOT	• watch points	BEHOLDEN
• sun *has* everybody *in* warm . . .	SHALLOT	• watch queen	BEHOLDER
• warm lugs	EARSHOT	watch	EYE
• warm rifles	GUNSHOT	• watches note	EYESTONE
and		watch cover	SENTRY BOX
• warm kitchen, *say*	GALLIOT	watch horse	HUNTER
warm coat	BLAZER	watch organ	TICKER
warm drink	CORDIAL, TOAST	watchchain	ALBERT
warm *environment*	(in) HO–T	watcher	ARGUS, EYE
• son *in* warm *environment*	HOST	watches crop	TURNIPS
warm front	W	watchful people	SPIES, SWISS
warm-hearted	CENTRALLY HEATED	watching cricket	ATTEST
wa*rm-hearted*	AR	watching slip	OVERSIGHT
warming up	OFFICE	watchman	ALBERT

Letter replaced \c\at; Omit (a); Pointers *out*; Retain a̲; Split B_ED; Down (D); Backwards <or ^

watchword	HUNTER, OMEGA, TURNIP	• way *to* beginner's . . .	VIAL
water		way out	omit N, S, E, W
water	ADAM'S ALE, ADAM'S WINE	• fi(n)d way *out*	FID
	AQ, EA, H–O	• (s)hoot out *out*	HOOT
water	NOTICE	ways *out*	omit NE, NW, SE, SW, etc
water at 0°C	JUSTICE	• fi(n)d(s) ways *out*	FID
water carrier	AQUEDUCT	• (sw)itch ways *out*	ITCH
	BUCKET	ways *out*	incl in N–E etc
	TEAR-DUCT	• all ways *out*	WALLS
water colour	LAKE, SEA-GREEN	• four ways *out*	WIVES
water pipe	HOOKAH, MAIN	**way³**	
water pipe, *say*	HOOKER, MANE	indicating highway:	
water rate	KNOT(S)	by the way	incl RD, ST
waterfall	EBB-TIDE, RAIN	• *by the* way, *the French* . . .	LARD
<u>water</u>*front*	W		LAST, LEST
Waterloo	ROUT, WC	• company, *by the* way, . . .	CORD
waterman	BARGEE, SAILOR		CEST
watermen	NAVY, RN	way	AVE, MALL, RD, ST
<u>water</u>*side*	W	• quiet way	PAVE
watersports champion	SURFACE	• Southern way is hard	SMALLISH
waterway	CANAL, RIVER	• he is *on* a way	HEARD
water(way)		• a way *to divide* h–en	HARDEN, HASTEN
indicating name of river,		way *back<*	DR, EVA, TS
sea, etc:		way *off*	omit RD, ST
• free *in* waterway	DERIDE	• report way *off*	HANSA(rd)
• learner *on* water	LOUSE	• fir(st) way *off*	FIR
• nine *in* water	MIXED	way *out*	omit RD, ST
watery [soup]	OPUS	• co(rd)on the way *out*	COON
watt	W	• way *out of* (St)afford	AFFORD
wave		way *out*	(in) R–D, S–T
[arm]-*waving*	MAR, RAM	• first-class way *out*	RAID
wave, *say*	WAIVE	• very small way *out*	SWEET
wave *to* sailor	FLAP-JACK		(*see also* street)
waving [to me]	MOTE	**way⁴**	
waver		indicating permanent way:	
waver [over sin]	VERSION	way	RLY, RY
wavering [voter]	OVERT, TROVE	• fellow *has* first-class way . . .	FAIRLY
way¹		• standard way	PARRY
way *back<*	YAW	**way⁵**	
way *out*	WA–Y	other uses:	
• right way *out*	WARY, WARTY	the way	HOW
[way]-*out*	YAW	way home	ROADHOUSE
way²		way of working	MO
indicating direction:		way *to* assess	MODERATE
way	L, R	*way to* [Paris]	PAIRS
• my way	MYR–	way out	EGRESS, EXIT
• no-way	NOR	*way-out* [design]	DEIGNS, SIGNED
• one way *and* another	LR, RL	way, *say*	WEIGH
• way above	LOVER, ROVER	way-out name	EGRESS, EXIT
way	N, S, E, W	*way-out* [name]	MANE, MEAN
• do *in* many ways	ENDOWS	*wayward* [boy]	YOB
• way *in* t–o . . .	TWO	**we**	
• ways *to* wrap . . .	ENFOLD	we	WE
way	VIA	• we are, *say*	WEIR, WERE
• a way *to* the hill	AVIATOR	• we had, *say*	WEED
• way *into* Sha–n . . .	SHAVIAN	• we have, *say*	WEAVE

Anag [cat]; Any *; Begin IGN–; Endings –ING; eg •; Hidden /cat/; Implied add (on); Implied in (in);

• we sell, *say*	WEASEL
• we, *say*	OUI, WEE
• we shall grow old, *say*	WHEELAGE
• we shall impose levy, *say*	WHEEL-TAX
• we *take* grave . . .	WESTERN
• we understood, *say*	WEAKENED
• we will, *say*	WEAL, WELL, WHEAL, WHEEL
• we would, *say*	WED, WEED
we *hear* talk	TORQUE
we object	US

weak

weak	LIMP
• b . . . . . weak	BLIMP
• weak alien	LIMPET
• weak ruler	LIMPER
weak	W
• no weak . . .	NOW
• weak beer	WALE
• weak member	WARM
weak	WET
• everybody *in* weak . . .	WALLET
• Henry *is in* weak . . .	WHET
• weak man	WETTED
weak acts	POOR LAWS
weak monarch	THINKING
weak, *say*	FEINT, PORE, POUR, WEEK

weapon

weapon carrier	FROG, HOLSTER, SCABBARD, SHEATH
weapon search	RIFLE
weapon-training school	COLLEGE OF ARMS

wear

[wear] *out*	WARE
wear out donkey, *say*	TIRASSE
wearing	IN
• wearing cooler hat	INFANTILE
• wearing dog's . . .	INCURS
• wearing tight . . .	INTENSE
• wearing undershirt	INVEST
• wearing uniform	INHABIT
wearing hat	CAPON
wearing headgear	(in) HA–T
wearing long hair	(in) MAN–E
wearing spots	(in) RA–SH
wearing stockings	(in) HOS–E
wearing undershirt	(in) V–EST
wearing vest	SINGLETON
wearing vest	(in) V–EST
wearing waistcoat	(in) V–EST
wearing waterproof	MACON
wearing women's clothes	DRAGON
wearing *	incl in *
• devil *wearing* hat	LIMPID
• he *is wearing* c–ap	CHEAP
• learner *wearing* ha–t	HALT

wears out overalls	FATIGUES
	(*see also* worn)

weary

wearied	BORED
• fish wearied, *say*	SKATEBOARD
• wearied her, *say*	BOARDER
• wearied him, *say*	BORDMAN
weary	BORE
weary	FLAG
• no weary . . .	OFLAG
• weary ensign	FLAG
• weary workers	FLAGSTAFF
weary band	TIRE
weary, *say*	BOAR, BOER

weather

weather permitting	WP
weatherstation	STANDPOINT
weather*talk*	WETHER, WHETHER
weathercock, *say*	VAIN, VEIN

weave

weave [satin]	STAIN
weave, *say*	BRAYED, NIT, WE'VE
weaver	BOTTOM
weaver-bird	WHIDAH, WHYDAH
weaver-bird, *say*	WIDER
woven [lace if] . . .	FACILE

wedding

wedding	UNION (MEETING)
wedding fixer	SHOTGUN

Wednesday — W, WED

weed

weed, *say*	TEAR
weedkiller	HOE
weeds	SACKCLOTH
weeds, *say*	HOSE, TEARS

week

week	WK
week-end	WE
wee_k_-end	K

weeper — CROCODILE, NIOBE

weigh

weigh down, *say*	ESCALATOR, STAIRCASE
weigh joint, *say*	WANEY
weigh up, *say*	ESCALATOR, STAIRCASE
weight	CT, G, GR, OZ, ST, TON(NE), WT
weight-lifter	ATLAS, CRANE, JACK
weight-*lifting*(D)^	NOT
weight*less* package	CAR(ton)
weighty harvest	STONECROP
weighty rollers	STONES

weird

weird sister	WITCH

weird [sister]	RESIST, RESITS
weird sisters	COVEN
weird [sisters]	RESISTS
well	
well (=not ill)	
• m(ill)et *well* . . .	MET
• *Well,* B(ill)y, . . .	BY
well	SPA
• well in . . .	SPAIN
• *Well,* 500 English . . .	SPADE
• well-run	SPAR
[well] *blended*	LLEW
well-blended [wines]	SINEW, SWINE
well-built structure	STAIRCASE
well content	TREACLE
well covered	CAPON
well drilled	INSTEP
well-earned money	PETRO-DOLLARS
well-favoured	IN
well-informed expert	WISECRACK
well-maintained road, *say*	TIDIEST
well-off	(SOUND) ASLEEP
well-placed	DROWNED
well-placed fluid	INK
well-produced material	GAS, OIL, WATER
well protected flight	STAIRCASE
well-provided area	OILFIELD
well qualified	BA, MA
well-run	SPAR
• state *has* well-run . . .	GASPAR
• English *in* well-run	SPEAR
• well-run brown . . .	SPARTAN
well-used equipment	(DRILLING) RIG
welsh	LEVANT, RAT
Welsh	
Welsh	CAMBRIAN, CYMRIC
Welsh	W
• no Welsh . . .	NOW
• Welsh language, *say*	WORSE
• Welsh member	WARM
Welsh girl	MEGAN
Welsh *leader*	W
Welshman	DAI
• Welshman's platform and	DAIS
• Welshman, *say*	DIE, DYE
Wembley game	FA, FOOTBALL
went	
went about in . . . <	NI
went, *say*	HIDE
[went] *wrong*	NEWT
went wrong [there]	ETHER, THREE
Wesleyan chapel	WC
west	
west	W
• West Country	WOMAN

• West has a very . . .	WAVERY
• West has no study	WODEN
• West in church	WINCE, WINCH
• west *to* east	WE
West Africa	WA
West Brom(wich Albion)	WBA
West Country	WOMAN
West Country trip	FLORAL DANCE
West *End*	T
west end of town	T
West Indies	WI
west-north-west	WNW
West Side girl	MARIA
west-south-west	WSW
western	W
• western aid	WHELP
• western art	WART
• western side	WEDGE
Western Australia	WA
Western Central	WC
Western European Union	WEU
Western *Front*	W
Western Region	WR
Western Samoa	SS
Westminster	WI
Westminster district	SW(I)
westwards	TOW
wet	
wet fat	DRIPPING
wet practice	BAPTISM
wet suit	BATHING COSTUME
	BIKINI
whack	QUARTER-HORSE
whale food	JONAH
	KRILL, PLANKTON
what	
what *did you say*	WATT, WOT
what *French* . . .	QUE
what *German* . . .	WAS
what *Italian* . . .	CHE
what *Spanish* . . .	CHE
what's-his-name, *say*	TYLER, WAT(T)
[What's] *new*?	SWATH, THAWS
What's the matter?	SUBSTANCE
wheel	
wheel rim, *say*	FELLOW
wheel round Eton<	NOTE
wheel spin<	NIPS
wheel [spin]	NIPS, PINS
wheeling [about]	U-BOAT
wheeling bats<	STAB
wheelwright	SPOKESMAN
when	
when	AS
• British when . . .	BRAS
• when alone	ASPERSE

Anag [cat]; Any *; Begin IGN–; Endings –ING; eg •; Hidden /cat/; Implied add (on); Implied in (in);

• when *in* church	CASE, CASH
• when put in order	ASSORTED
• when *short* film . . .	ASPIC
[when] *ordered*	HEWN
when, *say*	WEN
when speaking aloud	ALLOWED
when *speaking aloud*	WEN
when talking, Scandinavians . . .	LAPSE
where	
where *in ancient Rome*	UBI
where *in France*	OU
where *in Germany*	WO
where *in Italy*	DOVE
where *in Spain*	DONDE
where the sun rises	(in) EAS–T
where the sun sets	(in) W–EST
wherein w/e lan/guish	ELAN
which	
which is	QE
which *said*	WITCH
which see	QV
which was to be done	QEF
which was to be found	QEI
which was to be proved	QED
whichever way	
indicating palindrome:	
• a lady, *whichever way* . . .	MADAM
• grass *whichever way you look*	MARRAM
• *whichever way* it goes, boat . . .	KAYAK
whip	
whip	CAT
• whip a hairdresser	CATACOMB
• whip his mother	CATHISMA
• whip-round	CATO
whip cream	BEST
whip [cream]	CRAME, MACER
whip *round*	CA–T, LA–SH
• he *has* whip-*round*	CHEAT
• six *have* whip-*round*	LAVISH
whip *round*<	GOLF, TAC
whip, *say*	NOWT
whip soldiers, *say*	FLAMEN
whirl	
whirl [bone]	EBON
whirled [about]	U-BOAT
whirled about [in anger]	EARNING
	NEARING
*whirl*igig	GIGI
whirling [dervish]	SHRIVED
whirl[pool]	LOOP, POLO
*whirl*pool<	LOOP
whirlwind [romance]	CREMONA
whisk	
whisked [eggs]	SEGG
whisking [flies]	FILES
whistler	REF
white	
white	PALE
• white baby	PALETOT
• whiter doctor	PALERMO
white bowl	JACK
white charger	RHINO(CEROS)
white flower	NILE
white horse	BREAKER, WAVE
white lie	GROUND FROST
white rose bowl	YORK
whittle	
whittle down lis(t)	LIS
whittle down (s)tick	TICK
whittling [stick]	TICKS
who	
who	
–French	QUI
–German	WER
Italian	CHI, CHE
–Spanish	QUIENE
who, *say*	HOO
• who do . . . ?	HOODOO
• who expired?	HOODED
• who *has* the ruler?	HOOKING
whole	
the whole gamut	A–Z
whole numbers	W
whole *speech*	HOLE
wholly *observed in* . . .	incl ALL
• wholly *observed in* sh–ow	SHALLOW
wholly *sound*	HOLEY, HOLY
	MOTH-EATEN
why	
why answer	BECAUSE
why, *say*	
• why examine?	WHITEST
• why solicit?	WHITE-OUT
• why that number?	WHITEN
and	
• why make faces?	WIPE-OUT
• why no . . . ?	WINO
• why reel?	WIRE-HEEL
• why stained?	WIDE-EYED
• why that flower?	WILILY
why, *say*	WYE, Y
whys, *say*	WISE, YS, YY
wicked	
wicked graduate	BASINFUL
wicked ruler	SINKING
wicked sister	REGAN
wicked thing	CANDLE
wicket	
wicket	W
wicket-keeper	BAILSMAN
	DOORMAN, GATEMAN
wicket, *say*	GAIT

Letter replaced \c\at; Omit (a); Pointers *out*; Retain <u>a</u>; Split B_ED; Down (D); Backwards <or ^

wide

wide	BROAD
• a wide . . .	ABROAD
• wide characters	BROADCAST
• wide letter	BROADEN
• wide shed	BROADCAST
wide	THICK
• wide head	THICKNESS
• wide ruler	THICKER
• wide space	THICKEN
wide	W
wide clearing	SWEEPING
wide lid	SOMBRERO
wide *mouth*	W
wider, *say*	WHIDAH, WHYDAH

widespread

[it was] *widespread*	WAIST, WAITS
[wide]*spread*	DEWI
widespread [tales]	LEATS, SLATE, TEALS, STALE

widow

widow married, *say*	WIDOWED
widow's coin, *say*	MIGHT

wield

wielding [guns]	GNUS, SNUG
[that seer] *wielded*	THEATRES

wife

wife	BRIDE, DUTCH
wife	RIB
• 100 wives	CRIBS
• wife *takes* directions	RIBES
• wife's weight	RIBSTON
wife	UX
wife	W
• no wife	NOW
• pass *over* wife	COWL
• wife sick	WAILS, WILL
wife beater	PUNCH
wife of	
–Billy	NANNY
–Punch	JUDY

wigmaker — LOCKSMITH

wild

go wild [over]	ROVE
[region] *is wild*	IGNORE
wild abuse of [all the] . . .	LETHAL
wild *and* free	MADRID
wild [animal]	LAMINA, MANILA
wild [beast]	BASTE, BATES, BEATS
wild *flower*	RAPIDS, TORRENT
wild [flower]	FOWLER
wild [oats]	STOA
wild river	MANICURE
wild state of [garden]	DANGER
	GANDER, RANGED
Wild West (=America)	
• *Wild West* saloon	SEDAN

Wild [West]	STEW, WETS
wild[cat]	ACT
wildcat [strike]	TRIKES
wild[fowl]	FLOW, WOLF
wilder plant	MADDER
wilder [than ripe] . . .	PERIANTH
wild[fire]	RIFE
wild[life]	FILE, LIEF
wildlife sanctuary	NOAH'S ARK
wildly [rage]	GEAR
wilds of [Burma]	RUMBA

will[1]

will	
abbreviated to 'LL' or 'LE':	
• he will	HELL
• she will	SHELL
• we will	WELL
and	
• bat will, *say*	BATTLE
• cat will, *say*	CATTLE
• rat will, *say*	RATTLE
will Edward, *say*	WILTED
willing man	BARKIS
willing to take a job, *say*	WOODWORK
willingly, *say*	FANE, FEIGN

will[2]

willing	TESTATE
willing person	TESTATOR
willing recipient	TESTATEE
willing woman	TESTATRIX
Will's appendix	CODICIL

William

William	BILL
• William of Occam	RAZORBILL
William	WM
• gold *in* William's . . .	WORMS

willy-nilly

[went] *willy-nilly*	NEWT
willy-nilly [into an] . . .	NATION

wily

[men are] *wily*	MEANER
wily [stoat]	TOAST

win

win	GAIN
• prohibit winning . . .	BARGAINING
• win for example	GAINSAY
• wins support	GAINSAID
win	V
win five points	WINTRY
win gold	SUCCESSOR
winner	ACE
• 50 winners	LACES
• winner got up	ACEROSE

wind

wind	BLOW
wind	GALE

Anag [cat]; Any *; Begin IGN–; Endings –ING; eg •; Hidden /cat/; Implied add (on); Implied in (in);

• wind eroded . . .	GALEATE
• wind, *say*	GAEL
wind	WRAP
• wind, *say*	RAP
• wind through . . .	WRAPPER
wind circle	GUSTO
wind-sock	BLOW
wind [up an] . . .	PUNA
wind up an . . . (D)^	NA
winder, *say*	QUAY
winding lever<	REVEL
winding [stream]	MASTER, REMAST
windjammer	ANORAK, CAGOULE, PARKA
window	
window *doesn't open*	(d)ORMER, (o)RIEL
window *opening*	W
wine	
wine	ASTI
• compere *drinks* wine	MASTIC
• run *after* wine	ASTIR
• wine *in* company	PLASTIC
wine	HOCK
• a vessel *included in* the wine . . .	HASSOCK
• *son takes* wine	SHOCK
• wine *aboard*	SHOCKS
wine	PORT
• drink wine	SUPPORT
• *put* wine *before* the queen	PORTER
• ship *carrying* wine	SPORTS
• wine can	PORTABLE
• wine *vintage*	PORTAGE
wine	ROSE
• put *nothing in* wine	ROOSE
• soft wine	PROSE
• wine bowl	ROSEWOOD
• wine *goes by* rail	ROSERY
wine	TENT
• directions *about* wine	ENTENTE
• *put* wine *before* the queen	TENTER
• wine-grower	TENT-MAKER
• wine *without* an . . .	TENANT
wine container	SACK
wine, *say*	BONE, ROAN, WHINE
wine store, *say*	CELLA, SELLA, SELLER
winebearer	GANYMEDE
winebearer	HEBE
• winebearer ate, *say*	HEBETUDE
wing	
wide wings	WE
wingless	OWING
wingless, *say*	KNOWING
wings	ALA
wings of song	SG
wings off (r)oo(k)	OO
wingtip	W
wire gauge	WG

wise	
wise	SAGE
• father's wise . . .	PASSAGE
• wise Herb	SAGE
• wise saint	SAGEST
wise judge	DANIEL, SOLOMON
wise man	BALTHAZAR, GASPAR, MELCHIOR
	MAGUS, SAGE
	SOLON
Wise Men	MAGI
wise, *say*	WHYS, YS, YY
wit	
wit's end	T
wit*less*	omit WIT
• wit*less* bird	T(wit)E
witch	
witch	CIRCE
witch	HAG
• second witch	SHAG
• witch *has* protector, *say*	HAGGARD
witches	COVEN
• witches attempt . . .	COVENTRY
• witches *have* worker . . .	COVENANT
witchcraft	BROOMSTICK
Witchville	SALEM
with¹	
with	W
• contend with	VIEW
• with a bird	WHEN
with *French*	AVEC
with *German*	MIT
• with *German backing*<	TIM
• with *German* Communist	MITRED
• woman with *German* . . .	HERMIT
with *Italian*	CON
• graduate with *Italian* . . .	BACON
• with *Italian* kind	CONSORT
• with *Italian* sailors	CONCREW
with Latin	CUM
• *put* learner *in* with *Latin* . . .	CULM
• with *Latin*, GBS . . .	CUMSHAW
• with *Latin* in . . .	CUMIN
with *Spanish*	CON
• mother's with Spanish . . .	MASCON
• with *Spanish and*	
Italian leader	CONDUCE
• with *Spanish* in charge	CONIC
with²	
indicating addition:	
with hesitation	add ER
• two *with* hesitation	BOTHER
with much hesitation	add ERER
• two *with* much hesitation	BOTHERER
with nothing (on)	–O
• father *with* nothing	DADO
• Prince *with* nothing	HALO

• surgeon *with* nothing	VETO
with nothing on	–OON
• dance *with* nothing on	BALLOON
• girl *with* nothing on	GOON
• many *with* nothing on	LOON, MOON

with³

indicating inclusion:

with a . . .	incl A
with *a hole in*	incl O
with a name	incl AN
with *	incl *
• wea–r *with* the . . .	WEATHER
with an overdraft	(in) RE–D
with hesitation	incl ER
with love	incl O
• c–at *with* love . . .	COAT
with no . . .	incl O
with nothing *in*	incl O

with⁴

indicating omission:

with *a loss*	omit A
with *a missing* . . .	omit A
with *no aspiration*	omit H
with *no sides*	omit end letters
• (c)rat(e) *with no sides*	RAT
with *nothing in it*	omit centre
• c(rat)e *with nothing in it*	CE

with⁵

other uses:

[dance] *with abandon*	CANED
with a [grin]	RING
with a tenant	LET
with *difficulty* [masters]	REMASTS, STREAMS
with it	HIP
with love *for a* . . .	substitute O for A
• c\a\t *with* love *for a* . . .	COT
with one leg	-ION
• cat *with* one leg	CATION
with praise	CL
with string	CORDON

withdraw

withdraw	ATTRACTIVE
withdraw a . . .	omit A
withdraw money	omit L
withdraw part . . . <	TRAP
withdraw *	omit *
• in (cr)ash, *withdraw* credit	ASH
withdrawn from du/ty ro/ster	TYRO

withhold

withhold a . . .	omit A
withhold money	omit L
withhold *	omit *
• *withhold* everything from sh(all)ow . . .	SHOW
with*holding*	W–ITH
• with*holding* note	WIDTH, WITCH

within

call *within earshot*	CAUL
not *within hearing*	KNOT
within	incl IN
• mother *within*	MAIN
within 24 hours	(in) DA–Y
within bounds of Ol/d En/glish . . .	DEN
within call	R–ING
within earshot, hail	HALE
within his rights	R–R
• Is 'e *within his* rights?	RISER
within normal limits	N–L
within range, *say*	INCITE
within the limits of decency	D–Y
within these limits	T–E
within the/se w/alls	SEW
within limits, mo/st em/ployers	STEM
within view, *say*	INCITE
within *	incl in *
• learner *within* s–ight	SLIGHT

without¹

without a day fixed	SD, SINE DIE
without children	SINE PROLE, SP
without date	SA, SINE ANNO
without doubt	SINE DUBIO
without issue	SP, SINE PROLE

without²

indicating inclusion:

without a . . .	incl A
without hesitation	incl ER, UM
without money	incl L
without permission	incl OK
• *without* permission, ten . . .	TOKEN
without *	incl *
• w–e *without* her	WHERE

without³

indicating omission:

chips *without* fish	(carp)ENTER
without a . . .	omit A
without a head	omit 1st letter
without a key	omit A, B, C, D, E, F, G
• box *without* a key	(b)OX, (c)HEST (c)OFFER, (c)RATE
• gat(e) *without* a key	GAT
without a lead(er)	omit 1st letter
• (c)how *without a lead*	HOW
• (p)arty *without* a leader	ARTY
without a name	omit AN
without a penny	omit D, P
without a starter	omit 1st letter
• meal *without a starter*	(d)INNER (s)UPPER
without aspiration	omit H
without back	omit last letter
• sea(t) *without back*	SEA
without capital	omit 1st letter

without copyright	omit C
without direction	omit N, S, E, W
without end	omit last letter
• boo(k) *without* end	BOO
• composition *without* end	CONCERT(o)
without energy	omit E
without eyes, *say*	omit IS, ISE
without finalising agreement	TREAT(y)
without heart	
• was *without* heart	LI(v)ED
• without heart, Pe(t)er	PEER
without hesitation	omit ER
without honour	omit CH, OBE, OM
• *without* honour, (ch)eat	EAT
• fairy king *without* honour	(Obe)RON
• s(om)e *without* honour	SE
without introduction	omit 1st letter
• *without* introduction, actor	(p)LATER
• *without* introduction, (m)aster	ASTER
without king	omit ER, GR, R etc
without love	omit O
without money	omit L
without my . . .	omit MY
• *without* my fa(m)il(y)	FAIL
without name	omit N
without nothing	omit O
without notice	omit AD
• m(ad)e *without* notice	ME
without one . . .	omit A, I
without opening	omit 1st letter
• (w)all *without* opening	ALL
• window *without* opening	(o)RIEL
without oxygen	omit O
without passion	omit IRE
without rating	omit AB, TAR
• overseas *without* rating	(ab)ROAD
• s(tar)ting *without* rating	STING
without reaching a	
conclusion	omit last letter
without royal . . .	omit KING, R
• (r)ule(r) *without* royal . . .	ULE
• win(king) *without* royal . . .	WIN
without tail	omit last letter
• do(g) *without* tail	DO
without (t)he initiative	HE
without the initiative to (s)tart	TART
without the queen	omit ER
without victory	omit V
without[4]	
without (=having no)	
• noiseless	NOBEL
• without a parliament	NOTHING
• without ceremony	NORITE
• without furniture	NOTABLE
• without papers	–NOID
• without water	NOWELL

• without water, *say*	NOEL
and	
• without topping	NOTICED
• without the ability	NOTABLE
and	
• cannot fly	OPINIONS, OWING
• friendless	OPAL(S)
• noiseless	OBANG, ODIN
• unable to write	OPEN
without (=*with* out)	
• 150 *without*	CLOUT
• leaving *without*	OUTGOING
• sailor *without* . . .	ABOUT
without	–LESS
• without Lords	COUNTLESS, PEERLESS
• without proposals	MOTIONLESS
• without weapons	ARMLESS
and	
• without a jetty, *say*	PEERLESS
• without children, *say*	(H)AIRLESS
• without understanding, *say*	NOSE LESS
without[5]	
other uses:	
without a synonym	EXTERNAL, OUTSIDE
without end	ETERNAL, INFINITE
without *end*	T
without fully ap/pear/ing	PEAR
without punctuation	NON-STOP
without rank	NOTWITHSTANDING
withstanding	RESPECTED
witness	
witness	SEE
• witness in re–d	RESEED
• witness many . . .	SEED, SEEL, SEEM
• witness twice	LOOK-SEE
witnessed	SAW
• orchestra witnessed	BANDSAW
• witnessed fight	SAWMILL
• witnessed your, *say*	SAWYER
witty	
witty girl	SALLY
witty rhyme	BITTY, CITY
	DITTY, PITY
witty, *say*	WHITE
wizened	
wizened [hag sat] . . .	AGHAST
[skin is] *wizened*	SISKIN
wobble	
wobble boulder	ROCK
wobbling [chin]	INCH
wobbly dog	LURCHER
wobbly [dog]	GOD
wobbly note	QUAVER
wobbly [note]	ETON, TONE
woeful	
[plead] *woefully*	PALED

Letter replaced \c\at; Omit (a); Pointers *out*; Retain a; Split B_ED; Down (D); Backwards <or ^

woeful [plea]	LEAP, PALE, PEAL
wolf	
[wolf]	WILDFOWL
wolf pack	SUB-GROUP
wolf *returns<*	FLOW
wolfing, *say*	GOBLIN
woman[1]	
woman	ADA
• woman *follows* learner	LADA
• woman *with* child	ADAMITE
• woman *surrounded by*	
Frenchmen	MADAM
woman	EVE
• woman *is given* directions	EVENS
• woman *is neutral*	LEVER
• woman n(o)t *heartless*	EVENT
woman	F
• woman is hot	FISH
• woman or man	FORM
• woman *with* one aim	FIEND
woman	HER
• strike woman	HITHER
• tie *back<* woman . . .	EITHER
• woman with *German* . . .	HERMIT
woman	LADY
• woman is with it	LADYSHIP
• woman's joint	LADYSHIP
• woman's story, *say*	LADYSMITH
woman	RIB
• about a woman	CARIB
• b–e *without* a woman	BRIBE
• woman *with* good *French*	RIBBON
woman	SHE
• woman *has* a red . . .	SHEARED
• woman *is given* directions	SHEWN
• woman *with* learners	SHELL
woman	W
• woman *has* all . . .	WALL
• woman is queen	WISER
• woman's crew	WEIGHT
woman's	HER
• woman's age	HEREON
• woman's husband *and* father	HERMANDAD
• woman's working	HERON
and	
• woman's glove, *say*	HERMIT
• woman's outlook, *say*	HIRCINE
• woman's suit, *say*	HIRSUTE
	(*see also* girl[1, 2])
woman[2]	
Australian woman	ADELAIDE, SHEILA
Dutch woman	FROW, VROUW
Egyptian woman	BINT
French woman	FEMME
German woman	FRAU
Italian woman	DONNA

Spanish woman	MUJER
tragic woman	ELECTRA, HECUBA, MEROPE
woman[3]	
headless (w)oman	OMAN
short (w)omen	OMEN
woman *has* a kiss	THORAX
woman *losing her* head	(m)ARIA, (w)OMAN
woman *losing* <u>her</u> *head*	BET(h)
woman *with* man	EVADES, MANGAL
	SALTED, VIAL etc
woman's angle	NORMAL
woman's army	ATS
women excluded, *say*	FOREMAN
women *losing* their head	(w)OMEN
Women's	
–Institute	WI
–Land Army	WLA
–Liberal Federation	WLF
–Rural Institute	WRI
–Voluntary Service	WVS
women's extra	WX
women's magazine	POWDER ROOM
won't	
I *won't* be there	omit I
* *won't* be there	omit *
• p(r)ay king *won't be there*	PAY
wood	
wood	ASH, DEAL, FIR
• wooden measure	ASHEN
• wooden square	DEALT
• wooden saint	FIRST
wood	BOWL, JACK
wood processor	LATHE, TERMITE
wood, *say*	BOLE, TIMBRE, WOULD
woodcraft	ELDERSHIP
woodcut(ter)	SAW
woodcutter, *say*	FELLAH
wooden-faced	VENEERED
wooden junk	LUMBER
wooden vessel, *say*	TREPAN
Woodwork	EAST LYNNE
wool	
woollen fabric, *say*	RUSTLE
woolly [aphis]	SPAHI
woolly creature	GUERNSEY, JERSEY
woolly jumper	LAMB
word	
word of mouth news	GNUS
word processing	WP
word processor	ETYMOLOGIST, WP
word *sound*	WHIRRED
words per minute	WPM
wordsmith	PUNGENT
work	
work	ERG
• second-class work	BERG

Anag [cat]; Any *; Begin IGN–; Endings –ING; eg •; Hidden /cat/; Implied add (on); Implied in (in);

• work *in* an–y, *say*	ENERGY
• work *with* no . . .	ERGO
work	OP(US)
• church work	CHOP
• quiet work	SHOP
• see work	LOOP
• stop work	HOOP
• work a long time	OPERA
• work *at* laundry	OPPRESSING
• work *at* newspaper	OPPRESS
• work *by* painter, *say*	OPTICIAN
• work-force	OPPRESS
• work hard	OPH–
• work *over<*	PO
• work *overtime*(D)	OPERA, OPT
• work problems	OPPOSERS
• work-time	OPERA
• work together	COOP
• workman	OPAL
work	PLY
• admit *to* work	IMPLY
• work *after* the morning . . .	AMPLY
• work *with* timber and	PLYWOOD
• work about, *say*	PLICA
• work class, *say*	PLIFORM
• work well, *say*	PLIABLY
work *at* it, *say*	TOILET
work into [shape]	HEAPS, PHASE
wor(k) *not finished*	WOR
work on [road]	DORA
work out [sums]	MUSS
work record	BOOK OF JOB
worked out [in gym]	MINGY
worked [over]	ROVE
working	AT
working	ON
• girl working	SALON
• spacecraft working	LEMON
• vehicle working	CARTON
• working in hospital	ONWARDS
working	(in) HAR–NESS
• girl *working*	HARDINESS
working	INFIRM
working [men are] . . .	MEANER, RENAME
working [models]	SELDOM
working pupils	EYEING, LOOKING, SEEING
working well	INFORM
workman	GRAFTED
workout [when I] . . .	WHINE
work[rate]	TARE, TEAR
workshop striker	HAMMER, MALLET
worker	
worker	ANT
• defame worker	MALIGNANT
• ditch worker	TRENCHANT
• school worker	INFORMANT
• worker in charge	ANTIC
• worker *in* afterthought	PANTS
• worker's child	SONANT
worker	BEE
• worker *at* church	BEECH
• worker for each . . .	BEEPER
• worker on railway	BEERY
worker	HAND
• pack-worker	DECK-HAND
• worker *has* a few . . .	HANDSOME
• worker *on strike*	HANDOUT
worker	MAN
• worker and *French*	MANET
• worker *is given* directions	MANSE
• worker *has* unknown . . .	MANY
worker	TEMP
• worker *has* one . . .	TEMPI
• worker is *French*	TEMPEST
• worker *with* nothing . . .	TEMPO
worker in force	OPERATIVE
worker writing	HAND
Workers' Education Association	WEA
workers' group	BEE, TU
workers' store	HONEYCOMB
world	
world	EARTH
World	
–Bank	BIS
–Boxing Association	WBA
–Boxing Council	WBC
–Championship Tennis	WCT
–Council of Churches	WCC
–Health Organisation	WHO
–Meteorological Organisation	WMO
–Wildlife Fund	WWF
world, *say*	WHIRLED
world terminal	EARTH
worldwide	MONDIAL
worm catcher	EARLY BIRD
worn	
worn by	incl A
worn by *	incl *
• ha–t *worn by* learner	HALT
worn-down (m)at	AT
worn foundations	BRA(SSIERE)
	CORSETS, PANTS, VEST
	(*see also* wear)
worn-out horse	SHORE
worn [shoe]	HOES, HOSE
worry	
worried [mien]	MINE
worry badger, *say*	BAIT, HARASS
worry [over]	ROVE
worrying [sheep]	PHESE
Worshipful	WP

Letter replaced \c\at; Omit (a); Pointers *out*; Retain a; Split B_ED; Down (D); Backwards <or ^

worst	
[Coat] *Worsted*?	ATOC, CATO, TACO
worsted	BESTED
worsted [a Red] . . .	DARE, DEAR
	RADE, READ
worthless ship	JUNK
would	
would-be queen	PAWN
would he, say	WOODY
would you say	WOOD
would you say 'No'?	KNOW
would you say so?	SEW, SOW
wound	
wound	SCAR
• wound an insect	SCARABEE
• wound inflamed	SCARRED
• wound sailor	SCARAB
• wound stripe	SCAR
wound fly	WING
wound man with knife	STABLES
wounded	BULLETIN
wounded [deer that's] . . .	SHATTERED
woven	(*see* weave)
wrap	
wrapped in pa/per for	
m/y . . .	PERFORM
wrapped in *	incl in *
• is *wrapped in* hide	SISKIN
wrapping a . . .	incl A
wrapping *	incl A
• hide *wrapping* is . . .	SISKIN
wreathe	
[it was] *wreathed in* . . .	WAIST, WAITS
wreathed in [smoke]	MOKES
wreck	
wreckage of [yacht]	CATHY
wrecked [ship]	HIPS
Wren church	WRENCH
wrestle	
[arm]-*wrestling*	MAR, RAM
wrestling [ring is] . . .	RISING
wretched	
[lived] *wretchedly*	DEVIL
wretched [life]	FILE, LIEF
wriggle	
[eels] *wriggling*	ELSE, SEEL
wriggling [past]	PATS, SPAT, STAP
wriggly [adder]	DREAD
wring	
wring [neck or] . . .	RECKON
wring out [sheet]	THESE
wring [withers]	WRITHES
wringer, *say*	MANGEL
wrinkle	
wrinkle, *say*	PUKKA
wrinkled [skin]	INKS, SINK

wrinkles	HEADLINES
write[1]	
write	PEN
• mother writes	DAMPENS
• write a number . . .	PENNINE
• write songs	PENCHANTS
• write *to* Edward	PENNED
• write *to* Gotham	PENNY
and	
• write a little, *say*	PENSUM
• write riddle, *say*	PENSIVE
• write *to* a number, *say*	PENNATE
• write *to* worker, *say*	PENNANT
• writing material, *say*	PENTACLE
and	
• write *back*<	NEP
write-*up*(D)^	NEP
• write-*up* Greek letter	NEPETA
• write-*up* in i–t	INEPT
• write-*up* song	NEPTUNE
(*see also* writer)	
write[2]	
good writing	BIBLE, NT, OT
	SCRIPTURE(S)
write off [car]	ARC
write, *say*	INDICT, RITE, (W)RIGHT
write up notes(D)^	SETON
writing	HAND
• second writing	BACKHAND
• writing report	HANDCLAP
• writing *with* unknown . . .	HANDY
writing	MS
• he *has* writing	HEMS
• writing up . . . (D)^	SM
writing a synonym	INSCRIBING
writing cards	HAND
writing out [the list]	THISTLE
written about a . . .	incl A
written about *	incl *
• wor–ds *written about*	
out[set]	WORSTEDS
written in full	
• is *written in full*	ISLAND
• *written in full*, it . . .	ITALIAN
written in [prose]	PORES, POSER, SPORE
written in S/pan/ish	PAN
written in(to) *	incl in *
• out[set] *written in* wor–ds	WORSTEDS
(*see also* wrote)	
writer	
writer	ELIA
writer	NIB
• writer aboard	SNIBS
• writer beats . . .	NIBLICKS
• writer lost blood	NIBBLED
writer	I, ME

Anag [cat]; Any *; Begin IGN–; Endings –ING; eg •; Hidden /cat/; Implied add (on); Implied in (in);

writer	PEN	*wrong way* to VIP<	PIVOT
• lower writer	COW-PEN	*wrong way* up(D)^	PU
• writer *has* no *French*	PENNON	*wrong* [ways]	SWAY, YAWS
• writer *with* some . . .	PENNINE	*wrong,* [wrong]	GROWN
	(*see also* write¹)	*wrong*[doer]	ODER, RODE
writer	BUCHAN, POE, WELLS et al	*wrong*[doing]	DINGO
• writer present, *say*	BUCCANEER	*wrongfully* [the law] . . .	WEALTH
• writer *exactly* . . .	POET	*wrongly constructed* [arch]	CHAR
• writer *after 500* . . .	DWELLS	*wrongly executed* [turn]	RUNT
writer or two	TWAIN	**wrote**	
Writer to the Signet	WS	[wrote] *off*	TOWER
writer's block	PAD	*wrote off* [cars]	ARCS, SCAR
wrong		[wrote] *novel*	TOWER
wrong	TORT	[wrote] *out*	TOWER
• girl's wrong . . .	DISTORT	wrote, *say*	PEND
• when wrong	ASSORT	• wrote in Greece	PENDING
• *wrong* river	TORTOISE	• wrote *to* hospital department	PENDENT
• wrong *turning*<	TROT	• wrote *to* worker	PENDANT
wrong again	SECOND SLIP	wrote, *say*	ROTE
wrong fount	WF		(*see also* write)
wrong letters	TYPOS	**wrought**	
wrong [letters]	SETTLER	[over]*wrought*	ROVE
[wrong] *letters*	GROWN	*wrought* [iron panel]	NONPAREIL
wrong mark	(A)CROSS, X	**wry**	
[wrong] *parts*	GROWN	[spoke] *wryly*	POKES
wrong [parts]	PRATS, SPRAT, STRAP	*wry* [smile]	LIMES, MILES, SLIME
wrong sign	(A)CROSS, X	**w-worker**	WANT
wrong version of [song]	SNOG	**Wye**	
wrong way<	DR, EVA, TS	Wye, *say*	WHY, Y
	YAW	Wyeville	ROSS

Letter replaced \c\at; Omit (a); Pointers *out*; Retain a; Split B_ED; Down (D); Backwards <or ^

X

across, axis, body, chi, Christ, chromosome, craft, cross, draw, ex, Exe, factor, film, generation, height, *illiterate's sign*, kiss, particle, *PM's address*, ray, reactance, *sign of the times*, spot marked, takes, ten, ten thousand, times, unknown, variable, vitamin, vote, *wrong sign*, xi, Xian, Xmas

X		X-ray	CROSS-BEAM
X		Xantippe	SHREW
• related to x	TEN	Xeres	SHERRY
• x + 1	OFTEN	XLNC	EXCELLENCY
• x-square	TENACE	XPDNC	EXPEDIENCY
x + 1	TENT		
	XI		

Y

axis, alloy, chromosome, factor, level, moth, one hundred and fifty (thousand), track, unknown, variable, *why*, *Wye*, yard, year, yen, yes, yocto-, young, yttrium

y		**yew**	
Y-*front*	start with Y	yew, *say*	EU, EWE, U, YOU
• our Y-*front*	YOUR	yews, *say*	EUS, EWES, US, USE, UU, YOUSE
Y, *say*	WHY, WYE	**yield**	
yacht		*yield from* [shares]	SHEARS
[yacht]-*building*	CATHY	yield, *say*	SEED
yacht's *bow*	Y	*yielding* [oil]	OLI–
yacht's *stern*	T	yielding, *say*	SEEDING
yap		*yields* [much] . . .	CHUM
yap	PAY BACK, RETALIATE	**Yorkshire**	
yapping, *say*	BARKHAN	Yorkshire town, *say*	ARROGATE
yard		Yorkshire town, *say*	LEADS
yard	CID, Y, YD	• Yorkshire beauty queen, *say*	MISLEADS
yard measure	AREA	Yorkshireman	TYKE
year		**you**	
year	A(NNUS), Y, YR	you	THOU
year of reign	AR	• you *on* the beach	THOUSANDS
year *off*	omit Y	you	YE
• man(y) *take* year *off*	MAN	• you *exactly*	YET
[year] *off*	YARE	• you note	YETI
yearly	PA	• you soldiers	YEMEN
• yearly call	PARING	you are very generous, *say*	BEGONIA
• yearly employment	PAUSE	you are, *say*	UR, YORE, YOUR
• yearly expense	PARENTAL	*you can get* [wet in] . . .	TWINE
yearly meeting	AGM	you can *hear*	YUKON
yellow		*you can hear* a noise	ANNOYS
yellow	OR	*you can see* so/me ant/s . . .	MEANT
• yellow *in* m–e	MORE	you desert	THOUSAND
• yellow metal	ORAL	you *in France*	TU, VOUS
• yellow timber	ORDEAL	you *in Germany*	DU, DICH, SIE
yellow bird	CHICKEN	you *in Italy*	LEI, TU, VOI
yellow invertebrate	SPINELESS	you *in Spain*	TU, USTED, VOSOTROS
yellow plate	CHROME	you *in the middle*	O
yellow polish	BUFF	*you may have* [to shout]	OUTSHOT
yen	YN	*you might say* we . . .	OUI, WEE
yeomanry	YEO	you *no longer*	THEE, THOU, YE
yes		you *once*	THEE, THOU, YE
yes	AY, AYE	you queue	UQ
–*French*	OUI	you queue *up*(D)^	QU
–*French/German*	OUIJA	you, *say*	EU
–*German*	JA	• a girl *with* you	ADIEU
–*Italian*	SI	• you are a sham	EUPHONY
–*Russian*	DA	• you are from the East	EURASIAN
–*Spanish*	SI	• you dog!	EUCHRE

Letter replaced \c\at; Omit (a); Pointers *out*; Retain a̲; Split B_ED; Down (D); Backwards <or ^

you, *say*	EWE	young runner	ERRAND BOY
• you were	EWER	young sailor	SEASON
• you *in* telephone system	STEWED	young salmon, *say*	GRILL(E)S
you, *say*	U	young swan, *say*	SIGNET
• you fool!	UNIT	young swimmer	ELVER
• you get better	URALI	younger	YR
• you *have* a case	UKASE	younger brother	ABEL
• you make tidy	UNEATEN	youngest son	BENJAMIN
you, *say*	YEW	youngster	MINOR
you say no	KNOW	**your**	
you see, *say*	UC	your	YR
you *sound* . . .	EU, EWE, U, YEW	your *head*	Y
you will, *say*	YULE	Your Holiness	SV
• you will record	YULE-LOG	your *opposite*	MY
young		your *predecessor*	THY
young actress, *say*	MISLEAD(ING)	your room is No, 8, *say*	URINATE
young bird lost blood	SQUABBLED	your, *say*	THIGH, YORE
young bird, *say*	CHEAPER	your uncle	BOB
young bounder	JOEY, LAMB, LEVERET	yours	NOTOUR
young Conservative	BLUE BABY	yours truly	I, ME
young cook	FRY	**youth**	
young feller	WASHINGTON	youth	MINOR
young gangster	BOYHOOD	Youth Hosteller, *say*	CAMPANOLOGIST
young insect	LITTERBUG	youth leader	GUIDER
young lad *after* money	DOUGHBOY	youth *leader*	Y
young learner	BABEL	youth *leaders*	WISE, YS
young male fish	LADLING	youth *leaders*	YO
young male worker, *say*	BUOYANT	youth, *say*	BUOYAGE
young pi-dog, *say*	PIPE UP	**Yule log**	HOLLYWOOD
young refuse . . .	LITTER		

Z

atomic number, axis, bar, bend, boson, cedilla, contraction-mark, DNA, factor, impedance, integers, izzard, *last character*, last letter, omega, particle, proton number, two thousand, seven, seven thousand, two million, *sound of sleep*, unknown, variable, Zambia, zed, zee, zenith, zepto-, zero, zeta, zetta, zone

---

Zaire	ZR	zero *fall-out*	omit O
Zambia	Z	• bor(o)n *has* zero *fall-out*	BORN
Zamenhof's language	ESPERANTO	zero population growth	ZPG
Zantippe(Zentippe)	SHREW		*(see also* no², nothing)
zero		**zig-zag**	
zero	DUCK, LOVE	*zig-zag* [line]	LIEN, NEIL, NILE
	NIL, NO	*zig-zagging* [about]	U-BOAT
	NOTHING, NOUGHT	**Zone Standard Time**	ZST
zero	O	**zoo**	
• zero hour	OH	zoo-keeper	NOAH
• zero mark	OSCAR	zoo-keeper's assistant	HAM, JAPHET
• zero-rated	ORATED		SHEM
zero	OUGHT		

Letter replaced \c\at; Omit (a); Pointers *out*; Retain a̱; Split B_ED; Down (D); Backwards <or ^